Source Documents

2	GENERAL JOURNAL	PAGE 1

3	GENERAL LEDGER

7, 9

4

10

7

Name of Company
Work Sheet
For Period Ended

5

6

Name of Company
Post-Closing Trial Balance
Date

Adjusting

9

Closing

8

8

8

Name of Company
Income Statement
For Period Ended

Name of Company
Statement of Owner's Equity
For Period Ended

Name of Company
Balance Sheet
Date

Steps in the Accounting Cycle

During Accounting Period:
1. Analyze source documents.
2. Journalize the transactions.
3. Post to the ledger accounts.

End of Accounting Period:
4. Prepare a trial balance.
5. Determine and prepare the needed adjustments on the work sheet.
6. Complete an end-of-period work sheet.
7. Journalize and post the adjusting entries.
8. Prepare an income statement, statement of owner's equity, and balance sheet.
9. Journalize and post the closing entries.
10. Prepare a post-closing trial balance.

Heintz & Parry

COLLEGE ACCOUNTING

James A. Heintz, DBA, CPA

Professor of Accounting
School of Business
University of Kansas
Lawrence, Kansas

Robert W. Parry, Jr., Ph.D.

Professor of Accounting
Kelley School of Business
Indiana University
Bloomington, Indiana

20e

Chapters 1-15

SOUTH-WESTERN
CENGAGE Learning™

Australia • Brazil • Japan • Korea • Mexico • Singapore • Spain • United Kingdom • United States

SOUTH-WESTERN
CENGAGE Learning™

College Accounting, 20th edition, Chapters 1-15

James A. Heintz and Robert W. Parry, Jr.

Vice President of Editorial, Business: Jack W. Calhoun

Editor-in-Chief: Rob Dewey

Executive Editor: Sharon Oblinger

Developmental Editor: Sara Wilson, CPA,
   CATS Publishing

Associate Marketing Manager: Laura Stopa

Marketing Coordinator: Heather Mooney

Senior Content Project Manager: Tim Bailey

Director of Media Development: Rick Lindgren

Media Editor: Bryan England

Senior Frontlist Buyer, Manufacturing: Doug Wilke

Production Service: LEAP Publishing Services, Inc.

Compositor: KnowledgeWorks Global Limited

Senior Art Director: Stacy Jenkins Shirley

Cover and Internal Designer: Grannan Graphic
   Design

Cover Image: Digital Vision/Juice Images

Rights Acquisition Account Manager-Image:
   John Hill

Photo Researcher: Megan Lessard, Pre-PressPMG

For product information and technology assistance, contact us at
Cengage Learning Customer & Sales Support, 1-800-354-9706
For permission to use material from this text or product, submit all requests online at
www.cengage.com/permissions
Further permissions questions can be emailed to
permissionrequest@cengage.com

Library of Congress Control Number: 2009940238
ISBN-13: 978-0-538-74521-5
ISBN-10: 0-538-74521-5

South-Western Cengage Learning
5191 Natorp Boulevard
Mason, OH 45040
USA

Cengage Learning products are represented in Canada by Nelson Education, Ltd.

For your course and learning solutions, visit **www.cengage.com**
Purchase any of our products at your local college store or at our preferred online store
www.ichapters.com

Printed in the United States of America
1 2 3 4 5 6 7 13 12 11 10 09

Where Accounting Education and the Real World Meet

Be your best in the classroom *and* in the workplace with the accounting skills and confidence you'll achieve with Heintz/Parry's *College Accounting, 20e*!

The future belongs to those who possess the marketable skills learned from studying Heintz/Parry. With unmatched *clarity*, *accuracy*, and *technology*, our text provides you with the accounting knowledge you need to succeed. As you journey through this text, you will gain confidence as you learn accounting, which is the language of the business world.

Through 19 editions, we've fine-tuned the pedagogy in our text and supporting materials. Our proven step-by-step approach and inviting narrative style focus on the practical skills you'll need to transition from the classroom to the workplace. We've kept intact everything that has made *College Accounting* so successful and have added new features and ancillary materials to ensure that it remains **the best text** on the market.

We invite you to read the following preface, which serves as a guide to help you gain the most knowledge from this text and its supporting materials.

Best wishes to you for a successful college experience and business career!

Jim Heintz and Rob Parry

COLOR CODING GUIDES YOU

Throughout the text, you will see special color coding used to help you quickly know how accounts are classified and help you follow the key transactions presented. A quick reference to these colors can be found on the second page of each part opener. For example, page 2 shows the following chart for the chapters in Part 1:

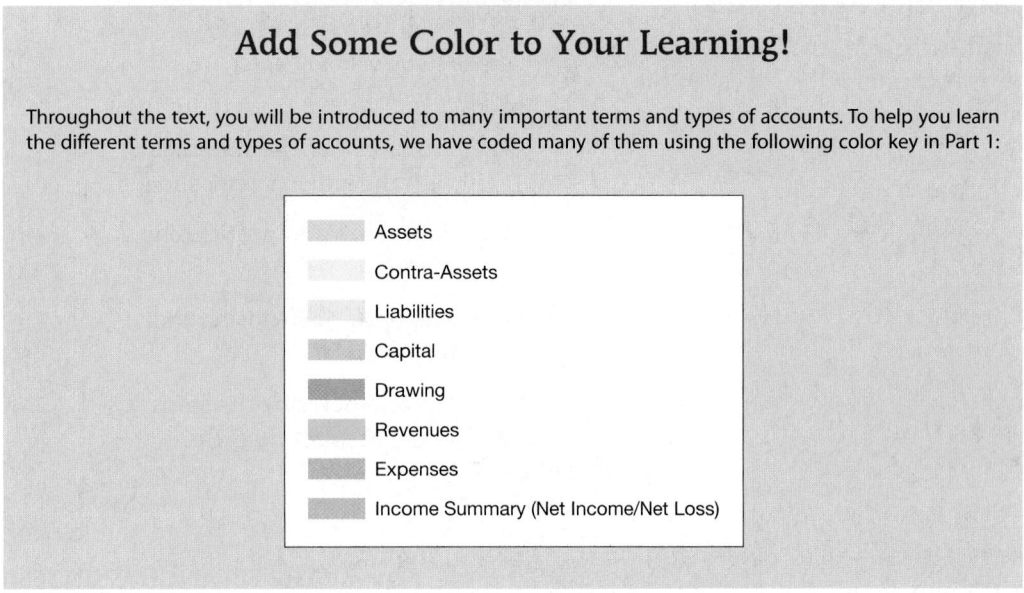

Add Some Color to Your Learning!

Throughout the text, you will be introduced to many important terms and types of accounts. To help you learn the different terms and types of accounts, we have coded many of them using the following color key in Part 1:

- Assets
- Contra-Assets
- Liabilities
- Capital
- Drawing
- Revenues
- Expenses
- Income Summary (Net Income/Net Loss)

As you move through the text, more color codes are added. So always check the Add Some Color To Your Learning! chart when you start a new part.

CHAPTER OPENERS PROVIDE CLUES

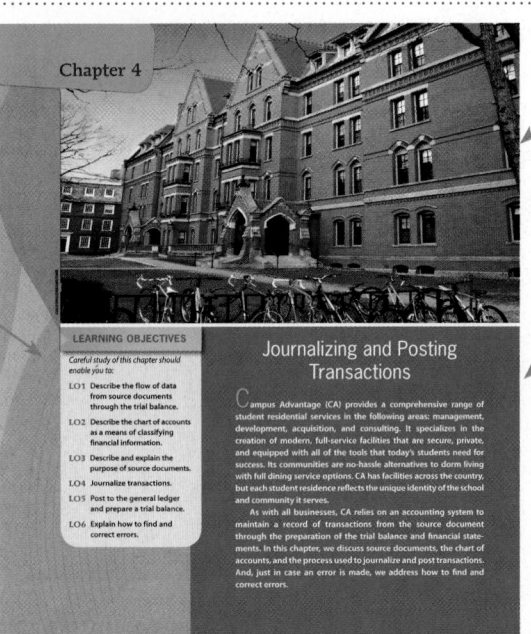

Don't miss the Learning Objectives! These tell you what you should know when you've completed studying the chapter.

Each chapter opens with a colorful image and a description of a real company. By reading the opening description, you will find out *why it's important* to master the information that is covered in the chapter. The openers can help you visualize how accounting is used in the business world and, therefore, why it's known as the "language of business."

LEARNING OBJECTIVES CONNECT THE CHAPTER COVERAGE FROM BEGINNING TO END

By paying attention to the Learning Objectives, you can focus on what is important. The Learning Objectives appear in many places throughout the chapter. Here's where you will find the Learning Objectives (LOs):

CHAPTER OPENER PAGE

The first page of the chapter lists all of the Learning Objectives for the chapter.

> ## LEARNING OBJECTIVES
>
> *Careful study of this chapter should enable you to:*
>
> **LO1** **Prepare financial statements with the aid of a work sheet.**
>
> **LO2** **Journalize and post closing entries.**
>
> **LO3** **Prepare a post-closing trial balance.**
>
> **LO4** **List and describe the steps in the accounting cycle.**

MARGINS

When the chapter is presenting coverage for a certain Learning Objective, the LO is stated at the beginning of the section.

LO1 Prepare financial statements with the aid of a work sheet.

THE FINANCIAL STATEMENTS

The work sheet prepared in Chapter 5 supplies most of the information needed to prepare an income statement, a statement of owner's equity, and a balance sheet. The statements and work sheet columns from which they are derived for Jessie Jane's Campus Delivery Service are shown in Figures 6-1 and 6-2.

As you refer to the financial statements in Figures 6-1 and 6-2, notice the placement of dollar signs, single rulings, and double rulings. Dollar signs are placed at the top of each column and beneath rulings. Single rulings indicate addition or subtraction, and double rulings are placed under totals. Notice that each statement heading contains three lines: (1) company name, (2) statement title, and (3) period ended or date.

KEY POINTS TO REMEMBER

At the beginning of the Self-Study section, each Learning Objective is stated along with the most important information covered in the chapter.

> **LEARNING OBJECTIVES**   Key Points to Remember
>
> **LO1** Prepare financial statements with the aid of a work sheet.
>
> The work sheet is used as an aid in preparing:
> 1. adjusting entries,
> 2. financial statements, and
> 3. closing entries.
>
> The following classifications are used for accounts reported on the balance sheet.
> - *Current assets* include cash and assets that will be converted into cash or consumed within either one year or the normal operating cycle of the business, whichever is longer. An *operating cycle* is the time required to purchase supplies and services and convert them back into cash.
> - *Property, plant, and equipment,* also called *plant assets* or *long-term assets,* represent assets that are expected to serve the business for many years.
> - *Current liabilities* are liabilities that are due within either one year or the normal operating cycle of the business, whichever is longer, and that are to be paid out of current assets.
> - *Long-term liabilities,* or *long-term debt,* are obligations that are not expected to be paid within a year and do not require the use of current assets.

U REVU BANNERS

Inside the banner, the Learning Objective number is indicated.

> **U REVU**   Complete U REVU-1 on **page 199** to test your basic understanding of LO1.

TRUE/FALSE AND MULTIPLE CHOICE QUESTIONS AND U REVU EXERCISES

Each of these Self-Study items indicates the related Learning Objective number(s). If you need to review the coverage in the chapter, use these LOs to guide you to the right place.

SELF-STUDY QUESTIONS AND EXERCISES

True/False Questions

1. LO1   Expenses are listed on the income statement as they appear in the chart of accounts or in descending order (by dollar amount).
2. LO1   Additional investments of capital during the month are not reported on the statement of owner's equity.
3. LO1   The income statement cannot be prepared using the work sheet alone.
4. LO1   A classified balance sheet groups similar items, such as current assets together.
5. LO2   Temporary accounts are closed at the end of each accounting period.

Multiple Choice Questions

1. LO2   Which of these types of accounts is considered a "permanent" account?

   (a) Revenue   (c) Drawing
   (b) Asset   (d) Expense

2. LO2   Which of these accounts is considered a "temporary" account?

   (a) Cash   (c) J. Jones, Capital
   (b) Accounts Payable   (d) J. Jones, Drawing

3. LO2   Which of these is the first step in the closing process?

   (a) Close revenue account(s).   (c) Close the income summary account.
   (b) Close expense accounts.   (d) Close the drawing account.

4. LO3   The _____ is prepared after closing entries are posted to prove the equality of debit and credit balances.

   (a) balance sheet   (c) post-closing trial balance
   (b) income statement   (d) statement of owner's equity

5. LO4   Steps that begin with analyzing source documents and conclude with the post-closing trial balance are called the

   (a) closing process.   (c) adjusting entries.
   (b) accounting cycle.   (d) posting process.

U REVU   Exercises

1. LO1   Joe Fisher operates Fisher Consulting. A partial work sheet for August 20-- is provided below. Fisher made no additional investments during the month. Prepare an income statement, statement of owner's equity, and balance sheet.

Fisher Consulting
Work Sheet (Partial)
For Month Ended August 31, 20--

	ACCOUNT TITLE	INCOME STATEMENT DEBIT	INCOME STATEMENT CREDIT	BALANCE SHEET DEBIT	BALANCE SHEET CREDIT	
1	Cash			2 5 0 0 00		1
2	Accounts Receivable			8 0 0 00		2
3	Equipment			3 8 0 0 00		3
4	Accum. Depr.— Equipment				2 0 0 00	4
5	Accounts Payable				1 0 0 0 00	5
6	Joe Fisher, Capital				3 0 0 0 00	6
7	Joe Fisher, Drawing			3 0 0 00		7
8	Professional Fees		5 0 0 0 00			8
9	Wages Expense	1 0 0 0 00				9
10	Rent Expense	7 0 0 00				10
11	Depreciation Expense	1 0 0 00				11
12	Net Income	1 8 0 0 00	5 0 0 0 00	7 4 0 0 00	4 2 0 0 00	12
13		3 2 0 0 00			3 2 0 0 00	13
14		5 0 0 0 00	5 0 0 0 00	7 4 0 0 00	7 4 0 0 00	14
15						15
16						16

2. LO2   Using the work sheet provided in U REVU Exercise 1, prepare closing entries in general journal form.
3. LO3   Using the work sheet provided in U REVU Exercise 1 and financial statements prepared for that exercise, prepare a post-closing trial balance.

The answers to the Self-Study Questions and Exercises are at the end of the chapter (page 213).

APPLYING YOUR KNOWLEDGE

REVIEW QUESTIONS

LO1   1. Identify the source of the information needed to prepare the income statement.

LO1   2. Describe two approaches to listing the expenses in the income statement.

LO1   3. Identify the sources of the information needed to prepare the statement of owner's equity.

LO1   4. If additional investments were made during the year, what information in addition to the work sheet would be needed to prepare the statement of owner's equity?

LO1   5. Identify the sources of the information needed to prepare the balance sheet.

LO2   6. What is a permanent account? On which financial statement are permanent accounts reported?

REVIEW QUESTIONS, A & B EXERCISES, AND A & B PROBLEMS

Each of these assignments indicates the related Learning Objective number. If you need to review the coverage in the chapter, use these LOs to guide you to the right place.

SERIES A EXERCISES

E 6-1A (LO1)
✓ Net income: $1,990

INCOME STATEMENT From the partial work sheet for Case Advising below, prepare an income statement.

E 6-2A (LO1)
✓ Capital 1/31: $5,190

STATEMENT OF OWNER'S EQUITY From the partial work sheet below, prepare a statement of owner's equity, assuming no additional investment was made by the owner.

SERIES A PROBLEMS

P 6-7A (LO1)
✓ Net income: $1,400; Capital 1/31: $7,400; Total assets: $8,650

FINANCIAL STATEMENTS Page 203 shows a work sheet for Monte's Repairs. No additional investments were made by the owner during the month.

REQUIRED

1. Prepare an income statement.
2. Prepare a statement of owner's equity.
3. Prepare a balance sheet.

CALLOUTS AND ARROWS HELP YOU NAVIGATE

Along with color coding, callouts and arrows help you quickly find important elements in a figure and know how different parts of a figure are connected.

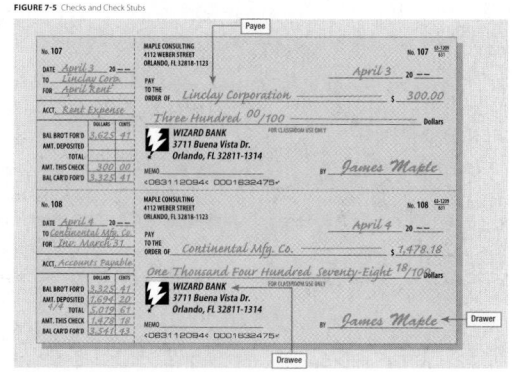

FIGURE 7-5 Checks and Check Stubs

THE STEPS LEAD THE WAY

Where it's most helpful, we provide step-by-step instructions. Related figures guide you visually through the steps to reinforce the process. When you see these, take the time to "walk" through each step to strengthen your understanding.

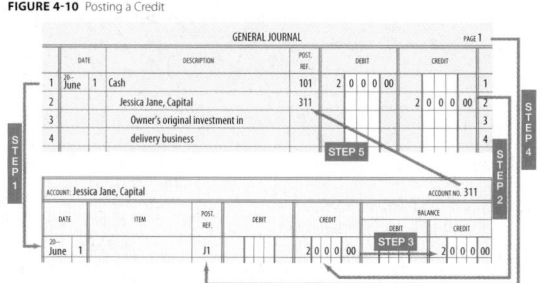

FIGURE 4-10 Posting a Credit

In the ledger account:

STEP 1   **Enter the date of the transaction in the Date column.** Enter the year, "20--," the month, "June," and the day, "1," in the Date column of the account Jessica Jane, Capital.

STEP 2   **Enter the credit.** Copy the $2,000 credit to Jessica Jane, Capital in the journal to the Credit column in the ledger.

STEP 3   **Enter the balance of the account.** Enter the $2,000 balance in the Balance columns under Credit. (If the balance of the account is zero, draw a line through the Debit and Credit columns.)

STEP 4   **Enter the journal page in the Posting Reference column.** Enter "J1" in the Posting Reference column since the posting came from page 1 of the journal.

LEARNING KEYS AND MARGIN NOTES REINFORCE AND EXPAND YOUR KNOWLEDGE

✎ LEARNING KEY

1. Find the row for wages.

2. Find the column for withholding allowances.

3. Find the amount where they cross.

Watch for Learning Keys. Make sure you understand them. Learning Keys reinforce basic content as it's covered in the chapter.

When the Social Security program was established in 1937, the tax was 1% on earnings up to $3,000 per year!

Watch for the margin notes. They give you more information so that you will have a greater understanding of the topic.

A BROADER VIEW WIDENS YOUR HORIZON

Each chapter expands your understanding by featuring a real situation or event. A Broader View puts accounting in perspective.

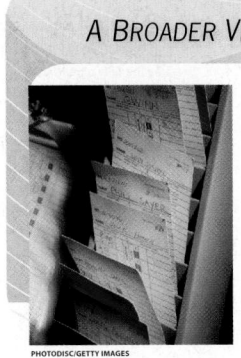

A BROADER VIEW

PHOTODISC/GETTY IMAGES

Payroll Fraud—Paying for Ghosts

A supervisor at Haas Transfer Warehouse embezzled $12,000 from the company by collecting paychecks for former employees. When an employee left the company, the supervisor continued to submit a department time report for the employee. This caused a paycheck to be generated for the "ghost" employee. The supervisor then simply kept this paycheck when others were distributed to actual employees.

This fraud shows the importance of two procedures that appear in this chapter: (1) a time card, plastic card, or badge should be used for each employee to keep an accurate record of time worked and (2) payment by direct deposit or electronic funds transfer to the employee's bank is a good internal control.

PROFILES IN ACCOUNTING LET YOU SEE WHAT OTHERS ARE DOING WITH THEIR ACCOUNTING EDUCATION

The individuals featured in Profiles in Accounting are real people who have learned the basics from the Heintz/Parry *College Accounting* text, continued their accounting and business education, and are now pursuing successful careers in the business world. As you will see, an accounting education can lead to a variety of careers.

Profiles in Accounting

Michael Burdish
Payroll Compliance
Auditor

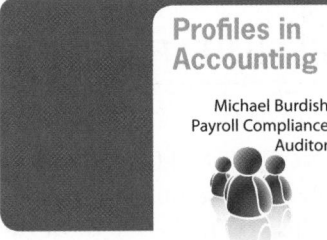

Michael Burdish graduated with an associate degree in accounting with honors from The College of Westchester. Michael excelled in his studies in accounting and knew this was the field for him. After graduation, Michael was hired as a payroll compliance auditor for an accounting firm. He is part of the team that audits companies and contractors that hire union members. The focus of the audits is to ensure that the correct amounts of benefits are paid. According to Michael he really enjoys his work. He especially likes meeting many new people and having new experiences. Michael intends to further his education and complete his baccalaureate degree in accounting.

SELF-STUDY QUESTIONS AND U REVU EXERCISES HELP YOU CHECK YOUR UNDERSTANDING

If you want to know how well you understand the chapter's information, watch for these banners and test yourself:

U REVU   Complete U REVU-1 on **page 154** to test your basic understanding of LO1

Throughout each chapter, the U REVU banners let you know when to test your basic understanding of the section you have completed.

SELF-STUDY QUESTIONS AND EXERCISES

Find the true/false and multiple choice questions and U REVU exercises section by looking for this banner. Be sure to note the "LO" by each question/exercise. That will help you find the coverage in the chapter.

ANSWERS TO SELF-STUDY QUESTIONS AND EXERCISES

Once you have tested yourself using the Self-Study Questions and Exercises, you will find the answers under this banner at the end of the chapter.

KEY POINTS TO REMEMBER HELP YOU REVIEW QUICKLY

In the end-of-chapter section, at the beginning of the Self-Study content, each of the chapter's Learning Objectives is repeated along with the core information covered in the chapter. This information will help you when you are working on your assignments and when you are studying for a test.

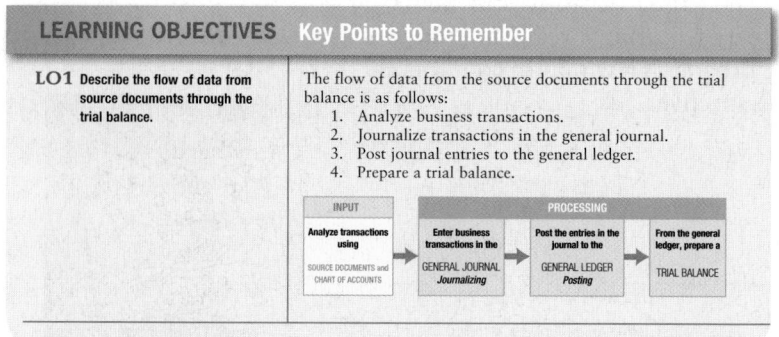

COMPREHENSIVE PROBLEMS PULL CONTENT ALTOGETHER

Following Chapter 6, the first Comprehensive Problem gives you a chance to see how well you understand the coverage of Part 1. After Chapter 15, the second Comprehensive Problem checks your understanding of the content in Parts 1–3. Depending on whether or not you've studied special journals (Chapter 12), this second one gives you two different choices for solving the problem.

CENGAGENOW HELPS YOU WORK AND LEARN MORE EFFICIENTLY

Ask your instructor about getting access to this powerful Web site.

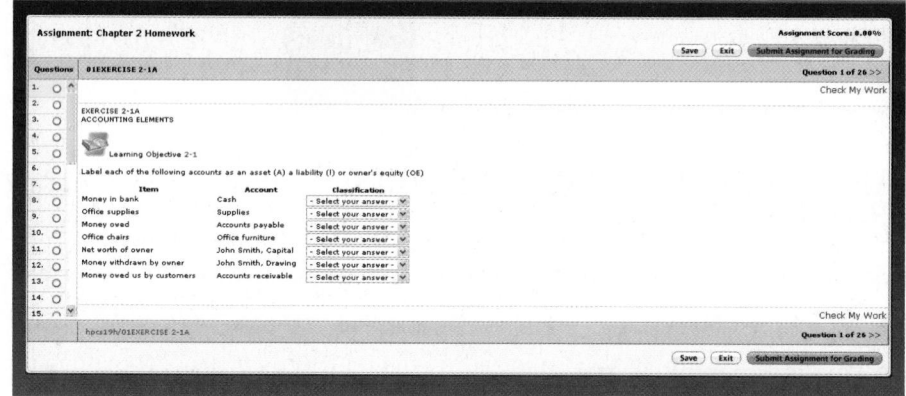

CengageNOW for Heintz/Parry's *College Accounting* online learning system helps you make the most of every minute of study and handle homework more efficiently. With CengageNOW's personalized study plans, you focus only on the areas of challenge to you with a variety of interactive learning tools to ensure you are prepared with the accounting skills most important for your future. Homework management tools help you efficiently complete homework assignments necessary to earn a successful grade in the course.

THE STUDY GUIDE PROVIDES MORE PRACTICE; WORKING PAPERS SHORTEN YOUR HOMEWORK TIME

The Heintz and Parry 20e Study Guide and Working Papers for Chapters 1–15 and the Combination Journal Module (ISBN-10: 0538737042, ISBN-13: 9780538737043) offers you the opportunity to reinforce your learning experience with brief discussions of each chapter's key points and learning objectives. In addition, the Study Guide provides a third set of "C" assignments, which consists of review questions, exercises, and problems similar to those at the end of each chapter. (The solutions to the Study Guide assignments are available separately, at the discretion of your instructor.) Included with the Study Guide are the Working Papers for the text's end-of-chapter assignments. Journals, ledgers, work sheets, and other documents are provided to make completing the assignments less time consuming for you. Ask your instructor about this helpful resource.

OTHER SUPPLEMENTAL MATERIALS ENHANCE YOUR UNDERSTANDING

Student Supplements and Resources	ISBN	Authors, Affiliations, Description
Student Web Site		Now mastering accounting concepts is easier than ever with the rich array of learning resources at the Heintz/Parry's *College Accounting*, 20e interactive companion Web site. Designed specifically to help you learn the most from your course and earn the grade you want, this Web site's interactive study center features chapter-by-chapter PowerPoint® lecture presentation slides, online quizzes, flashcards, outlines, key terms, and a final exam, as well as links to accounting resources, and more. These resources will help you develop the skills you need for progress now and success throughout the future!
Klooster & Allen General Ledger Software and Data Files CD-ROM	0538750693 9780538750691	Gain first-hand experience in working with full-functioning general ledger software. Use this proven software with selected problems in the main text that are clearly **identified by icons.** You'll learn to work with opening balances, to interpret a chart of accounts, and to set up functions to complete problems.
Peachtree and QuickBooks Data Files for Comprehensive Problems CD-ROM	0538476168 9780538476164	These data sets allow you to complete the requirements of the Comprehensive Problems using either Peachtree or QuickBooks software. (The software is not included on this CD-ROM.)
Online Excel Spreadsheet Templates	0538753595 9780538753593	These new templates are provided for selected end-of-chapter exercises and problems **(designated by an icon** in the text). They will assist you as you set up and work the assignment. To help you stay on track, certain cells are coded to display a red asterisk when an incorrect answer is entered.
Using Peachtree Complete for Accounting (w/ CD-ROM)	0324665512 9780324665512	Glenn Owen, Allan Hancock College The textbook takes a user perspective by illustrating how accounting information is both used and created. In addition, the text uses proven and successful pedagogy to demonstrate the software's features and elicit student interaction. The text's foremost goal is to help you learn fundamental accounting concepts through the use of Peachtree and the analysis of business events. The content complements the first course in accounting.
Using QuickBooks Pro for Accounting (w/ CD-ROM)	0324664044 9780324664041	Glenn Owen, Allan Hancock College Similar in description to the Peachtree text above, this book introduces QuickBooks Pro.
Using Excel and Access for Accounting	0324594399 9780324594393	Glenn Owen, Allan Hancock College This textbook teaches how businesses use spreadsheets and databases in accounting. It serves as a primer explaining how to use these tools in solving real accounting problems.

Student Supplements and Resources	ISBN	Authors, Affiliations, Description
Trey's Fast Cleaning Service Practice Set with Student CD **(Appropriate for use after Chapter 7)**	0538753226 9780538753227	**Toni R. Hartley, Laurel Business Institute** This practice set uses accrual-basis accounting and features a sole proprietorship service business simulation. It reviews the accounting cycle and accounting for cash. The practice set can be solved manually, with Klooster & Allen General Ledger software, or with Peachtree software. The Student CD includes the installation files for both software packages as well as the relevant data files.
Coolspring Furnitue Practice Set with Student CD **(Appropriate for use after Chapter 12)**	053875074X 9780538750745	**Toni R. Hartley, Laurel Business Institute** Practice your accounting success, including working with payroll taxes, within this sole proprietorship merchandising business. The accompanying CD contains both Klooster & Allen General Ledger software, Peachtree software, and the data files to complete the practice set using either software program. The practice set may also be completed manually.

SPECIAL INFORMATION FOR INSTRUCTORS

In addition to the important pedagogical elements introduced to your students above, we have some new features and key changes that will enhance your course. Overall, these are:

- A greater use of portrait presentation of figures wherever possible

FIGURE 6-2 Linkages Between the Work Sheet, Statement of Owner's Equity, and Balance Sheet

- Improved readability (shorter paragraphs, more listings/steps for easier understanding, etc.)

The adjustment for merchandise inventory is done in two steps.

1. Remove the beginning inventory from the merchandise inventory account by making the following entry:

Income Summary	old	
Merchandise Inventory		old

2. Enter the ending inventory in the merchandise inventory account by making the following entry:

Merchandise Inventory	new	
Income Summary		new

- The owner's initial investment is now shown as an investment during the period, instead of the beginning of the period

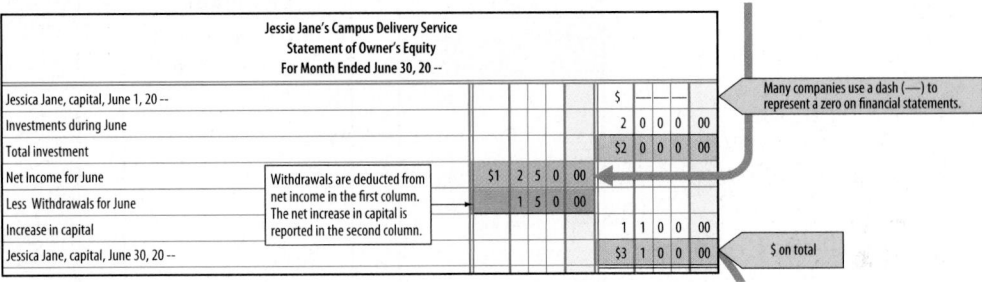

- New supplement—Excel templates (related exercises/problems are indicated by an icon in the text)

E 2-3A (LO3/4)

✓ Assets following (d): $22,000

EFFECTS OF TRANSACTIONS (BALANCE SHEET ACCOUNTS) Alice Stern started a business. During the first month (February 20--), the following transactions occurred. Show the effect of each transaction on the accounting equation: *Assets = Liabilities + Owner's Equity.* After each transaction, show the new totals.

(a) Invested cash in the business, $20,000.
(b) Bought office equipment on account, $3,500.
(c) Bought office equipment for cash, $1,200.
(d) Paid cash on account to supplier in transaction (b), $1,500.

By chapter:

Ch. 1—We have added brief coverage of International Financial Reporting Standards (IFRS) and forensic accounting.

- **Forensic Accounting.** Forensic accounting is a rapidly growing segment of accounting practice. It includes fraud detection, fraud prevention, litigation support, business valuations, expert witness services, and other investigative activities. Public accounting firms offer forensic accounting services, but forensic accountants also work for insurance companies, banks, law enforcement agencies, and other organizations. By meeting certain requirements, and passing the Certified Fraud Examiner exam, a forensic accountant may earn a **Certified Fraud Examiner (CFE)** designation.

Ch. 2—Redesigned accounting equation clarifies the expanded owner's equity after students gain an understanding of the basic equation (A = L + OE); new color coding highlights key accounts by category.

Assets (Items Owned)			=	Liabilities (Amounts Owed)	+	Owner's Equity (Owner's Investment)				(Earnings)		
Cash +	Accounts Receivable +	Delivery Equipment	=	Accounts Payable	+	Jessica Jane, Capital	−	Jessica Jane, Drawing	+	Revenues −	Expenses	Description
$750		$2,100		$600		$2,000				$ 500	$250	
(h)	+ $600									+ 600		Deliv. Fees
$750 +	$600 +	$2,100	=	$600	+	$2,000			+	$1,100 −	$250	
$3,450			=					$3,450				

Ch. 3—Redesigned owner's equity umbrella features new color coding for greater clarity.

FIGURE 3-2 The Accounting Equation and the Owner's Equity Umbrella

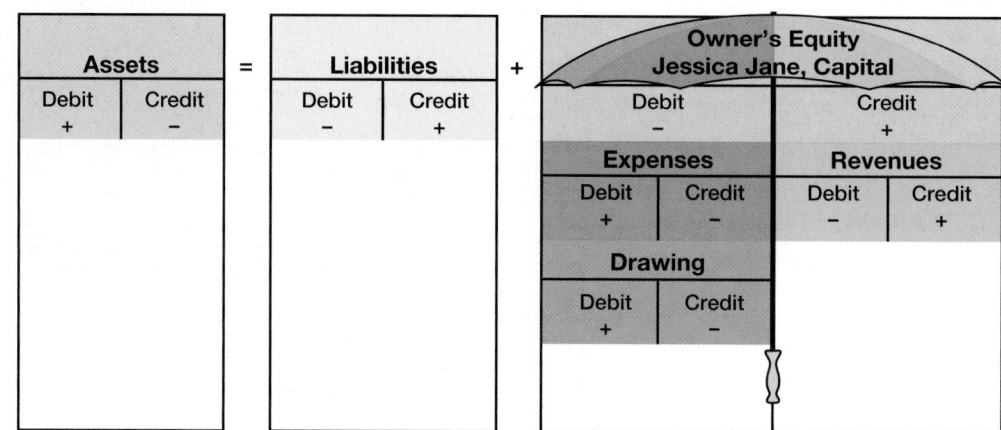

The color coding ties the narrative information with the T account presentation.

Analysis. This payment decreases the asset, Cash, and decreases the liability, Accounts Payable. Debit Accounts Payable and credit Cash for $300.

FIGURE 3-8 Transaction (d): Payment on Account

Assets		=	Liabilities		+	Owner's Equity	
Debit +	Credit −		Debit −	Credit +		Debit −	Credit +
Cash			Accounts Payable			Jessica Jane, Capital	
Bal. 800	(d) 300		(d) 300	Bal. 900			Bal. 2,000
Bal. 500				Bal. 600			
Delivery Equipment							
Bal. 2,100							
$2,600		=	$600		+	$2,000	
$2,600		=			$2,600		

Ch. 4—Financial statement illustration has been added to the demonstration problem. This helps students tie knowledge from earlier chapters together with information presented in the chapter.

4.

George Fielding, Financial Planning Consultant
Income Statement
For Month Ended December 31, 20 --

Revenue:													
Proffessional fees								$6	5	0	0	00	
Expenses:													
Wages expense	$1	2	0	0	00								
Rent expense	1	0	0	0	00								
Telephone expense		1	0	0	00								
Utilities expense			7	5	00								
Charitable contributions expense		1	0	0	00								
Automobile expense			6	0	00								
Total expenses								2	5	3	5	00	
Net income								$3	9	6	5	00	

George Fielding, Financial Planning Consultant
Statement of Owner's Equity
For Month Ended December 31, 20 --

George Fielding, capital, December 1, 20 --							$					
Investments during December							20	0	0	0	00	
Total investment							$20	0	0	0	00	
Net income for December	$3	9	6	5	00							
Less withdrawals for December	1	1	0	0	00							
Increase in capital							2	8	6	5	00	
George Fielding, Capital, December 1, 20 --							$22	8	6	5	00	

George Fielding, Financial Planning Consultant
Balance Sheet
December 31, 20 --

Assets						Liabilities					
Cash	$22	7	6	5	00	Accounts payable	$	1	8	0	00
Office Supplies		2	8	0	00	Owner's equity					
						George Fielding, capital	22	8	6	5	00
Total assets	$23	0	4	5	00	Total liabilities and owner's equity	$23	0	4	5	00

Ch. 5—Journal entries for the adjusting entries are now shown with T account presentations; chapter content presentation has been revised to cover posting of adjusting entries before work sheet coverage—this makes skipping work sheet coverage easier for those wanting to do so; for those using the work sheet, we enhanced the linkage between work sheet adjustments and adjusting entries. In the appendix, graphs have been added to the depreciation method examples to assist visual learners.

Ch. 6—Illustration of the closing process has been enhanced.

FIGURE 5-7 Adjustment for Unpaid Wages

FIGURE 6-8 Closing Entries in Journal Form

LEARNING KEY

Each individual revenue, expense, and drawing account must be closed.

Comprehensive Problem—New data sets have been added so that students can complete the problem using either Peachtree or QuickBooks software or the Klooster & Allen General Ledger software.

Ch. 7—Coverage of lapping and kiting has been added to the cash internal control section.

Ch. 8—Payroll information has been revised to be more current; to assist in understanding the link between the payroll register and related journal entries, cross-reference coding has been added.

PAYROLL REGISTER (RIGHT SIDE)   20--

	DEDUCTIONS								NET PAY
FEDERAL INCOME TAX	SOCIAL SECURITY TAX	MEDICARE TAX	HEALTH INSURANCE	UNITED WAY	OTHER		TOTAL		
4 7 6 00	2 9 9 77	8 4 61	4 6 00	4 0 00	0 00	0 00	9 4 6 38		4 8 8 8 62
(2)	(3)	(4)	(5)	(6)					(7)

		DATE		DESCRIPTION	POST REF.	DEBIT	CREDIT	
(1)	5	Dec.	19	Wages and Salaries Expense		5 8 3 5 00		5
(2)	6			Employee Income Tax Payable			4 7 6 00	6
(3)	7			Social Security Tax Payable			2 9 9 77	7
(4)	8			Medicare Tax Payable			8 4 61	8
(5)	9			Health Insurance Premiums Payable			4 6 00	9
(6)	10			United Way Contributions Payable			4 0 00	10
(7)	11			Cash			4 8 8 8 62	11
	12			Payroll for week ended Dec. 19				12

Ch. 9—Payroll information has been revised to be more current; brief coverage of Form I-9 (Employment Eligibility Verification) has been added; callouts have been added to several forms to enhance clarity.

FIGURE 9-10 Wage and Tax Statement (Form W-2)

Ch. 10—Expanded coverage of sales discounts, including a new figure illustrating the concept and accounting for sales when there are sales taxes and cash discounts.

Figure 10-11 shows how (1) a sale on account followed by (2) collection with a cash discount affects the accounts receivable, sales, and cash accounts.

FIGURE 10-11 Sales on Account → Collection with Cash Discount

In a more realistic situation, we must compute net sales and cost of goods sold, in order to compute gross profit. Multiple steps are involved. To illustrate, we use three of the four new accounts described in Chapter 10, the four new accounts described in this chapter, and the merchandise inventory balances. Assume that Northern Micro has the following sales, purchases, and merchandise inventory balances for the year ended December 31, 20--:

Ch. 11—Impact of sales discounts has been added to the gross profit coverage.

From Chapter 10	Sales	$201,500
	Sales returns and allowances	1,200
	Sales discounts	1,000

From Chapter 11	Purchases	105,000
	Purchases returns and allowances	800
	Purchases discounts	1,000
	Freight-in	300
	Merchandise inventory, January 1, 20--	26,000
	Merchandise inventory, December 31, 20--	18,000

Figure 11-7 uses these balances to compute net sales, net purchases, cost of goods sold, and gross profit. The following four steps in computing gross profit are labeled in the figure:

STEP 1 Compute net sales.

(Sales – Sales Returns and Allowances – Sales Discounts)

Ch. 14—Cost of goods sold illustration has been added to the demonstration problem.

3.

Ch. 15—Sales discounts has been added to the demonstration problem; unearned revenue has been added to selected problems.

P 15-10A (LO5/6)

✓ Net income: $10,610; Post-closing trial bal. col. totals: $79,650

WORK SHEET, ADJUSTING, CLOSING, AND REVERSING ENTRIES Ellis Fabric Store shows the trial balance on page 601 as of December 31, 20-1.

At the end of the year, the following adjustments need to be made:

(a and b) Merchandise inventory as of December 31, $28,900.
(c) Unused supplies on hand, $1,350.
(d) Insurance expired, $300.
(e) Depreciation expense for the year, $500.
(f) Wages earned but not paid (Wages Payable), $480.
(g) Unearned revenue on December 31, 20-1, $1,000.

Comprehensive Problem 2—A significant reduction in number of transactions required has been made in Part 1—thus decreasing redundancy.

COMPREHENSIVE PROBLEM 2: ACCOUNTING CYCLE WITH SUBSIDIARY LEDGERS, PART 1

During the second half of December 20-1, TJ's Specialty Shop engaged in the following transactions:

Dec. 16	Received payment from Lucy Greene on account, $1,960.
16	Sold merchandise on account to Kim Fields, $160, plus sales tax of $8. Sale No. 640.
17	Returned merchandise to Evans Essentials for credit, $150.
18	Issued Check No. 813 to Evans Essentials in payment of December 1 balance of $1,250, less the credit received on December 17.
19	Sold merchandise on account to Lucy Greene, $620, plus tax of $31. Sale No. 641.
22	Received payment from John Dempsey on account, $1,560.
23	Issued Check No. 814 for the purchase of supplies, $120. (Debit Supplies)
24	Purchased merchandise on account from West Wholesalers, $1,200. Invoice No. 465, dated December 24, terms n/30.

Instructor Supplements and Resources	ISBN	Authors, Affiliations, Description
CengageNOW		NEW CengageNOW for Heintz/Parry's College Accounting online teaching and learning system provides the ultimate in flexibility and ease of use with the results you want NOW to ensure your students are building skills for the future. Save time as you efficiently plan your course, teach and reinforce content with interactive learning tools and personalized study plans, and grade results based on AACSB accreditation standards.
Solutions Manual Chapters 1–15 + Combination Journal Module	053875088X 9780538750882	James Heintz and Robert Parry This printed version contains the complete, carefully verified solutions for all text assignments. Accounting rulings are used where appropriate. (*Note:* These are also the solutions to the working papers.) The solutions manual is also available on the Instructor's Resource CD-ROM and the Instructor's Web site, which are described below.
Study Guide Solutions Chapters 1–9 + Combination Journal Module Chapters 10-15	0538750715 9780538750714 0538750723 9780538750721	James Heintz and Robert Parry These solutions cover all set "C" assignments found in the Study Guide. **These may be packaged with the Study Guide at the instructor's discretion.**
Solution Transparencies Chapters 1–15 + Combination Journal Module	0538752521 9780538752527	James Heintz and Robert Parry Contains solutions for the Series A & B Exercises and Problems, Mastery Problems, Challenge Problems, and Comprehensive Problems in the text. Where appropriate, solutions appear on accounting rulings.

Instructor Supplements and Resources	ISBN	Authors, Affiliations, Description
Test Bank Chapters 1–15 + Combination Journal Module	0538752548 9780538752541	Revised and verified to ensure accuracy, this printed version of the test bank includes questions clearly identified by Learning Objectives, level of difficulty, and AACSB standards to allow greater guidance in developing assessments and evaluating student progress. Question types include true/false, multiple choice, and problems. The complete test bank in both the Microsoft Word and ExamView® testing software versions is available on the Instructor's Resource CD-ROM, which is listed below.
Instructor's Resource Guide Chapters 1–15 + Combination Journal Module	0538754389 9780538754385	This guide contains a wealth of resources to help instructors create an exciting and productive classroom experience. Included are enhanced chapter outlines and teaching tips; references to exhibits, PowerPoint® slides, and teaching transparencies; suggested enrichments and activities; check figures for text assignments; pretests tied to Learning Objectives; and Ten Questions Your Students Will Always Ask to help anticipate student learning needs. This guide is also available on the Instructor's Resource CD-ROM, which is listed below.
Instructor's Resource CD-ROM with ExamView®	0538750650 9780538750653	This all-in-one tool places the resources you need to plan and teach at your fingertips in one convenient CD-ROM. You'll find the Solutions Manual, Test Bank in Microsoft Word and Examview® testing software, PowerPoint® lecture presentation slides, Instructor's Resource Guide, Instructor's solutions, Excel template solutions, Teaching Transparencies, and Inspector software for checking solutions using the accompanying Klooster & Allen General Ledger software.
Instructor's Web Site		Ensure a higher level of understanding and success with this comprehensive, resource-rich text support site. An interactive student study center provides interactive quizzes and online tools that encourage learning. Password-protected teaching resources, including the Instructor's Manual, Teaching Transparencies, PowerPoint® lecture presentations, Test Bank, Instructor's solutions Excel templates, and Solutions Manual, are easy to download. You can link to Web Work assignments, ideal for Internet research, assign online quizzes with solutions, or assign other interactive assignments to help students test themselves during study. It's everything you need to deliver the skills your students need to enhance their future.
Trey's Fast Cleaning Service Practice Set Key + Inspector CD-ROM	0538753234 9780538753234	Toni R. Hartley, Laurel Business Institute This Instructor's Key for the Trey's Fast Cleaning Service practice set includes the inspector CD, which contains the Klooster & Allen General Ledger solutions software for the practice set.
Coolspring Furniture Practice Set Key + Inspector CD-ROM	0538752750 9780538752756	Toni R. Hartley, Laurel Business Institute This Instructor's Key for the Coolspring Furniture practice set includes the inspector CD, which contains the Klooster & Allen General Ledger solutions software for the practice set.

Additional Resources

Integrated Accounting for Windows (and software)	0538747978 9780538747974	Dale Klooster and Warren Allen Quite possibly the easiest-to-understand learning program on the market, this textbook, with accompanying software, teaches students all the aspects of computerized accounting and the operating procedures for all Windows-based programs at the same time. The software was designed to be very similar to the commercial software packages used in business, which will help students hit the ground running when they get that first real job. With its updated design and improved directions, students won't become overwhelmed with the program.

DEDICATION

We are grateful to our wives, Celia Heintz and Jane Parry, and our children, Andrea Heintz, John Heintz, Jessica Jane Parry, and Mitch Parry, for their love, support, and assistance during the creation of this 20th edition. We especially appreciate Jessie Parry's willingness to let us use her name throughout the first six chapters.

ACKNOWLEDGMENTS

We thank the following individuals for their helpful contributions in assisting us in this revision of College Accounting.

Allan N. Aspelund, *Century College*

Lelia Austin, *Lake City Community College*

Anne Bikofsky, *The College of Westchester*

Juanita Garza Blankenship, *Del Mar College*

Jane Bloom, *Palm Beach Community College*

Anna Boulware, *St. Charles Community College*

Dan Carroll, *Miami University—Hamilton and Middletown*

Susan S. Davis, *Green River Community College*

Judith A. Dixon, *York Technical College*

Sharon Doherty, *Lincoln College of Technology*

Larry J. Dragosavac, *Edison Community College*

Richard Dugger, *Kilgore College*

Charles D. Edwards, *Miami University—Hamilton and Middletown*

Marina Grau, *Houston Community College*

Becky Hancock, *El Paso Community College*

Toni R. Hartley, *Laurel Business Institute*

Patricia H. Holmes, *Des Moines Area Community College*

James Hurst, *National College—Lexington*

Dieter M. Kiefer, *American River College*

Susan S. Lafferty, *National College of Business and Technology*

Sonja Lolland, *Sierra College*

Ted Lynch, *Hocking College*

Alfonso J. Maldonado, *Laredo Community College*

Michael S. Manis, *College of the Desert*

James Mann, *Huntington Junior College*

Josephine M. Mathias, *Mercer County Community College*

Marc Newman, *Hocking College*

Sonia M. Gipson Rankin, *IIA College*

Aaron Reeves, *Saint Louis Community College—Forest Park*

Carolyn M. Seefer, *Diablo Valley College*

Tom Shaffer, *Spencerian College—Louisville*

Judy Toland, *Bucks County Community College*

Special recognition and thanks go to Anne Bikofsky, The College of Westchester, who provided the all-new Profiles in Accounting, which feature five of her former students. In addition, we express our appreciation to the following consultants for their quality assistance in providing supporting materials: Alice Sineath of Forsyth Technical Community College, Leonor Cabrera of Canada College of Business, James Emig of Villanova University, Susan Jefferson, Patti Hudepohl, and Mark Sears. We would also like to thank Richard Dugger of Kilgore College, Sheila Viel of the University of Wisconsin—Milwaukee, Bruce Gunning of Kent State University East Liverpool, and Robert Osborne of Ohio Dominican University for their diligent verification of the supplements.

CONTENTS IN BRIEF

CONTENTS

PART 2 ACCOUNTING FOR CASH AND PAYROLL 227

Practice Set: Trey's Fast Cleaning Service
This set uses accrual-basis accounting and features a service business operating as a sole proprietorship. It reviews the accounting cycle and accounting for cash, utilizing general journals. It can be solved manually, with Klooster and Allen General Ledger software (provided), or with Peachtree software (provided). (Appropriate for use after Chapter 7.)

Practice Set: Coolspring Furniture
This set is a merchandising business operating as a sole proprietorship. It includes accounting for payroll and can be solved using either general journals or special journals. It can be solved manually, with Klooster and Allen General Ledger software (provided), or Peachtree software (provided). Appropriate for use after Chapters 10 and 11, and Chapter 12 if special journals are being covered. The practice set includes content covered through Chapter 15, where students will be asked to prepare a simple income statement and balance sheet.

Accounting for a Service Business

PART 1

Add Some Color to Your Learning!

Throughout the text, you will be introduced to many important terms and types of accounts. To help you learn the different terms and types of accounts, we have coded many of them using the following color key in Part 1:

Introduction to Accounting

Need a private jet to get away for the weekend, attend a business meeting, or visit Mom? Call Jets.com. Established in 1999, Jets.com serves as a broker for private jet services. Call or go online, and its technology will automatically send your trip request/itinerary to a network of approved operators who will locate available aircraft. Operators will competitively bid for your business, resulting in significant savings and increased aircraft options for you.

In addition to a system that links customers with private jet service, Jets.com needs a system to account for its business transactions. Thus, it employs accounting professionals who understand the accounting process and generally accepted accounting principles.

Welcome to the world of accounting. We are delighted that you have decided to join us. A solid foundation in accounting concepts and techniques will serve you well. This is true whether you accept a professional position in accounting, work for or own a business, or simply seek a better understanding of your personal finances.

Oh, and what does it cost to take a private jet to the Super Bowl? Rates run from $2,000 to $7,000 per hour on the busiest weekend of the year.

LEARNING OBJECTIVES

Careful study of this chapter should enable you to:

LO1 Describe the purpose of accounting.

LO2 Describe the accounting process.

LO3 Define GAAP and describe the process used by FASB to develop these principles.

LO4 Define three types of business ownership structures.

LO5 Classify different types of businesses by activities.

LO6 Identify career opportunities in accounting.

Accounting is the language of business. You must learn this language to understand the impact of economic events on a specific company. Common, everyday terms have very precise meanings when used in accounting. For example, you have probably heard terms like asset, liability, revenue, expense, and net income. Take a moment to jot down how you would define each of these terms. After reading and studying Chapter 2, compare your definitions with those developed in this text. This comparison will show whether you can trust your current understanding of accounting terms. Whether you intend to pursue a career in accounting or simply wish to understand the impact of business transactions, you need a clear understanding of this language.

THE PURPOSE OF ACCOUNTING

LO1 Describe the purpose of accounting.

The purpose of accounting is to provide financial information about the current operations and financial condition of a business to individuals, agencies, and organizations. As shown in Figure 1-1, owners, managers, creditors, and government agencies all need accounting information. Other users of accounting information include customers, clients, labor unions, stock exchanges, and financial analysts.

FIGURE 1-1 Users of Accounting Information

USER	INFORMATION NEEDED	DECISIONS MADE BY USERS
Owners—Present and future	Company's profitability and current financial condition.	If business is good, owners may consider making additional investments for growth. If business is poor, they may want to talk to management to find out why and may consider closing the business.
Managers—May or may not own business	Detailed measures of business performance.	Managers need to make operating decisions. How much and what kinds of inventory should be carried? Is business strong enough to support higher wages for employees?
Creditors—Present and future	Company's profitability, debt outstanding, and assets that could be used to secure debt.	Should a loan be granted to this business? If so, what amount of debt can the business support, and what interest rate should be charged?
Government Agencies—National, state, and local	Company's profitability, cash flows, and overall financial condition.	The IRS will decide how much income tax the business must pay. Local governments may be willing to adjust property taxes paid by the business to encourage it to stay in town.

THE ACCOUNTING PROCESS

LO2 Describe the accounting process.

Accounting is a system of gathering financial information about a business and reporting this information to users. The six major steps of the accounting process are analyzing, recording, classifying, summarizing, reporting, and interpreting (Figure 1-2). Computers are often used in the recording, classifying, summarizing, and reporting steps. Whether or not computers are used, the accounting concepts and techniques are the same. Information entered into the computer system must reflect a proper application of these concepts. Otherwise, the output will be meaningless.

FIGURE 1-2 The Accounting Process

Analyzing → Recording → Classifying → Summarizing → Reporting → Interpreting

- **Analyzing** is looking at events that have taken place and thinking about how they affect the business.

- **Recording** is entering financial information about events into the accounting system. Although this can be done with paper and pencil, most businesses use computers to perform routine record-keeping operations.

- **Classifying** is sorting and grouping similar items together rather than merely keeping a simple, diary-like record of numerous events.

- **Summarizing** is the aggregation of many similar events to provide information that is easy to understand. For example, a firm may buy and sell baseballs during the year. Summarizing provides information on the total baseballs bought and sold and the change in the number of baseballs held from the beginning to the end of the period.

- **Reporting** is telling the results. In accounting, it is common to use tables of numbers to report results.

- **Interpreting** is deciding the meaning and importance of the information in various reports. This may include ratio analysis to help explain how pieces of information relate to one another.

GENERALLY ACCEPTED ACCOUNTING PRINCIPLES (GAAP)

LO3 Define GAAP and describe the process used by FASB to develop these principles.

Soon after the stock market crash of 1929, the federal government established the Securities and Exchange Commission (SEC). The purpose of this government agency is to help develop standards for reporting financial information to stockholders. The SEC currently has authority over 12,000 companies listed on the major stock exchanges (New York, American, and NASDAQ). It has the power to require these firms to follow certain rules when preparing their financial statements. These rules are referred to as **generally accepted accounting principles (GAAP)**.

Rather than developing GAAP on its own, the SEC encouraged the creation of a private standard-setting body. It did so because it believed the private sector had better access to the resources and talent necessary to develop these standards. Since 1973, the Financial Accounting Standards Board (FASB) has filled this role. In developing accounting standards, FASB follows a specific process and relies on the advice of many organizations. When an accounting issue is identified, the following steps are followed:

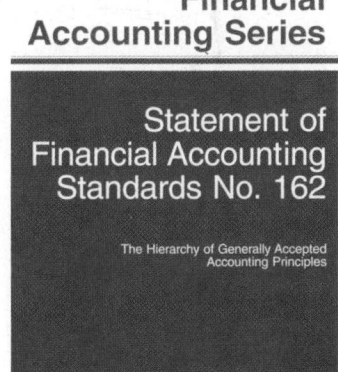

NO. 302 | MAY 2008
Financial Accounting Series

Statement of Financial Accounting Standards No. 162

The Hierarchy of Generally Accepted Accounting Principles

1. The issue is placed on FASB's agenda. This lets everyone know that the Board plans to develop a standard addressing this issue.

2. After researching an issue, FASB issues a **discussion memorandum**. This document identifies the pros and cons of various accounting treatments for an event.

3. To gather additional views on the issue, the Board will often hold **public hearings** around the country. Interested parties are invited to express their opinions at these hearings.

4. Following these hearings, the Board issues an **exposure draft**. This document explains the rules that FASB believes firms should follow in accounting for this event.

5. After considering feedback on the exposure draft, the Board issues a final **statement of financial accounting standards (SFAS)**.

Throughout this process, many parties participate by testifying at public hearings or by sending letters to the Board explaining why they agree or disagree with the proposed standard. These parties include the American Institute of Certified Public Accountants (AICPA), the American Accounting Association (AAA), the Institute of Management Accountants (IMA), the Financial Executives Institute (FEI), corporate executives and accountants, representatives from the investment community, analysts, bankers, industry associations, and the SEC and other government agencies. Clearly, FASB considers the views of a wide range of parties. By doing so, it maximizes the likelihood of developing and gaining acceptance of the most appropriate accounting and disclosure requirements.

The International Accounting Standards Board (IASB) issues accounting standards followed by many firms in countries outside the United States. These are called International Financial Reporting Standards (IFRS). In recent years, the IASB and FASB have worked together to try to minimize the differences in these standards. These standards may eventually converge into one set of standards used around the world.

THREE TYPES OF OWNERSHIP STRUCTURES

LO4 Define three types of business ownership structures.

One or more persons may own a business. Businesses are classified according to who owns them and the specific way they are organized. Three types of ownership structures are (1) sole proprietorship, (2) partnership, and (3) corporation (Figure 1-3). Accountants provide information to owners of all three types of ownership structures.

Most businesses in the United States operate as sole proprietorships or partnerships. However, corporations earn the highest amount of revenue.

FIGURE 1-3 Types of Ownership Structures—Advantages and Disadvantages

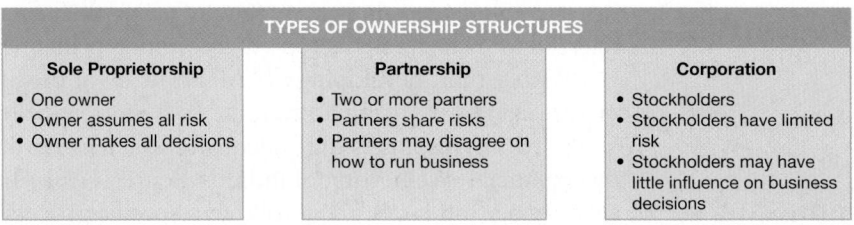

The largest corporations in the United States are known as the "Fortune 500."

SOLE PROPRIETORSHIP

A **sole proprietorship** is owned by one person. The owner is usually called a proprietor. The proprietor often manages the business. The owner assumes all risks for the business, and personal assets can be taken to pay creditors. The advantage of a sole proprietorship is that the owner can make all decisions.

PARTNERSHIP

A **partnership** is owned by more than one person. One or more partners may manage the business. Like proprietors, partners assume the risks for the business, and their assets may be taken to pay creditors. An advantage of a partnership is that owners share risks and decision making. A disadvantage is that partners may disagree about the best way to run the business.

CORPORATION

A **corporation** is owned by stockholders (or shareholders). Corporations may have many owners, and they usually employ professional managers. The owners' risk is usually limited to their initial investment, and they often have very little influence on the business decisions.

TYPES OF BUSINESSES

LO5 Classify different types of businesses by activities.

Businesses are classified according to the type of service or product provided. Some businesses provide a service. Others sell a product. A business that provides a service is called a **service business**. A business that buys a product from another business to sell to customers is called a **merchandising business**. A business that makes a product to sell is called a **manufacturing business**. You will learn about all three types of businesses in this book. Figure 1-4 lists examples of types of businesses organized by activity.

FIGURE 1-4 Types and Examples of Businesses Organized by Activities

SERVICE	MERCHANDISING	MANUFACTURING
Travel Agency	Department Store	Automobile Manufacturer
Computer Consultant	Pharmacy	Furniture Maker
Physician	Grocery Store	Toy Factory

A BROADER VIEW

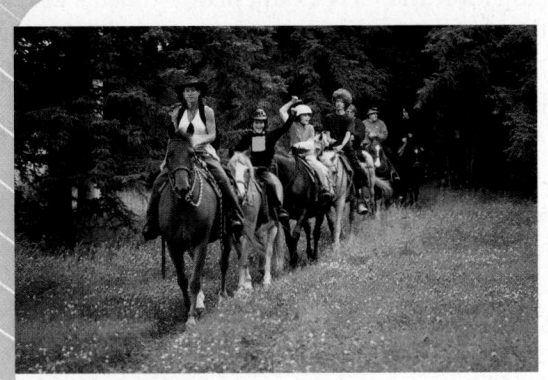

DESIGN PICS INC/PHOTOLIBRARY

All Kinds of Businesses Need Accounting Systems

Even small businesses like those that provide guided horse-back tours of the Rocky Mountains need good accounting systems. Proper records must be maintained for the cost of the horses, feed, food served, tour guides' salaries, and office expenses. Without this information, the company would not know how much to charge and whether a profit is made on these trips.

CAREER OPPORTUNITIES IN ACCOUNTING

LO6 Identify career opportunities in accounting.

Accounting offers many career opportunities. The positions described below require varying amounts of education, experience, and technological skill.

ACCOUNTING CLERKS

Businesses with large quantities of accounting tasks to perform daily often employ **accounting clerks** to record, sort, and file accounting information. Often, accounting clerks will specialize in cash, payroll, accounts receivable, accounts payable, inventory, or purchases. As a result, they are involved with only a small portion of the total accounting responsibilities for the firm. Accounting clerks usually have at least one year of accounting education.

BOOKKEEPERS AND PARA-ACCOUNTANTS

Bookkeepers generally supervise the work of accounting clerks, help with daily accounting work, and summarize accounting information. In small-to-medium-sized businesses, the bookkeeper may also help managers and owners interpret the accounting information. Bookkeepers usually have one to two years of accounting education and experience as an accounting clerk.

Para-accountants provide many accounting, auditing, or tax services under the direct supervision of an accountant. A typical para-accountant has a two-year degree or significant accounting and bookkeeping experience.

ACCOUNTANTS

The difference between accountants and bookkeepers is not always clear, particularly in smaller companies where bookkeepers also help interpret the accounting information. In large companies, the distinction is clearer. Bookkeepers focus on the processing of accounting data. **Accountants** design the accounting information system and focus on analyzing and interpreting information. They also look for important trends in the data and study the impact of alternative decisions.

Most accountants enter the field with a college degree in accounting. In fact, since many states require 150 credit hours to sit for the CPA exam, many students are also earning a master's degree in accounting before entering the profession. Accountants are employed in public accounting, private (managerial) accounting, and governmental and not-for-profit accounting (Figure 1-5).

FIGURE 1-5 Accounting Careers

ACCOUNTING CAREERS		
Public Accounting • Auditing • Taxation • Management Advisory services	**Private Accounting** • Accounting information systems • Financial Accounting • Cost Accounting • Budgeting • Tax Accounting • Internal Auditing	**Governmental and Not-for-Profit Accounting**

Public Accounting

Public accountants offer services in much the same way as doctors and lawyers. The public accountant can achieve professional recognition as a **Certified Public Accountant (CPA)**. This is done by meeting certain educational and experience requirements as determined by each state and passing a uniform examination prepared by the American Institute of Certified Public Accountants.

Many CPAs work alone, while others work for local, regional, or national accounting firms that vary in scope and size. The largest public accounting firms in the United States are known as the "Big Four." They are Deloitte, Ernst & Young, KPMG, and PricewaterhouseCoopers.

Services offered by public accountants are listed below.

- **Auditing.** Auditing involves the application of standard review and testing procedures to be certain that proper accounting policies and practices have been followed. The purpose of the audit is to provide an independent opinion that the financial information about a business is fairly presented in a manner consistent with generally accepted accounting principles.

- **Taxation.** Tax specialists advise on tax planning, prepare tax returns, and represent clients before governmental agencies such as the Internal Revenue Service.

- **Management Advisory Services.** Given the financial training and business experience of public accountants, many businesses seek their advice on a wide variety of managerial issues. Often, accounting firms are involved in designing computerized accounting systems.

- **Forensic Accounting.** Forensic accounting is a rapidly growing segment of accounting practice. It includes fraud detection, fraud prevention, litigation support, business valuations, expert witness services, and other investigative activities. Public accounting firms offer forensic accounting services, but forensic accountants also work for insurance companies, banks, law enforcement agencies, and other organizations. By meeting certain requirements, and passing the Certified Fraud Examiner exam, a forensic accountant may earn a **Certified Fraud Examiner (CFE)** designation.

In 2002, the **Sarbanes-Oxley Act (SOX)** was passed by Congress to help improve reporting practices of public companies. The act was in response to accounting scandals at firms like Enron, WorldCom, Cendant, Xerox, and others. Key provisions of SOX are listed below.

- The Public Company Accounting Oversight Board (PCAOB) was created to enforce SOX rules and regulations. The PCAOB also has authority to set auditing standards for public company audits and to perform inspections of auditing firms.

- External auditors are required to report on the effectiveness of a public company's accounting procedures.

- Auditing firms are prohibited from offering many nonaudit services to their public audit clients.

- Auditing firms must rotate audit partners off audit engagements every five years.

- The CEO and CFO must personally certify that the financial statements are accurate.

It is difficult to guarantee that information provided in financial statements is always complete and accurate. These measures are a step in the right direction. If our economy and financial markets are to function properly, information provided in financial statements must be reliable.

Private (Managerial) Accounting

Many accountants are employees of private business firms. The **controller** oversees the entire accounting process and is the principal accounting officer of the company. Private or managerial accountants perform a wide variety of services for the business. These services are listed below.

- **Accounting Information Systems.** Accountants in this area design and implement manual and computerized accounting systems.

- **Financial Accounting.** Based on the accounting data prepared by the bookkeepers and accounting clerks, accountants prepare various reports and financial statements and help in analyzing operating, investing, and financing decisions.

- **Cost Accounting.** The cost of producing specific products or providing services must be measured. Further analysis is also done to determine whether the products and services are produced in the most cost-effective manner.

- **Budgeting.** In the budgeting process, accountants help managers develop a financial plan.

- **Tax Accounting.** Instead of hiring a public accountant, a company may have its own accountants. They focus on tax planning, preparation of tax returns, and dealing with the Internal Revenue Service and other governmental agencies.

- **Internal Auditing.** Internal auditors review the operating and accounting control procedures adopted by management to make sure the controls are adequate and are being followed. They also monitor the accuracy and timeliness of the reports provided to management and to external parties.

A managerial accountant can achieve professional status as a **Certified Management Accountant (CMA)**. This is done by passing a uniform examination offered by the Institute of Management Accountants. An internal auditor can achieve professional recognition as a **Certified Internal Auditor (CIA)** by passing the uniform examination offered by the Institute of Internal Auditors.

Governmental and Not-for-Profit Accounting

Thousands of governmental and not-for-profit organizations (states, cities, schools, churches, and hospitals) gather and report financial information. These organizations employ a large number of accountants. Since these entities are not profit oriented, the rules are somewhat different for governmental and not-for-profit organizations. However, many accounting procedures are similar to those found in profit-seeking enterprises.

JOB OPPORTUNITIES

Job growth in some areas will be much greater than in others. Newspaper advertisements often indicate that accountants and accounting clerks are expected to have computer skills. Computer skills definitely increase the opportunities available to you in your career. Almost every business needs accountants, accounting clerks, and bookkeepers. Figure 1-6 shows the expected growth for different types of businesses. Notice that growth will be greatest in health care services. Chapters 2 through 9 introduce accounting skills that you will need to work in a service business, like health care. Chapter 10 begins the discussion of merchandising businesses. Accounting for manufacturing businesses is addressed in the last chapters of the book.

Figure 1-7 shows the expected demand for accounting skills. A 12.5% increase in demand is expected for bookkeeping, accounting, and auditing clerks. These types of

FIGURE 1-6 Expected Growth

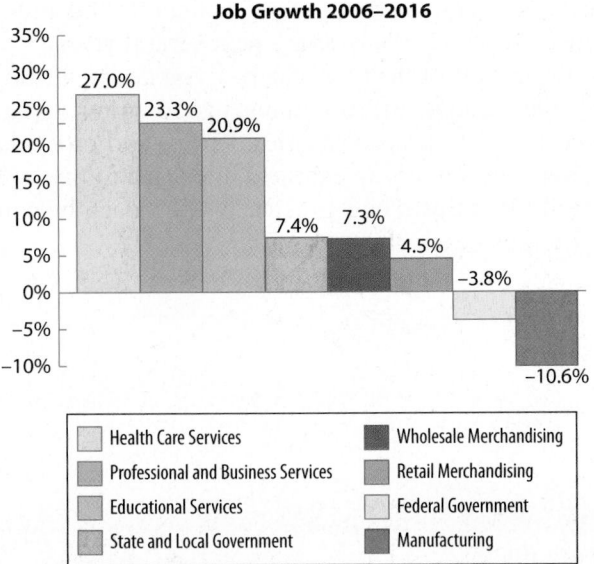

The growth in the number of new jobs from 2006 to 2016 will vary according to industry. The major area of growth will be in health care services. Businesses providing educational, health care, and professional/business services are expected to have the strongest employment growth. Moderate growth is expected in merchandising businesses and state and local governments. Employment in manufacturing and the federal government is expected to decline. Total employment for all industry sectors will increase 10.4%.

Source: U.S. Department of Labor—Bureau of Labor Statistics (http://www.bls.gov/news.release/ ecopro.t01.htm) as of January 20, 2009.

FIGURE 1-7 Expected Demand

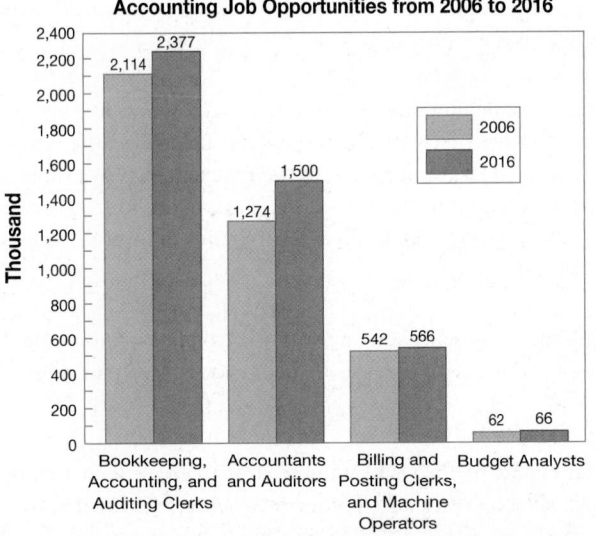

The highest number of jobs available will be for bookkeepers, accounting and auditing clerks, and accountants and auditors. The growth for each area shown from 2006 to 2016 will be as follows:

	Thousands	**Percentage**
Accountants and auditors	226	17.7%
Budget analysts	4	7.1%*
Bookkeeping, accounting, and auditing clerks	264*	12.5%*
Billing and posting clerks, and machine operators	24	4.4%

*Differences due to rounding.

Source: Arlene Dohm and Lynn Shniper, "Occupational Employment Projections to 2016," *Monthly Labor Review*, November 2007.

positions will offer the highest number of job opportunities over the next several years. The next highest demand is for accountants and auditors, and this demand is expected to increase by 17.7% over the next several years.

Regardless of the type of career you desire, writing skills are important in business and your personal life. Becoming a good writer requires practice and a strategy for the process used to prepare memos, letters, and other documents. On pages 12, 13, and 14, Ken Davis offers an excellent approach to managing your writing. Take a moment to read Ken's tips. Then, practice his approach by completing the writing assignments as you finish each chapter.

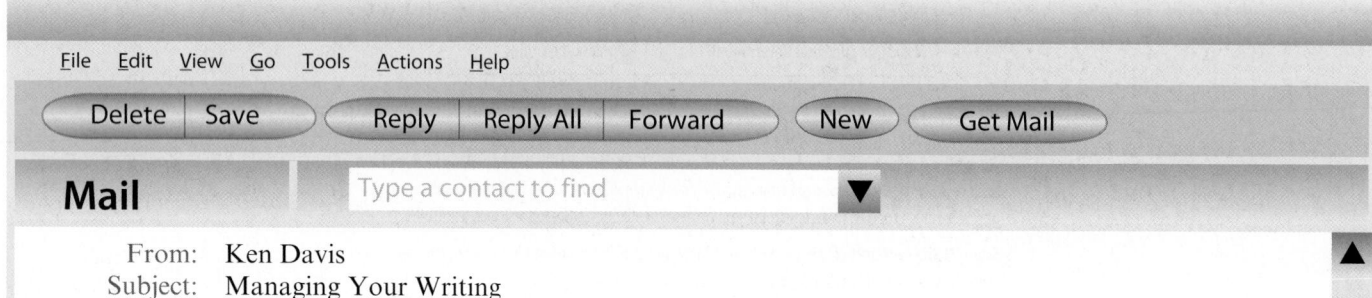

File   Edit   View   Go   Tools   Actions   Help

Delete | Save   Reply | Reply All | Forward   New   Get Mail

Mail   Type a contact to find   ▼

From: Ken Davis
Subject: Managing Your Writing
To: Accounting Students

Here's a secret: the business writing that you and I do—the writing that gets the world's work done—requires no special gift. It can be managed, like any other business process.

Managing writing is largely a matter of managing time. Writing is a process, and like any process it can be done efficiently or inefficiently. Unfortunately, most of us are pretty inefficient writers. That's because we try to get each word, each sentence, right the first time. Given a letter to write, we begin with the first sentence. We think about that sentence, write it, revise it, even check its spelling, before going on to the second sentence. In an hour of writing, we might spend 45 or 50 minutes doing this kind of detailed drafting. We spend only a few minutes on overall planning at the beginning and only a few minutes on overall revising at the end.

That approach to writing is like building a house by starting with the front door: planning, building, finishing—even washing the windows—before doing anything with the rest of the house. No wonder most of us have so much trouble writing.

Efficient, effective writers take better charge of their writing time. They *manage* their writing. Like building contractors, they spend time planning before they start construction. Once construction has started, they don't try to do all of the finishing touches as they go.

As the following illustration shows, many good writers break their writing process into three main stages: planning, drafting, and revising. They spend more time at the first and third stages than at the second. They also build in some "management" time at the beginning and the end, and some break time in the middle. To manage *your* writing time, try the following steps.

To Do List

✓ At the MANAGING stage (perhaps two or three minutes for a one-hour writing job), remind yourself that writing *can* be managed and that it's largely a matter of managing time. Plan your next hour.

At the PLANNING stage (perhaps 20 minutes out of the hour):

1. **Find the "we."** Define the community to which you and your reader belong. Then ask, "How are my reader and I alike and different?"—in knowledge, attitudes, and circumstances.

2. **Define your purpose.** Remember the advice a consultant once gave Stanley Tool executives: "You're not in the business of making drills: you're in the business of making holes." Too many of us lose sight of the difference between making drills and making holes when we write letters and memos. We focus on the piece of writing—the tool itself—not its purpose. The result: our writing often misses the chance to be as effective as it could be. When you're still at the planning stage, focus on the outcome you want, not on the means you will use to achieve it.

3. **Get your stuff together.** Learn from those times when you've turned a one-hour home-improvement project into a three- or four-hour job by having to make repeated trips to the hardware store for tools or parts. Before you start the drafting stage of writing, collect the information you need.

4. **Get your ducks in a row.** Decide on the main points you want to make. Then, make a list or rough outline placing your points in the most logical order.

At the DRAFTING STAGE (perhaps 5 minutes out of the hour):

5. **Do it wrong the first time.** Do a "quick and dirty" draft, without editing. Think of your draft as a "prototype," written not for the end user but for your own testing and improvement. Stopping to edit while you draft breaks your train of thought and keeps you from being a good writer. (*Hint:* If you are writing at a computer, try turning off the monitor during the drafting stage.)

At the BREAK STAGE (perhaps 5 minutes):

6. **Take a break and change hats.** Get away from your draft, even if for only a few minutes. Come back with a fresh perspective—the reader's perspective.

At the REVISING STAGE (perhaps 25 minutes):

7. **Signal your turns.** Just as if you were driving a car, you're leading your reader through new territory. Use "turn signals"—*and, in addition, but, however, or, therefore, because, for example*—to guide your reader from sentence to sentence.

8. **Say what you mean.** Put the point of your sentences in the subjects and verbs. For example, revise "There are drawbacks to using this accounting method" to "This accounting method has some drawbacks." You'll be saying what you mean, and you'll be a more effective communicator.

9. **Pay by the word.** Reading your memo requires work. If your sentences are wordy and you are slow to get to the point, the reader may decide that it is not worth the effort. Pretend you are paying the reader by the word to read your memo. Then, revise your memo to make it as short and to the point as possible.

10. **Translate into English.** Keep your words simple. (Lee Iacocca put both these tips in one "commandment of good management": "Say it in English and keep it short.") Remember that you write to express, not impress.

▼

11. **Finish the job.** Check your spelling, punctuation, and mechanics.

Finally, at the MANAGING STAGE again (2 to 3 minutes):

12. **Evaluate your writing process.** Figure out how to improve it next time.

By following these 12 steps, you can take charge of your writing time. Begin today to *manage your writing*. As a United Technologies Corporation advertisement in *The Wall Street Journal* admonished, "If you want to manage somebody, manage yourself. Do that well and you'll be ready to stop managing and start leading."

Dr. Kenneth W. Davis is Professor of English and Adjunct Professor of Communication Studies at Indiana University-Purdue University, Indianapolis. He is also president of Komei, Inc., a communication consulting and training company.

SELF-STUDY

LEARNING OBJECTIVES	Key Points to Remember
LO1 Describe the purpose of accounting.	The purpose of accounting is to provide financial information about a business to individuals and organizations.
LO2 Describe the accounting process.	The six major steps of the accounting process are analyzing, recording, classifying, summarizing, reporting, and interpreting.
LO3 Define GAAP and describe the process used by FASB to develop these principles.	Generally accepted accounting principles (GAAP) are the rules that businesses must follow when preparing financial statements. FASB takes the following steps to develop an accounting standard: 1. The issue is placed on the Board's agenda. 2. After researching the issue, a discussion memorandum is issued. 3. Public hearings are held. 4. An exposure draft is issued. 5. The statement of financial accounting standards is issued.
LO4 Define three types of business ownership structures.	Three types of business ownership structures are the sole proprietorship, the partnership, and the corporation.
LO5 Classify different types of businesses by activities.	Different types of businesses classified by activities are a service business, a merchandising business, and a manufacturing business.
LO6 Identify career opportunities in accounting.	Career opportunities in accounting include work in public accounting, private accounting, and governmental and not-for-profit accounting.

KEY TERMS

accountant (8)   Designs the accounting information system and focuses on analyzing and interpreting information.

accounting (4)   A system of gathering financial information about a business and reporting this information to users.

accounting clerk (8)   Records, sorts, and files accounting information.

accounting information systems (10)   Accountants in this area design and implement manual and computerized accounting systems.

analyzing (5)   Looking at events that have taken place and thinking about how they affect the business.

auditing (9)   Reviewing and testing to be certain that proper accounting policies and practices have been followed.

bookkeeper (8)   Generally supervises the work of accounting clerks, helps with daily accounting work, and summarizes accounting information.

budgeting (10)   The process in which accountants help managers develop a financial plan.

Certified Fraud Examiner (CFE) (9)   A forensic accountant who has passed the exam offered by the Association of Certified Fraud Examiners.

Certified Internal Auditor (CIA) (10)   An internal auditor who has achieved professional recognition by passing the uniform examination offered by the Institute of Internal Auditors.

Certified Management Accountant (CMA) (10)   An accountant who has passed an examination offered by the Institute of Management Accountants.

Certified Public Accountant (CPA) (9)   A public accountant who has met certain educational and experience requirements and has passed an examination prepared by the American Institute of Certified Public Accountants.

classifying (5)   Sorting and grouping similar items together rather than merely keeping a simple, diary-like record of numerous events.

controller (10)   The accountant who oversees the entire accounting process and is the principal accounting officer of a company.

corporation (7)   A type of ownership structure in which stockholders own the business. The owners' risk is usually limited to their initial investment, and they usually have very little influence on the business decisions.

cost accounting (10)   Determining the cost of producing specific products or providing services and analyzing for cost effectiveness.

discussion memorandum (5)   The first document issued by FASB when developing an accounting standard. This document identifies the pros and cons of various accounting treatments for an event.

exposure draft (6)   This document explains the rules that FASB believes firms should follow in accounting for a particular event. Based on the responses to the exposure draft, the Board will decide if any changes are necessary before issuing a final standard.

financial accounting (10)   Includes preparing various reports and financial statements and analyzing operating, investing, and financing decisions.

forensic accounting (9)   A specialized field that combines fraud detection, fraud prevention, litigation support, expert witnessing, business valuations, and other investigative activities.

generally accepted accounting principles (GAAP) (5)   Procedures and guidelines developed by the Financial Accounting Standards Board to be followed in the accounting and reporting process.

internal auditing (10)   Reviewing the operating and accounting control procedures adopted by management to make sure the controls are adequate and being followed; assuring that accurate and timely information is provided.

interpreting (5)   Deciding the meaning and importance of the information in various reports.

management advisory services (9)   Providing advice to businesses on a wide variety of managerial issues.

manufacturing business (7)   A business that makes a product to sell.

merchandising business (7)   A business that buys products to sell.

para-accountant (8)   A paraprofessional who provides many accounting, auditing, or tax services under the direct supervision of an accountant.

partnership (6)   A type of ownership structure in which more than one person owns the business.

public hearing (5)   Following the issuance of a discussion memorandum, public meetings are often held by FASB to gather opinions on the accounting issue.

recording (5)   Entering financial information about events affecting the company into the accounting system.

reporting (5)   Telling the results of the financial information.

Sarbanes-Oxley Act (SOX) (9)   An act passed by Congress to help improve reporting practices of public companies.

service business (7)   A business that provides a service.

sole proprietorship (6)   A type of ownership structure in which one person owns the business.

statement of financial accounting standards (SFAS) (6)   A standard issued by the Financial Accounting Standards Board. These standards must be followed when preparing financial statements.

summarizing (5)   Bringing the various items of information together to determine a result.

tax accounting (10)   Services focused on tax planning, preparing tax returns, and dealing with the Internal Revenue Service and other governmental agencies.

taxation (9)   See tax accounting.

APPLYING YOUR KNOWLEDGE

REVIEW QUESTIONS

LO1   1.   What is the purpose of accounting?

LO1   2.   Identify four user groups normally interested in financial information about a business.

LO2   3. Identify the six major steps of the accounting process and explain each step.

LO3   4. What are generally accepted accounting principles (GAAP)?

LO3   5. Describe the steps followed by the Financial Accounting Standards Board when developing an accounting standard.

LO3   6. What is the name of the organization that issues accounting standards followed by many firms in countries outside the United States?

LO4   7. Identify the three types of ownership structures and discuss the advantages and disadvantages of each.

LO5   8. Identify three types of businesses according to activities.

LO6   9. What are the main functions of an accounting clerk?

LO6   10. Name and describe three areas of specialization for a public accountant.

LO6   11. What is the purpose of the Sarbanes-Oxley Act?

LO6   12. Name and describe six areas of specialization for a managerial accountant.

SERIES A EXERCISES

E 1-1A (LO1)

PURPOSE OF ACCOUNTING Match the following users with the information needed.

1. Owners	a. Whether the firm can pay its bills on time
2. Managers	b. Detailed, up-to-date information to measure business performance (and plan for future operations)
3. Creditors	
4. Government agencies	c. To determine taxes to be paid and whether other regulations are met
	d. The firm's current financial condition

E 1-2A (LO2)

ACCOUNTING PROCESS List the six major steps of the accounting process in order (1–6) and define each.

_____	Recording
_____	Summarizing
_____	Reporting
_____	Analyzing
_____	Interpreting
_____	Classifying

SERIES B EXERCISES

E 1-1B (LO1)

PURPOSE OF ACCOUNTING Describe the kind of information needed by the users listed.

Owners (present and future)
Managers
Creditors (present and future)
Government agencies

E 1-2B **(LO2)**   **ACCOUNTING PROCESS** Match the following steps of the accounting process with
their definitions.

Analyzing	a. Telling the results
Recording	b. Looking at events that have taken place and thinking about
Classifying	how they affect the business
Summarizing	c. Deciding the importance of the various reports
Reporting	d. Aggregating many similar events to provide information that is
Interpreting	easy to understand
	e. Sorting and grouping like items together
	f. Entering financial information into the accounting system

 ## MANAGING YOUR WRITING

Take a moment to think about what it would be like to run your own business. If
you started a business, what would it be? Prepare a one-page memo that describes
the type of business you would enjoy the most. Would it be a service, merchandising,
or manufacturing business? Explain what form of ownership you would prefer
and why.

## Chapter 2

RICH ABRAHAMSON/FORT COLLINS COLORADOAN

Analyzing Transactions: The Accounting Equation

At Rob's Bike Courier Service in Fort Collins, Colorado, Rob believes "less is more." His small company doesn't "have a fleet of vehicles, just some pretty cool bicycles." His mission is providing successful bike delivery service, perfect for both traditional business delivery services and residential errands. Since January of 2005, Rob's Bike Courier Service has been the alternative to gas-powered vehicle delivery. Thus, besides great rates and friendly, reliable service, Rob offers earth-friendly service.

Currently, he delivers wholesale bagels from a mid-town baker to several downtown coffee shops. He does the same for another pastry chef. Rob also picks up recycling materials and will go to a customer's home to fix flat bike tires and make repairs.

Though his company is small, Rob still needs an accounting system to maintain records of his business transactions and to prepare financial statements. Currently, he uses Quickbooks®, an accounting program used by many small companies. In Chapters 2 through 6, we learn how to account for a service business like Rob's by using an example of a similar company: Jessie Jane's Campus Delivery Service.

LEARNING OBJECTIVES

Careful study of this chapter should enable you to:

LO1 Define the accounting elements.

LO2 Construct the accounting equation.

LO3 Analyze business transactions.

LO4 Show the effects of business transactions on the accounting equation.

LO5 Prepare and describe the purposes of a simple income statement, statement of owner's equity, and balance sheet.

LO6 Define the three basic phases of the accounting process.

The entire accounting process is based on one simple equation, called the accounting equation. In this chapter, you will learn how to use this equation to analyze business transactions. You also will learn how to prepare financial statements that report the effect of these transactions on the financial condition of a business.

THE ACCOUNTING ELEMENTS

LO1 Define the accounting elements.

Before the accounting process can begin, the entity to be accounted for must be defined. A **business entity** is an individual, association, or organization that engages in economic activities and controls specific economic resources. This definition allows the personal and business finances of an owner to be accounted for separately.

Three basic accounting elements exist for every business entity: assets, liabilities, and owner's equity. These elements are defined below.

ASSETS

LEARNING KEY

Pay close attention to the definitions for the basic accounting elements. A clear understanding of these definitions will help you analyze even the most complex business transactions.

Assets are items that are owned by a business and will provide future benefits. Examples of assets include cash, merchandise, furniture, fixtures, machinery, buildings, and land. Businesses may also have an asset called **accounts receivable**. This asset represents the amount of money owed to the business by its customers as a result of making sales "on account," or "on credit." Making sales on account simply means that the customers have promised to pay sometime in the future.

LIABILITIES

Liabilities represent something owed to another business entity. The amount owed represents a probable future outflow of assets as a result of a past event or transaction. Liabilities are debts or obligations of the business that can be paid with cash, goods, or services.

The most common liabilities are accounts payable and notes payable. An **account payable** is an unwritten promise to pay a supplier for assets purchased or services received. Acquiring assets or services by promising to make payments in the future is referred to as making a purchase "on account," or "on credit." Formal written promises to pay suppliers or lenders specified sums of money at definite future times are known as **notes payable**.

OWNER'S EQUITY

LEARNING KEY

The business entity's assets and liabilities are separate from the owner's nonbusiness assets and liabilities.

Owner's equity is the amount by which the business assets exceed the business liabilities. Other terms used for owner's equity include **net worth** and **capital**. If there are no business liabilities, the owner's equity is equal to the total assets.

The owner of a business may have business assets and liabilities as well as nonbusiness assets and liabilities. For example, the business owner probably owns a home, clothing, and a car, and perhaps owes the dentist for dental service. These are personal, nonbusiness assets and liabilities. According to the **business entity concept**, nonbusiness assets and liabilities are not included in the business entity's accounting records.

If the owner invests money or other assets in the business, the item invested is reclassified from a nonbusiness asset to a business asset. If the owner withdraws money or other assets from the business for personal use, the item withdrawn is reclassified from a business asset to a nonbusiness asset. These distinctions are important and allow the owner to make decisions based on the financial condition and results of the business apart from nonbusiness activities.

A BROADER VIEW

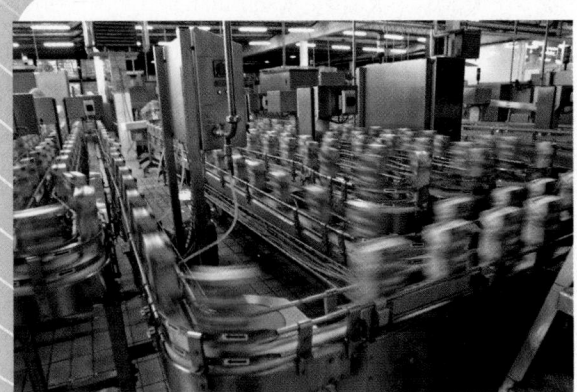

IMAGE COPYRIGHT MARK YUILL 2009. USED UNDER LICENSE FROM SHUTTERSTOCK.COM

Assets and the Cost of Products We Buy

Next time you buy something, think of all the assets a company needs to produce that product. If the product comes from a capital-intensive industry, one that requires heavy investments in assets, the company must price the product high enough to cover the cost of using the assets and replacing them when they wear out. For example, Procter & Gamble recently reported that the cost of property, plant, and equipment used for operating purposes came to over $38 billion.

U REVU

Complete U REVU-1 on **page 41** to test your basic understanding of LO1.

THE ACCOUNTING EQUATION

LO2 Construct the accounting equation.

The relationship between the three basic accounting elements—assets, liabilities, and owner's equity—can be expressed in the form of a simple equation known as the **accounting equation.**

Assets	=	Liabilities	+	Owner's Equity

This equation reflects the fact that both outsiders and insiders have an interest in the assets of a business.

- Liabilities represent the outside interests of creditors.

- Owner's equity represents the inside interests of owners.

Or, viewed another way,

The left side of the equation shows the assets.

The right side of the equation shows where the money came from to buy the assets.

When two elements are known, the third can always be calculated. For example, assume that assets on December 31 total $60,400. On that same day, the business liabilities consist of $5,400 owed for equipment. Owner's equity is calculated by subtracting total liabilities from total assets, $60,400 − $5,400 = $55,000.

LEARNING KEY

If you know two accounting elements, you can calculate the third element.

Total assets	$60,400
Total liabilities	−5,400
Owner's equity	$55,000

Assets	=	Liabilities	+	Owner's Equity
$60,400	=	$5,400	+	$55,000
$60,400	**=**	**$60,400**		

If during the next accounting period, assets increased by $10,000 and liabilities increased by $3,000, owner's equity must have increased by $7,000 ($10,000 – $3,000) as shown below.

	Assets	=	Liabilities	+	Owner's Equity
BB	$60,400		$5,400		$55,000
	+10,000	=	+3,000	+	+7,000
EB	$70,400	=	$8,400	+	$62,000
	$70,400	**=**	**$70,400**		

BB: Beginning balance
EB: Ending balance

Note also that after computing the ending balances for assets, liabilities, and owner's equity, the accounting equation remains in balance.

U REVU

Complete U REVU-2 on page 41 to test your basic understanding of LO2.

ANALYZING BUSINESS TRANSACTIONS

LO3 Analyze business transactions.

A **business transaction** is an economic event that has a direct impact on the business. A business transaction almost always requires an exchange between the business and another outside entity. We must be able to measure this exchange in dollars. Examples of business transactions include buying goods and services, selling goods and services, buying and selling assets, making loans, and borrowing money.

All business transactions affect the accounting equation through specific accounts. An **account** is a separate record used to summarize changes in each asset, liability, and owner's equity of a business. **Account titles** provide a description of the particular type of asset, liability, or owner's equity affected by a transaction.

Three basic questions must be answered when analyzing the effects of a business transaction on the accounting equation. These questions help address the steps in the accounting process discussed in Chapter 1.

1. **What happened?**
   - Make certain you understand the event that has taken place.

2. **Which accounts are affected?**
   - Identify the accounts that are affected.
   - Classify these accounts as assets, liabilities, or owner's equity.

3. **How is the accounting equation affected?**
   - Determine which accounts have increased or decreased.
   - Make certain that the accounting equation remains in balance after the transaction has been entered.

EFFECT OF TRANSACTIONS ON THE ACCOUNTING EQUATION

LO4 Show the effects of business transactions on the accounting equation.

In Chapters 2 through 6, we will focus on learning how to account for a business similar to Rob's Bike Courier Service, discussed in the chapter opener. In these chapters, we will focus on Jessie Jane's Campus Delivery Service. By studying Jessie's business transactions and accounting techniques, you will learn about business and accounting. A major advantage of studying accounting is that it helps you learn a great deal about business.

As explained above, we must first understand the economic substance of events. Then, we must determine how that information is entered into the accounting system. If Jessie does not understand the economic events affecting her delivery business and their impact on the accounting equation, the events will not be correctly entered into the accounting system.

Each transaction affects at least two accounts and one or more of the three basic accounting elements. A transaction increases or decreases specific asset, liability, or owner's equity accounts. Assume that the following transactions occurred during June 20--, the first month of operations for Jessie Jane's Campus Delivery Service.

Transaction (a): Investment by owner

> Remember, capital does not mean cash. The cash is shown in the cash account.

An Increase in an Asset Offset by an Increase in Owner's Equity. Jessica Jane opened a bank account with a deposit of $2,000 for her business. The new business now has $2,000 of the asset Cash. Since Jessie contributed the asset, the owner's equity element, Jessica Jane, Capital, increases by the same amount.

Assets (Items owned)	=	Liabilities (Amounts owed)	+	Owner's Equity (Owner's Investment)
Cash	=			Jessica Jane, Capital
(a) $2,000	=			$2,000

Transaction (b): Purchase of an asset for cash

An Increase in an Asset Offset by a Decrease in Another Asset. Jessie decided that the fastest and easiest way to get around campus and find parking is on a motor scooter. Thus, she bought a motor scooter (delivery equipment) for $1,200 cash. Jessie exchanged one asset, cash, for another, delivery equipment. This transaction reduces Cash and creates a new asset, Delivery Equipment.

LEARNING KEY

If transactions are entered correctly, the accounting equation always remains in balance.

Assets (Items owned)			=	Liabilities (Amounts owed)	+	Owner's Equity (Owner's Investment)
Cash	+	Delivery Equipment	=			Jessica Jane, Capital
$2,000						$2,000
(b) −1,200		+ $1,200				
$ 800	+	$1,200	=			$2,000
$2,000			=			$2,000

Transaction (c): Purchase of an asset on account

An Increase in an Asset Offset by an Increase in a Liability. Jessie hired a friend to work for her, which meant that a second scooter would be needed. Given Jessie's limited cash, she bought the dealer's demonstration model for $900. The seller agreed to allow Jessie to spread the payments over the next three months. This transaction increased an asset, Delivery Equipment, by $900 and increased the liability, Accounts Payable, by an equal amount.

	Assets (Items owned)		=	Liabilities (Amounts owed)	+	Owner's Equity (Owner's Investment)
	Cash +	Delivery Equipment	=	Accounts Payable	+	Jessica Jane, Capital
	$800	$1,200				$2,000
(c)		+ 900		+ $900		
	$800 +	$2,100	=	$900	+	$2,000
	$2,900		=	$2,900		

Transaction (d): Payment on a loan

A Decrease in an Asset Offset by a Decrease in a Liability. Jessie paid the first installment on the scooter of $300 [see transaction (c)]. This payment decreased the asset, Cash, and the liability, Accounts Payable, by $300.

	Assets (Items owned)		=	Liabilities (Amounts owed)	+	Owner's Equity (Owner's Investment)
	Cash +	Delivery Equipment	=	Accounts Payable	+	Jessica Jane, Capital
	$800	$2,100		$900		$2,000
(d)	− 300			− 300		
	$500 +	$2,100	=	$600	+	$2,000
	$2,600		=	$2,600		

EXPANDING THE ACCOUNTING EQUATION: REVENUES, EXPENSES, AND WITHDRAWALS

In the preceding sections, three key accounting elements of every business entity were defined and explained: assets, liabilities, and owner's equity. To complete the explanation of the accounting process, three additional elements must be added to the discussion: revenues, expenses, and withdrawals.

Revenues

Revenues represent the amount a business charges customers for products sold or services performed. Customers generally pay with cash or a credit card, or they promise to pay at a later date. Most businesses recognize revenues when earned, even if cash has not yet been received. Separate accounts are used to recognize different types of revenue. Examples include Delivery Fees; Consulting Fees; Rent Revenue, if the business rents space to others; Interest Revenue, for interest earned on bank deposits; and Sales, for sales of merchandise. *Revenues increase both assets and owner's equity.*

Expenses

Expenses represent the *decrease* in assets (or *increase* in liabilities) as a result of a company's efforts to produce revenues. Common examples of expenses are rent, salaries, supplies consumed, and taxes. As with revenues, separate accounts are used to keep the accounting records for each different type of expense. Expenses are "incurred" as

- assets are consumed (such as supplies), or

- services are provided (by employees, for example) to the business.

LEARNING KEY

It is important to remember that expenses do not always reduce cash and revenues do not always increase cash right away.

The two main purposes of recognizing an expense are (a) to keep track of the amount and types of expenses incurred and (b) to show the reduction in owner's equity. Again, an expense can cause a reduction in assets or an increase in liabilities. Wages earned by employees is a good example.

- If paid, the expense reduces owner's equity and an asset, Cash.

- If not paid, the expense reduces owner's equity and increases a liability, Wages Payable.

Either way, owner's equity is reduced. If total revenues are greater than total expenses for the period, the excess is the **net income,** or net profit, for the period. On the other hand, if total expenses are greater than total revenues for the period, the excess is a **net loss** for the period.

Revenues	$900		Revenues	$ 300
Expenses	500		Expenses	500
Net income	$400		Net loss	$(200)

The owner can determine the time period used in the measurement of net income or net loss. It may be a month, a quarter (three months), a year, or some other time period. The concept that income determination can be made on a periodic basis is known as the **accounting period concept.** Any accounting period of 12 months is called a **fiscal year.** The fiscal year frequently coincides with the calendar year.

Withdrawals

LEARNING KEY

Owner's Equity	
Decrease	Increase
Expenses	Revenues
Drawing	Investments

Withdrawals, or **drawing,** reduce owner's equity as a result of the owner taking cash or other assets out of the business for personal use. Since earnings are expected to offset withdrawals, this reduction is viewed as temporary.

The accounting equation is expanded to include revenues, expenses, and withdrawals. Note that revenues increase owner's equity, while expenses and drawing reduce owner's equity.

	Assets (Items Owned)			=	**Liabilities** (Amounts Owed)	+	**Owner's Equity** (Owner's Investment)				(Earnings)	
	Cash	+	Delivery Equipment	=	Accounts Payable	+	Jessica Jane, Capital	–	Jessica Jane, Drawing	+	Revenues	– Expenses
Balance	$500	+	$2,100	=	$600	+	$2,000					
		$2,600		=					$2,600			

EFFECT OF REVENUE, EXPENSE, AND WITHDRAWAL TRANSACTIONS ON THE ACCOUNTING EQUATION

To show the effects of revenue, expense, and withdrawal transactions, the example of Jessie Jane's Campus Delivery Service will be continued. Assume that the following transactions took place in Jessie's business during June 20--.

Transaction (e): Delivery revenues earned in cash

An Increase in an Asset Offset by an Increase in Owner's Equity Resulting from Revenue. Jessie received $500 cash from clients for delivery services. This transaction increased the asset, Cash, and increased owner's equity by $500. The increase in owner's equity is shown by increasing the revenue account, Delivery Fees, by $500.

	Assets (Items Owned)			=	Liabilities (Amounts Owed)	+	Owner's Equity						
							(Owner's Investment)		+	(Earnings)			
	Cash	+	Delivery Equipment	=	Accounts Payable	+	Jessica Jane, Capital	− Jessica Jane, Drawing	+	Revenues	−	Expenses	Description
	$ 500		$2,100		$600		$2,000						
(e)	+ 500									+ $500			Deliv. Fees
	$1,000	+	$2,100	=	$600	+	$2,000		+	$500			
	$3,100			=			**$3,100**						

Transaction (f): Paid rent for month

A Decrease in an Asset Offset by a Decrease in Owner's Equity Resulting from an Expense. Jessie rents a small office on campus. She paid $200 for office rent for June. This transaction decreased both Cash and owner's equity by $200. The decrease in owner's equity is shown by increasing an expense called Rent Expense by $200. An increase in an expense decreases owner's equity.

	Assets (Items Owned)			=	Liabilities (Amounts Owed)	+	Owner's Equity						
							(Owner's Investment)		+	(Earnings)			
	Cash	+	Delivery Equipment	=	Accounts Payable	+	Jessica Jane, Capital	− Jessica Jane, Drawing	+	Revenues	−	Expenses	Description
	$1,000	+	$2,100		$600		$2,000			$500			
(f)	− 200											+ $200	Rent Exp.
	$ 800	+	$2,100	=	$600	+	$2,000		+	$500	−	$200	
	$2,900			=			**$2,900**						

Transaction (g): Paid telephone bill

A Decrease in an Asset Offset by a Decrease in Owner's Equity Resulting from an Expense. Jessie paid $50 in cash for telephone service. This transaction, like the previous one, decreased both Cash and owner's equity. This decrease in owner's equity is shown by increasing an expense called Telephone Expense by $50.

Assets (Items Owned)		=	Liabilities (Amounts Owed)	+	Owner's Equity (Owner's Investment)		+	(Earnings)		
Cash +	Delivery Equipment	=	Accounts Payable	+	Jessica Jane, Capital −	Jessica Jane, Drawing	+	Revenues −	Expenses	Description
$800	$2,100		$600		$2,000			$500	$200	
(g) − 50									+ 50	Tele. Expense
$750 +	$2,100	=	$600	+	$2,000		+	$500 −	$250	
$2,850		=	$2,850							

LEARNING KEY

Revenue is recognized when it is earned even though cash is not received.

Transaction (h): Delivery revenues earned on account

An Increase in an Asset Offset by an Increase in Owner's Equity Resulting from Revenue. Jessie extends credit to regular customers. Often, delivery services are performed for which payment will be received later. Since revenues are recognized when earned, an increase in owner's equity must be reported by increasing the revenue account. Since no cash is received at this time, Cash cannot be increased. Instead, an increase is reported for another asset, Accounts Receivable. *The total of Accounts Receivable at any point in time reflects the amount owed to Jessie by her customers.* Deliveries made on account amounted to $600. Accounts Receivable and Delivery Fees are increased.

Assets (Items Owned)			=	Liabilities (Amounts Owed)	+	Owner's Equity (Owner's Investment)			+	(Earnings)		
Cash +	Accounts Receivable +	Delivery Equipment	=	Accounts Payable	+	Jessica Jane, Capital −	Jessica Jane, Drawing	+		Revenues −	Expenses	Description
$750		$2,100		$600		$2,000				$ 500	$250	
(h)	+ $600									+ 600		Deliv. Fees
$750 +	$600 +	$2,100	=	$600	+	$2,000		+		$1,100 −	$250	
$3,450			=	$3,450								

Transaction (i): Purchase of supplies

An Increase in an Asset Offset by a Decrease in an Asset. Jessie bought pens, paper, delivery envelopes, and other supplies for $80 cash. These supplies should last for several months. Since they will generate future benefits, the supplies should be recorded as an asset. The accounting equation will show an increase in an asset, Supplies, and a decrease in Cash.

Assets (Items Owned)				=	Liabilities (Amounts Owed)	Owner's Equity (Owner's Investment) +			(Earnings)		
Cash +	Accounts Receivable +	Supplies +	Delivery Equipment	=	Accounts Payable +	Jessica Jane, Capital −	Jessica Jane, Drawing	+ Revenues −	Expenses	Description
$750	$600		$2,100		$600	$2,000		$1,100	$250	
(i) − 80		+ $80								
$670 +	$600 +	$80 +	$2,100	=	$600 +	$2,000	+	$1,100 −	$250	
$3,450				=	$3,450					

LEARNING KEY

Both supplies and insurance are recorded as assets because they will provide benefits for several months.

Transaction (j): Payment of insurance premium

An Increase in an Asset Offset by a Decrease in an Asset. Since Jessie plans to graduate and sell the business next January, she paid $200 for an eight-month liability insurance policy. Insurance is paid in advance and will provide future benefits. Thus, it is treated as an asset. We must expand the equation to include another asset, Prepaid Insurance, and show that Cash has been reduced.

	Assets (Items Owned)					=	Liabilities (Amounts Owed)	+	Owner's Equity (Owner's Investment) + (Earnings)					
Cash +	Accounts Receivable	+ Supplies +	Prepaid Insurance	+	Delivery Equipment =		Accounts Payable	+	Jessica Jane, Capital	− Jessica Jane, Drawing	+	Revenues −	Expenses	Description
$670	$600	$80			$2,100		$600		$2,000			$1,100	$250	
(j) − 200			+ $200											
$470 +	$600	+ $80 +	$200	+	$2,100 =		$600	+	$2,000		+	$1,100 −	$250	
	$3,450					=			$3,450					

As shown in transactions (i), (j), and (k), transactions do not always affect both sides of the accounting equation.

Transaction (k): Cash receipts from prior sales on account

An Increase in an Asset Offset by a Decrease in an Asset. Jessie received $570 in cash for delivery services performed for customers earlier in the month [see transaction (h)]. Receipt of this cash increases the cash account and reduces the amount due from customers reported in the accounts receivable account. *Notice that owner's equity is not affected in this transaction. Owner's equity increased in transaction (h) when revenue was recognized as it was earned, rather than now when cash is received.*

	Assets (Items Owned)					=	Liabilities (Amounts Owed)	+	Owner's Equity (Owner's Investment) + (Earnings)					
Cash +	Accounts Receivable	+ Supplies +	Prepaid Insurance	+	Delivery Equipment =		Accounts Payable	+	Jessica Jane, Capital	− Jessica Jane, Drawing	+	Revenues −	Expenses	Description
$ 470	$600	$80	$200		$2,100		$600		$2,000			$1,100	$250	
(k) + 570	− 570													
$1,040 +	$ 30	+ $80 +	$200	+	$2,100 =		$600	+	$2,000		+	$1,100 −	$250	
	$3,450					=			$3,450					

Transaction (l): Purchase of an asset on account making a partial payment

An Increase in an Asset Offset by a Decrease in an Asset and an Increase in a Liability. With business increasing, Jessie hired a second employee and bought a third motor scooter. The scooter cost $1,500. Jessie paid $300 in cash and will spread the remaining payments over the next four months. The asset Delivery Equipment increases by $1,500, Cash decreases by $300, and the liability Accounts Payable increases by $1,200. *Note that this transaction changes three accounts. Even so, the accounting equation remains in balance.*

	Assets (Items Owned)				=	Liabilities (Amounts Owed)	+	Owner's Equity (Owner's Investment) + (Earnings)							
Cash +	Accounts Receivable +	Supplies +	Prepaid Insurance +	Delivery Equipment =		Accounts Payable +		Jessica Jane, Capital −	Jessica Jane, Drawing +	Revenues −	Expenses	Description
$1,040	$30	$80	$200	$2,100		$ 600		$2,000		$1,100	$250	
(l) − 300				**+ 1,500**		**+ 1,200**						
$ 740 +	$30 +	$80 +	$200 +	$3,600 =		$1,800 +		$2,000 +		$1,100 −	$250	
		$4,650			=			$4,650				

Transaction (m): Payment of wages

A Decrease in an Asset Offset by a Decrease in Owner's Equity Resulting from an Expense. Jessie paid her part-time employees $650 in wages. This represents an additional business expense. As with other expenses, Cash is reduced and owner's equity is reduced by increasing an expense.

	Assets (Items Owned)				=	Liabilities (Amounts Owed)	+	Owner's Equity (Owner's Investment) + (Earnings)							
Cash +	Accounts Receivable +	Supplies +	Prepaid Insurance +	Delivery Equipment =		Accounts Payable +		Jessica Jane, Capital −	Jessica Jane, Drawing +	Revenues −	Expenses	Description
$740	$30	$80	$200	$3,600		$1,800		$2,000		$1,100	$250	
(m) − 650											**+ 650**	**Wages Exp.**
$ 90 +	$30 +	$80 +	$200 +	$3,600 =		$1,800 +		$2,000 +		$1,100 −	$900	
		$4,000			=			$4,000				

Transaction (n): Deliveries made for cash and on account

An Increase in Two Assets Offset by an Increase in Owner's Equity. Total delivery fees for the remainder of the month amounted to $1,050: $430 in cash and $620 on account. Since all of these delivery fees have been earned, the revenue account increases by $1,050. Also, Cash increases by $430 and Accounts Receivable increases by $620. Thus, revenues increase assets and owner's equity. Note, once again, that one event impacts three accounts while the equation remains in balance.

	Assets (Items Owned)				=	Liabilities (Amounts Owed)	+	Owner's Equity (Owner's Investment) + (Earnings)							
Cash +	Accounts Receivable +	Supplies +	Prepaid Insurance +	Delivery Equipment =		Accounts Payable +		Jessica Jane, Capital −	Jessica Jane, Drawing +	Revenues −	Expenses	Description
$ 90	$ 30	$80	$200	$3,600		$1,800		$2,000		$1,100	$900	
(n) + 430	+ 620									**+1,050**		**Deliv. Fees**
$ 520 +	$ 650 +	$80 +	$200 +	$3,600 =		$1,800 +		$2,000 +		$2,150 −	$900	
		$5,050			=			$5,050				

LEARNING KEY

Withdrawals by the owner are reported in the drawing account. Withdrawals are the opposite of investments by the owner.

Transaction (o): Withdrawal of cash from business

A Decrease in an Asset Offset by a Decrease in Owner's Equity Resulting from a Withdrawal by the Owner. At the end of the month, Jessie took $150 in cash from the business to purchase books for her classes. Since the books are not business related, this is a withdrawal. Withdrawals can be viewed as the opposite of investments by the owner. Both owner's equity and Cash decrease.

Assets (Items Owned)					=	Liabilities (Amounts Owed)	+	Owner's Equity (Owner's Investment) + (Earnings)				
Cash +	Accounts Receivable	+ Supplies +	Prepaid Insurance	+ Delivery Equipment =		Accounts Payable	+	Jessica Jane, Capital	− Jessica Jane, Drawing	+ Revenues	− Expenses	Description
$520	$650	$80	$200	$3,600		$1,800		$2,000		$2,150	$900	
(o) − 150									+ $150			
$370 +	$650	+ $80 +	$200	+ $3,600 =		$1,800	+	$2,000	− $150	+ $2,150	− $900	
$4,900					=			**$4,900**				

Figure 2-1 shows a summary of the transactions. Use this summary to test your understanding of transaction analysis by describing the economic event represented by each transaction. At the bottom of Figure 2-1, the asset accounts and their totals are compared with the liability and owner's equity accounts and their totals.

U REVU

Complete U REVU-3 on **page 41** to test your basic understanding of LO3/4.

FINANCIAL STATEMENTS

LO5 Prepare and describe the purposes of a simple income statement, statement of owner's equity, and balance sheet.

Three financial statements commonly prepared by a business entity are the income statement, statement of owner's equity, and balance sheet. The transaction information gathered and summarized in the accounting equation may be used to prepare these financial statements. Figure 2-2 shows the following:

1. A summary of the specific revenue and expense transactions and the ending totals for the asset, liability, capital, and drawing accounts from the accounting equation.

2. The financial statements and their linkages with the accounting equation and each other.

Note that each of the financial statements in Figure 2-2 has a heading consisting of:

HEADING FOR FINANCIAL STATEMENTS	
1. The name of the company	Jessie Jane's Campus Delivery Service
2. The title of the statement	Income Statement, Statement of Owner's Equity, or Balance Sheet
3. The time period covered or the date of the statement	For Month Ended June 30, 20--, or June 30, 20--

FIGURE 2-1 Summary of Transactions Illustrated

Transaction	Cash	+ Accounts Receivable	+ Supplies	+ Prepaid Insurance	+ Delivery Equipment	= Accounts Payable	+ Jessica Jane, Capital	− Jessica Jane, Drawing	+ Revenues	− Expenses	Description
	Assets (Items Owned)					**Liabilities** (Amounts Owed)	**Owner's Equity** (Owner's Investment) +		(Earnings)		
Balance	2,000						2,000				
(a)											
Balance	2,000						2,000				
(b)	(1,200)				1,200						
Balance	800				1,200		2,000				
(c)					900	900					
Balance	800				2,100	900	2,000				
(d)	(300)					(300)					
Balance	500				2,100	600	2,000				
(e)	500								500		Deliv. Fees
Balance	1,000				2,100	600	2,000		500		
(f)	(200)									200	Rent Exp.
Balance	800				2,100	600	2,000		500	200	
(g)	(50)									50	Tele. Exp.
Balance	750				2,100	600	2,000		500	250	
(h)		600							600		Deliv. Fees
Balance	750	600			2,100	600	2,000		1,100	250	
(i)	(80)		80								
Balance	670	600	80		2,100	600	2,000		1,100	250	
(j)	(200)			200							
Balance	470	600	80	200	2,100	600	2,000		1,100	250	
(k)	570	(570)									
Balance	1,040	30	80	200	2,100	600	2,000		1,100	250	
(l)	(300)				1,500	1,200					
Balance	740	30	80	200	3,600	1,800	2,000		1,100	250	
(m)	(650)									650	Wages Exp.
Balance	90	30	80	200	3,600	1,800	2,000		1,100	900	
(n)	430	620							1,050		Deliv. Fees
Balance	520	650	80	200	3,600	1,800	2,000		2,150	900	
(o)	(150)							150			
Balance	**370** +	**650** +	**80** +	**200** +	**3,600** =	**1,800** +	**2,000** −	**150** +	**2,150** −	**900**	

Cash	$ 370	Accounts Payable	$ 1,800	
Accounts Receivable	650	Jessica Jane, Capital	2,000	
Supplies	80	Jessica Jane, Drawing	(150)	◁ Amounts in ( ) are subtracted
Prepaid Insurance	200	Delivery Fees	2,150	
Delivery Equipment	3,600	Rent Expense	(200)	
Total Assets	$ 4,900	Telephone Expense	(50)	
		Wages Expense	(650)	
		Total Liabilities and Owner's Equity	$ 4,900	

As with the running totals in the table, the listing immediately below the table provides proof that the accounting equation is in balance.

The income statement and statement of owner's equity provide information concerning events covering a period of time, in this case, *the month ended* June 30, 20--. The balance sheet, on the other hand, offers a picture of the business on *a specific date*, June 30, 20--.

FIGURE 2-2 Summary and Financial Statements

Trans-action	Cash	+	Accounts Receivable	+ Supplies +	Prepaid Insurance	+	Delivery Equipment	=	Accounts Payable	+	Jessica Jane, Capital	−	Jessica Jane, Drawing	+	Revenues−	Expenses	Description
Assets (Items Owned)								**= Liabilities + (Amounts Owed)**		**Owner's Equity (Owner's Investment) + (Earnings)**							
(e)															500		Deliv. Fees
(f)																200	Rent Exp.
(g)																50	Tele. Exp.
(h)															600		Deliv. Fees
(m)																650	Wages Exp.
(n)															1,050		Deliv. Fees
Balance	370	+	650	+ 80 +	200	+	3,600	=	1,800	+	2,000	−	150	+	2,150	− 900	

Jessie Jane's Campus Delivery Service
Income Statement
For Month Ended June 30, 20 --

Revenues:			
Delivery fees			$2 1 5 0 00

$ at top of columns

Expenses:			
Wages expense	$ 6 5 0 00		
Rent expense	2 0 0 00		
Telephone expense	5 0 00		
Total expenses		9 0 0 00	
Net income			$1 2 5 0 00

Expenses are listed in the first column and totaled in the second column under the revenues.

Subtotal underline

Jessie Jane's Campus Delivery Service
Statement of Owner's Equity
For Month Ended June 30, 20 --

Jessica Jane, capital, June 1, 20 --		$ — — —
Investments during June		2 0 0 0 00
Total investment		$2 0 0 0 00
Net Income for June	$1 2 5 0 00	
Less Withdrawals for June	1 5 0 00	
Increase in capital		1 1 0 0 00
Jessica Jane, capital, June 30, 20 --		$3 1 0 0 00

Many companies use a dash (—) to represent a zero on financial statements.

Withdrawals are deducted from net income in the first column. The net increase in capital is reported in the second column.

$ on total

Jessie Jane's Campus Delivery Service
Balance Sheet
June 30, 20 --

Assets		Liabilities	
Cash	$ 3 7 0 00	Accounts payable	$1 8 0 0 00
Accounts receivable	6 5 0 00		
Supplies	8 0 00	**Owner's Equity**	
Prepaid insurance	2 0 0 00	Jessica Jane, capital	3 1 0 0 00
Delivery equipment	3 6 0 0 00		
		Total liabilities and	
Total assets	$4 9 0 0 00	owner's equity	$4 9 0 0 00

Double underline totals

LEARNING KEY

Income Statement

Revenues	$500
Expenses	400
Net income	$100

Income Statement

Revenues	$ 500
Expenses	700
Net loss	$(200)

THE INCOME STATEMENT

The **income statement**, sometimes called the **profit and loss statement or operating statement**, reports the profitability of business operations for a specific period of time. Jessie's income statement shows the revenues earned for the month of June. Next, the expenses incurred as a result of the efforts made to earn these revenues are deducted. If the revenues are greater than the expenses, net income is reported. If the expenses are greater than the revenue, a net loss is reported.

By carefully studying the income statement, it is clear that Jessie earns revenues in only one way: by making deliveries. If other types of services were offered, these revenues would also be identified on the statement. Further, the reader can see the kinds of expenses that were incurred. The reader can make a judgment as to whether these seem reasonable given the amount of revenue earned. Finally, the most important number on the statement is the net income. This is known as the "bottom line."

THE STATEMENT OF OWNER'S EQUITY

The **statement of owner's equity** illustrated in Figure 2-2 reports on these activities for the month of June. Jessie started her business with an investment of $2,000. During the month of June, she earned $1,250 in net income and withdrew $150 for personal expenses. Jessie's $2,000 original investment, plus the net increase of $1,100, results in her ending capital of $3,100.

Note that Jessie's original investment and later withdrawal are taken from the accounting equation. *The net income figure could have been computed from information in the accounting equation. However, it is easier to simply transfer net income as reported on the income statement to the statement of owner's equity.* This is an important linkage between the income statement and statement of owner's equity.

If Jessie had a net loss of $500 for the month, the statement of owner's equity would be prepared as shown in Figure 2-3.

FIGURE 2-3 Statement of Owner's Equity with Net Loss

Jessie Jane's Campus Delivery Service Statement of Owner's Equity For Month Ended June 30, 20 --									
Jessica Jane, capital, June 1, 20 --						$	—	—	—	
Investments during June						2	0	0	0	00
Total investment						$2	0	0	0	00
Less: Net loss for June	$	5	0	0	00					
Withdrawals for June		1	5	0	00					
Decrease in capital							6	5	0	00
Jessica Jane, capital, June 30, 20 --						$1	3	5	0	00

THE BALANCE SHEET

The **balance sheet** reports a firm's assets, liabilities, and owner's equity on a specific date. It is called a balance sheet because it confirms that the accounting equation has remained in balance. It is also referred to as a **statement of financial position** or **statement of financial condition.**

As illustrated in Figure 2-2, the asset and liability accounts are taken from the accounting equation and reported on the balance sheet. *The total of Jessie's capital account on June 30 could have been computed from the owner's equity accounts in the accounting equation ($2,000 – $150 + $2,150 – $900). However, it is simpler to take the June 30, 20--, capital as computed on the statement of owner's equity and transfer it to the balance sheet.* This is an important linkage between these two statements.

> Most firms also prepare a statement of cash flows. Given the complexity of this statement, we will postpone its discussion until later in this text.

GUIDELINES FOR PREPARING FINANCIAL STATEMENTS

1. Financial statements are prepared primarily for users not associated with the company. To make a good impression and enhance understanding, financial statements must follow a standard form with careful attention to placement, spacing, and indentations.

2. All statements have a heading with the name of the company, name of the statement, and accounting period or date.

3. Single rules (lines) indicate that the numbers above the line have been added or subtracted. Double rules (double underlines) indicate a total.

4. Dollar signs are used at the top of columns and for the first amount entered in a column beneath a ruling.

5. On the income statement, some companies list expenses from highest to lowest dollar amount, with miscellaneous expense listed last.

6. On the balance sheet, assets are listed from most liquid to least liquid. **Liquidity** measures the ease with which the asset will be converted to cash. Liabilities are listed from most current to least current.

U REVU ▶   Complete U REVU-4 on **page 41** to test your basic understanding of LO5.

OVERVIEW OF THE ACCOUNTING PROCESS

LO6 Define the three basic phases of the accounting process.

Figure 2-4 shows the three basic phases of the accounting process in terms of input, processing, and output.

- **Input.** Business transactions provide the necessary *input.*
- **Processing.** Recognizing the effect of these transactions on the assets, liabilities, owner's equity, revenues, and expenses of a business is the *processing* function.
- **Output.** The financial statements are the *output.*

FIGURE 2-4 Input, Processing, and Output

INPUT	PROCESSING
Transactions	• Identify accounts • Classify accounts • Determine whether increase or decrease • Enter transaction and verify balance

OUTPUT

Income Statement	Statement of Owner's Equity	Balance Sheet
Revenues – Expenses = Net Income	Beginning Capital + Investments + Net Income – Withdrawals = Ending Capital	Assets = Liabilities + Owner's Equity

SELF-STUDY

LEARNING OBJECTIVES   Key Points to Remember

LO1 Define the accounting elements.

The three key accounting elements are assets, liabilities, and owner's equity. Owner's equity is expanded in LO4 to include revenues, expenses, and drawing.

LO2 Construct the accounting equation.

The accounting equation is:
Assets = Liabilities + Owner's Equity

LO3 Analyze business transactions.

Three questions must be answered in analyzing business transactions:
1. What happened?
2. Which accounts are affected?
3. How is the accounting equation affected?

LO4 Show the effects of business transactions on the accounting equation.

Each transaction affects at least two accounts and one or more of the three basic accounting elements. The transactions described in this chapter can be classified into five groups:
1. Increase in an asset offset by an increase in owner's equity.
2. Increase in an asset offset by a decrease in another asset.
3. Increase in an asset offset by an increase in a liability.
4. Decrease in an asset offset by a decrease in a liability.
5. Decrease in an asset offset by a decrease in owner's equity.

LO5 Prepare and describe the purposes of a simple income statement, statement of owner's equity, and balance sheet.

The purposes of the income statement, statement of owner's equity, and balance sheet can be summarized as follows:

STATEMENT	PURPOSE
Income statement	Reports net income or loss Revenues – Expenses = Net Income or Loss

(continued)

LEARNING OBJECTIVES   Key Points to Remember

LO5 (concluded)	Statement of owner's equity	Shows changes in the owner's capital account Beginning Capital + Investments + Net Income – Withdrawals = Ending Capital
	Balance sheet	Verifies balance of accounting equation Assets = Liabilities + Owner's Equity

LO6 Define the three basic phases of the accounting process.	The three basic phases of the accounting process are shown below. • **Input.** Business transactions provide the necessary input. • **Processing.** Recognizing the effect of these transactions on the assets, liabilities, owner's equity, revenues, and expenses of a business is the processing function. • **Output.** The financial statements are the output.

 DEMONSTRATION PROBLEM

Damon Young has started his own business, Home and Away Inspections. He inspects property for buyers and sellers of real estate. Young rents office space and has a part-time assistant to answer the phone and help with inspections. The transactions for the month of September are as follows:

(a) On the first day of the month, Young invested cash by making a deposit in a bank account for the business, $15,000.

(b) Paid rent for September, $300.

(c) Bought a used truck for cash, $8,000.

(d) Purchased tools on account from Crafty Tools, $3,000.

(e) Paid electricity bill, $50.

(f) Paid two-year premium for liability insurance on truck, $600.

(g) Received cash from clients for services performed, $2,000.

(h) Paid part-time assistant (wages) for first half of month, $200.

(i) Performed inspection services for clients on account, $1,000.

(j) Paid telephone bill, $35.

(k) Bought office supplies costing $300. Paid $100 cash and will pay the balance next month, $200.

(l) Received cash from clients for inspections performed on account in (i), $300.

(m) Paid part-time assistant (wages) for last half of month, $250.

(n) Made partial payment on tools bought in (d), $1,000.

(o) Earned additional revenues amounting to $2,000: $1,400 in cash and $600 on account.

(p) Young withdrew cash at the end of the month for personal expenses, $500.

REQUIRED

1. Enter the transactions in an accounting equation similar to the one illustrated on the following page.

Assets (Items Owned)						=	Liabilities (Amounts Owed)	+	Owner's Equity (Owner's Investment) + (Earnings)				
Cash +	Accounts Receivable +	Supplies +	Prepaid Insurance +	Tools +	Truck =		Accounts Payable	+	Damon Young, Capital	– Damon Young, Drawing	+ Revenues	– Expenses	Description

2. Compute the ending balances for all accounts.

3. Prepare an income statement for Home and Away Inspections for the month of September 20--.

4. Prepare a statement of owner's equity for Home and Away Inspections for the month of September 20--.

5. Prepare a balance sheet for Home and Away Inspections as of September 30, 20--.

Solution 1, 2.

	Cash +	Accounts Receivable +	Supplies +	Prepaid Insurance +	Tools +	Truck =	Accounts Payable	+ Damon Young, Capital	– Damon Young, Drawing	+ Revenues	– Expenses	Description
(a)	15,000							15,000				
(b)	(300)										300	Rent Exp.
(c)	(8,000)					8,000						
(d)					3,000		3,000					
(e)	(50)										50	Utilities Exp.
(f)	(600)		600									
(g)	2,000									2,000		Inspect. Fees
(h)	(200)										200	Wages Exp.
(i)		1,000								1,000		Inspect. Fees
(j)	(35)										35	Tele. Exp.
(k)	(100)		300				200					
(l)	300	(300)										
(m)	(250)										250	Wages Exp.
(n)	(1,000)						(1,000)					
(o)	1,400	600								2,000		Inspect. Fees
(p)	(500)								500			
Bal.	7,665 +	1,300 +	300 +	600 +	3,000 +	8,000 =	2,200	+ 15,000	– 500	+ 5,000	– 835	

(continued)

3.

Home and Away Inspections Income Statement For Month Ended September 30, 20 --									
Revenues:									
Inspection fees						$ 5	0	0	0	00
Expenses:									
Wages expense		$	4	5	0	00			
Rent expense			3	0	0	00			
Utilities expense				5	0	00			
Telephone expense				3	5	00			
Total expenses							8	3	5	00
Net income						$ 4	1	6	5	00

4.

Home and Away Inspections Statement of Owner's Equity For Month Ended September 30, 20 - -									
Damon Young, capital, September 1, 20 - -						$	—	—	—
Investment during September						15	0	0	0	00
Total investment						$15	0	0	0	00
Net income for September		$ 4	1	6	5	00			
Less withdrawals for September			5	0	0	00			
Increase in capital						3	6	6	5	00
Damon Young, capital, September 30, 20 - -						$18	6	6	5	00

5.

Home and Away Inspections Balance Sheet September 30, 20 --										
Assets						Liabilities				
Cash	$ 7	6	6	5	00	Accounts payable	$ 2	2	0	0	00
Accounts receivable	1	3	0	0	00					
Supplies		3	0	0	00	Owner's Equity				
Prepaid insurance		6	0	0	00	Damon Young, capital	18	6	6	5	00
Tools	3	0	0	0	00					
Truck	8	0	0	0	00					
						Total liabilities and				
Total assets	$20	8	6	5	00	owner's equity	$20	8	6	5	00

KEY TERMS

account (22)   A separate record used to summarize changes in each asset, liability, and owner's equity of a business.

account title (22)   Provides a description of the particular type of asset, liability, owner's equity, revenue, or expense.

accounting equation (21)   The accounting equation consists of the three basic accounting elements: Assets = Liabilities + Owner's Equity.

accounting period concept (25)   The concept that income determination can be made on a periodic basis.

accounts payable (20)   An unwritten promise to pay a supplier for assets purchased or services received.

accounts receivable (20)   An amount owed to a business by its customers as a result of the sale of goods or services.

asset (20)   An item that is owned by a business and will provide future benefits.

balance sheet (34)   Reports assets, liabilities, and owner's equity on a specific date. It is called a balance sheet because it confirms that the accounting equation is in balance.

business entity (20)   An individual, association, or organization that engages in economic activities and controls specific economic resources.

business entity concept (20)   The concept that nonbusiness assets and liabilities are not included in the business entity's accounting records.

business transaction (22)   An economic event that has a direct impact on the business.

capital (20)   Another term for owner's equity, the amount by which the business assets exceed the business liabilities.

drawing (25)   Withdrawals that reduce owner's equity as a result of the owner taking cash or other assets out of the business for personal use.

expenses (25)   The decrease in assets (or increase in liabilities) as a result of efforts to produce revenues.

fiscal year (25)   Any accounting period of 12 months' duration.

income statement (33)   Reports the profitability of business operations for a specific period of time.

input (34)   Business transactions provide the necessary input for the accounting information system.

liability (20)   Something owed to another business entity.

liquidity (34)   A measure of the ease with which an asset will be converted to cash.

net income (25)   The excess of total revenues over total expenses for the period.

net loss (25)   The excess of total expenses over total revenues for the period.

net worth (20)   Another term for owner's equity, the amount by which the business assets exceed the business liabilities.

notes payable (20)   A formal written promise to pay a supplier or lender a specified sum of money at a definite future time.

operating statement (33)   Another name for the income statement, which reports the profitability of business operations for a specific period of time.

output (34)   The financial statements are the output of the accounting information system.

owner's equity (20)   The amount by which the business assets exceed the business liabilities.

processing (34)   Recognizing the effect of transactions on the assets, liabilities, owner's equity, revenues, and expenses of a business.

profit and loss statement (33)   Another name for the income statement, which reports the profitability of business operations for a specific period of time.

revenues (24)   The amount a business charges customers for products sold or services performed.

statement of financial condition (34)   Another name for the balance sheet, which reports assets, liabilities, and owner's equity on a specific date.

statement of financial position (34)   Another name for the balance sheet, which reports assets, liabilities, and owner's equity on a specific date.

statement of owner's equity (33)   Reports beginning capital plus net income less withdrawals to compute ending capital.

withdrawals (25) Reduce owner's equity as a result of the owner taking cash or other assets out of the business for personal use.

SELF-STUDY QUESTIONS AND EXERCISES

True/False Questions

1. LO1   Assets are items that are owned by the business and are expected to provide future benefits.

2. LO1   Accounts Payable is an example of an asset account.

3. LO1   According to the business entity concept, nonbusiness assets and liabilities are not included in the business's accounting records.

4. LO2   The accounting equation (Assets = Liabilities + Owner's Equity) must always be in balance.

5. LO2   When an asset increases, a liability must also increase.

6. LO3   Expenses represent outflows of assets or increases in liabilities as a result of efforts to produce revenues.

7. LO5   When total revenues exceed total expenses, the difference is called net loss.

Multiple Choice Questions

1. LO4   An increase to which of these accounts will increase owner's equity?

   (a) Accounts Payable   (c) Client Fees
   (b) Drawing   (d) Rent Expense

2. LO4   When delivery revenue is earned in cash, which accounts increase or decrease?

   (a) Cash increases; Revenue increases.
   (b) Cash decreases; Revenue increases.
   (c) Cash decreases; Revenue decreases.
   (d) Cash does not change; owner's equity increases.

3. LO4   When delivery revenue is earned on account, which accounts increase or decrease?

    (a) Cash increases; Revenue increases.
    (b) Accounts Receivable increases; Revenue increases.
    (c) Accounts Receivable increases; Revenue decreases.
    (d) Accounts Receivable decreases; Revenue decreases.

4. LO4   When payment is made on an existing debt, which accounts increase or decrease?

    (a) Cash increases; Accounts Receivable increases.
    (b) Cash decreases; Accounts Payable increases.
    (c) Cash increases; Accounts Payable increases.
    (d) Cash decreases; Accounts Payable decreases.

5. LO5   Which of the following accounts does not appear on the income statement?

    (a) Delivery Fees   (c) Drawing
    (b) Wages Expense   (d) Rent Expense

U REVU   Exercises

1. LO1   Label each of the following accounts as an asset (A), a liability (L), or owner's equity (OE), using the following format:

Account	Classification
Accounts Receivable	_____
Accounts Payable	_____
Judy Smith, Capital	_____

2. LO2   What is missing from the accounting equation below?

_____?_____ = Liabilities + Owner's Equity

3. LO3/4   What are the effects of the following transactions on the accounting equation? Indicate an increase (+) or decrease (−) under the appropriate asset, liability, and owner's equity headings.

Transaction	Assets	Liabilities	Owner's Equity
a. Purchase of an asset on account.	_____	_____	_____
b. Made payment on account for transaction (a).	_____	_____	_____

4. LO5   Classify the following accounts as assets (A), liabilities (L), owner's equity (OE), revenue (R), or expense (E). Indicate the financial statement on which the account belongs—income statement (IS), statement of owner's equity (SOE), or balance sheet (BS).

Account	Classification	Financial Statement
Accounts Payable	_____	_____
Peggy Welsch, Drawing	_____	_____
Rent Expense	_____	_____
Sales	_____	_____
Equipment	_____	_____

The answers to the Self-Study Questions and Exercises are at the end of the chapter (page 49).

APPLYING YOUR KNOWLEDGE

REVIEW QUESTIONS

LO1   1.   Why is it necessary to distinguish between business assets and liabilities and nonbusiness assets and liabilities of a single proprietor?

LO1/4   2.   Name and define the six major elements of the accounting equation.

LO3   3.   List the three basic questions that must be answered when analyzing the effects of a business transaction on the accounting equation.

LO5   4.   What is the function of an income statement?

LO5   5.   What is the function of a statement of owner's equity?

LO5   6.   What is the function of a balance sheet?

LO6   7.   What are the three basic phases of the accounting process?

SERIES A EXERCISES

E 2-1A (LO1)

ACCOUNTING ELEMENTS Label each of the following accounts as an asset (A), a liability (L), or owner's equity (OE), using the following format:

Item	Account	Classification
Money in bank	Cash	
Office supplies	Supplies	
Money owed	Accounts Payable	
Office chairs	Office Furniture	
Net worth of owner	John Smith, Capital	
Money withdrawn by owner	John Smith, Drawing	
Money owed by customers	Accounts Receivable	

E 2-2A (LO2)

THE ACCOUNTING EQUATION Using the accounting equation, compute the missing elements.

Assets	=	Liabilities	+	Owner's Equity
_____	=	$24,000	+	$10,000
$25,000	=	$18,000	+	_____
$40,000	=	_____	+	$15,000

E 2-3A (LO3/4)

✓ Assets following (d): $22,000

EFFECTS OF TRANSACTIONS (BALANCE SHEET ACCOUNTS) Alice Stern started a business. During the first month (February 20--), the following transactions occurred. Show the effect of each transaction on the accounting equation: *Assets = Liabilities + Owner's Equity*. After each transaction, show the new totals.

(a)   Invested cash in the business, $20,000.
(b)   Bought office equipment on account, $3,500.
(c)   Bought office equipment for cash, $1,200.
(d)   Paid cash on account to supplier in transaction (b), $1,500.

E 2-4A (LO3/4)

✓ Assets following (k): $23,427

EFFECTS OF TRANSACTIONS (REVENUE, EXPENSE, WITHDRAWALS) This exercise is an extension of Exercise 2-3A. Assume Alice Stern completed the following additional transactions during February. Show the effect of each transaction on the basic elements of the expanded accounting equation: *Assets = Liabilities + Owner's Equity (Capital – Drawing + Revenues – Expenses)*. After transaction (k), report the totals for each element. Demonstrate that the accounting equation has remained in balance.

(e) Received cash from a client for professional services, $2,500.
(f) Paid office rent for February, $900.
(g) Paid February telephone bill, $73.
(h) Withdrew cash for personal use, $500.
(i) Performed services for clients on account, $1,000.
(j) Paid wages to part-time employee, $600.
(k) Received cash for services performed on account in transaction (i), $600.

E 2-5A (LO1/4/5)

FINANCIAL STATEMENT ACCOUNTS Label each of the following accounts as an asset (A), liability (L), owner's equity (OE), revenue (R), or expense (E). Indicate the financial statement on which the account belongs—income statement (IS), statement of owner's equity (SOE), or balance sheet (BS)—in a format similar to the following.

Account	Classification	Financial Statement
Cash		
Rent Expense		
Accounts Payable		
Service Fees		
Supplies		
Wages Expense		
Ramon Martinez, Drawing		
Ramon Martinez, Capital		
Prepaid Insurance		
Accounts Receivable		

E 2-6A (LO5)
✓ Capital, 6/30: $22,000

STATEMENT OF OWNER'S EQUITY REPORTING NET INCOME Betsy Ray started an accounting service on June 1, 20--, by investing $20,000. Her net income for the month was $10,000, and she withdrew $8,000. Prepare a statement of owner's equity for the month of June.

E 2-7A (LO5)
✓ Capital, 6/30: $9,000

STATEMENT OF OWNER'S EQUITY REPORTING NET LOSS Based on the information provided in Exercise 2-6A, prepare a statement of owner's equity assuming Ray had a net loss of $3,000.

SERIES A PROBLEMS

P 2-8A (LO1/2)
✓ 3: $34,920 = $12,570 + $22,350

THE ACCOUNTING EQUATION Dr. John Schleper is a chiropractor. As of December 31, he owned the following property that related to his professional practice.

Cash	$ 4,750
Office Equipment	6,200
X-ray Equipment	11,680
Laboratory Equipment	7,920

He also owes the following business suppliers:

Chateau Gas Company	$ 2,420
Aloe Medical Supply Company	3,740

(continued)

REQUIRED

1. From the preceding information, compute the accounting elements and enter them in the accounting equation shown as follows.

Assets	=	Liabilities	+	Owner's Equity
_____	=	_____	+	_____

2. During January, the assets increase by $7,290, and the liabilities increase by $4,210. Compute the resulting accounting equation.

3. During February, the assets decrease by $2,920, and the liabilities increase by $2,200. Compute the resulting accounting equation.

P 2-9A (LO3/4)

✓ Total cash following (g): $12,950

EFFECT OF TRANSACTIONS ON ACCOUNTING EQUATION Jay Pembroke started a business. During the first month (April 20--), the following transactions occurred.

(a) Invested cash in business, $18,000.
(b) Bought office supplies for $4,600: $2,000 in cash and $2,600 on account.
(c) Paid one-year insurance premium, $1,200.
(d) Earned revenues totaling $3,300: $1,300 in cash and $2,000 on account.
(e) Paid cash on account to the company that supplied the office supplies in transaction (b), $2,300.
(f) Paid office rent for the month, $750.
(g) Withdrew cash for personal use, $100.

REQUIRED

Show the effect of each transaction on the individual accounts of the expanded accounting equation: *Assets = Liabilities + Owner's Equity (Capital − Drawing + Revenues − Expenses)*. After transaction (g), report the totals for each element. Demonstrate that the accounting equation has remained in balance.

P 2-10A (LO5)

✓ Net income: $2,550

INCOME STATEMENT Based on Problem 2-9A, prepare an income statement for Jay Pembroke for the month of April 20--.

P 2-11A (LO5)

✓ Capital, 4/30: $20,450

STATEMENT OF OWNER'S EQUITY Based on Problem 2-9A, prepare a statement of owner's equity for Jay Pembroke for the month of April 20--.

P 2-12A (LO5)

✓ Total assets, 4/30: $20,750

BALANCE SHEET Based on Problem 2-9A, prepare a balance sheet for Jay Pembroke as of April 30, 20--.

SERIES B EXERCISES

E 2-1B (LO1)

ACCOUNTING ELEMENTS Label each of the following accounts as an asset (A), liability (L), or owner's equity (OE) using the following format.

Account	Classification
Cash	
Accounts Payable	
Supplies	
Bill Jones, Drawing	
Prepaid Insurance	
Accounts Receivable	
Bill Jones, Capital	

E 2-2B (LO2)

THE ACCOUNTING EQUATION Using the accounting equation, compute the missing elements.

Assets	=	Liabilities	+	Owner's Equity
_____	=	$20,000	+	$5,000
$30,000	=	$15,000	+	_____
$20,000	=	_____	+	$10,000

E 2-3B (LO3/4)

✓ Assets following (d): $32,500

EFFECTS OF TRANSACTIONS (BALANCE SHEET ACCOUNTS) Jon Wallace started a business. During the first month (March 20--), the following transactions occurred. Show the effect of each transaction on the accounting equation: *Assets = Liabilities + Owner's Equity*. After each transaction, show the new account totals.

(a) Invested cash in the business, $30,000.
(b) Bought office equipment on account, $4,500.
(c) Bought office equipment for cash, $1,600.
(d) Paid cash on account to supplier in transaction (b), $2,000.

E 2-4B (LO3/4)

✓ Assets following (k): $34,032

EFFECTS OF TRANSACTIONS (REVENUE, EXPENSE, WITHDRAWALS) This exercise is an extension of Exercise 2-3B. Assume Jon Wallace completed the following additional transactions during March. Show the effect of each transaction on the basic elements of the expanded accounting equation: *Assets = Liabilities + Owner's Equity (Capital – Drawing + Revenues – Expenses)*. After transaction (k), report the totals for each element. Demonstrate that the accounting equation has remained in balance.

(e) Performed services and received cash, $3,000.
(f) Paid rent for March, $1,000.
(g) Paid March telephone bill, $68.
(h) Jon Wallace withdrew cash for personal use, $800.
(i) Performed services for clients on account, $900.
(j) Paid wages to part-time employee, $500.
(k) Received cash for services performed on account in transaction (i), $500.

E 2-5B (LO1/4/5)

FINANCIAL STATEMENT ACCOUNTS Label each of the following accounts as an asset (A), liability (L), owner's equity (OE), revenue (R), or expense (E). Indicate the financial statement on which the account belongs—income statement (IS), statement of owner's equity (SOE), or balance sheet (BS)—in a format similar to the following.

(continued)

Account	Classification	Financial Statement
Cash		
Rent Expense		
Accounts Payable		
Service Fees		
Supplies		
Wages Expense		
Amanda Wong, Drawing		
Amanda Wong, Capital		
Prepaid Insurance		
Accounts Receivable		

E 2-6B (LO5)

✓ Capital, 6/30: $14,000

STATEMENT OF OWNER'S EQUITY REPORTING NET INCOME Efran Lopez started a financial consulting service on June 1, 20--, by investing $15,000. His net income for the month was $6,000, and he withdrew $7,000 for personal use. Prepare a statement of owner's equity for the month of June.

E 2-7B (LO5)

STATEMENT OF OWNER'S EQUITY REPORTING NET LOSS Based on the information provided in Exercise 2-6B, prepare a statement of owner's equity assuming Lopez had a net loss of $2,000.

SERIES B PROBLEMS

P 2-8B (LO1/2)

✓ 3: $25,235 = $10,165 + $15,070

THE ACCOUNTING EQUATION Dr. Patricia Parsons is a dentist. As of January 31, Parsons owned the following property that related to her professional practice:

Cash	$3,560
Office Equipment	4,600
X-ray Equipment	8,760
Laboratory Equipment	5,940

She also owes the following business suppliers:

Cupples Gas Company	$1,815
Swan Dental Lab	2,790

REQUIRED

1. From the preceding information, compute the accounting elements and enter them in the accounting equation as shown below.

Assets	=	Liabilities	+	Owner's Equity
_____	=	_____	+	_____

2. During February, the assets increase by $4,565, and the liabilities increase by $3,910. Compute the resulting accounting equation.

3. During March, the assets decrease by $2,190, and the liabilities increase by $1,650. Compute the resulting accounting equation.

P 2-9B (LO3/4)

✓ Total cash following (g): $11,300

EFFECT OF TRANSACTIONS ON ACCOUNTING EQUATION David Segal started a business. During the first month (October 20--), the following transactions occurred.
(a) Invested cash in the business, $15,000.
(b) Bought office supplies for $3,800: $1,800 in cash and $2,000 on account.
(c) Paid one-year insurance premium, $1,000.
(d) Earned revenues amounting to $2,700: $1,700 in cash and $1,000 on account.
(e) Paid cash on account to the company that supplied the office supplies in transaction (b), $1,800.
(f) Paid office rent for the month, $650.
(g) Withdrew cash for personal use, $150.

REQUIRED
Show the effect of each transaction on the individual accounts of the expanded accounting equation: *Assets = Liabilities + Owner's Equity (Capital – Drawing + Revenues – Expenses)*. After transaction (g), report the totals for each element. Demonstrate that the accounting equation has remained in balance.

P 2-10B (LO5)

✓ Net income: $2,050

INCOME STATEMENT Based on Problem 2-9B, prepare an income statement for David Segal for the month of October 20--.

P 2-11B (LO5)

✓ Capital, 10/31: $16,900

STATEMENT OF OWNER'S EQUITY Based on Problem 2-9B, prepare a statement of owner's equity for David Segal for the month of October 20--.

P 2-12B (LO5)

✓ Total assets, 10/31: $17,100

BALANCE SHEET Based on Problem 2-9B, prepare a balance sheet for David Segal as of October 31, 20--.

 MANAGING YOUR WRITING

Write a brief memo that explains the differences and similarities between expenses and withdrawals.

MASTERY PROBLEM

✓ Cash following (p): $3,105; Revenue following (p): $2,100

Lisa Vozniak started her own business, We Do Windows. She offers interior and exterior window cleaning for local area residents. Lisa rents a garage to store her tools and cleaning supplies and has a part-time assistant to answer the phone and handle third-story work. (Lisa is afraid of heights.) The transactions for the month of July are as follows:

(a) On the first day of the month, Vozniak invested cash by making a deposit in a bank account for the business, $8,000.

(continued)

(b) Paid rent for July, $150.

(c) Purchased a used van for cash, $5,000.

(d) Purchased tools on account from Clean Tools, $600.

(e) Purchased cleaning supplies that cost $300. Paid $200 cash and will pay the balance next month, $100.

(f) Paid part-time assistant (wages) for first half of month, $100.

(g) Paid for advertising, $75.

(h) Paid two-year premium for liability insurance on van, $480.

(i) Received cash from clients for services performed, $800.

(j) Performed cleaning services for clients on account, $500.

(k) Paid telephone bill, $40.

(l) Received cash from clients for window cleaning performed on account in transaction (j), $200.

(m) Paid part-time assistant (wages) for last half of month, $150.

(n) Made partial payment on tools purchased in transaction (d), $200.

(o) Earned additional revenues amounting to $800: $600 in cash and $200 on account.

(p) Vozniak withdrew cash at the end of the month for personal expenses, $100.

REQUIRED

1. Enter the above transactions in an accounting equation similar to the one illustrated below.

Assets (Items Owned)						=	Liabilities (Amounts Owed)	+	Owner's Equity				
									(Owner's Investment) +		(Earnings)		
Cash +	Accounts Receivable	+ Supplies +	Prepaid Insurance	+ Tools + Van		=	Accounts Payable	+	Lisa Vozniak, Capital	– Lisa Vozniak, Drawing	+ Revenues	– Expenses	Description

2. After transaction (p), compute the balance of each account.

3. Prepare an income statement for We Do Windows for the month of July 20--.

4. Prepare a statement of owner's equity for We Do Windows for the month of July 20--.

5. Prepare a balance sheet for We Do Windows as of July 31, 20--.

CHALLENGE PROBLEM

This problem challenges you to apply your cumulative accounting knowledge to move a step beyond the material in the chapter.

✓ Cash difference: $2,165

In this chapter, you learned about three important financial statements: the income statement, statement of owner's equity, and balance sheet. As mentioned in the margin note on page 34, most firms also prepare a statement of cash flows. Part of this statement reports the **cash received** from customers and **cash paid** for goods and services.

REQUIRED

Take another look at the Demonstration Problem for Damon Young's "Home and Away Inspections." Note that when revenues are measured based on the amount earned, and expenses are measured based on the amount incurred, net income for the period was $4,165. Now, compute the difference between cash received from customers and cash paid to suppliers of goods and services by completing the form provided below. Are these measures different? Which provides a better measure of profitability?

Cash from customers   _____
Cash paid for wages   _____
Cash paid for rent   _____
Cash paid for utilities   _____
Cash paid for insurance   _____
Cash paid for supplies   _____
Cash paid for telephone   _____
Total cash paid for operating items   _____

Difference between cash received from
    customers and cash paid for
    goods and services   _____

ANSWERS TO SELF-STUDY QUESTIONS AND EXERCISES

True/False Questions

1. T
2. F (Accounts Payable is a liability.)
3. T
4. T
5. F (Other changes could occur: capital could increase, revenue could increase, etc.)
6. T
7. F (net income)

Multiple Choice Questions

1. c   2. a   3. b   4. d   5. c

U REVU   Exercises

1.
Account	Classification
Accounts Receivable	A
Accounts Payable	L
Judy Smith, Capital	OE

2. Assets = Liabilities + Owner's Equity

3.
Transaction	Assets	Liabilities	Owner's Equity
a. Purchase of an asset on account.	+	+	
b. Made payment on account for transaction (a).	−	−	

4.
Account	Classification	Financial Statement
Accounts Payable	L	BS
Peggy Welsch, Drawing	OE	SOE
Rent Expense	E	IS
Sales	R	IS
Equipment	A	BS

Chapter 3

The Double-Entry Framework

Tired of receiving spam e-mail messages? Or, are you worried about your computer picking up a virus? Businesses have the same concerns. Computer viruses can cause serious financial damage to a business. In response to demand for e-mail security, AppRiver was founded in April of 2002 to provide simple, yet powerful e-mail security solutions to businesses of any size. The company is based in Gulf Breeze, Florida, and maintains multiple data centers at secure locations in the United States and Europe. AppRiver's 100 employees protect more than 35,000 customers around the world from spam, viruses, and Internet pollution.

Just as e-mail security is important to you in your personal life and to businesses, the same can be said about accounting. A solid understanding of financial accounting will help you manage your personal finances and help you understand business transactions in your professional life. In this chapter, you will learn about the double-entry framework used by businesses to enter transactions into an accounting system. You could use the same concepts for your personal transactions or for a business you might start.

The terms asset, liability, owner's equity, revenue, and expense were explained in Chapter 2. Examples showed how individual business transactions change one or more of these basic accounting elements. Each transaction had a dual effect. An increase or decrease in any asset, liability, owner's equity, revenue, or expense was *always* accompanied by an offsetting change within the basic accounting elements. The fact that each transaction has a dual effect upon the accounting elements provides the basis for what is called **double-entry accounting**. To understand double-entry accounting, it is important to learn how T accounts work and the role of debits and credits in accounting.

THE T ACCOUNT

LO1 Define the parts of a T account.

The assets of a business may consist of a number of items, such as cash, accounts receivable, equipment, buildings, and land. The liabilities may consist of one or more items, such as accounts payable and notes payable. Similarly, owner's equity may consist of the owner's investments and various revenue and expense items. A separate account is used to record the increases and decreases in each type of asset, liability, owner's equity, revenue, and expense.

The T account gets its name from the fact that it resembles the letter T. The three major parts of an account are as follows:

1. the title,
2. the debit, or left side, and
3. the credit, or right side.

Title	
Debit = Left	Credit = Right

The debit side is always on the left, and the credit side is always on the right. This is true for all types of asset, liability, owner's equity, revenue, and expense accounts.

BALANCING A T ACCOUNT

LO2 Foot and balance a T account

To determine the balance of a T account at any time, simply total the dollar amounts on the debit and credit sides. These totals are known as **footings**. The difference between the footings is called the **balance** of the account. This amount is then written on the side with the larger footing.

In Chapter 2, the accounting equation was used to analyze business transactions. This required columns in which to record the increases and decreases in various accounts. Let's compare this approach with the use of a T account for the transactions affecting cash. When a T account is used, increases in cash are recorded on the debit side and decreases are recorded on the credit side. Transactions for Jessie Jane's Campus Delivery Service are shown in Figure 3-1.

FIGURE 3-1 Cash T Account

COLUMNAR SUMMARY (From Chapter 2, page 31)		T ACCOUNT FORM				
Transaction	**Cash**		Cash			
(a)	2,000	(a)	2,000	(b)	1,200
(b)	(1,200)	(e)	500	(d)	300
(d)	(300)	(k)	570	(f)	200
(e)	500	(n)	430	(g)	50
(f)	(200)	footing ⟶	**3,500**	(i)	80
(g)	(50)			(j)	200
(i)	(80)			(l)	300
(j)	(200)			(m)	650
(k)	570			(o)	150
(l)	(300)	Balance ⟶	370		**3,130** ⟵ footing
(m)	(650)				
(n)	430				
(o)	(150)				
Balance	370				

U REVU Complete U REVU-1 on **page 74** to test your basic understanding of LO2.

DEBITS AND CREDITS

LO3 Describe the effects of debits and credits on specific types of accounts.

To **debit** an account means to enter an amount on the left or debit side of the account. To **credit** an account means to enter an amount on the right or credit side of the account. *Debits may increase or decrease the balances of specific accounts. This is also true for credits. To learn how to use debits and credits, it is best to focus on the accounting equation.*

Abbreviations:
Often debit and credit are abbreviated as: Dr. = Debit, Cr. = Credit (based on the Latin terms "debere" and "credere")

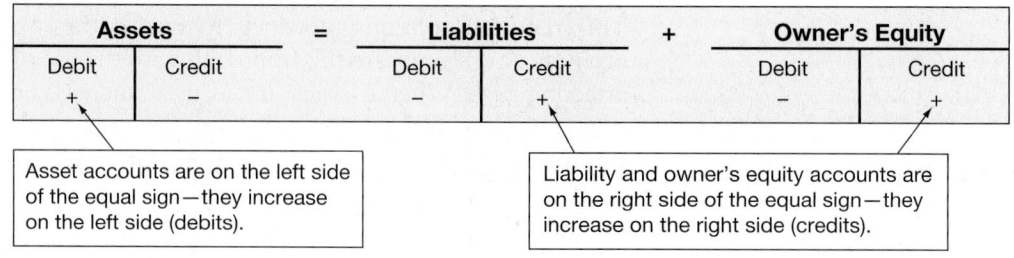

Assets		=	**Liabilities**		+	**Owner's Equity**	
Debit	Credit		Debit	Credit		Debit	Credit
+	–		–	+		–	+

Asset accounts are on the left side of the equal sign—they increase on the left side (debits).

Liability and owner's equity accounts are on the right side of the equal sign—they increase on the right side (credits).

ASSETS

Assets are on the left side of the accounting equation. Therefore, increases are entered on the left (debit) side of an asset account, and decreases are entered on the right (credit) side.

LIABILITIES AND OWNER'S EQUITY

Liabilities and owner's equity are on the right side of the equation. Therefore, increases are entered on the right (credit) side, and decreases are entered on the left (debit) side.

THE OWNER'S EQUITY UMBRELLA

Owner's equity includes four types of accounts: Owner's Capital, Revenues, Expenses, and Drawing. Expanding the accounting equation helps illustrate the use of debits and credits. Since these accounts affect owner's equity, they are shown under the "umbrella" of owner's equity in the accounting equation in Figure 3-2.

FIGURE 3-2 The Accounting Equation and the Owner's Equity Umbrella

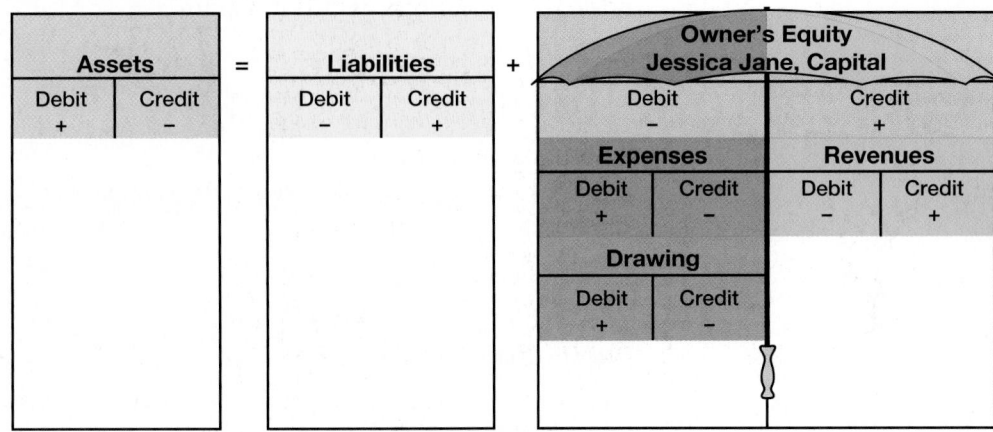

OWNER'S CAPITAL

The owner's capital account, Jessica Jane, Capital, in Figure 3-2 reports the amount the owner has invested in the business. These investments increase the owner's equity and are credited to the owner's capital account.

DRAWING

Withdrawals of cash and other assets by the owner for personal reasons decrease owner's equity. Withdrawals could be debited directly to the owner's capital account. However, readers of financial statements want to know the amount of withdrawals for the accounting period. Thus, as shown in Figure 3-2, withdrawals are debited to a separate account, Drawing.

REVENUES

Revenues increase owner's equity. Revenues could be recorded directly on the credit side of the owner's capital account. However, readers of financial statements are interested in the specific types of revenues earned. Therefore, specific revenue accounts, like Delivery Fees, Sales, and Service Fees, are used. These specific accounts are credited when revenue is earned.

EXPENSES

Expenses decrease owner's equity. Expenses could be recorded on the debit side of the owner's capital account. However, readers of financial statements want to see the types

LEARNING KEY

You could credit the owner's capital account for revenues and debit the capital account for expenses and withdrawals. However, this is not a good idea. Using specific accounts provides additional information. Remember: An increase in an expense decreases owner's equity.

of expenses incurred during the accounting period. Thus, specific expense accounts are maintained for items like rent, wages, advertising, and utilities. These specific accounts are debited as expenses are incurred.

NORMAL BALANCES

A **normal balance** is the side of an account that is used to increase the account. Thus, the normal balances for the accounts illustrated in Figure 3-2 are shown with a "+" sign. Since assets are debited for increases, these accounts normally have **debit balances**. Liability and owner's capital accounts are credited for increases; thus, these accounts normally have **credit balances**. Since expense and drawing accounts are debited for increases (reducing owner's equity), these accounts normally have debit balances. Finally, revenue accounts are credited for increases (increasing owner's equity); thus, these accounts normally have credit balances. A summary of normal balances is provided in Figure 3-3.

FIGURE 3-3 Normal Balances

ACCOUNT	INCREASE	DECREASE	NORMAL BALANCE
Assets	Debit	Credit	Debit
Liabilities	Credit	Debit	Credit
Owner's Capital	Credit	Debit	Credit
Revenues	Credit	Debit	Credit
Expenses	Debit	Credit	Debit
Drawing	Debit	Credit	Debit

U REVU ▶ Complete U REVU-2 on **page 74** to test your basic understanding of LO3.

TRANSACTION ANALYSIS

LO4 Use T accounts to analyze transactions.

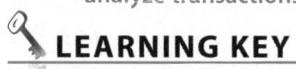
LEARNING KEY

If you have a debit, you must always have at least one credit. If you have a credit, you must always have at least one debit.

In Chapter 2, you learned how to analyze transactions by using the accounting equation. Here, we continue to use the accounting equation, but add debits and credits by using T accounts. As shown in Figure 3-4, the three basic questions that must be answered when analyzing a transaction are essentially the same but are expanded slightly to address the use of the owner's equity umbrella and T accounts. You must determine the location of the account within the accounting equation and/or the owner's equity umbrella. You must also determine whether the accounts should be debited or credited.

FIGURE 3-4 Steps in Transaction Analysis

1. **What happened?**
   Be sure you understand the event that has taken place.

2. **Which accounts are affected?**
   Once you understand what happened, you must:

   - Identify the accounts that are affected.
   - Classify these accounts as assets, liabilities, owner's equity, revenues, or expenses.
   - Identify the location of the accounts in the accounting equation and/or the owner's equity umbrella—left or right.

3. **How is the accounting equation affected?**

   - Determine whether the accounts have increased or decreased.
   - Determine whether the accounts should be debited or credited.
   - Make certain the accounting equation remains in balance after the transaction has been entered.
     (1) Assets = Liabilities + Owner's Equity.
     (2) Debits = Credits for every transaction.

DEBITS AND CREDITS: ASSET, LIABILITY, AND OWNER'S EQUITY ACCOUNTS

Transactions (a) through (d) from Jessie Jane's Campus Delivery Service (Chapter 2) demonstrate the double-entry process for transactions affecting asset, liability, and owner's equity accounts.

As you study each transaction, answer the three questions: (1) What happened? (2) Which accounts are affected? and (3) How is the accounting equation affected? The transaction statement tells you what happened. The analysis tells which accounts are affected. The illustration shows you how the accounting equation is affected.

Transaction (a): Investment by owner

Jessica Jane opened a bank account with a deposit of $2,000 for her business (Figure 3-5).

Analysis. As a result of this transaction, the business acquired an asset, Cash. In exchange for the asset, the business gave Jessica Jane owner's equity. The owner's equity account is called Jessica Jane, Capital. The transaction is entered as an increase in an asset and an increase in owner's equity. Debit **Cash** and credit **Jessica Jane, Capital** for $2,000.

FIGURE 3-5 Transaction (a): Investment by Owner

Assets		=	Liabilities		+	Owner's Equity	
Debit +	Credit −		Debit −	Credit +		Debit −	Credit +
Cash						**Jessica Jane, Capital**	
(a) 2,000							(a) 2,000
$2,000		=	$0		+	$2,000	
$2,000		=		$2,000			

Transaction (b): Purchase of an asset for cash

Jessie bought a motor scooter (delivery equipment) for $1,200 cash (Figure 3-6).

Analysis. Jessie exchanged one asset, Cash, for another, Delivery Equipment. Debit Delivery Equipment and credit Cash for $1,200. Notice that the total assets are still $2,000 as they were following transaction (a). Transaction (b) shifted assets from cash to delivery equipment, but total assets remained the same.

FIGURE 3-6 Transaction (b): Purchase of an Asset for Cash

Assets		=	Liabilities		+	Owner's Equity	
Debit	Credit	=	Debit	Credit	+	Debit	Credit
+	−		−	+		−	+
Cash						**Jessica Jane, Capital**	
Bal. 2,000							Bal. 2,000
	(b) 1,200						
Bal. 800							
Delivery Equipment							
(b) 1,200							
$2,000		=	$0		+	$2,000	
$2,000		=			$2,000		

Transaction (c): Purchase of an asset on account

Jessie bought a second motor scooter on account for $900 (Figure 3-7). Recall from chapter 2 that "on account" means Jessie will pay for the asset later.

Analysis. The asset, Delivery Equipment, increases by $900 and the liability, Accounts Payable, increases by the same amount. Thus, debit Delivery Equipment and credit Accounts Payable for $900.

FIGURE 3-7 Transaction (c): Purchase of an Asset on Account

Assets		=	Liabilities		+	Owner's Equity	
Debit	Credit	=	Debit	Credit	+	Debit	Credit
+	−		−	+		−	+
Cash			**Accounts Payable**			**Jessica Jane, Capital**	
Bal. 800				(c) 900			Bal. 2,000
Delivery Equipment							
Bal. 1,200							
(c) 900							
Bal. 2,100							
$2,900		=	$900		+	$2,000	
$2,900		=			$2,900		

Transaction (d): Payment on account

Jessie made the first $300 payment on the scooter purchased in transaction (c) (Figure 3-8).

Analysis. This payment decreases the asset, Cash, and decreases the liability, Accounts Payable. Debit Accounts Payable and credit Cash for $300.

FIGURE 3-8 Transaction (d): Payment on Account

Assets		=	Liabilities		+	Owner's Equity	
Debit +	Credit −		Debit −	Credit +		Debit −	Credit +
Cash			**Accounts Payable**			Jessica Jane, Capital	
Bal. 800				Bal. 900			Bal. 2,000
	(d) 300		(d) 300				
Bal. 500				Bal. 600			
Delivery Equipment							
Bal. 2,100							
$2,600		=	$600		+	$2,000	
$2,600		=		**$2,600**			

Notice that for transactions (a) through (d), the debits equal credits and the accounting equation is in balance. Review transactions (a) through (d). Again, identify the accounts that were affected and how they were classified (assets, liabilities, or owner's equity). Finally, note each account's location within the accounting equation.

DEBITS AND CREDITS: INCLUDING REVENUES, EXPENSES, AND DRAWING

Transactions (a) through (d) involved only assets, liabilities, and the owner's capital account. To complete the illustration of Jessie Jane's Campus Delivery Service, the equation is expanded to include revenues, expenses, and drawing. Remember, revenues increase owner's equity and are shown under the credit side of the capital account. Expenses and drawing decrease owner's equity and are shown under the debit side of the capital account. The expanded equation is shown in Figure 3-9.

LEARNING KEY

Credits increase the capital account. Revenues increase capital. Thus, revenues are shown under the credit side of the capital account. Debits decrease the capital account. Expenses and drawing reduce owner's equity. Thus, they are shown under the debit side of the capital account.

FIGURE 3-9 The Expanded Accounting Equation

Assets		=	Liabilities		+	Owner's Equity					
Debit +	Credit −		Debit −	Credit +		Debit −				Credit +	
						Drawing		**Expenses**		**Revenues**	
						Debit +	Credit −	Debit +	Credit −	Debit −	Credit +

Transaction (e): Delivery revenues earned in cash

Jessie made deliveries and received $500 cash from clients (Figure 3-10).

Analysis. The asset, Cash, and the revenue, Delivery Fees, increase. Debit Cash and credit Delivery Fees for $500.

FIGURE 3-10 Transaction (e): Delivery Revenues Earned in Cash

Assets		=	Liabilities		+	Owner's Equity			
Debit	Credit	=	Debit	Credit	+	Debit		Credit	
+	–		–	+		–		+	

Cash			Accounts Payable			Jessica Jane, Capital			
Bal. 500				Bal. 600				Bal. 2,000	
(e) 500									
Bal. 1,000									

					Drawing		Expenses		Revenues	
Delivery Equipment					Debit	Credit	Debit	Credit	Debit	Credit
Bal. 2,100					+	–	+	–	–	+

	Delivery Fees	
	(e)	500

$3,100	=	$600	+	$2,500
$3,100	=			**$3,100**

Transaction (f): Paid rent for month

Jessie paid $200 for office rent for June (Figure 3-11).

Analysis. Rent Expense increases and Cash decreases. Debit <mark>Rent Expense</mark> and credit <mark>Cash</mark> for $200.

A debit to an expense account *increases* that expense and *decreases* owner's equity. Notice that the placement of the plus and minus signs for expenses is opposite the placement of the signs for owner's equity. Note also that expenses are located on the left (debit) side of the owner's equity umbrella.

FIGURE 3-11 Transaction (f): Paid Rent for Month

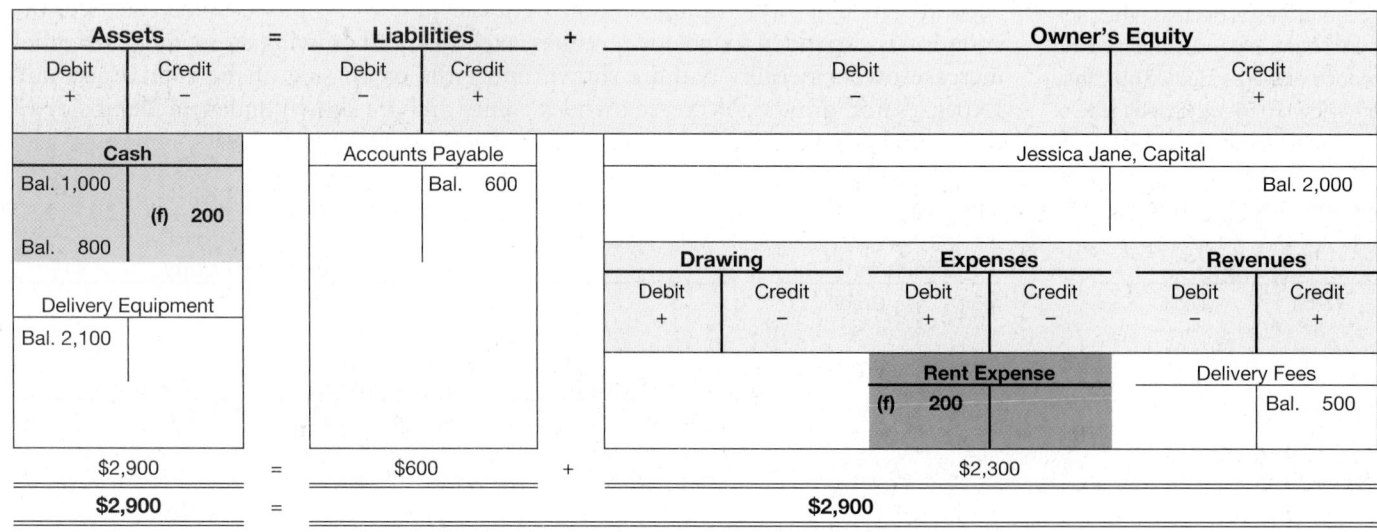

Transaction (g): Paid telephone bill

Jessie paid for telephone service, $50 (Figure 3-12).

Analysis. This transaction, like the previous one, increases an expense and decreases an asset. Debit <mark>Telephone Expense</mark> and credit <mark>Cash</mark> for $50.

FIGURE 3-12 Transaction (g): Paid Telephone Bill

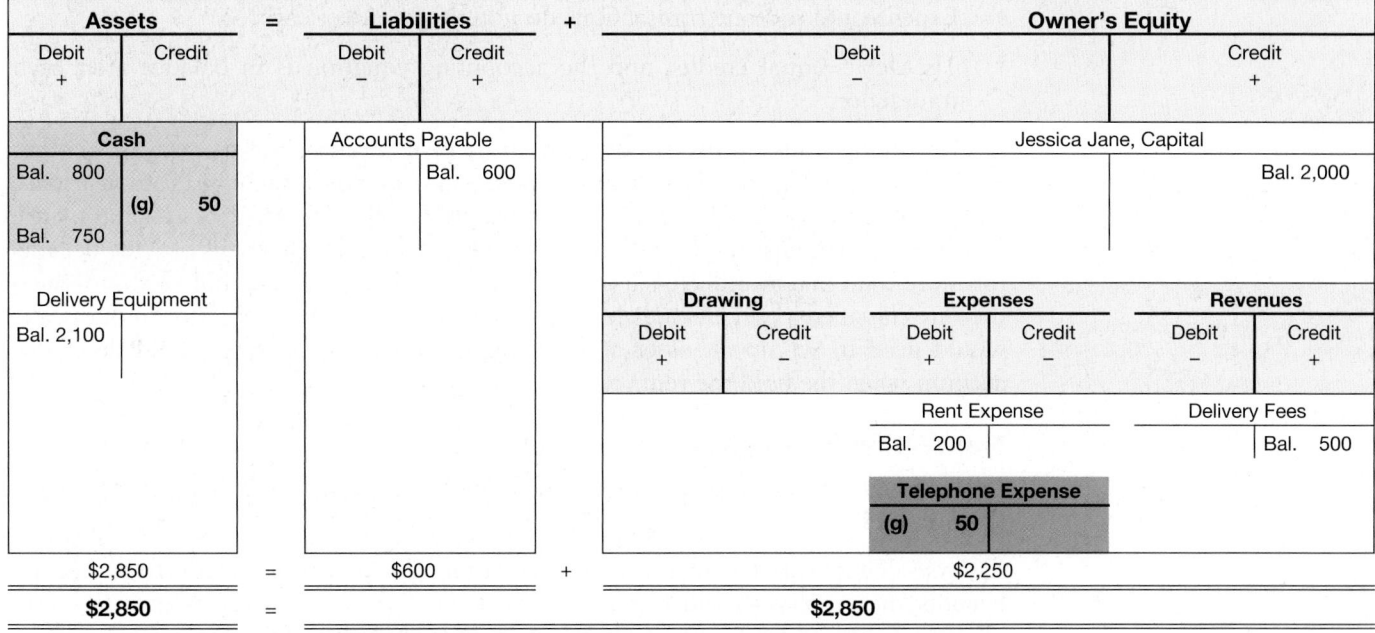

Transaction (h): Delivery revenues earned on account

Jessie made deliveries on account for $600 (Figure 3-13).

Analysis. As discussed in Chapter 2, delivery services are performed for which payment will be received later. This is called offering services "on account" or "on credit." Instead of receiving cash, Jessie receives a promise that her customers will pay cash in the future. Therefore, the asset, Accounts Receivable, increases. Since revenues are recognized when earned, the revenue account, Delivery Fees, also increases. Debit Accounts Receivable and credit Delivery Fees for $600.

FIGURE 3-13 Transaction (h): Delivery Revenues Earned on Account

Assets		=	Liabilities		+		Owner's Equity		
Debit +	Credit −		Debit −	Credit +			Debit −		Credit +

Cash			Accounts Payable				Jessica Jane, Capital		
Bal. 750				Bal. 600					Bal. 2,000

Accounts Receivable						Drawing		Expenses		Revenues	
(h) 600						Debit +	Credit −	Debit +	Credit −	Debit −	Credit +

Delivery Equipment							Rent Expense		Delivery Fees	
Bal. 2,100							Bal. 200		Bal. 500	
									(h) **600**	
									Bal. 1,100	

Telephone Expense
Bal. 50

$3,450	=	$600	+	$2,850
$3,450	=			**$3,450**

Review transactions (e) through (h). Note the following:

- Expense and revenue transactions do not always affect cash.
- The debits equal credits, and the accounting equation is in balance after each transaction.

Upcoming transactions (i) and (j) both involve an exchange of cash for another asset. As you analyze these two transactions, you may wonder why prepaid insurance and supplies are assets while the rent and telephone bill in transactions (f) and (g) are expenses. Prepaid insurance and supplies are assets because they will provide benefits for more than one month. Jessie pays her rent and her telephone bill each month so they are classified as expenses. If Jessie paid her rent only once every three months, she would need to set up an asset account called Prepaid Rent. She would debit this account when she paid the rent.

Transaction (i): Purchase of supplies

Jessie bought pens, paper, delivery envelopes, and other supplies for $80 cash (Figure 3-14).

Analysis. These supplies will last for several months. Since they will generate future benefits, the supplies should be recorded as an asset. An asset, Supplies, increases, and an asset, Cash, decreases. Debit Supplies and credit Cash for $80.

FIGURE 3-14 Transaction (i): Purchase of Supplies

A BROADER VIEW

MELANIE KINTZ / ISTOCKPHOTO.COM

Supplies—Asset or Expense?

When businesses buy office supplies from Staples or other suppliers, the supplies are initially recorded as assets. This is done because the supplies will provide future benefits. Those still remaining in inventory at the end of the accounting period are reported on the balance sheet as assets. Supplies actually used during the period are recognized as an expense on the income statement. We will discuss how to account for the expense in Chapter 5.

Transaction (j): Payment of insurance premium

Jessie paid $200 for an eight-month liability insurance policy (Figure 3-15).

Analysis. Since insurance is paid in advance and will provide future benefits, it is treated as an asset. Therefore, one asset, Prepaid Insurance, increases and another, Cash, decreases. Debit Prepaid Insurance and credit Cash for $200.

FIGURE 3-15 Transaction (j): Payment of Insurance Premium

Assets		=	Liabilities		+	Owner's Equity	
Debit +	Credit −		Debit −	Credit +		Debit −	Credit +

Cash			Accounts Payable			Jessica Jane, Capital	
Bal. 670	(j) 200			Bal. 600			Bal. 2,000
Bal. 470							

Accounts Receivable	
Bal. 600	

Drawing			Expenses			Revenues	
Debit +	Credit −		Debit +	Credit −		Debit −	Credit +

Supplies	
Bal. 80	

Rent Expense		Delivery Fees	
Bal. 200			Bal. 1,100

Prepaid Insurance	
(j) 200	

Telephone Expense	
Bal. 50	

Delivery Equipment	
Bal. 2,100	

$3,450	=	$600	+	$2,850
$3,450	=			**$3,450**

Transaction (k): Cash receipts from prior sales on account

Jessie received $570 in cash for delivery services performed for customers earlier in the month [see transaction (h)] (Figure 3-16).

Analysis. This transaction increases Cash and reduces the amount due from customers reported in Accounts Receivable. Debit Cash and credit Accounts Receivable $570.

As you analyze transaction (k), notice which accounts are affected and the location of these accounts in the accounting equation. Jessie received cash, but this transaction did not affect revenue. The revenue was recorded in transaction (h). Transaction (k) is an exchange of one asset (Accounts Receivable) for another asset (Cash).

FIGURE 3-16 Transaction (k): Cash Receipts from Prior Sales on Account

As you analyze transactions (l) through (o), make certain that you understand what has happened in each transaction. Identify the accounts that are affected and the locations of these accounts within the accounting equation. Notice that the accounting equation remains in balance after every transaction and debits equal credits for each transaction.

Transaction (l): Purchase of an asset on credit making a partial payment

Jessie bought a third motor scooter for $1,500. Jessie made a down payment of $300 and spread the remaining payments over the next four months (Figure 3-17).

Analysis. The asset, Delivery Equipment, increases by $1,500, Cash decreases by $300, and the liability, Accounts Payable, increases by $1,200. Thus, debit Delivery Equipment for $1,500, credit Cash for $300, and credit Accounts Payable for $1,200. This transaction requires one debit and two credits. Even so, total debits ($1,500) equal the total credits ($1,200 + $300) and the accounting equation remains in balance.

FIGURE 3-17 Transaction (l): Purchase of an Asset on Credit Making a Partial Payment

Assets		=	Liabilities		+	Owner's Equity	
Debit +	Credit −		Debit −	Credit +		Debit −	Credit +

Cash			Accounts Payable			Jessica Jane, Capital	
Bal. 1,040				Bal. 600			Bal. 2,000
	(l) 300			(l) 1,200			
Bal. 740				Bal. 1,800			

Accounts Receivable	
Bal. 30	

Drawing		Expenses		Revenues	
Debit +	Credit −	Debit +	Credit −	Debit −	Credit +

Supplies	
Bal. 80	

Rent Expense		Delivery Fees	
Bal. 200			Bal. 1,100

Prepaid Insurance	
Bal. 200	

Telephone Expense	
Bal. 50	

Delivery Equipment	
Bal. 2,100	
(l) 1,500	
Bal. 3,600	

$4,650	=	$1,800	+	$2,850
$4,650	=		**$4,650**	

Transaction (m): Payment of wages

Jessie paid her part-time employees $650 in wages (Figure 3-18).

Analysis. This is an additional business expense. Wages Expense increases and Cash decreases. Debit Wages Expense and credit Cash for $650.

FIGURE 3-18 Transaction (m): Payment of Wages

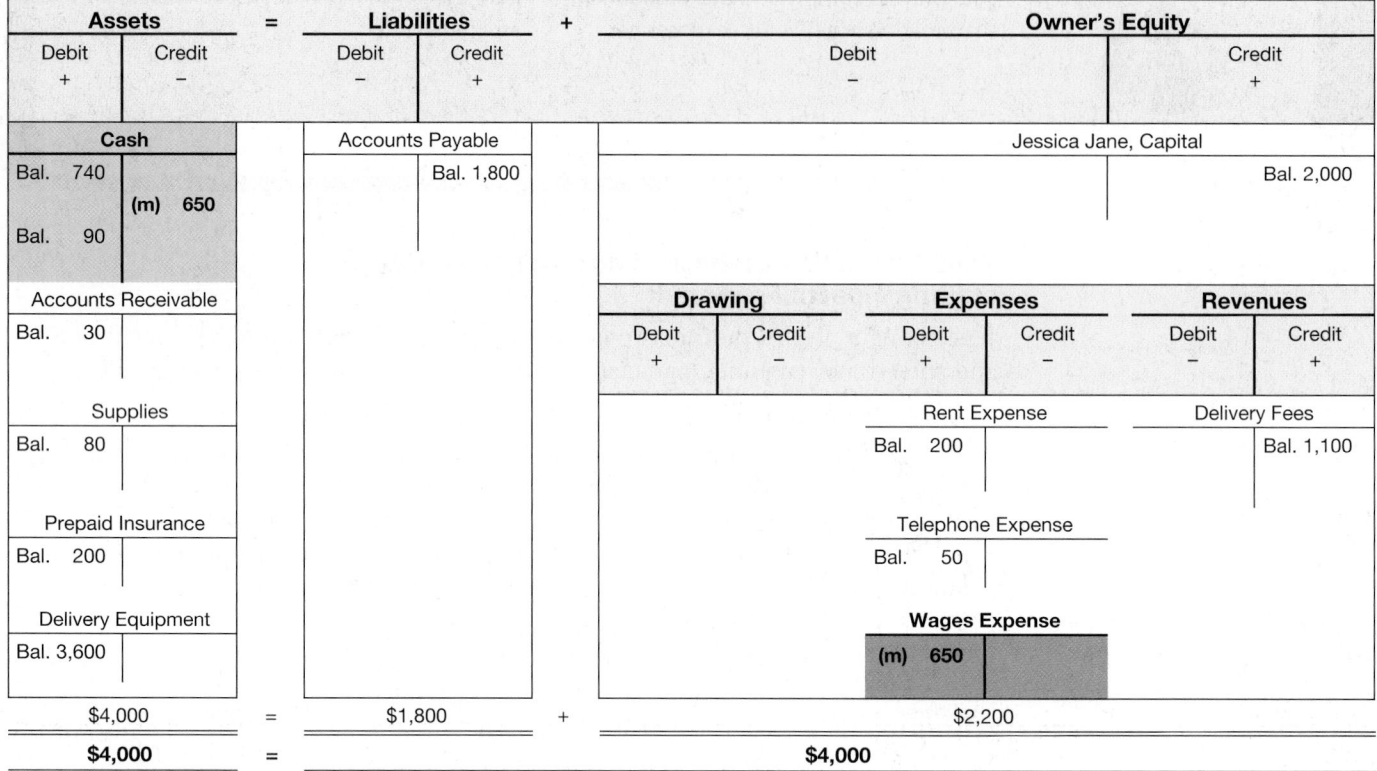

Transaction (n): Deliveries made for cash and credit

Total delivery fees for the remainder of the month amounted to $1,050: $430 in cash and $620 on account (Figure 3-19 on the next page).

Analysis. Since the delivery fees have been earned, the revenue account increases by $1,050. Also, Cash increases by $430 and Accounts Receivable increases by $620. Note once again that one event impacts three accounts. This time we have debits of $430 to Cash and $620 to Accounts Receivable, and a credit of $1,050 to Delivery Fees. As before, the total debits ($430 + $620) equal the total credits ($1,050) and the accounting equation remains in balance.

Transaction (o): Withdrawal of cash from business

At the end of the month, Jessie withdrew $150 in cash from the business to purchase books for her classes (Figure 3-20 on the next page).

Analysis. Cash withdrawals decrease owner's equity and decrease cash. Debit Jessica Jane, Drawing and credit Cash for $150.

Withdrawals are reported in the drawing account. Withdrawals by an owner are the opposite of an investment. You could debit the owner's capital account for withdrawals. However, using a specific account tells the user of the accounting information how much was withdrawn for the period.

FIGURE 3-19 Transaction (n): Deliveries Made for Cash and Credit

Assets		=	Liabilities		+	Owner's Equity	
Debit +	Credit −		Debit −	Credit +		Debit −	Credit +

Cash		Accounts Payable		Jessica Jane, Capital	
Bal. 90			Bal. 1,800		Bal. 2,000
(n) 430					
Bal. 520					

Drawing		Expenses		Revenues	
Debit +	Credit −	Debit +	Credit −	Debit +	Credit +

Accounts Receivable			Rent Expense		Delivery Fees	
Bal. 30			Bal. 200			Bal. 1,100
(n) 620						(n) 1,050
Bal. 650						Bal. 2,150

Supplies	
Bal. 80	

Prepaid Insurance			Telephone Expense	
Bal. 200			Bal. 50	

Delivery Equipment			Wages Expense	
Bal. 3,600			Bal. 650	

$5,050	=	$1,800	+	$3,250
$5,050	=		$5,050	

FIGURE 3-20 Transaction (o): Withdrawal of Cash from Business

Assets		=	Liabilities		+	Owner's Equity	
Debit +	Credit −		Debit −	Credit +		Debit −	Credit +

Cash		Accounts Payable		Jessica Jane, Capital	
Bal. 520			Bal. 1,800		Bal. 2,000
	(o) 150				
Bal. 370					

Drawing		Expenses		Revenues	
Debit +	Credit −	Debit +	Credit −	Debit −	Credit +

Accounts Receivable		Jessica Jane, Drawing		Rent Expense		Delivery Fees	
Bal. 650		(o) 150		Bal. 200			Bal. 2,150

Supplies	
Bal. 80	

Prepaid Insurance			Telephone Expense	
Bal. 200			Bal. 50	

Delivery Equipment			Wages Expense	
Bal. 3,600			Bal. 650	

$4,900	=	$1,800	+	$3,100
$4,900	=		$4,900	

SUMMARY OF TRANSACTIONS

In illustrating transactions (a) through (o), each T account for Jessie Jane's Campus Delivery Service shows a balance before and after each transaction. To focus your attention on the transaction being explained, only a single entry was shown. In practice, this is not done. Instead, each account gathers all transactions for a period. Jessie's accounts, with all transactions listed, are shown in Figure 3-21. Note the following four items:

1. The footings are directly under the debit (left) and credit (right) sides of the T account for those accounts with more than one debit or credit.

2. The balance is shown on the side with the larger footing.

3. The footing serves as the balance for accounts with entries on only one side of the account.

4. If an account has only a single entry, it is not necessary to enter a footing or balance.

FIGURE 3-21 Summary of Transactions (a) Through (o)

Assets			=	Liabilities		+	Owner's Equity		
Debit +	Credit −			Debit −	Credit +		Debit −		Credit +

Cash

(a)	2,000	(b)	1,200
(e)	500	(d)	300
(k)	570	(f)	200
(n)	430	(g)	50
	3,500	(i)	80
		(j)	200
		(l)	300
		(m)	650
		(o)	150
			3,130
Bal.	370		

Accounts Receivable

(h)	600	(k)	570
(n)	620		
	1,220		
Bal.	650		

Supplies

(i)	80	

Prepaid Insurance

(j)	200	

Delivery Equipment

(b)	1,200	
(c)	900	
(l)	1,500	
Bal.	3,600	

Accounts Payable

(d)	300	(c)	900
		(l)	1,200
			2,100
		Bal.	1,800

Jessica Jane, Capital

	(a)	2,000

Drawing			Expenses			Revenues	
Debit +	Credit −		Debit +	Credit −		Debit −	Credit +

Jessica Jane, Drawing

(o)	150	

Rent Expense

(f)	200	

Telephone Expense

(g)	50	

Wages Expense

(m)	650	

Delivery Fees

	(e)	500
	(h)	600
	(n)	1,050
	Bal.	2,150

$4,900	=	$1,800	+	$3,100
$4,900	=			**$4,900**

U REVU   Complete U REVU-3 on **page 74** to test your basic understanding of LO4.

THE TRIAL BALANCE

LO5 Prepare a trial balance and explain its purposes and linkages with the financial statements.

Recall the following two very important rules in double-entry accounting:

1. The sum of the debits must equal the sum of the credits.

    At least two accounts are affected by each transaction. This rule is so important that many computer accounting programs will not permit a transaction to be entered into the accounting system unless the debits equal the credits.

2. The accounting equation must remain in balance.

    In illustrating the transactions for Jessie Jane's Campus Delivery Service, the equality of the accounting equation was verified after each transaction. Because of the large number of transactions entered each day, this is not done in practice. Instead, a trial balance is prepared periodically to determine the equality of the debits and credits. A **trial balance** is a list of all accounts showing the title and balance of each account. By totaling the debits and credits, their equality can be tested.

    A trial balance of Jessie's accounts, taken on June 30, 20--, is shown in Figure 3-22. This date is shown on the third line of the heading. The trial balance shows that the debit and credit totals are equal in amount. This is proof that (1) in entering transactions (a) through (o), the total of the debits was equal to the total of the credits, and (2) the accounting equation has remained in balance.

    A trial balance is not a formal statement or report. Normally, only the accountant sees it. As shown in Figure 3-23, a trial balance can be used as an aid in preparing the financial statements.

LEARNING KEY

A trial balance provides proof that total debits equal total credits and shows that the accounting equation is in balance.

Since a trial balance is not a formal statement, dollar signs are not used.

FIGURE 3-22 Trial Balance

ACCOUNT TITLE	DEBIT BALANCE					CREDIT BALANCE				
Jessie Jane's Campus Delivery Service										
Trial Balance										
June 30, 20 --										
Cash		3	7	0	00					
Accounts Receivable		6	5	0	00					
Supplies			8	0	00					
Prepaid Insurance		2	0	0	00					
Delivery Equipment	3	6	0	0	00					
Accounts Payable						1	8	0	0	00
Jessica Jane, Capital						2	0	0	0	00
Jessica Jane, Drawing		1	5	0	00					
Delivery Fees						2	1	5	0	00
Rent Expense		2	0	0	00					
Telephone Expense			5	0	00					
Wages Expense		6	5	0	00					
	5	9	5	0	00	5	9	5	0	00

FIGURE 3-23 Linkages Between the Trial Balance and Financial Statements

Jessie Jane's Campus Delivery Service
Trial Balance
June 30, 20 --

ACCOUNT TITLE	DEBIT BALANCE	CREDIT BALANCE
Cash	3 7 0 00	
Accounts Receivable	6 5 0 00	
Supplies	8 0 00	
Prepaid Insurance	2 0 0 00	
Delivery Equipment	3 6 0 0 00	
Accounts Payable		1 8 0 0 00
Jessica Jane, Capital		2 0 0 0 00
Jessica Jane, Drawing	1 5 0 00	
Delivery Fees		2 1 5 0 00
Rent Expense	2 0 0 00	
Telephone Expense	5 0 00	
Wages Expense	6 5 0 00	
	5 9 5 0 00	5 9 5 0 00

Jessie Jane's Campus Delivery Service
Income Statement
For Month Ended June 30, 20 --

Revenue:		
Delivery fees		$2 1 5 0 00
Expenses:		
Wages expense	$ 6 5 0 00	
Rent expense	2 0 0 00	
Telephone expense	5 0 00	
Total expenses		9 0 0 00
Net income		$1 2 5 0 00

If the beginning capital balance was $2,000 and Jessie made no additional investments, the statement would be prepared as follows:

Jessie Jane's Campus Delivery Service
Statement of Owner's Equity
For Month Ended June 30, 20 --

Jessica Jane, capital, June 1, 20 --		$2 0 0 0 00
Net income for June	$1 2 5 0 00	
Less withdrawals for June	1 5 0 00	
Increase in capital		1 1 0 0 00
Jessica Jane, Capital, June 30, 20 --		$3 1 0 0 00

Jessie Jane's Campus Delivery Service
Statement of Owner's Equity
For Month Ended June 30, 20 --

Jessica Jane, capital, June 1, 20 --		$
Investments during June		2 0 0 0 00
Total investment		$2 0 0 0 00
Net income for June	$1 2 5 0 00	
Less withdrawals for June	1 5 0 00	
Increase in capital		1 1 0 0 00
Jessica Jane, capital, June 30, 20 --		$3 1 0 0 00

Jessie Jane's Campus Delivery Service
Balance Sheet
June 30, 20 --

Assets		Liabilities	
Cash	$ 3 7 0 00	Accounts payable	$1 8 0 0 00
Accounts receivable	6 5 0 00		
Supplies	8 0 00	Owner's Equity	
Prepaid insurance	2 0 0 00	Jessica Jane, capital	3 1 0 0 00
Delivery equipment	3 6 0 0 00		
Total assets	$4 9 0 0 00	Total liabilities and owner's equity	$4 9 0 0 00

U REVU

Complete U REVU-4 on **page 74** to test your basic understanding of LO5.

LEARNING OBJECTIVES	Key Points to Remember

LO1 **Define the parts of a T account.**

The parts of a T account are:
1. the title,
2. the debit or left side, and
3. the credit or right side.

Title	
Debit = Left	Credit = Right

LO2 **Foot and balance a T account.**

Rules for footing and balancing T accounts are:
1. The footings are directly under the debit (left) and credit (right) sides of the T account for those accounts with more than one debit or credit.
2. The balance is shown on the side with the larger footing.
3. The footing serves as the balance for accounts with entries on only one side of the account.
4. If an account has only a single entry, it is not necessary to enter a footing or balance.

LO3 **Describe the effects of debits and credits on specific types of accounts.**

Rules for debits and credits. (See illustration below.)
1. Assets are on the left side of the accounting equation. Therefore, increases are entered on the left (debit) side of an asset account and decreases are entered on the right (credit) side.
2. Liabilities and owner's equity are on the right side of the accounting equation. Therefore, increases are entered on the right (credit) side and decreases are entered on the left (debit) side.
3. Revenues increase owner's equity. Therefore, increases are entered on the right (credit) side and decreases are entered on the left (debit) side.
4. Expenses and drawing decrease owner's equity. Therefore, increases are entered on the left (debit) side and decreases are entered on the right (credit) side.

Accounting Equation with Owner's Equity Umbrella

Assets		=	Liabilities		+	Owner's Equity Jessica Jane, Capital	
Debit +	Credit −		Debit −	Credit +		Debit −	Credit +

Expenses		Revenues	
Debit +	Credit −	Debit −	Credit +

Drawing	
Debit +	Credit −

LO4 **Use T accounts to analyze transactions.**

Picture the accounting equation in your mind as you analyze transactions. When entering transactions in T accounts:
1. The sum of the debits must equal the sum of the credits.
2. At least two accounts are affected by each transaction.
3. When finished, the accounting equation must remain in balance.

LO5 **Prepare a trial balance and explain its purposes and linkages with the financial statements.**

A trial balance shows that the debit and credit totals are equal. A trial balance also can be used in preparing the financial statements.

DEMONSTRATION PROBLEM

Celia Pints opened We-Buy, You-Pay Shopping Services. For a fee that is based on the amount of research and shopping time required, Pints and her associates will shop for almost anything from groceries to home furnishings. Business is particularly heavy around Christmas and in early summer. The business operates from a rented store front. The associates receive a commission based on the revenues they produce and a mileage reimbursement for the use of their personal automobiles for shopping trips. Pints decided to use the following accounts to record transactions.

Assets	Owner's Equity
Cash	Celia Pints, Capital
Accounts Receivable	Celia Pints, Drawing
Office Equipment	Revenue
Computer Equipment	Shopping Fees
Liabilities	Expenses
Accounts Payable	Rent Expense
Notes Payable	Telephone Expense
	Commissions Expense
	Utilities Expense
	Travel Expense

The following transactions are for the month of December 20--.

(a) Pints invested cash in the business, $30,000.

(b) Bought office equipment for $10,000. Paid $2,000 in cash and promised to pay the balance over the next four months.

(c) Paid rent for December, $500.

(d) Provided shopping services for customers on account, $5,200.

(e) Paid telephone bill, $90.

(f) Borrowed cash from the bank by signing a note payable, $5,000.

(g) Bought a computer and printer, $4,800.

(h) Collected cash from customers for services performed on account, $4,000.

(i) Paid commissions to associates for revenues generated during the first half of the month, $3,500.

(j) Paid utility bill, $600.

(k) Paid cash on account for the office equipment purchased in transaction (b), $2,000.

(l) Earned shopping fees of $13,200: $6,000 in cash and $7,200 on account.

(m) Paid commissions to associates for last half of month, $7,000.

(n) Paid mileage reimbursements for the month, $1,500.

(o) Paid cash on note payable to bank, $1,000.

(p) Pints withdrew cash for personal use, $2,000.

REQUIRED

1. Enter the transactions for December in T accounts. Use the accounting equation as a guide for setting up the T accounts.

2. Foot the T accounts and determine their balances as necessary.

3. Prepare a trial balance of the accounts as of December 31 of the current year.

4. Prepare an income statement for the month ended December 31 of the current year.

5. Prepare a statement of owner's equity for the month ended December 31 of the current year.

6. Prepare a balance sheet as of December 31 of the current year.

Solution 1, 2.

Assets		=	Liabilities		+	Owner's Equity	
Debit +	Credit −		Debit −	Credit +		Debit −	Credit +

Cash

(a) 30,000	(b) 2,000		
(f) 5,000	(c) 500		
(h) 4,000	(e) 90		
(l) 6,000	(g) 4,800		
45,000	(i) 3,500		
	(j) 600		
	(k) 2,000		
	(m) 7,000		
	(n) 1,500		
	(o) 1,000		
	(p) 2,000		
	24,990		

Bal. 20,010

Accounts Receivable

(d) 5,200	(h) 4,000
(l) 7,200	
12,400	

Bal. 8,400

Office Equipment

(b) 10,000	

Computer Equipment

(g) 4,800	

$43,210

$43,210

Accounts Payable

(k) 2,000	(b) 8,000
	Bal. 6,000

Notes Payable

(o) 1,000	(f) 5,000
	Bal. 4,000

= $10,000 +

=

Celia Pints, Capital

	(a) 30,000

Drawing		Expenses		Revenues	
Debit +	Credit −	Debit +	Credit −	Debit −	Credit +

Celia Pints, Drawing

(p) 2,000	

Rent Expense

(c) 500	

Telephone Expense

(e) 90	

Commissions Expense

(i) 3,500	
(m) 7,000	
Bal. 10,500	

Utilities Expense

(j) 600	

Travel Expense

(n) 1,500	

Shopping Fees

	(d) 5,200
	(l) 13,200
	Bal. 18,400

$33,210

$43,210 = **$43,210**

(continued)

3.

We-Buy, You-Pay Shopping Services Trial Balance December 31, 20 --										
ACCOUNT TITLE	DEBIT BALANCE					CREDIT BALANCE				
Cash	20	0	1	0	00					
Accounts Receivable	8	4	0	0	00					
Office Equipment	10	0	0	0	00					
Computer Equipment	4	8	0	0	00					
Accounts Payable						6	0	0	0	00
Notes Payable						4	0	0	0	00
Celia Pints, Capital						30	0	0	0	00
Celia Pints, Drawing	2	0	0	0	00					
Shopping Fees						18	4	0	0	00
Rent Expense		5	0	0	00					
Telephone Expense			9	0	00					
Commissions Expense	10	5	0	0	00					
Utilities Expense		6	0	0	00					
Travel Expense	1	5	0	0	00					
	58	4	0	0	00	58	4	0	0	00

4.

We-Buy, You-Pay Shopping Services Income Statement For Month Ended December 31, 20 --										
Revenue:										
Shopping fees						$18	4	0	0	00
Expenses:										
Commissions expense	$10	5	0	0	00					
Travel expense	1	5	0	0	00					
Utilities expense		6	0	0	00					
Rent expense		5	0	0	00					
Telephone expense			9	0	00					
Total expenses						13	1	9	0	00
Net income						$ 5	2	1	0	00

5.

We-Buy, You-Pay Shopping Services Statement of Owner's Equity For Month Ended December 31, 20 - -										
Celia Pints, capital, December 1, 20 --						$				
Investments during December						30	0	0	0	00
Total investment						$30	0	0	0	00
Net income for December	$5	2	1	0	00					
Less withdrawals for December	2	0	0	0	00					
Increase in capital						3	2	1	0	00
Celia Pints, capital, December 31, 20 --						$33	2	1	0	00

6.

We-Buy, You-Pay Shopping Services Balance Sheet December 31, 20 - -												
Assets						Liabilities						
Cash	$20	0	1	0	00	Accounts payable	$ 6	0	0	0	00
Accounts receivable	8	4	0	0	00	Notes payable	4	0	0	0	00
Office equipment	10	0	0	0	00	Total liabilities	$10	0	0	0	00
Computer equipment	4	8	0	0	00						
						Owner's Equity					
						Celia Pints, capital	33	2	1	0	00
Total assets	$43	2	1	0	00	Total liabilities and owner's equity	$43	2	1	0	00

KEY TERMS

balance (51)   The difference between the footings of an account.

credit (52)   To enter an amount on the right side of an account.

credit balance (54)   The normal balance of liability, owner's equity, and revenue accounts.

debit (52)   To enter an amount on the left side of an account.

debit balance (54)   The normal balance of asset, expense, and drawing accounts.

double-entry accounting (51)   A system in which each transaction has a dual effect on the accounting elements.

footings (51)   The total dollar amounts on the debit and credit sides of an account.

normal balance (54)   The side of an account that is increased.

trial balance (67)   A list of all accounts, showing the title and balance of each account, used to prove that the sum of the debits equals the sum of the credits.

SELF-STUDY QUESTIONS AND EXERCISES

True/False Questions

1. LO3   To debit an account is to enter an amount on the left side of the account.

2. LO3   Liability accounts normally have debit balances.

3. LO3   Increases in owner's equity are entered as credits.

4. LO3   Revenue accounts normally have debit balances.

5. LO3   To credit an account is to enter an amount on the right side of the account.

6. LO3   A debit to an asset account will decrease it.

Multiple Choice Questions

1. LO3   A common example of an asset is

   (a) Professional Fees.
   (b) Rent Expense.
   (c) Accounts Receivable.
   (d) Accounts Payable.

2. **LO3**   The accounting equation may be expressed as

(a) Assets = Liabilities − Owner's Equity.
(b) Assets = Liabilities + Owner's Equity.
(c) Liabilities = Owner's Equity − Assets.
(d) all of the above.

3. **LO3**   Liability, owner's equity, and revenue accounts normally have

(a) debit balances.
(b) large balances.
(c) negative balances.
(d) credit balances.

4. **LO4**   To record the payment of rent expense, an accountant would

(a) debit Cash; credit Rent Expense.
(b) debit Rent Expense; debit Cash.
(c) debit Rent Expense; credit Cash.
(d) credit Rent Expense; credit Cash.

5. **LO4**   An investment of cash by the owner will

(a) increase assets and owner's equity.
(b) increase assets and liabilities.
(c) increase liabilities and owner's equity.
(d) increase owner's equity and decrease liabilities.

U REVU   **Exercises**

1. **LO2**   Foot and balance the accounts receivable T account shown below.

Accounts Receivable	
100	50
200	30

2. **LO3**   Complete the following questions using either "debit" or "credit":

(a) The asset account Supplies is increased with a _____.
(b) The owner's capital account is increased with a _____.
(c) The rent expense account is increased with a _____.

3. **LO4**   Analyze the following transaction using the T accounts provided below. Robb Todd purchased equipment for $300 cash.

Cash	Equipment

4. **LO5**   The following accounts have normal balances. Prepare a trial balance. Accounts Payable, $20; Accounts Receivable, $90; Capital, $40; Sales, $200; Cash, $100; Rent Expense, $70.

The answers to the Self-Study Questions and Exercises are at the end of the chapter (page 85).

REVIEW QUESTIONS

LO1 1. What are the three major parts of a T account?

LO1 2. What is the left side of the T account called? the right side?

LO2 3. What is a footing?

LO3 4. What is the relationship between the revenue and expense accounts and the owner's equity account?

LO5 5. What is the function of the trial balance?

SERIES A EXERCISES

E 3-1A (LO2)

✓ Cash bal.: $1,200 (Dr.)

FOOT AND BALANCE A T ACCOUNT Foot and balance the cash T account shown below.

Cash	
500	100
400	200
600	

E 3-2A (LO3)

DEBIT AND CREDIT ANALYSIS Complete the following statements using either "debit" or "credit":

(a) The cash account is increased with a _____.
(b) The owner's capital account is increased with a _____.
(c) The delivery equipment account is increased with a _____.
(d) The cash account is decreased with a _____.
(e) The liability account Accounts Payable is increased with a _____.
(f) The revenue account Delivery Fees is increased with a _____.
(g) The asset account Accounts Receivable is increased with a _____.
(h) The rent expense account is increased with a _____.
(i) The owner's drawing account is increased with a _____.

E 3-3A (LO2/3/4)

✓ Cash bal. after (c): $2,700 (Dr.)

ANALYSIS OF T ACCOUNTS Jim Arnold began a business called Arnold's Shoe Repair.

1. Create T accounts for Cash; Supplies; Jim Arnold, Capital; and Utilities Expense. Identify the following transactions by letter and place them on the proper side of the T accounts:

   (a) Invested cash in the business, $5,000.
   (b) Purchased supplies for cash, $800.
   (c) Paid utility bill, $1,500.

2. Foot the T account for cash and enter the ending balance.

E 3-4A (LO3)

NORMAL BALANCE OF ACCOUNT Indicate the normal balance (debit or credit) for each of the following accounts:

1. Cash	5. Supplies
2. Wages Expense	6. Owner's Capital
3. Accounts Payable	7. Equipment
4. Owner's Drawing	

E 3-5A (LO4)

TRANSACTION ANALYSIS Sheryl Hansen started a business on May 1, 20--. Analyze the following transactions for the first month of business using T accounts. Label each T account with the title of the account affected and then place the transaction letter and the dollar amount on the debit or credit side.

(a) Invested cash in the business, $4,000.
(b) Bought equipment for cash, $500.
(c) Bought equipment on account, $800.
(d) Paid cash on account for equipment purchased in transaction (c), $300.
(e) Withdrew cash for personal use, $700.

E 3-6A (LO2)
✓ Cash bal. after (e): $2,500 (Dr.)

FOOT AND BALANCE T ACCOUNTS Foot and balance the T accounts prepared in Exercise 3-5A if necessary.

E 3-7A (LO2/4)
✓ Cash bal. after (k): $24,400 (Dr.)

ANALYSIS OF TRANSACTIONS Charles Chadwick opened a business called Charlie's Detective Service in January 20--. Set up T accounts for the following accounts: Cash; Accounts Receivable; Office Supplies; Computer Equipment; Office Furniture; Accounts Payable; Charles Chadwick, Capital; Charles Chadwick, Drawing; Professional Fees; Rent Expense; and Utilities Expense.

The following transactions occurred during the first month of business. Record these transactions in T accounts. After all transactions are recorded, foot and balance the accounts if necessary.

(a) Invested cash in the business, $30,000.
(b) Bought office supplies for cash, $300.
(c) Bought office furniture for cash, $5,000.
(d) Purchased computer and printer on account, $8,000.
(e) Received cash from clients for services, $3,000.
(f) Paid cash on account for computer and printer purchased in transaction (d), $4,000.
(g) Earned professional fees on account during the month, $9,000.
(h) Paid cash for office rent for January, $1,500.
(i) Paid utility bills for the month, $800.
(j) Received cash from clients billed in transaction (g), $6,000.
(k) Withdrew cash for personal use, $3,000.

E 3-8A (LO5)
✓ Trial bal. total debits: $46,000

TRIAL BALANCE Based on the transactions recorded in Exercise 3-7A, prepare a trial balance for Charlie's Detective Service as of January 31, 20--.

E 3-9A (LO5)
✓ Trial bal. total debits: $42,800

TRIAL BALANCE The following accounts have normal balances. Prepare a trial balance for Damon's Lawn Service as of September 30, 20--.

Cash	$ 10,000
Accounts Receivable	6,000
Supplies	1,600
Prepaid Insurance	1,200
Delivery Equipment	16,000
Accounts Payable	4,000
Damon Young, Capital	20,000
Damon Young, Drawing	2,000
Delivery Fees	18,800
Wages Expense	4,200
Rent Expense	1,800

Provided below is a trial balance for Juanita's Delivery Service. **Use this trial balance for Exercises 3-10A, 3-11A, and 3-12A.**

	Juanita's Delivery Service Trial Balance September 30, 20--											
ACCOUNT TITLE	DEBIT BALANCE						CREDIT BALANCE				
Cash	5	0	0	0	00						
Accounts Receivable	3	0	0	0	00						
Supplies		8	0	0	00						
Prepaid Insurance		6	0	0	00						
Delivery Equipment	8	0	0	0	00						
Accounts Payable							2	0	0	0	00
Juanita Raye, Capital							10	0	0	0	00
Juanita Raye, Drawing	1	0	0	0	00						
Delivery Fees							9	4	0	0	00
Wage Expense	2	1	0	0	00						
Rent Expense		9	0	0	00						
	21	4	0	0	00		21	4	0	0	00

E 3-10A (LO5)

✓ Net income: $6,400

INCOME STATEMENT From the information in the trial balance presented above, prepare an income statement for Juanita's Delivery Service for the month ended September 30, 20--.

E 3-11A (LO5)

✓ Capital, 9/30: $15,400

STATEMENT OF OWNER'S EQUITY From the information in the trial balance presented above, prepare a statement of owner's equity for Juanita's Delivery Service for the month ended September 30, 20--.

E 3-12A (LO5)

✓ Total assets, 9/30: $17,400

BALANCE SHEET From the information in the trial balance presented above, prepare a balance sheet for Juanita's Delivery Service as of September 30, 20--.

SERIES A PROBLEMS

P 3-13A (LO2/4/5)

✓ Cash bal. after (p): $14,820 (Dr.);
Trial bal. total debits: $38,200

T ACCOUNTS AND TRIAL BALANCE Harold Long started a business in May 20-- called Harold's Home Repair. Long hired a part-time college student as an assistant. Long has decided to use the following accounts for recording transactions:

Assets
    Cash
    Accounts Receivable
    Office Supplies
    Prepaid Insurance
    Equipment
    Van
Liabilities
    Accounts Payable

Owner's Equity
    Harold Long, Capital
    Harold Long, Drawing
Revenue
    Service Fees
Expenses
    Rent Expense
    Wages Expense
    Telephone Expense
    Gas and Oil Expense

(continued)

The following transactions occurred during May:

(a) Invested cash in the business, $20,000.
(b) Purchased a used van for cash, $7,000.
(c) Purchased equipment on account, $5,000.
(d) Received cash for services rendered, $6,000.
(e) Paid cash on account owed from transaction (c), $2,000.
(f) Paid rent for the month, $900.
(g) Paid telephone bill, $200.
(h) Earned revenue on account, $4,000.
(i) Purchased office supplies for cash, $120.
(j) Paid wages to student, $600.
(k) Purchased a one-year insurance policy, $1,200.
(l) Received cash from services performed in transaction (h), $3,000.
(m) Paid cash for gas and oil expense on the van, $160.
(n) Purchased additional equipment for $3,000, paying $1,000 cash and spreading the remaining payments over the next 10 months.
(o) Earned service fees for the remainder of the month of $3,200: $1,800 in cash and $1,400 on account.
(p) Withdrew cash at the end of the month, $2,800.

REQUIRED

1. Enter the transactions in T accounts, identifying each transaction with its corresponding letter.

2. Foot and balance the accounts where necessary.

3. Prepare a trial balance as of May 31, 20--.

P 3-14A (LO5)

✓ Net income: $11,340

✓ Owner's equity, 5/31: $28,540

✓ Total assets, 5/31: $33,540

NET INCOME AND CHANGE IN OWNER'S EQUITY Refer to the trial balance of Harold's Home Repair in Problem 3-13A to determine the following information. Use the format provided below.

1. a. Total revenue for the month   _____

    b. Total expenses for the month   _____

    c. Net income for the month   _____

2. a. Harold Long's original investment _____
        in the business

        + Net income for the month   _____

        − Owner's drawing   _____

        Increase (decrease) in capital   _____

        = Ending owner's equity   _____

    b. End of month accounting equation:

Assets	=	Liabilities	+	Owner's Equity
_____	=	_____	+	_____

P 3-15A (LO5)

✓ NI: $11,340; Capital, 5/31/20--:

$28,540; Total assets: $33,540

FINANCIAL STATEMENTS Refer to the trial balance in Problem 3-13A and to the analysis of the change in owner's equity in Problem 3-14A.

REQUIRED

1. Prepare an income statement for Harold's Home Repair for the month ended May 31, 20--.

2. Prepare a statement of owner's equity for Harold's Home Repair for the month ended May 31, 20--.

3. Prepare a balance sheet for Harold's Home Repair as of May 31, 20--.

SERIES B EXERCISES

E 3-1B (LO2)
✓ Accts. Pay: $400 (Cr.)

FOOT AND BALANCE A T ACCOUNT Foot and balance the accounts payable T account shown below.

Accounts Payable	
300	450
250	350
	150

E 3-2B (LO3)

DEBIT AND CREDIT ANALYSIS Complete the following statements using either "debit" or "credit":

(a) The asset account Prepaid Insurance is increased with a _____.
(b) The owner's drawing account is increased with a _____.
(c) The asset account Accounts Receivable is decreased with a _____.
(d) The liability account Accounts Payable is decreased with a _____.
(e) The owner's capital account is increased with a _____.
(f) The revenue account Professional Fees is increased with a _____.
(g) The expense account Repair Expense is increased with a _____.
(h) The asset account Cash is decreased with a _____.
(i) The asset account Delivery Equipment is decreased with a _____.

E 3-3B (LO2/3/4)
✓ Cash bal. after (c): $3,900 (Dr.)

ANALYSIS OF T ACCOUNTS Roberto Alvarez began a business called Roberto's Fix-It Shop.

1. Create T accounts for Cash; Supplies; Roberto Alvarez, Capital; and Utilities Expense. Identify the following transactions by letter and place them on the proper side of the T accounts:

   (a) Invested cash in the business, $6,000.
   (b) Purchased supplies for cash, $1,200.
   (c) Paid utility bill, $900.

2. Foot the T account for cash and enter the ending balance.

E 3-4B (LO3)

NORMAL BALANCE OF ACCOUNT Indicate the normal balance (debit or credit) for each of the following accounts:

1. Cash
2. Rent Expense
3. Notes Payable
4. Owner's Drawing
5. Accounts Receivable
6. Owner's Capital
7. Tools

E 3-5B (LO4)

TRANSACTION ANALYSIS George Atlas started a business on June 1, 20--. Analyze the following transactions for the first month of business using T accounts. Label each T account with the title of the account affected and then place the transaction letter and the dollar amount on the debit or credit side.

(a) Invested cash in the business, $7,000.

(b) Purchased equipment for cash, $900.

(c) Purchased equipment on account, $1,500.

(d) Paid cash on account for equipment purchased in transaction (c), $800.

(e) Withdrew cash for personal use, $1,100.

E 3-6B (LO2)
✓ Cash bal. after (e): $4,200 (Dr.)

FOOT AND BALANCE T ACCOUNTS Foot and balance the T accounts prepared in Exercise 3-5B if necessary.

E 3-7B (LO2/4)
✓ Cash bal. after (k): $9,000 (Dr.)

ANALYSIS OF TRANSACTIONS Nicole Lawrence opened a business called Nickie's Neat Ideas in January 20--. Set up T accounts for the following accounts: Cash; Accounts Receivable; Office Supplies; Computer Equipment; Office Furniture; Accounts Payable; Nicole Lawrence, Capital; Nicole Lawrence, Drawing; Professional Fees; Rent Expense; and Utilities Expense.

The following transactions occurred during the first month of business. Record these transactions in T accounts. After all transactions have been recorded, foot and balance the accounts if necessary.

(a) Invested cash in the business, $18,000.

(b) Purchased office supplies for cash, $500.

(c) Purchased office furniture for cash, $8,000.

(d) Purchased computer and printer on account, $5,000.

(e) Received cash from clients for services, $4,000.

(f) Paid cash on account for computer and printer purchased in transaction (d), $2,000.

(g) Earned professional fees on account during the month, $7,000.

(h) Paid office rent for January, $900.

(i) Paid utility bills for the month, $600.

(j) Received cash from clients that were billed previously in transaction (g), $3,000.

(k) Withdrew cash for personal use, $4,000.

E 3-8B (LO5)
✓ Trial bal. total debits: $32,000

TRIAL BALANCE Based on the transactions recorded in Exercise 3-7B, prepare a trial balance for Nickie's Neat Ideas as of January 31, 20--.

E 3-9B (LO5)
✓ Trial bal. total debits: $55,000

TRIAL BALANCE The following accounts have normal balances. Prepare a trial balance for Betty's Cleaning Service as of September 30, 20--.

Cash	$14,000	Betty Par, Capital	$24,000
Accounts Receivable	8,000	Betty Par, Drawing	4,000
Supplies	1,200	Delivery Fees	25,000
Prepaid Insurance	1,800	Wages Expense	6,000
Delivery Equipment	18,000	Rent Expense	2,000
Accounts Payable	6,000		

Provided below is a trial balance for Bill's Delivery Service. **Use this trial balance for Exercises 3-10B, 3-11B, and 3-12B.**

	Bill's Delivery Service Trial Balance September 30, 20 --									
ACCOUNT TITLE		DEBIT BALANCE					CREDIT BALANCE			
Cash	7	0	0	0	00					
Accounts Receivable	4	0	0	0	00					
Supplies		6	0	0	00					
Prepaid Insurance		9	0	0	00					
Delivery Equipment	9	0	0	0	00					
Accounts Payable							3	0	0	0	00
Bill Swift, Capital							12	0	0	0	00
Bill Swift, Drawing	2	0	0	0	00					
Delivery Fees							12	5	0	0	00
Wage Expense	3	0	0	0	00					
Rent Expense	1	0	0	0	00					
	27	5	0	0	00		27	5	0	0	00

E 3-10B (LO5)

✓ Net income: $8,500

INCOME STATEMENT From the information in the trial balance presented above, prepare an income statement for Bill's Delivery Service for the month ended September 30, 20--.

E 3-11B (LO5)

✓ Capital, 9/30: $18,500

STATEMENT OF OWNER'S EQUITY From the information in the trial balance presented above, prepare a statement of owner's equity for Bill's Delivery Service for the month ended September 30, 20--.

E 3-12B (LO5)

✓ Total assets, 9/30: $21,500

BALANCE SHEET From the information in the trial balance presented above, prepare a balance sheet for Bill's Delivery Service as of September 30, 20--.

SERIES B PROBLEMS

P 3-13B (LO2/4/5)

✓ Cash bal. after (p): $20,200 (Dr.); Trial bal. total debits: $44,300

T ACCOUNTS AND TRIAL BALANCE Sue Jantz started a business in August 20-- called Jantz Plumbing Service. Jantz hired a part-time college student as an administrative assistant. Jantz has decided to use the following accounts:

Assets
    Cash
    Accounts Receivable
    Office Supplies
    Prepaid Insurance
    Plumbing Equipment
    Van
Liabilities
    Accounts Payable

Owner's Equity
    Sue Jantz, Capital
    Sue Jantz, Drawing
Revenue
    Service Fees
Expenses
    Rent Expense
    Wages Expense
    Telephone Expense
    Advertising Expense

(continued)

The following transactions occurred during August:

(a) Invested cash in the business, $30,000.

(b) Purchased a used van for cash, $8,000.

(c) Purchased plumbing equipment on account, $4,000.

(d) Received cash for services rendered, $3,000.

(e) Paid cash on account owed from transaction (c), $1,000.

(f) Paid rent for the month, $700.

(g) Paid telephone bill, $100.

(h) Earned revenue on account, $4,000.

(i) Purchased office supplies for cash, $300.

(j) Paid wages to student, $500.

(k) Purchased a one-year insurance policy, $800.

(l) Received cash from services performed in transaction (h), $3,000.

(m) Paid cash for advertising expense, $2,000.

(n) Purchased additional plumbing equipment for $2,000, paying $500 cash and spreading the remaining payments over the next six months.

(o) Earned revenue from services for the remainder of the month of $2,800: $1,100 in cash and $1,700 on account.

(p) Withdrew cash at the end of the month, $3,000.

REQUIRED

1. Enter the transactions in T accounts, identifying each transaction with its corresponding letter.

2. Foot and balance the accounts where necessary.

3. Prepare a trial balance as of August 31, 20--.

P 3-14B (LO5)

✓ Net income: $6,500

✓ Owner's equity, 8/31: $33,500

✓ Total assets, 8/31: $38,000

NET INCOME AND CHANGE IN OWNER'S EQUITY Refer to the trial balance of Jantz Plumbing Service in Problem 3-13B to determine the following information. Use the format provided below.

1. a. Total revenue for the month   _____

   b. Total expenses for the month   _____

   c. Net income for the month   _____

2. a. Sue Jantz's original investment in the business

     + Net income for the month   _____

     – Owner's drawing   _____   _____

     Increase (decrease) in capital   _____

     = Ending owner's equity   _____

   b. End of month accounting equation:

Assets	=	Liabilities	+	Owner's Equity
_____	=	_____	+	_____

P 3-15B (LO5)

✓ NI: $6,500

✓ Capital, 8/31/20--: $33,500

✓ Total assets: $38,000

FINANCIAL STATEMENTS Refer to the trial balance in Problem 3-13B and to the analysis of the change in owner's equity in Problem 3-14B.

REQUIRED

1. Prepare an income statement for Jantz Plumbing Service for the month ended August 31, 20--.

2. Prepare a statement of owner's equity for Jantz Plumbing Service for the month ended August 31, 20--.

3. Prepare a balance sheet for Jantz Plumbing Service as of August 31, 20--.

MANAGING YOUR WRITING

Write a one-page memo to your instructor explaining how you could use the double-entry system to maintain records of your personal finances. What types of accounts would you use for the accounting elements?

MASTERY PROBLEM

✓ Cash bal. after (p): $1,980 (Dr.);

Trial bal. debit total: $5,840; Net income: $500; Total assets: $4,300

Craig Fisher started a lawn service called Craig's Quick Cut to earn money over the summer months. Fisher has decided to use the following accounts for recording transactions:

Assets	Revenue
Cash	Lawn Fees
Accounts Receivable	Expenses
Mowing Equipment	Rent Expense
Lawn Tools	Wages Expense
Liabilities	Telephone Expense
Accounts Payable	Gas and Oil Expense
Notes Payable	Transportation Expense
Owner's Equity	
Craig Fisher, Capital	
Craig Fisher, Drawing	

Transactions for the month of June are listed below.

(a) Invested cash in the business, $3,000.

(b) Bought mowing equipment for $1,000: paid $200 in cash and promised to pay the balance over the next four months.

(c) Paid garage rent for June, $50.

(d) Provided lawn services for customers on account, $520.

(e) Paid telephone bill, $30.

(f) Borrowed cash from the bank by signing a note payable, $500.

(g) Bought lawn tools, $480.

(h) Collected cash from customers for services performed on account in transaction (d), $400.

(i) Paid associates for lawn work done during the first half of the month, $350.

(j) Paid for gas and oil for the equipment, $60.

(k) Paid cash on account for the mowing equipment purchased in transaction (b), $200.

(l) Earned lawn fees of $1,320: $600 in cash and $720 on account.

(m) Paid associates for last half of month, $700.

(continued)

(n) Reimbursed associates for costs incurred using their own vehicles for transportation, $150.

(o) Paid on note payable to bank, $100.

(p) Withdrew cash for personal use, $200.

REQUIRED

1. Enter the transactions for June in T accounts. Use the accounting equation as a guide for setting up the T accounts.

2. Foot and balance the T accounts where necessary.

3. Prepare a trial balance of the accounts as of June 30, 20--.

4. Prepare an income statement for the month ended June 30, 20--.

5. Prepare a statement of owner's equity for the month ended June 30, 20--.

6. Prepare a balance sheet as of June 30, 20--.

This problem challenges you to apply your cumulative accounting knowledge to move a step beyond the material in the chapter.

✓ **Capital, 8/31/20--: $600**

CHALLENGE PROBLEM

Your friend Chris Stevick started a part-time business in June and has been keeping her own accounting records. She has been preparing monthly financial statements. At the end of August, she stopped by to show you her performance for the most recent month. She prepared the following income statement and balance sheet:

Income Statement		Balance Sheet	End of Month	Beginning of Month
Revenues	$500	Cash	$600	$400
Expenses	200	Capital	600	400
Net income	$300			

Chris has also heard that there is a statement of owner's equity, but she is not familiar with that statement. She asks if you can help her prepare one. After confirming that she has no assets other than cash, no liabilities, and made no additional investments in the business in August, you agree.

REQUIRED

1. Prepare the statement of owner's equity for your friend's most recent month.

2. What suggestions might you give to Chris that would make her income statement more useful?

ANSWERS TO SELF-STUDY QUESTIONS AND EXERCISES

True/False Questions

1. T   2. F (Liability accounts normally have credit balances.)   3. T   4. F (credit balances)   5. T   6. F (increase)

Multiple Choice Questions

1. c   2. b   3. d   4. c   5. a

U REVU   **Exercises**

1.
Accounts Receivable	
100	50
200	30
300	80
220	

2. (a) The asset account Supplies is increased with a <u>debit</u>.
   (b) The owner's capital account is increased with a <u>credit</u>.
   (c) The rent expense account is increased with a <u>debit</u>.

3.
Cash		Equipment	
	300	300	

4.

Trial Balance		
Cash	100	
Accounts Receivable	90	
Accounts Payable		20
Capital		40
Sales		200
Rent Expense	70	
	260	260

Chapter 4

COLEONG/DREAMSTIME

LEARNING OBJECTIVES

Careful study of this chapter should enable you to:

LO1 Describe the flow of data from source documents through the trial balance.

LO2 Describe the chart of accounts as a means of classifying financial information.

LO3 Describe and explain the purpose of source documents.

LO4 Journalize transactions.

LO5 Post to the general ledger and prepare a trial balance.

LO6 Explain how to find and correct errors.

Journalizing and Posting Transactions

Campus Advantage (CA) provides a comprehensive range of student residential services in the following areas: management, development, acquisition, and consulting. It specializes in the creation of modern, full-service facilities that are secure, private, and equipped with all of the tools that today's students need for success. Its communities are no-hassle alternatives to dorm living with full dining service options. CA has facilities across the country, but each student residence reflects the unique identity of the school and community it serves.

As with all businesses, CA relies on an accounting system to maintain a record of transactions from the source document through the preparation of the trial balance and financial statements. In this chapter, we discuss source documents, the chart of accounts, and the process used to journalize and post transactions. And, just in case an error is made, we address how to find and correct errors.

The double-entry framework of accounting was explained and illustrated in Chapter 3. To demonstrate the use of debits and credits, business transactions were entered directly into T accounts. Now we will take a more detailed look at the procedures used to account for business transactions.

FLOW OF DATA

LO1 Describe the flow of data from source documents through the trial balance.

This chapter traces the flow of financial data from the source documents through the accounting information system. This process includes the following steps:

1. Analyze what happened by using information from source documents and the firm's chart of accounts.

2. Enter business transactions in the general journal in the form of journal entries.

3. Post these journal entries to the accounts in the general ledger.

4. Prepare a trial balance.

The flow of data from the source documents through the preparation of a trial balance is shown in Figure 4-1.

FIGURE 4-1 Flow of Data from Source Documents through Trial Balance

THE CHART OF ACCOUNTS

LO2 Describe the chart of accounts as a means of classifying financial information.

You learned in Chapters 2 and 3 that there are three basic questions that must be answered when analyzing transactions.

1. What happened?

2. Which accounts are affected?

3. How is the accounting equation affected?

To determine which accounts are affected (step 2), the accountant must know the accounts being used by the business. A list of all accounts used by a business is called a **chart of accounts**.

The chart of accounts includes the account titles in numeric order for all assets, liabilities, owner's equity, revenues, and expenses. The numbering should follow a consistent pattern. In Jessie Jane's Campus Delivery Service, asset accounts begin with "1," liability accounts begin with "2," owner's equity accounts begin with "3," revenue accounts begin with "4," and expense accounts begin with "5." Jessie uses three-digit numbers for all accounts.

A chart of accounts for Jessie Jane's Campus Delivery Service is shown in Figure 4-2. Jessie would not need many accounts initially because the business is new. Additional accounts can easily be added as needed. Note that the accounts are arranged according to the accounting equation.

FIGURE 4-2 Chart of Accounts

JESSIE JANE'S CAMPUS DELIVERY SERVICE CHART OF ACCOUNTS				
Assets	**(100–199)**	**Revenues**	**(400–499)**	
101	Cash	401	Delivery Fees	*Revenues begin with 4*
122	Accounts Receivable			
Assets begin with 1 141	Supplies	**Expenses**	**(500–599)**	
145	Prepaid Insurance	511	Wages Expense	*Expenses begin with 5*
185	Delivery Equipment	521	Rent Expense	
		525	Telephone Expense	
Liabilities	**(200–299)**			
Liabilities begin with 2 202	Accounts Payable			
Owner's Equity	**(300–399)**			
311	Jessica Jane, Capital			
Owner's Equity begin with 3 312	Jessica Jane, Drawing			

SOURCE DOCUMENTS

LO3 Describe and explain the purpose of source documents.

Almost any document that provides information about a business transaction can be called a **source document**. A source document triggers the analysis of what happened. It begins the process of entering transactions in the accounting system. Examples of source documents are shown in Figure 4-3. These source documents provide information that is useful in determining the effect of business transactions on specific accounts.

In addition to serving as input for transaction analysis, source documents serve as objective evidence of business transactions. If anyone questions the accounting records, these documents may be used as objective, verifiable evidence of the accuracy of the accounting records. For this reason, source documents are filed for possible future reference. *Having objective, verifiable evidence that a transaction occurred is an important accounting concept.*

FIGURE 4-3 Source Documents

1	2	3	4

Check Stubs

Cash Register Tape Summary

Sales Ticket

Purchase Invoice

SOURCE DOCUMENTS	
Example	**Provides Information About**
1. Check stubs or copies of checks	Cash payments
2. Receipt stubs, copies of receipts, cash register tapes, or memos of cash register totals	Cash receipts
3. Copies of sales tickets or sales invoices issued to customers or clients	Sales of goods or services
4. Purchase invoices received from suppliers	Purchase of goods or services

A BROADER VIEW

Electronic Source Documents

With the ability to go shopping in cyberspace, more transactions are being initiated electronically. Even Best Buy, known for its low prices and excellent in-store service, has "online" shopping at http://www.bestbuy.com. Customers can place orders and these orders can be filled, all based on electronic communications. This means that more and more "source documents" will be in an electronic form.

U REVU

Complete U REVU-1 on **page 114** to test your basic understanding of LO3.

THE GENERAL JOURNAL

LO4 Journalize transactions.

LEARNING KEY

A journal provides a day-by-day listing of all transactions completed by the business.

A day-by-day listing of the transactions of a business is called a **journal**. The purpose of a journal is to provide a record of all transactions completed by the business. The journal shows the date of each transaction, titles of the accounts to be debited and credited, and the amounts of the debits and credits.

A journal is commonly referred to as a **book of original entry** because it is here that the first formal accounting record of a transaction is made. Although many types of journals are used in business, the simplest journal form is a two-column general journal (Figure 4-4). Any kind of business transaction may be entered into a general journal.

A **two-column general journal** is so-named because it has only two amount columns, one for debit amounts and one for credit amounts. Journal pages are numbered in the upper right-hand corner. The five column numbers in Figure 4-4 are explained in Figure 4-5.

FIGURE 4-4 Two-Column General Journal

	DATE	DESCRIPTION	POST. REF.	DEBIT	CREDIT	
1	20-- ①	②	③	④	⑤	1
2						2
3						3

FIGURE 4-5 The Columns in a Two-Column General Journal

Column 1 Date	The year is entered in small figures at the top of the column immediately below the column heading. The year is repeated only at the top of each new page. The month is entered for the first entry on the page and for the first transaction of the month. The day of the month is recorded for every transaction, even if it is the same as the prior entry.
Column 2 Description	The *Description* or *Explanation* column is used to enter the titles of the accounts affected by each transaction and to provide a very brief description of the transaction. Each transaction affects two or more accounts. The account(s) to be debited are entered first at the extreme left of the column. The account(s) to be credited are listed after the debits and indented. The description should be entered immediately following the last credit entry with an additional indentation.
Column 3 Posting Reference	No entries are made in the *Posting Reference* column during journalizing. Entries are made in this column when the debits and credits are copied to the proper accounts in the ledger. This process will be explained in detail later in this chapter.
Column 4 Debit Amount	The *Debit amount column* is used to enter the amount to be debited to an account. The amount should be entered on the same line as the title of that account.
Column 5 Credit Amount	The *Credit amount column* is used to enter the amount to be credited to an account. The amount should be entered on the same line as the title of that account.

LEARNING KEY

When journalizing, the exact account titles shown in the chart of accounts must be used. Refer to the chart of accounts in Figure 4-2 as you review the entries for Jessie Jane's Campus Delivery Service.

JOURNALIZING

Entering the transactions in a journal is called **journalizing**. For every transaction, the entry should include the date, the title of each account affected, the amounts, and a brief description.

To illustrate the journalizing process, transactions for the first month of operations of Jessie Jane's Campus Delivery Service will be journalized. The transactions are listed in Figure 4-6. Since you analyzed these transactions in Chapters 2 and 3, the journalizing process should be easier to understand. Let's start with a close look at the steps followed when journalizing the first transaction, Jessie's initial investment of $2,000.

FIGURE 4-6 Summary of Transactions

	SUMMARY OF TRANSACTIONS JESSIE JANE'S CAMPUS DELIVERY SERVICE	
	Transaction	
(a)	June 1	Jessica Jane invested cash in her business, $2,000.
(b)	3	Bought delivery equipment for cash, $1,200.
(c)	5	Bought delivery equipment on account from Big Red Scooters, $900.
(d)	6	Paid first installment from transaction (c) to Big Red Scooters, $300.
(e)	6	Received cash for delivery services rendered, $500.
(f)	7	Paid cash for June office rent, $200.
(g)	15	Paid telephone bill, $50.
(h)	15	Made deliveries on account for a total of $600: Accounting Department ($400) and the School of Music ($200).
(i)	16	Bought supplies for cash, $80.
(j)	18	Paid cash for an eight-month liability insurance policy, $200. Coverage began on June 1.
(k)	20	Received $570 in cash for services performed in transaction (h): $400 from the Accounting Department and $170 from the School of Music.
(l)	25	Bought a third scooter from Big Red Scooters, $1,500. Paid $300 cash, with the remaining payments expected over the next four months.
(m)	27	Paid wages of part-time employees, $650.
(n)	30	Earned delivery fees for the remainder of the month amounting to $1,050: $430 in cash and $620 on account. Deliveries on account: Accounting Department ($250) and Athletic Ticket Office ($370).
(o)	30	Jessie withdrew cash for personal use, $150.

Transaction (a)

June 1   Jessica Jane opened a bank account with a deposit of $2,000 for her business.

STEP 1   **Enter the date.** Since this is the first entry on the journal page, the year is entered on the first line of the Date column (in small print at the top of the line). The month and day are entered on the same line, below the year, in the Date column.

		GENERAL JOURNAL				PAGE 1	
	DATE	DESCRIPTION	POST. REF.	DEBIT		CREDIT	
1	20-- June 1						1
2							2

STEP 2   **Enter the debit.** Cash is entered on the first line at the extreme left of the Description column. The amount of the debit, $2,000, is entered on the same line in the Debit column. Since this is not a formal financial statement, dollar signs are not used.

In Chapter 3, we simply debited the T account.

Cash

(a) 2,000 |

GENERAL JOURNAL — PAGE 1

	DATE		DESCRIPTION	POST. REF.	DEBIT	CREDIT	
1	20-- June	1	Cash		2 0 0 0 00		1
2							2

STEP 3   **Enter the credit.** The title of the account to be credited, Jessica Jane, Capital, is entered on the second line, **indented one-half inch from the left side of the Description column.** The amount of the credit, $2,000, is entered on the same line in the Credit column.

In Chapter 3, we simply credited the T account.

Jessica Jane, Capital

| (a) 2,000

GENERAL JOURNAL — PAGE 1

	DATE		DESCRIPTION	POST. REF.	DEBIT	CREDIT	
1	20-- June	1	Cash		2 0 0 0 00		1
2			Jessica Jane, Capital			2 0 0 0 00	2

STEP 4   **Enter the explanation.** The explanation of the entry is entered on the next line, **indented an additional one-half inch.** The second line of the explanation, if needed, is also indented the same distance as the first.

GENERAL JOURNAL — PAGE 1

	DATE		DESCRIPTION	POST. REF.	DEBIT	CREDIT	
1	20-- June	1	Cash		2 0 0 0 00		1
2			Jessica Jane, Capital			2 0 0 0 00	2
3			Owner's original investment in				3
4			delivery business				4

Enter the next transaction. To enter transaction (b), the purchase of a motor scooter for $1,200 cash, we skip a line and follow the same four steps. Note that the month and year do not need to be repeated. The day of the month must, however, be entered.

GENERAL JOURNAL — PAGE 1

	DATE		DESCRIPTION	POST. REF.	DEBIT	CREDIT	
1	20-- June	1	Cash		2 0 0 0 00		1
2			Jessica Jane, Capital			2 0 0 0 00	2
3			Owner's original investment in				3
4			delivery business				4
Skip a line → 5							5
6		3	Delivery Equipment		1 2 0 0 00		6
7			Cash			1 2 0 0 00	7
8			Purchased delivery equipment for cash				8

The journal entries for the month of June are shown in Figure 4-7. Note that the entries on June 25 and June 30 affect more than two accounts. Entries requiring more than one debit and/or one credit are called **compound entries**. The entry on June 25 has two credits. The credits are listed after the debit, indented and listed one under the other. The entry on June 30 has two debits. They are aligned with the left margin of the Description column and listed one under the other. In both cases, the debits equal the credits.

FIGURE 4-7 General Journal Entries

	DATE		DESCRIPTION	POST. REF.	DEBIT	CREDIT	
1	20-- June	1	Cash — List debits first.		2 0 0 0 00		1
2			Jessica Jane, Capital			2 0 0 0 00	2
3			Owner's original investment in				3
4			delivery business				4
5							5
6			Delivery Equipment		1 2 0 0 00		6
7			Cash			1 2 0 0 00	7
8			Purchased delivery equipment for cash				8
9							9
10		5	Delivery Equipment		9 0 0 00		10
11			Accounts Payable			9 0 0 00	11
12			Purchased delivery equipment on account				12
13			from Big Red Scooters				13
14							14
15		6	Accounts Payable		3 0 0 00		15
16			Cash			3 0 0 00	16
17			Made partial payment to Big Red Scooters				17
18							18
19		6	Cash		5 0 0 00		19
20			Delivery Fees			5 0 0 00	20
21			Received cash for delivery services				21
22							22
23		7	Rent Expense		2 0 0 00		23
24			Cash			2 0 0 00	24
25			Paid office rent for June				25
26							26
27		15	Telephone Expense		5 0 00		27
28			Cash			5 0 00	28
29			Paid telephone bill for June				29
30							30
31		15	Accounts Receivable		6 0 0 00		31
32			Delivery Fees			6 0 0 00	32
33			Deliveries made on account for Accounting				33
34			Department ($400) and School of Music ($200)				34
35							35

GENERAL JOURNAL PAGE 1

List credits second and indented.

Explanation is third and indented.

Space to make entries easier to read. To prevent improper changes to entries, the extra spacing might not be used in practice.

(continued)

FIGURE 4-7 General Journal Entries (concluded)

	DATE		DESCRIPTION	POST. REF.	DEBIT	CREDIT	
1	20-- June	16	Supplies		8 0 00		1
2			Cash			8 0 00	2
3			Purchased supplies for cash				3
4							4
5		18	Prepaid Insurance		2 0 0 00		5
6			Cash			2 0 0 00	6
7			Paid premium for eight-month				7
8			insurance policy				8
9							9
10		20	Cash		5 7 0 00		10
11			Accounts Receivable			5 7 0 00	11
12			Received cash on account from Accounting				12
13			Department ($400) and School of Music ($170)				13
14							14
15		25	Delivery Equipment		1 5 0 0 00		15
16	Line up credits		Accounts Payable	Compound entry	Debits = Credits	1 2 0 0 00	16
17			Cash			3 0 0 00	17
18			Purchased scooter with down payment;				18
19			balance on account with Big Red Scooters				19
20							20
21		27	Wages Expense		6 5 0 00		21
22			Cash			6 5 0 00	22
23			Paid employees				23
24							24
25		30	Cash		4 3 0 00		25
26	Line up debits		Accounts Receivable	Compound entry	6 2 0 00		26
27			Delivery Fees			1 0 5 0 00	27
28			Deliveries made for cash and on account to	Debits = Credits			28
29			Accounting Department ($250) and				29
30			Athletic Ticket Office ($370)				30
31							31
32		30	Jessica Jane, Drawing		1 5 0 00		32
33			Cash			1 5 0 00	33
34			Owner's withdrawal				34

GENERAL JOURNAL — PAGE 2

U REVU

Complete U REVU-2 on page 114 to test your basic understanding of LO4.

THE GENERAL LEDGER

LO5 Post to the general ledger and prepare a trial balance.

The journal provides a day-by-day record of business transactions. To determine the current balance of specific accounts, however, the information in the journal must be transferred to accounts similar to the T accounts illustrated in Chapter 3. This process is called posting.

A complete set of all the accounts used by a business is known as the **general ledger**. The general ledger accumulates a complete record of the debits and credits made to each account as a result of entries made in the journal. The accounts are numbered and arranged in the same order as the chart of accounts. That is, accounts are numbered and grouped by classification: assets, liabilities, owner's equity, revenues, and expenses.

GENERAL LEDGER ACCOUNT

For purposes of illustration, the T account was introduced in Chapter 3. In practice, businesses are more likely to use a version of the account called the **general ledger account**. Figure 4-8 compares the cash T account from Chapter 3 for Jessie Jane's Campus Delivery Service and a general ledger account summarizing the same cash transactions.

A four-column general ledger account contains columns for the debit or credit transaction and columns for the debit or credit running balance. In addition, there are columns for the date, description of the item, and posting reference.

The Item column is used to provide descriptions of special entries. For example, "Balance" is written in this column when the balance of an account is transferred to a new page. In addition, "Correcting," "Adjusting," "Closing," or "Reversing" may be written in this column when these types of entries are made. Correcting entries are described later in the chapter. Adjusting, closing, and reversing entries are illustrated in Chapters 5, 6, and 15, respectively.

The Posting Reference (Post. Ref.) column is used to indicate the journal page from which an entry was posted, or a check mark (✔) is inserted to indicate that no posting was required.

As shown in Figure 4-8, the primary advantage of the T account is that the debit and credit sides of the account are easier to identify. Thus, for demonstration purposes

FIGURE 4-8 Comparison of T Account and General Ledger Account

Cash			
(a) 2,000	(b) 1,200		
(e) 500	(d) 300		
(k) 570	(f) 200		
(n) 430	(g) 50		
3,500	(i) 80		
	(j) 200		
	(l) 300		
	(m) 650		
	(o) 150		
Bal. 370	3,130		

GENERAL LEDGER

ACCOUNT: Cash   ACCOUNT NO. 101

DATE	ITEM	POST. REF.	DEBIT	CREDIT	BALANCE DEBIT	BALANCE CREDIT
20-- June 1			2 0 0 0 00		2 0 0 0 00	
3				1 2 0 0 00	8 0 0 00	
6				3 0 0 00	5 0 0 00	
6			5 0 0 00		1 0 0 0 00	
7				2 0 0 00	8 0 0 00	
15				5 0 00	7 5 0 00	
16				8 0 00	6 7 0 00	
18				2 0 0 00	4 7 0 00	
20			5 7 0 00		1 0 4 0 00	
25				3 0 0 00	7 4 0 00	
27				6 5 0 00	9 0 00	
30			4 3 0 00		5 2 0 00	
30				1 5 0 00	3 7 0 00	

└── Transaction Amount ──┘ └── Running Balance ──┘

and analyzing what happened, T accounts are very helpful. However, computing the balance of a T account is cumbersome. The primary advantage of the general ledger account is that it maintains a running balance.

Note that the heading for the general ledger account has the account title and an account number. The account number is taken from the chart of accounts and is used in the posting process.

POSTING TO THE GENERAL LEDGER

The process of copying the debits and credits from the journal to the ledger accounts is known as **posting**. All amounts entered in the journal must be posted to the general ledger accounts. Posting from the journal to the ledger is done daily or at frequent intervals.

To illustrate the posting process, the first journal entry for Jessie Jane's Campus Delivery Service will be posted step by step. There are five steps in the process of posting each debit and credit. First, let's post the debit to Cash (Figure 4-9).

FIGURE 4-9 Posting a Debit

In the ledger account:

STEP 1 **Enter the date of the transaction in the Date column.** Enter the year, "20--," the month, "June," and the day, "1," in the Date column of the cash account.

STEP 2 **Enter the debit.** Copy the $2,000 debit to Cash in the journal to the Debit column of the ledger. Since this is not a formal financial statement, dollar signs are not used.

STEP 3 **Enter the balance of the account.** Enter the $2,000 balance in the Balance columns under Debit. (If the balance of the account is zero, draw a line through the Debit and Credit columns.)

STEP 4 **Enter the journal page in the Posting Reference column.** Enter "J1" in the Posting Reference column since the posting came from page 1 of the journal.

The Item column is left blank, except for special reasons such as indicating the beginning balance, adjusting, correcting, closing, or reversing entries.

In the journal:

STEP 5 **Enter the ledger account number in the Posting Reference column.** Enter the account number for Cash, 101 (see chart of accounts in Figure 4-2 on page 88), in the Posting Reference column of the journal on the same line as the debit to Cash for $2,000.

Step 5 is the last step in the posting process. After this step is completed, the posting references will indicate which journal entries have been posted to the ledger accounts. This is very helpful, particularly if you are interrupted during the posting process. The information in the Posting Reference columns of the journal and ledger provides a link between the journal and ledger known as a **cross-reference.**

Now let's post the credit portion of the first entry (Figure 4-10).

FIGURE 4-10 Posting a Credit

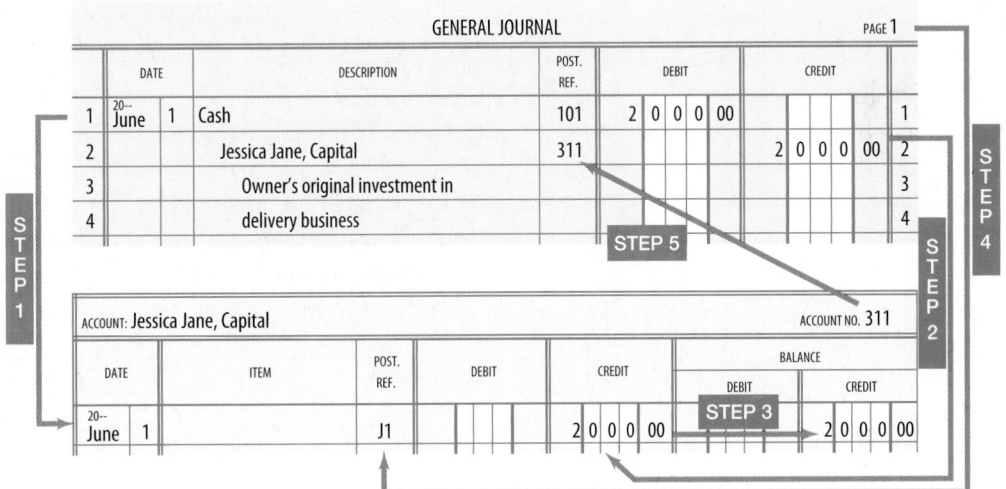

In the ledger account:

STEP 1 **Enter the date of the transaction in the Date column.** Enter the year, "20--," the month, "June," and the day, "1," in the Date column of the account Jessica Jane, Capital.

STEP 2 **Enter the credit.** Copy the $2,000 credit to Jessica Jane, Capital in the journal to the Credit column in the ledger.

STEP 3 **Enter the balance of the account.** Enter the $2,000 balance in the Balance columns under Credit. (If the balance of the account is zero, draw a line through the Debit and Credit columns.)

STEP 4 **Enter the journal page in the Posting Reference column.** Enter "J1" in the Posting Reference column since the posting came from page 1 of the journal.

In the journal:

STEP 5 **Enter the ledger account number in the Posting Reference column.** Enter the account number for Jessica Jane, Capital, 311, in the Posting Reference column. Again, this last step indicates that the credit has been posted to the general ledger.

After posting the journal entries for Jessie Jane's Campus Delivery Service for the month of June, the general journal and general ledger should appear as illustrated in Figures 4-11 and 4-12 on pages 98–101. *Note that the Posting Reference column of the journal has been filled in because the entries have been posted.*

FIGURE 4-11 General Journal After Posting

GENERAL JOURNAL   PAGE 1

	DATE		DESCRIPTION	POST. REF.	DEBIT					CREDIT					
1	20-- June	1	Cash	101	2	0	0	0	00						1
2			Jessica Jane, Capital	311						2	0	0	0	00	2
3			Owner's original investment in												3
4			delivery business												4
5															5
6		3	Delivery Equipment	185	1	2	0	0	00						6
7			Cash	101						1	2	0	0	00	7
8			Purchased delivery equipment for cash												8
9															9
10		5	Delivery Equipment	185		9	0	0	00						10
11			Accounts Payable	202							9	0	0	00	11
12			Purchased delivery equipment on account												12
13			from Big Red Scooters												13
14															14
15		6	Accounts Payable	202		3	0	0	00						15
16			Cash	101							3	0	0	00	16
17			Made partial payment to Big Red Scooters												17
18															18
19		6	Cash	101		5	0	0	00						19
20			Delivery Fees	401							5	0	0	00	20
21			Received cash for delivery services												21
22															22
23		7	Rent Expense	521		2	0	0	00						23
24			Cash	101							2	0	0	00	24
25			Paid office rent for June												25
26															26
27		15	Telephone Expense	525			5	0	00						27
28			Cash	101								5	0	00	28
29			Paid telephone bill for June												29
30															30
31		15	Accounts Receivable	122		6	0	0	00						31
32			Delivery Fees	401							6	0	0	00	32
33			Deliveries made on account for Accounting												33
34			Department ($400) and School of Music ($200)												34
35															35

FIGURE 4-11 General Journal After Posting *(concluded)*

	DATE		DESCRIPTION	POST. REF.	DEBIT				CREDIT				
1	20-- June	16	Supplies	141		8	0	00					1
2			Cash	101						8	0	00	2
3			Purchased supplies for cash										3
4													4
5		18	Prepaid Insurance	145	2	0	0	00					5
6			Cash	101					2	0	0	00	6
7			Paid premium for eight-month										7
8			insurance policy										8
9													9
10		20	Cash	101	5	7	0	00					10
11			Accounts Receivable	122					5	7	0	00	11
12			Received cash on account from Accounting										12
13			Department ($400) and School of Music ($170)										13
14													14
15		25	Delivery Equipment	185	1 5	0	0	00					15
16			Accounts Payable	202					1 2	0	0	00	16
17			Cash	101					3	0	0	00	17
18			Purchased scooter with down payment;										18
19			balance on account with Big Red Scooters										19
20													20
21		27	Wages Expense	511	6	5	0	00					21
22			Cash	101					6	5	0	00	22
23			Paid employees										23
24													24
25		30	Cash	101	4	3	0	00					25
26			Accounts Receivable	122	6	2	0	00					26
27			Delivery Fees	401					1 0	5	0	00	27
28			Deliveries made for cash and on account to										28
29			Accounting Department ($250) and										29
30			Athletic Ticket Office ($370)										30
31													31
32		30	Jessica Jane, Drawing	312	1	5	0	00					32
33			Cash	101					1	5	0	00	33
34			Owner's withdrawal										34
35													35

GENERAL JOURNAL   PAGE 2

FIGURE 4-12 General Ledger After Posting

GENERAL LEDGER

ACCOUNT: **Cash**   ACCOUNT NO. **101**

DATE		ITEM	POST. REF.	DEBIT	CREDIT	BALANCE DEBIT	BALANCE CREDIT
20-- June	1		J1	2 0 0 0 00		2 0 0 0 00	
	3		J1		1 2 0 0 00	8 0 0 00	
	6		J1		3 0 0 00	5 0 0 00	
	6		J1	5 0 0 00		1 0 0 0 00	
	7		J1		2 0 0 00	8 0 0 00	
	15		J1		5 0 00	7 5 0 00	
	16		J2		8 0 00	6 7 0 00	
	18		J2		2 0 0 00	4 7 0 00	
	20		J2	5 7 0 00		1 0 4 0 00	
	25		J2		3 0 0 00	7 4 0 00	
	27		J2		6 5 0 00	9 0 00	
	30		J2	4 3 0 00		5 2 0 00	
	30		J2		1 5 0 00	3 7 0 00	

> For asset, expense, and drawing accounts, a running balance is maintained by adding the debit or subtracting the credit from the balance shown on the line above.

ACCOUNT: **Accounts Receivable**   ACCOUNT NO. **122**

DATE		ITEM	POST. REF.	DEBIT	CREDIT	BALANCE DEBIT	BALANCE CREDIT
20-- June	15		J1	6 0 0 00		6 0 0 00	
	20		J2		5 7 0 00	3 0 00	
	30		J2	6 2 0 00		6 5 0 00	

ACCOUNT: **Supplies**   ACCOUNT NO. **141**

DATE		ITEM	POST. REF.	DEBIT	CREDIT	BALANCE DEBIT	BALANCE CREDIT
20-- June	16		J2	8 0 00		8 0 00	

ACCOUNT: **Prepaid Insurance**   ACCOUNT NO. **145**

DATE		ITEM	POST. REF.	DEBIT	CREDIT	BALANCE DEBIT	BALANCE CREDIT
20-- June	18		J2	2 0 0 00		2 0 0 00	

ACCOUNT: **Delivery Equipment**   ACCOUNT NO. **185**

DATE		ITEM	POST. REF.	DEBIT	CREDIT	BALANCE DEBIT	BALANCE CREDIT
20-- June	3		J1	1 2 0 0 00		1 2 0 0 00	
	5		J1	9 0 0 00		2 1 0 0 00	
	25		J2	1 5 0 0 00		3 6 0 0 00	

FIGURE 4-12 General Ledger After Posting *(concluded)*

ACCOUNT: Accounts Payable ACCOUNT NO. 202

DATE		ITEM	POST. REF.	DEBIT	CREDIT	BALANCE DEBIT	BALANCE CREDIT
20-- June	5		J1		9 0 0 00		9 0 0 00
	6		J1	3 0 0 00			6 0 0 00
	25		J2		1 2 0 0 00		1 8 0 0 00

> For liability, revenue, and capital accounts, a running balance is maintained by adding the credit or subtracting the debit from the balance shown on the line above.

ACCOUNT: Jessica Jane, Capital ACCOUNT NO. 311

DATE		ITEM	POST. REF.	DEBIT	CREDIT	BALANCE DEBIT	BALANCE CREDIT
20-- June	1		J1		2 0 0 0 00		2 0 0 0 00

ACCOUNT: Jessica Jane, Drawing ACCOUNT NO. 312

DATE		ITEM	POST. REF.	DEBIT	CREDIT	BALANCE DEBIT	BALANCE CREDIT
20-- June	30		J2	1 5 0 00		1 5 0 00	

ACCOUNT: Delivery Fees ACCOUNT NO. 401

DATE		ITEM	POST. REF.	DEBIT	CREDIT	BALANCE DEBIT	BALANCE CREDIT
20-- June	6		J1		5 0 0 00		5 0 0 00
	15		J1		6 0 0 00		1 1 0 0 00
	30		J2		1 0 5 0 00		2 1 5 0 00

ACCOUNT: Wages Expense ACCOUNT NO. 511

DATE		ITEM	POST. REF.	DEBIT	CREDIT	BALANCE DEBIT	BALANCE CREDIT
20-- June	27		J2	6 5 0 00		6 5 0 00	

ACCOUNT: Rent Expense ACCOUNT NO. 521

DATE		ITEM	POST. REF.	DEBIT	CREDIT	BALANCE DEBIT	BALANCE CREDIT
20-- June	7		J1	2 0 0 00		2 0 0 00	

ACCOUNT: Telephone Expense ACCOUNT NO. 525

DATE		ITEM	POST. REF.	DEBIT	CREDIT	BALANCE DEBIT	BALANCE CREDIT
20-- June	15		J1	5 0 00		5 0 00	

THE TRIAL BALANCE

In Chapter 3, a **trial balance** was used to prove that the totals of the debit and credit balances in the T accounts were equal. In this chapter, a trial balance is used to prove the equality of the debits and credits in the ledger accounts. A trial balance can be prepared daily, weekly, monthly, or whenever desired. Before preparing a trial balance, all transactions should be journalized and posted so that the effect of all transactions will be reflected in the ledger accounts.

The trial balance for Jessie Jane's Campus Delivery Service shown in Figure 4-13 was prepared from the balances in the general ledger in Figure 4-12. The accounts are listed in the order used in the chart of accounts. This order is also often used when preparing financial statements. In Chapter 2, we pointed out that many firms list expenses from highest to lowest amounts. Some firms list expenses according to the chart of accounts, which is the method we will follow.

🔑 **LEARNING KEY**

The chart of accounts determines the order for listing accounts in the general ledger and trial balance. This order may also be used when preparing financial statements.

FIGURE 4-13 Trial Balance

			DEBIT BALANCE					CREDIT BALANCE				
ACCOUNT TITLE	ACCOUNT NO.											
Cash	101		3	7	0	00						
Accounts Receivable	122		6	5	0	00						
Supplies	141			8	0	00						
Prepaid Insurance	145		2	0	0	00						
Delivery Equipment	185	3	6	0	0	00						
Accounts Payable	202							1	8	0	0	00
Jessica Jane, Capital	311							2	0	0	0	00
Jessica Jane, Drawing	312		1	5	0	00						
Delivery Fees	401							2	1	5	0	00
Wages Expense	511		6	5	0	00						
Rent Expense	521		2	0	0	00						
Telephone Expense	525			5	0	00						
		5	9	5	0	00		5	9	5	0	00

Table title: Jessie Jane's Campus Delivery Service / Trial Balance / June 30, 20 - -

Even though the trial balance indicates that the ledger is in balance, the ledger can still contain errors. For example, if a journal entry was made debiting or crediting the wrong accounts, or if an item was posted to the wrong account, the ledger will still be in balance. It is important, therefore, to be very careful in preparing the journal entries and in posting them to the ledger accounts.

U REVU ▸   Complete U REVU-3 on **page 114** to test your basic understanding of LO5.

FINDING AND CORRECTING ERRORS IN THE TRIAL BALANCE

LO6 Explain how to find and correct errors.

Tips are available to help if your trial balance has an error. Figure 4-14 offers hints for finding the error when your trial balance does not balance.

FIGURE 4-14 Tips for Finding Errors in the Trial Balance

1. Double check your addition. Review balances to see if they are too large or small, relative to other accounts, or entered in the wrong column.

2. Find the difference between the debits and the credits.

    a. If the difference is equal to the amount of a specific transaction, perhaps you forgot to post the debit or credit portion of this transaction.

    b. Divide the difference by 2. If the difference is evenly divisible by 2, you may have posted two debits or two credits for a transaction. If a debit was posted as a credit, it would mean that one transaction had two credits and no debits. The difference between the total debits and credits would be twice the amount of the debit that was posted as a credit.

    c. Divide the difference by 9. If the difference is evenly divisible by 9, you may have committed a **slide error** or a **transposition error**. A slide occurs when debit or credit amounts "slide" a digit or two to the left or right when entered. For example, if *$250* was entered as *$25*:

$250	–	$25	=	$225
$225	÷	9	=	$25

    The difference is evenly divisible by 9.

    A transposition occurs when two digits are reversed. For example, if *$250* was entered as *$520*:

$520	–	$250	=	$270
$270	÷	9	=	$30

    Again, the difference is evenly divisible by 9.

If the tips in Figure 4-14 don't work, you must retrace your steps through the accounting process. Double check your addition for the ledger accounts. Also trace all postings. Be patient as you search for your error. Use this process as an opportunity to reinforce your understanding of the flow of information through the accounting system. Much can be learned while looking for an error.

Once you have found an error, there are two methods of making the correction. Although you may want to erase when correcting your homework, this is not acceptable in practice. An erasure may suggest that you are trying to hide something. You should use the ruling method or make a correcting entry instead.

RULING METHOD

The **ruling method** should be used to correct two types of errors.

1. When an incorrect journal entry has been made, but not yet posted.

2. When a proper entry has been made but posted to the wrong account or for the wrong amount.

When using the ruling method, draw a single line through the incorrect account title or amount and write the correct information directly above the line. Corrections should be initialed by someone authorized to make such changes. This is done so the source and reason for the correction can be traced. This type of correction may be made in the journal or ledger accounts, as shown in Figure 4-15.

FIGURE 4-15 Ruling Method of Making a Correction

	DATE		DESCRIPTION	POST. REF.	DEBIT	CREDIT	
1	20-- Sept.	17	~~Wages Expense MP~~ ~~Entertainment Expense~~		6 5 0 00		1
2			Cash			6 5 0 00	2
3			Paid employees				3
4							4
5		18	Prepaid Insurance		MP 2 0 0 00 ~~2 0 00~~		5
6			Cash			MP 2 0 0 00 ~~2 0 00~~	6
7			Paid premium for eight-month				7
8			insurance policy				8
9							9

Slide

GENERAL LEDGER

ACCOUNT: Accounts Payable — ACCOUNT NO. 202

DATE		ITEM	POST. REF.	DEBIT	CREDIT	BALANCE DEBIT	BALANCE CREDIT	
20-- Sept.	8		J1		7 0 0 00		7 0 0 00	
	15		J1	2 0 0 00			5 0 0 00	
	25		J2	~~1 2 0 0 00~~ MP ~~2 1 0 0 00~~			MP 1 7 0 0 00 ~~2 6 0 0 00~~	

Transposition

CORRECTING ENTRY METHOD

If an incorrect entry has been journalized and posted to the wrong account, a **correcting entry** should be made. For example, assume that a $400 payment for Rent Expense was incorrectly debited to Repair Expense and correctly credited to Cash. This requires a correcting entry and explanation as shown in Figure 4-16. Figure 4-17 shows the effects of the correcting entry on the ledger accounts. Generally, "Correcting" is written in the Item column of the general ledger account.

FIGURE 4-16 Correcting Entry Method

	DATE		DESCRIPTION	POST. REF.	DEBIT	CREDIT	
1	20-- Sept.	25	Rent Expense	521	4 0 0 00		1
2			Repair Expense	537		4 0 0 00	2
3			To correct error in which payment for rent				3
4			was debited to Repair Expense				4
5							5

FIGURE 4-17 Effects of Correcting Entry on Ledger Accounts

GENERAL LEDGER

ACCOUNT: Rent Expense   ACCOUNT NO. 521

DATE		ITEM	POST. REF.	DEBIT	CREDIT	BALANCE	
						DEBIT	CREDIT
20-- Sept.	25	Correcting	J6	4 0 0 00		4 0 0 00	

ACCOUNT: Repair Expense   ACCOUNT NO. 537

DATE		ITEM	POST. REF.	DEBIT	CREDIT	BALANCE	
						DEBIT	CREDIT
20-- Sept.	10		J5	5 0 00		5 0 00	
	15		J5	4 0 0 00		4 5 0 00	
	25	Correcting	J6		4 0 0 00	5 0 00	

U REVU

Complete U REVU-4 on **page 114** to test your basic understanding of LO6

SELF-STUDY

LEARNING OBJECTIVES   Key Points to Remember

LO1 Describe the flow of data from source documents through the trial balance.

The flow of data from the source documents through the trial balance is as follows:

1. Analyze business transactions.
2. Journalize transactions in the general journal.
3. Post journal entries to the general ledger.
4. Prepare a trial balance.

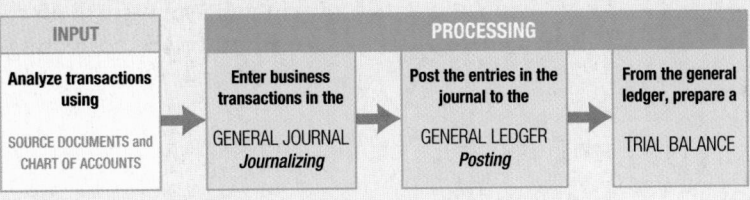

LEARNING OBJECTIVES   Key Points to Remember

LO2 Describe the chart of accounts as a means of classifying financial information.	The chart of accounts includes the account titles in numerical order for all assets, liabilities, owner's equity, revenues, and expenses. The chart of accounts is used in classifying information about transactions.
LO3 Describe and explain the purpose of source documents.	Source documents trigger the analysis of business transactions and the entries into the accounting system.
LO4 Journalize transactions.	A journal provides a day-by-day listing of transactions. The journal shows the date, titles of the accounts to be debited or credited, and the amounts of the debits and credits. The steps in the journalizing process are as follows: 1. Enter the date. 2. Enter the debit. Accounts to be debited are entered first. 3. Enter the credit. Accounts to be credited are entered after the debits and are indented one-half inch. 4. Enter the explanation. A brief explanation of the transaction should be entered in the description column on the line following the last credit. The explanation should be indented an additional one-half inch.
LO5 Post to the general ledger and prepare a trial balance.	The general ledger is a complete set of all accounts used by the business. The steps in posting from the general journal to the general ledger are as follows: In the general ledger: 1. Enter the date of each transaction. 2. Enter the amount of each debit or credit in the Debit or Credit column. 3. Enter the new balance. 4. Enter the journal page number from which each transaction is posted in the Posting Reference column. In the journal: 5. Enter the account number to which each transaction is posted in the Posting Reference column. The trial balance provides a check to make sure the total of all debit balances in the ledger accounts equals the total of all credit balances in the ledger accounts.
LO6 Explain how to find and correct errors.	Errors may be found by verifying your addition, by dividing the difference between the debits and credits by 2 or 9, and by retracing your steps through the accounting process. Use the ruling method or the correcting entry method to correct the error.

DEMONSTRATION PROBLEM

George Fielding is a financial planning consultant. He provides budgeting, estate planning, tax planning, and investing advice for professional golfers. He developed the following chart of accounts for his business:

Assets	Revenues
101 Cash	401 Professional Fees
142 Office Supplies	
	Expenses
Liabilities	511 Wages Expense
202 Accounts Payable	521 Rent Expense
	525 Telephone Expense
Owner's Equity	533 Utilities Expense
311 George Fielding, Capital	534 Charitable Contributions Expense
312 George Fielding, Drawing	538 Automobile Expense

The following transactions took place during the month of December of the current year:

Dec. 1   Fielding invested cash to start the business, $20,000.

3   Paid Bollhorst Real Estate for December office rent, $1,000.

4   Received cash from Aaron Patton, a client, for services, $2,500.

6   Paid T. Z. Anderson Electric for December heating and light, $75.

7   Received cash from Andrew Conder, a client, for services, $2,000.

12   Paid Fichter's Super Service for gasoline and oil purchases for the company car, $60.

14   Paid Hillenburg Staffing for temporary secretarial services during the past two weeks, $600.

17   Bought office supplies from Bowers Office Supply on account, $280.

20   Paid Mitchell Telephone Co. for business calls during the past month, $100.

21   Fielding withdrew cash for personal use, $1,100.

24   Made donation to the National Multiple Sclerosis Society, $100.

27   Received cash from Billy Walters, a client, for services, $2,000.

28   Paid Hillenburg Staffing for temporary secretarial services during the past two weeks, $600.

29   Made payment on account to Bowers Office Supply, $100.

REQUIRED

1.   Record the preceding transactions in a general journal.

2.   Post the entries to the general ledger.

3.   Prepare a trial balance.

4.   Prepare an income statement, statement of owner's equity, and balance sheet for the month of December.

(continued)

Solution 1, 2.

	DATE		DESCRIPTION	POST. REF.	DEBIT					CREDIT					
1	20-- Dec.	1	Cash	101	20	0	0	0	00						1
2			George Fielding, Capital	311						20	0	0	0	00	2
3			Owner's original investment in												3
4			consulting business												4
5															5
6		3	Rent Expense	521	1	0	0	0	00						6
7			Cash	101						1	0	0	0	00	7
8			Paid rent for December												8
9															9
10		4	Cash	101	2	5	0	0	00						10
11			Professional Fees	401						2	5	0	0	00	11
12			Received cash for services rendered												12
13															13
14		6	Utilities Expense	533			7	5	00						14
15			Cash	101								7	5	00	15
16			Paid utilities												16
17															17
18		7	Cash	101	2	0	0	0	00						18
19			Professional Fees	401						2	0	0	0	00	19
20			Received cash for services rendered												20
21															21
22		12	Automobile Expense	538			6	0	00						22
23			Cash	101								6	0	00	23
24			Paid for gas and oil												24
25															25
26		14	Wages Expense	511		6	0	0	00						26
27			Cash	101							6	0	0	00	27
28			Paid temporary secretaries												28
29															29
30		17	Office Supplies	142		2	8	0	00						30
31			Accounts Payable	202							2	8	0	00	31
32			Purchased office supplies on account from												32
33			Bowers Office Supply												33
34															34
35															35

GENERAL JOURNAL — PAGE 1

GENERAL JOURNAL PAGE 2

	DATE		DESCRIPTION	POST. REF.	DEBIT	CREDIT	
1	20-- Dec.	20	Telephone Expense	525	1 0 0 00		1
2			Cash	101		1 0 0 00	2
3			Paid telephone bill				3
4							4
5		21	George Fielding, Drawing	312	1 1 0 0 00		5
6			Cash	101		1 1 0 0 00	6
7			Owner's withdrawal				7
8							8
9		24	Charitable Contributions Expense	534	1 0 0 00		9
10			Cash	101		1 0 0 00	10
11			Contribution to National Multiple				11
12			Sclerosis Society				12
13							13
14		27	Cash	101	2 0 0 0 00		14
15			Professional Fees	401		2 0 0 0 00	15
16			Received cash for services rendered				16
17							17
18		28	Wages Expense	511	6 0 0 00		18
19			Cash	101		6 0 0 00	19
20			Paid temporary secretaries				20
21							21
22		29	Accounts Payable	202	1 0 0 00		22
23			Cash	101		1 0 0 00	23
24			Payment on account to Bowers Office Supply				24

2.

GENERAL LEDGER

ACCOUNT: Cash   ACCOUNT NO. 101

DATE		ITEM	POST. REF.	DEBIT	CREDIT	BALANCE DEBIT	BALANCE CREDIT
20-- Dec.	1		J1	20 0 0 0 00		20 0 0 0 00	
	3		J1		1 0 0 0 00	19 0 0 0 00	
	4		J1	2 5 0 0 00		21 5 0 0 00	
	6		J1		7 5 00	21 4 2 5 00	
	7		J1	2 0 0 0 00		23 4 2 5 00	
	12		J1		6 0 00	23 3 6 5 00	
	14		J1		6 0 0 00	22 7 6 5 00	
	20		J2		1 0 0 00	22 6 6 5 00	
	21		J2		1 1 0 0 00	21 5 6 5 00	
	24		J2		1 0 0 00	21 4 6 5 00	
	27		J2	2 0 0 0 00		23 4 6 5 00	
	28		J2		6 0 0 00	22 8 6 5 00	
	29		J2		1 0 0 00	22 7 6 5 00	

(continued)

ACCOUNT: Office Supplies   ACCOUNT NO. 142

DATE		ITEM	POST. REF.	DEBIT	CREDIT	BALANCE	
						DEBIT	CREDIT
20-- Dec.	17		J1	2 8 0 00		2 8 0 00	

ACCOUNT: Accounts Payable   ACCOUNT NO. 202

DATE		ITEM	POST. REF.	DEBIT	CREDIT	BALANCE	
						DEBIT	CREDIT
20-- Dec.	17		J1		2 8 0 00		2 8 0 00
	29		J2	1 0 0 00			1 8 0 00

ACCOUNT: George Fielding, Capital   ACCOUNT NO. 311

DATE		ITEM	POST. REF.	DEBIT	CREDIT	BALANCE	
						DEBIT	CREDIT
20-- Dec.	1		J1		20 0 0 0 00		20 0 0 0 00

ACCOUNT: George Fielding, Drawing   ACCOUNT NO. 312

DATE		ITEM	POST. REF.	DEBIT	CREDIT	BALANCE	
						DEBIT	CREDIT
20-- Dec.	21		J2	1 1 0 0 00		1 1 0 0 00	

ACCOUNT: Professional Fees   ACCOUNT NO. 401

DATE		ITEM	POST. REF.	DEBIT	CREDIT	BALANCE	
						DEBIT	CREDIT
20-- Dec.	4		J1		2 5 0 0 00		2 5 0 0 00
	7		J1		2 0 0 0 00		4 5 0 0 00
	27		J2		2 0 0 0 00		6 5 0 0 00

ACCOUNT: Wages Expense   ACCOUNT NO. 511

DATE		ITEM	POST. REF.	DEBIT	CREDIT	BALANCE	
						DEBIT	CREDIT
20-- Dec.	14		J1	6 0 0 00		6 0 0 00	
	28		J2	6 0 0 00		1 2 0 0 00	

ACCOUNT: Rent Expense   ACCOUNT NO. 521

DATE		ITEM	POST. REF.	DEBIT	CREDIT	BALANCE	
						DEBIT	CREDIT
20-- Dec.	3		J1	1 0 0 0 00		1 0 0 0 00	

ACCOUNT: Telephone Expense   ACCOUNT NO. 525

DATE		ITEM	POST. REF.	DEBIT	CREDIT	BALANCE	
						DEBIT	CREDIT
20-- Dec.	20		J2	1 0 0 00		1 0 0 00	

ACCOUNT: Utilities Expense   ACCOUNT NO. 533

DATE		ITEM	POST. REF.	DEBIT	CREDIT	BALANCE	
						DEBIT	CREDIT
20-- Dec.	6		J1	7 5 00		7 5 00	

ACCOUNT: Charitable Contributions Expense   ACCOUNT NO. 534

DATE		ITEM	POST. REF.	DEBIT	CREDIT	BALANCE	
						DEBIT	CREDIT
20-- Dec.	24		J2	1 0 0 00		1 0 0 00	

ACCOUNT: Automobile Expense   ACCOUNT NO. 538

DATE		ITEM	POST. REF.	DEBIT	CREDIT	BALANCE	
						DEBIT	CREDIT
20-- Dec.	12		J1	6 0 00		6 0 00	

3.

George Fielding, Financial Planning Consultant
Trial Balance
December 31, 20 --

ACCOUNT TITLE	ACCOUNT NO.	DEBIT BALANCE	CREDIT BALANCE
Cash	101	22 7 6 5 00	
Office Supplies	142	2 8 0 00	
Accounts Payable	202		1 8 0 00
George Fielding, Capital	311		20 0 0 0 00
George Fielding, Drawing	312	1 1 0 0 00	
Professional Fees	401		6 5 0 0 00
Wages Expense	511	1 2 0 0 00	
Rent Expense	521	1 0 0 0 00	
Telephone Expense	525	1 0 0 00	
Utilities Expense	533	7 5 00	
Charitable Contributions Expense	534	1 0 0 00	
Automobile Expense	538	6 0 00	
		26 6 8 0 00	26 6 8 0 00

(continued)

4.

George Fielding, Financial Planning Consultant Income Statement For Month Ended December 31, 20 --										
Revenue:										
Proffessional fees							$6	5	0	0	00
Expenses:										
Wages expense	$1	2	0	0	00					
Rent expense	1	0	0	0	00					
Telephone expense		1	0	0	00					
Utilities expense			7	5	00					
Charitable contributions expense		1	0	0	00					
Automobile expense			6	0	00					
Total expenses							2	5	3	5	00
Net income							$3	9	6	5	00

George Fielding, Financial Planning Consultant Statement of Owner's Equity For Month Ended December 31, 20 --										
George Fielding, capital, December 1, 20 --						$				
Investments during December						20	0	0	0	00
Total investment						$20	0	0	0	00
Net income for December	$3	9	6	5	00					
Less withdrawals for December	1	1	0	0	00					
Increase in capital							2	8	6	5	00
George Fielding, Capital, December 1, 20 --						$22	8	6	5	00

George Fielding, Financial Planning Consultant Balance Sheet December 31, 20 --										
Assets						**Liabilities**				
Cash	$22	7	6	5	00	Accounts payable	$	1	8	0	00
Office Supplies		2	8	0	00	Owner's equity					
						George Fielding, capital	22	8	6	5	00
Total assets	$23	0	4	5	00	Total liabilities and owner's equity	$23	0	4	5	00

KEY TERMS

book of original entry (90)   The journal or the first formal accounting record of a transaction.

chart of accounts (87)   A list of all accounts used by a business.

compound entry (93)   A general journal entry that affects more than two accounts.

correcting entry (104)   An entry to correct an incorrect entry that has been journalized and posted to the wrong account.

cross-reference (97)   The information in the Posting Reference columns of the journal and ledger that provides a link between the journal and ledger.

general ledger (95)   A complete set of all the accounts used by a business. The general ledger accumulates a complete record of the debits and credits made to each account as a result of entries made in the journal.

general ledger account (95)   An account with columns for the debit or credit transaction and columns for the debit or credit running balance.

journal (90)   A day-by-day listing of the transactions of a business.

journalizing (90)   Entering the transactions in a journal.

posting (96)   Copying the debits and credits from the journal to the ledger accounts.

ruling method (103)   A method of correcting an entry in which a line is drawn through the error and the correct information is placed above it.

slide error (103)   An error that occurs when debit or credit amounts "slide" a digit or two to the left or right.

source document (88)   Any document that provides information about a business transaction.

transposition error (103)   An error that occurs when two digits are reversed.

trial balance (102)   A list used to prove that the totals of the debit and credit balances in the ledger accounts are equal.

two-column general journal (90)   A journal with only two amount columns, one for debit amounts and one for credit amounts.

SELF-STUDY QUESTIONS AND EXERCISES

True/False Questions

1. **LO2**   The chart of accounts lists capital accounts first, followed by liabilities, assets, expenses, and revenue.

2. **LO3**   Source documents serve as historical evidence of business transactions.

3. **LO4**   No entries are made in the Posting Reference column at the time of journalizing.

4. **LO4**   When entering the credit item in a general journal, it should be listed after all debits and indented.

5. **LO6**   When an incorrect entry has been journalized and posted to the wrong account, a correcting entry should be made.

Multiple Choice Questions

1. **LO2**   A revenue account will begin with the number _____ in the chart of accounts.

   (a) 1   (c) 3
   (b) 2   (d) 4

(continued)

2. **LO3** Which of the following is not a source document?

(a) Check stub
(b) Cash register tape
(c) Journal entry
(d) Purchase invoice

3. **LO4** To purchase an asset such as office equipment on account, you would credit which account?

(a) Cash
(b) Accounts Receivable

(c) Accounts Payable
(d) Capital

4. **LO4** When fees are earned and the customer promises to pay later, which account is debited?

(a) Cash
(b) Accounts Receivable

(c) Accounts Payable
(d) Capital

5. **LO6** When the correct numbers are used but are in the wrong order, the error is called a

(a) transposition.
(b) slide.

(c) ruling.
(d) correcting entry.

U REVU Exercises

1. **LO3** A check stub serves as a source document for what kind of transaction?

2. **LO4** Indicate the information that would be entered for each of the lettered items in the general journal provided below.

		GENERAL JOURNAL			PAGE
	DATE	DESCRIPTION	POST. REF.	DEBIT	CREDIT
1	A B	C D	G	H	1
2		E	J	I	2
3		F			3
4					4
5					5

3. **LO5** Indicate the information that would be entered for each of the lettered items in the general ledger account provided below.

		GENERAL LEDGER					
ACCOUNT: A						ACCOUNT NO. B	
DATE	ITEM	POST. REF.	DEBIT	CREDIT	BALANCE		
					DEBIT		CREDIT
C D	E	F	G	H	I	J	K

4. **LO6** Dunkin Company made the following entry for the payment of $500 cash for rent expense:

Rent Expense   500
   Rent Payable   500

Prepare a correcting entry.

The answers to the Self-Study Questions and Exercises are at the end of the chapter (pages 128–129).

REVIEW QUESTIONS

LO1   1. Trace the flow of accounting information through the accounting system.

LO2   2. Explain the purpose of a chart of accounts.

LO2   3. Name the five types of financial statement classifications for which it is ordinarily desirable to keep separate accounts.

LO3   4. Name a source document that provides information about each of the following types of business transactions:
   a. Cash payment
   b. Cash receipt
   c. Sale of goods or services
   d. Purchase of goods or services

LO4   5. Where is the first formal accounting record of a business transaction usually made?

LO4   6. Describe the four steps required to journalize a business transaction in a general journal.

LO5   7. In what order are the accounts customarily placed in the ledger?

LO5   8. Explain the primary advantage of a general ledger account.

LO5   9. Explain the five steps required when posting the journal to the ledger.

LO5 10. What information is entered in the Posting Reference column of the journal as an amount is posted to the proper account in the ledger?

LO6 11. Explain why the ledger can still contain errors even though the trial balance is in balance. Give examples of two such types of errors.

LO6 12. What is a slide error?

LO6 13. What is a transposition error?

LO6 14. What is the ruling method of correcting an error?

LO6 15. What is the correcting entry method?

SERIES A EXERCISES

E 4-1A (LO3)

SOURCE DOCUMENTS Source documents trigger the analysis of events requiring an accounting entry. Match the following source documents with the type of information they provide.

1. Check stubs or check register
2. Purchase invoice from suppliers (vendors)
3. Sales tickets or invoices to customers
4. Receipts or cash register tapes

a. A good or service has been sold.
b. Cash has been received by the business.
c. Cash has been paid by the business.
d. Goods or services have been purchased by the business.

E 4-2A (LO4)

GENERAL JOURNAL ENTRIES For each of the following transactions, list the account to be debited and the account to be credited in the general journal.

(continued)

1. Invested cash in the business, $5,000.

2. Paid office rent, $500.

3. Purchased office supplies on account, $300.

4. Received cash for services rendered (fees), $400.

5. Paid cash on account, $50.

6. Rendered services on account, $300.

7. Received cash for an amount owed by a customer, $100.

E 4-3A (LO5)

✓ Final Cash bal.: $4,950

GENERAL LEDGER ACCOUNTS Set up T accounts for each of the general ledger accounts needed for Exercise 4-2A and post debits and credits to the accounts. Foot the accounts and enter the balances. Prove that total debits equal total credits.

E 4-4A (LO4)

GENERAL JOURNAL ENTRIES Jean Jones has opened Jones Consulting. Journalize the following transactions that occurred during January of the current year. Use the following journal pages: January 1–10, page 1, and January 11–29, page 2. Use the following chart of accounts:

Chart of Accounts

Assets
101 Cash
142 Office Supplies
181 Office Equipment

Liabilities
202 Accounts Payable

Owner's Equity
311 Jean Jones, Capital
312 Jean Jones, Drawing

Revenues
401 Consulting Fees

Expenses
511 Wages Expense
521 Rent Expense
525 Telephone Expense
533 Utilities Expense
549 Miscellaneous Expense

Jan. 1 Jones invested cash in the business, $10,000.

2 Paid office rent, $500.

3 Purchased office equipment on account, $1,500.

5 Received cash for services rendered, $750.

8 Paid telephone bill, $65.

10 Paid for a magazine subscription (miscellaneous expense), $15.

11 Purchased office supplies on account, $300.

15 Made a payment on account (see Jan. 3 transaction), $150.

18 Paid part-time employee, $500.

21 Received cash for services rendered, $350.

25 Paid utilities bill, $85.

27 Jones withdrew cash for personal use, $100.

29 Paid part-time employee, $500.

E 4-5A (LO5)

✓ Final Cash bal.: $9,185;
Trial bal. total debits: $12,750

GENERAL LEDGER ACCOUNTS; TRIAL BALANCE Set up general ledger accounts using the chart of accounts provided in Exercise 4-4A. Post the transactions from Exercise 4-4A to the general ledger accounts and prepare a trial balance.

E 4-6A (LO5)

✓ Total assets, Jan. 31: $10,985

FINANCIAL STATEMENTS From the information in Exercises 4-4A and 4-5A, prepare an income statement, a statement of owner's equity, and a balance sheet.

E 4-7A (LO5)

✓ Total assets, July 31: $7,100

FINANCIAL STATEMENTS From the following trial balance taken after one month of operation, prepare an income statement, a statement of owner's equity, and a balance sheet.

<table>
<tr><td colspan="5" align="center">TJ's Paint Service
Trial Balance
July 31, 20 - -</td></tr>
<tr><th>ACCOUNT TITLE</th><th>ACCOUNT NO.</th><th>DEBIT BALANCE</th><th>CREDIT BALANCE</th></tr>
<tr><td>Cash</td><td>101</td><td>4 3 0 0 00</td><td></td></tr>
<tr><td>Accounts Receivable</td><td>122</td><td>1 1 0 0 00</td><td></td></tr>
<tr><td>Supplies</td><td>141</td><td>8 0 0 00</td><td></td></tr>
<tr><td>Paint Equipment</td><td>183</td><td>9 0 0 00</td><td></td></tr>
<tr><td>Accounts Payable</td><td>202</td><td></td><td>2 1 5 0 00</td></tr>
<tr><td>TJ Ulza, Capital</td><td>311</td><td></td><td>3 2 0 5 00</td></tr>
<tr><td>TJ Ulza, Drawing</td><td>312</td><td>5 0 0 00</td><td></td></tr>
<tr><td>Painting Fees</td><td>401</td><td></td><td>3 6 0 0 00</td></tr>
<tr><td>Wages Expense</td><td>511</td><td>9 0 0 00</td><td></td></tr>
<tr><td>Rent Expense</td><td>521</td><td>2 5 0 00</td><td></td></tr>
<tr><td>Telephone Expense</td><td>525</td><td>5 0 00</td><td></td></tr>
<tr><td>Transportation Expense</td><td>526</td><td>6 0 00</td><td></td></tr>
<tr><td>Utilities Expense</td><td>533</td><td>7 0 00</td><td></td></tr>
<tr><td>Miscellaneous Expense</td><td>549</td><td>2 5 00</td><td></td></tr>
<tr><td></td><td></td><td>8 9 5 5 00</td><td>8 9 5 5 00</td></tr>
</table>

E 4-8A (LO6)

FINDING AND CORRECTING ERRORS Joe Adams bought $500 worth of office supplies on account. The following entry was recorded on May 17. Find the error(s) and correct it (them) using the ruling method.

<table>
<tr><td>14</td><td></td><td></td><td></td><td></td><td></td><td>14</td></tr>
<tr><td>15</td><td>20--
May</td><td>17</td><td>Office Equipment</td><td>4 0 0 00</td><td></td><td>15</td></tr>
<tr><td>16</td><td></td><td></td><td>Cash</td><td></td><td>4 0 0 00</td><td>16</td></tr>
<tr><td>17</td><td></td><td></td><td>Purchased copy paper</td><td></td><td></td><td>17</td></tr>
</table>

On May 25, after the transactions had been posted, Adams discovered that the following entry contains an error. The cash received represents a collection on account, rather than new service fees. Correct the error in the general journal using the correcting entry method.

<table>
<tr><td>22</td><td></td><td></td><td></td><td></td><td></td><td></td><td>22</td></tr>
<tr><td>23</td><td>20--
May</td><td>23</td><td>Cash</td><td>101</td><td>1 0 0 0 00</td><td></td><td>23</td></tr>
<tr><td>24</td><td></td><td></td><td>Service Fees</td><td>401</td><td></td><td>1 0 0 0 00</td><td>24</td></tr>
<tr><td>25</td><td></td><td></td><td>Received cash for services previously earned</td><td></td><td></td><td></td><td>25</td></tr>
</table>

SERIES A PROBLEMS

P 4-9A (LO4/5)

✓ Cash bal., Jan. 31: $10,021;
Trial bal. total debits: $13,460

JOURNALIZING AND POSTING TRANSACTIONS Annette Creighton opened Creighton Consulting. She rented a small office and paid a part-time worker to answer the telephone and make deliveries. Her chart of accounts is as follows:

Chart of Accounts

Assets
101   Cash
142   Office Supplies
181   Office Equipment

Liabilities
202   Accounts Payable

Owner's Equity
311   Annette Creighton, Capital
312   Annette Creighton, Drawing

Revenues
401   Consulting Fees

Expenses
511   Wages Expense
512   Advertising Expense
521   Rent Expense
525   Telephone Expense
526   Transportation Expense
533   Utilities Expense
549   Miscellaneous Expense

Creighton's transactions for the first month of business are as follows:

Jan. 1   Creighton invested cash in the business, $10,000.
      1   Paid rent, $500.
      2   Purchased office supplies on account, $300.
      4   Purchased office equipment on account, $1,500.
      6   Received cash for services rendered, $580.
      7   Paid telephone bill, $42.
      8   Paid utilities bill, $38.
     10   Received cash for services rendered, $360.
     12   Made payment on account, $50.
     13   Paid for car rental while visiting an out-of-town client (transportation expense), $150.
     15   Paid part-time worker, $360.
     17   Received cash for services rendered, $420.
     18   Creighton withdrew cash for personal use, $100.
     20   Paid for a newspaper ad, $26.
     22   Reimbursed part-time employee for cab fare incurred delivering materials to clients (transportation expense), $35.
     24   Paid for books on consulting practices (miscellaneous expense), $28.
     25   Received cash for services rendered, $320.
     27   Made payment on account for office equipment purchased, $150.
     29   Paid part-time worker, $360.
     30   Received cash for services rendered, $180.

REQUIRED

1. Set up general ledger accounts from the chart of accounts.

2. Journalize the transactions for January in a two-column general journal. Use the following journal page numbers: January 1–10, page 1; January 12–24, page 2; January 25–30, page 3.

3. Post the transactions to the general ledger.

4. Prepare a trial balance.

5. Prepare an income statement and a statement of owner's equity for the month of January and a balance sheet as of January 31, 20--.

P 4-10A (LO4/5)

✓ Cash bal., June 30: $3,958;
Trial bal. total debits: $22,358

JOURNALIZING AND POSTING TRANSACTIONS Jim Andrews opened a delivery business in March. He rented a small office and has a part-time assistant. His trial balance shows accounts for the first three months of business.

<table>
<tr><td colspan="4" align="center">Jim's Quick Delivery
Trial Balance
May 31, 20 - -</td></tr>
<tr><td>ACCOUNT TITLE</td><td>ACCOUNT NO.</td><td>DEBIT BALANCE</td><td>CREDIT BALANCE</td></tr>
<tr><td>Cash</td><td>101</td><td>3 8 2 6 00</td><td></td></tr>
<tr><td>Accounts Receivable</td><td>122</td><td>1 2 1 2 00</td><td></td></tr>
<tr><td>Office Supplies</td><td>142</td><td>6 4 8 00</td><td></td></tr>
<tr><td>Office Equipment</td><td>181</td><td>2 1 0 0 00</td><td></td></tr>
<tr><td>Delivery Truck</td><td>185</td><td>8 0 0 0 00</td><td></td></tr>
<tr><td>Accounts Payable</td><td>202</td><td></td><td>6 0 0 0 00</td></tr>
<tr><td>Jim Andrews, Capital</td><td>311</td><td></td><td>4 4 7 8 00</td></tr>
<tr><td>Jim Andrews, Drawing</td><td>312</td><td>1 8 0 0 00</td><td></td></tr>
<tr><td>Delivery Fees</td><td>401</td><td></td><td>9 8 8 0 00</td></tr>
<tr><td>Wages Expense</td><td>511</td><td>1 2 0 0 00</td><td></td></tr>
<tr><td>Advertising Expense</td><td>512</td><td>9 0 00</td><td></td></tr>
<tr><td>Rent Expense</td><td>521</td><td>9 0 0 00</td><td></td></tr>
<tr><td>Telephone Expense</td><td>525</td><td>1 2 6 00</td><td></td></tr>
<tr><td>Electricity Expense</td><td>533</td><td>9 8 00</td><td></td></tr>
<tr><td>Charitable Contributions Expense</td><td>534</td><td>6 0 00</td><td></td></tr>
<tr><td>Gas and Oil Expense</td><td>538</td><td>1 8 6 00</td><td></td></tr>
<tr><td>Miscellaneous Expense</td><td>549</td><td>1 1 2 00</td><td></td></tr>
<tr><td></td><td></td><td>20 3 5 8 00</td><td>20 3 5 8 00</td></tr>
</table>

Andrews' transactions for the month of June are as follows:

June 1 Paid rent, $300.

    2 Performed delivery services for $300: $100 in cash and $200 on account.

    4 Paid for newspaper advertising, $15.

    6 Purchased office supplies on account, $180.

    7 Received cash for delivery services rendered, $260.

    9 Paid cash on account (truck payment), $200.

   10 Purchased a copier (office equipment) for $700: paid $100 in cash and put $600 on account.

   11 Made a contribution to the Red Cross (charitable contributions), $20.

   12 Received cash for delivery services rendered, $380.

   13 Received cash on account for services previously rendered, $100.

   15 Paid a part-time worker, $200.

   16 Paid electric bill, $36.

   18 Paid telephone bill, $46.

   19 Received cash on account for services previously rendered, $100.

(continued)

June 20	Andrews withdrew cash for personal use, $200.	
21	Paid for gas and oil, $32.	
22	Made payment on account (for office supplies), $40.	
24	Received cash for services rendered, $340.	
26	Paid for a magazine subscription (miscellaneous expense), $15.	
27	Received cash for services rendered, $180.	
27	Received cash on account for services previously rendered, $100.	
29	Paid for gasoline, $24.	
30	Paid a part-time worker, $200.	

REQUIRED

1. Set up general ledger accounts by entering the balances as of June 1.

2. Journalize the transactions for June in a two-column general journal. Use the following journal pages: June 1–10, page 7; June 11–20, page 8; June 21–30, page 9.

3. Post the entries to the general ledger.

4. Prepare a trial balance.

P 4-11A (LO6)

CORRECTING ERRORS Assuming that all entries have been posted, prepare correcting entries for each of the following errors.

1. The following entry was made to record the purchase of $500 in supplies on account:

Supplies	142	500	
Cash	101		500

2. The following entry was made to record the payment of $300 in wages:

Rent Expense	521	300	
Cash	101		300

3. The following entry was made to record a $200 payment to a supplier on account:

Supplies	142	100	
Cash	101		100

SERIES B EXERCISES

E 4-1B (LO3)

SOURCE DOCUMENTS What type of information is found on each of the following source documents?

1. Cash register tape
2. Sales ticket (issued to customer)
3. Purchase invoice (received from supplier or vendor)
4. Check stub

E 4-2B (LO4)

GENERAL JOURNAL ENTRIES For each of the following transactions, list the account to be debited and the account to be credited in the general journal.

1. Invested cash in the business, $1,000.
2. Performed services on account, $200.

3. Purchased office equipment on account, $500.

4. Received cash on account for services previously rendered, $200.

5. Made a payment on account, $100.

E 4-3B (LO5)

✓ Final Cash bal.: $1,100

GENERAL LEDGER ACCOUNTS Set up T accounts for each of the general ledger accounts needed for Exercise 4-2B and post debits and credits to the accounts. Foot the accounts and enter the balances. Prove that total debits equal total credits.

E 4-4B (LO4)

GENERAL JOURNAL ENTRIES Sengel Moon opened The Bike Doctor. Journalize the following transactions that occurred during the month of October of the current year. Use the following journal pages: October 1–12, page 1, and October 14–29, page 2. Use the following chart of accounts:

Chart of Accounts

Assets
101 Cash
141 Bicycle Parts
142 Office Supplies

Liabilities
202 Accounts Payable

Owner's Equity
311 Sengel Moon, Capital
312 Sengel Moon, Drawing

Revenues
401 Repair Fees

Expenses
511 Wages Expense
521 Rent Expense
525 Telephone Expense
533 Utilities Expense
549 Miscellaneous Expense

Oct. 1 Moon invested cash in the business, $15,000.
2 Paid shop rental for the month, $300.
3 Purchased bicycle parts on account, $2,000.
5 Purchased office supplies on account, $250.
8 Paid telephone bill, $38.
9 Received cash for services, $140.
11 Paid a sports magazine subscription (miscellaneous expense), $15.
12 Made payment on account (see Oct. 3 transaction), $100.
14 Paid part-time employee, $300.
15 Received cash for services, $350.
16 Paid utilities bill, $48.
19 Received cash for services, $250.
23 Moon withdrew cash for personal use, $50.
25 Made payment on account (see Oct. 5 transaction), $50.
29 Paid part-time employee, $300.

E 4-5B (LO5)

✓ Final Cash bal.: $14,539;
Trial bal. total debits: $17,840

GENERAL LEDGER ACCOUNTS; TRIAL BALANCE Set up general ledger accounts using the chart of accounts provided in Exercise 4-4B. Post the transactions from Exercise 4-4B to the general ledger accounts and prepare a trial balance.

E 4-6B (LO5)

✓ Total assets, Oct. 31: $16,789

FINANCIAL STATEMENTS From the information in Exercises 4-4B and 4-5B, prepare an income statement, a statement of owner's equity, and a balance sheet.

E 4-7B (LO5)
✓ Total assets, Mar. 31: $11,900

FINANCIAL STATEMENTS From the following trial balance taken after one month of operation, prepare an income statement, a statement of owner's equity, and a balance sheet.

ACCOUNT TITLE	ACCOUNT NO.	DEBIT BALANCE	CREDIT BALANCE
Cash	101	6 6 0 0 00	
Accounts Receivable	122	2 8 0 0 00	
Office Supplies	142	1 0 0 0 00	
Office Equipment	181	1 5 0 0 00	
Accounts Payable	202		3 0 0 0 00
AT Speaker, Capital	311		6 0 9 8 00
AT Speaker, Drawing	312	8 0 0 00	
Speaking Fees	401		4 8 0 0 00
Wages Expense	511	4 0 0 00	
Rent Expense	521	2 0 0 00	
Telephone Expense	525	3 5 00	
Travel Expense	526	4 5 0 00	
Utilities Expense	533	8 8 00	
Miscellaneous Expense	549	2 5 00	
		13 8 9 8 00	13 8 9 8 00

AT Speaker's Bureau / Trial Balance / March 31, 20 - -

E 4-8B (LO6)

FINDING AND CORRECTING ERRORS Mary Smith purchased $350 worth of office equipment on account. The following entry was recorded on April 6. Find the error(s) and correct it (them) using the ruling method.

7						7
8	20-- Apr.	6	Office Supplies	5 3 0 00		8
9			Cash		5 3 0 00	9
10			Purchased office equipment			10

On April 25, after the transactions had been posted, Smith discovered the following entry contains an error. When her customer received services, Cash was debited, but no cash was received. Correct the error in the journal using the correcting entry method.

27							27
28	20-- Apr.	21	Cash	101	3 0 0 00		28
29			Service Fees	401		3 0 0 00	29
30			Revenue earned from services				30
31			previously rendered				31

SERIES B PROBLEMS

P 4-9B **(LO4/5)**

✓ Cash bal., May 31: $4,500;
Trial bal. total debits: $8,790

JOURNALIZING AND POSTING TRANSACTIONS Benito Mendez opened Mendez Appraisals. He rented office space and has a part-time secretary to answer the telephone and make appraisal appointments. His chart of accounts is as follows:

Chart of Accounts

Assets
101 Cash
122 Accounts Receivable
142 Office Supplies
181 Office Equipment

Liabilities
202 Accounts Payable

Owner's Equity
311 Benito Mendez, Capital
312 Benito Mendez, Drawing

Revenues
401 Appraisal Fees

Expenses
511 Wages Expense
512 Advertising Expense
521 Rent Expense
525 Telephone Expense
526 Transportation Expense
533 Electricity Expense
549 Miscellaneous Expense

Mendez's transactions for the first month of business are as follows:

May 1   Mendez invested cash in the business, $5,000.

2   Paid rent, $500.

3   Purchased office supplies, $100.

4   Purchased office equipment on account, $2,000.

5   Received cash for services rendered, $280.

8   Paid telephone bill, $38.

9   Paid electric bill, $42.

10   Received cash for services rendered, $310.

13   Paid part-time employee, $500.

14   Paid car rental for out-of-town trip, $200.

15   Paid for newspaper ad, $30.

18   Received cash for services rendered, $620.

19   Paid mileage reimbursement for part-time employee's use of personal car for business deliveries (transportation expense), $22.

21   Mendez withdrew cash for personal use, $50.

23   Made payment on account for office equipment purchased earlier, $200.

24   Earned appraisal fee, which will be paid in a week, $500.

26   Paid for newspaper ad, $30.

27   Paid for local softball team sponsorship (miscellaneous expense), $15.

28   Paid part-time employee, $500.

29   Received cash on account, $250.

30   Received cash for services rendered, $280.

31   Paid cab fare (transportation expense), $13.

(continued)

REQUIRED

1. Set up general ledger accounts from the chart of accounts.

2. Journalize the transactions for May in a two-column general journal. Use the following journal page numbers: May 1–10, page 1; May 13–24, page 2; May 26–31, page 3.

3. Post the transactions to the general ledger.

4. Prepare a trial balance.

5. Prepare an income statement and a statement of owner's equity for the month of May, and a balance sheet as of May 31, 20--.

P 4-10B (LO4/5)

✓ Cash bal., Nov. 30: $7,012;
Trial bal. total debits: $16,105

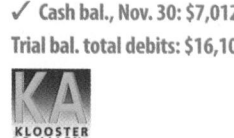

JOURNALIZING AND POSTING TRANSACTIONS Ann Taylor owns a suit tailoring shop. She opened business in September. She rented a small work space and has an assistant to receive job orders and process claim tickets. Her trial balance shows her account balances for the first two months of business.

ACCOUNT TITLE	ACCOUNT NO.	DEBIT BALANCE					CREDIT BALANCE				
Taylor Tailoring											
Trial Balance											
October 31, 20 --											
Cash	101	6	2	1	1	00					
Accounts Receivable	122		4	8	4	00					
Tailoring Supplies	141	1	0	0	0	00					
Tailoring Equipment	183	3	8	0	0	00					
Accounts Payable	202						4	1	2	5	00
Ann Taylor, Capital	311						6	1	3	0	00
Ann Taylor, Drawing	312		8	0	0	00					
Tailoring Fees	401						3	6	0	0	00
Wages Expense	511		8	0	0	00					
Advertising Expense	512			3	4	00					
Rent Expense	521		6	0	0	00					
Telephone Expense	525			6	0	00					
Electricity Expense	533			4	4	00					
Miscellaneous Expense	549			2	2	00					
		13	8	5	5	00	13	8	5	5	00

Taylor's transactions for November are as follows:

Nov. 1   Paid rent, $300.

2   Purchased tailoring supplies on account, $150.

3   Purchased a new button hole machine on account, $300.

5   Earned first week's revenue, $400: $100 in cash and $300 on account.

8   Paid for newspaper advertising, $13.

9   Paid telephone bill, $28.

10   Paid electric bill, $21.

11   Received cash on account from customers, $200.

12   Earned second week's revenue, $450: $200 in cash and $250 on account.

15   Paid assistant, $400.

16   Made payment on account, $100.

17   Paid for magazine subscription (miscellaneous expense), $12.

Nov. 19   Earned third week's revenue, $450: $300 in cash, $150 on account.

    23   Received cash on account from customers, $300.

    24   Paid for newspaper advertising, $13.

    26   Paid for postage (miscellaneous expense), $12.

    27   Earned fourth week's revenue, $600: $200 in cash and $400 on account.

    30   Received cash on account from customers, $400.

REQUIRED

1. Set up general ledger accounts by entering the balances as of November 1, 20--.

2. Journalize the transactions for November in a two-column general journal. Use the following journal page numbers: November 1–11, page 7; November 12–24, page 8; November 26–30, page 9.

3. Post the entries to the general ledger.

4. Prepare a trial balance.

P 4-11B (LO6)

CORRECTING ERRORS Assuming that all entries have been posted, prepare correcting entries for each of the following errors.

1. The following entry was made to record the purchase of $400 in equipment on account:

Supplies	142	400	
Cash	101		400

2. The following entry was made to record the payment of $200 for advertising:

Repair Expense	537	200	
Cash	101		200

3. The following entry was made to record a $600 payment to a supplier on account:

Prepaid Insurance	145	400	
Cash	101		400

 # MANAGING YOUR WRITING

You are a public accountant with many small business clients. During a recent visit to a client's business, the bookkeeper approached you with a problem. The columns of the trial balance were not equal. You helped the bookkeeper find and correct the error, but believe you should go one step further. Write a memo to all of your clients that explains the purpose of the double-entry framework, the importance of maintaining the equality of the accounting equation, the errors that might cause an inequality, and suggestions for finding the errors.

MASTERY PROBLEM

✓ Cash bal., June 30: $45,495;
Trial bal. total debits: $96,200

Barry Bird opened the Barry Bird Basketball Camp for children ages 10 through 18. Campers typically register for one week in June or July, arriving on Sunday and returning home the following Saturday. College players serve as cabin counselors and assist the local college and high school coaches who run the practice sessions. The registration fee includes a room, meals at a nearby restaurant, and basketball instruction.

(continued)

In the off-season, the facilities are used for weekend retreats and coaching clinics. Bird developed the following chart of accounts for his service business:

Chart of Accounts

Assets	Revenues
101 Cash	401 Registration Fees
142 Office Supplies	
183 Athletic Equipment	Expenses
184 Basketball Facilities	511 Wages Expense
	512 Advertising Expense
Liabilities	524 Food Expense
202 Accounts Payable	525 Telephone Expense
	533 Utilities Expense
	536 Postage Expense
Owner's Equity	
311 Barry Bird, Capital	
312 Barry Bird, Drawing	

The following transactions took place during the month of June:

June	1	Bird invested cash in the business, $10,000.
	1	Purchased basketballs and other athletic equipment, $3,000.
	2	Paid Hite Advertising for flyers that had been mailed to prospective campers, $5,000.
	2	Collected registration fees, $15,000.
	2	Rogers Construction completed work on a new basketball court that cost $12,000. Arrangements were made to pay the bill in July.
	5	Purchased office supplies on account from Gordon Office Supplies, $300.
	6	Received bill from Magic's Restaurant for meals served to campers on account, $5,800.
	7	Collected registration fees, $16,200.
	10	Paid wages to camp counselors, $500.
	14	Collected registration fees, $13,500.
	14	Received bill from Magic's Restaurant for meals served to campers on account, $6,200.
	17	Paid wages to camp counselors, $500.
	18	Paid postage, $85.
	21	Collected registration fees, $15,200.
	22	Received bill from Magic's Restaurant for meals served to campers on account, $6,500.
	24	Paid wages to camp counselors, $500.
	28	Collected registration fees, $14,000.
	30	Received bill from Magic's Restaurant for meals served to campers on account, $7,200.
	30	Paid wages to camp counselors, $500.
	30	Paid Magic's Restaurant on account, $25,700.
	30	Paid utility bill, $500.
	30	Paid telephone bill, $120.
	30	Bird withdrew cash for personal use, $2,000.

REQUIRED

1. Enter the transactions in a general journal. Use the following journal pages: June 1–6, page 1; June 7–22, page 2; June 24–30, page 3.

2. Post the entries to the general ledger.

3. Prepare a trial balance.

CHALLENGE PROBLEM

This problem challenges you to apply your cumulative accounting knowledge to move a step beyond the material in the chapter.

✓ **Total debits: $19,150**

Journal entries and a trial balance for Fred Phaler Consulting follow. As you will note, the trial balance does not balance, suggesting that there are errors. Recall that the chapter offers tips on identifying individual posting errors. These techniques are not as effective when there are two or more errors. Thus, you will need to first carefully inspect the trial balance to see if you can identify any obvious errors due to amounts that either look out of proportion or are simply reported in the wrong place. Then, you will need to carefully evaluate the other amounts by using the techniques offered in the text, or tracing the journal entries to the amounts reported on the trial balance. (*Hint*: Four errors were made in the posting process and preparation of the trial balance.)

GENERAL JOURNAL   PAGE 1

	DATE		DESCRIPTION	POST. REF.	DEBIT	CREDIT	
1	20-- June	1	Cash	101	10 0 0 0 00		1
2			Fred Phaler, Capital	311		10 0 0 0 00	2
3							3
4		2	Rent Expense	521	5 0 0 00		4
5			Cash	101		5 0 0 00	5
6							6
7		3	Cash	101	4 0 0 0 00		7
8			Professional Fees	401		4 0 0 0 00	8
9							9
10		4	Utilities Expense	533	1 0 0 00		10
11			Cash	101		1 0 0 00	11
12							12
13		7	Cash	101	3 0 0 0 00		13
14			Professional Fees	401		3 0 0 0 00	14
15							15
16		12	Automobile Expense	526	5 0 00		16
17			Cash	101		5 0 00	17
18							18
19		14	Wages Expense	511	5 0 0 00		19
20			Cash	101		5 0 0 00	20
21							21
22		14	Office Supplies	142	2 5 0 00		22
23			Accounts Payable	202		2 5 0 00	23
24							24
25		20	Telephone Expense	525	1 0 0 00		25
26			Cash	101		1 0 0 00	26
27							27
28		21	Fred Phaler, Drawing	312	1 2 0 0 00		28
29			Cash	101		1 2 0 0 00	29
30							30
31		24	Accounts Receivable	122	2 0 0 0 00		31
32			Professional Fees	401		2 0 0 0 00	32
33							33
34		25	Accounts Payable	202	1 0 0 00		34
35			Cash	101		1 0 0 00	35
36							36
37		30	Wages Expense	511	3 0 0 00		37
38			Cash	101		3 0 0 00	38

(continued)

Fred Phaler Consulting
Trial Balance
June 30, 20 - -

ACCOUNT TITLE	ACCOUNT NO.	DEBIT BALANCE	CREDIT BALANCE
Cash	101		13 9 0 0 00
Accounts Receivable	122	2 0 0 0 00	
Office Supplies	142	2 5 0 00	
Accounts Payable	202	1 0 0 00	
Fred Phaler, Capital	311		10 0 0 0 00
Fred Phaler, Drawing	312	2 1 0 0 00	
Professional Fees	401		9 0 0 0 00
Wages Expense	511	8 0 0 00	
Rent Expense	521	5 0 0 00	
Telephone Expense	525	1 0 0 00	
Automobile Expense	526	50 0 0 0 00	
Utilities Expense	533	1 0 0 00	
		55 9 5 0 00	32 9 0 0 00

REQUIRED

1. Find the errors.

2. Explain what caused the errors.

3. Prepare a corrected trial balance.

ANSWERS TO SELF-STUDY QUESTIONS AND EXERCISES

True/False Questions

1. F (A, L, OE, R, E)

2. T

3. T

4. T

5. T

Multiple Choice Questions

1. d

2. c

3. c

4. b

5. a

U REVU   Exercises

1. A cash payment.

2. A   Year in which entry was made. (Needed for first transaction on this page.)

    B   Month in which entry was made. (Needed for first transaction on this page.)

    C   Day of the month entry was made. (Needed for every transaction.)

    D   Account debited.

    E   Account credited.

    F   Description of transaction.

    G   Account number for account debited to indicate the debit has been posted.

    H   Amount for account debited.

    I   Amount for account credited.

    J   Account number for account credited to indicate the credit has been posted.

3. A   Account title.

    B   Account number.

    C   Year of transaction. (Needed for first transaction on this page.)

    D   Month of transaction. (Needed for first transaction on this page.)

    E   Day of month transaction was made. (Needed for every transaction.)

    F   Generally left blank, except for special reasons such as indicating the beginning balance, adjusting, correcting, closing, or reversing entries.

    G   Journal page from which entry was posted.

    H   Dollar amount of debit.

    I   Dollar amount of credit.

    J   Balance if account has a debit balance.

    K   Balance if account has a credit balance.

4.

	DATE	DESCRIPTION	POST. REF.	DEBIT	CREDIT	
1		Rent Payable		5 0 0 00		1
2		Cash			5 0 0 00	2
3		To correct error in which payment for rent				3
4		was credited to Rent Payable rather than Cash.				4
5						5

GENERAL JOURNAL   PAGE 1

Chapter 5

COURTESY OF FLOYD'S 99 BARBERSHOPS

LEARNING OBJECTIVES

Careful study of this chapter should enable you to:

LO1 Prepare end-of-period adjustments.

LO2 Post adjusting entries to the general ledger.

LO3 Prepare a work sheet.

LO4 Describe methods for finding errors on the work sheet.

LO5 Journalize adjusting entries from the work sheet.

LO6 Explain the cash, modified cash, and accrual bases of accounting.

Adjusting Entries and the Work Sheet

Floyd's 99 Barbershops was founded in 2001 and currently has 350 employees. The company generates over $15 million in revenues annually. Floyd's 99 is a contemporary full-service barbershop/hair-care concept offering haircuts, coloring, styling, and shaves. In a setting where *Hard Rock* meets haircuts, customers listen to custom designed Floyd's 99 Radio, watch TV, surf the internet, and get a signature shoulder massage and hot lather neck shave all as a part of their overall haircut experience. About 80% of Floyd's 99 customers are male. The company has an aggressive expansion program and requires that franchisees be able to immediately fund and open three to five branches. Headquartered in Greenwood Village, Colorado, Floyd's 99 has shops in nine states, primarily Colorado, California, and Texas. Over half of the current 40 locations are corporately owned, and the rest are franchise owned.

As a rapidly growing company, Floyd's 99 uses the accrual basis of accounting, which requires making end-of-period adjusting entries. In this chapter, you will learn why adjusting entries are important, how they are made, and how they affect the financial statements. In addition, you will learn how to use a work sheet to help in the preparation of adjusting entries and the financial statements.

U p to this point, you have learned how to journalize business transactions, post to the ledger, and prepare a trial balance. Now it is time to learn how to make end-of-period adjustments to the accounts listed in the trial balance. This chapter explains the need for adjustments and illustrates how they are made with or without the use of a work sheet.

END-OF-PERIOD ADJUSTMENTS

LO1 Prepare end-of-period adjustments.

Transactions are entered as they occur throughout the year. Adjustments are made at the end of the accounting period for items that do not involve exchanges with an outside party.

Throughout the accounting period, business transactions are entered in the accounting system. These transactions are based on exchanges between the business and other companies and individuals. During the accounting period, other changes occur that affect the business's financial condition. For example, equipment is wearing out, prepaid insurance and supplies are being used up, and employees are earning wages that have not yet been paid. Since these events have not been entered into the accounting system, **adjusting entries** must be made prior to the preparation of financial statements.

The **matching principle** in accounting requires the matching of revenues earned during an accounting period with the expenses incurred to produce the revenues. This approach offers the best measure of net income. The income statement reports earnings for a specific period of time, and the balance sheet reports the assets, liabilities, and owner's equity on a specific date. Thus, to follow the matching principle, the accounts must be brought up to date before financial statements are prepared. This requires adjusting some of the accounts listed in the trial balance. Figure 5-1 lists reasons to adjust the trial balance.

LEARNING KEY

Matching revenues earned with expenses incurred to produce those revenues offers the best measure of net income.

FIGURE 5-1   Reasons to Adjust the Trial Balance

1. To report all revenues earned during the accounting period.
2. To report all expenses incurred to produce the revenues earned in the accounting period.
3. To accurately report the assets on the balance sheet date. Some assets may have been used up during the accounting period.
4. To accurately report the liabilities on the balance sheet date. Expenses may have been incurred but not yet paid.

Generally, adjustments are made and financial statements prepared at the end of a 12-month period called a **fiscal year**. This period does not need to be the same as a calendar year. In fact, many businesses schedule their fiscal year-end for a time when business is slow. In this chapter, we continue the illustration of Jessie Jane's Campus Delivery Service and will prepare adjustments at the end of the first month of operations. We will focus on the following accounts: Supplies, Prepaid Insurance, Wages Expense, and Delivery Equipment.

A BROADER VIEW

TRISH LEASE/GETTY IMAGES

Adjusting Entries

Are adjusting entries important? The Walt Disney Company and Mattel, Inc., probably think so. The Walt Disney Company granted Mattel, Inc., the right to make and sell toys based on Disney characters. In return, Mattel agreed to make payments to Disney as the toys were sold. One of the issues in a court case was whether Mattel should have made an adjusting entry when it fell behind on these payments. The entry would have been:

Royalty Expense	17,000,000	
Accounts Payable (Disney)		17,000,000

This adjusting entry would have reduced Mattel's fourth-quarter earnings for that year by more than 15%. Following an investigation by the Securities and Exchange Commission, Mattel eventually agreed to make an adjustment to later financial statements.

SUPPLIES

During June, Jessie purchased supplies consisting of paper, pens, and delivery envelopes for $80. *Since these supplies were expected to provide future benefits, Supplies, an asset, was debited at the time of the purchase.* No other entries were made to the supplies account during June. As reported on the trial balance in Figure 5-2, the $80 balance remains in the supplies account at the end of the month.

FIGURE 5-2 Trial Balance

Jessie Jane's Campus Delivery Service
Trial Balance
June 30, 20 - -

ACCOUNT TITLE	ACCOUNT NO	DEBIT BALANCE	CREDIT BALANCE
Cash	101	3 7 0 00	
Accounts Receivable	122	6 5 0 00	
Supplies	141	8 0 00	
Prepaid Insurance	145	2 0 0 00	
Delivery Equipment	185	3 6 0 0 00	
Accounts Payable	202		1 8 0 0 00
Jessica Jane, Capital	311		2 0 0 0 00
Jessica Jane, Drawing	312	1 5 0 00	
Delivery Fees	401		2 1 5 0 00
Wages Expense	511	6 5 0 00	
Rent Expense	521	2 0 0 00	
Telephone Expense	525	5 0 00	
		5 9 5 0 00	5 9 5 0 00

As supplies are used, an expense is incurred. However, it is not practical to make a journal entry to recognize this expense and the reduction in the supplies account every time someone uses an envelope. It is more efficient to wait until the end of the accounting period to make one adjusting entry to reflect the expense incurred for the use of supplies for the entire month.

At the end of the month, an inventory, or physical count, of the remaining supplies is taken. The inventory shows that supplies costing $20 were still unused at the end of June. Since Jessie bought supplies costing $80, and only $20 worth remain, supplies costing $60 must have been used ($80 – $20 = $60). Thus, supplies expense for the month is $60.

Since $60 worth of supplies have been used, Supplies Expense is debited and Supplies (asset) is credited for $60. This entry is illustrated in Figure 5-3 in T account and general journal form. Thus, as shown in Figure 5-4, supplies with a cost of $20 will be reported as an asset on the balance sheet and a supplies expense of $60 will be reported on the income statement. The adjusting entry affected an income statement account (Supplies Expense) and a balance sheet account (Supplies).

FIGURE 5-3   Adjustment for Supplies

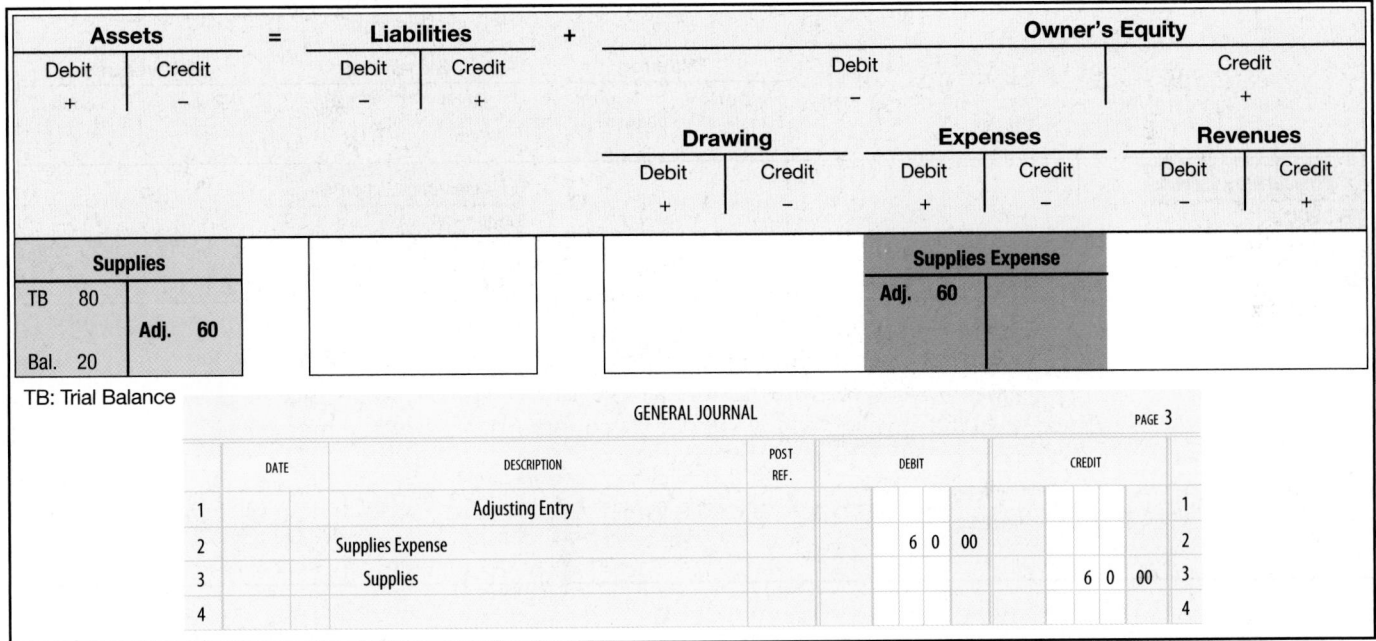

FIGURE 5-4   Effect of Adjusting Entry for Supplies on Financial Statements

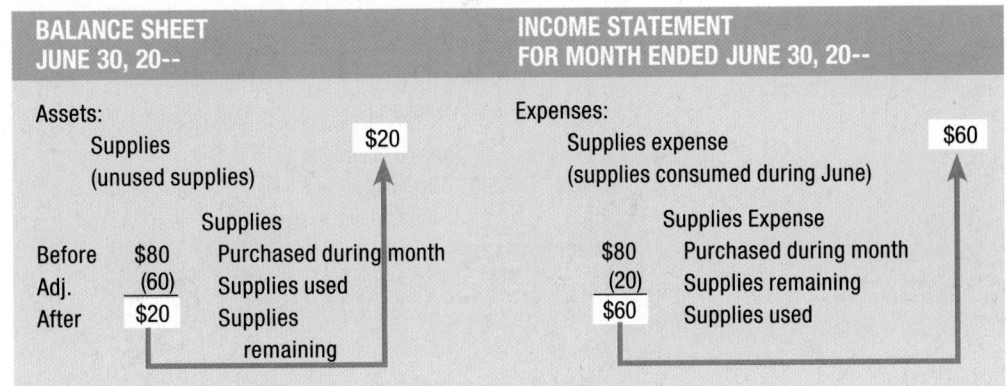

PREPAID INSURANCE

On June 18, Jessie paid $200 for an eight-month liability insurance policy with coverage beginning on June 1. *Prepaid Insurance, an asset, was debited because the insurance policy is expected to provide future benefits.* The $200 balance is reported on the trial balance. As the insurance policy expires with the passage of time, the asset should be reduced and an expense recognized.

Since the $200 premium covers eight months, the cost of the expired coverage for June is $25 ($200 ÷ 8 months). As shown in Figure 5-5, the adjusting entry is to debit Insurance Expense for $25 and credit Prepaid Insurance for $25. Figure 5-6 shows that the unexpired portion of the insurance premium will be reported on the balance sheet as Prepaid Insurance of $175. The expired portion will be reported on the income statement as Insurance Expense of $25.

FIGURE 5-5 Adjustment for Expired Insurance

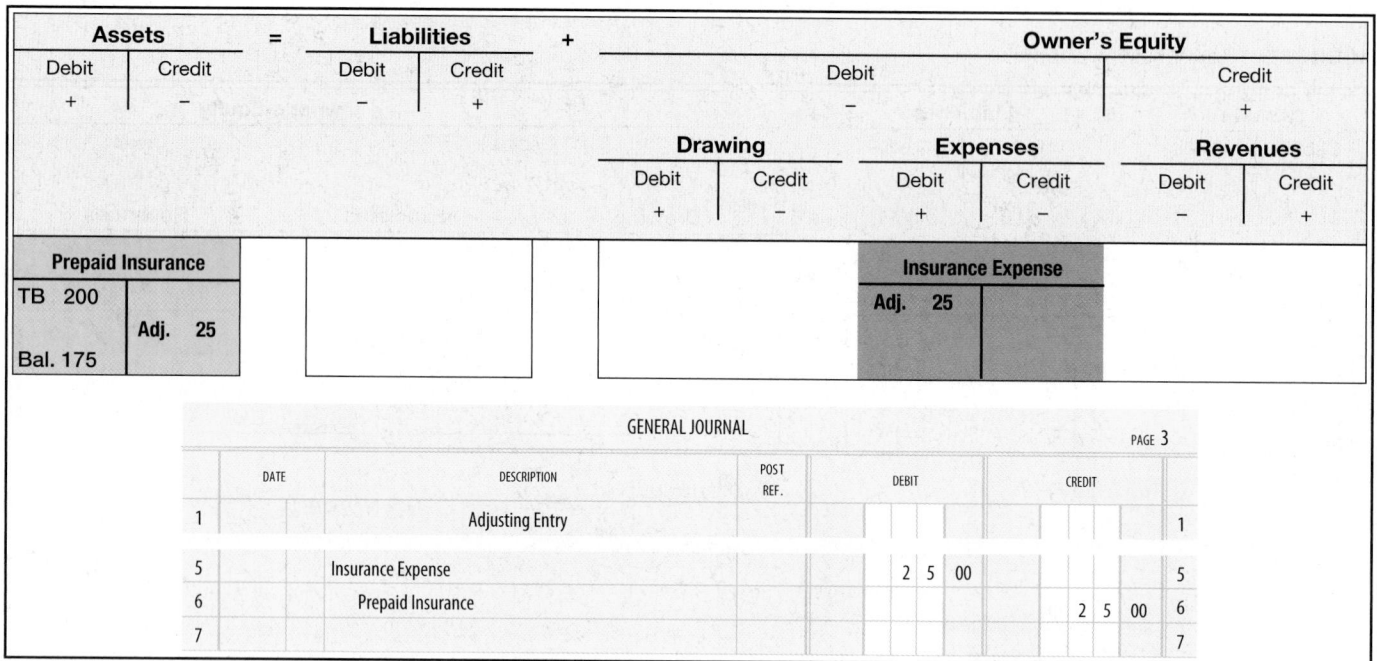

FIGURE 5-6 Effect of Adjusting Entry for Prepaid Insurance on Financial Statements

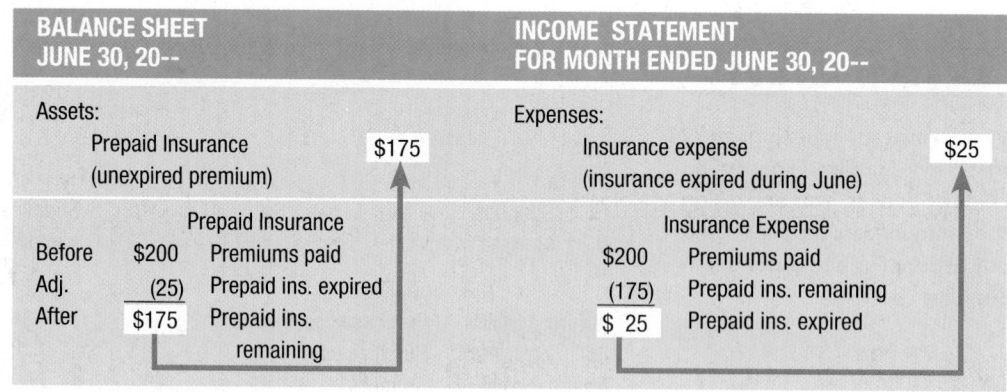

WAGES EXPENSE

Jessie paid her part-time employees $650 on June 27. Since then, they have earned an additional $50, but have not yet been paid. The additional wages expense must be recognized.

Since the employees have not been paid, Wages Payable, a liability, should be established. Thus, Wages Expense is debited and Wages Payable is credited for $50 in

Figure 5-7. Note in Figure 5-8 that Wages Expense of $700 is reported on the income statement and Wages Payable of $50 is reported on the balance sheet.

FIGURE 5-7 Adjustment for Unpaid Wages

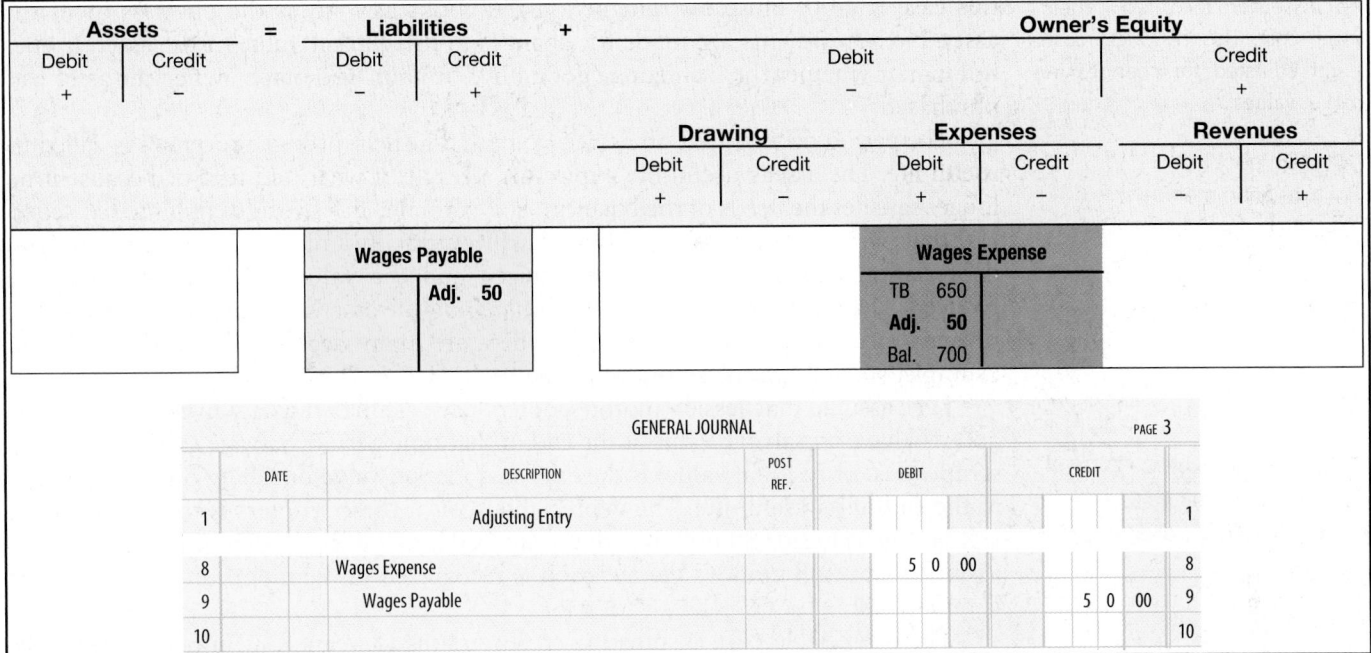

FIGURE 5-8 Effect of Adjusting Entry for Wages on Financial Statements

Profiles in Accounting

Mezaun Akeera Ramjohn, Accounts Payable Coordinator

Mezaun Akeera Ramjohn has an AAS degree in accounting and is currently completing her baccalaureate degree at The College of Westchester at night. She is a member of Sigma Beta Delta and is on the President's List. Mezaun is employed full time as accounts payable coordinator at an international importing/exporting company located in Westchester, NY. According to Mezaun, she loves her job and is learning a lot. Working full time and going to school at night is a challenge, which she enjoys. Mezaun's educational goal is to acquire her master's degree in accounting and sit for the CPA exam.

LEARNING KEY

The historical cost principle is an important accounting concept. Assets are recorded at their actual cost. This historical cost is not adjusted for changes in market values.

To learn about other depreciation methods, see the appendix to this chapter.

Depreciation expense is based on estimates of useful lives and salvage values.

DEPRECIATION EXPENSE

During the month of June, Jessie purchased three motor scooters. Since the scooters will provide future benefits, they were recorded as assets in the delivery equipment account. Under the **historical cost principle**, assets are recorded at their actual cost, in this case $3,600. This cost remains on the books as long as the business owns the asset. No adjustments are made for changes in the market value of the asset. It does not matter whether the firm got a "good buy" or paid "too much" when the asset was purchased.

The period of time that an asset is expected to help produce revenues is called its **useful life**. The asset's useful life expires as a result of wear and tear or because it no longer satisfies the needs of the business. For example, as Jessie adds miles to her scooters, they will become less reliable and will eventually fail to run. As this happens, depreciation expense should be recognized and the value of the asset should be reduced. **Depreciation** is a method of *matching* an asset's original cost against the revenues produced over its useful life. There are many depreciation methods. In our example, we will use the **straight-line method**.

Let's assume that Jessie's motor scooters have estimated useful lives of three years and will have no salvage value at the end of that time period. **Salvage value** (also called scrap value, or residual value) is the expected **market value** or selling price of the asset at the end of its useful life. The **depreciable cost** of these scooters is the original cost, less salvage value, or $3,600. It is this amount that is subject to depreciation. Let's also assume that a full month's depreciation is recognized in the month in which an asset is purchased.

The depreciable cost is spread over 36 months (3 years × 12 months). Thus, the straight-line depreciation expense for the month of June is $100 ($3,600 ÷ 36 months).

STRAIGHT-LINE DEPRECIATION				
Original Cost	–	Salvage Value	=	Depreciable Cost
$\dfrac{\text{Depreciable Cost}}{\text{Estimated Useful Life}}$	=	$\dfrac{\$3,600}{36\ \text{months}}$	=	$100 per month

LEARNING KEY

Depreciable assets provide benefits over more than one year. Therefore, the historical cost of the asset remains in the asset account. To show that it has been depreciated, a *contra-asset* account is used.

When we made adjustments for supplies and prepaid insurance, the asset accounts were credited to show that they had been consumed. Assets of a durable nature that are expected to provide benefits over several years or more, called **plant assets**, require a different approach. The business maintains a record of the original cost and the amount of depreciation taken since the asset was acquired. By comparing these two amounts, the reader can estimate the relative age of the assets. Thus, instead of crediting Delivery Equipment for the amount of depreciation, a contra-asset account, Accumulated Depreciation—Delivery Equipment, is credited. "Contra" means opposite or against. Thus, a **contra-asset** has a credit balance (the opposite of an asset) and is deducted from the related asset account on the balance sheet.

As shown in Figure 5-9, the appropriate adjusting entry consists of a debit to Depreciation Expense—Delivery Equipment and a credit to Accumulated Depreciation—Delivery Equipment. Note the position of the accumulated depreciation account in the accounting equation. It is shown in the assets section, directly beneath Delivery Equipment. Contra-asset accounts should always be shown along with the related asset account. Therefore, Delivery Equipment and Accumulated Depreciation—Delivery Equipment are shown together.

FIGURE 5-9   Adjustment for Depreciation of Delivery Equipment

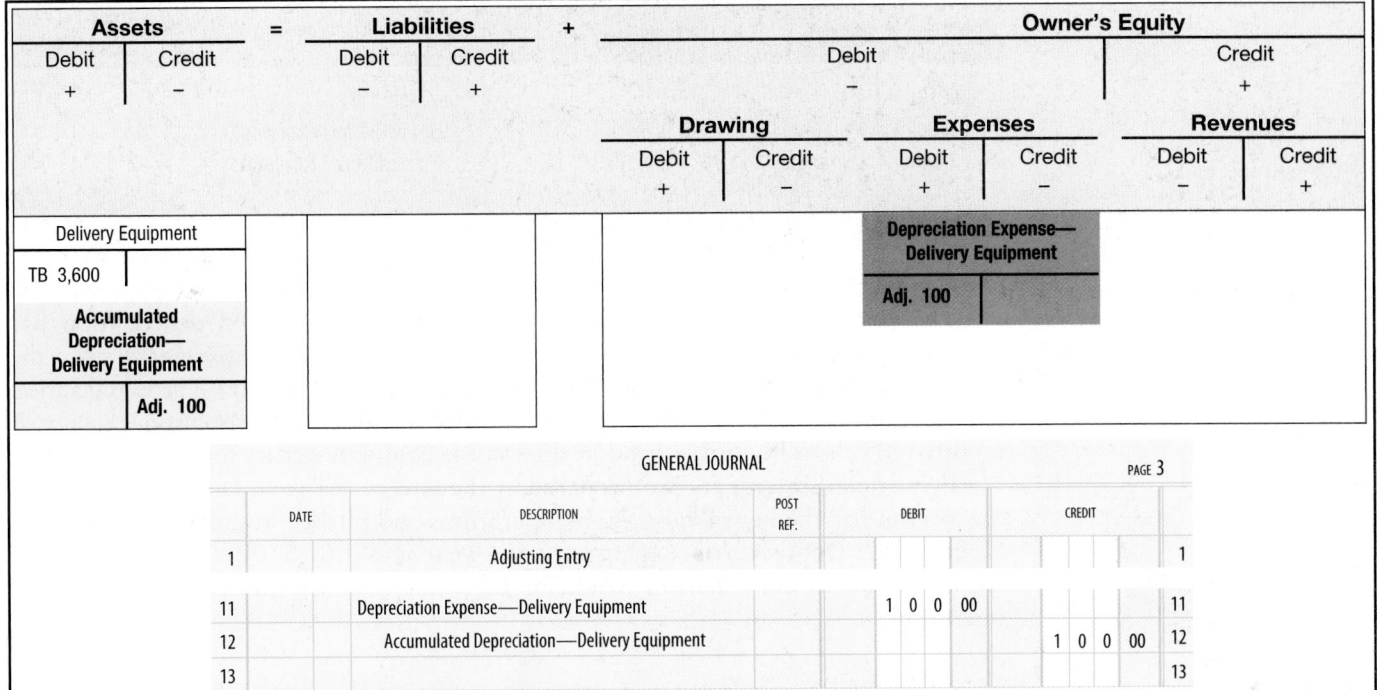

LEARNING KEY

There is no individual account that reports book value. It must be computed.

Cost of Plant Assets
− Accumulated Depreciation
= Book Value

The same concept is used on the balance sheet. Note in Figure 5-10 that Accumulated Depreciation is reported immediately beneath Delivery Equipment as a deduction. The difference between these accounts is known as the **book value,** or **undepreciated cost,** of the delivery equipment. Book value simply means the value carried on the books or in the accounting records. It does *not* represent the market value, or selling price, of the asset.

FIGURE 5-10   Effect of Adjusting Entry for Depreciation on Financial Statements for June

BALANCE SHEET JUNE 30, 20--		INCOME STATEMENT FOR MONTH ENDED JUNE 30, 20--	
Assets:		Expenses:	
Delivery equipment	$3,600	Depreciation expense	$100
Less: Accumulated		(Expired cost for June)	
depreciation	100 $3,500		
	(Book value)		

If no delivery equipment is bought or sold during the next month, the same adjusting entry would be made at the end of July. If an income statement for the month of July and a balance sheet as of July 31 were prepared, the amounts shown in Figure 5-11 would be reported for the delivery equipment.

FIGURE 5-11 Effect of Adjusting Entry for Depreciation on Financial Statements for July

BALANCE SHEET JULY 31, 20--			INCOME STATEMENT FOR MONTH ENDED JULY 31, 20--	
Assets:			Expenses:	
Delivery equipment	$3,600		Depreciation expense	$100
Less: Accumulated			(Expired cost for July)	
depreciation	200	$3,400		
		(Book value)		

The cost ($3,600) remains unchanged, but the accumulated depreciation has increased to $200. This represents *the depreciation that has accumulated* since the delivery equipment was purchased ($100 in June and $100 in July). The depreciation expense for July is $100, the same as reported for June. Depreciation expense is reported for a specific time period. It does not accumulate across reporting periods.

If financial statements are prepared at the end of the year, December 31, 20--, the results for the seven months of operations would be presented as shown in Figure 5-12. Depreciation expense for the year is $700 ($100 × 7 months), and the accumulated depreciation would be the same because this is the first year of operation.

Cost	$3,600	= $100
Useful life	36 months	
Dep./month	$100	
Months in service	× 7	
Dep. June–Dec.	$700	

FIGURE 5-12 Straight-Line Depreciation for Seven Months

BALANCE SHEET DECEMBER 31, 20--			INCOME STATEMENT FOR YEAR ENDED DECEMBER 31, 20--	
Assets:			Expenses:	
Delivery equipment	$3,600		Depreciation expense	$700
Less: Accumulated			(Expired cost from June	
depreciation	700	$2,900	through December)	
		(Book value)		

EXPANDED CHART OF ACCOUNTS

Several new accounts were needed to make the adjusting entries. New accounts are easily added to the chart of accounts, as shown in Figure 5-13. Note the close relationship between assets and contra-assets in the numbering of the accounts. Contra-accounts carry the same number as the related asset account with a ".1" suffix. For example, Delivery Equipment is account number 185 and the contra-asset account, Accumulated Depreciation—Delivery Equipment, is account number 185.1.

U REVU

Complete U REVU-1 on **page 154** to test your basic understanding of LO1

POSTING ADJUSTING ENTRIES

LO2 Post adjusting entries to the general ledger.

Adjusting entries are posted to the general ledger in the same manner as all other entries, except that "*Adjusting*" is written in the Item column of the general ledger. Figure 5-14 shows the posting of the adjusting entries. The posting reference numbers are inserted as each entry is posted.

FIGURE 5-13 Expanded Chart of Accounts

JESSIE JANE'S CAMPUS DELIVERY SERVICE
CHART OF ACCOUNTS

Assets		Revenues	
101	Cash	401	**Delivery Fees**
122	Accounts Receivable		
141	Supplies	**Expenses**	
145	Prepaid Insurance	511	Wages Expense
185	Delivery Equipment	521	Rent Expense
185.1	Accumulated Depr.—	523	Supplies Expense
	Delivery Equipment	525	Telephone Expense
		535	Insurance Expense
Liabilities		541	Depr. Expense —
202	Accounts Payable		Delivery Equipment
219	Wages Payable		
Owner's Equity			
311	Jessica Jane, Capital		
312	Jessica Jane, Drawing		

FIGURE 5-14 Posting the Adjusting Entries

(continued)

FIGURE 5-14 Posting the Adjusting Entries (*concluded*)

U REVU

Complete U REVU-2 on **page 154** to test your basic understanding of LO2

THE WORK SHEET

LO3 Prepare a work sheet.

A **work sheet** pulls together all of the information needed to enter adjusting entries and prepare the financial statements. Work sheets are not financial statements, are not a formal part of the accounting system, and are not a required part of the accounting process. However, many accountants prepare them because they are very helpful in planning the adjustments and preparing the financial statements. Ordinarily, only the accountant uses a work sheet. For this reason, a work sheet is usually prepared in pencil or as a computer spreadsheet. As computer use has become more common, the term "spreadsheet" is often used in place of "work sheet."

THE 10-COLUMN WORK SHEET

Although a work sheet can take several forms, a common format has a column for account titles and 10 amount columns grouped into five pairs. The work sheet format and the five steps in preparing the work sheet are illustrated in Figure 5-15 on page 142A. As with financial statements, the work sheet has a heading consisting of the name of the company, name of the working paper, and the date of the accounting period just ended. The five major column headings for the work sheet are Trial Balance, Adjustments, Adjusted Trial Balance, Income Statement, and Balance Sheet.

PREPARING THE WORK SHEET

Let's apply the five steps required for the preparation of a work sheet to Jessie Jane's Campus Delivery Service.

STEP 1 **Prepare the Trial Balance.** As shown in Figure 5-16 on page 142B, the first pair of amount columns is for the trial balance. The trial balance assures the equality of the debits and credits before the adjustment process begins. The columns should be double ruled to show that they are equal.

Note that all accounts listed in the expanded chart of accounts are included in the Trial Balance columns of the work sheet. This is done even though some accounts have zero balances. The accounts with zero balances could be added to the bottom of the list as they are needed for adjusting entries. However, it is easier to include them now, especially if preparing the work sheet on an electronic spreadsheet. Listing the accounts within their proper classifications (assets, liabilities, etc.) also makes it easier to extend the amounts to the proper columns.

STEP 2 **Prepare the Adjustments.** As shown in Figure 5-17 on page 142C, the second pair of amount columns is used to prepare the adjusting entries. Enter the adjustments directly in these columns. When an account is debited or credited, the amount is entered on the same line as the name of the account and in the appropriate Adjustments Debit or Credit column. A small letter in parentheses identifies each adjusting entry made on the work sheet.

ADJUSTMENT (a):

Supplies costing $60 were used during June.

	Debit	Credit
Supplies Expense	60	
Supplies		60

ADJUSTMENT (b):

One month's insurance premium has expired.

	Debit	Credit
Insurance Expense	25	
Prepaid Insurance		25

ADJUSTMENT (c):

Employees earned $50 that has not yet been paid.

	Debit	Credit
Wages Expense	50	
Wages Payable		50

ADJUSTMENT (d):

Depreciation on the motor scooters is recognized.

	Debit	Credit
Depreciation Expense—Delivery Equipment	100	
Accumulated Depreciation—Delivery Equipment		100

When all adjustments have been entered on the work sheet, each column should be totaled to assure that the debits equal the credits for all entries. After balancing the columns, they should be double ruled.

STEP 3 **Prepare the Adjusted Trial Balance.** As shown in Figure 5-18 on page 142D, the third pair of amount columns on the work sheet is the **Adjusted Trial Balance columns**.

- When an account balance is not affected by entries in the Adjustments columns, the amount in the Trial Balance columns is extended directly to the Adjusted Trial Balance columns.

- *When affected by an entry in the Adjustments columns, the account balance to be entered in the Adjusted Trial Balance columns increases or decreases by the amount of the adjusting entry.*

For example, in Jessica Jane's business, Supplies is listed in the Trial Balance Debit column as $80. Since the entry of $60 is in the Adjustments Credit column, the amount extended to the Adjusted Trial Balance Debit column is $20 ($80 − $60).

Wages Expense is listed in the Trial Balance Debit column as $650. Since $50 is in the Adjustments Debit column, the amount extended to the Adjusted Trial Balance Debit column is $700 ($650 + $50).

After all extensions have been made, the Adjusted Trial Balance columns are totaled to prove the equality of the debits and the credits. Once balanced, the columns are double ruled.

STEP 4 **Extend Adjusted Balances to the Income Statement and Balance Sheet Columns.** As shown in Figure 5-19 on page 142E, each account listed in the Adjusted Trial Balance must be extended to either the Income Statement or Balance Sheet columns. The **Income Statement columns** show the amounts that will be reported in the income statement. All revenue accounts are extended to the Income Statement Credit column and expense accounts are extended to the Income Statement Debit column.

The asset, liability, drawing, and capital accounts are extended to the **Balance Sheet columns**. Although called the Balance Sheet columns, these columns of the work sheet show the amounts that will be reported in the balance sheet and the statement of owner's equity. The asset and drawing accounts are extended to the Balance Sheet Debit column. The liability and owner's capital accounts are extended to the Balance Sheet Credit column.

> **🔑 LEARNING KEY**
>
> The Balance Sheet columns show the amounts for both the balance sheet and the statement of owner's equity.

STEP 5 **Complete the Work Sheet.** To complete the work sheet, first total the Income Statement columns. If the total of the credits (revenues) exceeds the total of the debits (expenses), the difference represents net income. If the total of the debits exceeds the total of the credits, the difference represents a net loss.

The Income Statement columns of Jessie's work sheet in Figure 5-20 on page 142F show total credits of $2,150 and total debits of $1,135. The difference, $1,015, is the net income for the month of June. This amount should be added to the Debit column to balance the Income Statement columns. "Net Income" should be written on the same line in the Account Title column. If the business had a net loss, the amount of the loss would be added to the Income Statement Credit column and the words "Net Loss" would be written in the Account Title column. Once balanced, the columns should be double ruled.

Finally, the Balance Sheet columns are totaled. The difference between the totals of these columns also is the amount of net income or net loss for the accounting period. If the total debits exceed the total credits, the difference is net income. If the total credits exceed the total debits, the difference is a net loss. This difference should be the same as the difference we found for the Income Statement columns.

> **🔑 LEARNING KEY**
>
> In the Balance Sheet columns of the work sheet, total debits minus total credits equals net *income* if greater than zero and equals net *loss* if less than zero.

FIGURE 5-15   Steps In Preparing The Work Sheet

Name of Company
Work Sheet
For Month Ended June 30, 20 --

ACCOUNT TITLE	TRIAL BALANCE		ADJUSTMENTS		ADJUSTED TRIAL BALANCE		INCOME STATEMENT		BALANCE SHEET	
	DEBIT	CREDIT	DEBIT	CREDIT	DEBIT	CREDIT	DEBIT	CREDIT	DEBIT	CREDIT

Insert ledger account titles

STEP 1
Prepare the trial balance

STEP 2
Prepare the adjustments

STEP 3
Prepare the adjusted trial balance

STEP 4
Extend adjusted account balances

STEP 5
Complete the work sheet
1. Sum columns
2. Compute net income (loss)

Trial Balance — Debit: Assets, Drawing, Expenses
Trial Balance — Credit: Liabilities, Capital, Revenues

Adjusted Trial Balance — Debit: Assets, Drawing, Expenses
Adjusted Trial Balance — Credit: Liabilities, Capital, Revenues

Income Statement — Debit: Expenses
Income Statement — Credit: Revenues

Balance Sheet — Debit: Assets, Drawing
Balance Sheet — Credit: Liabilities, Capital

Net Income / Net Loss
Net Loss / Net Income

Rows numbered 1–30

FIGURE 5-16 Step 1—Prepare the Trial Balance

Jessica Jane's Campus Delivery Service
Work Sheet
For Month Ended June 30, 20 - -

	ACCOUNT TITLE	TRIAL BALANCE DEBIT	TRIAL BALANCE CREDIT	ADJUSTMENTS DEBIT	ADJUSTMENTS CREDIT	ADJUSTED TRIAL BALANCE DEBIT	ADJUSTED TRIAL BALANCE CREDIT	INCOME STATEMENT DEBIT	INCOME STATEMENT CREDIT	BALANCE SHEET DEBIT	BALANCE SHEET CREDIT	
1	Cash	3 7 0 00										1
2	Accounts Receivable	6 5 0 00										2
3	Supplies	8 0 00										3
4	Prepaid Insurance	2 0 0 00										4
5	Delivery Equipment	3 6 0 0 00										5
6	Accum. Depr.—Delivery Equipment											6
7	Accounts Payable		1 8 0 0 00									7
8	Wages Payable											8
9	Jessica Jane, Capital		2 0 0 0 00									9
10	Jessica Jane, Drawing	1 5 0 00										10
11	Delivery Fees		2 1 5 0 00									11
12	Wages Expense	6 5 0 00										12
13	Rent Expense	2 0 0 00										13
14	Supplies Expense											14
15	Telephone Expense	5 0 00										15
16	Insurance Expense											16
17	Depr. Expense—Delivery Equipment											17
18		5 9 5 0 00	5 9 5 0 00									18
19												19
20												20
21												21
22												22
23												23
24												24
25												25
26												26
27												27
28												28
29												29
30												30

STEP 1

Preparing the Work Sheet

STEP 1 Prepare the Trial Balance.

- Write the heading, account titles, and the debit and credit amounts from the general ledger.
- Place a single rule across the Trial Balance columns and total the debit and credit amounts.
- Place a double rule under the totals for each column.
- Total debits must equal total credits.

STEP 2 Prepare the Adjustments.

- Record the adjustments.
  Hint: Make certain that each adjustment is on the same line as the account name and in the appropriate column.
  Hint: Identify each adjusting entry by a letter in parentheses.
- Rule the Adjustments columns.
- Total the Debit and Credit columns and double rule the columns.
- Total debits must equal total credits.

STEP 3 Prepare the Adjusted Trial Balance.

- Extend those debits and credits that are not adjusted directly to the appropriate Adjusted Trial Balance column.
  Hint: If an account has a debit and a credit, subtract the adjustment. If an account has two debits or two credits, add the adjustment.
- Enter the adjusted balances in the appropriate Adjusted Trial Balance column.
- Single rule the Adjusted Trial Balance columns. Total and double rule the Debit and Credit columns.
- Total debits must equal total credits.

STEP 4 Extend Adjusted Balances to the Income Statement and Balance Sheet Columns.

- Extend all revenue accounts to the Income Statement Credit column.
- Extend all expense accounts to the Income Statement Debit column.
- Extend the asset and drawing accounts to the Balance Sheet Debit column.
- Extend the liability and owner's capital accounts to the Balance Sheet Credit column.

STEP 5 Complete the Work Sheet.

- Rule and total the Income Statement and Balance Sheet columns.
- Calculate the difference between the Income Statement Debit and Credit columns.
- Calculate the difference between the Balance Sheet Debit and Credit columns.
  Hint: If the Income Statement credits exceed debits, net income has occurred; otherwise, a net loss has occurred. If the Balance Sheet debits exceed the credits, the difference is net income; otherwise, a net loss has occurred.
- Add the net income to the Income Statement Debit column or add the net loss to the Income Statement Credit column. Add the net income to the Balance Sheet Credit column or the net loss to the Balance Sheet Debit column. Write "Net Income" or "Net Loss" in the Account Title column.
  Hint: The difference between the Balance Sheet columns should be the same as the difference between the Income Statement columns.
- Total and double rule the columns.

The Balance Sheet columns of Jessie's work sheet show total debits of $4,965 and total credits of $3,950. The difference of $1,015 represents the amount of net income for the month. This amount is added to the Credit column to balance the Balance Sheet columns. If the business had a net loss, this amount would be added to the Balance Sheet Debit column. Once balanced, the columns should be double ruled.

A trick for remembering the appropriate placement of the net income and net loss is the following: Net Income *apart*; Net Loss *together*. Figure 5-21 illustrates this learning aid.

FIGURE 5-21 Net Income Apart, Net Loss Together

| U REVU | Complete U REVU-3 on **page 154** to test your basic understanding of LO3. |

FINDING ERRORS ON THE WORK SHEET

LO4 Describe methods for finding errors on the work sheet.

If any of the columns on the work sheet do not balance, you must find the error before you continue. Once you are confident that the work sheet is accurate, you are ready to journalize the adjusting entries and prepare financial statements. Figure 5-22 offers tips for finding errors on the work sheet.

FIGURE 5-22 Finding Errors on the Work Sheet

TIPS FOR FINDING ERRORS ON THE WORK SHEET

1. Check the addition of all columns.

2. Check the addition and subtraction required when extending to the Adjusted Trial Balance columns.

3. Make sure the adjusted account balances have been extended to the appropriate columns.

4. Make sure that the net income or net loss has been added to the appropriate columns.

| U REVU | Complete U REVU-4 on **page 154** to test your basic understanding of LO4. |

JOURNALIZING ADJUSTING ENTRIES FROM THE WORK SHEET

LO5 Journalize adjusting entries from the work sheet.

Keep in mind that the work sheet simply helps the accountant organize the end-of-period work. *Writing the adjustments on the work sheet has no effect on the ledger accounts in the accounting system. The only way to change the balance of a ledger account is to make a journal entry.* Once the work sheet has been completed, simply copy the adjustments from the work sheet to the journal, as shown in Figure 5-23.

FIGURE 5-23 Journalizing Adjusting Entries from the Work Sheet

Jessica Jane's Campus Delivery Service
Work Sheet (Partial)
For Month Ended June 30, 20--

	ACCOUNT TITLE	TRIAL BALANCE DEBIT	TRIAL BALANCE CREDIT	ADJUSTMENTS DEBIT	ADJUSTMENTS CREDIT
1	Cash	3 7 0 00			
2	Accounts Receivable	6 5 0 00			
3	Supplies	8 0 00			(a) 6 0 00
4	Prepaid Insurance	2 0 0 00			(b) 2 5 00
5	Delivery Equipment	3 6 0 0 00			
6	Accum. Depr.—Delivery Equipment				(d) 1 0 0 00
7	Accounts Payable		1 8 0 0 00		
8	Wages Payable				(c) 5 0 00
9	Jessica Jane, Capital		2 0 0 0 00		
10	Jessica Jane, Drawing	1 5 0 00			
11	Delivery Fees		2 1 5 0 00		
12	Wages Expense	6 5 0 00		(c) 5 0 00	
13	Rent Expense	2 0 0 00			
14	Supplies Expense			(a) 6 0 00	
15	Telephone Expense	5 0 00			
16	Insurance Expense			(b) 2 5 00	
17	Depr. Expense—Delivery Equipment			(d) 1 0 0 00	
18		5 9 5 0 00	5 9 5 0 00	2 3 5 00	2 3 5 00

		GENERAL JOURNAL				PAGE 3
		DATE	DESCRIPTION	POST. REF.	DEBIT	CREDIT
1			Adjusting Entries				1
(a)	2	20-- June 30	Supplies Expense	523	6 0 00		2
	3		Supplies	141		6 0 00	3
	4						4
(b)	5	30	Insurance Expense	535	2 5 00		5
	6		Prepaid Insurance	145		2 5 00	6
	7						7
(c)	8	30	Wages Expense	511	5 0 00		8
	9		Wages Payable	219		5 0 00	9
	10						10
(d)	11	30	Depr. Expense—Delivery Equipment	541	1 0 0 00		11
	12		Accum. Depr.—Delivery Equipment	185.1		1 0 0 00	12

Jessie's adjusting entries are illustrated in Figure 5-23 as they would appear in a general journal. Note that the last day of the accounting period, June 30, has been entered in the date column and "*Adjusting Entries*" is written in the Description column prior to the first adjusting entry. No explanation is required in the Description column for individual adjusting entries. We simply label them as adjusting entries.

U REVU

Complete U REVU-5 on **page 155** to test your basic understanding of LO5.

METHODS OF ACCOUNTING: CASH, MODIFIED CASH, AND ACCRUAL

LO6 Explain the cash, modified cash, and accrual bases of accounting.

The accrual basis of accounting offers the best matching of revenues and expenses and is required under generally accepted accounting principles. GAAP financial statements prepared using the accrual method are particularly important when major businesses want to raise large amounts of money. Investors and creditors expect GAAP financial statements and generally will not invest or make loans without them.

However, many small professional service organizations are not concerned with raising large amounts of money from investors and creditors. These organizations include CPAs, doctors, dentists, lawyers, engineers, and architects. Since these organizations do not need to prepare GAAP financial statements, they often use the cash or modified cash basis. If one of these organizations needs to borrow money from a bank that requires GAAP financial statements, an accountant can convert the financial statements to the accrual basis.

Under the **accrual basis of accounting**, revenues are recorded when earned. Revenues are considered earned when a service is provided or a product sold, regardless of whether cash is received. If cash is not received, a receivable is set up.

The accrual basis also assumes that expenses are recorded when incurred. Expenses are incurred when a service is received or an asset consumed, regardless of when cash is paid. If cash is not paid when a service is received, a payable is set up. When assets are consumed, prepaid assets are decreased or long-term assets are depreciated. Since the accrual basis accounts for long-term assets, prepaid assets, receivables, and payables, it is the most comprehensive system and best method of measuring income for the vast majority of businesses.

 LEARNING KEY

Accrual Basis		
Accounting for:		
Revenues and Expenses	**Assets and Liabilities**	
Record revenue when earned.	Accounts receivable:	Yes
Record expenses when incurred.	Accounts payable:	Yes
	Prepaid assets:	Yes
	Long-term assets:	Yes

Under the **cash basis of accounting**, revenues are recorded when cash is received and expenses are recorded when cash is paid. This method will provide results that are similar to the accrual basis if there are few receivables, payables, and assets. However, as shown in Figure 5-24, the cash and accrual bases can result in very different measures of net income if a business has significant amounts of receivables, payables, and assets.

LEARNING KEY

Cash Basis		
Accounting for:	**Assets and Liabilities**	
Revenues and Expenses	Accounts receivable:	No
Record revenue when cash is received.	Accounts payable:	No
Record expenses when cash is paid.	Prepaid assets:	No
	Long-term assets:	No

FIGURE 5-24 Cash versus Accrual Accounting

RECOGNITION OF REVENUES AND EXPENSES: ACCRUAL BASIS VS. CASH BASIS

		Method of Accounting			
		Accrual Basis		Cash Basis	
	Transaction	Expense	Revenue	Expense	Revenue
(a)	Provided services on account, $600.		$600		
(b)	Paid wages earned this period, $300	$300		$300	
(c)	Received cash for services performed on account last month, $200				$ 200
(d)	Received cleaning bill for month, $250	250			
(e)	Paid on account for last month's advertising, $100			100	
(f)	Purchase of supplies, $50			50	
(g)	Supplies used during month, $40	40			
		$590	$600	$450	$ 200
Revenue			$600		$ 200
Expense			590		450
Net Income (Loss)			$ 10		$(250)
Revenues are recognized when:			earned		cash is received
Expenses are recognized when:			incurred		cash is paid

A third method of accounting combines aspects of the cash and accrual methods. With the **modified cash basis**, a business uses the cash basis for recording revenues and most expenses. Exceptions are made when cash is paid for assets with useful lives greater than one accounting period. For example, under a strict cash basis, if cash is paid for equipment, buildings, supplies, or insurance, the amount is immediately recorded as an expense. This approach could cause major distortions when measuring net income. Under the modified cash basis, cash payments like these are recorded as assets, and adjustments are made each period as under the accrual basis. Liabilities associated with the acquisition of these assets are also recognized.

> The modified cash basis is the same as the accrual basis, except receivables and payables are not recognized for revenues and operating expenses.

Although similar to the accrual basis, the modified cash basis does not account for receivables or for payables for services received. Thus, the modified cash basis is a combination of the cash and accrual methods of accounting. The differences and similarities among the cash, modified cash, and accrual methods of accounting are demonstrated in Figure 5-25.

🔑 LEARNING KEY

Modified Cash Basis

Accounting for:	Assets and Liabilities	
Revenues and Expenses	Accounts receivable:	No
Record revenue when cash is received.	Accounts payable	
Record expenses when cash is paid, except	for purchase of assets:	Yes
for assets with useful lives greater than	for services received:	No
one accounting period. Accrual accounting	Prepaid assets:	Yes
is used for prepaid assets (insurance and		
supplies) and long-term assets.	Long-term assets:	Yes

If all businesses were the same, only one method of accounting would be needed. However, businesses vary in their need for major assets like buildings and equipment, the amount of customer receivables, and payables to suppliers. For example, if a business were rather small with no major assets, receivables, or payables, it would be simpler to use the cash basis of accounting. In addition, under these circumstances, the difference in net income under the accrual and cash bases of accounting would be small. Most individuals fit this description and use the cash basis on their tax returns.

Businesses with buildings and equipment, but few receivables and payables, might use the modified cash basis. Again, the accounting would be a little simpler and differences between net income computed under the modified cash and accrual bases would be small. Finally, businesses with buildings and equipment, and receivables and payables, should use the accrual basis of accounting to achieve the best matching of revenues and expenses.

🔑 LEARNING KEY

The shaded areas in Figure 5-25 show that sometimes the modified cash basis is the same as the cash basis and sometimes it is the same as the accrual basis. For some transactions, all methods are the same.

FIGURE 5-25 Comparison of Cash, Modified Cash, and Accrual Methods

ENTRIES MADE UNDER EACH ACCOUNTING METHOD			
Event	**Cash**	**Modified Cash**	**Accrual**

Revenues:
Perform services for cash
	Cash
	    Professional Fees
		Cash
		    Professional Fees
			Cash
			    Professional Fees

Perform services on account	No entry	No entry	Accounts Receivable Professional Fees

Expenses:
Pay cash for operating expenses:
wages, advertising, rent,
telephone, etc.
	Expense
	    Cash
		Expense
		    Cash
			Expense
			    Cash

Pay cash for prepaid items:
insurance, supplies, etc.
	Expense
	    Cash
		Prepaid Asset
		    Cash
			Prepaid Asset
			    Cash

Pay cash for property, plant, and
equipment (PP&E)
	Expense
	    Cash
		PP&E Asset
		    Cash
			PP&E Asset
			    Cash

Receive bill for services received	No entry	No entry	Expense Accounts Payable
End-of-period adjustments: Wages earned by employees but not paid	No entry	No entry	Wages Expense Wages Payable

Prepaid items used	No entry	Expense
		    Prepaid Asset
			Expense
			    Prepaid Asset

Depreciation on property,
plant, and equipment
	No entry	Depreciation Expense
		    Accumulated Depreciation
			Depreciation Expense
			    Accumulated Depreciation

Other:
Purchase of assets
on account
	No entry	Asset
		    Accounts Payable
			Asset
			    Accounts Payable

Payments for assets
purchased on account
	Expense
	    Cash
		Accounts Payable
		    Cash
			Accounts Payable
			    Cash

U REVU   Complete U REVU-6 on **page 155** to test your basic understanding of LO6.

LEARNING OBJECTIVES Key Points to Remember

LO1 Prepare end-of-period adjustments.

End-of-period adjustments are necessary to bring the general ledger accounts up to date prior to preparing financial statements. Reasons to adjust the trial balance are as follows:

1. To report all revenues earned during the accounting period.
2. To report all expenses incurred to produce the revenues during the accounting period.
3. To accurately report the assets on the balance sheet. Some assets may have expired, depreciated, or been used up during the accounting period.
4. To accurately report the liabilities on the balance sheet date. Expenses may have been incurred, but not yet paid.

LO2 Post adjusting entries to the general ledger.

Adjusting entries are posted to the general ledger in the same manner as all other entries, except that "Adjusting" is written in the Item column of the general ledger.

LO3 Prepare a work sheet.

Steps in preparing the work sheet are as follows:

1. Prepare the trial balance.
2. Prepare the adjustments.
3. Prepare the adjusted trial balance.
4. Extend the adjusted account balances to the Income Statement and Balance Sheet columns.
5. Total the Income Statement and Balance Sheet columns to compute the net income or net loss.

LO4 Describe methods for finding errors on the work sheet.

Tips for finding errors on the work sheet include the following:

1. Check the addition of all columns.
2. Check the addition and subtraction required when extending to the Adjusted Trial Balance columns.
3. Make sure the adjusted account balances have been extended to the appropriate columns.
4. Make sure that the net income or net loss has been added to the appropriate columns.

LO5 Journalize adjusting entries from the work sheet.

The adjustments are copied from the work sheet to the journal. The last day of the accounting period is entered in the Date column and "Adjusting Entries" is written in the Description column.

LO6 Explain the cash, modified cash, and accrual bases of accounting.

Cash Basis—Record revenues when cash is received and expenses when cash is paid.

Accrual Basis—Record revenues when earned and expenses as incurred.

Modified Cash Basis—Same as accrual, except no accounts receivable and no accounts payable for operating expenses.

DEMONSTRATION PROBLEM

Justin Park is a lawyer specializing in corporate tax law. He began his practice on January 1. A chart of accounts and trial balance taken on December 31, 20--, are provided below.

Information for year-end adjustments is as follows:

(a)   Office supplies on hand at year-end amounted to $300.

(b)   On January 1, 20--, Park purchased office equipment costing $15,000 with an expected life of five years and no salvage value.

(c)   Computer equipment costing $6,000 with an expected life of three years and no salvage value was purchased on July 1, 20--. Assume that Park computes depreciation to the nearest full month.

(d)   A premium of $1,200 for a one-year insurance policy was paid on December 1, 20--.

(e)   Wages earned by Park's part-time secretary, which have not yet been paid, amount to $300.

REQUIRED

1.   Prepare the work sheet for the year ended December 31, 20--.

2.   Prepare adjusting entries in a general journal.

JUSTIN PARK LEGAL SERVICES CHART OF ACCOUNTS				
Assets		**Revenue**		
101	Cash	401	Client Fees	
142	Office Supplies			
145	Prepaid Insurance	**Expenses**		
181	Office Equipment	511	Wages Expense	
181.1	Accumulated Depr.—	521	Rent Expense	
	Office Equipment	523	Office Supplies Expense	
187	Computer Equipment	525	Telephone Expense	
187.1	Accumulated Depr.—	533	Utilities Expense	
	Computer Equipment	535	Insurance Expense	
Liabilities		541	Depr. Expense—	
201	Notes Payable		Office Equipment	
202	Accounts Payable	542	Depr. Expense—	
219	Wages Payable		Computer Equipment	
Owner's Equity				
311	Justin Park, Capital			
312	Justin Park, Drawing			

(continued)

Justin Park Legal Services
Trial Balance
December 31, 20 --

ACCOUNT TITLE	ACCOUNT NO.	DEBIT BALANCE	CREDIT BALANCE
Cash	101	7 0 0 0 00	
Office Supplies	142	8 0 0 00	
Prepaid Insurance	145	1 2 0 0 00	
Office Equipment	181	15 0 0 0 00	
Computer Equipment	187	6 0 0 0 00	
Notes Payable	201		5 0 0 0 00
Accounts Payable	202		5 0 0 00
Justin Park, Capital	311		11 4 0 0 00
Justin Park, Drawing	312	5 0 0 0 00	
Client Fees	401		40 0 0 0 00
Wages Expense	511	12 0 0 0 00	
Rent Expense	521	5 0 0 0 00	
Telephone Expense	525	1 0 0 0 00	
Utilities Expense	533	3 9 0 0 00	
		56 9 0 0 00	56 9 0 0 00

The solution to part (1) is found on page 151.

2.

			GENERAL JOURNAL			PAGE 11	
	DATE		DESCRIPTION	POST. REF.	DEBIT	CREDIT	
1			**Adjusting Entries**				1
2	20-- Dec.	31	Office Supplies Expense		5 0 0 00		2
3			Office Supplies			5 0 0 00	3
4							4
5		31	Depr. Expense—Office Equipment		3 0 0 0 00		5
6			Accum. Depr.—Office Equipment			3 0 0 0 00	6
7							7
8		31	Depr. Expense—Computer Equipment		1 0 0 0 00		8
9			Accum. Depr.—Computer Equipment			1 0 0 0 00	9
10							10
11		31	Insurance Expense		1 0 0 00		11
12			Prepaid Insurance			1 0 0 00	12
13							13
14		31	Wages Expense		3 0 0 00		14
15			Wages Payable			3 0 0 00	15

SOLUTION 1.

Justin Park Legal Services
Work Sheet
For Year Ended December 31, 20--

	ACCOUNT TITLE	TRIAL BALANCE DEBIT	TRIAL BALANCE CREDIT	ADJUSTMENTS DEBIT	ADJUSTMENTS CREDIT	ADJUSTED TRIAL BALANCE DEBIT	ADJUSTED TRIAL BALANCE CREDIT	INCOME STATEMENT DEBIT	INCOME STATEMENT CREDIT	BALANCE SHEET DEBIT	BALANCE SHEET CREDIT	
1	Cash	7 0 0 0 00				7 0 0 0 00				7 0 0 0 00		1
2	Office Supplies	8 0 0 00			(a) 5 0 0 00	3 0 0 00				3 0 0 00		2
3	Prepaid Insurance	1 2 0 0 00			(d) 1 0 0 00	1 1 0 0 00				1 1 0 0 00		3
4	Office Equipment	15 0 0 0 00				15 0 0 0 00				15 0 0 0 00		4
5	Accum. Depr.—Office Equip.				(b) 3 0 0 0 00		3 0 0 0 00				3 0 0 0 00	5
6	Computer Equipment	6 0 0 0 00				6 0 0 0 00				6 0 0 0 00		6
7	Accum. Depr.—Computer Equip.				(c) 1 0 0 0 00		1 0 0 0 00				1 0 0 0 00	7
8	Notes Payable		5 0 0 0 00				5 0 0 0 00				5 0 0 0 00	8
9	Accounts Payable		5 0 0 0 00				5 0 0 0 00				5 0 0 0 00	9
10	Wages Payable				(e) 3 0 0 00		3 0 0 00				3 0 0 00	10
11	Justin Park, Capital		11 4 0 0 00				11 4 0 0 00				11 4 0 0 00	11
12	Justin Park, Drawing	5 0 0 0 00				5 0 0 0 00				5 0 0 0 00		12
13	Client Fees		40 0 0 0 00				40 0 0 0 00		40 0 0 0 00			13
14	Wages Expense	12 0 0 0 00		(e) 3 0 0 00		12 3 0 0 00		12 3 0 0 00				14
15	Rent Expense	5 0 0 0 00				5 0 0 0 00		5 0 0 0 00				15
16	Office Supplies Expense			(a) 5 0 0 00		5 0 0 00		5 0 0 00				16
17	Telephone Expense	1 0 0 0 00				1 0 0 0 00		1 0 0 0 00				17
18	Utilities Expense	3 9 0 0 00				3 9 0 0 00		3 9 0 0 00				18
19	Insurance Expense			(d) 1 0 0 00		1 0 0 00		1 0 0 00				19
20	Depr. Expense—Office Equip.			(b) 3 0 0 0 00		3 0 0 0 00		3 0 0 0 00				20
21	Depr. Expense—Computer Equip.			(c) 1 0 0 0 00		1 0 0 0 00		1 0 0 0 00				21
22		56 9 0 0 00	56 9 0 0 00	4 9 0 0 00	4 9 0 0 00	61 2 0 0 00	61 2 0 0 00	26 8 0 0 00	40 0 0 0 00	34 4 0 0 00	21 2 0 0 00	22
23	Net Income							13 2 0 0 00			13 2 0 0 00	23
24								40 0 0 0 00	40 0 0 0 00	34 4 0 0 00	34 4 0 0 00	24
25												25
26												26
27												27
28												28
29												29
30												30

KEY TERMS

accrual basis of accounting (144)   A method of accounting under which revenues are recorded when earned and expenses are recorded when incurred.

Adjusted Trial Balance columns (142)   The third pair of amount columns on the work sheet. They are used to prove the equality of the debits and credits in the general ledger accounts after making all end-of-period adjustments.

adjusting entries (131)   Journal entries made at the end of an accounting period to reflect changes in account balances that are not the direct result of an exchange with an outside party.

Balance Sheet columns (142)   The work sheet columns that show the amounts that will be reported in the balance sheet and the statement of owner's equity.

book value (137)   The difference between the asset account and its related accumulated depreciation account. The value reflected by the accounting records.

cash basis of accounting (145)   A method of accounting under which revenues are recorded when cash is received and expenses are recorded when cash is paid.

contra-asset (136)   An account with a credit balance that is deducted from the related asset account on the balance sheet.

depreciable cost (136) The cost of an asset that is subject to depreciation.

depreciation (136)   A method of matching an asset's original cost against the revenues produced over its useful life.

fiscal year (131)   A 12-month period for which financial reports are prepared.

historical cost principle (136)   A principle that requires assets to be recorded at their actual cost.

Income Statement columns (142)   The work sheet columns that show the amounts that will be reported in the income statement.

market value (136)   The amount an item can be sold for under normal economic conditions.

matching principle (131)   A principle that requires the matching of revenues earned during an accounting period with the expenses incurred to produce the revenues.

modified cash basis (145)   A method of accounting that combines aspects of the cash and accrual methods. It uses the cash basis for recording revenues and most expenses. Exceptions are made when cash is paid for assets with useful lives greater than one accounting period.

plant assets (136)   Assets of a durable nature that will be used for operations over several years. Examples include buildings and equipment.

salvage value (136)   The expected market value of an asset at the end of its useful life.

straight-line method (136)   A depreciation method in which the depreciable cost is divided by the estimated useful life.

undepreciated cost (137)   The difference between the asset account and its related accumulated depreciation account. Also known as book value.

useful life (136)   The period of time that an asset is expected to help produce revenues.

work sheet (140)   A form used to pull together all of the information needed to enter adjusting entries and prepare the financial statements.

SELF-STUDY QUESTIONS AND EXERCISES

True/False Questions

1. LO1   The matching principle in accounting requires the matching of debits and credits.

2. LO1   Adjusting entries are required at the end of the accounting period because of mistakes in the journal and ledger.

3. LO1   As part of the adjustment of supplies, an expense account is debited and Supplies is credited for the amount of supplies used during the accounting period.

4. LO1   Depreciable cost is the difference between the original cost of the asset and its accumulated depreciation.

5. LO1   The purpose of depreciation is to record the asset's market value in the accounting records.

Multiple Choice Questions

1. LO1   The purpose of depreciation is to

   (a) spread the cost of an asset over its useful life.
   (b) show the current market value of an asset.
   (c) set up a reserve fund to purchase a new asset.
   (d) expense the asset in the year it was purchased.

2. LO1   Depreciable cost is the

   (a) difference between original cost and accumulated depreciation.
   (b) difference in actual cost and true market value.
   (c) difference between original cost and estimated salvage value.
   (d) difference between estimated salvage value and the actual salvage value.

3. LO1   Book value is the

   (a) difference between market value and estimated value.
   (b) difference between market value and historical cost.
   (c) difference between original cost and salvage value.
   (d) difference between original cost and accumulated depreciation.

4. LO1   The adjustment for wages earned by employees but not yet paid is

   (a) debit Wages Payable and credit Wages Expense.
   (b) debit Wages Expense and credit Cash.
   (c) debit Wages Expense and credit Wages Payable.
   (d) debit Wages Expense and credit Accounts Receivable.

5. LO3   The first step in preparing a work sheet is to

   (a) prepare the trial balance.
   (b) prepare the adjustments.
   (c) prepare the adjusted trial balance.
   (d) extend the amounts from the Adjusted Trial Balance to the Income Statement and Balance Sheet columns.

U REVU Exercises

1. LO1 On December 31, the trial balance indicates that the supplies account has a balance, prior to the adjusting entry, of $100. A physical count of the supplies inventory shows that $70 of supplies remain. What adjustment should be made to the supplies account?

2. LO2 When posting adjusting entries to the general ledger, what is written in the Item column?

3. LO3 Indicate the heading for the columns of the work sheet A through F below.

A	B		C		D		E		F	
	DEBIT	CREDIT	DEBIT	CREDIT	DEBIT	CREDIT	DEBIT	CREDIT	DEBIT	CREDIT
1										
2										

4. LO4 Find the error(s) in the work sheet below.

	ACCOUNT TITLE	TRIAL BALANCE DEBIT	TRIAL BALANCE CREDIT	ADJUSTMENTS DEBIT	ADJUSTMENTS CREDIT	ADJUSTED TRIAL BALANCE DEBIT	ADJUSTED TRIAL BALANCE CREDIT	INCOME STATEMENT DEBIT	INCOME STATEMENT CREDIT	BALANCE SHEET DEBIT	BALANCE SHEET CREDIT	
1	Cash	370 00				370 00				370 00		1
2	Accounts Receivable	650 00				650 00				650 00		2
3	Supplies	80 00			(a) 60 00	140 00				140 00		3
4	Prepaid Insurance	200 00			(b) 25 00	175 00				175 00		4
5	Delivery Equipment	3600 00				3600 00				3600 00		5
6	Accum. Depr.—Delivery Equipment				(d) 100 00		100 00				100 00	6
7	Accounts Payable		1800 00				1800 00				1800 00	7
8	Wages Payable				(c) 50 00		50 00				50 00	8
9	Jessica Jane, Capital		2000 00				2000 00				2000 00	9
10	Jessica Jane, Drawing	150 00				150 00				150 00		10
11	Delivery Fees		2150 00				2150 00		2150 00			11
12	Wages Expense	650 00		(c) 50 00		700 00		700 00				12
13	Rent Expense	200 00				200 00		200 00				13
14	Supplies Expense			(a) 60 00		60 00		60 00				14
15	Telephone Expense		50 00			50 00		50 00				15
16	Insurance Expense			(b) 25 00		25 00		25 00				16
17	Depr. Expense—Delivery Equipment			(d) 100 00		100 00		100 00				17
18		5950 00	5950 00	235 00	235 00	6220 00	6100 00	1135 00	2150 00	5085 00	3950 00	18
19								1015 00			1135 00	19
20								2150 00	2150 00	5085 00	5085 00	20
21												21
22												22
23												23
24												24

5. **LO5**   Using the following partial work sheet prepared on December 31, 20--, journalize the adjusting entry.

	ACCOUNT TITLE	TRIAL BALANCE				ADJUSTMENTS			
		DEBIT		CREDIT		DEBIT		CREDIT	
1	Cash	3 7 0 00							
2	Accounts Receivable	6 5 0 00							
3	Supplies	8 0 00							
4	Prepaid Insurance	2 0 0 00						(b)	5 0 00
5	Delivery Equipment	3 6 0 0 00							
6	Accum. Depr.—Delivery Equipment								
7	Accounts Payable			1 8 0 0 00					
8	Wages Payable								
9	Jessica Jane, Capital			2 0 0 0 00					
10	Jessica Jane, Drawing	1 5 0 00							
11	Delivery Fees			2 1 5 0 00					
12	Wages Expense	6 5 0 00							
13	Rent Expense	2 0 0 00							
14	Supplies Expense								
15	Telephone Expense	5 0 00							
16	Insurance Expense					(b)	5 0 00		
17	Depr. Expense—Delivery Equipment								
18		5 9 5 0 00		5 9 5 0 00			5 0 00		5 0 00
19									

6. **LO6**   Bill Roberts provided legal advice to a client for $500 on account. Roberts paid a legal assistant $50 for research on this engagement and used office supplies costing $10. If these are the only transactions for the period, compute net income under the cash, accrual, and modified cash bases.

The answers to the Self-Study Questions and Exercises are at the end of the chapter (pages 173–174).

APPLYING YOUR KNOWLEDGE

REVIEW QUESTIONS

LO1   1. Explain the matching principle.

LO1   2. Explain the historical cost principle.

LO1   3. Describe a plant asset.

LO1   4. What is a contra-asset?

LO1   5. What is the useful life of an asset?

LO1   6. What is the purpose of depreciation?

LO1   7. What is an asset's depreciable cost?

LO1   8. What is the book value of an asset?

LO3   9. Explain the purpose of the work sheet.

LO3   10. Identify the five major column headings on a work sheet.

LO3   11. List the five steps taken in preparing a work sheet.

LO4   12. Describe four tips for finding errors on the work sheet.

LO6   13. Explain when revenues are recorded under the cash basis, modified cash basis, and accrual basis of accounting.

LO6   14. Explain when expenses are recorded under the cash basis, modified cash basis, and accrual basis of accounting.

SERIES A EXERCISES

E 5-1A (LO1)   **ADJUSTMENT FOR SUPPLIES** On December 31, the trial balance indicates that the supplies account has a balance, prior to the adjusting entry, of $320. A physical count of the supplies inventory shows that $90 of supplies remain. Analyze this adjustment for supplies using T accounts, and then formally enter this adjustment in the general journal.

E 5-2A (LO1)   **ADJUSTMENT FOR INSURANCE** On December 1, a six-month liability insurance policy was purchased for $900. Analyze the required adjustment as of December 31 using T accounts, and then formally enter this adjustment in the general journal.

E 5-3A (LO1)   **ADJUSTMENT FOR WAGES** On December 31, the trial balance shows wages expense of $600. An additional $200 of wages was earned by the employees, but has not yet been paid. Analyze this adjustment for wages using T accounts, and then formally enter this adjustment in the general journal.

E 5-4A (LO1)   **ADJUSTMENT FOR DEPRECIATION OF ASSET** On December 1, delivery equipment was purchased for $7,200. The delivery equipment has an estimated useful life of four years (48 months) and no salvage value. Using the straight-line depreciation method, analyze the necessary adjusting entry as of December 31 (one month) using T accounts, and then formally enter this adjustment in the general journal.

E 5-5A (LO1)   **CALCULATION OF BOOK VALUE** On June 1, 20--, a depreciable asset was acquired for $5,400. The asset has an estimated useful life of five years (60 months) and no salvage value. Using the straight-line depreciation method, calculate the book value as of December 31, 20--.

E 5-6A (LO1)

ANALYSIS OF ADJUSTING ENTRY FOR SUPPLIES Analyze each situation and indicate the correct dollar amount for the adjusting entry. (Trial balance is abbreviated as TB.)

1. Ending inventory of supplies is $130.

(Balance Sheet) Supplies		(Income Statement) Supplies Expense	
TB 460			
	Adj. _____	Adj. _____	
Bal. _____			

2. Amount of supplies used is $320.

(Balance Sheet) Supplies		(Income Statement) Supplies Expense	
TB 545			
	Adj. _____	Adj. _____	
Bal. _____			

E 5-7A (LO1)

ANALYSIS OF ADJUSTING ENTRY FOR INSURANCE Analyze each situation and indicate the correct dollar amount for the adjusting entry.

1. Amount of insurance expired is $900.

(Balance Sheet) Prepaid Insurance		(Income Statement) Insurance Expense	
TB 1,300			
	Adj. _____	Adj. _____	
Bal. _____			

2. Amount of unexpired insurance is $185.

(Balance Sheet) Prepaid Insurance		(Income Statement) Insurance Expense	
TB 860			
	Adj. _____	Adj. _____	
Bal. _____			

E 5-8A (LO2)

POSTING ADJUSTING ENTRIES Two adjusting entries are in the following general journal. Post these adjusting entries to the four general ledger accounts. The following account numbers were taken from the chart of accounts: 141, Supplies; 219, Wages Payable; 511, Wages Expense; and 523, Supplies Expense. If you are not using the working papers that accompany this text, enter the following balances before posting the entries: Supplies, $200 Dr.; Wages Expense, $1,200 Dr.

(continued)

GENERAL JOURNAL

PAGE 9

	DATE		DESCRIPTION	POST. REF.	DEBIT	CREDIT	
1			Adjusting Entries				1
2	20-- Dec.	31	Supplies Expense		8 5 00		2
3			Supplies			8 5 00	3
4							4
5		31	Wages Expense		2 2 0 00		5
6			Wages Payable			2 2 0 00	6

E 5-9A (LO3)

✓ Adjustments col. total: $1,550

WORK SHEET AND ADJUSTING ENTRIES A partial work sheet for Jim Jacobs' Furniture Repair is shown as follows. Indicate by letters (a) through (d) the four adjustments in the Adjustments columns of the work sheet, properly matching each debit and credit. Complete the Adjustments columns.

Jim Jacobs' Furniture Repair
Work Sheet (Partial)
For Year Ended December 31, 20 - -

	ACCOUNT TITLE	TRIAL BALANCE		ADJUSTMENTS		ADJUSTED TRIAL BALANCE		
		DEBIT	CREDIT	DEBIT	CREDIT	DEBIT	CREDIT	
1	Cash	1 0 0 00				1 0 0 00		1
2	Supplies	8 5 0 00				2 0 0 00		2
3	Prepaid Insurance	9 0 0 00				3 0 0 00		3
4	Delivery Equipment	3 6 0 0 00				3 6 0 0 00		4
5	Accum. Depr.—Delivery Equipment		6 0 0 00				8 0 0 00	5
6	Wages Payable						1 0 0 00	6
7	Jim Jacobs, Capital		4 0 0 0 00				4 0 0 0 00	7
8	Repair Fees		1 6 5 0 00				1 6 5 0 00	8
9	Wages Expense	6 0 0 00				7 0 0 00		9
10	Advertising Expense	2 0 0 00				2 0 0 00		10
11	Supplies Expense					6 5 0 00		11
12	Insurance Expense					6 0 0 00		12
13	Depr. Expense—Delivery Equipment					2 0 0 00		13
14		6 2 5 0 00	6 2 5 0 00			6 5 5 0 00	6 5 5 0 00	14

E 5-10A (LO5)

JOURNALIZING ADJUSTING ENTRIES From the adjustments columns in Exercise 5-9A, journalize the four adjusting entries, as of December 31, in proper general journal format.

E 5-11A (LO3)

EXTENDING ADJUSTED BALANCES TO THE INCOME STATEMENT AND BALANCE SHEET COLUMNS Indicate with an "X" whether each account total should be extended to the Income Statement Debit or Credit or to the Balance Sheet Debit or Credit columns on the work sheet.

	Income Statement		Balance Sheet	
	Debit	Credit	Debit	Credit
Cash	___	___	___	___
Accounts Receivable	___	___	___	___
Supplies	___	___	___	___
Prepaid Insurance	___	___	___	___
Delivery Equipment	___	___	___	___
Accum. Depr.—Delivery Equipment	___	___	___	___
Accounts Payable	___	___	___	___
Wages Payable	___	___	___	___
Owner, Capital	___	___	___	___
Owner, Drawing	___	___	___	___
Delivery Fees	___	___	___	___
Wages Expense	___	___	___	___
Rent Expense	___	___	___	___
Supplies Expense	___	___	___	___
Insurance Expense	___	___	___	___
Depr. Exp.—Delivery Equipment	___	___	___	___

E 5-12A (LO3)

ANALYSIS OF NET INCOME OR NET LOSS ON THE WORK SHEET Indicate with an "X" in which columns, Income Statement Debit or Credit or Balance Sheet Debit or Credit, a net income or a net loss would appear on a work sheet.

	Income Statement		Balance Sheet	
	Debit	Credit	Debit	Credit
Net Income	___	___	___	___
Net Loss	___	___	___	___

E 5-13A (LO6)

✓ See Figure 5-25 in text

CASH, MODIFIED CASH, AND ACCRUAL BASES OF ACCOUNTING Prepare the entry for each of the following transactions, using the (a) cash basis, (b) modified cash basis, and (c) accrual basis of accounting.

1. Purchase supplies on account.
2. Make payment on asset previously purchased.
3. Purchase supplies for cash.
4. Purchase insurance for cash.
5. Pay cash for wages.
6. Pay cash for telephone expense.
7. Pay cash for new equipment.

End-of-Period Adjusting Entries:

8. Wages earned but not paid.
9. Prepaid item purchased, partly used.
10. Depreciation on long-term assets.

SERIES A PROBLEMS

P 5-14A (LO1/3)

✓ **Adjustments col. total: $1,895;**

Net income: $1,060

ADJUSTMENTS AND WORK SHEET SHOWING NET INCOME The trial balance after one month of operation for Mason's Delivery Service as of September 30, 20--, is shown below. Data to complete the adjustments are as follows:

(a) Supplies inventory as of September 30, $165.
(b) Insurance expired (used), $800.
(c) Depreciation on delivery equipment, $400.
(d) Wages earned by employees but not paid as of September 30, $225.

REQUIRED

1. Enter the adjustments in the Adjustments columns of the work sheet.

2. Complete the work sheet.

Mason's Delivery Service
Work Sheet (Partial)
For Month Ended September 30, 20 - -

	ACCOUNT TITLE	TRIAL BALANCE DEBIT	TRIAL BALANCE CREDIT	ADJUSTMENTS DEBIT	ADJUSTMENTS CREDIT	
1	Cash	1 6 0 0 00				1
2	Accounts Receivable	9 4 0 00				2
3	Supplies	6 3 5 00				3
4	Prepaid Insurance	1 2 0 0 00				4
5	Delivery Equipment	6 4 0 0 00				5
6	Accum. Depr.—Delivery Equipment					6
7	Accounts Payable		1 2 2 0 00			7
8	Wages Payable					8
9	Jill Mason, Capital		8 0 0 0 00			9
10	Jill Mason, Drawing	1 4 0 0 00				10
11	Delivery Fees		6 2 0 0 00			11
12	Wages Expense	1 5 0 0 00				12
13	Advertising Expense	4 6 0 00				13
14	Rent Expense	8 0 0 00				14
15	Supplies Expense					15
16	Telephone Expense	1 6 5 00				16
17	Insurance Expense					17
18	Repair Expense	2 3 0 00				18
19	Oil and Gas Expense	9 0 00				19
20	Depr. Expense—Delivery Equipment					20
21		15 4 2 0 00	15 4 2 0 00			21

P 5-15A (LO1/3)

✓ **Adjustments col. total: $1,380;**

Net loss: $2,495

ADJUSTMENTS AND WORK SHEET SHOWING A NET LOSS Jason Armstrong started a business called Campus Delivery Service. After the first month of operations, the trial balance as of November 30, 20--, is as shown on the next page.

REQUIRED

1. Analyze the following adjustments and enter them on the work sheet.

    (a) Ending inventory of supplies on November 30, $185.
    (b) Unexpired (remaining) insurance as of November 30, $800.
    (c) Depreciation expense on van, $300.
    (d) Wages earned but not paid as of November 30, $190.

2. Complete the work sheet.

Campus Delivery Service
Work Sheet (Partial)
For Month Ended November 30, 20 - -

	ACCOUNT TITLE	TRIAL BALANCE DEBIT	TRIAL BALANCE CREDIT	ADJUSTMENTS DEBIT	ADJUSTMENTS CREDIT	
1	Cash	9 8 0 00				1
2	Accounts Receivable	5 9 0 00				2
3	Supplies	5 7 5 00				3
4	Prepaid Insurance	1 3 0 0 00				4
5	Van	5 8 0 0 00				5
6	Accum. Depr.—Van					6
7	Accounts Payable		9 6 0 00			7
8	Wages Payable					8
9	Jason Armstrong, Capital		10 0 0 0 00			9
10	Jason Armstrong, Drawing	6 0 0 00				10
11	Delivery Fees		2 6 0 0 00			11
12	Wages Expense	1 8 0 0 00				12
13	Advertising Expense	3 8 0 00				13
14	Rent Expense	9 0 0 00				14
15	Supplies Expense					15
16	Telephone Expense	2 2 0 00				16
17	Insurance Expense					17
18	Repair Expense	3 1 5 00				18
19	Oil and Gas Expense	1 0 0 00				19
20	Depr. Expense—Van					20
21		13 5 6 0 00	13 5 6 0 00			21

P 5-16A (LO2/5)

JOURNALIZE AND POST ADJUSTING ENTRIES FROM THE WORK SHEET
Refer to Problem 5-15A and the following additional information:

Account Name	Account Number	Balance in Account Before Adjusting Entry
Supplies	141	$ 575
Prepaid Insurance	145	1,300
Accum. Depr.—Van	185.1	0
Wages Payable	219	0
Wages Expense	511	1,800
Supplies Expense	523	0
Insurance Expense	535	0
Depr. Expense—Van	541	0

(continued)

1. Journalize the adjusting entries on page 5 of the general journal.

2. Post the adjusting entries to the general ledger. (If you are not using the working papers that accompany this text, enter the balances provided in this problem before posting the adjusting entries.)

P 5-17A (LO4)

✓ Adjustments col. total: $1,160; Net income: $1,575

CORRECTING WORK SHEET WITH ERRORS A beginning accounting student tried to complete a work sheet for Joyce Lee's Tax Service. The following adjusting entries were to have been analyzed and entered onto the work sheet. The work sheet is shown on page 163.

(a) Ending inventory of supplies as of March 31, $160.
(b) Unexpired insurance as of March 31, $520.
(c) Depreciation of office equipment, $275.
(d) Wages earned, but not paid as of March 31, $110.

REQUIRED

The accounting student made a number of errors. Review the work sheet for addition mistakes, transpositions, and other errors and make all necessary corrections.

SERIES B EXERCISES

E 5-1B (LO1)

ADJUSTMENT FOR SUPPLIES On July 31, the trial balance indicates that the supplies account has a balance, prior to the adjusting entry, of $430. A physical count of the supplies inventory shows that $120 of supplies remain. Analyze the adjustment for supplies using T accounts, and then formally enter this adjustment in the general journal.

E 5-2B (LO1)

ADJUSTMENT FOR INSURANCE On July 1, a six-month liability insurance policy was purchased for $750. Analyze the required adjustment as of July 31 using T accounts, and then formally enter this adjustment in the general journal.

E 5-3B (LO1)

ADJUSTMENT FOR WAGES On July 31, the trial balance shows wages expense of $800. An additional $150 of wages was earned by the employees but has not yet been paid. Analyze the required adjustment using T accounts, and then formally enter this adjustment in the general journal.

E 5-4B (LO1)

ADJUSTMENT FOR DEPRECIATION OF ASSET On July 1, delivery equipment was purchased for $4,320. The delivery equipment has an estimated useful life of three years (36 months) and no salvage value. Using the straight-line depreciation method, analyze the necessary adjusting entry as of July 31 (one month) using T accounts, and then formally enter this adjustment in the general journal.

E 5-5B (LO1)

CALCULATION OF BOOK VALUE On January 1, 20--, a depreciable asset was acquired for $5,760. The asset has an estimated useful life of four years (48 months) and no salvage value. Use the straight-line depreciation method to calculate the book value as of July 1, 20--.

PROBLEM 5-17A

Joyce Lee's Tax Service
Work Sheet
For Month Ended March 31, 20--

	ACCOUNT TITLE	TRIAL BALANCE DEBIT	TRIAL BALANCE CREDIT	ADJUSTMENTS DEBIT	ADJUSTMENTS CREDIT	ADJUSTED TRIAL BALANCE DEBIT	ADJUSTED TRIAL BALANCE CREDIT	INCOME STATEMENT DEBIT	INCOME STATEMENT CREDIT	BALANCE SHEET DEBIT	BALANCE SHEET CREDIT
1	Cash	1 7 2 5 00				1 7 2 5 00				1 7 5 2 00	
2	Accounts Receivable	9 6 0 0 00				9 6 0 0 00				9 6 0 0 00	
3	Supplies	5 2 5 0 00			(a) 1 6 0 0 00	3 6 5 0 00				3 6 5 0 00	
4	Prepaid Insurance	9 3 0 0 00			(b) 4 1 0 0 00	5 4 0 0 00				5 4 0 0 00	
5	Office Equipment	5 4 5 0 00			(c) 2 7 5 0 00	5 1 7 5 00				5 1 7 5 00	
6	Accum. Depr.– Office Equipment										
7	Accounts Payable		4 8 0 0 00				4 8 0 0 00				4 8 0 0 00
8	Wages Payable				(d) 1 1 0 0 00		1 1 0 0 00		1 1 0 0 00		
9	Joyce Lee, Capital		7 5 0 0 00				7 5 0 0 00				7 5 0 0 00
10	Joyce Lee, Drawing	1 1 2 5 00				1 1 2 5 00		1 1 2 5 00			
11	Professional Fees		5 7 0 0 00				5 7 0 0 00		5 7 0 0 00		
12	Wages Expense	1 4 2 0 00		(d) 1 1 0 0 00		1 4 2 0 00		1 4 2 0 00			
13	Advertising Expense	3 5 0 00				3 5 0 00		3 5 0 00			
14	Rent Expense	7 0 0 00				7 0 0 00		7 0 0 00			
15	Supplies Expense			(a) 1 6 0 0 00		1 6 0 0 00		1 6 0 0 00			
16	Telephone Expense	1 3 0 00				1 3 0 00		1 3 0 00			
17	Utilities Expense	1 9 0 00				1 9 0 00		1 9 0 00			
18	Insurance Expense			(b) 4 1 0 00		4 1 0 00		4 1 0 00			
19	Depr. Expense–Office Equipment			(c) 2 7 5 00		2 7 5 00		2 7 5 00			
20	Miscellaneous Expense	1 7 5 00				1 7 5 00		1 7 5 00			
21											
22		13 6 8 0 00	13 6 8 0 00	9 5 00	9 5 00	13 1 6 0 00	13 7 9 0 00	4 5 6 6 00	5 8 1 0 00	9 5 0 8 00	7 9 8 0 00
23								1 2 4 4 00			1 5 2 8 00
24								5 8 1 0 00	5 8 1 0 00	9 5 0 8 00	9 5 0 8 00

E 5-6B (LO1)

ANALYSIS OF ADJUSTING ENTRY FOR SUPPLIES Analyze each situation and indicate the correct dollar amount for the adjusting entry.

1. Ending inventory of supplies is $95.

(Balance Sheet) Supplies		(Income Statement) Supplies Expense
TB 540	Adj. _____	Adj. _____
Bal. _____		

2. Amount of supplies used is $280.

(Balance Sheet) Supplies		(Income Statement) Supplies Expense
TB 330	Adj. _____	Adj. _____
Bal. _____		

E 5-7B (LO1)

ANALYSIS OF ADJUSTING ENTRY FOR INSURANCE Analyze each situation and indicate the correct dollar amount for the adjusting entry.

1. Amount of insurance expired (used) is $830.

(Balance Sheet) Prepaid Insurance		(Income Statement) Insurance Expense
TB 960	Adj. _____	Adj. _____
Bal. _____		

2. Amount of unexpired (remaining) insurance is $340.

(Balance Sheet) Prepaid Insurance		(Income Statement) Insurance Expense
TB 1,135	Adj. _____	Adj. _____
Bal. _____		

E 5-8B (LO2)

POSTING ADJUSTING ENTRIES Two adjusting entries are shown in the following general journal. Post these adjusting entries to the four general ledger accounts. The following account numbers were taken from the chart of accounts: 145, Prepaid Insurance; 183.1, Accumulated Depreciation—Cleaning Equipment; 541, Depreciation Expense—Cleaning Equipment; and 535, Insurance Expense. If you are not using the working papers that accompany this text, enter the following balances before posting the entries: Prepaid Insurance, $960 Dr.; Accumulated Depreciation—Cleaning Equipment, $870 Cr.

		GENERAL JOURNAL									PAGE 7	
	DATE	DESCRIPTION	POST. REF.		DEBIT				CREDIT			
1		Adjusting Entries										1
2	20-- July	31 Insurance Expense			3	2	0	00				2
3		Prepaid Insurance							3	2	0	00	3
4												4
5		31 Depr. Expense—Cleaning Equipment			1	4	5	00				5
6		Accum. Depr.—Cleaning Equipment							1	4	5	00	6

E 5-9B (LO3)

✓ Adjustments col. total: $1,530

WORK SHEET AND ADJUSTING ENTRIES A partial work sheet for Jasmine Kah's Auto Detailing is shown below. Indicate by letters (a) through (d) the four adjustments in the Adjustments columns of the work sheet, properly matching each debit and credit. Complete the Adjustments columns.

Jasmine Kah's Auto Detailing
Work Sheet (Partial)
For Month Ended June 30, 20 - -

	ACCOUNT TITLE	TRIAL BALANCE				ADJUSTMENTS				ADJUSTED TRIAL BALANCE				
		DEBIT			CREDIT		DEBIT		CREDIT		DEBIT		CREDIT	
1	Cash	1	5	0	00						1	5	0	00				1
2	Supplies	5	2	0	00							9	0	00				2
3	Prepaid Insurance	7	5	0	00						2	0	0	00				3
4	Cleaning Equipment	5	4	0	0	00					5	4	0	0	00				4
5	Accum. Depr.— Cleaning Equipment			8	5	0	00						1	1	5	0	00	5
6	Wages Payable												2	5	0	00	6
7	Jasmine Kah, Capital			4	6	0	0	00					4	6	0	0	00	7
8	Detailing Fees			2	2	2	0	00					2	2	2	0	00	8
9	Wages Expense	7	0	0	00						9	5	0	00				9
10	Advertising Expense	1	5	0	00						1	5	0	00				10
11	Supplies Expense										4	3	0	00				11
12	Insurance Expense										5	5	0	00				12
13	Depr. Expense—Cleaning Equipment										3	0	0	00				13
14		7	6	7	0	00	7	6	7	0	00						8	2	2	0	00	8	2	2	0	00	14

E 5-10B (LO5)

JOURNALIZING ADJUSTING ENTRIES From the Adjustments columns in Exercise 5-9B, journalize the four adjusting entries as of June 30, in proper general journal format.

E 5-11B (LO3)

EXTENDING ADJUSTED BALANCES TO THE INCOME STATEMENT AND BALANCE SHEET COLUMNS Indicate with an "X" whether each account total should be extended to the Income Statement Debit or Credit or to the Balance Sheet Debit or Credit columns on the work sheet.

(continued)

	Income Statement		Balance Sheet	
	Debit	Credit	Debit	Credit
Cash	_____	_____	_____	_____
Accounts Receivable	_____	_____	_____	_____
Supplies	_____	_____	_____	_____
Prepaid Insurance	_____	_____	_____	_____
Automobile	_____	_____	_____	_____
Accum. Depr.—Automobile	_____	_____	_____	_____
Accounts Payable	_____	_____	_____	_____
Wages Payable	_____	_____	_____	_____
Owner, Capital	_____	_____	_____	_____
Owner, Drawing	_____	_____	_____	_____
Service Fees	_____	_____	_____	_____
Wages Expense	_____	_____	_____	_____
Supplies Expense	_____	_____	_____	_____
Utilities Expense	_____	_____	_____	_____
Insurance Expense	_____	_____	_____	_____
Depr. Exp.—Automobile	_____	_____	_____	_____

E 5-12B (LO3)

ANALYSIS OF NET INCOME OR NET LOSS ON THE WORK SHEET Insert the dollar amounts where the net income or net loss would appear on the work sheet.

	Income Statement		Balance Sheet	
	Debit	Credit	Debit	Credit
Net Income: $2,500	_____	_____	_____	_____
Net Loss: $1,900	_____	_____	_____	_____

E 5-13B (LO6)

✓ See Figure 5-25 in text

CASH, MODIFIED CASH, AND ACCRUAL BASES OF ACCOUNTING For each journal entry shown below, indicate the accounting method(s) for which the entry would be appropriate. If the journal entry is not appropriate for a particular accounting method, explain the proper accounting treatment for that method.

1. Office Equipment
   Cash
   Purchased equipment for cash

2. Office Equipment
   Accounts Payable
   Purchased equipment on account

3. Cash
   Revenue
   Cash receipts for week

4. Accounts Receivable
   Revenue
   Services performed on account

5. Prepaid Insurance
   Cash
   Purchased prepaid asset

6. Supplies
   Accounts Payable
   Purchased prepaid asset

    7. Telephone Expense
        Cash
            Paid telephone bill

    8. Wages Expense
        Cash
            Paid wages for month

    9. Accounts Payable
        Cash
            Made payment on account

Adjusting Entries:
10. Supplies Expense
        Supplies

11. Wages Expense
        Wages Payable

12. Depreciation Expense—Office Equipment
        Accumulated Depreciation—Office Equipment

SERIES B PROBLEMS

P 5-14B (LO1/3)

✓ Adjustments col. total: $805;
Net income: $2,410

ADJUSTMENTS AND WORK SHEET SHOWING NET INCOME Louie Long started a business called Louie's Lawn Service. The trial balance as of March 31, after the first month of operation, is as follows:

Louie's Lawn Service
Work Sheet
For Month Ended March 31, 20 --

	ACCOUNT TITLE	TRIAL BALANCE		ADJUSTMENTS		
		DEBIT	CREDIT	DEBIT	CREDIT	
1	Cash	1 3 7 5 00				1
2	Accounts Receivable	8 8 0 00				2
3	Supplies	4 9 0 00				3
4	Prepaid Insurance	8 0 0 00				4
5	Lawn Equipment	5 7 0 0 00				5
6	Accum. Depr.—Lawn Equipment					6
7	Accounts Payable		7 8 0 00			7
8	Wages Payable					8
9	Louie Long, Capital		6 5 0 0 00			9
10	Louie Long, Drawing	1 2 5 0 00				10
11	Lawn Service Fees		6 1 0 0 00			11
12	Wages Expense	1 1 4 5 00				12
13	Advertising Expense	5 4 0 00				13
14	Rent Expense	7 2 5 00				14
15	Supplies Expense					15
16	Telephone Expense	1 6 0 00				16
17	Insurance Expense					17
18	Repair Expense	2 5 0 00				18
19	Depr. Expense—Lawn Equipment					19
20	Miscellaneous Expense	6 5 00				20
21		13 3 8 0 00	13 3 8 0 00			21

(continued)

REQUIRED

1. Analyze the following adjustments and enter them on a work sheet.

   (a) Ending supplies inventory as of March 31, $165.
   (b) Insurance expired (used), $100.
   (c) Depreciation of lawn equipment, $200.
   (d) Wages earned but not paid as of March 31, $180.

2. Complete the work sheet.

P 5-15B (LO1/3)

✓ Adjustments col. total: $990;

Net loss: $1,625

ADJUSTMENTS AND WORK SHEET SHOWING A NET LOSS Val Nolan started a business called Nolan's Home Appraisals. The trial balance as of October 31, after the first month of operations, is as follows:

Nolan's Home Appraisals
Work Sheet
For Month Ended October 31, 20 - -

	ACCOUNT TITLE	TRIAL BALANCE DEBIT	TRIAL BALANCE CREDIT	ADJUSTMENTS DEBIT	ADJUSTMENTS CREDIT	
1	Cash	8 3 0 00				1
2	Accounts Receivable	7 6 0 00				2
3	Supplies	6 2 5 00				3
4	Prepaid Insurance	9 5 0 00				4
5	Automobile	6 5 0 0 00				5
6	Accum. Depr.—Automobile					6
7	Accounts Payable		1 5 0 0 00			7
8	Wages Payable					8
9	Val Nolan, Capital		9 9 0 0 00			9
10	Val Nolan, Drawing	1 1 0 0 00				10
11	Appraisal Fees		3 0 0 0 00			11
12	Wages Expense	1 5 6 0 00				12
13	Advertising Expense	4 2 0 00				13
14	Rent Expense	1 0 5 0 00				14
15	Supplies Expense					15
16	Telephone Expense	2 5 5 00				16
17	Insurance Expense					17
18	Repair Expense	2 7 0 00				18
19	Oil and Gas Expense	8 0 00				19
20	Depr. Expense—Automobile					20
21		14 4 0 0 00	14 4 0 0 00			21

REQUIRED

1. Analyze the following adjustments and enter them on the work sheet.

   (a) Supplies inventory as of October 31, $210.
   (b) Unexpired (remaining) insurance as of October 31, $800.
   (c) Depreciation of automobile, $250.
   (d) Wages earned but not paid as of October 31, $175.

2. Complete the work sheet.

P 5-16B (LO2/5)

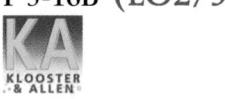

JOURNALIZE AND POST ADJUSTING ENTRIES FROM THE WORK SHEET
Refer to Problem 5-15B and the following additional information:

Account Name	Account Number	Balance in Account Before Adjusting Entry
Supplies	141	$ 625
Prepaid Insurance	145	950
Accum. Depr.—Automobile	185.1	0
Wages Payable	219	0
Wages Expense	511	1,560
Supplies Expense	523	0
Insurance Expense	535	0
Depr. Expense—Automobile	541	0

REQUIRED

1. Journalize the adjusting entries on page 3 of the general journal.

2. Post the adjusting entries to the general ledger. (If you are not using the working papers that accompany this text, enter the balances provided in this problem before posting the adjusting entries.)

P 5-17B (LO4)

✓ Adjustments col. total: $1,640;
Net income: $1,405

CORRECTING WORK SHEET WITH ERRORS A beginning accounting student tried to complete a work sheet for Dick Ady's Bookkeeping Service. The following adjusting entries were to have been analyzed and entered in the work sheet:

(a) Ending inventory of supplies on July 31, $130.
(b) Unexpired insurance on July 31, $420.
(c) Depreciation of office equipment, $325.
(d) Wages earned, but not paid as of July 31, $95.

REQUIRED

Review the work sheet shown on page 170 for addition mistakes, transpositions, and other errors and make all necessary corrections.

MANAGING YOUR WRITING

Delia Alvarez, owner of Delia's Lawn Service, wants to borrow money to buy new lawn equipment. A local bank has asked for financial statements. Alvarez has asked you to prepare financial statements for the year ended December 31, 20--. You have been given the unadjusted trial balance on page 171 and suspect that Alvarez expects you to base your statements on this information. You are concerned, however, that some of the account balances may need to be adjusted. Write a memo to Alvarez explaining what additional information you need before you can prepare the financial statements. Alvarez is not familiar with accounting issues. Therefore, explain in your memo why you need this information, the potential impact of this information on the financial statements, and the importance of making these adjustments before approaching the bank for a loan.

(continued)

PROBLEM 5-17B

Dick Ady's Bookkeeping Service
Work Sheet
For Month Ended July 31, 20--

	ACCOUNT TITLE	TRIAL BALANCE DEBIT	TRIAL BALANCE CREDIT	ADJUSTMENTS DEBIT	ADJUSTMENTS CREDIT	ADJUSTED TRIAL BALANCE DEBIT	ADJUSTED TRIAL BALANCE CREDIT	INCOME STATEMENT DEBIT	INCOME STATEMENT CREDIT	BALANCE SHEET DEBIT	BALANCE SHEET CREDIT	
1	Cash	1 3 6 5 00				1 3 6 5 00				1 3 5 6 00		1
2	Accounts Receivable	8 4 5 00				8 4 5 00			8 4 5 00			2
3	Supplies	6 2 0 00			(a) 4 9 0 00	1 3 0 00				1 3 0 00		3
4	Prepaid Insurance	1 1 5 00			(b) 4 2 0 00	7 3 0 00				7 3 0 00		4
5	Office Equipment	6 4 0 00			(c) 3 2 5 00	6 7 2 5 00				6 7 2 5 00		5
6	Accum. Depr.—Office Equipment											6
7	Accounts Payable		7 3 5 00				7 3 5 00				7 3 5 00	7
8	Wages Payable				(d) 9 5 00		9 5 00				5 9 00	8
9	Dick Ady, Capital		7 8 0 0 00				7 8 0 0 00				7 8 0 0 00	9
10	Dick Ady, Drawing	1 2 0 0 00				1 2 0 0 00				1 2 0 0 00		10
11	Professional Fees		6 3 5 0 00				6 3 5 0 00		6 3 5 0 00			11
12	Wages Expense	1 4 9 5 00		(d) 9 5 00		1 5 9 0 00		1 5 9 0 00				12
13	Advertising Expense	3 8 0 00				3 8 0 00		3 8 0 00				13
14	Rent Expense	8 5 0 00				8 5 0 00		8 5 0 00				14
15	Supplies Expense			(a) 4 9 0 00		4 9 0 00		4 9 0 00				15
16	Telephone Expense	2 0 5 00				2 0 5 00		2 0 5 00				16
17	Utilities Expense	2 8 5 00				2 8 5 00		2 8 5 00				17
18	Insurance Expense			(b) 4 2 0 00		4 2 0 00		4 2 0 00				18
19	Depr. Expense—Office Equipment			(c) 3 2 5 00		3 2 5 00		3 2 5 00				19
20	Miscellaneous Expense	9 0 00				9 0 00		9 0 00				20
21		14 8 8 5 00	14 8 8 5 00	1 3 3 0 00	1 3 3 0 00	15 6 3 0 00	14 9 8 0 00	4 8 8 0 00	7 1 9 5 00	10 1 4 1 00	8 5 9 4 00	21
22	Net Income							2 3 1 5 00			1 5 4 7 00	22
23								7 1 9 5 00	7 1 9 5 00	10 1 4 1 00	10 1 4 1 00	23
24												24
25												25
26												26
27												27
28												28
29												29
30												30

Contains Errors

This work sheet contains errors.

Delia's Lawn Service Trial Balance December 31, 20 - -												
ACCOUNT TITLE	ACCOUNT NO.	DEBIT BALANCE					CREDIT BALANCE					
Cash	101			7	7	0	00					
Accounts Receivable	122		1	7	0	0	00					
Supplies	142			2	8	0	00					
Prepaid Insurance	145			4	0	0	00					
Lawn Equipment	183		13	8	0	0	00					
Accounts Payable	202								2	2	0	0	00
Delia Alvarez, Capital	311								3	0	0	0	00
Delia Alvarez, Drawing	312			3	5	0	00					
Lawn Cutting Fees	401								52	4	0	0	00
Wages Expense	511		35	8	5	0	00					
Rent Expense	521		1	2	0	0	00					
Gas and Oil Expense	538		3	2	5	0	00					
			57	6	0	0	00		57	6	0	0	00

MASTERY PROBLEM

✓ Adjusted Trial Bal. total: $58,500;
Net income: $13,630

Kristi Williams offers family counseling services specializing in financial and marital problems. A chart of accounts and a trial balance taken on December 31, 20--, follow.

KRISTI WILLIAMS FAMILY COUNSELING SERVICES CHART OF ACCOUNTS			
Assets		**Revenue**	
101	Cash	401	Client Fees
142	Office Supplies		
145	Prepaid Insurance	**Expenses**	
181	Office Equipment	511	Wages Expense
181.1	Accumulated Depr.—	521	Rent Expense
	Office Equipment	523	Office Supplies Expense
187	Computer Equipment	533	Utilities Expense
187.1	Accumulated Depr.—	535	Insurance Expense
	Computer Equipment	541	Depr. Expense—
Liabilities			Office Equipment
201	Notes Payable	542	Depr. Expense—
202	Accounts Payable		Computer Equipment
		549	Miscellaneous Expense
Owner's Equity			
311	Kristi Williams, Capital		
312	Kristi Williams, Drawing		

(continued)

Kristi Williams Family Counseling Services Trial Balance December 31, 20 - -													
ACCOUNT TITLE	ACCOUNT NO.	DEBIT BALANCE					CREDIT BALANCE					
Cash	101	8	7	3	0	00					
Office Supplies	142		7	0	0	00					
Prepaid Insurance	145		6	0	0	00					
Office Equipment	181	18	0	0	0	00					
Computer Equipment	187	6	0	0	0	00					
Notes Payable	201						8	0	0	0	00
Accounts Payable	202							5	0	0	00
Kristi Williams, Capital	311						11	4	0	0	00
Kristi Williams, Drawing	312	3	0	0	0	00					
Client Fees	401						35	8	0	0	00
Wages Expense	511	9	5	0	0	00					
Rent Expense	521	6	0	0	0	00					
Utilities Expense	533	2	1	7	0	00					
Miscelleneous Expense	549	1	0	0	0	00					
		55	7	0	0	00	55	7	0	0	00

Information for year-end adjustments is as follows:

(a) Office supplies on hand at year-end amounted to $100.

(b) On January 1, 20--, Williams purchased office equipment that cost $18,000. It has an expected useful life of 10 years and no salvage value.

(c) On July 1, 20--, Williams purchased computer equipment costing $6,000. It has an expected useful life of three years and no salvage value. Assume that Williams computes depreciation to the nearest full month.

(d) On December 1, 20--, Williams paid a premium of $600 for a six-month insurance policy.

REQUIRED

1. Prepare the work sheet for the year ended December 31, 20--.

2. Prepare adjusting entries in a general journal.

CHALLENGE PROBLEM

This problem challenges you to apply your cumulative accounting knowledge to move a step beyond the material in the chapter.

KA
KLOOSTER
& ALLEN

Your friend, Diane Kiefner, teaches elementary school and operates her own wilderness kayaking tours in the summers. She thinks she has been doing fine financially, but has never really measured her profits. Until this year, her business has always had more money at the end of the summer than at the beginning. She enjoys kayaking and as long as she came out a little ahead, that was fine. Unfortunately, Diane had to dip into her savings to make up for "losses" on her kayaking tours this past summer. Hearing that you have been studying accounting, she brought a list of cash receipts and expenditures and would like you to try to figure out what happened.

Cash balance beginning of summer		$15,000
Cash receipts from kayakers over the summer	$10,000	
Cash expenditures over the summer	13,500	
Amount taken from savings		(3,500)
Cash balance end of summer		$11,500

When asked for more details on the expenditures and the kayaking gear that you saw in her garage, Diane provided the following information:

Expenditures were made on the following items:

Brochures used to advertise her services (Diane only used about 1/4 of them and plans to use the remainder over the next three summers.)	$1,000
Food for trips (nothing left)	2,000
Rent on equipment used by kayakers on trips	3,000
Travel expenses	4,000
A new kayak and paddles (At the beginning of the summer, Diane bought a new kayak and paddles. Up to this time, she had always borrowed her father's. Diane expects to use the equipment for about five years. At that time, she expects it to have no value.)	3,500

A trial balance based on this information follows. As you will note, Diane's trial balance is not consistent with some of the concepts discussed in this chapter.

Diane Kiefner's Wilderness Kayaking Tours
Work Sheet
For Summer Ended 20 - -

	ACCOUNT TITLE	TRIAL BALANCE DEBIT	TRIAL BALANCE CREDIT	ADJUSTMENTS DEBIT	ADJUSTMENTS CREDIT	ADJUSTED TRIAL BALANCE DEBIT	ADJUSTED TRIAL BALANCE CREDIT	INCOME STATEMENT DEBIT	INCOME STATEMENT CREDIT	BALANCE SHEET DEBIT	BALANCE SHEET CREDIT	
1	Cash	11 5 0 0 00										1
2	Diane Kiefner, Capital		15 0 0 0 00									2
3	Tour Revenue		10 0 0 0 00									3
4	Advertising Supplies Expense	1 0 0 0 00										4
5	Food Expense	2 0 0 0 00										5
6	Equipment Rental Expense	3 0 0 0 00										6
7	Travel Expense	4 0 0 0 00										7
8	Kayak Expense	3 5 0 0 00										8
9		25 0 0 0 00	25 0 0 0 00									9

REQUIRED

1. Complete Diane's work sheet by making appropriate adjustments and extensions. *Note:* (a) You may need to add new accounts. (b) Some of the adjustments you need to make are actually "corrections of errors" Diane has made in classifying certain items.

2. What is your best measure of Diane's net income for the summer of 20--?

ANSWERS TO SELF-STUDY QUESTIONS AND EXERCISES

True/False Questions

1. F (match revenues and expenses)   2. F (to bring accounts up to date)   3. T
4. F (depreciable cost = cost – salvage value)   5. F (to match cost of asset against revenues it will help generate)

Multiple Choice Questions

1. a   2. c   3. d   4. c   5. a

U REVU Exercises

1. Supplies should be reduced (credited) for $30.

2. Adjusting.

3. A. Account Title
   B. Trial Balance
   C. Adjustments
   D. Adjusted Trial Balance
   E. Income Statement
   F. Balance Sheet

4. Errors are highlighted in yellow.

ACCOUNT TITLE	TRIAL BALANCE DEBIT	TRIAL BALANCE CREDIT	ADJUSTMENTS DEBIT	ADJUSTMENTS CREDIT	ADJUSTED TRIAL BALANCE DEBIT	ADJUSTED TRIAL BALANCE CREDIT	INCOME STATEMENT DEBIT	INCOME STATEMENT CREDIT	BALANCE SHEET DEBIT	BALANCE SHEET CREDIT	
1 Cash	3 7 0 0 00				3 7 0 0 00				3 7 0 0 00		1
2 Accounts Receivable	6 5 0 0 00				6 5 0 0 00				6 5 0 0 00		2
3 Supplies	8 0 00			(a) 6 0 00	1 4 0 00				1 4 0 00		3
4 Prepaid Insurance	2 0 0 00			(b) 2 5 00	1 7 5 00				1 7 5 00		4
5 Delivery Equipment	3 6 0 0 00				3 6 0 0 00				3 6 0 0 00		5
6 Accum. Depr.—Delivery Equipment				(d) 1 0 0 00		1 0 0 00				1 0 0 00	6
7 Accounts Payable		1 8 0 0 00				1 8 0 0 00				1 8 0 0 00	7
8 Wages Payable				(c) 5 0 00		5 0 00				5 0 00	8
9 Jessica Jane, Capital		2 0 0 0 00				2 0 0 0 00				2 0 0 0 00	9
10 Jessica Jane, Drawing	1 5 0 00				1 5 0 00				1 5 0 00		10
11 Delivery Fees		2 1 5 0 00				2 1 5 0 00		2 1 5 0 00			11
12 Wages Expense	6 5 0 00		(c) 5 0 00		7 0 0 00		7 0 0 00				12
13 Rent Expense	2 0 0 00				2 0 0 00		2 0 0 00				13
14 Supplies Expense			(a) 6 0 00		6 0 00		6 0 00				14
15 Telephone Expense	5 0 00				5 0 00		5 0 00				15
16 Insurance Expense			(b) 2 5 00		2 5 00		2 5 00				16
17 Depr. Expense—Delivery Equipment			(d) 1 0 0 00		1 0 0 00		1 0 0 00				17
18	5 9 5 0 00	5 9 5 0 00	2 3 5 00	2 3 5 00	6 2 2 0 00	6 1 0 0 00	1 1 3 5 00	2 1 5 0 00	5 0 8 5 00	3 9 5 0 00	18
19 Net Income							1 0 1 5 00			1 1 3 5 00	19
20							2 1 5 0 00	2 1 5 0 00	5 0 8 5 00	5 0 8 5 00	20
21											21

5.
                     Adjusting Entry
Dec. 31   Insurance Expense   50.00
                     Prepaid Insurance   50.00

6.

Transaction	Cash Basis	Accrual Basis	Modified Cash Basis
Services on account,	$ —	$500.00	$ —
Payment for legal research assistance	(50.00)	(50.00)	(50.00)
Office supplies used		(10.00)	(10.00)
Net Income (Net Loss)	$(50.00)	$440.00	$(60.00)

Chapter 5 Appendix
Depreciation Methods

LEARNING OBJECTIVES

Careful study of this appendix should enable you to:

LO1 Prepare a depreciation schedule using the straight-line method.

LO2 Prepare a depreciation schedule using the sum-of-the-years'-digits method.

LO3 Prepare a depreciation schedule using the double-declining-balance method.

LO4 Prepare a depreciation schedule for tax purposes using the Modified Accelerated Cost Recovery System.

In Chapter 5, we introduced the straight-line method of depreciation. Here, we will review this method and illustrate three others: sum-of-the-years'-digits; double-declining-balance; and, for tax purposes, the Modified Accelerated Cost Recovery System. For all illustrations, we will assume that a delivery van was purchased for $40,000. It has a five-year useful life and salvage value of $4,000.

STRAIGHT-LINE METHOD

LO1 Prepare a depreciation schedule using the straight-line method.

Under the **straight-line depreciation method,** an equal amount of depreciation will be taken each period. First, compute the depreciable cost by subtracting the salvage value from the cost of the asset. This is done because we expect to sell the asset for $4,000 at the end of its useful life. Thus, the total cost to be recognized as an expense over the five years is $36,000, not $40,000.

Cost	–	Salvage Value	=	Depreciable Cost
$40,000	–	$4,000	=	$36,000

Next, we divide the depreciable cost by the expected life of the asset, five years.

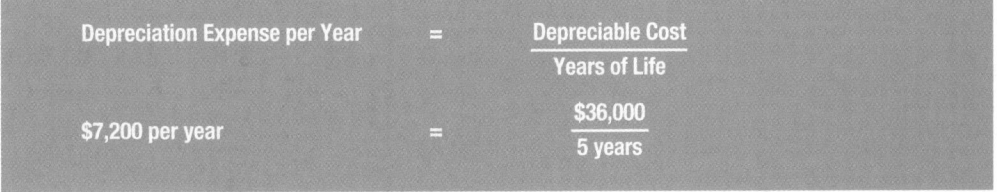

Depreciation Expense per Year	=	Depreciable Cost / Years of Life
$7,200 per year	=	$36,000 / 5 years

When preparing a depreciation schedule, it is often convenient to use a depreciation rate per year. In this case, it would be 20% (100% ÷ 5 years of life). Figure 5A-1 shows the depreciation expense, accumulated depreciation, and book value for each of the five years.

FIGURE 5A-1 Depreciation Schedule Using Straight-Line Method

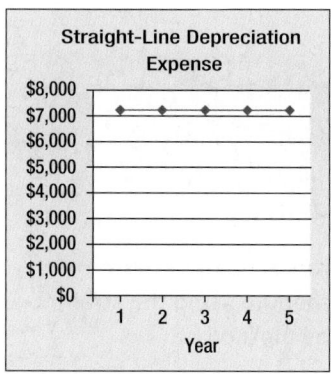

Straight-Line Depreciation Expense

STRAIGHT-LINE DEPRECIATION

Year	Depreciable Cost	×	Rate	=	Depreciation Expense	Accumulated Depreciation (End of Year)	Book Value (End of Year)
1	$36,000		20%		$7,200	$ 7,200	$32,800
2	36,000		20%		7,200	14,400	25,600
3	36,000		20%		7,200	21,600	18,400
4	36,000		20%		7,200	28,800	11,200
5	36,000		20%		7,200	36,000	4,000

Cost	$40,000
− Salvage Value	4,000
Depreciable Cost	$36,000

100%
5 Years
= 20%

Same amount each year

Accum. Depr. increases by the same amount each year, $7,200.

Cost
−Accum. Depr.
Book Value

SUM-OF-THE-YEARS'-DIGITS

LO2 Prepare a depreciation schedule using the sum-of-the-years'-digits method.

Under the **sum-of-the-years'-digits depreciation method,** depreciation is determined by multiplying the depreciable cost by a schedule of fractions. The numerator of the fraction for a specific year is the number of years of remaining useful life for the asset, measured from the beginning of the year. The denominator for all fractions is determined by adding the digits that represent the years of the estimated life of the asset. The calculation of the **sum-of-the-years'-digits** for our delivery van with a five-year useful life is shown below.

Sum-of-the-Years'-Digits = 5 + 4 + 3 + 2 + 1 = 15

A depreciation schedule using these fractions is shown in Figure 5A-2.

FIGURE 5A-2 Depreciation Schedule Using Sum-of-the-Years'-Digits Method

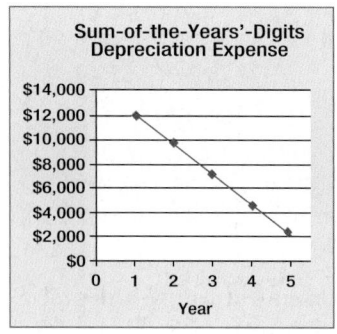

Sum-of-the-Years'-Digits Depreciation Expense

SUM-OF-THE-YEARS'-DIGITS

Year	Depreciable Cost	×	Rate	=	Depreciation Expense	Accumulated Depreciation (End of Year)	Book Value (End of Year)
1	$36,000		5/15		$12,000	$12,000	$28,000
2	36,000		4/15		9,600	21,600	18,400
3	36,000		3/15		7,200	28,800	11,200
4	36,000		2/15		4,800	33,600	6,400
5	36,000		1/15		2,400	36,000	4,000

Cost	$40,000
− Salvage Value	4,000
Depreciable Cost	$36,000

Remaining life from
beginning of period
SYD

Expense gets smaller each year

Accum. Depr. increases by amount of current year's depreciation expense.

Cost
− Accum. Depr.
Book Value

DOUBLE-DECLINING-BALANCE METHOD

LO3 Prepare a depreciation schedule using the double-declining-balance method.

Under the **double-declining-balance depreciation method**, the book value is multiplied by a fixed rate, often double the straight-line rate. The van has a five-year life, so the straight-line rate is 1 ÷ 5, or 20%. Double the straight-line rate is 2 × 20%, or 40%. The double-declining-balance depreciation schedule is shown in Figure 5A-3. Note that the rate is applied to the book value of the asset. Once the book value is reduced to the expected salvage value, $4,000, no more depreciation may be recognized.

FIGURE 5A-3   Depreciation Schedule Using Double-Declining-Balance Method

DOUBLE-DECLINING-BALANCE METHOD

Year	Book Value (Beginning of Year)	× Rate =	Depreciation Expense	Accumulated Depreciation (End of Year)	Book Value (End of Year)
1	$40,000	40%	$16,000	$16,000	$24,000
2	24,000	40%	9,600	25,600	14,400
3	14,400	40%	5,760	31,360	8,640
4	8,640	40%	3,456	34,816	5,184
5	5,184		1,184	36,000	4,000

Cost
− Accum.Depr.
Book Value

Double the Straight Line
Rate 1/5 x 2
= 2/5 = 40%

🔑 LEARNING KEY

Double means double the straight-line rate. Declining-balance means that the rate is multiplied by the *book value* (not depreciable cost) at the beginning of each year. This amount is *declining* each year.

MODIFIED ACCELERATED COST RECOVERY SYSTEM

LO4 Prepare a depreciation schedule for tax purposes using the Modified Accelerated Cost Recovery System.

For assets purchased since 1986, many firms use the **Modified Accelerated Cost Recovery System (MACRS)** for tax purposes. Under this method, the Internal Revenue Service (IRS) classifies various assets according to useful life and sets depreciation rates for each year of the asset's life. These rates are then multiplied by the cost of the asset. Even though the van is expected to have a useful life of five years, and a salvage value of $4,000, the IRS schedule, shown in Figure 5A-4, spreads the depreciation over a six-year period and assumes no salvage value.

FIGURE 5A-4   Depreciation Schedule Using Modified Accelerated Cost Recovery System

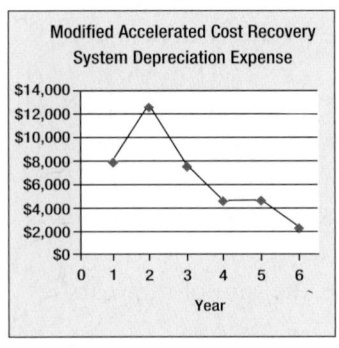

MODIFIED ACCELERATED COST RECOVERY SYSTEM

Year	Cost	× Rate =	Depreciation Expense	Accumulated Depreciation (End of Year)	Book Value (End of Year)
1	$40,000	20.00%	$ 8,000	$ 8,000	$32,000
2	40,000	32.00%	12,800	20,800	19,200
3	40,000	19.20%	7,680	28,480	11,520
4	40,000	11.52%	4,608	33,088	6,912
5	40,000	11.52%	4,608	37,696	2,304
6	40,000	5.76%	2,304	40,000	0

Rate set by
IRS

Cost
−Accum. Depr.
Book Value

LEARNING OBJECTIVES   Key Points to Remember

LO1 Prepare a depreciation schedule using the straight-line method.	Under straight-line depreciation, an equal amount of depreciation is taken each period. Depreciation expense for each year is computed as follows:

Cost – Salvage Value = Depreciable Cost/Expected Years of Life = Depreciation Expense per Year

LO2 Prepare a depreciation schedule using the sum-of-the-years'-digits method.

Under the sum-of-the-years'-digits method, the depreciable cost is multiplied by a fraction. The fraction consists of the following:

$$\frac{\text{Remaining Years of Life Measured from the Beginning of the Current Year}}{\text{Sum-of-the-Years'-Digits}}$$

If an asset has a life of three years, the sum-of-the-years'-digits is equal to:

$$3 + 2 + 1 = 6$$

Depreciation would be computed as follows:

Year 1: 3/6 × Depreciable Cost
Year 2: 2/6 × Depreciable Cost
Year 3: 1/6 × Depreciable Cost

LO3 Prepare a depreciation schedule using the double-declining-balance method.

Under this method, the book value (the declining balance) is multiplied by a fixed rate, often double the straight-line rate.

LO4 Prepare a depreciation schedule for tax purposes using the Modified Accelerated Cost Recovery System.

Under this method, the IRS provides the depreciation rates to be applied to the cost of the asset. Simply multiply the rate provided by the IRS by the cost of the asset.

KEY TERMS

double-declining-balance depreciation method (177) A depreciation method that recognizes depreciation each year by multiplying a rate (typically double the straight-line rate) by the book value of the asset.

Modified Accelerated Cost Recovery System (MACRS) (177) A depreciation method in which rates determined by the IRS are multiplied by the cost of the asset to determine depreciation expense for the year.

straight-line depreciation method (175) A depreciation method that recognizes an equal amount of depreciation each year.

sum-of-the-years'-digits (176) If an asset has a five-year life, the sum-of-the-years'-digits is computed as follows: 5 + 4 + 3 + 2 + 1 = 15.

sum-of-the-years'-digits depreciation method (176) A depreciation method that recognizes depreciation each year by multiplying a fraction by the depreciable cost. The numerator of the fraction is the remaining life of the asset, measured from the beginning of the year. The denominator is the sum-of-the-years'-digits.

REVIEW QUESTIONS

1. List three depreciation methods used for financial reporting.

2. Which depreciation method is used for tax purposes?

SERIES A EXERCISES

E 5Apx-1A (LO1)
✓ Accum. depr. end of Yr. 2:
$10,000

STRAIGHT-LINE DEPRECIATION A small delivery truck was purchased on January 1 at a cost of $25,000. It has an estimated useful life of four years and an estimated salvage value of $5,000. Prepare a depreciation schedule showing the depreciation expense, accumulated depreciation, and book value for each year under the straight-line method.

E 5Apx-2A (LO2)
✓ Accum. depr. end of Yr. 2:
$14,000

SUM-OF-THE-YEARS'-DIGITS DEPRECIATION Using the information given in Exercise 5Apx-1A, prepare a depreciation schedule showing the depreciation expense, accumulated depreciation, and book value for each year under the sum-of-the-years'-digits method.

E 5Apx-3A (LO3)
✓ Accum. depr. end of Yr. 2:
$18,750

DOUBLE-DECLINING-BALANCE DEPRECIATION Using the information given in Exercise 5Apx-1A, prepare a depreciation schedule showing the depreciation expense, accumulated depreciation, and book value for each year under the double-declining-balance method.

E 5Apx-4A (LO4)
✓ Accum. depr. end of Yr. 2:
$13,000

MODIFIED ACCELERATED COST RECOVERY SYSTEM Using the information given in Exercise 5Apx-1A and the rates shown in Figure 5A-4, prepare a depreciation schedule showing the depreciation expense, accumulated depreciation, and book value for each year under the Modified Accelerated Cost Recovery System. For tax purposes, assume that the truck has a useful life of five years. (The IRS schedule will spread depreciation over six years.)

SERIES B EXERCISES

E 5Apx-1B (LO1)
✓ Accum. depr. end of Yr. 2:
$1,800

STRAIGHT-LINE DEPRECIATION A computer was purchased on January 1 at a cost of $5,000. It has an estimated useful life of five years and an estimated salvage value of $500. Prepare a depreciation schedule showing the depreciation expense, accumulated depreciation, and book value for each year under the straight-line method.

E 5Apx-2B (LO2)
✓ Accum. depr. end of Yr. 2:
$2,700

SUM-OF-THE-YEARS'-DIGITS DEPRECIATION Using the information given in Exercise 5Apx-1B, prepare a depreciation schedule showing the depreciation expense, accumulated depreciation, and book value for each year under the sum-of-the-years'-digits method.

E 5Apx-3B (LO3)
✓ Accum. depr. end of Yr. 2:
$3,200

DOUBLE-DECLINING-BALANCE DEPRECIATION Using the information given in Exercise 5Apx-1B, prepare a depreciation schedule showing the depreciation expense, accumulated depreciation, and book value for each year under the double-declining-balance method.

E 5Apx-4B (LO4)
✓ Accum. depr. end of Yr. 2:
$2,600

MODIFIED ACCELERATED COST RECOVERY SYSTEM Using the information given in Exercise 5Apx-1B and the rates shown in Figure 5A-4, prepare a depreciation schedule showing the depreciation expense, accumulated depreciation, and book value for each year under the Modified Accelerated Cost Recovery System. For tax purposes, assume that the computer has a useful life of five years. (The IRS schedule will spread depreciation over six years.)

Chapter 6

LEARNING OBJECTIVES

Careful study of this chapter should enable you to:

LO1 Prepare financial statements with the aid of a work sheet.

LO2 Journalize and post closing entries.

LO3 Prepare a post-closing trial balance.

LO4 List and describe the steps in the accounting cycle.

Financial Statements and the Closing Process

Indy Express Band is central Indiana's premier variety band. It offers a popular mix of musical styles from Top 40 to Big Band. The eight-piece band is led by Greg Imboden, fronted by Cozette Myers, driven by a three-piece horn section, and backed by a tight rhythm section. The **Indy Express Band is** perfect for a wedding reception, corporate function, conference event, dinner dance, or charity ball. Members of Indy Express Band have provided music for entertainers such as Jay Leno, Rod Stewart, Natalie Cole, Dionne Warwick, and Al Jarreau.

In addition to playing at Jessie Jane's wedding and other events, the band generally performs on New Year's Eve, the same day many businesses prepare closing entries. In this chapter, we complete the accounting cycle by demonstrating how to make closing entries and prepare the Post-Closing Trial Balance.

The work sheet, introduced in Chapter 5, is used for three major end-of-period activities:

1. journalizing adjusting entries,

2. preparing financial statements, and

3. journalizing closing entries.

This chapter illustrates the use of the work sheet for preparing financial statements and closing entries. In addition, the post-closing trial balance is explained and illustrated. All of these activities take place at the end of the firm's fiscal year. However, to continue our illustration of Jessie Jane's Campus Delivery Service, we demonstrate these activities at the end of the first month of operations.

THE FINANCIAL STATEMENTS

LO1 Prepare financial statements with the aid of a work sheet.

The work sheet prepared in Chapter 5 supplies most of the information needed to prepare an income statement, a statement of owner's equity, and a balance sheet. The statements and work sheet columns from which they are derived for Jessie Jane's Campus Delivery Service are shown in Figures 6-1 and 6-2.

As you refer to the financial statements in Figures 6-1 and 6-2, notice the placement of dollar signs, single rulings, and double rulings. Dollar signs are placed at the top of each column and beneath rulings. Single rulings indicate addition or subtraction, and double rulings are placed under totals. Notice that each statement heading contains three lines: (1) company name, (2) statement title, and (3) period ended or date.

THE INCOME STATEMENT

Multiple columns are used on the financial statements to make them easier to read. There are no debit or credit columns on the financial statements.

Figure 6-1 shows how the Income Statement columns of the work sheet provide the information needed to prepare an income statement. Revenue is shown first, followed by an itemized and totaled list of expenses. Then, net income is calculated to double check the accuracy of the work sheet. It is presented with a double ruling as the last item in the statement.

The expenses could be listed in the same order that they appear in the chart of accounts or in descending order by dollar amount. The second approach helps the reader identify the most important expenses.

THE STATEMENT OF OWNER'S EQUITY

LEARNING KEY

The owner's capital account in the general ledger must be reviewed to determine if additional investments were made during the accounting period.

The Balance Sheet columns of the work sheet provide most of the information needed to prepare a statement of owner's equity. Figure 6-2 shows that Jessie's capital account balance and the drawing account balance are in the Balance Sheet columns. Be careful, however, when using the capital account balance reported on the work sheet. This account balance is the beginning balance *plus any investments made during the period*. Recall that Jessie's beginning capital balance was zero. During June, she made an investment of $2,000. Thus, as reported previously, the beginning balance on the statement of owner's equity must be zero with the $2,000 reported as an investment during June. The net income for the month can be found either on the work sheet at the bottom of the Income Statement (see Figure 6-1) and Balance Sheet columns or on the income statement itself. With these items of information, the statement of owner's equity can be prepared.

FIGURE 6-1 Linkages Between the Work Sheet and Income Statement

	Jessie Jane's Campus Delivery Service Work Sheet (Partial) For Month Ended June 30, 20 - -				
	ACCOUNT TITLE	INCOME STATEMENT			
		DEBIT		CREDIT	
1	Cash				
2	Accounts Receivable				
3	Supplies				
4	Prepaid Insurance				
5	Delivery Equipment				
6	Accum. Depr.—Delivery Equipment				
7	Accounts Payable				
8	Wages Payable				
9	Jessica Jane, Capital				
10	Jessica Jane, Drawing				
11	Delivery Fees			2 1 5 0 00	
12	Wages Expense	7 0 0 00			
13	Rent Expense	2 0 0 00			
14	Supplies Expense	6 0 00			
15	Telephone Expense	5 0 00			
16	Insurance Expense	2 5 00			
17	Depr. Expense—Delivery Equipment	1 0 0 00			
18		1 1 3 5 00		2 1 5 0 00	
19	Net Income	1 0 1 5 00			
20		2 1 5 0 00		2 1 5 0 00	
21					
22					
23					

Formatting Reminders:
Statement Heading
   Name of company
   Title of statement
   Accounting period ended
Revenues listed first
Expenses listed second by amount (largest to smallest), or in chart of accounts order. Amounts are itemized in left column, subtotaled in right column.

Prepare Income Statement First

Jessie Jane's Campus Delivery Service Income Statement For Month Ended June 30, 20 --		
Revenue:		
Delivery fees		$ 2 1 5 0 00
Expenses:		
Wages expense	$ 7 0 0 00	
Rent expense	2 0 0 00	
Supplies expense	6 0 00	
Telephone expense	5 0 00	
Insurance expense	2 5 00	
Depr. expense—delivery equip.	1 0 0 00	
Total expenses		1 1 3 5 00
Net income		$ 1 0 1 5 00

Dollar signs used at top of columns and under rulings.
Single rulings indicate addition or subtraction.
Double rulings indicate totals.

THE BALANCE SHEET

As shown in Figure 6-2, the work sheet and the statement of owner's equity are used to prepare Jessie's balance sheet. The asset and liability amounts can be found in the Balance Sheet columns of the work sheet. The ending balance in Jessica Jane, Capital has been computed on the statement of owner's equity. This amount should be copied from the statement of owner's equity to the balance sheet.

Two important features of the balance sheet in Figure 6-2 should be noted. First, it is a **report form of balance sheet**, which means that the liabilities and owner's equity sections are shown below the assets section. It differs from an **account form of balance sheet** in which the assets are on the left and the liabilities and owner's equity sections are on the right. (See Jessie's balance sheet illustrated in Figure 2-2 on page 32 in Chapter 2.)

Second, it is a **classified balance sheet**, which means that similar items are grouped together on the balance sheet. Assets are classified as current assets and property, plant, and equipment. Similarly, liabilities are broken down into current and long-term sections. The following major balance sheet classifications are generally used.

FIGURE 6-2 Linkages Between the Work Sheet, Statement of Owner's Equity, and Balance Sheet

Statement Heading
   Name of company
   Title of statement
   Accounting period ended
Current assets: cash and items that will be converted to cash or consumed within a year.
Property, plant, and equipment: durable assets that will help produce revenues for several years.
Current liabilities: amounts owed that will be paid within a year (will require the use of current assets).

Note: The statement of owner's equity is prepared before the balance sheet. The S.O.E. is shown below the B.S. to enhance the illustration of the linkages between the work sheet and financial statements.

Jessie Jane's Campus Delivery Service — Work Sheet (Partial) — For Month Ended June 30, 20 - -

	ACCOUNT TITLE	BALANCE SHEET DEBIT	BALANCE SHEET CREDIT
1	Cash	3 7 0 00	
2	Accounts Receivable	6 5 0 00	
3	Supplies	2 0 00	
4	Prepaid Insurance	1 7 5 00	
5	Delivery Equipment	3 6 0 0 00	
6	Accum. Depr.—Delivery Equip.		1 0 0 00
7	Accounts Payable		1 8 0 0 00
8	Wages Payable		5 0 00
9	Jessica Jane, Capital		2 0 0 0 00
10	Jessica Jane, Drawing	1 5 0 00	
11	Delivery Fees		
12	Wages Expense		
13	Rent Expense		
14	Supplies Expense		
15	Telephone Expense		
16	Insurance Expense		
17	Depr. Expense—Delivery Equip.		
18		4 9 6 5 00	3 9 5 0 00
19	Net Income		1 0 1 5 00
20		4 9 6 5 00	4 9 6 5 00
21			

Prepare BS Third

Jessie Jane's Campus Delivery Service — Balance Sheet — June 30, 20 --

Assets				
Current assets:				
Cash	$ 3 7 0 00			
Accounts receivable	6 5 0 00			
Supplies	2 0 00			
Prepaid insurance	1 7 5 00			
Total current assets			$ 1 2 1 5 00	
Property, plant, and equipment:				
Delivery equipment	$3 6 0 0 00			
Less accumulated depreciation	1 0 0 00		3 5 0 0 00	
Total assets			$ 4 7 1 5 00	
Liabilities				
Current liabilities:				
Accounts payable	$1 8 0 0 00			
Wages payable	5 0 00			
Total current liabilities			$ 1 8 5 0 00	
Owner's Equity				
Jessica Jane, capital			2 8 6 5 00	
Total liabilities and owner's equity			$ 4 7 1 5 00	

Prepare SOE Second

Jessie Jane's Campus Delivery Service — Statement of Owner's Equity — For Month Ended June 30, 20 --

Jessica Jane, capital, June 1, 20--		$	
Investments during June		2 0 0 0 00	
Total investment		$2 0 0 0 00	
Net income for June	$1 0 1 5 00		
Less: withdrawals for June	1 5 0 00		
Increase in capital		8 6 5 00	
Jessica Jane, capital, June 30, 20--		$2 8 6 5 00	

Ending capital is not taken from the work sheet. It is computed on the statement of owner's equity.
Dollar signs used at top of columns and under rulings.
Single rulings indicate addition or subtraction.
Double rulings indicate totals.

Current Assets

Current assets include cash and assets that will be converted into cash or consumed within either one year or the normal operating cycle of the business, whichever is longer. Examples include cash, accounts receivable, supplies, and prepaid insurance. As shown in Figure 6-3, an **operating cycle** is the period of time required to purchase supplies and services and convert them back into cash.

FIGURE 6-3 Operating Cycle

Operating Cycle for a Service Business

| Start with Cash | → | Purchase Supplies and Services | → | Provide Services for Cash and "On Account" | → | Collect Receivables | → | Back to Cash |

Property, Plant, and Equipment

Property, plant, and equipment, also called **plant assets** or **long-term assets,** represent assets that are expected to serve the business for many years. Examples include land, buildings, and equipment.

Current Liabilities

Current liabilities are due within either one year or the normal operating cycle of the business, whichever is longer. They will be paid out of current assets. Accounts payable and wages payable are classified as current liabilities.

Long-Term Liabilities

Long-term liabilities, or **long-term debt,** are obligations that are not expected to be paid within a year and do not require the use of current assets. A mortgage on an office building is an example of a long-term liability. Jessie has no long-term debts. If she did, they would be listed on the balance sheet in the long-term liabilities section immediately following the current liabilities.

ADDITIONAL INVESTMENTS BY THE OWNER (REVISITED)

If the owner of a business made additional investments during the accounting period, the owner's capital reported in the Balance Sheet columns of the work sheet represents the beginning balance plus any additional investments made during the accounting period. If this amount were used as the beginning balance on the statement of owner's equity, it would not equal the ending balance from last period and would create confusion for those comparing the two statements. In addition, the statement would not reflect all of the activities affecting the owner's capital account during the period.

Thus, we must also review the owner's capital account in the general ledger to get the information needed to prepare the statement of owner's equity. Figure 6-4 illustrates this situation for another business, Ramon's Shopping Service. The $5,000 balance of July 1, 20--, in Ramon Balboa's general ledger capital account is used as the beginning balance on the statement of owner's equity. Note that this is also the ending balance on June 30, 20--. The additional investment of $3,000 made on July 5 and posted to Balboa's general ledger capital account is reported by writing "Investments during period" on the line immediately after the beginning balance. The beginning

FIGURE 6-4 Statement of Owner's Equity with Additional Investment

GENERAL LEDGER

ACCOUNT: Ramon Balboa, Capital   ACCOUNT NO. 311

DATE		ITEM	POST. REF.	DEBIT	CREDIT	BALANCE DEBIT	BALANCE CREDIT
20-- July	1	Balance	J5		5 0 0 0 00		5 0 0 0 00
	5		J5		3 0 0 0 00		8 0 0 0 00

Additional investment

Amount reported on work sheet

Ramon's Shopping Service
Statement of Owner's Equity
For Months Ended June 30 and July 31, 20 - -

	June		July	
Ramon Balboa, beginning capital		$ 4 0 0 0 00		$ 5 0 0 0 00
Investments during period				3 0 0 0 00
Total investment				$ 8 0 0 0 00
Net income for the month	$ 1 5 0 0 00		$ 2 1 0 0 00	
Less withdrawals for the month	5 0 0 00		2 5 0 00	
Increase in capital		1 0 0 0 00		1 8 5 0 00
Ramon Balboa, ending capital		$ 5 0 0 0 00		$ 9 8 5 0 00

From general ledger

From work sheet

balance plus investments during the period equals the total investment by the owner in the business and is the amount reported in the Balance Sheet columns of the work sheet. From this point, the preparation of the statement is the same as for businesses without additional investments.

U REVU

Complete U REVU-1 on **page 199** to test your basic understanding of LO1.

THE CLOSING PROCESS

LO2 Journalize and post closing entries.

Assets, liabilities, and the owner's capital account accumulate information across accounting periods. For example, the cash balance at the end of one accounting period must be the same as the cash balance at the beginning of the next period. Thus, the balance reported for Cash is a result of all cash transactions since the business first opened. This is true for all accounts reported on the balance sheet. For this reason, they are called **permanent accounts**.

LEARNING KEY

Permanent accounts contain the results of all transactions since the business started. Their balances are carried forward to each new accounting period.

Revenue, expense, and drawing accounts accumulate information *for only a specific accounting period*. When preparing the financial statements, only revenues, expenses, and withdrawals for *this year* should be reported. Revenues, expenses, and withdrawals from prior years should not be included in *this year's* financial statements. Similarly, *this year's* revenues, expenses, and withdrawals should not be included in next year's financial statements. Thus, at the end of the fiscal year, these accounts must be *closed*. The **closing process** gives these accounts zero balances so they are prepared to accumulate new information for the next accounting period. Since these accounts are closed at the end of each period, they are called **temporary accounts**.

The accounting records are closed "as of" December 31, or another fiscal year-end chosen by the business. The actual adjusting entries, closing entries, and financial statements are generally prepared several weeks after the official closing date. However, it is important to include all transactions occurring prior to year-end in the *current* year's financial statements. Similarly, transactions taking place after year-end must be included in the *next* year's financial statements. Improper timing of the recognition of transactions taking place around the end of the year can have major effects on the reported profits. For example, some businesses have been found to "leave the books open" for a few days to include a major sale, or other profitable transactions, that actually took place after the end of the fiscal year. Thus, proper treatment of transactions taking place around the end of the year is carefully monitored by auditors.

The closing process is most clearly demonstrated by returning to the accounting equation and T accounts. As shown in Figure 6-5, revenue, expense, and drawing accounts impact owner's equity and should be considered "under the umbrella" of the capital account. The effect of these accounts on owner's equity is formalized at the end of the accounting period when the balances of the temporary accounts are transferred to the owner's capital account (a permanent account) during the closing process.

The four basic steps in the closing process are illustrated in Figure 6-5. As you can see, a new account, **Income Summary**, is used in the closing process. This account may also be called *Expense and Revenue Summary*. This temporary account is used to close the revenue and expense accounts. After closing the revenues and expenses to Income Summary, the balance of this account is equal to the net income. This is why it is called Income Summary. Income Summary is opened during the closing process. Then it is closed to the owner's capital account. It does not appear on any financial statement. The four steps in the closing process are explained on page 197.

FIGURE 6-5 The Closing Process

STEPS IN THE CLOSING PROCESS

Dashes are entered on the debit and credit sides of the T accounts to indicate a zero balance.

STEP 1 **Close Revenue Accounts to Income Summary.** Revenues have credit balances and increase owner's equity. Therefore, the revenue account is debited to create a zero balance. Income Summary is credited for the same amount.

STEP 2 **Close Expense Accounts to Income Summary.** Expenses have debit balances and reduce owner's equity. Therefore, the expense accounts are credited to create a zero balance. Income Summary must be debited for the total of the expenses.

STEP 3 **Close Income Summary to the Owner's Capital Account.** The balance in Income Summary represents the net income (credit balance) or net loss (debit balance). If net income has been earned, Income Summary is debited to create a zero balance, and the owner's capital account is credited. If a net loss has been incurred, the owner's capital account is debited and Income Summary is credited to create a zero balance. Figure 6-6 shows examples for closing net income and net loss.

FIGURE 6-6 Step 3: Closing Net Income and Closing Net Loss

NET INCOME			
Capital			
		1,000	STEP 3
			(Net Income)
Income Summary			
(Expenses)	4,000	5,000	(Revenues)
STEP 3 to close	1,000	1,000	(Bal. before closing)
	—	—	

NET LOSS			
Capital			
STEP 3	2,000		
(Net Loss)			
Income Summary			
(Expenses)	6,000	4,000	(Revenues)
(Bal. before closing)	2,000	2,000	STEP 3 to close
	—	—	

LEARNING KEY

The owner can make withdrawals from the business at any time, as long as the assets are available. These withdrawals have nothing to do with measuring the profitability of the firm. Thus, they are closed directly to the owner's capital account.

STEP 4 **Close Drawing to the Owner's Capital Account.** Drawing has a debit balance and reduces owner's equity. Therefore, it is credited to create a zero balance. The owner's capital account is debited.

Upon completion of these four steps, all temporary accounts have zero balances. The earnings and withdrawals for the period have been transferred to the owner's capital account. Closing entries for Jessie Jane's Campus Delivery Service, in T account form, are illustrated in Figure 6-7.

JOURNALIZE CLOSING ENTRIES

Of course, to actually change the ledger accounts, the closing entries must be journalized and posted to the general ledger. As shown in Figure 6-8, the balances of the accounts to be closed are readily available from the Income Statement and Balance Sheet columns of the work sheet. These balances are used to illustrate the closing entries for Jessie Jane's Campus Delivery Service, in general journal form. Remember: Closing entries are made at the end of the *fiscal year*. Closing entries made at the end of June are illustrated here so you can see the completion of the accounting cycle for Jessie Jane's Campus Delivery Service. Like adjusting entries, the closing entries are made on the last day of the accounting period. "Closing Entries" is written in the Description column before the first entry and no explanations are required. Note that it is best to make one compound entry to close the expense accounts.

FIGURE 6-7 Closing Entries in T Account Form

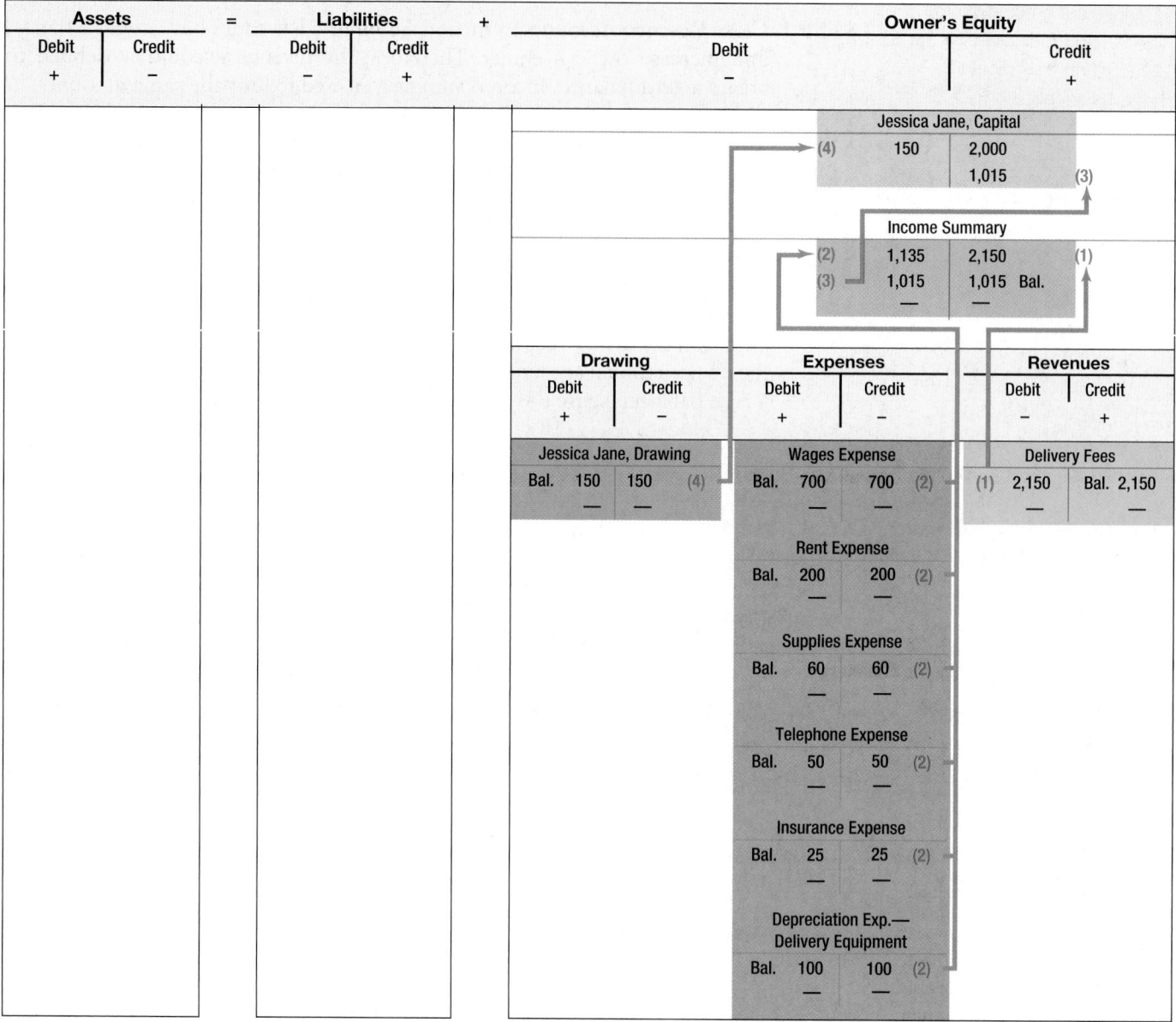

Dashes (—) in the T Accounts indicate zero balances

POST THE CLOSING ENTRIES

Computer programs post the closing entries to the owner's capital account automatically.

The account numbers have been entered in the Posting Reference column of the journal to show that the entries have been posted to the ledger accounts illustrated in Figure 6-9. Note that "Closing" has been written in the Item column of each account to identify the closing entries. Zero account balances are recorded by entering dashes in both the Balance Debit and Credit columns.

FIGURE 6-8 Closing Entries in Journal Form

LEARNING KEY

Each individual revenue, expense, and drawing account must be closed.

FIGURE 6-9 Closing Entries Posted to the General Ledger

FIGURE 6-9 Closing Entries Posted to the General Ledger (continued)

ACCOUNT: Income Summary ACCOUNT NO. 313

DATE		ITEM	POST. REF.	DEBIT	CREDIT	BALANCE DEBIT	BALANCE CREDIT
20-- June	30	Closing	J4		2 1 5 0 00		2 1 5 0 00
	30	Closing	J4	1 1 3 5 00			1 0 1 5 00
	30	Closing	J4	1 0 1 5 00			

ACCOUNT: Delivery Fees ACCOUNT NO. 401

DATE		ITEM	POST. REF.	DEBIT	CREDIT	BALANCE DEBIT	BALANCE CREDIT
20-- June	6		J1		5 0 0 00		5 0 0 00
	15		J1		6 0 0 00		1 1 0 0 00
	30		J2		1 0 5 0 00		2 1 5 0 00
	30	Closing	J4	2 1 5 0 00			

ACCOUNT: Wages Expense ACCOUNT NO. 511

DATE		ITEM	POST. REF.	DEBIT	CREDIT	BALANCE DEBIT	BALANCE CREDIT
20-- June	27		J2	6 5 0 00		6 5 0 00	
	30	Adjusting	J3	5 0 00		7 0 0 00	
	30	Closing	J4		7 0 0 00		

ACCOUNT: Rent Expense ACCOUNT NO. 521

DATE		ITEM	POST. REF.	DEBIT	CREDIT	BALANCE DEBIT	BALANCE CREDIT
20-- June	7		J1	2 0 0 00		2 0 0 00	
	30	Closing	J4		2 0 0 00		

ACCOUNT: Supplies Expense ACCOUNT NO. 523

DATE		ITEM	POST. REF.	DEBIT	CREDIT	BALANCE DEBIT	BALANCE CREDIT
20-- June	30	Adjusting	J3	6 0 00		6 0 00	
	30	Closing	J4		6 0 00		

ACCOUNT: Telephone Expense ACCOUNT NO. 525

DATE		ITEM	POST. REF.	DEBIT	CREDIT	BALANCE DEBIT	BALANCE CREDIT
20-- June	15		J1	5 0 00		5 0 00	
	30	Closing	J4		5 0 00		

ACCOUNT: Insurance Expense ACCOUNT NO. 535

DATE		ITEM	POST. REF.	DEBIT	CREDIT	BALANCE DEBIT	BALANCE CREDIT
20-- June	30	Adjusting	J3	2 5 00		2 5 00	
	30	Closing	J4		2 5 00		

FIGURE 6-9 Closing Entries Posted to the General Ledger *(concluded)*

ACCOUNT: Depreciation Expense—Delivery Equipment										ACCOUNT NO. 541		
DATE	ITEM	POST. REF.	DEBIT		CREDIT		BALANCE					
							DEBIT			CREDIT		
20-- June 30	Adjusting	J3	1 0 0 00				1 0 0 00					
30	Closing	J4			1 0 0 00							

U REVU   Complete U REVU-2 on **page 199** to test your basic understanding of LO2.

POST-CLOSING TRIAL BALANCE

LO3 Prepare a post-closing trial balance.

After posting the closing entries, a **post-closing trial balance** should be prepared to prove the equality of the debit and credit balances in the general ledger accounts. The ending balance of each general ledger account that remains open at the end of the year is listed. Remember: Only the permanent accounts remain open after the closing process is completed. Figure 6-10 shows the post-closing trial balance for Jessie's ledger.

LEARNING KEY

Once the closing entries are posted, the general ledger capital account balance will agree with the amount reported on the balance sheet.

Note that all amounts reflected on the post-closing trial balance are the same as reported in the Balance Sheet columns of the work sheet except Drawing and Owner's Capital. Drawing was closed. Owner's Capital was updated to reflect revenues, expenses, and drawing for the accounting period.

FIGURE 6-10 Post-Closing Trial Balance

Jessie Jane's Campus Delivery Service
Post-Closing Trial Balance
June 30, 20 - -

ACCOUNT TITLE	ACCOUNT NO.	DEBIT BALANCE	CREDIT BALANCE
Cash	101	3 7 0 00	
Accounts Receivable	122	6 5 0 00	
Supplies	141	2 0 00	
Prepaid Insurance	145	1 7 5 00	
Delivery Equipment	185	3 6 0 0 00	
Accumulated Depreciation—Delivery Equipment	185.1		1 0 0 00
Accounts Payable	202		1 8 0 0 00
Wages Payable	219		5 0 00
Jessica Jane, Capital	311		2 8 6 5 00
		4 8 1 5 00	4 8 1 5 00

U REVU   Complete U REVU-3 on **page 199** to test your basic understanding of LO3.

A BROADER VIEW

Importance of Earnings to the Stock Market

Investors in the stock market pay close attention to earnings reported on the income statement. This information is so important that corporate officials often announce expected earnings before the financial statements are actually distributed to the public. If the announcement is different from what investors are expecting, the price of the stock may go up or down. For example, when Aetna, a leader in the managed health care industry, warned that earnings would be about 27% lower than expected by stock analysts, its stock price fell more than 10%.

THE ACCOUNTING CYCLE

LO4 List and describe the steps in the accounting cycle.

The steps involved in accounting for all of the business activities during an accounting period are called the **accounting cycle**. The cycle begins with the analysis of source documents and ends with a post-closing trial balance. A brief summary of the steps in the cycle follows.

STEPS IN THE ACCOUNTING CYCLE

During Accounting Period

STEP 1   Analyze source documents.

STEP 2   Journalize the transactions.

STEP 3   Post to the general ledger accounts.

End of Accounting Period

STEP 4   Prepare a trial balance.

STEP 5   Determine and prepare the needed adjustments on the work sheet.

STEP 6   Complete an end-of-period work sheet.

STEP 7   Journalize and post the adjusting entries.

STEP 8   Prepare an income statement, a statement of owner's equity, and a balance sheet.

STEP 9   Journalize and post the closing entries.

STEP 10   Prepare a post-closing trial balance.

Steps 4 through 10 in the preceding list are performed *as of* the last day of the accounting period. This does not mean that they are actually done on the last day. The accountant may not be able to do any of these things until the first few days (sometimes weeks) of the next period. Nevertheless, the work sheet, statements, and entries are prepared as of the closing date.

LEARNING KEY

Properly analyzing and journalizing transactions is very important. A mistake made in step 1 is carried through the entire accounting cycle.

LEARNING OBJECTIVES   Key Points to Remember

LO1 Prepare financial statements with the aid of a work sheet.

The work sheet is used as an aid in preparing:
1. adjusting entries,
2. financial statements, and
3. closing entries.

The following classifications are used for accounts reported on the balance sheet.

- *Current assets* include cash and assets that will be converted into cash or consumed within either one year or the normal operating cycle of the business, whichever is longer. An *operating cycle* is the time required to purchase supplies and services and convert them back into cash.
- *Property, plant, and equipment*, also called *plant assets* or *long-term assets*, represent assets that are expected to serve the business for many years.
- *Current liabilities* are liabilities that are due within either one year or the normal operating cycle of the business, whichever is longer, and that are to be paid out of current assets.
- *Long-term liabilities*, or *long-term debt*, are obligations that are not expected to be paid within a year and do not require the use of current assets.

LO2 Journalize and post closing entries.

Steps in the closing process are:
1. Close revenue accounts to Income Summary.
2. Close expense accounts to Income Summary.
3. Close Income Summary to the owner's capital account.
4. Close Drawing to the owner's capital account.

LEARNING OBJECTIVES   Key Points to Remember

LO3 Prepare a post-closing trial balance.	After posting the closing entries, a post-closing trial balance should be prepared to prove the equality of the debit and credit balances in the general ledger accounts. The accounts shown in the post-closing trial balance are the permanent accounts.
LO4 List and describe the steps in the accounting cycle.	Steps in the accounting cycle are: *During Accounting Period* 1. Analyze source documents. 2. Journalize the transactions. 3. Post to the general ledger accounts. *End of Accounting Period* 4. Prepare a trial balance. 5. Determine and prepare the needed adjustments on the work sheet. 6. Complete an end-of-period work sheet. 7. Journalize and post the adjusting entries. 8. Prepare an income statement, a statement of owner's equity, and a balance sheet. 9. Journalize and post the closing entries. 10. Prepare a post-closing trial balance.

DEMONSTRATION PROBLEM

Timothy Chang owns and operates Hard Copy Printers. A work sheet for the year ended December 31, 20--, is provided on the next page. Chang made no additional investments during the year.

REQUIRED

1.   Prepare financial statements.

2.   Prepare closing entries.

Hard Copy Printers
Work Sheet
For Year Ended December 31, 20--

	ACCOUNT TITLE	TRIAL BALANCE DEBIT	TRIAL BALANCE CREDIT	ADJUSTMENTS DEBIT	ADJUSTMENTS CREDIT	ADJUSTED TRIAL BALANCE DEBIT	ADJUSTED TRIAL BALANCE CREDIT	INCOME STATEMENT DEBIT	INCOME STATEMENT CREDIT	BALANCE SHEET DEBIT	BALANCE SHEET CREDIT	
1	Cash	1 1 8 0 00				1 1 8 0 00				1 1 8 0 00		1
2	Paper Supplies	3 6 0 0 00			(a) 3 5 5 0 00	5 0 00				5 0 00		2
3	Prepaid Insurance	1 0 0 0 00			(b) 5 0 5 00	4 9 5 00				4 9 5 00		3
4	Printing Equipment	5 8 0 0 00				5 8 0 0 00				5 8 0 0 00		4
5	Accum. Depr.—Printing Equipment				(d) 1 2 0 0 00		1 2 0 0 00				1 2 0 0 00	5
6	Accounts Payable		5 0 0 00				5 0 0 00				5 0 0 00	6
7	Wages Payable				(c) 3 0 00		3 0 00				3 0 00	7
8	Timothy Chang, Capital		1 0 0 0 0 00				1 0 0 0 0 00				1 0 0 0 0 00	8
9	Timothy Chang, Drawing	1 3 0 0 0 00				1 3 0 0 0 00				1 3 0 0 0 00		9
10	Printing Fees		3 5 1 0 0 00				3 5 1 0 0 00		3 5 1 0 0 00			10
11	Wages Expense	1 1 9 7 0 00		(c) 3 0 00		1 2 0 0 0 00		1 2 0 0 0 00				11
12	Rent Expense	7 5 0 0 00				7 5 0 0 00		7 5 0 0 00				12
13	Paper Supplies Expense			(a) 3 5 5 0 00		3 5 5 0 00		3 5 5 0 00				13
14	Telephone Expense	5 5 0 00				5 5 0 00		5 5 0 00				14
15	Utilities Expense	1 0 0 0 00				1 0 0 0 00		1 0 0 0 00				15
16	Insurance Expense			(b) 5 0 5 00		5 0 5 00		5 0 5 00				16
17	Depr. Expense—Printing Equipment			(d) 1 2 0 0 00		1 2 0 0 00		1 2 0 0 00				17
18		4 5 6 0 0 00	4 5 6 0 0 00	5 2 8 5 00	5 2 8 5 00	4 6 8 3 0 00	4 6 8 3 0 00	2 6 3 0 5 00	3 5 1 0 0 00	2 0 5 2 5 00	1 1 7 3 0 00	18
19	Net Income							8 7 9 5 00			8 7 9 5 00	19
20								3 5 1 0 0 00	3 5 1 0 0 00	2 0 5 2 5 00	2 0 5 2 5 00	20
21												21
22												22
23												23
24												24
25												25
26												26
27												27
28												28
29												29
30												30

(continued)

Solution 1.

Hard Copy Printers
Income Statement
For Year Ended December 31, 20 --

Revenue:									
Printing fees						$ 35	1	0 0	00
Expenses:									
Wages expense	$ 12	0	0 0	00					
Rent expense	7	5	0 0	00					
Paper supplies expense	3	5	5 0	00					
Telephone expense		5	5 0	00					
Utilities expense	1	0	0 0	00					
Insurance expense		5	0 5	00					
Depreciation expense—printing equipment	1	2	0 0	00					
Total expenses						26	3	0 5	00
Net income						$ 8	7	9 5	00

Hard Copy Printers
Statement of Owner's Equity
For Year Ended December 31, 20 --

Timothy Chang, capital, January 1, 20 - -						$ 10	0	0 0	00
Net income for 20 - -	$ 8	7	9 5	00					
Less withdrawals for 20 - -	13	0	0 0	00					
Decrease in capital						(4	2	0 5	00)
Timothy Chang, capital, December 31, 20 - -						$ 5	7	9 5	00

Hard Copy Printers
Balance Sheet
December 31, 20 - -

Assets									
Current assets:									
Cash	$ 1	1	8 0	00					
Paper supplies			5 0	00					
Prepaid insurance		4	9 5	00					
Total current assets						$ 1	7	2 5	00
Property, plant, and equipment:									
Printing equipment	$ 5	8	0 0	00					
Less accumulated depreciation	1	2	0 0	00		4	6	0 0	00
Total assets						$ 6	3	2 5	00
Liabilities									
Current liabilities:									
Accounts payable	$	5	0 0	00					
Wages payable			3 0	00					
Total current liabilities						$	5	3 0	00
Owner's Equity									
Timothy Chang, capital							5	7 9 5	00
Total liabilities and owner's equity						$ 6	3	2 5	00

2.

	DATE		DESCRIPTION	POST. REF.	DEBIT					CREDIT					
1			Closing Entries												1
2	20-- Dec.	31	Printing Fees		35	1	0	0	00						2
3			Income Summary							35	1	0	0	00	3
4															4
5		31	Income Summary		26	3	0	5	00						5
6			Wages Expense							12	0	0	0	00	6
7			Rent Expense							7	5	0	0	00	7
8			Paper Supplies Expense							3	5	5	0	00	8
9			Telephone Expense								5	5	0	00	9
10			Utilities Expense							1	0	0	0	00	10
11			Insurance Expense								5	0	5	00	11
12			Depr. Expense—Printing Equipment							1	2	0	0	00	12
13															13
14		31	Income Summary		8	7	9	5	00						14
15			Timothy Chang, Capital							8	7	9	5	00	15
16															16
17		31	Timothy Chang, Capital		13	0	0	0	00						17
18			Timothy Chang, Drawing							13	0	0	0	00	18
19															19

GENERAL JOURNAL PAGE 4

KEY TERMS

account form of balance sheet (182) A balance sheet in which the assets are on the left and the liabilities and the owner's equity sections are on the right.

accounting cycle (192) The steps involved in accounting for all of the business activities during an accounting period.

classified balance sheet (182) A balance sheet with separate categories for current assets; property, plant, and equipment; current liabilities; and long-term liabilities.

closing process (185) The process of giving zero balances to the temporary accounts so that they can accumulate information for the next accounting period.

current assets (184) Cash and assets that will be converted into cash or consumed within either one year or the normal operating cycle of the business, whichever is longer.

current liabilities (184) Liabilities that are due within either one year or the normal operating cycle of the business, whichever is longer, and that are to be paid out of current assets.

Income Summary (186) A temporary account used in the closing process to summarize the effects of all revenue and expense accounts.

long-term assets (184) See property, plant, and equipment.

long-term debt (184) See long-term liabilities.

long-term liabilities (184) Obligations that are not expected to be paid within a year and do not require the use of current assets. Also called long-term debt.

operating cycle (184)   The period of time required to purchase supplies and services and convert them back into cash.

permanent accounts (185)   Accounts that accumulate information across accounting periods; all accounts reported on the balance sheet.

plant assets (184)   See property, plant, and equipment.

post-closing trial balance (191)   Prepared after posting the closing entries to prove the equality of the debit and credit balances in the general ledger accounts.

property, plant, and equipment (184)   Assets that are expected to serve the business for many years. Also called plant assets or long-term assets.

report form of balance sheet (182)   A balance sheet in which the liabilities and the owner's equity sections are shown below the assets section.

temporary accounts (185)   Accounts that do not accumulate information across accounting periods but are closed, such as the drawing account and all income statement accounts.

SELF-STUDY QUESTIONS AND EXERCISES

True/False Questions

1. **LO1**   Expenses are listed on the income statement as they appear in the chart of accounts or in descending order (by dollar amount).

2. **LO1**   Additional investments of capital during the month are not reported on the statement of owner's equity.

3. **LO1**   The income statement cannot be prepared using the work sheet alone.

4. **LO1**   A classified balance sheet groups similar items, such as current assets together.

5. **LO2**   Temporary accounts are closed at the end of each accounting period.

Multiple Choice Questions

1. **LO2**   Which of these types of accounts is considered a "permanent" account?

   (a) Revenue
   (b) Asset
   (c) Drawing
   (d) Expense

2. **LO2**   Which of these accounts is considered a "temporary" account?

   (a) Cash
   (b) Accounts Payable
   (c) J. Jones, Capital
   (d) J. Jones, Drawing

3. **LO2**   Which of these is the first step in the closing process?

   (a) Close revenue account(s).
   (b) Close expense accounts.
   (c) Close the income summary account.
   (d) Close the drawing account.

4. **LO3**   The _____ is prepared after closing entries are posted to prove the equality of debit and credit balances.

   (a) balance sheet
   (b) income statement
   (c) post-closing trial balance
   (d) statement of owner's equity

5. **LO4**   Steps that begin with analyzing source documents and conclude with the post-closing trial balance are called the

   (a) closing process.
   (b) accounting cycle.
   (c) adjusting entries.
   (d) posting process.

U REVU Exercises

1. **LO1** Joe Fisher operates Fisher Consulting. A partial work sheet for August 20-- is provided below. Fisher made no additional investments during the month. Prepare an income statement, statement of owner's equity, and balance sheet.

Fisher Consulting
Work Sheet (Partial)
For Month Ended August 31, 20- -

	ACCOUNT TITLE	INCOME STATEMENT DEBIT	INCOME STATEMENT CREDIT	BALANCE SHEET DEBIT	BALANCE SHEET CREDIT	
1	Cash			2 5 0 0 00		1
2	Accounts Receivable			8 0 0 00		2
3	Equipment			3 8 0 0 00		3
4	Accum. Depr.— Equipment				2 0 0 00	4
5	Accounts Payable				1 0 0 0 00	5
6	Joe Fisher, Capital				3 0 0 0 00	6
7	Joe Fisher, Drawing			3 0 0 00		7
8	Professional Fees		5 0 0 0 00			8
9	Wages Expense	1 0 0 0 00				9
10	Rent Expense	7 0 0 00				10
11	Depreciation Expense	1 0 0 00				11
12	Net Income	1 8 0 0 00	5 0 0 0 00	7 4 0 0 00	4 2 0 0 00	12
13		3 2 0 0 00			3 2 0 0 00	13
14		5 0 0 0 00	5 0 0 0 00	7 4 0 0 00	7 4 0 0 00	14
15						15
16						16

2. **LO2** Using the work sheet provided in U REVU Exercise 1, prepare closing entries in general journal form.

3. **LO3** Using the work sheet provided in U REVU Exercise 1 and financial statements prepared for that exercise, prepare a post-closing trial balance.

The answers to the Self-Study Questions and Exercises are at the end of the chapter (pages 213–215).

APPLYING YOUR KNOWLEDGE

REVIEW QUESTIONS

LO1 1. Identify the source of the information needed to prepare the income statement.

LO1 2. Describe two approaches to listing the expenses in the income statement.

LO1 3. Identify the sources of the information needed to prepare the statement of owner's equity.

LO1 4. If additional investments were made during the year, what information in addition to the work sheet would be needed to prepare the statement of owner's equity?

LO1 5. Identify the sources of the information needed to prepare the balance sheet.

LO2 6. What is a permanent account? On which financial statement are permanent accounts reported?

LO2 7. Name three types of temporary accounts.

LO2 8. List the four steps for closing the temporary accounts.

LO2 9. Describe the net effect of the four closing entries on the balance of the owner's capital account. Where else is this same amount calculated?

LO3 10. What is the purpose of the post-closing trial balance?

LO4 11. List the 10 steps in the accounting cycle.

SERIES A EXERCISES

E 6-1A (LO1)

✓ Net income: $1,990

INCOME STATEMENT From the partial work sheet for Case Advising below, prepare an income statement.

E 6-2A (LO1)

✓ Capital 1/31: $5,190

STATEMENT OF OWNER'S EQUITY From the partial work sheet below, prepare a statement of owner's equity, assuming no additional investment was made by the owner.

E 6-3A (LO1)

✓ Total assets: $6,390

BALANCE SHEET From the partial work sheet below, prepare a balance sheet.

(FOR EXERCISES 6-1A, 6-2A, AND 6-3A)

Case Advising
Work Sheet (Partial)
For Month Ended January 31, 20 - -

	ACCOUNT TITLE	INCOME STATEMENT DEBIT	INCOME STATEMENT CREDIT	BALANCE SHEET DEBIT	BALANCE SHEET CREDIT	
1	Cash			1 2 1 2 00		1
2	Accounts Receivable			8 9 6 00		2
3	Supplies			4 8 2 00		3
4	Prepaid Insurance			9 0 0 00		4
5	Office Equipment			3 0 0 0 00		5
6	Accum. Depr.—Office Equipment				1 0 0 00	6
7	Accounts Payable				1 0 0 0 00	7
8	Wages Payable				2 0 0 00	8
9	Bill Case, Capital				4 0 0 0 00	9
10	Bill Case, Drawing			8 0 0 00		10
11	Advising Fees		3 7 9 3 00			11
12	Wages Expense	8 0 0 00				12
13	Advertising Expense	8 0 00				13
14	Rent Expense	5 0 0 00				14
15	Supplies Expense	1 2 0 00				15
16	Telephone Expense	5 8 00				16
17	Electricity Expense	4 4 00				17
18	Insurance Expense	3 0 00				18
19	Gas and Oil Expense	3 8 00				19
20	Depr. Expense—Office Equipment	1 0 0 00				20
21	Miscellaneous Expense	3 3 00				21
22		1 8 0 3 00	3 7 9 3 00	7 2 9 0 00	5 3 0 0 00	22
23	Net Income	1 9 9 0 00			1 9 9 0 00	23
24		3 7 9 3 00	3 7 9 3 00	7 2 9 0 00	7 2 9 0 00	24

E 6-4A (LO2)

✓ Capital 1/31: $5,190

CLOSING ENTRIES (NET INCOME) Set up T accounts for Case Advising based on the work sheet in Exercise 6-1A and the chart of accounts provided below. Enter the existing balance for each account. Prepare closing entries in general journal form. Then post the closing entries to the T accounts.

Chart of Accounts

Assets
101   Cash
122   Accounts Receivable
141   Supplies
145   Prepaid Insurance
181   Office Equipment
181.1 Accum. Depr.—Office Equip.

Liabilities
202   Accounts Payable
219   Wages Payable

Owner's Equity
311   Bill Case, Capital
312   Bill Case, Drawing
313   Income Summary

Revenues
401   Advising Fees

Expenses
511   Wages Expense
512   Advertising Expense
521   Rent Expense
524   Supplies Expense
525   Telephone Expense
533   Electricity Expense
535   Insurance Expense
538   Gas and Oil Expense
541   Depr. Exp.—Office Equip.
549   Miscellaneous Expense

E 6-5A (LO2)

CLOSING ENTRIES (NET INCOME) Using the following partial listing of T accounts, prepare closing entries in general journal form dated April 30, 20--. Then post the closing entries to the T accounts.

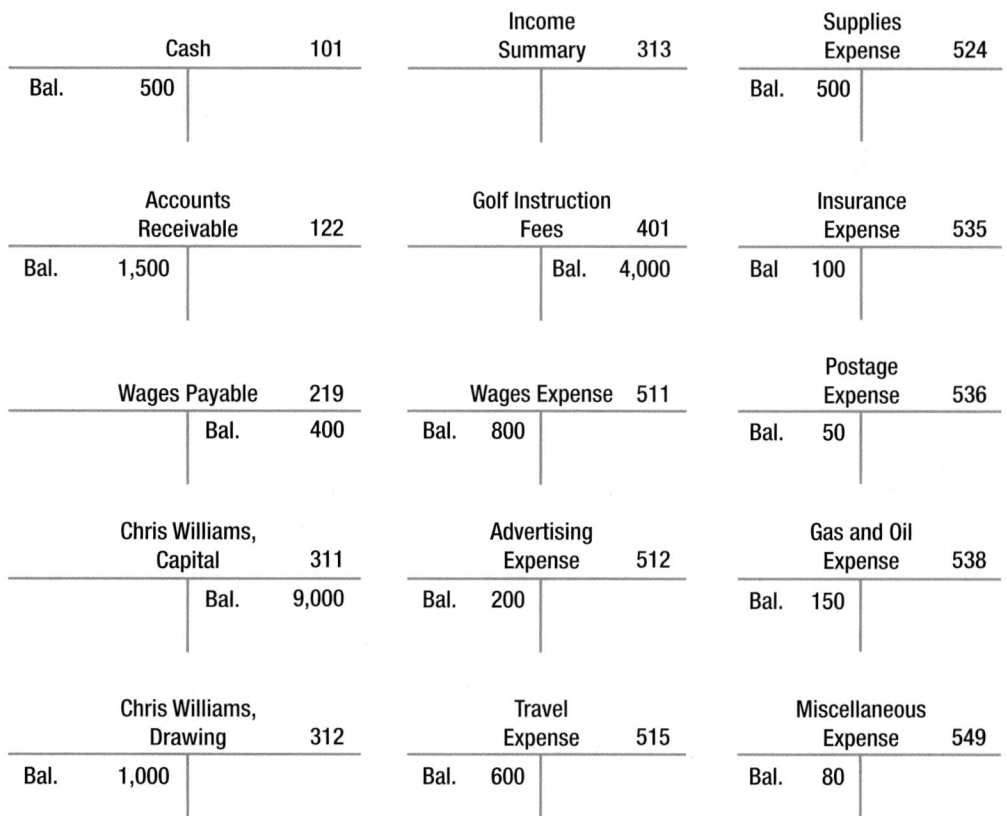

E 6-6A (LO2)

✓ Capital 1/31: $2,597

CLOSING ENTRIES (NET LOSS) Using the following partial listing of T accounts, prepare closing entries in general journal form dated January 31, 20--. Then post the closing entries to the T accounts.

Accum. Depr.— Del. Equip.	185.1		Wages Expense	511		Electricity Expense	533
	Bal. 100		Bal. 1,800			Bal. 44	

Wages Payable	219		Advertising Expense	512		Insurance Expense	535
	Bal. 200		Bal. 80			Bal 30	

Saburo Goto, Capital	311		Rent Expense	521		Gas and Oil Expense	538
	Bal. 4,000		Bal. 500			Bal. 38	

Saburo Goto, Drawing	312		Supplies Expense	523		Depr. Exp.— Del. Equip.	541
Bal. 800			Bal. 120			Bal. 100	

Income Summary	313		Telephone Expense	525		Miscellaneous Expense	549
			Bal. 58			Bal. 33	

Delivery Fees	401
	Bal. 2,200

SERIES A PROBLEMS

P 6-7A (LO1)

✓ Net income: $1,400; Capital 1/31: $7,400; Total assets: $8,650

FINANCIAL STATEMENTS Page 203 shows a work sheet for Monte's Repairs. No additional investments were made by the owner during the month.

REQUIRED

1.   Prepare an income statement.

2.   Prepare a statement of owner's equity.

3.   Prepare a balance sheet.

PROBLEM 6-7A

Monte's Repairs
Work Sheet
For Month Ended January 31, 20--

ACCOUNT TITLE	TRIAL BALANCE DEBIT	TRIAL BALANCE CREDIT	ADJUSTMENTS DEBIT	ADJUSTMENTS CREDIT	ADJUSTED TRIAL BALANCE DEBIT	ADJUSTED TRIAL BALANCE CREDIT	INCOME STATEMENT DEBIT	INCOME STATEMENT CREDIT	BALANCE SHEET DEBIT	BALANCE SHEET CREDIT	
1 Cash	3 0 8 0 00				3 0 8 0 00				3 0 8 0 00		1
2 Accounts Receivable	1 2 0 0 00				1 2 0 0 00				1 2 0 0 00		2
3 Supplies	8 0 0 00			(a) 2 0 0 00	6 0 0 00				6 0 0 00		3
4 Prepaid Insurance	9 0 0 00			(b) 1 0 0 00	8 0 0 00				8 0 0 00		4
5 Delivery Equipment	3 0 0 0 00				3 0 0 0 00				3 0 0 0 00		5
6 Accum. Depr.—Delivery Equipment				(d) 3 0 00		3 0 00				3 0 00	6
7 Accounts Payable		1 1 0 0 00				1 1 0 0 00				1 1 0 0 00	7
8 Wages Payable				(c) 1 5 0 00		1 5 0 00				1 5 0 00	8
9 Monte Eli, Capital		7 0 0 0 00				7 0 0 0 00				7 0 0 0 00	9
10 Monte Eli, Drawing	1 0 0 0 00				1 0 0 0 00				1 0 0 0 00		10
11 Repair Fees		4 2 3 0 00				4 2 3 0 00		4 2 3 0 00			11
12 Wages Expense	1 6 5 0 00		(c) 1 5 0 00		1 8 0 0 00		1 8 0 0 00				12
13 Advertising Expense	1 7 0 00				1 7 0 00		1 7 0 00				13
14 Rent Expense	4 2 0 00				4 2 0 00		4 2 0 00				14
15 Supplies Expense			(a) 2 0 0 00		2 0 0 00		2 0 0 00				15
16 Telephone Expense	4 9 00				4 9 00		4 9 00				16
17 Insurance Expense			(b) 1 0 0 00		1 0 0 00		1 0 0 00				17
18 Gas and Oil Expense	3 3 00				3 3 00		3 3 00				18
19 Depr. Expense—Delivery Equipment			(d) 3 0 00		3 0 00		3 0 00				19
20 Miscellaneous Expense	2 8 00				2 8 00		2 8 00				20
21	12 3 3 0 00	12 3 3 0 00	4 8 0 00	4 8 0 00	12 5 1 0 00	12 5 1 0 00	2 8 3 0 00	4 2 3 0 00	9 6 8 0 00	8 2 8 0 00	21
22 Net Income							1 4 0 0 00			1 4 0 0 00	22
23							4 2 3 0 00	4 2 3 0 00	9 6 8 0 00	9 6 8 0 00	23
24											24
25											25
26											26
27											27
28											28
29											29
30											30

P 6-8A (LO1)

✓ Capital 1/31: $6,820

STATEMENT OF OWNER'S EQUITY The capital account for Autumn Chou, including an additional investment, and a partial work sheet are shown below.

REQUIRED

Prepare a statement of owner's equity.

GENERAL LEDGER

ACCOUNT: Autumn Chou, Capital   ACCOUNT NO. 311

DATE		ITEM	POST. REF.	DEBIT	CREDIT	BALANCE DEBIT	BALANCE CREDIT
20-- Jan.	1	Balance	✔				4 8 0 0 00
	18		J 1		1 2 0 0 00		6 0 0 0 00

Autumn's Home Designs
Work Sheet (Partial)
For Month Ended January 31, 20 --

	ACCOUNT TITLE	INCOME STATEMENT DEBIT	INCOME STATEMENT CREDIT	BALANCE SHEET DEBIT	BALANCE SHEET CREDIT	
1	Cash			3 2 0 0 00		1
2	Accounts Receivable			1 6 0 0 00		2
3	Supplies			8 0 0 00		3
4	Prepaid Insurance			9 0 0 00		4
5	Office Equipment			2 5 0 0 00		5
6	Accum. Depr.—Office Equipment				5 0 00	6
7	Accounts Payable				1 9 5 0 00	7
8	Wages Payable				1 8 0 00	8
9	Autumn Chou, Capital				6 0 0 0 00	9
10	Autumn Chou, Drawing			1 0 0 0 00		10
11	Design Fees		4 8 6 6 00			11
12	Wages Expense	1 9 0 0 00				12
13	Advertising Expense	2 1 00				13
14	Rent Expense	6 0 0 00				14
15	Supplies Expense	2 0 0 00				15
16	Telephone Expense	8 5 00				16
17	Electricity Expense	4 8 00				17
18	Insurance Expense	6 0 00				18
19	Gas and Oil Expense	3 2 00				19
20	Depr. Expense—Office Equipment	5 0 00				20
21	Miscellaneous Expense	5 0 00				21
22		3 0 4 6 00	4 8 6 6 00	10 0 0 0 00	8 1 8 0 00	22
23	Net Income	1 8 2 0 00			1 8 2 0 00	23
24		4 8 6 6 00	4 8 6 6 00	10 0 0 0 00	10 0 0 0 00	24

P 6-9A (LO2/3)

✓ Capital 1/31:$7,400; Post-closing trial
bal. total debits: $8,680

CLOSING ENTRIES AND POST-CLOSING TRIAL BALANCE Refer to the work sheet in Problem 6-7A for Monte's Repairs. The trial balance amounts (before adjustments) have been entered in the ledger accounts provided in the working papers. If you are not using the working papers that accompany this book, set up ledger accounts and enter these balances as of January 31, 20--. A chart of accounts is provided below.

Monte's Repairs
Chart of Accounts

Assets		Revenues	
101	Cash	401	Repair Fees
122	Accounts Receivable		
141	Supplies	Expenses	
145	Prepaid Insurance	511	Wages Expense
185	Delivery Equipment	512	Advertising Expense
185.1	Accum. Depr.—Delivery Equip.	521	Rent Expense
		523	Supplies Expense
Liabilities		525	Telephone Expense
202	Accounts Payable	535	Insurance Expense
219	Wages Payable	538	Gas and Oil Expense
		541	Depr. Exp.--Delivery Equip.
Owner's Equity		549	Miscellaneous Expense
311	Monte Eli, Capital		
312	Monte Eli, Drawing		
313	Income Summary		

REQUIRED

1. Journalize (page 10) and post the adjusting entries.

2. Journalize (page 11) and post the closing entries.

3. Prepare a post-closing trial balance.

SERIES B EXERCISES

E 6-1B (LO1)
✓ Net income: $1,826

INCOME STATEMENT From the partial work sheet for Adams' Shoe Shine below, prepare an income statement.

E 6-2B (LO1)
✓ Capital 6/30: $5,826

STATEMENT OF OWNER'S EQUITY From the partial work sheet below, prepare a statement of owner's equity, assuming no additional investment was made by the owner.

E 6-3B (LO1)
✓ Total assets: $7,936

BALANCE SHEET From the partial work sheet below, prepare a balance sheet for Adams' Shoe Shine.

(FOR EXERCISES 6-1B, 6-2B, AND 6-3B)

Adams' Shoe Shine
Work Sheet (Partial)
For Month Ended June 30, 20 - -

	ACCOUNT TITLE	INCOME STATEMENT DEBIT	INCOME STATEMENT CREDIT	BALANCE SHEET DEBIT	BALANCE SHEET CREDIT	
1	Cash			3 2 6 2 00		1
2	Accounts Receivable			1 2 4 4 00		2
3	Supplies			8 0 0 00		3
4	Prepaid Insurance			6 4 0 00		4
5	Office Equipment			2 1 0 0 00		5
6	Accum. Depr.—Office Equipment				1 1 0 00	6
7	Accounts Payable				1 8 5 0 00	7
8	Wages Payable				2 6 0 00	8
9	Mary Adams, Capital				6 0 0 0 00	9
10	Mary Adams, Drawing			2 0 0 0 00		10
11	Service Fees		4 8 1 3 00			11
12	Wages Expense	1 0 8 0 00				12
13	Advertising Expense	3 4 00				13
14	Rent Expense	9 0 0 00				14
15	Supplies Expense	3 2 2 00				15
16	Telephone Expense	1 3 3 00				16
17	Utilities Expense	1 0 2 00				17
18	Insurance Expense	1 2 0 00				18
19	Gas and Oil Expense	8 8 00				19
20	Depr. Expense—Office Equipment	1 1 0 00				20
21	Miscellaneous Expense	9 8 00				21
22		2 9 8 7 00	4 8 1 3 00	10 0 4 6 00	8 2 2 0 00	22
23	Net Income	1 8 2 6 00			1 8 2 6 00	23
24		4 8 1 3 00	4 8 1 3 00	10 0 4 6 00	10 0 4 6 00	24

E 6-4B (LO2)
✓ Capital 6/30: $5,826

CLOSING ENTRIES (NET INCOME) Set up T accounts for Adams' Shoe Shine based on the work sheet above and the chart of accounts provided on the next page. Enter the existing balance for each account. Prepare closing entries in general journal form. Then post the closing entries to the T accounts.

Chart of Accounts

Assets
101   Cash
122   Accounts Receivable
141   Supplies
145   Prepaid Insurance
181   Office Equipment
181.1 Accum. Depr.—Office Equip.

Liabilities
202   Accounts Payable
219   Wages Payable

Owner's Equity
311   Mary Adams, Capital
312   Mary Adams, Drawing
313   Income Summary

Revenues
401   Service Fees

Expenses
511   Wages Expense
512   Advertising Expense
521   Rent Expense
523   Supplies Expense
525   Telephone Expense
533   Utilities Expense
535   Insurance Expense
538   Gas and Oil Expense
542   Depr. Exp.—Office Equip.
549   Miscellaneous Expense

E 6-5B (LO2)

CLOSING ENTRIES (NET INCOME) Using the following partial listing of T accounts, prepare closing entries in general journal form dated May 31, 20--. Then post the closing entries to the T accounts.

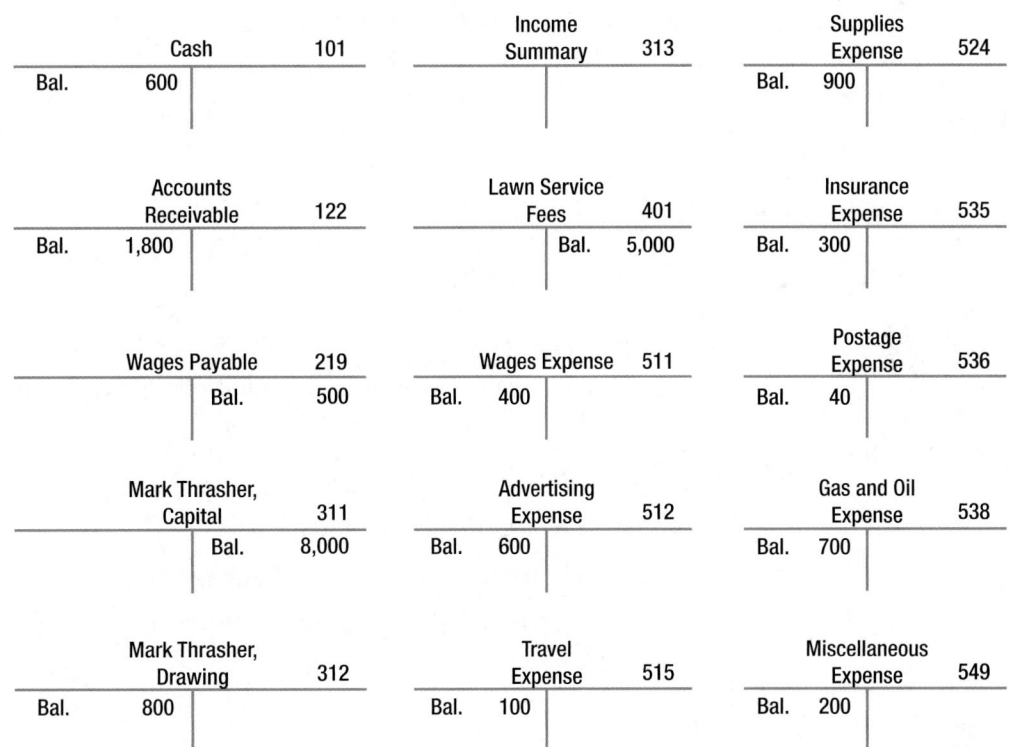

E 6-6B (LO2)

✓ Capital 6/30: $3,826

CLOSING ENTRIES (NET LOSS) Using the following partial listing of T accounts, prepare closing entries in general journal form dated June 30, 20--. Then post the closing entries to the T accounts.

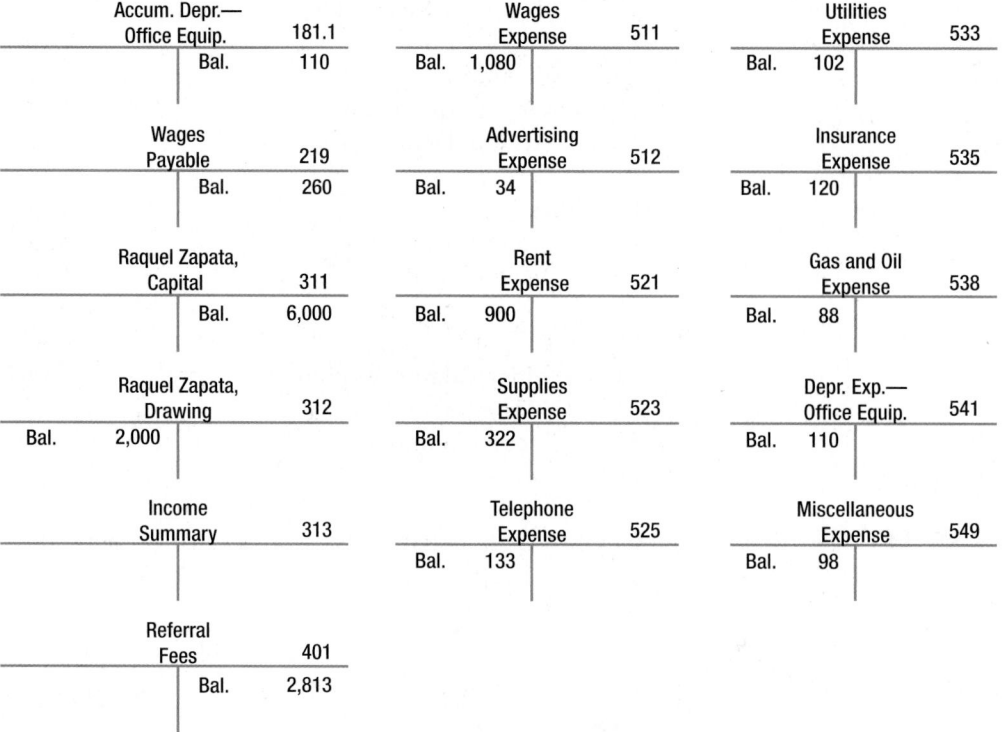

Accum. Depr.—Office Equip.	181.1		Wages Expense	511		Utilities Expense	533
Bal.	110	Bal.	1,080		Bal.	102	

Wages Payable	219		Advertising Expense	512		Insurance Expense	535
Bal.	260	Bal.	34		Bal.	120	

Raquel Zapata, Capital	311		Rent Expense	521		Gas and Oil Expense	538
Bal.	6,000	Bal.	900		Bal.	88	

Raquel Zapata, Drawing	312		Supplies Expense	523		Depr. Exp.—Office Equip.	541
Bal. 2,000		Bal.	322		Bal.	110	

Income Summary	313		Telephone Expense	525		Miscellaneous Expense	549
		Bal.	133		Bal.	98	

Referral Fees	401
Bal.	2,813

SERIES B PROBLEMS

P 6-7B (LO1)

✓ Net income: $1,450;
Capital 6/30: $7,650;
Total assets: $9,350

FINANCIAL STATEMENTS A work sheet for Juanita's Consulting is shown on the following page. There were no additional investments made by the owner during the month.

REQUIRED

1. Prepare an income statement.

2. Prepare a statement of owner's equity.

3. Prepare a balance sheet.

PROBLEM 6-7B

Juanita's Consulting
Work Sheet
For Month Ended June 30, 20--

	ACCOUNT TITLE	TRIAL BALANCE DEBIT	TRIAL BALANCE CREDIT	ADJUSTMENTS DEBIT	ADJUSTMENTS CREDIT	ADJUSTED TRIAL BALANCE DEBIT	ADJUSTED TRIAL BALANCE CREDIT	INCOME STATEMENT DEBIT	INCOME STATEMENT CREDIT	BALANCE SHEET DEBIT	BALANCE SHEET CREDIT	
1	Cash	5 2 8 5 00				5 2 8 5 00				5 2 8 5 00		1
2	Accounts Receivable	1 0 7 5 00				1 0 7 5 00				1 0 7 5 00		2
3	Supplies	7 5 0 00			(a) 2 5 0 00	5 0 0 00				5 0 0 00		3
4	Prepaid Insurance	5 0 0 00			(b) 1 0 0 00	4 0 0 00				4 0 0 00		4
5	Office Equipment	2 2 0 0 00				2 2 0 0 00				2 2 0 0 00		5
6	Accum. Depr.—Office Equipment				(d) 1 1 0 00		1 1 0 00				1 1 0 00	6
7	Accounts Payable		1 5 0 0 00				1 5 0 0 00				1 5 0 0 00	7
8	Wages Payable				(c) 2 0 0 00		2 0 0 00				2 0 0 00	8
9	Juanita Alvarez, Capital		7 0 0 0 00				7 0 0 0 00				7 0 0 0 00	9
10	Juanita Alvarez, Drawing	8 0 0 00				8 0 0 00				8 0 0 00		10
11	Consulting Fees		4 2 0 4 00				4 2 0 4 00		4 2 0 4 00			11
12	Wages Expense	1 4 0 0 00		(c) 2 0 0 00		1 6 0 0 00		1 6 0 0 00				12
13	Advertising Expense	6 0 00				6 0 00		6 0 00				13
14	Rent Expense	5 0 0 00				5 0 0 00		5 0 0 00				14
15	Supplies Expense			(a) 2 5 0 00		2 5 0 00		2 5 0 00				15
16	Telephone Expense	4 6 00				4 6 00		4 6 00				16
17	Electricity Expense	3 9 00				3 9 00		3 9 00				17
18	Insurance Expense			(b) 1 0 0 00		1 0 0 00		1 0 0 00				18
19	Gas and Oil Expense	2 8 00				2 8 00		2 8 00				19
20	Depr. Expense—Office Equipment			(d) 1 1 0 00		1 1 0 00		1 1 0 00				20
21	Miscellaneous Expense	2 1 00				2 1 00		2 1 00				21
22		12 7 0 4 00	12 7 0 4 00	6 6 0 00	6 6 0 00	13 0 1 4 00	13 0 1 4 00	2 7 5 4 00	4 2 0 4 00	10 2 6 0 00	8 8 1 0 00	22
23	Net Income							1 4 5 0 00			1 4 5 0 00	23
24								4 2 0 4 00	4 2 0 4 00	10 2 6 0 00	10 2 6 0 00	24
25												25
26												26
27												27
28												28
29												29
30												30

P 6-8B (LO1)

✓ Capital 1/31: $9,975

STATEMENT OF OWNER'S EQUITY The capital account for Minta's Editorial Services, including an additional investment, and a partial work sheet are shown below.

GENERAL LEDGER

ACCOUNT: Minta Berry, Capital   ACCOUNT NO. 311

DATE		ITEM	POST. REF.	DEBIT	CREDIT	BALANCE DEBIT	BALANCE CREDIT
20-- Jan.	1	Balance	✔				3 6 0 0 00
	22		J 1		2 9 0 0 00		6 5 0 0 00

Minta's Editorial Services
Work Sheet (Partial)
For Month Ended January 31, 20 --

	ACCOUNT TITLE	INCOME STATEMENT DEBIT	INCOME STATEMENT CREDIT	BALANCE SHEET DEBIT	BALANCE SHEET CREDIT	
1	Cash			3 8 0 0 00		1
2	Accounts Receivable			2 2 0 0 00		2
3	Supplies			1 0 0 0 00		3
4	Prepaid Insurance			9 5 0 00		4
5	Computer Equipment			4 5 0 0 00		5
6	Accum. Depr.—Computer Equipment				2 2 5 00	6
7	Accounts Payable				2 1 0 0 00	7
8	Wages Payable				1 5 0 00	8
9	Minta Berry, Capital				6 5 0 0 00	9
10	Minta Berry, Drawing			1 7 0 0 00		10
11	Editing Fees		7 0 1 2 00			11
12	Wages Expense	6 0 0 00				12
13	Advertising Expense	4 9 00				13
14	Rent Expense	4 5 0 00				14
15	Supplies Expense	2 8 8 00				15
16	Telephone Expense	4 4 00				16
17	Utilities Expense	3 8 00				17
18	Insurance Expense	1 2 5 00				18
19	Depr. Expense—Computer Equipment	2 2 5 00				19
20	Miscellaneous Expense	1 8 00				20
21		1 8 3 7 00	7 0 1 2 00	14 1 5 0 00	8 9 7 5 00	21
22	Net Income	5 1 7 5 00			5 1 7 5 00	22
23		7 0 1 2 00	7 0 1 2 00	14 1 5 0 00	14 1 5 0 00	23

REQUIRED

Prepare a statement of owner's equity.

P 6-9B (LO2/3)

✓ Capital 6/30: $7,650;
Post-closing trial bal.
total debits: $9,460

CLOSING ENTRIES AND POST-CLOSING TRIAL BALANCE Refer to the work sheet for Juanita's Consulting in Problem 6-7B. The trial balance amounts (before adjustments) have been entered in the ledger accounts provided in the working papers. If you are not using the working papers that accompany this book, set up ledger accounts and enter these balances as of June 30, 20--. A chart of accounts is provided below.

Juanita's Consulting
Chart of Accounts

Assets		Revenues	
101	Cash	401	Consulting Fees
122	Accounts Receivable		
141	Supplies		Expenses
145	Prepaid Insurance	511	Wages Expense
181	Office Equipment	512	Advertising Expense
181.1	Accum. Depr.—Office Equip.	521	Rent Expense
		523	Supplies Expense
Liabilities		525	Telephone Expense
202	Accounts Payable	533	Electricity Expense
219	Wages Payable	535	Insurance Expense
		538	Gas and Oil Expense
Owner's Equity		541	Depr. Exp.—Office Equip.
311	Juanita Alvarez, Capital	549	Miscellaneous Expense
312	Juanita Alvarez, Drawing		
313	Income Summary		

REQUIRED

1. Journalize (page 10) and post the adjusting entries.

2. Journalize (page 11) and post the closing entries.

3. Prepare a post-closing trial balance.

MANAGING YOUR WRITING

At lunch, two bookkeepers got into a heated discussion about whether closing entries should be made before or after preparing the financial statements. They have come to you to resolve this issue and have agreed to accept your position. Write a memo explaining the purpose of closing entries and whether they should be made before or after preparing the financial statements.

MASTERY PROBLEM

✓ Total assets: $4,740;
E. Soltis, capital, Dec. 31: $4,475

Elizabeth Soltis owns and operates Aunt Ibby's Styling Salon. A year-end work sheet is provided on the next page. Using this information, prepare adjusting entries, financial statements, and closing entries. Soltis made no additional investments during the year.

(continued)

MASTERY PROBLEM

Aunt Ibby's Styling Salon
Work Sheet
For Year Ended December 31, 20--

#	ACCOUNT TITLE	Trial Balance Debit	Trial Balance Credit	Adjustments Debit	Adjustments Credit	Adjusted Trial Balance Debit	Adjusted Trial Balance Credit	Income Statement Debit	Income Statement Credit	Balance Sheet Debit	Balance Sheet Credit
1	Cash	9 4 0 00				9 4 0 00				9 4 0 00	
2	Styling Supplies	15 0 0 00			(a) 1 4 5 0 00	5 0 00				5 0 00	
3	Prepaid Insurance	8 0 0 00			(b) 6 5 0 00	1 5 0 00				1 5 0 00	
4	Salon Equipment	45 0 0 00				45 0 0 00				45 0 0 00	
5	Accum. Depr.—Salon Equipment				(d) 9 0 0 00		9 0 0 00				9 0 0 00
6	Accounts Payable		2 2 5 00				2 2 5 00				2 2 5 00
7	Wages Payable				(c) 4 0 00		4 0 00				4 0 00
8	Elizabeth Soltis, Capital		27 6 5 00				27 6 5 00				27 6 5 00
9	Elizabeth Soltis, Drawing	12 0 0 0 00				12 0 0 0 00				12 0 0 0 00	
10	Styling Fees		32 0 0 0 00				32 0 0 0 00		32 0 0 0 00		
11	Wages Expense	8 0 0 0 00		(c) 4 0 00		8 0 4 0 00		8 0 4 0 00			
12	Rent Expense	6 0 0 0 00				6 0 0 0 00		6 0 0 0 00			
13	Styling Supplies Expense			(a) 1 4 5 0 00		1 4 5 0 00		1 4 5 0 00			
14	Telephone Expense	4 5 0 00				4 5 0 00		4 5 0 00			
15	Utilities Expense	8 0 0 00				8 0 0 00		8 0 0 00			
16	Insurance Expense			(b) 6 5 0 00		6 5 0 00		6 5 0 00			
17	Depr. Expense—Salon Equipment			(d) 9 0 0 00		9 0 0 00		9 0 0 00			
18		34 9 9 0 00	34 9 9 0 00	3 0 4 0 00	3 0 4 0 00	35 9 3 0 00	35 9 3 0 00	18 2 9 0 00	32 0 0 0 00	17 6 4 0 00	3 9 3 0 00
19	Net Income							13 7 1 0 00			13 7 1 0 00
20								32 0 0 0 00	32 0 0 0 00	17 6 4 0 00	17 6 4 0 00

CHALLENGE PROBLEM

This problem challenges you to apply your cumulative accounting knowledge to move a step beyond the material in the chapter.

✓ **Net loss: $2,100;**

Capital, 1/31/20--: ($700)

Provided below is a partial work sheet for Ardery Advising.

Ardery Advising
Work Sheet (Partial)
For Month Ended January 31, 20 - -

	ACCOUNT TITLE	INCOME STATEMENT DEBIT	INCOME STATEMENT CREDIT	BALANCE SHEET DEBIT	BALANCE SHEET CREDIT	
1	Cash			2 4 1 2 00		1
2	Accounts Receivable			8 9 6 00		2
3	Supplies			4 8 2 00		3
4	Prepaid Insurance			9 0 0 00		4
5	Office Equipment			3 0 0 0 00		5
6	Accum. Depr.—Office Equipment				2 0 0 0 00	6
7	Accounts Payable				2 1 9 0 00	7
8	Wages Payable				1 2 0 0 00	8
9	Notes Payable				3 0 0 0 00	9
10	Sam Ardery, Capital				2 2 0 0 00	10
11	Sam Ardery, Drawing			8 0 0 00		11
12	Advising Fees		3 8 0 2 00			12
13	Wages Expense	1 8 0 0 00				13
14	Advertising Expense	4 0 0 00				14
15	Rent Expense	1 5 0 0 00				15
16	Supplies Expense	1 2 0 00				16
17	Telephone Expense	3 0 0 00				17
18	Electricity Expense	4 4 00				18
19	Insurance Expense	2 0 0 00				19
20	Gas and Oil Expense	3 8 00				20
21	Depr. Expense—Office Equipment	1 0 0 0 00				21
22	Miscellaneous Expense	5 0 0 00				22
23		5 9 0 2 00	3 8 0 2 00	8 4 9 0 00	10 5 9 0 00	23
24	Net Loss		2 1 0 0 00	2 1 0 0 00		24
25		5 9 0 2 00	5 9 0 2 00	10 5 9 0 00	10 5 9 0 00	25

REQUIRED

During January, Ardery made an additional investment of $1,200. Prepare an income statement, statement of owner's equity, and balance sheet for Ardery Advising.

ANSWERS TO SELF-STUDY QUESTIONS AND EXERCISES

True/False Questions

1. T
2. F (additional investments are shown as an addition to the beginning balance)
3. F 4. T 5. T

Multiple Choice Questions

1. b 2. d 3. a 4. c 5. b

U REVU Exercises

1.

Fisher Consulting Income Statement For Month Ended August 31, 20 --										
Revenue:										
Professional fees							$ 5	0	0	0	00
Expenses:										
Wages expense	$ 1	0	0	0	00					
Rent expense		7	0	0	00					
Depreciation expense		1	0	0	00					
Total expenses							1	8	0	0	00
Net income							$ 3	2	0	0	00

Fisher Consulting Statement of Owner's Equity For Month Ended August 31, 20 --										
Joe Fisher, capital, August 1, 20 - -							$ 3	0	0	0	00
Net income for August	$3	2	0	0	00					
Less withdrawals for August		3	0	0	00					
Increase in capital							2	9	0	0	00
Joe Fisher, capital, August 31, 20 - -							$ 5	9	0	0	00

Fisher Consulting Balance Sheet August 31, 20 --										
Assets										
Current assets:										
Cash	$2	5	0	0	00					
Accounts receivable		8	0	0	00					
Total current assets							$ 3	3	0	0	00
Property, plant, and equipment:										
Equipment	$3	8	0	0	00					
Less accumulated depreciation		2	0	0	00		3	6	0	0	00
Total assets							$ 6	9	0	0	00
Liabilities										
Current liabilities:										
Accounts payable							$ 1	0	0	0	00
Owner's Equity										
Joe Fisher, capital, August 31, 20--								5	9	0	0	00
Total liabilities and owner's equity							$ 6	9	0	0	00

2.

DATE		DESCRIPTION	POST. REF.	DEBIT					CREDIT				
		Closing Entries											
20-- Aug.	31	Professional Fees		5	0	0	0	00					
		Income Summary							5	0	0	0	00
	31	Income Summary		1	8	0	0	00					
		Wages Expense							1	0	0	0	00
		Rent Expense								7	0	0	00
		Depreciation Expense								1	0	0	00
	31	Income Summary		3	2	0	0	00					
		Joe Fisher, capital							3	2	0	0	00
	31	Joe Fisher, Capital			3	0	0	00					
		Joe Fisher, Drawing								3	0	0	00

3

Joe Fisher, Consulting Post-Closing Trial Balance August 31, 20 - -										
ACCOUNT TITLE	ACCOUNT NO	DEBIT BALANCE					CREDIT BALANCE			
Cash		2	5	0	0	00				
Accounts Receivable			8	0	0	00				
Equipment		3	8	0	0	00				
Accumulated Depr.—Equipment								2	0	0	00
Accounts Payable							1	0	0	0	00
Joe Fisher, Capital							5	9	0	0	00
		7	1	0	0	00	7	1	0	0	00

Chapter 6 Appendix
Statement of Cash Flows

Thus far, we have discussed three financial statements: the income statement, the statement of owner's equity, and the balance sheet. A fourth statement, the statement of cash flows, is also very important. It explains what the business did to generate cash and how the cash was used. This is done by categorizing all cash transactions into three types of activities: operating, investing, and financing.

LEARNING OBJECTIVES

Careful study of this appendix should enable you to:

LO1 Classify business transactions as operating, investing, or financing.

LO2 Prepare a statement of cash flows by analyzing and categorizing a series of business transactions.

TYPES OF BUSINESS ACTIVITIES

LO1 Classify business transactions as operating, investing, or financing.

LEARNING KEY

There are three types of business activities: operating, investing, and financing.

Cash flows from **operating activities** are related to the revenues and expenses reported on the income statement. Examples include cash received for services performed and the payment of cash for expenses.

Investing activities are those transactions involving the purchase and sale of long-term assets, lending money, and collecting the principal on the related loans.

Financing activities are those transactions dealing with the exchange of cash between the business and its owners and creditors. Examples include cash received from the owner to finance the operations and cash paid to the owner as withdrawals. Financing activities also include borrowing cash and repaying the loan principal.

Figure 6A-1 provides a review of the transactions for Jessie Jane's Campus Delivery Service for the month of June. The transactions are classified as operating, investing, or financing, and an explanation for the classification is provided.

LEARNING KEY

Lending money to another entity is an outflow of cash from investing activities. The collection of the principal when the loan is due is an inflow of cash from investing activities. Borrowing cash is an inflow from financing activities. Repayment of the loan principal is an outflow from financing activities.

FIGURE 6A-1 Summary of Transactions for Jessie Jane's Campus Delivery Service

SUMMARY OF TRANSACTIONS FOR JESSIE JANE'S CAMPUS DELIVERY SERVICE	TYPE OF TRANSACTION	EXPLANATION
(a) Jessica Jane invested cash in her business, $2,000.	Financing	Cash received from the owner is an inflow from financing activities. Don't be fooled by the word "invested." From the company's point of view, this is a way to *finance* the business.
(b) Purchased delivery equipment for cash, $1,200.	Investing	Purchases of long-term assets are investments.
(c) Purchased delivery equipment on account from Big Red Scooters, $900. (*Note*: Big Red has loaned Jane $900.)	No cash involved	This transaction will not affect the main sections of the statement of cash flows. (This is a noncash investing and financing activity.)
(d) Paid first installment to Big Red Scooters, $300. [See transaction (c).]	Financing	Repayments of loans are financing activities.
(e) Received cash for delivery services rendered, $500.	Operating	Cash received as a result of providing services is classified as an operating activity.
(f) Paid cash for June office rent, $200.	Operating	Cash payments for expenses are classified as operating activities.
(g) Paid telephone bill, $50.	Operating	Cash payments for expenses are classified as operating activities.
(h) Made deliveries on account for a total of $600: $400 for the Accounting Department and $200 for the School of Music.	No cash involved	This transaction will not affect the statement of cash flows.
(i) Purchased supplies for cash, $80.	Operating	Cash payments for expenses are classified as operating activities. Most of these supplies were used up. Those that remain will be used in the near future. These are not long-term assets and, thus, do not qualify as investments.
(j) Paid cash for an eight-month liability insurance policy, $200. Coverage began on June 1.	Operating	Cash payments for expenses are classified as operating activities. Prepaid Insurance is not considered a long-term asset and, thus, does not qualify as an investment.
(k) Received $570 in cash for services performed in transaction (h): $400 from the Accounting Department and $170 from the School of Music.	Operating	Cash received as a result of providing services is classified as an operating activity.
(l) Purchased a third scooter from Big Red Scooters, $1,500. A down payment of $300 was made with the remaining payments expected over the next four months.	Investing	Purchases of long-term assets are investments. Only the $300 cash paid will be reported on the statement of cash flows.
(m) Paid wages of part-time employees, $650.	Operating	Cash payments for expenses are classified as operating activities.
(n) Earned delivery fees for the remainder of the month amounting to $1,050: $430 in cash and $620 on account. Deliveries on account: $250 for the Accounting Department and $370 for the Athletic Ticket Office.	Operating	Cash received ($430) as a result of providing services is classified as an operating activity.
(o) Jane withdrew cash for personal use, $150.	Financing	Cash payments to owners are classified as a financing activity.

PREPARING THE STATEMENT OF CASH FLOWS

LO2 Prepare a statement of cash flows by analyzing and categorizing a series of business transactions.

The classifications of the cash transactions for Jessie Jane's Campus Delivery Service are summarized in the expanded cash T account shown in Figure 6A-2. Using this information, we can prepare a statement of cash flows. As shown in Figure 6A-3, the heading is similar to that used for the income statement. Since the statement of cash flows reports on the flow of cash for a period of time, the statement is dated for the month ended June 30, 20--.

FIGURE 6A-2 Cash T Account for Jessie Jane's Campus Delivery Service with Classifications of Cash Transactions

CASH						
Event	**Classification**	**Amount**	**Amount**	**Classification**	**Event**	
(a) Investment by Jessie.	Financing	2,000	1,200	Investing	Purchased delivery equipment.	(b)
(e) Cash received for services.	Operating	500	300	Financing	Made payment on loan.	(d)
(k) Cash received for services.	Operating	570	200	Operating	Paid office rent.	(f)`
(n) Cash received for services.	Operating	430	50	Operating	Paid telephone bill.	(g)
		3,500	80	Operating	Purchased supplies.	(i)
			200	Operating	Paid for insurance.	(j)
			300	Investing	Purchased delivery equipment.	(l)
			650	Operating	Paid wages.	(m)
			150	Financing	Withdrawal by owner.	(o)
			3,130			
	Bal.	370				

FIGURE 6A-3 Statement of Cash Flows for Jessie Jane's Campus Delivery Service

Jessie Jane's Campus Delivery Service
Statement of Cash Flows
For Month Ended June 30, 20 - -

Cash flows from operating activities:			
Cash received from customers for delivery services			$ 1 5 0 0 00
Cash paid for wages	$ (6 5 0 00)		
Cash paid for rent	(2 0 0 00)		
Cash paid for supplies	(8 0 00)		
Cash paid for telephone	(5 0 00)		
Cash paid for insurance	(2 0 0 00)		
Total cash paid for operations		(1 1 8 0 00)	
Net cash provided by operating activities		$ 3 2 0 00	
Cash flows from investing activities:			
Cash paid for delivery equipment	$(1 5 0 0 00)		
Net cash used for investing activities		(1 5 0 0 00)	
Cash flows from financing activities:			
Cash investment by owner	$ 2 0 0 0 00		
Cash withdrawal by owner	(1 5 0 00)		
Payment made on loan	(3 0 0 00)		
Net cash provided by financing activities		1 5 5 0 00	
Net increase in cash		$ 3 7 0 00	

The main body of the statement is arranged in three sections: operating, investing, and financing activities. First, cash received from customers is listed under operating activities. Then, cash payments for operating activities are listed and totaled. The net amount is reported as net cash provided by operating activities. Since this is the main purpose of the business, it is important to be able to generate positive cash flows from operating activities.

The next two sections list the inflows and outflows from investing and financing activities. Debits to the cash account are inflows and credits are outflows. Note that there was an outflow, or net use of cash, from investing activities resulting from the purchase of the motor scooters. In addition, cash was provided from financing activities because Jessie's initial investment more than covered her withdrawal and the payment on the loan. These investing and financing activities are typical for a new business.

LEARNING KEY

To prove the accuracy of the statement of cash flows, compare the net increase or decrease reported on the statement with the change in the balance of the cash account.

The sum of the inflows and outflows from operating, investing, and financing activities equals the net increase (or decrease) in the cash account during the period. Since this is a new business, the cash account had a beginning balance of zero. The ending balance is $370. This agrees with the net increase in cash of $370 reported on the statement of cash flows.

This appendix introduces you to the purpose and format of the statement of cash flows. Here, we classified entries made to the cash account as operating, investing, or financing. These classifications were then used to prepare the statement. Businesses have thousands of entries to the cash account. Thus, this approach to preparing the statement is not really practical. Other approaches to preparing the statement will be discussed in Chapter 23. However, the purpose and format of the statements are the same.

LEARNING OBJECTIVES   Key Points to Remember

LO1 Classify business transactions as operating, investing, or financing.

The purpose of the statement of cash flows is to report what the firm did to generate cash and how the cash was used. Business transactions are classified as operating, investing, and financing activities.

Operating activities are those transactions related to the revenues and expenses reported on the income statement.

Investing activities are those transactions involving the purchase and sale of long-term assets, lending money, and collecting the principal on the related loans.

Financing activities are those transactions dealing with the exchange of cash between the business and its owners and creditors.

LO2 Prepare a statement of cash flows by analyzing and categorizing a series of business transactions.

The main body of the statement of cash flows consists of three sections: operating, investing, and financing activities.

Name of Business Statement of Cash Flows For Period Ended Date										
Cash flows from operating activities:										
Cash received from customers						$x	x	x	x	xx
List cash paid for various expenses	$	(x	x	x	xx)					
Total cash paid for operations						(x	x	x	x	xx)
Net cash provided by (used for) operating activities						$	x	x	x	xx
Cash flows from investing activities:										
List cash received from the sale of long-term assets and other investing activities	$x	x	x	x	xx					
List cash paid for the purchase of long-term assets and other investing activities	(x	x	x	x	xx)					
Net cash provided by (used for) investing activities						x	x	x	x	xx
Cash flows from financing activities:										
List cash received from owners and creditors	$x	x	x	x	xx					
List cash paid to owners and creditors		(x	x	x	xx)					
Net cash provided by (used for) financing activities						x	x	x	x	xx
Net increase (decrease) in cash						$	x	x	x	xx

KEY TERMS

financing activities (216)   Those transactions dealing with the exchange of cash between the business and its owners and creditors.

investing activities (216)   Those transactions involving the purchase and sale of long-term assets, lending money, and collecting the principal on the related loans.

operating activities (216)   Those transactions related to the revenues and expenses reported on the income statement.

REVIEW QUESTIONS

LO1   1.   Explain the purpose of the statement of cash flows.

LO1   2.   Define and provide examples of the three types of business activities.

SERIES A EXERCISE

E 6Apx-1A (LO1)

CLASSIFYING BUSINESS TRANSACTIONS Dolores Lopez opened a new consulting business. The following transactions occurred during January of the current year. Classify each transaction as an operating, an investing, or a financing activity.

(a)   Invested cash in the business, $10,000.
(b)   Paid office rent, $500.
(c)   Purchased office equipment. Paid $1,500 cash and agreed to pay the balance of $2,000 in four monthly installments.
(d)   Received cash for services rendered, $900.
(e)   Paid telephone bill, $65.
(f)   Made payment on loan in transaction (c), $500.
(g)   Paid wages to part-timse employee, $500.
(h)   Received cash for services rendered, $800.
(i)   Paid electricity bill, $85.
(j)   Withdrew cash for personal use, $100.
(k)   Paid wages to part-time employee, $500.

SERIES A PROBLEM

P 6Apx-2A (LO2)

✓ Operating activities: $50;
Investing activities: ($1,500);
Financing activities: $9,400

PREPARING A STATEMENT OF CASH FLOWS Prepare a statement of cash flows based on the transactions reported in Exercise 6Apx-1A.

SERIES B EXERCISE

E 6Apx-1B (LO1)

CLASSIFYING BUSINESS TRANSACTIONS Bob Jacobs opened an advertising agency. The following transactions occurred during January of the current year. Classify each transaction as an operating, an investing, or a financing activity.

(a) Invested cash in the business, $5,000.
(b) Purchased office equipment. Paid $2,500 cash and agreed to pay the balance of $2,000 in four monthly installments.
(c) Paid office rent, $400.
(d) Received cash for services rendered, $700.
(e) Paid telephone bill, $95.
(f) Received cash for services rendered, $600.
(g) Made payment on loan in transaction (b), $500.
(h) Paid wages to part-time employee, $800.
(i) Paid electricity bill, $100.
(j) Withdrew cash for personal use, $500.
(k) Paid wages to part-time employee, $600.

SERIES B PROBLEM

P 6Apx-2B (LO2)

✓ Operating activities: ($695);
Investing activities: ($2,500);
Financing activities: $4,000

PREPARING A STATEMENT OF CASH FLOWS Prepare a statement of cash flows based on the transactions reported in Exercise 6Apx-1B.

This comprehensive problem is intended to serve as a mini-practice set without the source documents. As such, students should plan on about three to four hours to complete this problem.

COMPREHENSIVE PROBLEM 1: THE ACCOUNTING CYCLE

Bob Night opened "The General's Favorite Fishing Hole." The fishing camp is open from April through September and attracts many famous college basketball coaches during the off-season. Guests typically register for one week, arriving on Sunday afternoon and returning home the following Saturday afternoon. The registration fee includes room and board, the use of fishing boats, and professional instruction in fishing techniques. The chart of accounts for the camping operations is provided below.

The General's Favorite Fishing Hole
Chart of Accounts

Assets		Revenues	
101	Cash	401	Registration Fees
142	Office Supplies		
144	Food Supplies		Expenses
145	Prepaid Insurance	511	Wages Expense
181	Fishing Boats	521	Rent Expense
181.1	Accum. Depr.—Fishing Boats	523	Office Supplies Expense
		524	Food Supplies Expense
Liabilities		525	Telephone Expense
202	Accounts Payable	533	Utilities Expense
219	Wages Payable	535	Insurance Expense
		536	Postage Expense
Owner's Equity		542	Depr. Exp.—Fishing Boats
311	Bob Night, Capital		
312	Bob Night, Drawing		
313	Income Summary		

The following transactions took place during April 20--.

Apr. 1 Night invested cash in business, $90,000.

1 Paid insurance premium for six-month camping season, $9,000.

2 Paid rent for lodge and campgrounds for the month of April, $40,000.

2 Deposited registration fees, $35,000.

2 Purchased 10 fishing boats on account for $60,000. The boats have estimated useful lives of five years, at which time they will be donated to a local day camp. Arrangements were made to pay for the boats in July.

3 Purchased food supplies from Acme Super Market on account, $7,000.

5 Purchased office supplies from Gordon Office Supplies on account, $500.

7 Deposited registration fees, $38,600.

10 Purchased food supplies from Acme Super Market on account, $8,200.

10 Paid wages to fishing guides, $10,000.

14 Deposited registration fees, $30,500.

16 Purchased food supplies from Acme Super Market on account, $9,000.

17 Paid wages to fishing guides, $10,000.

18 Paid postage, $150.

Apr. 21   Deposited registration fees, $35,600.

24   Purchased food supplies from Acme Super Market on account, $8,500.

24   Paid wages to fishing guides, $10,000.

28   Deposited registration fees, $32,000.

29   Paid wages to fishing guides, $10,000.

30   Purchased food supplies from Acme Super Market on account, $6,000.

30   Paid Acme Super Market on account, $32,700.

30   Paid utilities bill, $2,000.

30   Paid telephone bill, $1,200.

30   Bob Night withdrew cash for personal use, $6,000.

Adjustment information for the end of April is provided below.

(a)   Office supplies remaining on hand, $100.
(b)   Food supplies remaining on hand, $8,000.
(c)   Insurance expired during the month of April, $1,500.
(d)   Depreciation on the fishing boats for the month of April, $1,000.
(e)   Wages earned, but not yet paid, at the end of April, $500.

REQUIRED

1.   Enter the transactions in a general journal. Enter transactions from April 1–5 on page 1, April 7–18 on page 2, April 21–29 and the first two entries for April 30 on page 3, and the remaining entries for April 30 on page 4.

2.   Post the entries to the general ledger. (If you are not using the working papers that accompany this text, you will need to enter the account titles and account numbers in the general ledger accounts.)

3.   Prepare a trial balance on a work sheet.

4.   Complete the work sheet.

5.   Journalize the adjusting entries (page 5).

6.   Post the adjusting entries to the general ledger.

7.   Prepare the income statement.

8.   Prepare the statement of owner's equity.

9.   Prepare the balance sheet.

10.   Journalize the closing entries (pages 5 and 6).

11.   Post the closing entries to the general ledger.

12.   Prepare a post-closing trial balance.

COMPREHENSIVE PROBLEM 1, PERIOD 2: THE ACCOUNTING CYCLE

During the month of May 20--, The General's Favorite Fishing Hole engaged in the following transactions. These transactions required an expansion of the chart of accounts as shown below.

Assets
101	Cash
122	Accounts Receivable
142	Office Supplies
144	Food Supplies
145	Prepaid Insurance
146	Prepaid Subscriptions
161	Land
171	Buildings
171.1	Accum. Depr.—Buildings
181	Fishing Boats
181.1	Accum. Depr.—Fishing Boats
182	Surround Sound System
182.1	Accum. Depr.—Surround Sound Sys.
183	Big Screen TV
183.1	Accum. Depr.—Big Screen TV

Liabilities
202	Accounts Payable
219	Wages Payable

Owner's Equity
311	Bob Night, Capital
312	Bob Night, Drawing
313	Income Summary

Revenues
401	Registration Fees
404	Vending Commission Revenue

Expenses
511	Wages Expense
512	Advertising Expense
521	Rent Expense
523	Office Supplies Expense
524	Food Supplies Expense
525	Telephone Expense
533	Utilities Expense
535	Insurance Expense
536	Postage Expense
537	Repair Expense
540	Depr. Exp.—Buildings
541	Depr. Exp.—Surround Sound Sys.
542	Depr. Exp.—Fishing Boats
543	Depr. Exp.—Big Screen TV
546	Satellite Programming Exp.
548	Subscriptions Expense

> This comprehensive problem is intended to serve as a mini-practice set without the source documents. As such, students should plan on about three to four hours to complete this problem.

May 1   In order to provide snacks for guests on a 24-hour basis, Night signed a contract with Snack Attack. Snack Attack will install vending machines with food and drinks and pay a 10% commission on all sales. Estimated payments are made at the beginning of each month. Night received a check for $200, the estimated commission on sales for May.

2   Night purchased a surround sound system and big screen TV with a digital satellite system for the guest lounge. The surround sound system cost $3,600 and has an estimated useful life of five years and no salvage value. The TV cost $8,000, has an estimated useful life of eight years, and has a salvage value of $800. Night paid cash for both items.

2   Paid for May's programming on the new digital satellite system, $125.

3   Night's office manager returned $100 worth of office supplies to Gordon Office Supply. Night received a $100 reduction on the account.

3   Deposited registration fees, $52,700.

3   Paid rent for lodge and campgrounds for the month of May, $40,000.

3   In preparation for the purchase of a nearby campground, Night invested an additional $600,000.

May 4	Paid Gordon Office Supply on account, $400.
4	Purchased the assets of a competing business and paid cash for the following: land, $100,000; lodge, $530,000; and fishing boats, $9,000. The lodge has a remaining useful life of 50 years and a $50,000 salvage value. The boats have remaining lives of five years and no salvage value.
5	Paid May's insurance premium for the new camp, $1,000. (See above transaction.)
5	Purchased food supplies from Acme Super Market on account, $22,950.
5	Purchased office supplies from Gordon Office Supplies on account, $1,200.
7	Night paid $40 each for one-year subscriptions to *Fishing Illustrated*, *Fishing Unlimited*, and *Fish Master*. The magazines are published monthly.
10	Deposited registration fees, $62,750.
13	Paid wages to fishing guides, $30,000. (Don't forget wages payable.)
14	A guest became ill and was unable to stay for the entire week. A refund was issued in the amount of $1,000.
17	Deposited registration fees, $63,000.
19	Purchased food supplies from Acme Super Market on account, $18,400.
21	Deposited registration fees, $63,400.
23	Paid $2,500 for advertising spots on National Sports Talk Radio.
25	Paid repair fee for damaged boat, $850.
27	Paid wages to fishing guides, $30,000.
28	Paid $1,800 for advertising spots on billboards.
29	Purchased food supplies from Acme Super Market on account, $14,325.
30	Paid utilities bill, $3,300.
30	Paid telephone bill, $1,800.
30	Paid Acme Super Market on account, $47,350.
31	Bob Night withdrew cash for personal use, $7,500.

Adjustment information at the end of May is provided below.

(a) Total vending machine sales were $2,300 for the month of May.
(b) Straight-line depreciation is used for the 10 boats purchased on April 2 for $60,000. The useful life for these assets is five years and there is no salvage value. A full month's depreciation was taken in April on these boats. Straight-line depreciation is also used for the two boats purchased in May. Make one adjusting entry for all depreciation on the boats.
(c) Straight-line depreciation is used to depreciate the surround sound system.
(d) Straight-line depreciation is used to depreciate the big screen TV.
(e) Straight-line depreciation is used for the building purchased in May.
(f) On April 2, Night paid $9,000 for insurance during the six-month camping season. May's portion of this premium was used up during this month.

(continued)

(g) Night received his May issues of *Fishing Illustrated*, *Fishing Unlimited*, and *Fish Master*.

(h) Office supplies remaining on hand, $150.

(i) Food supplies remaining on hand, $5,925.

(j) Wages earned, but not yet paid, at the end of May, $6,000.

REQUIRED

1. Enter the transactions in a general journal. Enter transactions from May 1–4 on page 5, May 5–28 on page 6, and the remaining entries on page 7. To save time and space, don't enter descriptions for the journal entries.

2. Post the entries to the general ledger. (If you are not using the working papers that accompany this text, you will need to enter the account titles, account numbers, and balances from April 30 in the general ledger accounts.)

3. Prepare a trial balance on a work sheet.

4. Complete the work sheet.

5. Journalize the adjusting entries on page 8 of the general journal.

6. Post the adjusting entries to the general ledger.

7. Prepare the income statement.

8. Prepare the statement of owner's equity.

9. Prepare the balance sheet.

10. Journalize the closing entries on page 9 of the general journal.

11. Post the closing entries to the general ledger.

12. Prepare a post-closing trial balance.

Accounting for Cash and Payroll

PART
2

ADRIAN PEACOCK/DIGITAL VISION/JUPITER IMAGES

Add Some Color to Your Learning!

Throughout the text, you will be introduced to many important terms and types of accounts. To help you learn the different terms and types of accounts, we have coded many of them using the following color key in Part 2:

Assets

Contra-Assets

Liabilities

Capital

Drawing

Revenues

Expenses

Income Summary (Net Income/Net Loss)

COURTESY OF H₂O AUDIO

Accounting for Cash

H₂O Audio was founded in 2003 and has its home office in San Diego, California. Its key products are waterproof headphones, armbands and cases, and headsets designed to enable swimmers, surfers, and divers to use their iPods underwater. H2O sells its merchandise online, in major electronics stores such as Best Buy, and in many outdoor and sports shops throughout the United States. The company started quite small, but its revenues increased from $440,000 in 2004 to $4 million in 2008, for a growth of over 800% in just four years.

Two of the challenges for a company growing as fast as H2O Audio are managing and protecting its cash. H2O has multiple checking accounts, receives cash receipts from multiple sources, and makes cash payments for many different bills. The company must have clear procedures and complete and accurate records in order to properly control cash and to plan for future needs. In this chapter, you will learn some of the ways to manage this critical business asset.

LEARNING OBJECTIVES

Careful study of this chapter should enable you to:

LO1 Describe how to open and use a checking account.

LO2 Prepare a bank reconciliation and related journal entries.

LO3 Establish and use a petty cash fund.

LO4 Establish a change fund and use the cash short and over account.

Cash is an asset that is quite familiar and important to all of us. We generally think of **cash** as the currency and coins in our pockets and the money we have in our checking accounts. To a business, cash also includes checks received from customers, money orders, and bank cashier's checks.

Because it plays such a central role in operating a business, cash must be carefully managed and controlled. A business should have a system of **internal control**—a set of policies and procedures designed to ensure proper accounting for transactions. For good internal control of cash transactions, all cash received should be deposited daily in a bank. All disbursements, except for payments from petty cash, should be made by check.

CHECKING ACCOUNT

LO1 Describe how to open and use a checking account.

The key documents and forms required in opening and using a checking account are the signature card, deposit tickets, checks, and bank statements.

OPENING A CHECKING ACCOUNT

To open a checking account, each person authorized to sign checks must complete and sign a **signature card** (Figure 7-1). The bank uses this card to verify the depositor's

FIGURE 7-1 Signature Card

signature on any banking transactions. The taxpayer identification number (TIN) is the depositor's social security number or employer identification number (EIN). This number is shown on the card to identify the depositor for income tax purposes. An EIN can be obtained from the Internal Revenue Service.

MAKING DEPOSITS

A **deposit ticket** (Figure 7-2) is a form showing a detailed listing of items being deposited. Currency, coins, and checks are listed separately. Each check should be identified by its **ABA (American Bankers Association) Number**. This number is the small fraction printed in the upper right-hand corner of each check (see Figure 7-5 on page 233). Part of this number also appears in **magnetic ink character recognition (MICR) code** on the lower left side of the front of each check. The code is used to sort and route checks throughout the U.S. banking system. Normally, only the numerator of the fraction is used in identifying checks on the deposit ticket.

FIGURE 7-2 Deposit Ticket

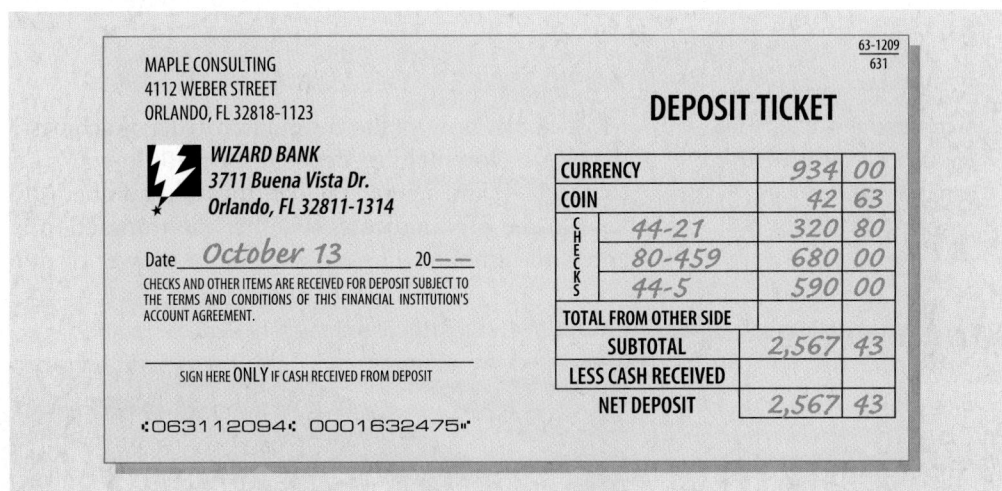

The depositor delivers or mails the deposit ticket and all items being deposited to the bank. The bank then gives or mails a receipt to the depositor. The deposit also can be made after business hours by using the night depository provided by most banks. The deposit is put in a locked bag, which is placed in a secure drawer or chute at the bank, for processing the following morning.

ENDORSEMENTS

Each check being deposited must be endorsed by the depositor. The **endorsement** consists of stamping or writing the depositor's name and sometimes other information on the back of the check, in the space provided near the left end. There are two basic types of endorsements.

1. **Blank endorsement**—the depositor simply signs the back of the check. This makes the check payable to any bearer.

2. **Restrictive endorsement**—the depositor adds words such as "For deposit," "Pay to any bank," or "Pay to Daryl Beck only" to restrict the payment of the check.

Businesses commonly use a rubber stamp to endorse checks for deposit. The check shown in Figure 7-3 has been stamped with a restrictive endorsement.

FIGURE 7-3 Restrictive Endorsement

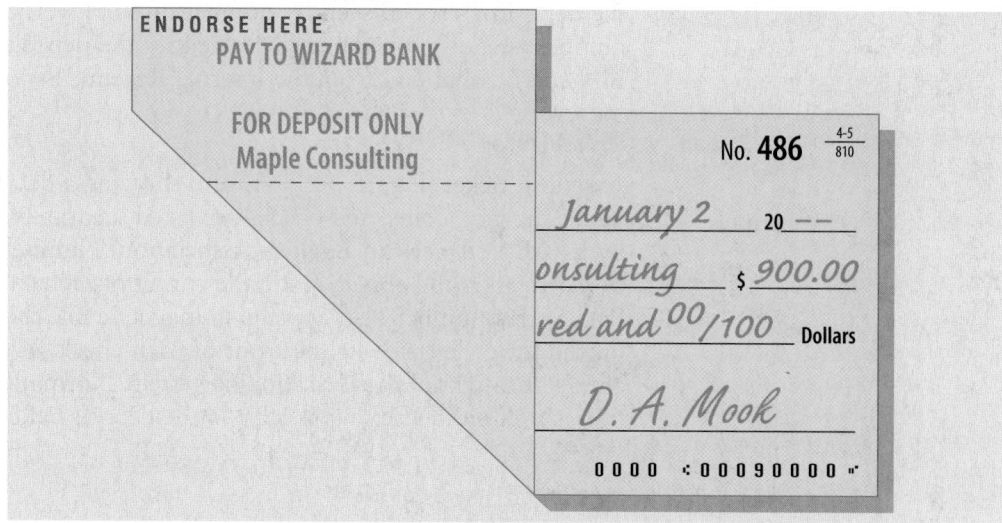

AUTOMATED TELLER MACHINES

Postage stamps can be purchased at some ATMs. For deposits, some ATMs can provide an image of any checks being deposited.

Most banks now make **automated teller machines** (ATMs) available at all times to depositors for making deposits or withdrawals. Each depositor has a plastic card (Figure 7-4) and a personal identification number (PIN). The depositor inserts the card, keys in the PIN, indicates whether the transaction is a withdrawal or a deposit, and enters the amount. The machine has a drawer or door for the withdrawal or deposit.

FIGURE 7-4 Automated Teller Machine Card

Most ATMs are now on a system such as Cirrus that allows noncustomers to use other ATMs in both the United States and foreign countries. There are also "cash machines" that supply only cash and do not take deposits. These are often found at airports and convenience stores.

It is important for the depositor to keep an accounting record of ATM withdrawals and deposits. This is done on the check stub or register described in the following section, and with an appropriate journal entry.

WRITING CHECKS

A **check** is a document ordering a bank to pay cash from a depositor's account. There are three parties to every check.

1. **Drawer**—the depositor who orders the bank to pay the cash.

2. **Drawee**—the bank on which the check is drawn.

3. **Payee**—the person being paid the cash.

Checks used by businesses are usually bound in the form of a book. In some checkbooks, each check is attached to a **check stub** (Figure 7-5) that contains space to record all relevant information about the check. Other checkbooks are accompanied by a small register book in which the relevant information is noted. If a financial computer software package is used, both the check and the register can be prepared electronically.

Note that the check stubs in Figure 7-5 contain space to record amounts deposited. It generally is a good idea also to indicate the date of the deposit, as shown on check stub No. 108.

Use the following three steps in preparing a check:

STEP 1   Complete the check stub or register.

STEP 2   Enter the date, payee name, and amount on the check.

STEP 3   Sign the check.

It is sometimes necessary to void a check. Proper procedures for doing so are to tear off or deface the signature box and to file the voided check numerically with the canceled checks.

FIGURE 7-5 Checks and Check Stubs

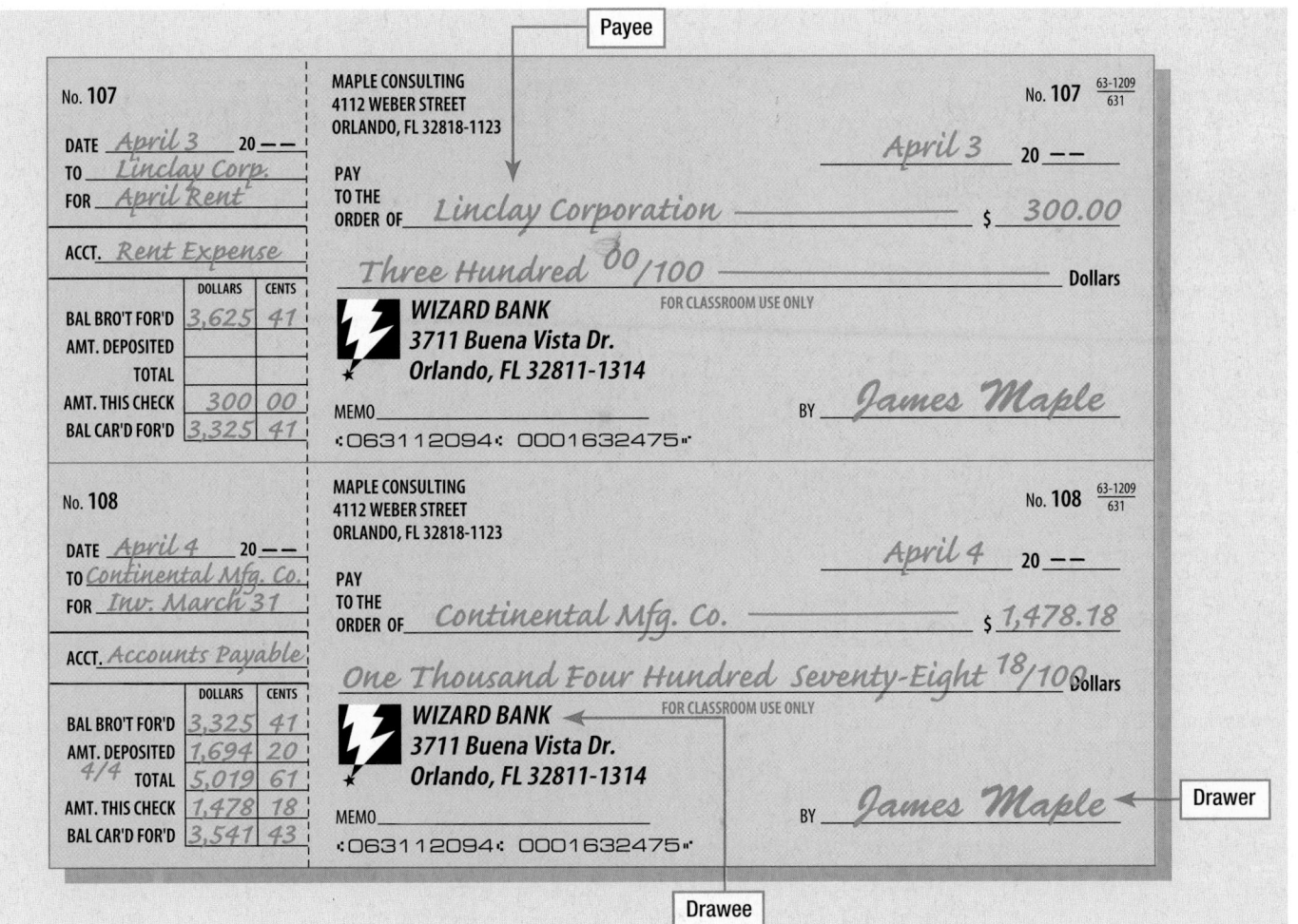

The check stub is completed first so that the drawer retains a record of each check issued. This information is needed to determine the proper journal entry for the transaction.

The payee name is entered on the first long line on the check, followed by the amount in figures. The amount in words is then entered on the second long line. If the amount in figures does not agree with the amount in words, the bank usually contacts the drawer for the correct amount or returns the check unpaid.

The most critical point in preparing a check is signing it, and this should be done last. The signature authorizes the bank to pay cash from the drawer's account. The check signer should make sure that all other aspects of the check are correct before signing it.

> The payee and amount written in words should be followed by something, such as a line, to make it difficult to alter the payee or the amount.

LEARNING KEY

The check should not be signed until the check signer has verified that all aspects of the check are correct.

BANK STATEMENT

A statement of account issued by a bank to each depositor once a month is called a **bank statement**. Figure 7-6 is a bank statement for a checking account. The statement shows the following:

1. The balance at the beginning of the period.

2. Deposits and other amounts added during the period.

3. Checks and other amounts subtracted during the period.

4. The balance at the end of the period.

FIGURE 7-6 Bank Statement

STATEMENT — WIZARD BANK

MAPLE CONSULTING
4112 WEBER STREET
ORLANDO, FL 32818-1123

Account Number: 16 3247 5
Statement Date: Nov. 21, 20—
Page Number: 1

Beginning Balance	No. of Deposits and Credits	We Have Added these Deposits and Credits Totaling	No. of Withdrawals and Charges	We Have Subtracted these Withdrawals and Charges Totaling	Resulting in a Statement Balance of
$2,721.51	2	$2,599.31	17	$3,572.73	$1,748.09

Beginning balance → $2,721.51   Ending balance → $1,748.09

Document Count | Average Daily Balance this Statement Period | Minimum Balance this Statement Period | Date | Amount

If Your Account does not Balance, Please See Reverse Side and Report any Discrepancies to our Customer Service Department.

DATE	DESCRIPTION	AMOUNT	BALANCE
10/20	Beginning Balance		2,721.51
10/27	Check No. 207	−242.00	2,479.51
10/28	Check No. 212	−68.93	2,410.58
10/28	Check No. 213	−58.00	2,352.58
10/29	Deposit	867.00	3,219.58
11/3	Deposit	1,732.31	4,951.89
11/3	Check No. 214	−18.98	4,932.91
11/3	Check No. 215	−229.01	4,703.90
11/3	Check No. 216	−452.13	4,251.77
11/3	Check No. 217	−94.60	4,157.17
11/10	Check No. 218	−1,800.00	2,357.17
11/10	DM: NSF	−200.00	2,157.17
11/10	Check No. 220	−32.42	2,124.75
11/10	Check No. 221	−64.08	2,060.67
11/10	Check No. 222	−110.87	1,949.80
11/13	ATM Withdrawal	−100.00	1,849.80
11/18	Check No. 223	−18.00	1,831.80
11/18	Check No. 225	−23.31	1,808.49
11/18	Check No. 226	−58.60	1,749.89
11/19	DM: Service Charge	−1.80	1,748.09

An amount added → Deposit (10/29)
An amount subtracted → Check No. 220 (11/10)

EC – Error Correction
CM – Credit Memo
DM – Debit Memo
NSF – Not Sufficient Funds
ATM – Automated Teller Machine
TR – Wire Transfer

It is increasingly common for banks to return only a listing of checks with the bank statement. A check "image" can be obtained by making a special request to the bank.

With the bank statement, the bank normally sends the following to the depositor:

1. **Canceled checks**—the depositor's checks paid by the bank during the period. The bank may send the checks themselves, "imaged" sheets showing only the faces of the checks, or simply a listing of the checks on the bank statement.

2. Any other forms representing items added to or subtracted from the account.

U REVU

Complete U REVU-1 on **page 252** to test your basic understanding of LO1.

RECONCILING THE BANK STATEMENT

LO2 Prepare a bank reconciliation and related journal entries.

On any given day, the balance in the cash account on the depositor's books (the book balance) is unlikely to be the same as that on the bank's books (the bank balance). This difference can be due to errors, but it usually is caused by timing. Transactions generally are recorded by the business at a time that is different from when the bank records them.

DEPOSITS

Suppose there are cash receipts of $600 on April 30. These cash receipts would be recorded on the depositor's books on April 30, and a deposit of $600 would be sent to the bank. The deposit would not reach the bank, however, until at least the following day, May 1. This timing difference in recording the $600 of cash receipts is illustrated in Figure 7-7. Notice that on April 30, the balances in the depositor's books and in the bank's books would be different.

FIGURE 7-7 Depositor and Bank Records—Deposits

CASH PAYMENTS

Similar timing differences occur with cash payments. Suppose a check for $350 is written on April 30. This cash payment would be recorded on the depositor's books on April 30 and the check mailed to the payee. The check probably would not be received by the payee until May 3. If the payee deposited the check promptly, it still would not clear the bank until May 4. This timing difference in recording the $350 cash payment is illustrated in Figure 7-8. Notice once again that on April 30, the balances in the depositor's books and in the bank's books would be different.

FIGURE 7-8 Depositor and Bank Records—Cash Payments

REASONS FOR DIFFERENCES BETWEEN BANK AND BOOK BALANCES

When the bank statement is received, the depositor examines the records to identify the items that explain the difference between the book and bank balances. This process of bringing the book and bank balances into agreement is called preparing a **bank reconciliation**.

The most common reasons for differences between the book and bank balances are the following:

1. **Deposits in transit.** Deposits that have not reached or been recorded by the bank before the statement is prepared.

2. **Outstanding checks.** Checks issued that have not been presented to the bank for payment before the statement is prepared.

3. **Service charges.** Bank charges for services such as check printing and processing.

4. **Collections.** Collections of promissory notes or charge accounts made by the bank on behalf of the depositor.

5. **Not sufficient funds (NSF) checks.** Checks deposited by the depositor that are not paid because the drawer did not have sufficient funds.

6. **Errors.** Errors made by the bank or the depositor in recording cash transactions.

STEPS IN PREPARING THE BANK RECONCILIATION

Use the following three steps in preparing the bank reconciliation:

STEP 1 Identify deposits in transit and any related errors.

STEP 2 Identify outstanding checks and any related errors.

STEP 3 Identify additional reconciling items.

Deposits in Transit and Related Errors

Follow these steps:

STEP 1 Compare deposits listed on the bank statement with deposits in transit on last month's bank reconciliation. All of last month's deposits in transit should appear on the current month's bank statement.

STEP 2 Compare the remaining deposits on the bank statement with deposits listed in the accounting records. Any deposits listed in the accounting records but not on the bank statement are deposits in transit on the current bank reconciliation.

STEP 3   Compare the individual deposit amounts on the bank statement and in the accounting records. If they differ, the error needs to be corrected.

Outstanding Checks and Related Errors

Follow these steps:

STEP 1   Compare canceled checks with the bank statement and the accounting records. If the amounts differ, the error needs to be corrected.

STEP 2   As each canceled check is compared with the accounting records, place a check mark on the check stub or other accounting record to indicate that the check has cleared.

STEP 3   Any checks written that have not been checked off represent outstanding checks on the bank reconciliation. This includes outstanding checks from last month's bank reconciliation that have not yet cleared.

Additional Reconciling Items

Some banks pay interest on checking account balances. This reconciling item would be handled in the same manner as a bank credit memo.

Compare any additions and deductions on the bank statement that are not deposits or checks with the accounting records. Items that the bank adds to the account are called **credit memos**. Items that the bank deducts from the account are called **debit memos**. Remember that a depositor's account is a liability to the bank. Thus, a credit memo increases this liability; a debit memo reduces the liability. Any of these items not appearing in the accounting records represent additional items on the bank reconciliation.

ILLUSTRATION OF A BANK RECONCILIATION

A general format for the bank reconciliation is shown in Figure 7-9. Not every item shown in this illustration would be in every bank reconciliation, but this format is helpful in determining where to put items. A bank reconciliation form also can be found on the back of most bank statements. Some banks also include a reconciliation form on their Web site.

FIGURE 7-9 Bank Reconciliation Format

BANK RECONCILIATION		
Bank statement balance		$xxxx
Add: Deposits in transit	$xxxx	
Bank errors (that understate balance)	xxxx	xxxx
		$xxxx
Deduct: Outstanding checks	$xxxx	
Bank errors (that overstate balance)	xxxx	xxxx
Adjusted bank balance		$xxxx
Book balance		$xxxx
Add: Bank credit memos	$xxxx	
Book errors (that understate balance)	xxxx	xxxx
		$xxxx
Deduct: Bank debit memos	$xxxx	
Book errors (that overstate balance)	xxxx	xxxx
Adjusted book balance		$xxxx

To illustrate the preparation of a bank reconciliation, we will use the Maple Consulting bank statement shown in Figure 7-6. That statement shows a balance of $1,748.09 as of November 21. The balance in Maple's check stubs and general ledger cash account is $2,393.23. The three steps described on page 236 were used to identify the following items, and the reconciliation in Figure 7-10 was prepared.

1. A deposit of $637.02 recorded on November 21 had not been received by the bank. Maple has received the funds but the amount has not yet been counted by the bank. This deposit in transit is added to the bank statement balance.

2. Check numbers 219, 224, and 227 are outstanding. The funds have been disbursed by Maple but have not yet been paid out by the bank. The amount of these outstanding checks is subtracted from the bank statement balance.

3. Check number 214 was written for $18.98 but was entered on the check stub and on the books as $19.88. This $0.90 error is added to the book balance because $0.90 too much had been deducted from the book balance.

4. Maple made an ATM withdrawal of $100.00 on November 13 for personal use but did not record the withdrawal on the books. The bank has reduced Maple's balance by this amount. Thus, this amount is deducted from the book balance.

5. The bank returned an NSF check of $200.00. This was a check received by Maple from a customer. The bank has reduced Maple's balance by $200.00, but Maple has not yet recorded it. This amount is deducted from the book balance.

6. The bank service charge was $1.80. The bank has reduced Maple's balance by this amount, but Maple has not yet recorded it. This amount is deducted from the book balance.

FIGURE 7-10 Bank Reconciliation

Maple Consulting Bank Reconciliation November 21, 20 - -			
Bank statement balance, November 21			$1,748.09
Add deposit in transit			637.02
			$2,385.11
Deduct outstanding checks:			
No. 219	$200.00		
No. 224	25.00		
No. 227	67.78	292.78	
Adjusted bank balance			$2,092.33
Book balance, November 21			$2,393.23
Add error on Check No. 214			0.90
			$2,394.13
Deduct:			
Unrecorded ATM withdrawal	$100.00		
NSF check	200.00		
Bank service charge	1.80	301.80	
Adjusted book balance			$2,092.33

Requires journal entry (1)

Require journal entries (2), (3), and (4)

Reconciled balances

LEARNING KEY

Journal entries are needed to correct errors in the books and to record bank additions and deductions that are not in the books.

JOURNAL ENTRIES

Only two kinds of items appearing on a bank reconciliation require journal entries.

1. Errors in the depositor's books.

2. Bank additions and deductions that do not already appear in the books.

Note the four items in the lower portion of the bank reconciliation in Figure 7-10. A journal entry always is required for each item in this book balance portion of the bank reconciliation. The four journal entries for Maple Consulting are shown below, using entry numbers matching those noted in Figure 7-10.

The $0.90 item is an error in the accounting records that occurred when the check amount was incorrectly entered. Assume the $18.98 was in payment of an account payable which had been incorrectly debited for $19.88. The entry to correct this error is as follows:

4		(1)	Cash				0	90						4
5			Accounts Payable							0	90	5
6			Error in recording check									6

The $100.00 ATM withdrawal has been deducted from Maple's account by the bank. Maple has not yet recorded the withdrawal. Maple withdrew the funds for personal use, so the following journal entry is required:

8		(2)	James Maple, Drawing		1	0	0	00						8
9			Cash						1	0	0	00	9
10			Unrecorded ATM withdrawal									10

The $200.00 NSF check is a deduction by the bank for a check deposited by Maple that proved to be worthless. This amount must be deducted from the book balance. Assuming the $200.00 was received from a customer on account, the following journal entry is required:

12		(3)	Accounts Receivable		2	0	0	00						12
13			Cash						2	0	0	00	13
14			Unrecorded NSF check									14

The $1.80 bank service charge is a fee for bank services received by Maple. The bank has deducted this amount from Maple's account. Bank service charges are usually small and are charged to Miscellaneous Expense.

16		(4)	Miscellaneous Expense			1	80						16
17			Cash							1	80	17
18			Bank service charge									18

Figure 7-11 contains a detailed list of items that require journal entries.

FIGURE 7-11 Bank Reconciliation Items that Require Journal Entries

ADDITIONS TO CASH BALANCE	DEDUCTIONS FROM CASH BALANCE

* Unrecorded deposits (including ATM)
* Note collected by bank
* Interest earned
* Errors:
  1. Added too little as a deposit
  2. Deducted too much as a check
	* Unrecorded ATM withdrawals
	* NSF checks
	* Bank service charges
	* Deposits recorded twice
	* Unrecorded checks
	* Loan payments
	* Interest payments
	* Errors:
	  1. Added too much as a deposit
	  2. Deducted too little as a check

ELECTRONIC FUNDS TRANSFER

Electronic funds transfer (EFT) uses a computer rather than paper checks to complete transactions with the bank. This technique is being used increasingly today. Applications of EFT include payrolls, social security payments, retail purchases, mortgage payments, and the ATM transactions described earlier in the chapter.

Heavy use of EFT can present a challenge in preparing bank reconciliations. Many of the documents handled in a purely manual environment disappear when EFT is used. Bank accounts are just one of many areas where computers require accountants to think in new ways. Regardless of what system is used, the key point to remember is that the accounting records must be correctly updated.

U REVU

Complete U REVU-2 on **page 252** to test your basic understanding of LO2.

A BROADER VIEW

DON FARRALL/PHOTODISC/GETTY IMAGES

Fraud—A Real Threat to Small Business

Every two years, the Association of Certified Fraud Examiners (ACFE) surveys its members on the occupational fraud they have investigated during the preceding two years. The most recent survey showed that 40% of the frauds occurred in private companies. In addition, the median loss suffered by small businesses was $200,000. The most commonly cited factor that allowed the fraud to occur was a lack of adequate internal control. And 85% of the asset misappropriation cases involved theft or misuse of cash.

These survey findings show the importance of the kinds of internal controls over cash described in this chapter and the appendix.

THE PETTY CASH FUND

LO3 Establish and use a petty cash fund.

For good control over cash, payments generally should be made by check. Unfortunately, payments of very small amounts by check can be both inconvenient and inefficient. For example, the time and cost required to write a check for $0.70 to mail a letter might be greater than the cost of the postage. Therefore, businesses customarily establish a **petty cash fund** to pay for small items with cash. "Petty" means small, and both the amount of the fund and the maximum amount of any bill that can be paid from the fund are small.

ESTABLISHING A PETTY CASH FUND

To establish a petty cash fund, a check is written to the petty cash custodian for the amount to be set aside in the fund. The amount may be $50.00, $100.00, $200.00, or any amount considered necessary. The journal entry to establish a petty cash fund of $100.00 would be as follows:

4		Petty Cash		1 0 0 00			4
5		Cash			1 0 0 00	5
6		Establish petty cash fund				6

Petty Cash is an asset that is listed immediately below Cash on the balance sheet.

The custodian cashes the check and places the money in a petty cash box. For good control, the custodian should be the only person authorized to make payments from the fund. The custodian should be able to account for the full amount of the fund at any time.

MAKING PAYMENTS FROM A PETTY CASH FUND

A receipt called a **petty cash voucher** (Figure 7-12) should be prepared for every payment from the fund. The voucher shows the name of the payee, the purpose of the payment, and the account to be charged for the payment. Each voucher should be signed by the custodian and by the person receiving the cash. The vouchers should be numbered consecutively so that all vouchers can be accounted for.

FIGURE 7-12 Petty Cash Voucher

PETTY CASH PAYMENTS RECORD

When a petty cash fund is maintained, a formal record is often kept of all payments from the fund. The **petty cash payments record** (Figure 7-13) is a special multi-column record that supplements the regular accounting records. It is not a journal. The headings of the Distribution of Payments columns may vary, depending upon the types of expenditures.

The petty cash payments record of Maple Consulting is shown in Figure 7-13. A narrative of the petty cash transactions shown in Figure 7-13 is as follows:

Dec. 1   Maple issued a check for $200.00 payable to Tina Blank, Petty Cash Custodian. Blank cashed the check and placed the money in a secure cash box.

A notation of the amount received is made in the Description column of the petty cash payments record. In addition, this transaction is entered in the journal as follows:

8	Dec. 1	Petty Cash		2 0 0 00		8
9		Cash			2 0 0 00	9
10		Establish petty cash fund				10

During the month of December, the following payments were made from the petty cash fund:

Dec. 5   Paid $32.80 to Jerry's Auto for servicing the company automobile. Voucher No. 1.

8   Reimbursed Maple $15.75 for the amount spent for lunch with a client. Voucher No. 2.

9   Gave Maple $30.00 for personal use. Voucher No. 3.

There is no special Distribution column for entering amounts withdrawn by the owner for personal use. Therefore, this payment is entered by writing the account name in the Account column and $30.00 in the Amount column at the extreme right of the petty cash payments record.

15   Paid $38.25 for printer repairs. Voucher No. 4.

17   Reimbursed Maple $14.50 for travel expenses. Voucher No. 5.

19   Paid $8.00 to Big Red Car Care for washing the company automobile. Voucher No. 6.

22   Paid $9.50 for mailing a package. Voucher No. 7.

29   Paid $30.00 for postage stamps. Voucher No. 8.

REPLENISHING THE PETTY CASH FUND

The petty cash fund should be replenished whenever the fund runs low and at the end of each accounting period, so that the accounts are brought up to date. The amount columns of the petty cash payments record are totaled to verify that the total of the Total Amount column equals the total of the Distribution columns. The amount columns are then ruled as shown in Figure 7-13.

FIGURE 7-13 Maple Consulting's Petty Cash Payments Record

PETTY CASH PAYMENTS FOR THE MONTH OF December 20--   PAGE 1

DAY		DESCRIPTION	VOU. NO.	TOTAL AMOUNT	AUTO EXP.	POST. EXP.	TRAVEL/ ENTERT. EXP.	MISC. EXP.	ACCOUNT	AMOUNT	
1	1	Received in fund 200.00									1
2	5	Automobile repairs	1	3 2 80	3 2 80						2
3	8	Client luncheon	2	1 5 75			1 5 75				3
4	9	James Maple, personal use	3	3 0 00					James Maple, Drawing	3 0 00	4
5	15	Printer repairs	4	3 8 25				3 8 25			5
6	17	Traveling expenses	5	1 4 50			1 4 50				6
7	19	Washing automobile	6	8 00	8 00						7
8	22	Postage expense	7	9 50		9 50					8
9	29	Postage stamps	8	3 0 00		3 0 00					9
10				1 7 8 80	4 0 80	3 9 50	3 0 25	3 8 25		3 0 00	10
11	31	Balance 21.20									11
12	31	Replenished fund 178.80									12
13		Total 200.00									13

DISTRIBUTION OF PAYMENTS

Credit to replenish petty cash fund and reduce Cash.

Debits to replenish petty cash fund and recognize expenses paid out of petty cash.

The information in the petty cash payments record is then used to replenish the petty cash fund. On December 31, a check for $178.80 is issued to the petty cash custodian. The journal entry to record the replenishment of the fund is as follows:

18	Dec.	31	Automobile Expense				4	0	80						18
19			Postage Expense				3	9	50						19
20			Travel and Entertainment Expense				3	0	25						20
21			Miscellaneous Expense				3	8	25						21
22			James Maple, Drawing				3	0	00						22
23			Cash							1	7	8	80		23
24			Replenishment of petty cash fund												24

Note two important aspects of the functioning of a petty cash fund.

LEARNING KEY

Once the petty cash fund is established, an entry is made to Petty Cash only if the amount of the fund is being changed.

1. Once the fund is established by debiting Petty Cash and crediting Cash, no further entries are made to Petty Cash. Notice in the journal entry to replenish the fund that the debits are to appropriate expense accounts and the credit is to Cash. Only if the amount of the fund itself is being changed would there be a debit or credit to Petty Cash.

2. The petty cash payments record is strictly a supplement to the regular accounting records. Because it is not a journal, no posting is done from this record. A separate entry must be made in the journal to replenish the fund and update the expense accounts.

U REVU

Complete U REVU-3 on **page 252** to test your basic understanding of LO3.

THE CHANGE FUND AND CASH SHORT AND OVER

LO4 Establish a change fund and use the cash short and over account.

Businesses generally must be able to make change when customers use cash to pay for goods or services received. To do so, generally it is a good idea to establish a **change fund**. A change fund is a supply of currency and coins kept in a cash register or cash drawer for use in handling cash sales.

ESTABLISHING AND OPERATING THE CHANGE FUND

The journal entries for establishing and maintaining a change fund are very similar to the ones just used for petty cash. To establish a change fund of $200.00 on June 1, the following entry would be made:

8	June 1	Change Fund			2	0	0	00						8
9		Cash							2	0	0	00		9
10		Establish change fund												10

At the end of the day, cash received during the day is deposited, but the change fund is held back for use the following business day. For example, if cash of $1,250.00 was received on June 3 for services provided, the cash drawer would contain $1,450.00, as follows:

Change fund	$ 200.00
Cash sales	1,250.00
Total cash on hand	$1,450.00

The $1,250 would be deposited in the bank, and the following journal entry would be made:

12	June 3	Cash				1	2	5	0	00					12
13		Service Fees									1	2	5	0	00	13
14		Cash received for services														14

LEARNING KEY

Once the change fund is established, an entry is made to Change Fund only if the amount of the fund is being changed.

Notice the additional similarity between the change fund and the petty cash fund. Once the change fund is established by a debit to Change Fund and a credit to Cash, no further entries are made to the change fund. Only if the amount of the change fund itself is being changed would there be a debit or credit to Change Fund.

CASH SHORT AND OVER

An unavoidable part of the change-making process is that errors can occur. It is important to know whether such errors have occurred and how to account for them.

Businesses commonly use cash registers with tapes that accumulate a record of the day's receipts. The amount of cash according to the tapes plus the amount of the change fund can be compared with the amount of cash in the register to determine any error. For example, assume a cash shortage is identified for June 19.

Change fund	$ 200.00
Receipts per register tapes	963.00
Total	$1,163.00
Cash count	1,161.00
Cash shortage	$ 2.00

Similarly, assume a cash overage is identified for June 20.

Change fund	$ 200.00
Receipts per register tapes	814.00
Total	$1,014.00
Cash count	1,015.00
Cash overage	$ 1.00

We account for such errors by using an account called Cash Short and Over. In T account form, Cash Short and Over appears as follows:

Cash Short and Over

Shortage (Expense)	Overage (Revenue)

The register tapes on June 19 showed receipts of $963.00 and the change fund was $200.00, but only $1,161.00 in cash was counted. The journal entry on June 19 to record the revenues and cash shortage (remember that we hold back the change fund) would be as follows:

18	June	19	Cash					9	6	1	00					18
19			Cash Short and Over						2	00						19
20			Service Fees									9	6	3	00	20
21			Record service fees and cash shortage													21

The entry on June 20 to record the revenues and cash overage (holding back the change fund) would be as follows:

23	June	20	Cash					8	1	5	00					23
24			Service Fees									8	1	4	00	24
25			Cash Short and Over											1	00	25
26			Record service fees and cash overage													26

The cash short and over account is used to accumulate cash shortages and overages throughout the accounting period. At the end of the period, a debit balance in the account (a net shortage) is treated as an expense. A credit balance in the account (a net overage) is treated as revenue.

U REVU

Complete U REVU-4 on **page 252** to test your basic understanding of LO4.

SELF-STUDY

LEARNING OBJECTIVES   Key Points to Remember

LO1 Describe how to open and use a checking account.

Three steps to follow in preparing a check are as follows:
1. Complete the check stub or register.
2. Enter the date, payee name, and amount on the check.
3. Sign the check.

LEARNING OBJECTIVES   Key Points to Remember

LO2 **Prepare a bank reconciliation and related journal entries.**

The most common reasons for differences between the book and bank cash balances are as follows:
1. Deposits in transit
2. Outstanding checks
3. Bank service charges
4. Bank collections for the depositor
5. NSF checks
6. Errors by the bank or the depositor

Three steps to follow in preparing a bank reconciliation are as follows:
1. Identify deposits in transit and any related errors.
2. Identify outstanding checks and any related errors.
3. Identify additional reconciling items.

Only two kinds of items on a bank reconciliation require journal entries.
1. Errors in the depositor's books.
2. Bank additions and deductions that do not already appear in the books.

LO3 **Establish and use a petty cash fund.**

Two important aspects of the functioning of a petty cash fund are as follows:
1. Once the fund is established, subsequent entries do not affect the petty cash account balance, unless the size of the fund itself is being changed.
2. The petty cash payments record is supplemental to the regular accounting records. No posting is done from this record.

LO4 **Establish a change fund and use the cash short and over account.**

A change fund is established by debiting Change Fund and crediting Cash. Cash shortages and overages are accounted for using the cash short and over account. A debit balance in this account represents expense; a credit balance represents revenue.

DEMONSTRATION PROBLEM

Jason Kuhn's check stubs indicated a balance of $4,565.12 for Kuhn's Wilderness Outfitters on March 31. This included a record of a deposit of $926.10 mailed to the bank on March 30, but not credited to Kuhn's account until April 1. In addition, the following checks were outstanding on March 31:

No. 462	$524.26
No. 465	$213.41
No. 473	$543.58
No. 476	$351.38
No. 477	$197.45

(continued)

The bank statement showed a balance of $5,419.00 as of March 31. The bank statement included a service charge of $4.10 with the date of March 29. In matching the canceled checks and record of deposits with the stubs, it was discovered that Check No. 456, a payment on account to Office Suppliers, Inc., for $39.00 was erroneously recorded on the stub as $93.00. This caused the bank balance on that stub and those following to be $54.00 too small. It was also discovered that an ATM withdrawal of $100.00 for personal use was not recorded on the books.

Kuhn maintains a $200.00 petty cash fund. His petty cash payments record showed the following totals at the end of March of the current year:

Automobile expense	$ 32.40
Postage expense	27.50
Charitable contributions expense	35.00
Telephone expense	6.20
Travel and entertainment expense	38.60
Miscellaneous expense	17.75
Jason Kuhn, drawing	40.00
Total	$197.45

This left a balance of $2.55 in the petty cash fund, and the fund was replenished.

REQUIRED

1. Prepare a bank reconciliation for Jason Kuhn as of March 31, 20--.

2. Journalize the entries that should be made by Kuhn on his books as of March 31, 20--, (a) as a result of the bank reconciliation and (b) to replenish the petty cash fund.

3. Show proof that, after these entries, the total of the cash and petty cash account balances equals $4,715.02.

Solution

1.

Kuhn's Wilderness Outfitters Bank Reconciliation March 31, 20 --			
Bank statement balance, March 31			$5 4 1 9 00
Add deposit in transit			9 2 6 10
			$6 3 4 5 10
Deduct outstanding checks:			
No. 462	$ 5 2 4 26		
No. 465	2 1 3 41		
No. 473	5 4 3 58		
No. 476	3 5 1 38		
No. 477	1 9 7 45	1 8 3 0 08	
Adjusted bank balance			$4 5 1 5 02
Book balance, March 31			$4 5 6 5 12
Add error on Check No. 456			5 4 00
			$4 6 1 9 12
Deduct: Bank service charge	$ 4 10		
Unrecorded ATM withdrawal	1 0 0 00	1 0 4 10	
Adjusted book balance			$4 5 1 5 02

2a.

3																		3
4	Mar.	31	Miscellaneous Expense						4	10								4
5			Cash										4	10				5
6			Bank service charge															6
7																		7
8			Cash					5	4	00								8
9			Accounts Payable—Office Suppliers, Inc.									5	4	00				9
10			Error on Check No. 456															10
11																		11
12			Jason Kuhn, Drawing				1	0	0	00								12
13			Cash								1	0	0	00				13
14			Unrecorded ATM withdrawal															14
15																		15
16		31	Automobile Expense					3	2	40								16
17			Postage Expense					2	7	50								17
18			Charitable Contributions Expense					3	5	00								18
19			Telephone Expense						6	20								19
20			Travel and Entertainment Expense					3	8	60								20
21			Miscellaneous Expense					1	7	75								21
22			Jason Kuhn, Drawing					4	0	00								22
23			Cash								1	9	7	45				23
24			Replenishment of petty cash fund															24
25																		25

b. (rows 16–25)

3. Cash in bank:
Check stub balance, March 31	$4,565.12
Plus error on Ck. No. 456	54.00
Less bank charges	(104.10)
Adjusted cash in bank	$4,515.02

   Cash on hand:
Petty cash fund	$ 2.55
Add replenishment	197.45
Adjusted cash on hand	200.00
Total cash in bank and petty cash on hand	$4,715.02

KEY TERMS

ABA (American Bankers Association) Number (231) The small fraction printed in the upper right-hand corner of each check.

automated teller machine (ATM) (232) A machine used by depositors to make withdrawals or deposits at any time.

bank reconciliation (236) A report used to bring the book and bank balances into agreement.

bank statement (234) A statement of account issued by a bank to each depositor once a month.

blank endorsement (231) An endorsement where the depositor simply signs the back of the check, making the check payable to any bearer.

canceled check (235) A depositor's check paid by the bank during the bank statement period.

cash (230) To a business, cash includes currency, coins, checks received from customers, money orders, and bank cashier's checks.

change fund (244) A supply of currency and coins kept in a cash register or cash drawer for use in handling cash sales.

check (233) A document ordering a bank to pay cash from a depositor's account.

check stub (233) In some checkbooks, a document attached to a check that contains space for relevant information about the check.

credit memo (237) An item that the bank adds to the account.

debit memo (237) An item that the bank deducts from the account.

deposit ticket (231) A form showing a detailed listing of items being deposited.

deposits in transit (236) Deposits that have not reached or been recorded by the bank before the bank statement is prepared.

drawee (233) The bank on which the check is drawn.

drawer (233) The depositor who orders the bank to pay the cash.

electronic funds transfer (EFT) (240) A process using a computer rather than paper checks to complete transactions with the bank.

endorsement (231) Stamping or writing the depositor's name and sometimes other information on the back of the check.

internal control (230) A set of procedures designed to ensure proper accounting for transactions.

magnetic ink character recognition (MICR) code (231) The character code used to print identifying information on the lower left front side of each check.

not sufficient funds (NSF) check (236) A check deposited by the depositor that is not paid because the drawer did not have sufficient funds.

outstanding check (236) A check issued that has not been presented to the bank for payment before the statement is prepared.

payee (233) The person being paid the cash.

petty cash fund (241) A fund established to pay for small items with cash.

petty cash payments record (242) A special multi-column record that supplements the regular accounting records.

petty cash voucher (241) A receipt that is prepared for every payment from the petty cash fund.

restrictive endorsement (231)   An endorsement where the depositor adds words such as "For deposit" to restrict the payment of the check.

service charge (236)   A bank charge for services such as check printing and processing.

signature card (230)   A card that is completed and signed by each person authorized to sign checks.

SELF-STUDY QUESTIONS AND EXERCISES

True/False Questions

1. LO2   The primary purpose of a bank reconciliation is to detect and correct errors made by the bank in its records.

2. LO2   NSF checks are subtracted from the bank's ending balance on the bank reconciliation.

3. LO2   The bank service charge requires a journal entry to record its effects on the cash account.

4. LO2   Unrecorded ATM withdrawals are added to the checkbook balance on the bank reconciliation.

5. LO3   The petty cash record is a journal of original entry (entries are posted from it to the general ledger accounts).

Multiple Choice Questions

1. LO2   Which of these could be *added* to the ending checkbook balance?

   (a) service charges
   (b) NSF check
   (c) checkbook errors
   (d) outstanding checks

2. LO2   Which of these is *subtracted* from the ending checkbook balance?

   (a) deposits in transit
   (b) service charges
   (c) note collection
   (d) bank errors

3. LO2   Which of these is *added* to the ending bank statement balance?

   (a) outstanding checks
   (b) service charges
   (c) checkbook errors
   (d) deposits in transit

4. LO3   To establish a petty cash fund, which account is debited?

   (a) Cash
   (b) Petty Cash
   (c) Miscellaneous Expense
   (d) Revenue

5. LO4   When the cash short and over account has a debit balance at the end of the month, it is considered

   (a) an expense.
   (b) an asset.
   (c) revenue.
   (d) a liability.

U REVU Exercises

1. **LO1** Match the following words with their definitions by entering the correct number in the spaces below.

    1. deposit ticket
    2. ATM
    3. check
    4. bank statement
    5. blank endorsement

    _____ a. A document ordering a bank to pay cash from a depositor's account.

    _____ b. An endorsement where the depositor simply signs the back of the check, making the check payable to any bearer.

    _____ c. Automated teller machine—a machine used by depositors to make withdrawals or deposits at any time.

    _____ d. A statement of account issued by a bank to each depositor once a month.

    _____ e. A form showing a detailed listing of items being deposited.

2. **LO2** Indicate how each of the following items should be treated in a bank reconciliation by entering the correct letter in the spaces provided.

    a. Add to bank statement balance
    b. Subtract from bank statement balance
    c. Add to book balance
    d. Subtract from book balance

    _____ 1. Interest earned on checking account balance

    _____ 2. Error in checkbook whereby a check for $82 was entered in the checkbook as $28

    _____ 3. Deposit in transit

    _____ 4. Outstanding checks

3. **LO3** A petty cash fund established for $200 had the following cash payments during the month:

Telephone expense	$23.50
Automobile expense	49.10
H. Appy, drawing	50.00

    Prepare the journal entry to replenish the petty cash fund at the end of the month.

4. **LO4** The cash register tape for June 30 showed cash receipts of $876, and the cash in the register drawer was $1,070. A change fund of $200 is maintained.

    Prepare the journal entry for service fees and cash short and over at June 30.

The answers to the Self-Study Questions and Exercises are at the end of the chapter (page 265).

APPLYING YOUR KNOWLEDGE

REVIEW QUESTIONS

LO1 1. Why must a signature card be filled out and signed to open a checking account?

LO1 2. Explain the difference between a blank endorsement and a restrictive endorsement.

LO1 3. Who are the three parties to every check?

LO1 4. What are the three steps to follow in preparing a check?

LO2 5. What are the most common reasons for differences between the book and bank cash balances?

LO2 6. What are the three steps to follow in preparing a bank reconciliation?

LO2 7. What two kinds of items on a bank reconciliation require journal entries?

LO2 8. Name five applications of electronic funds transfer in current use.

LO3 9. What is the purpose of a petty cash fund?

LO3 10. What should be prepared every time a petty cash payment is made?

LO3 11. At what two times should the petty cash fund be replenished?

LO3 12. From what source is the information obtained for issuing a check to replenish the petty cash fund?

LO4 13. At what two times would an entry be made affecting the change fund?

LO4 14. What does a debit balance in the cash short and over account represent? What does a credit balance in this account represent?

SERIES A EXERCISES

E 7-1A (LO1) **CHECKING ACCOUNT TERMS** Match the following words with their definitions:

1. An endorsement where the depositor simply signs on the back of the check
2. An endorsement that contains words like "For Deposit Only" together with the signature
3. A card filled out and signed by each person authorized to sign checks on an account
4. The depositor who orders the bank to pay cash from the depositor's account
5. The bank on which the check is drawn
6. The person being paid the cash
7. A check that has been paid by the bank and is being returned to the depositor

a. signature card
b. canceled check
c. blank endorsement
d. drawer
e. restrictive endorsement
f. drawee
g. payee

E 7-2A (LO1)

✓ Total deposit: $817.00

PREPARE DEPOSIT TICKET Based on the following information, prepare a deposit ticket:

Date:		January 15, 20--
Currency:		$334.00
Coin:		26.00
Checks:	No. 4-11	311.00
	No. 80-322	108.00
	No. 3-9	38.00

E 7-3A (LO1)

PREPARE CHECK AND STUB Based on the following information, prepare a check and stub:

Date:	January 15, 20--
Balance brought forward:	$2,841.50
Deposit:	(from Exercise 7-2A)
Check to:	J. M. Suppliers
Amount:	$150.00
For:	Office Supplies
Signature:	Sign your name

E 7-4A (LO2)

BANK RECONCILIATION PROCEDURES In a format similar to the following, indicate whether the action at the left will result in an addition to (+) or subtraction from (−) the ending bank balance or the ending checkbook balance.

	Ending Bank Balance	Ending Checkbook Balance
1. Deposits in transit to the bank	_____	_____
2. Error in checkbook: check recorded as $32.00 but was actually for $23.00	_____	_____
3. Service fee charged by bank	_____	_____
4. Outstanding checks	_____	_____
5. NSF check deposited earlier	_____	_____
6. Error in checkbook: check recorded as $22.00 but was actually for $220.00	_____	_____
7. Bank credit memo advising a note was collected for us	_____	_____

E 7-5A (LO2)

✓ NSF check: Dr. Accounts
Receivable, $390.00

PREPARE JOURNAL ENTRIES FOR BANK RECONCILIATION Based on the following bank reconciliation, prepare the journal entries:

Lisa Chai Associates Bank Reconciliation July 31, 20 - -															
Bank statement balance, July 31								$2	7	6	4	40
Add deposits in transit	$	2	5	0	00							
			9	8	00				3	4	8	00
						$3	1	1	2	40
Deduct outstanding checks:												
No. 387	$	3	5	3	50							
No. 393			1	7	80							
No. 398			3	3	20			4	0	4	50
Adjusted bank balance								$2	7	0	7	90
Book balance, July 31								$3	0	8	4	90
Add error on Check No. 394*										2	3	00
								$3	1	0	7	90
Deduct: NSF check	$	3	9	0	00							
Bank service charge			1	0	00				4	0	0	00
Adjusted book balance								$2	7	0	7	90
*Accounts Payable was debited in original entry.												

E 7-6A (LO3)

✓ Replenishment: Cr. Cash, $197.00

PETTY CASH JOURNAL ENTRIES Based on the following petty cash information, prepare (a) the journal entry to establish a petty cash fund, and (b) the journal entry to replenish the petty cash fund.

On January 1, 20--, a check was written in the amount of $200.00 to establish a petty cash fund. During January, the following vouchers were written for cash removed from the petty cash drawer:

Voucher No.	Account Debited	Amount
1	Telephone Expense	$17.50
2	Automobile Expense	33.00
3	Joseph Levine, Drawing	70.00
4	Postage Expense	12.50
5	Charitable Contributions Expense	15.00
6	Miscellaneous Expense	49.00

E 7-7A (LO4)

✓ Apr. 16: Cr. Cash Short
and Over, $1.75

CASH SHORT AND OVER ENTRIES Based on the following information, prepare the weekly entries for cash receipts from service fees and cash short and over. A change fund of $100.00 is maintained.

Date	Change Fund	Cash Register Receipt Amount	Actual Cash Counted
Apr. 2	$100.00	$268.50	$366.50
9	100.00	237.75	333.50
16	100.00	309.25	411.00
23	100.00	226.50	324.00
30	100.00	318.00	422.00

SERIES A PROBLEMS

P 7-8A (LO2)

✓ Adjusted book balance: $4,182.00

BANK RECONCILIATION AND RELATED JOURNAL ENTRIES The book balance in the checking account of Volman Enterprises as of October 31 is $4,765.00. The bank statement shows an ending balance of $4,348.00. The following information is discovered by (1) comparing last month's deposits in transit and outstanding checks with this month's bank statement, (2) comparing deposits and checks written per books and per bank in the current month, and (3) noting service charges and other debit and credit memos shown on the bank statement.

Deposits in transit:	10/29	$175.00
	10/30	334.00
Outstanding checks:	No. 1764	47.00
	No. 1767	146.00
	No. 1772	113.00
	No. 1781	369.00
Unrecorded ATM withdrawal:*		180.00
Bank service charge:		43.00
NSF check:		370.00

Error on Check No. 1754   Checkbook shows it was for $72.00, but it was actually written for $62.00. Accounts Payable was debited.

*Funds were withdrawn by Gary Volman for personal use.

REQUIRED

1. Prepare a bank reconciliation as of October 31, 20--.

2. Prepare the required journal entries.

P 7-9A (LO2)

✓ Adjusted bank balance: $3,069.95

BANK RECONCILIATION AND RELATED JOURNAL ENTRIES The book balance in the checking account of Lyle's Salon as of November 30 is $3,282.95. The bank statement shows an ending balance of $2,127.00. By examining last month's bank reconciliation, comparing the deposits and checks written per books and per bank in November, and noting the service charges and other debit and credit memos shown on the bank statement, the following were found:

(a) An ATM withdrawal of $150.00 on November 18 by Lyle for personal use was not recorded on the books.

(b) A bank debit memo issued for an NSF check from a customer of $19.50.

(c) A bank credit memo issued for interest of $19.00 earned during the month.

(d) On November 30, a deposit of $1,177.00 was made, which is not shown on the bank statement.

(e) A bank debit memo issued for $17.50 for bank service charges.

(f) Checks No. 549, 561, and 562 for the amounts of $185.00, $21.00, and $9.40, respectively, were written during November but have not yet been received by the bank.

(g) The reconciliation from the previous month showed outstanding checks totaling $271.95. One of those checks, No. 471 for $18.65, has not yet been received by the bank.

(h) Check No. 523 written to a creditor in the amount of $372.90 was recorded in the books as $327.90.

REQUIRED

1. Prepare a bank reconciliation as of November 30.

2. Prepare the required journal entries.

P 7-10A (LO3)

✓ Replenishment: Cr. Cash, $149.00

PETTY CASH RECORD AND JOURNAL ENTRIES On May 1, a petty cash fund was established for $150.00. The following vouchers were issued during May:

Date	Voucher No.	Purpose	Amount
May 1	1	postage due	$ 3.50
3	2	office supplies	11.00
5	3	auto repair (miscellaneous)	43.00
7	4	drawing (Joy Adams)	25.00
11	5	donation (Red Cross)	10.00
15	6	travel expenses	28.00
22	7	postage stamps	3.50
26	8	telephone call	5.00
30	9	donation (Boy Scouts)	20.00

REQUIRED

1. Prepare the journal entry to establish the petty cash fund.

2. Record the vouchers in the petty cash record. Total and rule the petty cash record.

3. Prepare the journal entry to replenish the petty cash fund. Make the appropriate entry in the petty cash record.

P 7-11A (LO4)

✓ July 23: Dr. Cash Short and Over, $2.50

CASH SHORT AND OVER ENTRIES Listed below are the weekly cash register tape amounts for service fees and the related cash counts during the month of July. A change fund of $100.00 is maintained.

Date	Change Fund	Cash Register Receipt Amount	Actual Cash Counted
July 2	$100.00	$289.50	$387.00
9	100.00	311.50	411.50
16	100.00	306.00	408.50
23	100.00	317.50	415.00
30	100.00	296.00	399.50

REQUIRED

1. Prepare the journal entries to record the cash service fees and cash short and over for each of the five weeks.

2. Post to the cash short and over account (use Account No. 516).

3. Determine the ending balance of the cash short and over account. Does it represent an expense or revenue?

SERIES B EXERCISES

E 7-1B (LO1)

CHECKING ACCOUNT TERMS Match the following words with their definitions:

1. Banking number used to identify checks for deposit tickets
2. A card filled out to open a checking account
3. A machine from which withdrawals can be taken or deposits made to accounts
4. A place where relevant information is recorded about a check
5. A set of procedures designed to ensure proper accounting for transactions
6. A statement of account issued to each depositor once a month
7. A detailed listing of items being deposited to an account

a. bank statement
b. deposit ticket
c. signature card
d. internal control
e. check stub
f. ATM
g. ABA number

E 7-2B (LO1)

✓ Total deposit: $645.00

PREPARE DEPOSIT TICKET Based on the following information, prepare a deposit ticket:

Date:		November 15, 20--
Currency:		$283.00
Coin:		19.00
Checks:	No. 3-22	201.00
	No. 19-366	114.00
	No. 3-2	28.00

E 7-3B (LO1)

PREPARE CHECK AND STUB Based on the following information, prepare a check and stub:

Date:	November 15, 20--
Balance brought forward:	$3,181.00
Deposit:	(from Exercise 7-2B)
Check to:	R. J. Smith Co.
Amount:	$120.00
For:	Payment on account
Signature:	Sign your name

E 7-4B (LO2)

BANK RECONCILIATION PROCEDURES In a format similar to the following, indicate whether the action at the left will result in an addition to (+) or subtraction from (−) the ending bank balance or the ending checkbook balance.

		Ending Bank Balance	Ending Checkbook Balance
1.	Service fee of $12 charged by bank	_____	_____
2.	Outstanding checks_____	_____	_____
3.	Error in checkbook: check recorded as $36.00 was actually for $28.00	_____	_____
4.	NSF check deposited earlier	_____	_____
5.	Bank credit memo advising a note was collected for us	_____	_____
6.	Deposits in transit to the bank	_____	_____
7.	Error in checkbook: check recorded as $182.00 was actually for $218.00	_____	_____

E 7-5B (LO2)

✓ NSF check: Dr. Accounts Receivable, $66.00

PREPARE JOURNAL ENTRIES FOR BANK RECONCILIATION Based on the following bank reconciliation, prepare the journal entries:

Ruggero Celini Associates Bank Reconciliation July 31, 20 --			
Bank statement balance, July 31			$1,784 00
Add deposits in transit	$418 50		
	100 50		519 00
			$2,303 00
Deduct outstanding checks:			
No. 185	$206 50		
No. 203	317 40		
No. 210	56 10		580 00
Adjusted bank balance			$1,723 00
Book balance, July 31			$1,792 00
Add: Error on Check No. 191*	10 00		
Interest earned	2 00		12 00
			$1,804 00
Deduct: NSF check	$66 00		
Bank service charge	15 00		81 00
Adjusted book balance			$1,723 00
*Accounts Payable was debited in original entry.			

E 7-6B (LO3)

✓ Replenishment: Cr. Cash, $190.00

PETTY CASH JOURNAL ENTRIES Based on the following petty cash information, prepare (a) the journal entry to establish a petty cash fund, and (b) the journal entry to replenish the petty cash fund.

On October 1, 20--, a check was written in the amount of $200.00 to establish a petty cash fund. During October, the following vouchers were written for cash taken from the petty cash drawer:

(continued)

Voucher No.	Account Debited	Amount
1	Postage Expense	$13.00
2	Miscellaneous Expense	17.00
3	John Flanagan, Drawing	45.00
4	Telephone Expense	36.00
5	Charitable Contributions Expense	50.00
6	Automobile Expense	29.00

E 7-7B (LO4)

✓ June 15: Dr. Cash Short and Over, $2.00

CASH SHORT AND OVER ENTRIES Based on the following information, prepare the weekly entries for cash receipts from service fees and cash short and over. A change fund of $100.00 is maintained.

Date	Change Fund	Cash Register Receipt Amount	Actual Cash Counted
June 1	$100.00	$330.00	$433.00
8	100.00	297.00	400.00
15	100.00	233.00	331.00
22	100.00	302.00	396.50
29	100.00	316.00	412.00

SERIES B PROBLEMS

P 7-8B (LO2)

✓ Adjusted book balance: $2,674.00

BANK RECONCILIATION AND RELATED JOURNAL ENTRIES The book balance in the checking account of Kyri Enterprises as of November 30 is $2,964.00. The bank statement shows an ending balance of $2,525.00. The following information is discovered by (1) comparing last month's deposits in transit and outstanding checks with this month's bank statement, (2) comparing deposits and checks written per books and per bank in the current month, and (3) noting service charges and other debit and credit memos shown on the bank statement.

Deposits in transit:	11/29	$125.00
	11/30	200.00
Outstanding checks:	No. 322	17.00
	No. 324	105.00
	No. 327	54.00
Unrecorded ATM withdrawal:*		100.00
Bank service charge:		25.00
NSF check:		185.00

Error on Check No. 321   Checkbook shows it was for $64.00, but it was actually written for $44.00. Accounts Payable was debited.

*Funds were withdrawn by Susan Kyri for personal use.

REQUIRED

1. Prepare a bank reconciliation as of November 30, 20--.

2. Prepare the required journal entries.

P 7-9B (LO2)

✓ **Adjusted bank balance: $4,518.70**

BANK RECONCILIATION AND RELATED JOURNAL ENTRIES The book balance in the checking account of Tori's Health Center as of April 30 is $4,690.30. The bank statement shows an ending balance of $3,275.60. By examining last month's bank reconciliation, comparing the deposits and checks written per books and per bank in April, and noting the service charges and other debit and credit memos shown on the bank statement, the following were found:

(a) An ATM withdrawal of $200.00 on April 20 by Tori for personal use was not recorded on the books.

(b) A bank debit memo issued for an NSF check from a customer of $29.10.

(c) A bank credit memo issued for interest of $28.00 earned during the month.

(d) On April 30, a deposit of $1,592.00 was made, which is not shown on the bank statement.

(e) A bank debit memo issued for $24.50 for bank service charges.

(f) Checks No. 481, 493, and 494 for the amounts of $215.00, $71.00, and $24.30, respectively, were written during April but have not yet been received by the bank.

(g) The reconciliation from the previous month showed outstanding checks totaling $418.25. One of these checks, No. 397 for $38.60, has not yet been received by the bank.

(h) Check No. 422 written to a creditor in the amount of $217.90 was recorded in the books as $271.90.

REQUIRED

1. Prepare a bank reconciliation as of April 30.

2. Prepare the required journal entries.

P 7-10B (LO3)

✓ **Replenishment: Cr. Cash, $87.00**

PETTY CASH RECORD AND JOURNAL ENTRIES On July 1, a petty cash fund was established for $100.00. The following vouchers were issued during July:

Date	Voucher No.	Purpose	Amount
July 1	1	office supplies	$ 3.00
3	2	donation (Goodwill)	15.00
5	3	travel expenses	5.00
7	4	postage due	2.00
8	5	office supplies	4.00
11	6	postage due	3.50
15	7	telephone call	5.00
21	8	travel expenses	11.00
25	9	withdrawal by owner (L. Ortiz)	20.00
26	10	copier repair (miscellaneous)	18.50

REQUIRED

1. Prepare the journal entry to establish the petty cash fund.

2. Record the vouchers in the petty cash record. Total and rule the petty cash record.

3. Prepare the journal entry to replenish the petty cash fund. Make the appropriate entry in the petty cash record.

P 7-11B (LO4)

✓ Aug. 8: Dr. Cash Short and
Over, $3.50

CASH SHORT AND OVER ENTRIES Listed below are the weekly cash register tape amounts for service fees and the related cash counts during the month of July. A change fund of $200.00 is maintained.

Date	Change Fund	Cash Register Receipt Amount	Actual Cash Counted
Aug. 1	$200.00	$292.50	$495.00
8	200.00	305.00	501.50
15	200.00	286.00	486.00
22	200.00	330.25	532.75
29	200.00	299.20	495.00

REQUIRED

1. Prepare the journal entries to record the cash service fees and cash short and over for each of the five weeks.

2. Post to the cash short and over account (use Account No. 516).

3. Determine the ending balance of the cash short and over account. Does it represent an expense or revenue?

MANAGING YOUR WRITING

The current month's bank statement for your account arrives in the mail. In reviewing the statement, you notice a deposit listed for $400.00 that you did not make. It has been credited in error to your account.

Discuss whether you have an ethical or legal obligation to inform the bank of the error. What action should you take?

ETHICS CASE

Ben Thomas works as a teller for First National Bank. When he arrived at work on Friday, the branch manager, Frank Mills, asked him to get his cash drawer out early because the head teller, Naomi Ray, was conducting a surprise cash count for all the tellers. Surprise cash counts are usually done four or five times a year by the branch manager or the head teller and once or twice a year by internal auditors. Ben's drawer was $100.00 short and his reconciliation tape showed that he was in balance on Thursday night. Naomi asked Ben for an explanation, and Ben immediately took $100.00 out of his pocket and handed it to her. He went on to explain he needed the cash to buy prescriptions for his son and pay for groceries and intended to put the $100.00 back in his cash drawer on Monday, which was pay day. He also told Naomi that this was the first time he had ever "borrowed" money from his cash drawer and that he would never do it again.

1. What are the ethical considerations in this case from both Ben's and Naomi's perspectives?

2. What options does Naomi have to address this problem?

3. Assume Naomi chooses to inform the branch manager. Write a short incident report describing the findings.

4. In small groups, come up with as many ideas as possible on how to safeguard cash on hand in a bank (petty cash, teller drawer cash, and vault cash) from employee theft and mismanagement.

MASTERY PROBLEM

✓ Adjusted bank balance: $4,324.05

Turner Excavation maintains a checking account and has decided to open a petty cash fund. The following petty cash fund transactions occurred during July:

July 2   Established a petty cash fund by issuing Check No. 301 for $100.00.

5   Paid $25.00 from the petty cash fund for postage. Voucher No. 1.

7   Paid $30.00 from the petty cash fund for delivery of flowers (Miscellaneous Expense). Voucher No. 2.

8   Paid $20.00 from the petty cash fund to repair a tire on the company truck. Voucher No. 3.

12   Paid $22.00 from the petty cash fund for a newspaper advertisement. Voucher No. 4.

13   Issued Check No. 303 to replenish the petty cash fund. (Total and rule the petty cash payments record. Record the balance and the amount needed to replenish the fund in the Description column of the petty cash payments record.)

20   Paid $26.00 from the petty cash fund to reimburse an employee for expenses incurred to repair the company truck. Voucher No. 5.

24   Paid $12.50 from the petty cash fund for telephone calls made from a phone booth. Voucher No. 6.

28   Paid $25.00 from the petty cash fund as a contribution to the YMCA. Voucher No. 7.

31   Issued Check No. 308 to replenish the petty cash fund. (Total and rule the petty cash payments record. Record the balance and the amount needed to replenish the fund in the Description column of the petty cash payments record.)

The following additional transactions occurred during July:

July 5   Issued Check No. 302 to pay office rent, $650.00.

15   Issued Check No. 304 for office equipment, $525.00.

17   Issued Check No. 305 for the purchase of supplies, $133.00.

18   Issued Check No. 306 to pay attorney fees, $1,000.00.

30   Issued Check No. 307 to pay newspaper for an advertisement, $200.20.

REQUIRED

1. Record the petty cash transactions in a petty cash payments record.

2. Make all required general journal entries for the cash transactions. (*Note*: The petty cash fund was established and replenished twice during July.)

3. The bank statement on page 264 was received in the mail. Deposits were made on July 6 for $3,500.00 and on July 29 for $2,350.00. The checkbook balance on July 31 is $4,331.55. Notice the discrepancy in Check No. 302 that cleared the bank for $655.00. This check was written on July 5 for rent expense, but was incorrectly entered on the check stub and in the journal as $650.00. Prepare a bank reconciliation and make any necessary journal entries as of July 31.

(continued)

STATEMENT

Merchant's
National Bank

TURNER EXCAVATION
220 MAIN STREET
OAKHURST, NJ 07755-1461

TE

Account Number	16 3247 5
Statement Date	July 31, 20—
Statement Instructions	

Page Number

Beginning Balance	No. of Deposits and Credits	We have added these deposits and credits totaling	No. of withdrawals and charges	We have subtracted these withdrawals and charges totaling	Resulting in a statement balance of
$1,250.25	1	$3,500.00	6	$1,512.50	$3,237.75

Document Count	Average Daily Balance this Statement Period	Minimum Balance this Statement Period	Date	Amount

If Your Account does not Balance, Please See Reverse Side and Report any Discrepancies to our Customer Service Department.

7/1	Beginning Balance			1,250.25
7/5	Check No. 301		−100.00	1,150.25
7/8	Check No. 302		−655.00	495.25
7/9	Deposit		3,500.00	3,995.25
7/15	Check No. 303		−97.00	3,898.25
7/20	Check No. 304		−525.00	3,373.25
7/28	Check No. 305		−133.00	3,240.25
7/31	Service Charge		−2.50	3,237.75

EC – Error Correction	**OD** – Overdrawn	**RC** – Return Check Charge
ATM – Automated Teller Machine	**TR** – Wire Transfer	**D/N** – Day/Night

Depositor Agrees and Bank Accepts Business Upon the Terms and Conditions of Bank's Rules and Regulations Now in Effect or as May be Hereafter Adopted.

CHALLENGE PROBLEM

This problem challenges you to apply your cumulative accounting knowledge to move a step beyond the material in the chapter.

✓ **2. Item 4: Dr. Depositor Accounts, $350.00**

Susan Panera is preparing the June 30 bank reconciliation for Panera Bakery. She discovers the following items that explain the difference between the cash balance on her books and the balance as reported by Lawrence Bank:

1. An ATM withdrawal of $200.00 for personal use was not recorded by Susan.

2. A deposit of $850.00 was recorded by Susan but has not been received by Lawrence Bank as of June 30.

3. A check written in payment on account to Jayhawk Supply for $340.00 was recorded by Susan as $430.00 and by Lawrence Bank as $530.00.

4. An ATM deposit of $350.00 was recorded twice by Lawrence Bank.

5. An electronic funds transfer of $260.00 to Sunflower Mills as a payment on account was not recorded by Susan.

6. Checks No. 103 for $235.00 and No. 110 for $127.00 had not cleared Lawrence Bank as of June 30.

REQUIRED

1. Prepare the journal entries required to correct Panera Bakery's books as of June 30.

2. Prepare the journal entries required to correct Lawrence Bank's books as of June 30.

ANSWERS TO SELF-STUDY QUESTIONS AND EXERCISES

True/False Questions

1. F (primary purpose is to reconcile book balance with bank balance)
2. F (deducted from book balance)
3. T
4. F (deducted from book balance)
5. F (entries are not posted from petty cash record to general ledger)

Multiple Choice Questions

1. c   2. b   3. d   4. b   5. a

U REVU   Exercises

1. __3__ a. A document ordering a bank to pay cash from a depositor's account.

    __5__ b. An endorsement where the depositor simply signs the back of the check, making the check payable to any bearer.

    __2__ c. Automated teller machine—a machine used by depositors to make withdrawals or deposits at any time.

    __4__ d. A statement of account issued by a bank to each depositor once a month.

    __1__ e. A form showing a detailed listing of items being deposited.

2. __c__ 1. Interest earned on checking account balance

    __d__ 2. Error in checkbook whereby a check for $82 was entered in the checkbook as $28

    __a__ 3. Deposit in transit

    __b__ 4. Outstanding checks

3. | | | |
    |---|---|---|
    | Telephone Expense | 23.50 | |
    | Automobile Expense | 49.10 | |
    | H. Appy, Drawing | 50.00 | |
    | Cash | | 122.60 |
    | Replenished petty cash fund | | |

4. | | | |
    |---|---|---|
    | Cash | 870.00 | |
    | Cash Short and Over | 6.00 | |
    | Service Fees | | 876.00 |
    | Recorded service fees and cash shortage | | |

Chapter 7 Appendix
Internal Controls

LEARNING OBJECTIVES

Careful study of this appendix should enable you to:

LO1 Explain the importance of internal control.

LO2 Define internal control and describe its key components.

LO3 Describe selected internal controls over cash receipts.

LO4 Describe selected internal controls over cash payments and the use of a voucher system.

In Chapter 7, we introduced the concept of internal control and provided some examples of good internal control over cash transactions. Here, we examine internal control in greater depth.

We do the following:

1. Explain why internal control has achieved greater importance today.

2. Identify the key components of internal control.

3. Give examples of internal control over cash receipts.

4. Describe internal control of cash payments using a voucher system.

IMPORTANCE OF INTERNAL CONTROL

LO1 Explain the importance of internal control.

To be successful, management must have adequate control of the operations of the business. For example, the records of business activities must be reliable and timely, so that management has the information it needs to take necessary actions. The assets of the business must be known and protected. Employees must follow the rules and procedures defined by management. Accurate information must be available to report to owners, lenders, and regulatory bodies, such as the IRS. Without good internal control, it simply would not be possible to effectively and efficiently run a business.

The importance of strong internal control for managing a business has been known for years. But in 2002, the importance of internal control was raised to a whole new level. In July 2002, Congress passed the Sarbanes-Oxley Act (SOX). SOX applies to all **publicly held companies**—companies whose stock is traded on the major stock exchanges. Section 404 of SOX requires these companies to report annually on the effectiveness of internal control over financial reporting. For decades, these corporations have been required to provide audited financial statements. Now, they must also report on the quality of their internal control system. Figure 7A-1 provides an example of management's Section 404 report for Microsoft.

One of the interesting effects of SOX is how widely its rules are being felt. Officially, SOX applies to all publicly held companies and their external auditors. But SOX is causing many other companies and managements to look closely at the quality of their internal controls. The logic is simple: if internal controls are so important for publicly held companies, they probably deserve attention in other companies as well. Clearly, internal controls are a hot topic today.

FIGURE 7A-1 Section 404 Internal Control Report

> ### REPORT OF MANAGEMENT ON INTERNAL CONTROL OVER FINANCIAL REPORTING
>
> Our management [of Microsoft] is responsible for establishing and maintaining adequate internal control over financial reporting for the company. Internal control over financial reporting is a process to provide reasonable assurance regarding the reliability of our financial reporting for external purposes in accordance with accounting principles generally accepted in the United States of America. Internal control over financial reporting includes maintaining records that in reasonable detail accurately and fairly reflect our transactions; providing reasonable assurance that transactions are recorded as necessary for preparation of our financial statements; providing reasonable assurance that receipts and expenditures of company assets are made in accordance with management authorization; and providing reasonable assurance that unauthorized acquisition, use, or disposition of company assets that could have a material effect on our financial statements would be prevented or detected on a timely basis. Because of its inherent limitations, internal control over financial reporting is not intended to provide absolute assurance that a misstatement of our financial statements would be prevented or detected.
>
> Management conducted an evaluation of the effectiveness of our internal control over financial reporting based on the framework in Internal Control—Integrated Framework issued by the Committee of Sponsoring Organizations of the Treadway Commission. Based on this evaluation, management concluded that the company's internal control over financial reporting was effective as of June 30, 2008. There were no changes in our internal control over financial reporting during the quarter ended June 30, 2008 that have materially affected, or are reasonably likely to materially affect, our internal control over financial reporting. Deloitte & Touche LLP has audited our internal control over financial reporting as of June 30, 2008; their report follows.

KEY COMPONENTS OF INTERNAL CONTROL

LO2 Define internal control and describe its key components.

Internal control is really important. So what exactly do we mean by internal control? Both the concept and attempts to define it have existed for many years. For our purposes, the following is a good definition:

> Internal control is a system developed by a company to provide reasonable assurance of achieving (1) effective and efficient operations, (2) reliable financial reporting, and (3) compliance with laws and regulations.

Several internal control frameworks have been developed that are consistent with this definition. The most widely accepted framework in the United States contains the following five components:

- Control environment
- Risk assessment
- Control activities
- Information and communication system
- Monitoring processes

CONTROL ENVIRONMENT

The control environment is the policies, procedures, and attitudes of the top management and owners of the business. It is often referred to as the "tone at the top." It includes the organization structure, management's philosophy and operating style, integrity and ethical values, and commitment to competent, trustworthy employees. The control environment provides the foundation for all other components of internal control.

RISK ASSESSMENT

Risk assessment is management's process for identifying, analyzing, and responding to its business risks. All businesses face various and changing risks from both external and internal sources. These risks include error and fraud. As part of the risk assessment component of internal control, management must deal with these risks. For example, if a business sells products like computers that are affected by rapid technology changes, its marketing and inventory plans should carefully guard against obsolete inventory. If a business has high employee turnover, its employee screening and training programs should be very thorough and up to date. If a business is growing rapidly, it should regularly review its internal controls to see that they fit the size and activities of the business.

CONTROL ACTIVITIES

Control activities are the policies and procedures established to help management meet its control objectives. Control activities can be classified in various ways. Four types of control activities are particularly important for our purposes.

1. Segregation of duties

2. Authorization procedures and related responsibilities

3. Adequate documents and records

4. Protection of assets and records

   Segregation of *duties* means that:

   1. Different employees should be responsible for different parts of a transaction; and

   2. Employees who account for transactions should not also have custody of the assets.

For example, one employee should be responsible for ordering goods and another employee should be responsible for issuing the check to pay for them. One employee should be responsible for recording the purchase of goods and another employee should be responsible for receiving and placing the goods in inventory. This segregation of duties provides a built-in check by one employee on another. One employee cannot obtain goods for personal use without being caught by another employee.

Authorization procedures and related responsibilities means that every business activity should be properly authorized. In addition, it should be possible to identify who is responsible for every activity that has occurred. For example, to acquire new equipment, a signed document should authorize the purchase. After the purchase is made, this signed document shows who is responsible for the action.

Adequate documents and records means that accounting documents and records should be used so that all business transactions are recorded. For example, every purchase that occurs should be supported by a document. These documents should be:

- prenumbered,

- used in sequence, and

- subsequently accounted for.

In this way, the business can be sure that it has made a record of each transaction.

Protection of assets and records means that assets and records should be physically and logically protected. For assets, this generally means physical protection. Some examples are vaults for cash, securities and precious gems, or secure storage rooms for inventory. For records, this can mean storing journals, ledgers, and key documents in physically secure locations. In computerized systems, both physical and logical protection are needed. Passwords are a common form of logical protection of data files and processing programs.

INFORMATION AND COMMUNICATION SYSTEM

The information and communication system is the set of procedures, processes, and records used to initiate, process, record, and report the business's transactions. In addition, the system accounts for the related assets and liabilities. Typically, the system has several subcomponents for different business processes, such as:

- sales,
- cash receipts,
- purchases, and
- cash payments.

The journals and ledgers we learned to use in the previous chapters would be part of an information and communication system.

MONITORING PROCESSES

Monitoring processes are the methods used by management to determine that controls are operating properly, and that the controls are modified in response to changes in assessed risks. Figure 7A-2 provides some examples of such processes. Monitoring can be part of the ongoing activities of the business or a separate process. One ongoing activity could be comparisons of financial reports with expectations. If financial reports differ from expectations, it could indicate internal control failures. Follow-up on customer complaints regarding account balances might also uncover internal control weaknesses. The most common form of separate process is the work of the internal audit department. Internal auditors evaluate the design of the internal control system in light of the business risks. They also perform specific tests to determine whether internal controls are operating properly. If a business is not large enough to have an internal audit department, these responsibilities must be assumed by top management.

FIGURE 7A-2 Sample Monitoring Processes

- Comparison of results with expectations
- Review of customer correspondence
- Internal audit

INTERNAL CONTROLS OVER CASH RECEIPTS

LO3 Describe selected internal controls over cash receipts.

The main purposes of internal controls over cash receipts are to make sure that

- all cash received by the business is recorded in the accounts, and
- the cash is promptly deposited in the business bank account.

The exact form of some of these controls will vary depending on whether the cash is received directly from customers for sales, or is received by mail as a collection on account. Some of the key internal controls are shown in Figure 7A-3 and described in the following paragraphs.

FIGURE 7A-3 Sample Controls over Cash Receipts

Do these three amounts agree?

| Cash receipts per register record | = | Cash receipts per register drawer | = | Cash receipts per bank deposit |

Do these two amounts agree?

| Cash receipts per remittance list | = | Cash receipts per bank deposit |

Do transactions and balances per books and bank agree?

Monthly bank reconciliation

If cash is received directly from customers, the use of a cash register or terminal with a printed receipt is essential. Only authorized employees should be allowed to operate the register. The register should generate an internal record of all transactions entered, including a total of cash receipts. This amount should be reconciled with the actual cash (and checks) in the register drawer. Any differences greater than a small amount to allow for errors in making change should be investigated. All cash receipts should be deposited daily in the business bank account. The total deposited and the total cash receipts according to the register should be reconciled and any differences investigated.

If cash is received as collections on account, the mail room should be supervised and employees who handle the cash (checks) should have no access to the accounting records. One reason for separating the handling of cash from the accounting records is to prevent lapping. **Lapping** means stealing cash received on account from one customer and hiding the theft by applying the cash received on account from another customer to the first customer's account. For example, assume customer A sends a check for $500 as a payment on account and that the employee keeps the $500 for him/herself. This causes customer A's account to be in error by $500. So when customer B makes a $500 payment on account, the employee applies this cash receipt to customer A's account. The dishonest employee must continue lapping the accounts receivable in this manner to continue to conceal the theft.

When the mail is opened, a remittance list should be prepared showing all amounts received and from whom they are received. Checks should be immediately endorsed "For deposit" to the business bank account.

The remittance list is sent to the accounting department for use in recording the collections in the journal and ledgers. The cash is sent to the cash receipts department to deposit in the business bank account. The total of the remittance list and the amount of the bank deposit should be independently verified and any differences investigated.

An additional internal control common to both systems described above is the independent monthly preparation of a bank reconciliation. Procedures for preparing the bank reconciliation are described in Chapter 7. The cash receipts, cash payments, and beginning and ending balances per bank and per books must be reconciled. The reconciliation should be prepared by employees who have no access to cash. Any differences should be investigated.

Many businesses have multiple bank accounts and transfer cash among them. When there are multiple bank accounts, it is possible to overstate the cash balance by engaging in kiting. **Kiting** consists of recording a transfer of cash *into* one bank account in the current period, but not recording the transfer *out of* another bank account until the following period. For example, assume a $1,000 check is written on bank account A on June 30, but not recorded as a cash payment until July 1. This check is deposited in bank account B and recorded as a cash receipt on June 30. By recording the transaction in this manner, the cash balance in both bank accounts includes the $1,000 at June 30. The total cash balance is thus overstated by $1,000 on June 30.

One of the reasons internal controls over cash are so important is that they help businesses manage their cash resources. Naturally, it is important to plan to have sufficient cash to meet current obligations. But it is also important not to allow too much cash to lie idle. Management should carefully monitor and plan for its cash needs. Strong internal controls help with this process.

INTERNAL CONTROLS OVER CASH PAYMENTS

LO4 Describe selected internal controls over cash payments and the use of a voucher system.

The main purpose of internal controls over cash payments is to make sure cash is paid only for goods and services received by the business, consistent with its best interests. To achieve this objective, controls are needed from the beginning of the process of acquiring goods and services through the payment of cash for those goods and services. An effective way to do so is with a voucher system.

VOUCHER SYSTEM

The three control activities described above can be combined to control cash payments by using a **voucher system**. A voucher system is a control technique that requires every acquisition and subsequent payment to be supported by an approved voucher. A **voucher** is a document which shows that an acquisition is proper and that payment is authorized.

THE PURCHASING PROCESS

Figure 7A-4 is a simplified illustration of how the purchasing portion of a voucher system operates. An authorized person or department prepares a purchase requisition to indicate the need for goods. The purchasing department reviews and approves the purchase requisition and prepares a purchase order to send to the supplier. When the goods are received, a receiving report is prepared. A copy of each of these documents is sent to the vouchers payable section in the accounting department.

When the purchase invoice arrives, it is compared with the purchase requisition, purchase order, and receiving report. If the purchase invoice is

- for the goods ordered (purchase requisition and purchase order),

- at the correct price (purchase order),

- and for the correct quantity (receiving report),

then a voucher like the one in Figure 7A-5 on page 273 is prepared. This is the first key control provided by the voucher system. If any aspect of the purchase is improper, it will be caught when the voucher is prepared.

FIGURE 7A-4 Voucher System—Purchasing Process

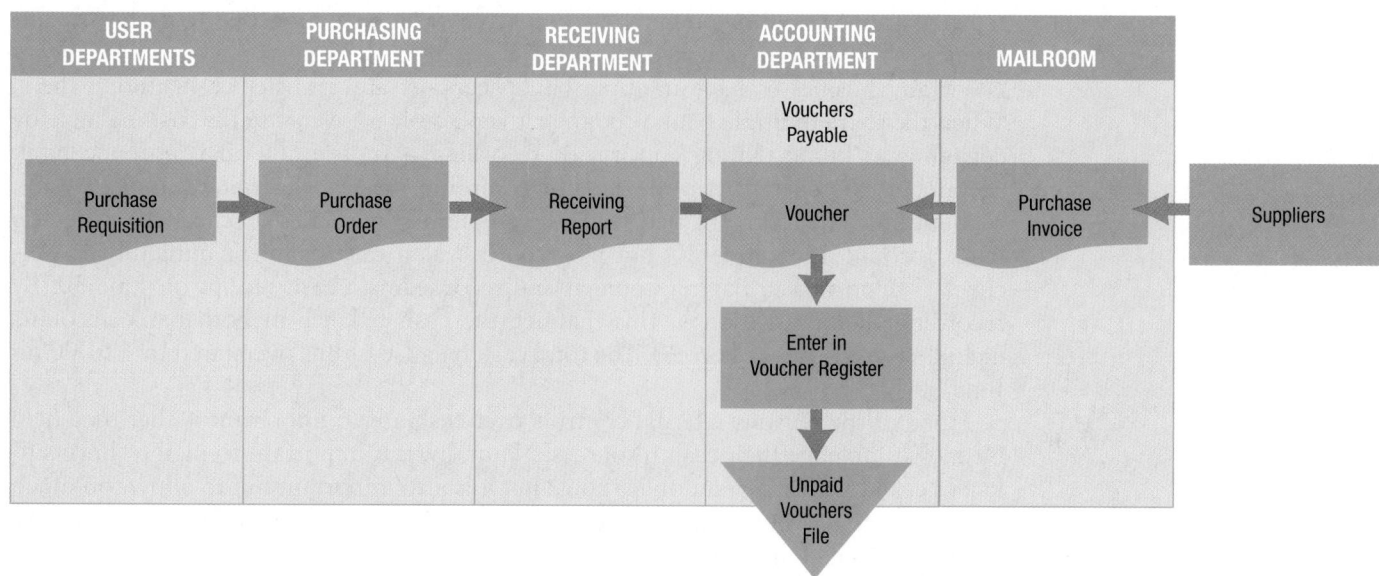

The front of the voucher usually shows the voucher number, date, supplier, and what was purchased. The back indicates the accounts to be debited and the payment date, check number, and amount.

After the voucher is prepared and approved, it is entered in a special journal called a **voucher register**. A voucher register is used to record purchases of all types of assets and services.

After the voucher is entered in the voucher register, the voucher and supporting documents (purchase requisition, purchase order, receiving report, and purchase invoice) are stapled together. This "voucher packet" is then filed in an **unpaid vouchers file**, normally by due date. Alternatively, vouchers can be filed by supplier name. Filing by due date is preferred because this helps management plan for cash needs. It also helps ensure that vouchers are paid on the due date and cash discounts are taken.

The completed voucher provides the basis for paying the supplier's invoice on the due date. This is the second key control provided by the voucher system. No payment may be made without an approved voucher.

Notice how three of the four control activities that are part of an internal control system can be seen in this system.

- *Duties are segregated* because different employees order, receive, and record the purchases.

- *Authorization* is required to order the goods and to prepare the voucher.

- The *documents and records* include purchase requisitions, purchase orders, receiving reports, and vouchers that are prenumbered and accounted for. This means that every recorded purchase is supported by the following five documents:

1. Voucher

2. Purchase invoice

3. Receiving report

4. Purchase order

5. Purchase requisition

LEARNING KEY

The voucher system contains elements of internal control such as segregation of duties, authorization to order the goods and prepare the voucher, and accounting procedures that require prenumbering and accounting for the supporting documents.

This provides management with strong assurance that purchasing activities are properly controlled.

FIGURE 7A-5 Voucher

NORTHERN MICRO
1099 E. Louisiana, Indianapolis, IN 46217-3322

Voucher No. **111**

Date 4/11/--   Terms: 1/15, n/30   Due: 4/24/--
To: EZX Corp.
    2928 Rhodes Ave.
    Chicago, IL 60658

Invoice Date	Invoice No.	Description	Amount
4/9/--	4973	P75 Computers-3	$5,700.00
		Q19 Laser Printers-3	3,000.00
			$8,700.00

Authorization _J. Jensen_ (Supervisor)   Prepared By _B. Zimmer_ (Clerk)

Front

Voucher No. **111**

Account Debited	Account No.	Amount	Summary	
Purchases	501	$8,700.00	Invoice	$8,700.00
			Discount	87.00
			Net	$8,613.00

Payment   Date 4/24/--   Check No. 437   Amount $8,613.00

Approved   Distribution _J. G._   Payment _____

Back

THE PAYMENT PROCESS

Figure 7A-6 on page 274 is a simplified illustration of the payment process when a voucher system is used. On the due date, the voucher is pulled from the unpaid vouchers file. The voucher is given to the person responsible for preparing and signing checks (the cashier in this illustration). The cashier reviews each voucher and supporting documents to see that the expenditure is proper. The cashier then prepares and signs the check and sends it to the supplier. It is important for internal control that no check be prepared without a supporting voucher and that the check be mailed as soon as it is signed.

Ordinary checks may be used to make payments, but under the voucher system, voucher checks often are used. A **voucher check** is a check with space for entering data about the voucher being paid. Figure 7A-7 on page 274 shows a voucher check used to pay Voucher No. 111 (Figure 7A-5).

The voucher check has two parts:

1. The check itself, which is similar to an ordinary check, and

2. An attached statement, which indicates the invoice being paid and any deductions.

In addition, the voucher check stub identifies the voucher number being paid.

LEARNING KEY

For good internal control of cash payments, it is important for the check to be mailed as soon as it is signed.

FIGURE 7A-6 Voucher System—Payment Process

1 Pull Voucher and Supporting Documents; Send to Cashier.
2 Review Voucher and Documents; Prepare and Sign Check.
3 Send Check to Supplier.
4 Cancel Voucher and Documents.
5 Return Voucher and Documents to Vouchers Payable; Record Payment in Voucher Register.
6 File Voucher and Documents in Paid Vouchers File.
7 Record Payment in Check Register.

FIGURE 7A-7 Voucher Check

After the voucher has been paid, the cashier completes the "Payment" information and approval on the back of the voucher. The voucher and supporting documents are then canceled to indicate payment. The canceling can be done with a rubber stamp, by perforating, or by simply writing "paid" on all relevant documents. This prevents a voucher from being processed again to create a duplicate payment. The canceled voucher and supporting documents are then returned to the vouchers payable section. The canceled voucher is used to record the payment of the voucher in the voucher register. The voucher and supporting documents are then filed either numerically or by supplier in a **paid vouchers file.** In either case, the numerical sequence should be accounted for to identify possible missing or duplicate vouchers.

A copy of the check is used to enter the payment in a check register. A **check register** is a special journal used to record all checks written in a voucher system. This completes the payment process using the voucher system.

This appendix provides an introduction to internal control concepts and procedures. We have focused on cash here, but internal controls are important in every area of the business. Internal controls can be a very complicated subject, particularly in dealing with computerized operations. More thorough analysis of internal controls is a subject for a more advanced text.

LEARNING OBJECTIVES   Key Points to Remember

LO1 Explain the importance of internal control.	Internal controls help assure management that it has reliable records to run the business and prepare needed reports. In addition, SOX requires publicly held companies to report annually on the quality of their internal control system.
LO2 Define internal control and describe its key components.	Internal control is a system developed by a company to provide reasonable assurance of achieving (1) effective and efficient operations, (2) reliable financial reporting, and (3) compliance with laws and regulations. The key components are as follows: <ul><li>Control environment</li><li>Risk assessment</li><li>Control activities</li><li>Information and communication system</li><li>Monitoring processes</li></ul>
LO3 Describe selected internal controls over cash receipts.	If cash is received directly from customers, a cash register should be used. The record of cash receipts per the register should be reconciled with the actual cash in the drawer. If cash is received by mail, a remittance list should be prepared and sent to accounting. The checks should be endorsed immediately "For deposit" and sent to the cash receipts department for deposit in the bank. The remittance list and bank deposit should be independently reconciled.
LO4 Describe selected internal controls over cash payments and the use of a voucher system.	Every acquisition and subsequent payment should be supported by an approved voucher. The voucher should be supported by a purchase requisition, purchase order, receiving report, and purchase invoice. On the due date, checks are written only for approved vouchers, and vouchers and supporting documents are canceled to prevent reuse.

KEY TERMS

check register (275)   A special journal used to record all checks written in a voucher system.

kiting (271)   Recording a transfer of cash *into* one bank account in the current period, but not recording the transfer *out of* another bank account until the following period.

lapping (270)   Stealing cash received on account from one customer and hiding the theft by applying the cash received on account from another customer to the first customer's account.

paid vouchers file (275)   A file in which paid vouchers and supporting documents are placed, organized either numerically or by supplier.

publicly held companies (266)   Companies whose stock is traded on the major stock exchanges.

unpaid vouchers file (272)   A file in which unpaid voucher packets are placed, normally organized by due date.

voucher (271)   A document that shows that an acquisition is proper and that payment is authorized.

voucher check (273)   A check with space for entering data about the voucher being paid.

voucher register (272)   A special journal used to record purchases of all types of assets and services.

voucher system (271)   A control technique that requires that every acquisition and subsequent payment be supported by an approved voucher.

REVIEW QUESTIONS

LO1   1. What does Section 404 of the Sarbanes-Oxley Act require?

LO2   2. What is the meaning of internal control?

LO2   3. What are the five components of internal control?

LO2   4. What are the four types of control activities?

LO3   5. What are the main purposes of internal controls over cash receipts?

LO4   6. What is the main purpose of internal controls over cash payments?

LO4   7. What is a voucher system?

LO4   8. In a voucher system, each recorded purchase is supported by what five documents?

LO4   9. What is the purpose of canceling the voucher and supporting documents when a payment is made?

SERIES A EXERCISES

E 7Apx-1A (LO2)

INTERNAL CONTROL COMPONENTS The most widely accepted internal control framework in the United States contains the following five components. Describe each of them.

1. Control environment
2. Risk assessment
3. Control activities
4. Information and communication system
5. Monitoring processes

E 7Apx-2A (LO2)

INTERNAL CONTROL PROCEDURES AND PROCESSES In the left column below, five different internal control procedures and processes are described. In the right column, the five components of internal control are listed. Match the procedures and processes with the components by placing the letter of the appropriate component on the blank provided.

1. _____ A company publishes and uses a code of ethical conduct.
2. _____ The accounting system automatically generates monthly sales reports for each product line.
3. _____ A company has established an internal audit department.
4. _____ All purchases above $5,000 must be approved in writing by the head of the purchasing department.
5. _____ A company invests heavily in employee training programs because of the technical nature of its products.

a. Control environment
b. Risk assessment
c. Control activities
d. Information and communication system
e. Monitoring processes

E 7Apx-3A (LO4)

PURCHASING PROCESS USING A VOUCHER SYSTEM In the following flowchart, identify the documents, records, and procedures that illustrate the purchasing process in a voucher system.

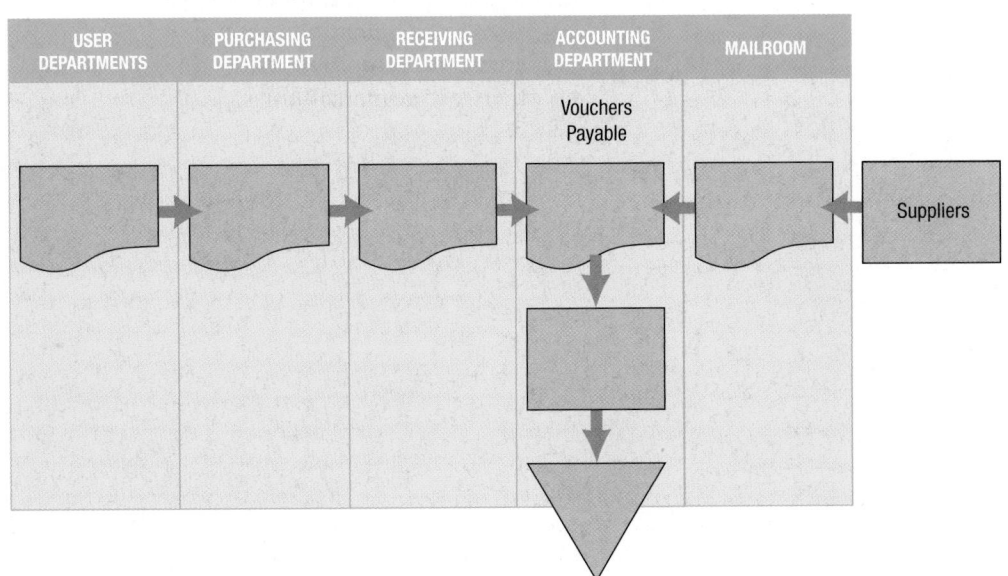

SERIES A PROBLEM

P 7Apx-4A (LO2/3/4)   **USING INTERNAL CONTROLS TO PREVENT ERRORS.** The following misstatements occurred in the records of ICW Company. For each misstatement, suggest a control to prevent it from happening.

1.   A bill from a supplier was paid even though the shipment was not received.
2.   A supplier's bill was paid twice for the same purchase.
3.   A plant employee increased his pay rate by entering the computer system using a plant terminal and altering the payroll records.
4.   The cash receipts clerk kept a portion of the regular bank deposits for personal use and concealed the theft by manipulating the monthly bank reconciliation she prepared.

SERIES B EXERCISES

E 7Apx-1B (LO2)   **INTERNAL CONTROL COMPONENTS** Four types of internal control activities are listed below. Describe each of them.

1.   Segregation of duties
2.   Authorization procedures and related responsibilities
3.   Adequate documents and records
4.   Protection of assets and records

E 7Apx-2B (LO2)   **INTERNAL CONTROL PROCEDURES AND PROCESSES** In the left column below, four different internal control procedures are described. In the right column, the four basic types of internal control activities are listed. Match the procedures with the activities by placing the letter of the appropriate activity on the blank provided.

1.   ____ All passwords for access to sales and inventory databases must be changed monthly.
2.   ____ All new hires must be approved by the department of human resources.
3.   ____ All sales invoices are prenumbered and accounted for.
4.   ____ Bank reconciliations are prepared by an employee with no other cash responsibilities.

a.   Segregation of duties
b.   Authorization procedures and related responsibilities
c.   Adequate documents and records
d.   Protection of assets and records

E 7Apx-3B (LO4)   **PAYMENT PROCESS USING A VOUCHER SYSTEM** In the following flowchart, identify the documents, records, and procedures that illustrate the payment process using a voucher system.

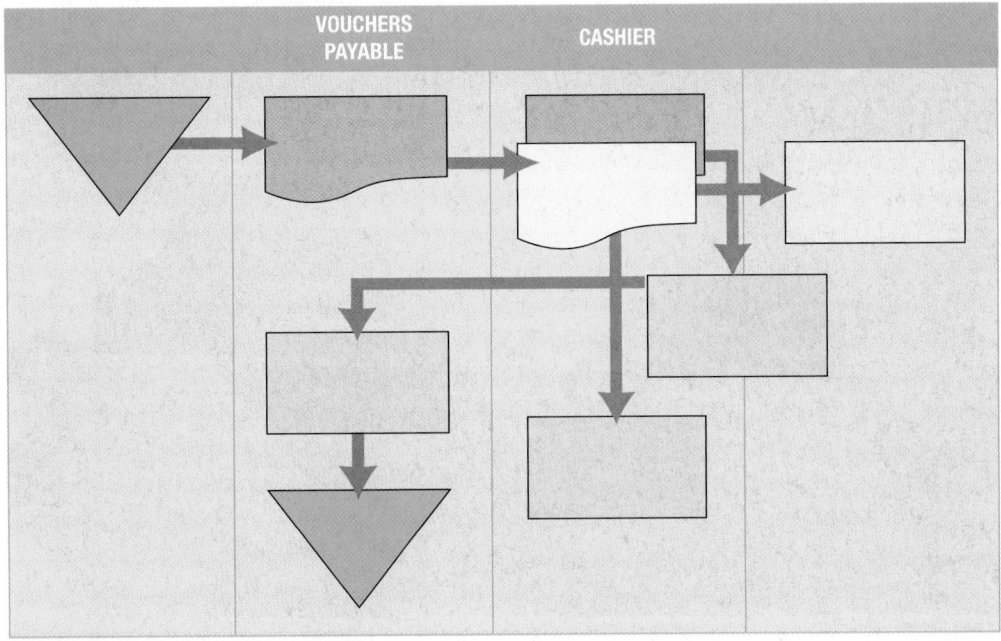

SERIES B PROBLEM

P 7Apx-4B (LO2/3/4)   **USING INTERNAL CONTROLS TO PREVENT ERRORS** The following misstatements occurred in the records of MW Company. For each misstatement, suggest a control to prevent it from happening.

1. A bill from a supplier was paid for goods that had not been ordered.
2. A supplier's bill for 50 boxes of materials was paid even though only 40 boxes were received.
3. Expensive product components were stolen by an employee from a loading dock area after hours.
4. No bill was sent to a customer for a shipment because the shipping document was lost after the shipment was made.

Chapter 8

EJLA/DREAMSTIME

Payroll Accounting: Employee Earnings and Deductions

Intechra provides computer hardware, software, and database disposal and recycling services. The company has grown rapidly in response to environmental and privacy concerns about the use of IT assets. Founded in 2004, Intechra has already become the largest electronics life cycle management company in the United States. The company currently recycles more than 200,000 units per month. With more than 600 employees, it offers both on-site services and secure transport of assets to its locations. The recycling function provides companies with value recovery for used IT products. And this enables other users to acquire name-brand computer equipment at greatly reduced prices. Consistent with environmental concerns, the entire recycling operation is performed under a zero-landfill policy for e-waste.

A company such as Intechra requires a variety of employees—from highly technical to basic materials handling staff—with very different rates of pay. For legal and operating efficiency reasons, a company must accurately track and control its payroll costs. It needs to know not only what to pay its people, but also what taxes to withhold from their wages. In this chapter, you will learn how to identify and account for payroll expenses for multiple employees.

The only contact most of us have with payroll is receiving a paycheck. Few of us have seen the large amount of record keeping needed to produce that paycheck.

Employers maintain complete payroll accounting records for two reasons. First, payroll costs are major expenditures for most companies. Payroll accounting records provide data useful in analyzing and controlling these expenditures. Second, federal, state, and local laws require employers to keep payroll records. Companies must accumulate payroll data both for the business as a whole and for each employee.

There are two major types of payroll taxes: those paid by the employee and those paid by the employer. In this chapter, we discuss employee taxes. In Chapter 9, we address payroll taxes paid by the employer.

EMPLOYEES AND INDEPENDENT CONTRACTORS

LO1 Distinguish between employees and independent contractors.

Not every person who performs services for a business is considered an employee. An **employee** works under the control and direction of an employer. Examples include secretaries, maintenance workers, salesclerks, and plant supervisors. In contrast, an **independent contractor** performs a service for a fee and does not work under the control and direction of the company paying for the service. Examples of independent contractors include public accountants, real estate agents, and lawyers.

The distinction between an employee and an independent contractor is important for payroll purposes. Government laws and regulations regarding payroll are much more complex for employees than for independent contractors. Employers must deduct certain taxes, maintain payroll records, and file numerous reports for all employees. Only one form (Form 1099) must be filed for independent contractors. The payroll accounting procedures described in this chapter apply only to employer/employee relationships.

EMPLOYEE EARNINGS AND DEDUCTIONS

LO2 Calculate employee earnings and deductions.

Three steps are required to determine how much to pay an employee for a pay period:

1. Calculate total earnings.

2. Determine the amounts of deductions.

3. Subtract deductions from total earnings to compute net pay.

SALARIES AND WAGES

Compensation for managerial or administrative services usually is called **salary**. A salary normally is expressed in biweekly (every two weeks), monthly, or annual terms. Compensation for skilled or unskilled labor usually is referred to as **wages**. Wages ordinarily are expressed in terms of hours, weeks, or units produced. The terms "salaries" and "wages" often are used interchangeably in practice.

The **Fair Labor Standards Act (FLSA)** requires employers to pay overtime at 1½ times the regular rate to any hourly employee who works over 40 hours in a week. Some companies pay a higher rate for hours worked on Saturday or Sunday, but this is not required by the FLSA. Some salaried employees are exempt from the FLSA rules and are not paid overtime.

COMPUTING TOTAL EARNINGS

Compensation usually is based on the time worked during the payroll period. Sometimes it is based on sales or units of output during the period. When compensation is based on time, a record must be kept of the time worked by each employee. Time cards (Figure 8-1) are helpful for this purpose. In large businesses with computer-based timekeeping systems, plastic cards or badges with special magnetic strips or bar codes (Figure 8-2) can be used. Employees use the cards to clock in and out at terminals with card readers. For increased security, these terminals also are available with fingerprint readers.

FIGURE 8-1 Time Card

Westly, Inc.
Time Card — Hourly Payroll

Emp. Name **Kuzmik, Helen**   Base Dept.: **Sales**

Emp. ID: **359-47-1138**   Pay Per. End: **12/19/20--**

					HOURS			
Date	**Time In**	**Time Out**	**Time In**	**Time Out**	**Reg**	**OT**	**DT**	**Total**
12/13	8:00	12:30	13:00	17:30	8	1		9
12/14	8:00	12:30	13:00	17:30	8	1		9
12/15	8:00	12:30	13:00	17:30	8	1		9
12/16	8:00	12:30	13:00	17:30	8	1		9
12/17	8:00	12:30	13:00	17:30	8	1		9
12/18	10:00	16:00				6		6
12/19	13:00	17:00					4	4
TOTAL					40	11	4	55

Remarks _____

_____

Approval _____ TM _____
        Dept. Head

To illustrate the computation of total earnings, look at the time card of Helen Kuzmik in Figure 8-1. The card shows that Kuzmik worked 55 hours for the week.

Regular hours	40 hours
Overtime	11
Double time	4
Total hours worked	55 hours

Kuzmik's regular rate of pay is $12 per hour. She is paid 1½ times the regular rate for hours in excess of 8 on Monday through Friday and any hours worked on

FIGURE 8-2 Time Cards and Clock Terminal

Saturday, and twice the regular rate for hours on Sunday. Kuzmik's total earnings for the week ended December 19 are computed as follows:

40 hours × $12	$480
11 hours × $18 (1½ × $12 = $18)	198
4 hours (on Sunday) × $24 (2 × $12 = $24)	96
Total earnings for the week	$774

Salaried employees who are not exempt from the FSLA rules may also be entitled to premium pay for overtime. If this is the case, it is necessary to compute the regular hourly rate of pay before computing the overtime rate. To illustrate, assume that Linda Swaney has a salary of $2,288 a month plus 1½ times the regular hourly rate for hours in excess of 40 per week. Swaney's overtime rate of pay is computed as follows:

$2,288 × 12 months	$27,456 annual pay
$27,456 ÷ 52 weeks	$528.00 pay per week
$528.00 ÷ 40 hours	$13.20 pay per regular hour
$13.20 × 1½	$19.80 overtime pay per hour

There are 52 weeks in each year but not 4 weeks in each month. That is why monthly salaries must be annualized in order to determine the hourly rate.

If Swaney worked 50 hours during the week ended December 19, her total earnings for the week would be computed as follows:

40 hours × $13.20	$528.00
10 hours × $19.80	198.00
Total earnings for the week	$726.00

DEDUCTIONS FROM TOTAL EARNINGS

An employee's total earnings are called **gross pay**. Various deductions are made from gross pay to yield take-home or **net pay**. Deductions from gross pay fall into three major categories:

1. Federal (and possibly state and city) income tax withholding

2. Employee FICA tax withholding

3. Voluntary deductions

Income Tax Withholding

Federal law requires employers to withhold certain amounts from the total earnings of each employee. These withholdings are applied toward the payment of the employee's federal income tax. Four factors determine the amount to be withheld from an employee's gross pay each pay period:

1. Total earnings

2. Marital status

3. Number of withholding allowances claimed

4. Length of the pay period

Withholding Allowances. Each employee is required to furnish the employer an Employee's Withholding Allowance Certificate, Form W-4 (Figure 8-3). The marital status of the employee and the number of allowances claimed on Form W-4 determine the dollar amount of earnings subject to withholding. A **withholding allowance** exempts a specific dollar amount of an employee's gross pay from federal income tax withholding. In general, each employee is permitted one personal withholding allowance, one for a spouse who does not also claim an allowance, and one for each dependent.

FIGURE 8-3 Employee's Withholding Allowance Certificate (Form W-4)

A withholding certificate completed by Ken Istone is shown in Figure 8-3. Istone is married, has a spouse who does not claim an allowance, and has two dependent children. On line 5 of the W-4 form, Istone claims four allowances, calculated as follows:

Personal allowance	1
Spouse allowance	1
Allowances for dependents	2
Total withholding allowances	4

Wage-Bracket Method. Employers generally use the **wage-bracket method** to determine the amount of tax to be withheld from an employee's pay. The employee's gross pay for a specific time period is traced into the appropriate wage-bracket table provided by the Internal Revenue Service (IRS). These tables cover various time periods, and there are separate tables for single and married taxpayers. Copies are provided in *Circular E—Employer's Tax Guide,* which may be obtained from any local IRS office or at the IRS Internet site.

Portions of weekly income tax wage-bracket withholding tables for single and married persons are illustrated in Figure 8-4. Assume that Ken Istone (who claims 4 allowances) had gross earnings of $545 for the week ending December 19, 20--. The amount to withhold for Istone is determined by using the following steps, as shown in Figure 8-4 for married persons (on page 287):

1. Find the row for wages of "at least $540, but less than $550."

2. Find the column headed "4 withholding allowances."

3. Where the row and column cross, $11.00 is given as the amount to be withheld.

For state or city income taxes, withholding generally is handled in one of two ways: (1) forms and tables similar to those provided by the IRS are used or (2) an amount equal to a percentage of the federal withholding amount is withheld.

Employee FICA Tax Withholding

The Federal Insurance Contributions Act requires employers to withhold **FICA taxes** from employees' earnings. FICA taxes include amounts for both Social Security and Medicare programs. Social Security provides pensions and disability benefits. Medicare provides health insurance.

Congress has frequently changed the tax rates and the maximum amounts of earnings subject to FICA taxes. For this text, we assume the Social Security rate is 6.2% on maximum earnings of $106,800. The Medicare rate is 1.45% on all earnings; there is no maximum.

To illustrate the calculation of FICA taxes, assume the following earnings for Sarah Cadrain:

	Earnings	
Pay Period	Week	Year-to-Date
Dec. 6–12	$2,000	$106,140
Dec. 13–19	$1,660	$107,800

For the week of December 6–12, FICA taxes on Cadrain's earnings would be:

Gross Pay	×	Tax Rate		=	Tax
$2,000		Social Security	6.2%		$124.00
		Medicare	1.45%		29.00
					$153.00

A large number of IRS publications and forms can be found at the IRS Web site: http://www.irs.gov

LEARNING KEY

1. Find the row for wages.

2. Find the column for withholding allowances.

3. Find the amount where they cross.

When the Social Security program was established in 1937, the tax was 1% on earnings up to $3,000 per year!

FIGURE 8-4 Federal Withholding Tax Table: Single Persons

SINGLE Persons—WEEKLY Payroll Period

(For Wages Paid in 2009)

If the wages are–		And the number of withholding allowances claimed is–										
At least	But less than	0	1	2	3	4	5	6	7	8	9	10
		The amount of income tax to be withheld is–										
$200	$210	$16	$8	$1	$0	$0	$0	$0	$0	$0	$0	$0
210	220	17	9	2	0	0	0	0	0	0	0	0
220	230	19	10	3	0	0	0	0	0	0	0	0
230	240	20	11	4	0	0	0	0	0	0	0	0
240	250	22	12	5	0	0	0	0	0	0	0	0
250	260	23	13	6	0	0	0	0	0	0	0	0
260	270	25	14	7	0	0	0	0	0	0	0	0
270	280	26	16	8	1	0	0	0	0	0	0	0
280	290	28	17	9	2	0	0	0	0	0	0	0
290	300	29	19	10	3	0	0	0	0	0	0	0
300	310	31	20	11	4	0	0	0	0	0	0	0
310	320	32	22	12	5	0	0	0	0	0	0	0
320	330	34	23	13	6	0	0	0	0	0	0	0
330	340	35	25	14	7	0	0	0	0	0	0	0
340	350	37	26	16	8	1	0	0	0	0	0	0
350	360	38	28	17	9	2	0	0	0	0	0	0
360	370	40	29	19	10	3	0	0	0	0	0	0
370	380	41	31	20	11	4	0	0	0	0	0	0
380	390	43	32	22	12	5	0	0	0	0	0	0
390	400	44	34	23	13	6	0	0	0	0	0	0
400	410	46	35	25	14	7	0	0	0	0	0	0
410	420	47	37	26	16	8	1	0	0	0	0	0
420	430	49	38	28	17	9	2	0	0	0	0	0
430	440	50	40	29	19	10	3	0	0	0	0	0
440	450	52	41	31	20	11	4	0	0	0	0	0
450	460	53	43	32	22	12	5	0	0	0	0	0
460	470	55	44	34	23	13	6	0	0	0	0	0
470	480	56	46	35	25	14	7	0	0	0	0	0
480	490	58	47	37	26	16	8	1	0	0	0	0
490	500	59	49	48	28	17	9	2	0	0	0	0
500	510	61	50	40	29	19	10	3	0	0	0	0
510	520	62	52	41	31	20	11	4	0	0	0	0
520	530	64	53	43	32	22	12	5	0	0	0	0
530	540	65	55	44	34	23	13	6	0	0	0	0
540	550	67	56	46	35	25	14	7	0	0	0	0
550	560	68	58	47	37	26	16	8	1	0	0	0
560	570	70	59	49	38	28	17	9	2	0	0	0
570	580	71	61	50	40	29	19	10	3	0	0	0
580	590	73	62	52	41	31	20	11	4	0	0	0
590	600	74	64	53	43	32	22	12	5	0	0	0
600	610	76	65	55	44	34	23	13	6	0	0	0
610	620	77	67	56	46	35	25	14	7	0	0	0
620	630	79	68	58	47	37	26	15	8	1	0	0
630	640	80	70	59	49	38	28	17	9	2	0	0
640	650	82	71	61	50	40	29	18	10	3	0	0
650	660	83	73	62	52	41	31	20	11	4	0	0
660	670	85	74	64	53	43	32	21	12	5	0	0
670	680	86	76	65	55	44	34	23	13	6	0	0
680	690	88	77	67	56	46	35	24	14	7	0	0
690	700	91	79	68	58	47	37	26	15	8	1	0
700	710	93	80	70	59	49	38	27	17	9	2	0
710	720	96	82	71	61	50	40	29	18	10	3	0
720	730	98	83	73	62	52	41	30	20	11	4	0
730	740	101	85	74	64	53	43	32	21	12	5	0
740	750	103	86	76	65	55	44	33	23	13	6	0
750	760	106	88	77	67	56	46	35	24	14	7	0
760	770	108	91	79	68	58	47	36	26	15	8	1
770	780	111	93	80	70	59	49	38	27	17	9	2
780	790	113	96	82	71	61	50	39	29	18	10	3
790	800	116	98	83	73	62	52	41	30	20	11	4

FIGURE 8-4 Federal Withholding Tax Table: (*concluded*) Married Persons

MARRIED Persons—WEEKLY Payroll Period

(For Wages Paid in 2009)

If the wages are—		And the number of withholding allowances claimed is—										
At least	But less than	0	1	2	3	(2) 4	5	6	7	8	9	10
		The amount of income tax to be withheld is—										
$200	$210	$5	$0	$0	$0	$0	$0	$0	$0	$0	$0	$0
210	220	6	0	0	0	0	0	0	0	0	0	0
220	230	7	0	0	0	0	0	0	0	0	0	0
230	240	8	1	0	0	0	0	0	0	0	0	0
240	250	9	2	0	0	0	0	0	0	0	0	0
250	260	10	3	0	0	0	0	0	0	0	0	0
260	270	11	4	0	0	0	0	0	0	0	0	0
270	280	12	5	0	0	0	0	0	0	0	0	0
280	290	13	6	0	0	0	0	0	0	0	0	0
290	300	14	7	0	0	0	0	0	0	0	0	0
300	310	15	8	1	0	0	0	0	0	0	0	0
310	320	16	9	2	0	0	0	0	0	0	0	0
320	330	17	10	3	0	0	0	0	0	0	0	0
330	340	18	11	4	0	0	0	0	0	0	0	0
340	350	19	12	5	0	0	0	0	0	0	0	0
350	360	20	13	6	0	0	0	0	0	0	0	0
360	370	21	14	7	0	0	0	0	0	0	0	0
370	380	22	15	8	1	0	0	0	0	0	0	0
380	390	23	16	9	2	0	0	0	0	0	0	0
390	400	24	17	10	3	0	0	0	0	0	0	0
400	410	25	18	11	4	0	0	0	0	0	0	0
410	420	26	19	12	5	0	0	0	0	0	0	0
420	430	27	20	13	6	0	0	0	0	0	0	0
430	440	28	21	14	7	0	0	0	0	0	0	0
440	450	29	22	15	8	1	0	0	0	0	0	0
450	460	30	23	16	9	2	0	0	0	0	0	0
460	470	31	24	17	10	3	0	0	0	0	0	0
470	480	33	25	18	11	4	0	0	0	0	0	0
480	490	34	26	19	12	5	0	0	0	0	0	0
490	500	35	27	20	13	6	0	0	0	0	0	0
500	510	37	28	21	14	7	0	0	0	0	0	0
510	520	39	29	22	15	8	1	0	0	0	0	0
520	530	40	30	23	16	9	2	0	0	0	0	0
530	540	42	31	24	17	10	3	0	0	0	0	0
(1) 540	550	43	33	25	18	(3) 11	4	0	0	0	0	0
550	560	45	34	26	19	12	5	0	0	0	0	0
560	570	46	36	27	20	13	6	0	0	0	0	0
570	580	48	37	28	21	14	7	0	0	0	0	0
580	590	49	39	29	22	15	8	1	0	0	0	0
590	600	51	40	30	23	16	9	2	0	0	0	0
600	610	52	42	31	24	17	10	3	0	0	0	0
610	620	54	43	33	25	18	11	4	0	0	0	0
620	630	55	45	34	26	19	12	5	0	0	0	0
630	640	57	46	36	27	20	13	6	0	0	0	0
640	650	58	48	37	28	21	14	7	0	0	0	0
650	660	60	49	39	29	22	15	8	1	0	0	0
660	670	61	51	40	30	23	16	9	2	0	0	0
670	680	63	52	42	31	24	17	10	3	0	0	0
680	690	64	54	43	33	25	18	11	4	0	0	0
690	700	66	55	45	34	26	19	12	5	0	0	0
1,300	1,310	157	147	136	126	115	105	94	84	73	63	52
1,310	1,320	159	148	138	127	117	106	96	85	75	64	54
1,320	1,330	160	150	139	129	118	108	97	87	76	66	55
1,330	1,340	162	151	141	130	120	109	99	88	78	67	57
1,340	1,350	163	153	142	132	121	111	100	90	79	69	58
1,350	1,360	165	154	144	133	123	112	102	91	81	70	60
1,360	1,370	166	156	145	135	124	114	103	93	82	72	61
1,370	1,380	168	157	147	136	126	115	105	94	84	73	63
1,380	1,390	169	159	148	138	127	117	106	96	85	75	64
1,390	1,400	171	160	150	139	129	118	108	97	87	76	66

During the week of December 13–19, Cadrain's earnings for the calendar year went over the $106,800 Social Security maximum by $1,000 ($107,800 – $106,800). Therefore, $1,000 of her $1,660 earnings for the week would not be subject to the Social Security tax.

Year-to-date earnings	$107,800
Social Security maximum	106,800
Amount not subject to Social Security tax	$ 1,000

The Social Security tax on Cadrain's December 13–19 earnings would be:

Gross pay	$1,660.00
Amount not subject to Social Security tax	1,000.00
Amount subject to Social Security tax	$ 660.00
Tax rate	6.2%
Social Security tax	$ 40.92

Since there is no Medicare maximum, all of Cadrain's December 13–19 earnings would be subject to the Medicare tax.

Gross pay	$1,660.00
Tax rate	1.45%
Medicare tax	$ 24.07

The total FICA tax would be:

Social Security tax	$40.92
Medicare tax	24.07
Total FICA tax	$64.99

For the rest of the calendar year through December 31, Cadrain's earnings would be subject only to Medicare taxes.

Voluntary Deductions

In addition to the mandatory deductions from employee earnings for income and FICA taxes, many other deductions are possible. These deductions are usually voluntary and depend on specific agreements between the employee and employer. Examples of voluntary deductions are:

1. U.S. savings bond purchases

2. Health insurance premiums

3. Credit union deposits

4. Pension plan payments

5. Charitable contributions

COMPUTING NET PAY

If you use computer software, such as Microsoft® Excel, to create a payroll register, you may notice a column or row that is off by a penny or two. Usually, this occurs in the Social Security and Medicare tax calculations. These are not errors. They are simply differences caused when rounding numbers to the nearest penny.

To compute an employee's net pay for the period, subtract all tax withholdings and voluntary deductions from the gross pay. Ken Istone's net pay for the week ended December 19 would be calculated as follows:

Gross pay		$545.00
Deductions:		
Federal income tax withholding	$11.00	
Social Security tax withholding	33.79	
Medicare tax withholding	7.90	
Health insurance premiums	10.00	
Total deductions		62.69
Net pay		$482.31

U REVU   Complete U REVU-1 on **page 303** to test your basic understanding of LO2.

PAYROLL RECORDS

LO3 Describe and prepare payroll records.

Payroll records should provide the following information for each employee:

1. Name, address, occupation, social security number, marital status, and number of withholding allowances

2. Gross amount of earnings, date of payment, and period covered by each payroll

3. Gross amount of earnings accumulated for the year

4. Amounts of taxes and other items withheld

Three types of payroll records are used to accumulate this information:

1. The payroll register

2. The payroll check with earnings statement attached

3. The employee earnings record

These records can be prepared by either manual or automated methods. The illustrations in this chapter are based on a manual system. The forms and procedures illustrated are equally applicable to both manual and automated systems.

PAYROLL REGISTER

A good example of a deduction column that could be added is State Income Tax. In the payroll register in Figure 8-5, the column could be inserted immediately after Federal Income Tax.

A **payroll register** is a form used to assemble the data required at the end of each payroll period. Figure 8-5 on pages 290 and 291 illustrates Westly, Inc.'s payroll register for the payroll period ended December 19, 20--. Detailed information on earnings, taxable earnings, deductions, and net pay is provided for each employee. Column headings for deductions may vary, depending on which deductions are commonly used by a particular business. The sources of key information in the register are indicated in Figure 8-5.

Note four important things about Westly's payroll register:

1. The first $106,800 of earnings of each employee is subject to Social Security tax. The Cumulative Total column, under the Earnings category, shows that Sarah Cadrain has exceeded this limit during the period. Thus, only $660 of her earnings for this pay period is subject to Social Security tax, as shown in the Taxable Earnings columns.

2. There are two Taxable Earnings columns: Unemployment Compensation and Social Security. Only one of these columns (Social Security) is needed to determine employee taxes. Both columns are shown here because they are a standard part of a payroll register. The Unemployment Compensation column is needed to determine this payroll tax on employers. The Social Security column is needed to determine both employee and employer Social Security taxes. The two employer taxes (Unemployment Compensation and Social Security) are discussed in Chapter 9.

3. Regular deductions are made from employee earnings for federal income tax and Social Security and Medicare taxes.

FIGURE 8-5 Payroll Register (left side)

PAYROLL

	NAME	ALLOWANCES	MARITAL STATUS	EARNINGS				TAXABLE EARNINGS		
				REGULAR	OVERTIME	TOTAL	CUMULATIVE TOTAL	UNEMPLOYMENT COMPENSATION	SOCIAL SECURITY	
1	Cadrain, Sarah	4	M	1 600 00	60 00	1 660 00	107 800 00	0 00	660 00	1
2	Gruder, James	1	S	760 00	140 00	900 00	43 400 00	0 00	900 00	2
3	Istone, Ken	4	M	545 00		545 00	27 025 00	0 00	545 00	3
4	Kuzmik, Helen	2	M	480 00	294 00	774 00	31 000 00	0 00	774 00	4
5	Lee, Hoseoup	3	M	440 00		440 00	22 340 00	0 00	440 00	5
6	Swaney, Linda	2	S	528 00	198 00	726 00	27 500 00	0 00	726 00	6
7	Tucci, Paul	3	M	490 00		490 00	25 050 00	0 00	490 00	7
8	Wiles, Harry	1	S	300 00		300 00	6 300 00	300 00	300 00	8
9				5 143 00	692 00	5 835 00	290 415 00	300 00	4 835 00	9
10										10

Time cards, pay rates

Prior period total + current period earnings

Current below $7,000 cumul. total

Current below $106,800 cumul. total

Discussed in Chapter 9

4. Voluntary deductions are made for health insurance and United Way contributions, based on agreements with individual employees.

After the data for each employee have been entered, the amount columns in the payroll register should be totaled and the totals verified as follows:

Regular earnings		$5,143.00
Overtime earnings		692.00
Gross earnings		$5,835.00
Deductions:		
Federal income tax	$476.00	
Social Security tax	299.77	
Medicare tax	84.61	
Health insurance premiums	46.00	
United Way	40.00	946.38
Net amount of payroll		$4,888.62

In a computerized accounting system, the payroll software performs this proof. An error in the payroll register could cause the payment of an incorrect amount to an employee. It also could result in sending an incorrect amount to the government or other agencies for whom funds are withheld.

PAYROLL CHECK

Employees may be paid in cash or by check. Data needed to prepare a paycheck for each employee are contained in the payroll register. In a computer-based system, the paychecks and payroll register normally are prepared at the same time. The employer furnishes an earnings statement to each employee along with each paycheck. Paychecks with detachable earnings statements, like the one for Ken Istone illustrated in Figure 8-6, are widely used for this purpose. Before the check is deposited or cashed, the employee should detach the stub and keep it.

FIGURE 8-5 Payroll Register (right side)

REGISTER—WEEK ENDED 12/19/--

	FEDERAL INCOME TAX	SOCIAL SECURITY TAX	MEDICARE TAX	HEALTH INSURANCE	UNITED WAY	OTHER	TOTAL	NET PAY	CHECK NO.	
1	168 00	40 92	24 07				232 99	1 427 01	409	1
2	126 00	55 80	13 05		20 00		214 85	685 15	410	2
3	11 00	33 79	7 90	10 00			62 69	482 31	411	3
4	57 00	47 99	11 22	13 00	20 00		149 21	624 79	412	4
5	8 00	27 28	6 38	13 00			54 66	385 34	413	5
6	73 00	45 01	10 53				128 54	597 46	414	6
7	13 00	30 38	7 11	10 00			60 49	429 51	415	7
8	20 00	18 60	4 35				42 95	257 05	416	8
9	476 00	299 77	84 61	46 00	40 00		946 38	4 888 62		9
10										10

- Withholding Tax Table → (Federal Income Tax)
- 6.2% × Social Security taxable earnings → (Social Security Tax)
- 1.45% × total earnings → (Medicare Tax)
- Specific employer–employee agreements → (Health Insurance / United Way)
- Total earnings – total deductions → (Net Pay)

FIGURE 8-6 Paycheck and Earnings Statement

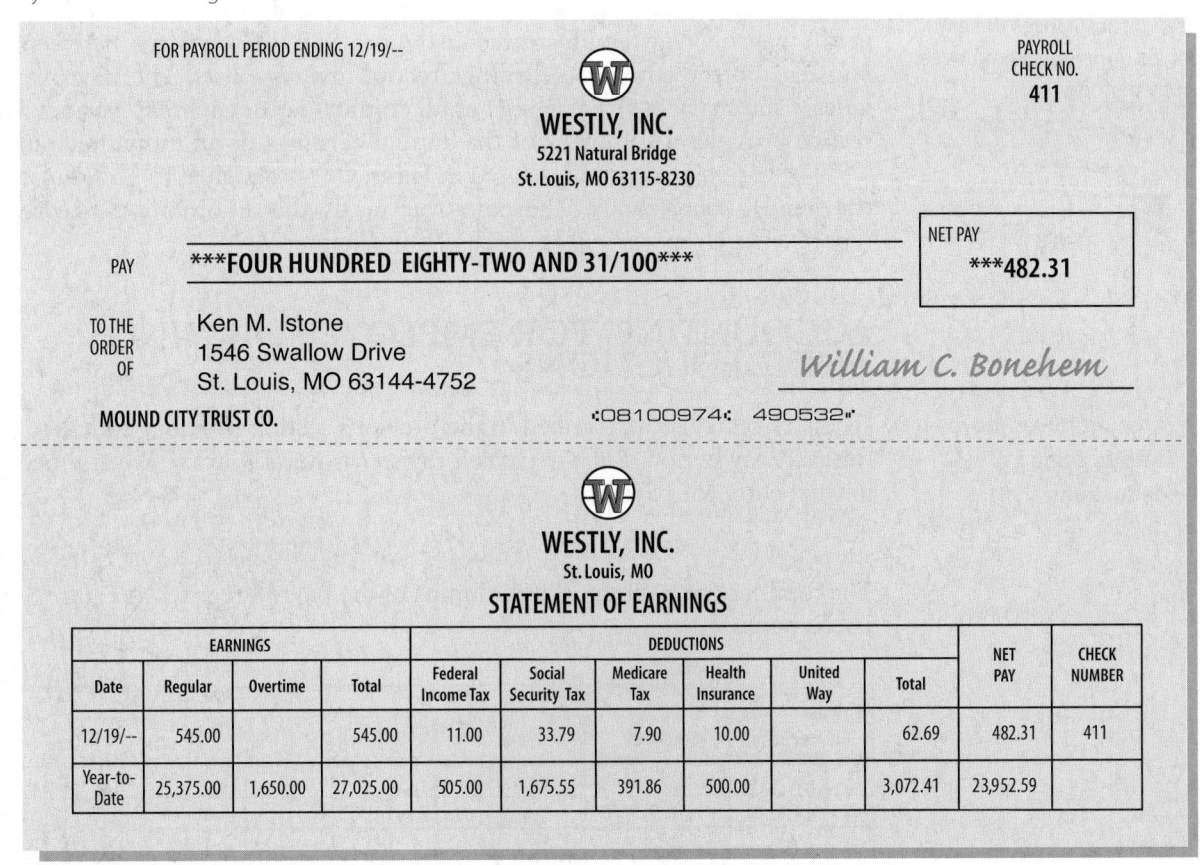

FOR PAYROLL PERIOD ENDING 12/19/--

PAYROLL CHECK NO. **411**

WESTLY, INC.
5221 Natural Bridge
St. Louis, MO 63115-8230

PAY   ***FOUR HUNDRED EIGHTY-TWO AND 31/100***

NET PAY ***482.31

TO THE ORDER OF   Ken M. Istone
1546 Swallow Drive
St. Louis, MO 63144-4752

William C. Bonehem

MOUND CITY TRUST CO.   ⑆08100974⑆   490532⑈

WESTLY, INC.
St. Louis, MO
STATEMENT OF EARNINGS

	EARNINGS			DEDUCTIONS						NET PAY	CHECK NUMBER
Date	Regular	Overtime	Total	Federal Income Tax	Social Security Tax	Medicare Tax	Health Insurance	United Way	Total		
12/19/--	545.00		545.00	11.00	33.79	7.90	10.00		62.69	482.31	411
Year-to-Date	25,375.00	1,650.00	27,025.00	505.00	1,675.55	391.86	500.00		3,072.41	23,952.59	

FIGURE 8-7 Employee Earnings Record (left side)

EMPLOYEE EARNINGS RECORD

PERIOD ENDED	EARNINGS			TAXABLE EARNINGS	
	REGULAR	OVERTIME	TOTAL	CUMULATIVE TOTAL	UNEMPLOYMENT COMPENSATION	SOCIAL SECURITY
11/28	5 4 5 00	7 5 00	6 2 0 00	25 2 4 0 00		6 2 0 00
12/5	5 4 5 00	7 5 00	6 2 0 00	25 8 6 0 00		6 2 0 00
12/12	5 4 5 00	7 5 00	6 2 0 00	26 4 8 0 00		6 2 0 00
12/19	5 4 5 00		5 4 5 00	27 0 2 5 00		5 4 5 00

GENDER	DEPARTMENT	OCCUPATION	SOCIAL SECURITY NUMBER	MARITAL STATUS	ALLOWANCES
M ✔ F	Maintenance	Service	393-58-8194	M	4

In many cases, the employee does not even handle the paycheck. Rather, payment is made by **direct deposit** or electronic funds transfer (EFT) by the employer to the employee's bank. The employee receives only the earnings statement from the check indicating the deposit has been made. Payment by check or direct deposit provides better internal accounting control than payment by cash.

EMPLOYEE EARNINGS RECORD

LEARNING KEY

The payroll register and employee earnings record are linked. The payroll register shows the earnings of all employees for a single pay period. The employee earnings record summarizes the earnings of an individual employee for all pay periods.

A separate record of each employee's earnings is called an **employee earnings record**. An employee earnings record for Ken M. Istone for a portion of the last quarter of the calendar year is illustrated in Figure 8-7 above.

The information in this record is obtained from the payroll register. In a computer-based system, the employee earnings record can be updated at the same time the payroll register is prepared.

Istone's earnings for four weeks of the last quarter of the year are shown on this form. Note that the entry for the pay period ended December 19 is the same as that in the payroll register illustrated in Figure 8-5. This linkage between the payroll register and the employee earnings record always exists. The payroll register provides a summary of the earnings of all employees for each pay period. The earnings record provides a summary of the annual earnings of an individual employee.

The earnings record illustrated in Figure 8-7 is designed to accumulate both quarterly and annual totals. The employer needs this information to prepare several reports. These reports will be discussed in Chapter 9.

ACCOUNTING FOR EMPLOYEE EARNINGS AND DEDUCTIONS

LO4 Account for employee earnings and deductions.

The payroll register described in the previous section provides complete payroll data for each pay period. But the payroll register is not a journal. We still need to make a journal entry for payroll.

JOURNALIZING PAYROLL TRANSACTIONS

The totals at the bottom of the columns of the payroll register in Figure 8-5 are reproduced here.

PAYROLL REGISTER (LEFT SIDE)

EARNINGS				TAXABLE EARNINGS	
REGULAR	OVERTIME	TOTAL	CUMULATIVE TOTAL	UNEMPLOYMENT COMPENSATION	SOCIAL SECURITY
5 1 4 3 00	6 9 2 00	5 8 3 5 00	290 4 1 5 00	3 0 0 00	4 8 3 5 00

(1)

FIGURE 8-7 Employee Earnings Record (right side)

FOR PERIOD ENDED   20--

FEDERAL INCOME TAX	SOCIAL SECURITY TAX	MEDICARE TAX	HEALTH INSURANCE	UNITED WAY	OTHER		TOTAL	CHECK NO.	AMOUNT
1 9 00	3 8 44	8 99	1 0 00				7 6 43	387	5 4 3 57
1 9 00	3 8 44	8 99	1 0 00				7 6 43	395	5 4 3 57
1 9 00	3 8 44	8 99	1 0 00				7 6 43	403	5 4 3 57
1 1 00	3 3 79	7 90	1 0 00				6 2 69	411	4 8 2 31

PAY RATE	DATE OF BIRTH	DATE HIRED	NAME/ADDRESS	EMPLOYEE NUMBER
$545/wk	8/17/64	1/3/87	Ken M. Istone 1546 Swallow Drive St. Louis, MO 63144-4752	3

A BROADER VIEW

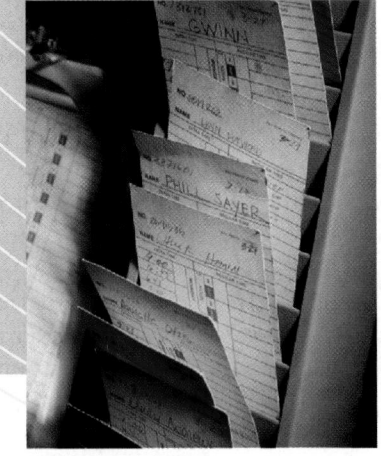

PHOTODISC/GETTY IMAGES

Payroll Fraud—Paying for Ghosts

A supervisor at Haas Transfer Warehouse embezzled $12,000 from the company by collecting paychecks for former employees. When an employee left the company, the supervisor continued to submit a department time report for the employee. This caused a paycheck to be generated for the "ghost" employee. The supervisor then simply kept this paycheck when others were distributed to actual employees.

This fraud shows the importance of two procedures that appear in this chapter: (1) a time card, plastic card, or badge should be used for each employee to keep an accurate record of time worked and (2) payment by direct deposit or electronic funds transfer to the employee's bank is a good internal control.

The numbered amounts in the payroll register column totals thus provide the basis for recording the payroll. If the employee paychecks are written from the regular bank account, the following journal entry is made:

PAYROLL REGISTER (RIGHT SIDE)   20--

FEDERAL INCOME TAX	SOCIAL SECURITY TAX	MEDICARE TAX	HEALTH INSURANCE	UNITED WAY	OTHER		TOTAL		NET PAY
4 7 6 00	2 9 9 77	8 4 61	4 6 00	4 0 00	0 00	0 00	9 4 6 38		4 8 8 8 62
(2)	(3)	(4)	(5)	(6)					(7)

		DATE		DESCRIPTION	POST REF.	DEBIT					CREDIT					
(1)	5	Dec.	19	Wages and Salaries Expense		5	8	3	5	00						5
(2)	6			Employee Income Tax Payable								4	7	6	00	6
(3)	7			Social Security Tax Payable								2	9	9	77	7
(4)	8			Medicare Tax Payable									8	4	61	8
(5)	9			Health Insurance Premiums Payable									4	6	00	9
(6)	10			United Way Contributions Payable									4	0	00	10
(7)	11			Cash							4	8	8	8	62	11
	12			Payroll for week ended Dec. 19												12

Employee paychecks also can be written from a special payroll bank account. Large businesses with many employees commonly use a payroll bank account. If Westly used a payroll bank account, it first would have made the following entry on December 19 to transfer funds from the regular bank account to the payroll bank account:

	DATE		DESCRIPTION	POST REF.	DEBIT					CREDIT					
1	Dec.	19	Payroll Cash		4	8	8	8	62						1
2			Cash							4	8	8	8	62	2
3			Cash for Dec. 19 payroll												3

Then, the payroll entry shown above would be made, except that the credit of $4,888.62 would be to Payroll Cash rather than Cash.

If a payroll bank account is used, individual checks totaling $4,888.62 are written to the employees from that account. Otherwise, individual checks totaling that amount are written to the employees from the regular bank account.

Notice two important facts about the payroll entry. First, Wages and Salaries Expense is debited for the gross pay of the employees. The expense to the employer is the gross pay, not the employees' net pay after deductions. Second, a separate account is kept for each deduction.

The accounts needed in entering deductions depend upon the deductions involved. To understand the accounting for these deductions, consider what the employer is doing. By deducting amounts from employees' earnings, the employer is simply serving as an agent for the government and other groups. Amounts that are deducted from an employee's gross earnings must be paid by the employer to these groups. Therefore, a separate account should be kept for the liability for each type of deduction.

To help us understand the journal entry for payroll, let's use the accounting equation to examine the accounts involved. The seven accounts affected by the payroll entry above are shown in the accounting equation in Figure 8-8.

🔑 LEARNING KEY

Wages and Salaries Expense is debited for the gross pay. A separate account is kept for each earnings deduction. Cash is credited for the net pay.

FIGURE 8-8 Accounting for Payroll

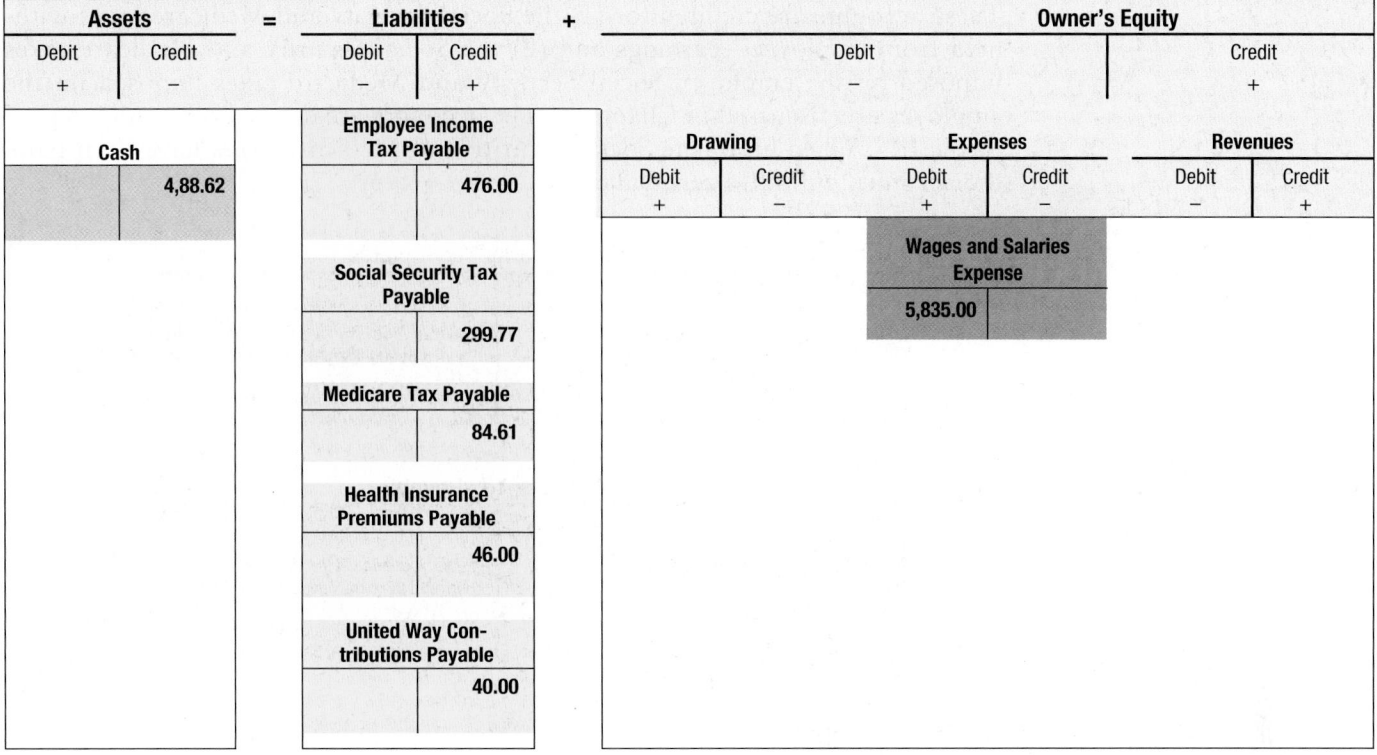

WAGES AND SALARIES EXPENSE

This account is debited for the gross pay of all employees for each pay period. Sometimes separate expense accounts are kept for the employees of different departments. Thus, separate accounts may be kept for Office Salaries Expense, Sales Salaries Expense, and Factory Wages Expense.

Wages and Salaries Expense

Debit	Credit
gross pay of employees for each pay period	

EMPLOYEE INCOME TAX PAYABLE

This account is credited for the total federal income tax withheld from employees' earnings. The account is debited for amounts paid to the IRS. When all of the income taxes withheld have been paid, the account will have a zero balance. A state or city income tax payable account is used in a similar manner.

Employee Income Tax Payable

Debit	Credit
payment of income tax previously withheld	federal income tax withheld from employees' earnings

SOCIAL SECURITY AND MEDICARE TAXES PAYABLE

These accounts are credited for (1) the Social Security and Medicare taxes withheld from employees' earnings and (2) the Social Security and Medicare taxes imposed on the employer. Social Security and Medicare taxes imposed on the employer are discussed in Chapter 9. The accounts are debited for amounts paid to the IRS. When all of the Social Security and Medicare taxes have been paid, the accounts will have zero balances.

Social Security Tax Payable

Debit	Credit
payment of Social Security tax previously withheld or imposed	Social Security taxes (1) withheld from employees' earnings and (2) imposed on the employer

Medicare Tax Payable

Debit	Credit
payment of Medicare tax previously withheld or imposed	Medicare taxes (1) withheld from employees' earnings and (2) imposed on the employer

OTHER DEDUCTIONS

Health Insurance Premiums Payable is credited for health insurance contributions deducted from an employee's pay. The account is debited for the subsequent payment of these amounts to the health insurer. United Way Contributions Payable is handled in a similar manner.

> **U REVU**
>
> Complete U REVU-2 on **page 303** to test your basic understanding of LO4.

PAYROLL RECORD-KEEPING METHODS

LO5 Describe various payroll record-keeping methods.

Payroll typically is one of the first functions to be computerized by businesses.

You probably noticed that the same information appears in several places in the payroll records—in the payroll register, paycheck and stub, and employee earnings records. If all records are prepared by hand (a **manual system**), the same information would be recorded several times. Unless an employer has only a few employees, this can be very inefficient. Various approaches are available to make payroll accounting more efficient and accurate.

Both medium- and large-size businesses commonly use two approaches for payroll record keeping: payroll processing centers and electronic systems. A **payroll processing center** is a business that sells payroll record-keeping services. The employer provides the center with all basic employee data and each period's report of hours worked. The processing center maintains all payroll records and prepares each period's payroll checks. Payroll processing center fees tend to be much less than the cost to an employer of handling payroll internally.

An **electronic system** is a computer system based on a software package that performs all payroll record keeping and prepares payroll checks. In this system, only the employee number and hours worked need to be entered into a computer each pay period, as shown in Figure 8-9. All other payroll data needed to prepare the payroll records can be stored in the computer. The computer uses the employee number and hours worked to determine the gross pay, deductions, and net pay. The payroll register, checks, and employee earnings records are provided as outputs.

FIGURE 8-9 Electronic Payroll System

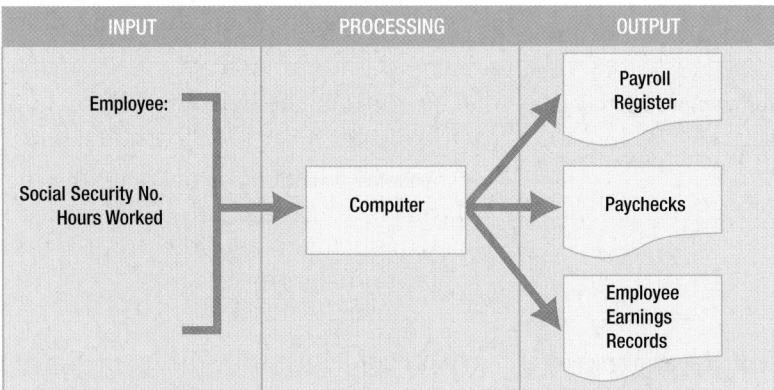

The same inputs and outputs are required in all payroll systems. Even with a computer, the data required for payroll processing have to be entered into the system at some point. The outputs—the payroll register, paychecks, and employee earnings records—are basically the same under each system.

SELF-STUDY

LEARNING OBJECTIVES	Key Points to Remember
LO1 **Distinguish between employees and independent contractors.**	Employees work under the control and direction of an employer. Independent contractors perform a service for a fee and do not work under the control and direction of the company paying for the service. Payroll accounting procedures apply only to employees, not to independent contractors.
LO2 **Calculate employee earnings and deductions.**	Three steps are required to determine how much to pay an employee for a pay period: 1. Calculate total earnings. 2. Determine the amounts of deductions. 3. Subtract deductions from total earnings to compute net pay. Deductions from gross pay fall into three categories: 1. Income tax withholding 2. Employee Social Security and Medicare taxes withholding 3. Voluntary deductions Four factors determine the amount to be withheld from an employee's gross pay each pay period: 1. Total earnings 2. Marital status 3. Number of withholding allowances claimed 4. Length of the pay period

LEARNING OBJECTIVES   Key Points to Remember

LO3 Describe and prepare payroll records.	The payroll register and the employee earnings record are linked. The payroll register provides a summary of earnings of all employees for each pay period. The earnings record provides a summary of the annual earnings of an individual employee.
LO4 Account for employee earnings and deductions.	The totals at the bottom of the columns of the payroll register provide the basis for the journal entry for payroll.
	Amounts withheld or deducted by the employer from employee earnings are credited to liability accounts. The employer must pay these amounts to the proper government groups and other appropriate groups.
LO5 Describe various payroll record-keeping methods.	In a manual payroll system, the same information needs to be recorded several times. An electronic payroll system is much more efficient.

DEMONSTRATION PROBLEM

Carole Vohsen operates a pet grooming salon called Canine Coiffures. She has five employees, all of whom are paid on a weekly basis. Canine Coiffures uses a payroll register, individual employee earnings records, a journal, and a general ledger.

The payroll data for each employee for the week ended January 21, 20--, are given below. Employees are paid 1½ times the regular rate for work over 40 hours a week and double time for work on Sunday.

Name	Employee No.	No. of Allowances	Marital Status	Total Hours Worked Jan. 15–21	Rate	Total Earnings Jan. 1–14
DeNourie, Katie	1	2	S	44	$11.50	$1,058.00
Garriott, Pete	2	1	M	40	12.00	1,032.00
Martinez, Sheila	3	3	M	39	12.50	987.50
Parker, Nancy	4	4	M	42	11.00	957.00
Shapiro, John	5	2	S	40	11.50	931.50

Sheila Martinez is the manager of the Shampooing Department. Her social security number is 500-88-4189, and she was born April 12, 1969. She lives at 46 Darling Crossing, Norwich, CT 06360. Martinez was hired September 1 of last year.

Canine Coiffures uses a federal income tax withholding table. A portion of this weekly table is provided in Figure 8-4 on pages 286 and 287. Social Security tax is withheld at the rate of 6.2% of the first $106,800 earned. Medicare tax is withheld at the rate of 1.45%, and city earnings tax at the rate of 1%, both applied to gross pay. Garriott and Parker each have $14.00 and DeNourie and Martinez each have $4.00 withheld for health insurance. DeNourie, Martinez, and Shapiro each have $15.00 withheld to be invested in the groomers' credit union. Garriott and Shapiro each have $18.75 withheld under a savings bond purchase plan.

Canine Coiffures' payroll is met by drawing checks on its regular bank account. This week, the checks were issued in sequence, beginning with No. 811.

REQUIRED

1. Prepare a payroll register for Canine Coiffures for the week ended January 21, 20--. (In the Taxable Earnings/Unemployment Compensation column, enter the same amounts as in the Social Security column.) Total the amount columns, verify the totals, and rule with single and double lines.

2. Prepare an employee earnings record for Sheila Martinez for the week ended January 21, 20--.

3. Assuming that the wages for the week ended January 21 were paid on January 23, prepare the journal entry for the payment of this payroll.

4. Post the entry in requirement (3) to the affected accounts in the ledger of Canine Coiffures. Do not enter any amounts in the Balance columns. Use account numbers as follows: Cash—101; Employee Income Tax Payable—211; Social Security Tax Payable—212; Medicare Tax Payable—213; City Earnings Tax Payable—215; Health Insurance Premiums Payable—216; Credit Union Payable—217; Savings Bond Deductions Payable—218; Wages and Salaries Expense—511.

Solution 1.

PAYROLL

	NAME	EMPLOYEE NO.	ALLOWANCES	MARITAL STATUS	EARNINGS REGULAR	EARNINGS OVERTIME	EARNINGS TOTAL	CUMULATIVE TOTAL	TAXABLE EARNINGS UNEMPLOYMENT COMPENSATION	TAXABLE EARNINGS SOCIAL SECURITY	
1	DeNourie, Katie	1	2	S	460 00	69 00	529 00	1 587 00	529 00	529 00	1
2	Garriott, Pete	2	1	M	480 00		480 00	1 512 00	480 00	480 00	2
3	Martinez, Sheila	3	3	M	487 50		487 50	1 475 00	487 50	487 50	3
4	Parker, Nancy	4	4	M	440 00	33 00	473 00	1 430 00	473 00	473 00	4
5	Shapiro, John	5	2	S	460 00		460 00	1 391 50	460 00	460 00	5
6					2 327 50	102 00	2 429 50	7 395 50	2 429 50	2 429 50	6
7											7

REGISTER—WEEK ENDED January 21, 20--

	DEDUCTIONS FEDERAL INCOME TAX	SOCIAL SECURITY TAX	MEDICARE TAX	CITY TAX	HEALTH INSURANCE	CREDIT UNION	OTHER	TOTAL	NET PAY	CHECK NO.	
1	43 00	32 80	7 67	5 29	4 00	15 00		107 76	421 24	811	1
2	26 00	29 76	6 96	4 80	14 00		18 75	100 27	379 73	812	2
3	12 00	30 23	7 07	4 88	4 00	15 00		73 18	414 32	813	3
4	4 00	29 33	6 86	4 73	14 00			58 92	414 08	814	4
5	34 00	28 52	6 67	4 60		15 00	18 75	107 54	352 46	815	5
6	119 00	150 64	35 23	24 30	36 00	45 00	37 50	447 67	1 981 83		6
7											7

(continued)

2.

EMPLOYEE EARNINGS RECORD

20-- PERIOD ENDED	EARNINGS				TAXABLE EARNINGS	
	REGULAR	OVERTIME	TOTAL	CUMULATIVE TOTAL	UNEMPLOYMENT COMPENSATION	SOCIAL SECURITY
1/7						
1/14						
1/21	4 8 7 50		4 8 7 50	1 4 7 5 00	4 8 7 50	4 8 7 50
1/28						

GENDER	DEPARTMENT	OCCUPATION	SOCIAL SECURITY NUMBER	MARITAL STATUS	ALLOWANCES
M F ✔	Shampooing	Manager	500-88-4189	M	3

FOR PERIOD ENDED   20--

FEDERAL INCOME TAX	SOCIAL SECURITY TAX	MEDICARE TAX	CITY TAX	HEALTH INSURANCE	CREDIT UNION	OTHER	TOTAL	CHECK NO.	AMOUNT
1 2 00	3 0 23	7 07	4 88	4 00	1 5 00		7 3 18	813	4 1 4 32

PAY RATE	DATE OF BIRTH	DATE HIRED	NAME/ADDRESS	EMPLOYEE NUMBER
$12.50	4/12/69	9/1/--	Sheila Martinez 46 Darling Crossing Norwich, CT 06360	3

3.

GENERAL JOURNAL   PAGE 1

	DATE		DESCRIPTION	POST. REF.	DEBIT	CREDIT	
1	20-- Jan.	23	Wages and Salaries Expense	511	2 4 2 9 50		1
2			Employee Income Tax Payable	211		1 1 9 00	2
3			Social Security Tax Payable	212		1 5 0 64	3
4			Medicare Tax Payable	213		3 5 23	4
5			City Earnings Tax Payable	215		2 4 30	5
6			Health Insurance Premiums Payable	216		3 6 00	6
7			Credit Union Payable	217		4 5 00	7
8			Savings Bond Deductions Payable	218		3 7 50	8
9			Cash	101		1 9 8 1 83	9
10			Payroll for week ended Jan. 21				10

4.

GENERAL LEDGER

ACCOUNT: Cash **ACCOUNT NO.** 101

DATE	ITEM	POST. REF.	DEBIT	CREDIT	BALANCE DEBIT	BALANCE CREDIT
20-- Jan. 23		J1		1 9 8 1 83		

ACCOUNT: Employee Income Tax Payable **ACCOUNT NO.** 211

DATE	ITEM	POST. REF.	DEBIT	CREDIT	BALANCE DEBIT	BALANCE CREDIT
20-- Jan. 23		J1		1 1 9 00		

ACCOUNT: Social Security Tax Payable **ACCOUNT NO.** 212

DATE	ITEM	POST. REF.	DEBIT	CREDIT	BALANCE DEBIT	BALANCE CREDIT
20-- Jan. 23		J1		1 5 0 64		

ACCOUNT: Medicare Tax Payable **ACCOUNT NO.** 213

DATE	ITEM	POST. REF.	DEBIT	CREDIT	BALANCE DEBIT	BALANCE CREDIT
20-- Jan. 23		J1		3 5 23		

ACCOUNT: City Earnings Tax Payable **ACCOUNT NO.** 215

DATE	ITEM	POST. REF.	DEBIT	CREDIT	BALANCE DEBIT	BALANCE CREDIT
20-- Jan. 23		J1		2 4 30		

ACCOUNT: Health Insurance Premiums Payable **ACCOUNT NO.** 216

DATE	ITEM	POST. REF.	DEBIT	CREDIT	BALANCE DEBIT	BALANCE CREDIT
20-- Jan. 23		J1		3 6 00		

ACCOUNT: Credit Union Payable **ACCOUNT NO.** 217

DATE	ITEM	POST. REF.	DEBIT	CREDIT	BALANCE DEBIT	BALANCE CREDIT
20-- Jan. 23		J1		4 5 00		

ACCOUNT: Savings Bond Deductions Payable **ACCOUNT NO.** 218

DATE	ITEM	POST. REF.	DEBIT	CREDIT	BALANCE DEBIT	BALANCE CREDIT
20-- Jan. 23		J1		3 7 50		

ACCOUNT: Wages and Salaries Expense **ACCOUNT NO.** 511

DATE	ITEM	POST. REF.	DEBIT	CREDIT	BALANCE DEBIT	BALANCE CREDIT
20-- Jan. 23		J1	2 4 2 9 50			

KEY TERMS

direct deposit (292)   A payroll method in which the employee does not handle the paycheck; payment is made by the employer directly to the employee's bank.

electronic system (296)   A computer system based on a software package that performs all payroll record keeping and prepares payroll checks.

employee (281)   Someone who works under the control and direction of an employer.

employee earnings record (292)   A separate record of each employee's earnings.

Fair Labor Standards Act (FLSA) (281)   A law that requires employers to pay overtime at 1½ times the regular rate to any hourly employee who works over 40 hours in a week.

FICA taxes (285)   Payroll taxes withheld to provide Social Security and Medicare benefits.

gross pay (284)   An employee's total earnings.

independent contractor (281)   Someone who performs a service for a fee and does not work under the control and direction of the company paying for the service.

manual system (296)   Payroll system in which all records are prepared by hand.

net pay (284)   Gross pay less mandatory and voluntary deductions.

payroll processing center (296)   A business that sells payroll record-keeping services.

payroll register (289)   A form used to assemble the data required at the end of each payroll period.

salary (281)   Compensation for managerial or administrative services.

wage-bracket method (285)   A method of determining the amount to withhold from an employee's gross pay for a specific time period. Wage-bracket tables are provided by the Internal Revenue Service.

wages (281)   Compensation for skilled or unskilled labor.

withholding allowance (284)   A specific dollar amount of an employee's gross pay that is exempt from federal income tax withholding.

SELF-STUDY QUESTIONS AND EXERCISES

True/False Questions

1. LO1   An independent contractor is one who works under the control and direction of an employer.

2. LO1   Government laws and regulations regarding payroll are more complex for employees than for independent contractors.

3. LO2   Compensation for skilled or unskilled labor expressed in terms of hours, weeks, or units is called salary.

4. LO2   An employee's total earnings is called gross pay.

5. LO3   A payroll register is a multi-column form used to assemble the data required at the end of each payroll period.

Multiple Choice Questions

1. LO2   Jack Smith is married, has a spouse who is not employed and has five dependent children. How many withholding allowances is Smith entitled to?

   (a) 5   (c) 7
   (b) 6   (d) 8

2. LO2   Nancy Summers worked 44 hours during the past week. She is entitled to 1½ times her regular pay for all hours worked in excess of 40 during the week. Her regular rate of pay is $12.00. Social Security tax is withheld at the rate of 6.2% and Medicare tax is withheld at the rate of 1.45%; federal income tax withheld is $68; and $5 of union dues are withheld. Her net pay for the week is

   (a) $440.89.   (c) $552.00.
   (b) $472.00.   (d) $436.78.

3. LO2   Which of the following is *not* a factor that determines the amount of federal income tax to be withheld from an employee's gross pay?

   (a) marital status   (c) total earnings
   (b) number of withholding allowances claimed   (d) age of employee

4. LO3   A separate record of each employee's earnings is called a(n)

   (a) payroll register.   (c) W-4.
   (b) employee earnings record.   (d) earnings statement.

5. LO4   Social Security Tax Payable and Medicare Tax Payable are classified as

   (a) liabilities.   (c) owner's equity.
   (b) assets.   (d) expenses.

U REVU   Exercises

1. LO2   Qian Wang is paid a regular rate of $14 per hour and 1½ times the regular rate for hours worked over 40 in a week. During the past week, Qian worked 45 hours.

   (a) Compute Qian's gross pay for the week.
   (b) Assume Qian is married and claims two withholding allowances. Compute the amount of federal income tax her employer should withhold for the week.

2. LO4   The column totals from the payroll register of Jawhawk Supplies for the week ended February 9 were as follows:

Total earnings	$4,600.00
Federal income tax	417.00
Social Security tax	285.20
Medicare tax	66.70
State income tax	46.00
Health insurance	181.00

   Prepare the journal entry to record the payroll, crediting Cash for the net pay.

The answers to the Self-Study Questions and Exercises are at the end of the chapter (page 314).

REVIEW QUESTIONS

LO1 1. Why is it important for payroll accounting purposes to distinguish between an employee and an independent contractor?

LO2 2. Name three major categories of deductions from an employee's gross pay.

LO2 3. Identify the four factors that determine the amount of federal income tax that is withheld from an employee's pay each pay period.

LO2 4. In general, an employee is entitled to withholding allowances for what purposes?

LO3 5. Identify the three payroll records usually needed by an employer.

LO3 6. Describe the information contained in the payroll register.

LO3 7. Why is it important to total and verify the totals of the payroll register after the data for each employee have been entered?

LO3 8. Distinguish between the payroll register and the employee earnings record.

LO4 9. Explain what an employer does with the amounts withheld from an employee's pay.

LO5 10. Explain why payroll processing centers and electronic systems are commonly used in payroll accounting.

SERIES A EXERCISES

E 8-1A (LO2)

✓ Net pay: $446.51

COMPUTING NET PAY Mary Sue Guild works for a company that pays its employees 1½ times the regular rate for all hours worked in excess of 40 per week. Guild's pay rate is $10.00 per hour. Her wages are subject to deductions for federal income tax, Social Security tax, and Medicare tax. She is married and claims four withholding allowances. Guild has a ½-hour lunch break during an 8½-hour day. Her time card is shown below.

Name	Mary Sue Guild					
Week Ending	March 30, 20--					
					Hours Worked	
Day	In	Out	In	Out	Regular	Overtime
M	7:57	12:05	12:35	4:33	8	
T	7:52	12:09	12:39	5:05	8	½
W	7:59	12:15	12:45	5:30	8	1
T	8:00	12:01	12:30	6:31	8	2
F	7:56	12:05	12:34	4:30	8	
S	8:00	10:31				2½

Complete the following:

(a) _____ regular hours × $10.00 per hour $_____

(b) _____ overtime hours × $15.00 per hour $_____

(c) Total gross wages $_____

(d) Federal income tax withholding (from tax tables in Figure 8-4, pages 286 and 287) $_____

(e) Social Security withholding at 6.2% $_____

(f) Medicare withholding at 1.45% $_____

(g) Total withholding $_____

(h) Net pay $_____

E 8-2A (LO2)
✓ Gross pay: $795.00

COMPUTING WEEKLY GROSS PAY Ryan Lawrence's regular hourly rate is $15.00. He receives 1½ times the regular rate for any hours worked over 40 a week and double the rate for work on Sunday. During the past week, Lawrence worked 8 hours each day Monday through Thursday, 10 hours on Friday, and 5 hours on Sunday. Compute Lawrence's gross pay for the past week.

E 8-3A (LO2)
✓ b: $712.50

COMPUTING OVERTIME RATE OF PAY AND GROSS WEEKLY PAY Rebecca Huang receives a regular salary of $2,600 a month and is paid 1½ times the regular hourly rate for hours worked in excess of 40 per week.

(a) Calculate Huang's overtime rate of pay.
(b) Calculate Huang's total gross weekly pay if she works 45 hours during the week.

E 8-4A (LO2)
✓ e: $10.00

COMPUTING FEDERAL INCOME TAX Using the table in Figure 8-4 on pages 286 and 287, determine the amount of federal income tax an employer should withhold weekly for employees with the following marital status, earnings, and withholding allowances:

	Marital Status	Total Weekly Earnings	Number of Allowances	Amount of Withholding
(a)	S	$327.90	2	_____
(b)	S	410.00	1	_____
(c)	M	438.16	3	_____
(d)	S	518.25	0	_____
(e)	M	603.98	5	_____

E 8-5A (LO2)
✓ 3d row, Soc. Sec. tax: $161.20

CALCULATING SOCIAL SECURITY AND MEDICARE TAXES Assume a Social Security tax rate of 6.2% is applied to maximum earnings of $106,800 and a Medicare tax rate of 1.45% is applied to all earnings. Calculate the Social Security and Medicare taxes for the following situations:

Cumul. Pay Before Current Weekly Payroll	Current Gross Pay	Year-to-Date Earnings	Soc. Sec. Maximum	Amount Over Max. Soc. Sec.	Amount Subject to Soc. Sec.	Soc. Sec. Tax Withheld	Medicare Tax Withheld
$ 22,000	$1,200	____	$106,800	____	____	____	____
54,000	4,200	____	106,800	____	____	____	____
104,200	3,925	____	106,800	____	____	____	____
106,200	4,600	____	106,800	____	____	____	____

E 8-6A (LO4)

✓ Med. tax: $126.15

JOURNALIZING PAYROLL TRANSACTIONS On December 31, the payroll register of Hamstreet Associates indicated the following information:

Wages and Salaries Expense	$8,700.00
Employee Income Tax Payable	920.00
United Way Contributions Payable	200.00
Earnings subject to Social Security tax	8,000.00

Determine the amount of Social Security and Medicare taxes to be withheld and record the journal entry for the payroll, crediting Cash for the net pay.

E 8-7A (LO4)

✓ Cr. Cash: $4,756.49

PAYROLL JOURNAL ENTRY Journalize the following data taken from the payroll register of University Printing as of April 15, 20—:

Regular earnings	$5,418.00
Overtime earnings	824.00
Deductions:	
Federal income tax	593.00
Social Security tax	387.00
Medicare tax	90.51
Pension plan	90.00
Health insurance premiums	225.00
United Way contributions	100.00

SERIES A PROBLEMS

P 8-8A (LO2/4)

✓ Net pay: $180.19

GROSS PAY, DEDUCTIONS, AND NET PAY Donald Chin works for Northwest Supplies. His rate of pay is $8.50 per hour, and he is paid 1½ times the regular rate for all hours worked in excess of 40 per week. During the last week of January of the current year, he worked 48 hours. Chin is married and claims three withholding allowances on his W-4 form. His weekly wages are subject to the following deductions:

(a) Employee income tax (use Figure 8-4 on pages 286 and 287)
(b) Social Security tax at 6.2%
(c) Medicare tax at 1.45%
(d) Health insurance premium, $85.00
(e) Credit union, $125.00
(f) United Way contribution, $10.00

REQUIRED

1. Compute Chin's regular pay, overtime pay, gross pay, and net pay.

2. Journalize the payment of his wages for the week ended January 31, crediting Cash for the net amount.

P 8-9A (LO2/3/4)

✓ Cr. Cash: $1,827.03

PAYROLL REGISTER AND PAYROLL JOURNAL ENTRY Don McCullum operates a travel agency called Don's Luxury Travel. He has five employees, all of whom are paid on a weekly basis. The travel agency uses a payroll register, individual employee earnings records, and a general journal.

Don's Luxury Travel uses a weekly federal income tax withholding table. The payroll data for each employee for the week ended March 22, 20—, are given on the following page. Employees are paid 1½ times the regular rate for working over 40 hours a week.

Name	No. of Allowances	Marital Status	Total Hours Worked Mar. 16–22	Rate	Total Earnings Jan. 1–Mar. 15
Ali, Loren	4	M	45	$11.00	$5,280.00
Carson, Judy	1	S	40	12.00	5,760.00
Hernandez, Maria	3	M	43	9.50	4,560.00
Knox, Wayne	1	S	39	11.00	5,125.50
Paglione, Jim	2	M	40	10.50	4,720.50

Social Security tax is withheld from the first $106,800 of earnings at the rate of 6.2%. Medicare tax is withheld at the rate of 1.45%, and city earnings tax at the rate of 1%, both applied to gross pay. Ali and Knox have $15.00 withheld and Carson and Hernandez have $5.00 withheld for health insurance. Ali and Knox have $20.00 withheld to be invested in the travel agency's credit union. Carson has $38.75 withheld and Hernandez has $18.75 withheld under a savings bond purchase plan.

Don's Luxury Travel's payroll is met by drawing checks on its regular bank account. The checks were issued in sequence, beginning with Check No. 423.

REQUIRED

1. Prepare a payroll register for Don's Luxury Travel for the week ended March 22, 20--. (In the Taxable Earnings/Unemployment Compensation column, enter the same amounts as in the Social Security column.) Total the amount columns, verify the totals, and rule with single and double lines.

2. Assuming that the wages for the week ended March 22 were paid on March 24, prepare the journal entry for the payment of the payroll.

P 8-10A (LO3)

✓ Soc. Sec. tax: $29.76

EMPLOYEE EARNINGS RECORD Don's Luxury Travel in Problem 8-9A keeps employee earnings records. Judy Carson, employee number 62, is employed as a manager in the ticket sales department. She was born on May 8, 1959, and was hired on June 1 of last year. Her social security number is 544-67-1283. She lives at 28 Quarry Drive, Vernon, CT 06066.

REQUIRED

For the week ended March 22, complete an employee earnings record for Judy Carson. (Insert earnings data only for the week of March 22.)

SERIES B EXERCISES

E 8-1B (LO2)

✓ Net pay: $527.70

COMPUTING NET PAY Tom Hallinan works for a company that pays its employees 1½ times the regular rate for all hours worked in excess of 40 per week. Hallinan's pay rate is $12.00 per hour. His wages are subject to deductions for federal income tax, Social Security tax, and Medicare tax. He is married and claims five withholding allowances. Hallinan has a ½-hour lunch break during an 8½-hour day. His time card is shown on page 308.

(continued)

Name	Tom Hallinan					
Week Ending	March 30, 20--					
Day	In	Out	In	Out	Hours Worked	
					Regular	Overtime
M	7:55	12:02	12:32	5:33	8	1
T	7:59	12:04	12:34	6:05	8	1½
W	7:59	12:05	12:35	4:30	8	
T	8:00	12:01	12:30	5:01	8	½
F	7:58	12:02	12:31	5:33	8	1
S	7:59	9:33				1½

Complete the following:

(a) _____ regular hours × $12.00 per hour $_____

(b) _____ overtime hours × $18.00 per hour $_____

(c) Total gross wages $_____

(d) Federal income tax withholding (from tax tables in Figure 8-4, pages 286 and 287) $_____

(e) Social Security withholding at 6.2% $_____

(f) Medicare withholding at 1.45% $_____

(g) Total withholding $_____

(h) Net pay $_____

E 8-2B (LO2)

✓ Gross pay: $678.00

COMPUTING WEEKLY GROSS PAY Manuel Soto's regular hourly rate is $12.00. He receives 1½ times the regular rate for hours worked in excess of 40 a week and double the rate for work on Sunday. During the past week, Soto worked 8 hours each day Monday through Thursday, 11 hours on Friday, and 6 hours on Sunday. Compute Soto's gross pay for the past week.

E 8-3B (LO2)

✓ b: $918.75

COMPUTING OVERTIME RATE OF PAY AND GROSS WEEKLY PAY Mike Fritz receives a regular salary of $3,250 a month and is paid 1½ times the regular hourly rate for hours worked in excess of 40 per week.

(a) Calculate Fritz's overtime rate of pay. (Compute to the nearest half cent.)
(b) Calculate Fritz's total gross weekly pay if he works 46 hours during the week.

E 8-4B (LO2)

✓ e: $77.00

COMPUTING FEDERAL INCOME TAX Using the table in Figure 8-4 on pages 286 and 287, determine the amount of federal income tax an employer should withhold weekly for employees with the following marital status, earnings, and withholding allowances:

	Marital Status	Total Weekly Earnings	Number of Allowances	Amount of Withholding
(a)	M	$546.00	4	_____
(b)	M	390.00	3	_____
(c)	S	461.39	2	_____
(d)	M	522.88	2	_____
(e)	S	612.00	0	_____

E 8-5B (LO2)

✓ 3rd row, Soc. Sec. tax: $179.80

CALCULATING SOCIAL SECURITY AND MEDICARE TAXES Assume a Social Security tax rate of 6.2% is applied to maximum earnings of $106,800 and a Medicare tax rate of 1.45% is applied to all earnings. Calculate the Social Security and Medicare taxes for the following situations:

Cumul. Pay Before Current Weekly Payroll	Current Gross Pay	Year-to-Date Earnings	Soc. Sec. Maximum	Amount Over Max. Soc. Sec.	Amount Subject to Soc. Sec.	Soc. Sec. Tax Withheld	Medicare Tax Withheld
$ 31,000	$1,500	_____	$106,800	_____	_____	_____	_____
53,000	2,860	_____	106,800	_____	_____	_____	_____
103,900	3,140	_____	106,800	_____	_____	_____	_____
106,200	2,920	_____	106,800	_____	_____	_____	_____

E 8-6B (LO4)

✓ Med. tax: $136.30

JOURNALIZING PAYROLL TRANSACTIONS On November 30, the payroll register of Webster & Smith indicated the following information:

Wages and Salaries Expense	$9,400.00
Employee Income Tax Payable	985.00
United Way Contributions Payable	200.00
Earnings subject to Social Security tax	9,400.00

Determine the amount of Social Security and Medicare taxes to be withheld and record the journal entry for the payroll, crediting Cash for the net pay.

E 8-7B (LO4)

✓ Cr. Cash: $5,696.54

PAYROLL JOURNAL ENTRY Journalize the following data taken from the payroll register of Himes Bakery as of June 12, 20--:

Regular earnings	$6,520.00
Overtime earnings	950.00
Deductions:	
Federal income tax	782.00
Social Security tax	463.14
Medicare tax	108.32
Pension plan	80.00
Health insurance premiums	190.00
United Way contributions	150.00

SERIES B PROBLEMS

P 8-8B (LO2/4)

✓ Net pay: $185.27

GROSS PAY, DEDUCTIONS, AND NET PAY Elyse Lin works for Columbia Industries. Her rate of pay is $9.00 per hour, and she is paid 1½ times the regular rate for all hours worked in excess of 40 per week. During the last week of January of the current year, she worked 46 hours. Lin is married and claims two withholding allowances on her W-4 form. Her weekly wages are subject to the following deductions:

(a) Employee income tax (use Figure 8-4 on pages 286 and 287)
(b) Social Security tax at 6.2%
(c) Medicare tax at 1.45%
(d) Health insurance premium, $92.00
(e) Credit union, $110.00
(f) United Way contribution, $5.00

(continued)

1.   Compute Lin's regular pay, overtime pay, gross pay, and net pay.

2.   Journalize the payment of her wages for the week ended January 31, crediting Cash for the net amount.

P 8-9B (LO2/3/4)

✓ Cr. Cash: $1,777.42

PAYROLL REGISTER AND PAYROLL JOURNAL ENTRY Karen Jolly operates a bakery called Karen's Cupcakes. She has five employees, all of whom are paid on a weekly basis. Karen's Cupcakes uses a payroll register, individual employee earnings records, and a general journal.

Karen's Cupcakes uses a weekly federal income tax withholding table. The payroll data for each employee for the week ended February 15, 20--, are given below. Employees are paid 1½ times the regular rate for working over 40 hours a week.

Name	No. of Allowances	Marital Status	Total Hours Worked Feb. 9–15	Rate	Total Earnings Jan. 1–Feb. 8
Barone, William	1	S	40	$10.00	$2,400.00
Hastings, Gene	4	M	45	12.00	3,360.00
Nitobe, Isako	3	M	46	8.75	2,935.00
Smith, Judy	4	M	42	11.00	2,745.00
Tarshis, Dolores	1	S	39	10.50	2,650.75

Social Security tax is withheld from the first $106,800 of earnings at the rate of 6.2%. Medicare tax is withheld at the rate of 1.45%, and city earnings tax at the rate of 1%, both applied to gross pay. Hastings and Smith have $35.00 withheld and Nitobe and Tarshis have $15.00 withheld for health insurance. Nitobe and Tarshis have $25.00 withheld to be invested in the bakers' credit union. Hastings has $18.75 withheld and Smith has $43.75 withheld under a savings bond purchase plan.

Karen's Cupcakes' payroll is met by drawing checks on its regular bank account. The checks were issued in sequence, beginning with No. 365.

REQUIRED

1.   Prepare a payroll register for Karen's Cupcakes for the week ended February 15, 20--. (In the Taxable Earnings/Unemployment Compensation column, enter the same amounts as in the Social Security column.) Total the amount columns, verify the totals, and rule with single and double lines.

2.   Assuming that the wages for the week ended February 15 were paid on February 17, prepare the journal entry for the payment of this payroll.

P 8-10B (LO3)

✓ Soc. Sec. tax: $24.80

EMPLOYEE EARNINGS RECORD Karen's Cupcakes in Problem 8-9B keeps employee earnings records. William Barone, employee number 19, is employed as a baker in the desserts department. He was born on August 26, 1959, and was hired on October 1 of last year. His social security number is 342-73-4681. He lives at 30 Timber Lane, Willington, CT 06279.

REQUIRED

For the week ended February 15, complete an employee earnings record for William Barone. (Insert earnings data only for the week of February 15.)

MANAGING YOUR WRITING

The minimum wage originally was only 25 cents an hour. Today it is $7.25 an hour. Assume that Congress is considering raising the minimum wage again and your U.S. representative is asking for public opinion on this issue. Write a letter to your representative with arguments for and against a higher minimum wage.

ETHICS CASE

Maura Lowe is a payroll accountant for N & L Company. She prepares and processes the company's payroll on a weekly basis and has been at N & L for only three months. All employees are paid on Friday. On Wednesday afternoon, Simon Lentz, one of the company's top sales associates, asks Maura to not take out any payroll deductions from his pay this week. He explains that he is short of cash and needs the full amount of his gross salary just to put food on the table and make his past-due car payment. He promises Maura that she can catch up on the deductions over the next month. The deductions include employee income tax, Social Security tax, Medicare tax, and health insurance premiums.

1. Is Simon's request of Maura ethical? Why or why not?

2. If this were the first pay period of the year and Maura agreed not to take out deductions from Simon's pay, what effect would this have on the liabilities section of the balance sheet?

3. Write a short paragraph from Maura to Simon explaining how omitting deductions from a pay period will cause errors in the company's financial statements.

4. In small groups, discuss what action Maura should take regarding Simon's request.

MASTERY PROBLEM

✓ Cr. Cash: $4,253.54

Abigail Trenkamp owns and operates the Trenkamp Collection Agency. Listed on the following page are the name, number of allowances claimed, marital status, information from time cards on hours worked each day, and the hourly rate of each employee. All hours worked in excess of 40 hours for Monday through Friday are paid at 1½ times the regular rate. All weekend hours are paid at double the regular rate.

Trenkamp uses a weekly federal income tax withholding table (see Figure 8-4 on pages 286 and 287). Social Security tax is withheld at the rate of 6.2% for the first $106,800 earned. Medicare tax is withheld at 1.45% and state income tax at 3.5%. Each employee has $5.00 withheld for health insurance. All employees use payroll deduction to the credit union for varying amounts as listed.

(continued)

Trenkamp Collection Agency
Payroll Information for the Week Ended November 18, 20--

Name	Employee No.	No of Allow.	Marital Status	Regular Hours Worked							Hourly Rate	Credit Union Deposit	Total Earnings 1/1–11/11
				S	S	M	T	W	T	F			
Berling, James	1	3	M	2	2	9	8	8	9	10	$12.00	$149.60	$24,525.00
Merz, Linda	2	4	M	4	3	8	8	8	8	11	10.00	117.00	20,480.00
Goetz, Ken	3	2	M	0	0	6	7	8	9	10	11.00	91.30	21,500.00
Menick, Judd	4	2	S	8	8	0	0	8	8	9	11.00	126.50	22,625.00
Morales, Eva	5	3	M	0	0	8	8	8	6	8	13.00	117.05	24,730.00
Heimbrock, Jacob	6	5	M	0	0	8	8	8	8	8	34.00	154.25	105,840.00
Townsley, Sarah	7	2	M	4	0	6	6	6	6	4	9.00	83.05	21,425.00
Salzman, Ben	8	4	M	6	2	8	8	6	6	6	11.00	130.00	6,635.00
Layton, Esther	9	3	M	0	0	8	8	8	8	8	11.00	88.00	5,635.00
Thompson, David	10	5	M	0	2	10	9	7	7	10	11.00	128.90	21,635.00
Vadillo, Carmen	11	2	S	8	0	4	8	8	8	9	13.00	139.11	24,115.00

The Trenkamp Collection Agency follows the practice of drawing a single check for the net amount of the payroll and depositing the check in a special payroll account at the bank. Individual checks issued were numbered consecutively, beginning with No. 331.

REQUIRED

1. Prepare a payroll register for Trenkamp Collection Agency for the week ended November 18, 20--. (In the Taxable Earnings/Unemployment Compensation column, enter $365 for Salzman and $440 for Layton. Leave this column blank for all other employees.) Total the amount columns, verify the totals, and rule with single and double lines.

2. Assuming that the wages for the week ended November 18 were paid on November 21, prepare the journal entry for the payment of this payroll.

3. The current employee earnings record for Ben Salzman is provided in the working papers. Update Salzman's earnings record to reflect the November 18 payroll. Although this information should have been entered earlier, complete the required information on the earnings record. The necessary information is as follows:

Name	Ben F. Salzman
Address	12 Windmill Lane
	Trumbull, CT 06611
Employee No.	8
Gender	Male
Department	Administration
Occupation	Office Manager
Social Security No.	446-46-6321
Marital Status	Married
Allowances	4
Pay Rate	$11.00 per hour
Date of Birth	4/5/64
Date Hired	7/22/--

CHALLENGE PROBLEM

This problem challenges you to apply your cumulative accounting knowledge to move a step beyond the material in the chapter.

✓ **Dr. Wages and Salaries Expense: $1,596**

Irina Company pays its employees weekly. The last pay period for 20-1 was on December 28. From December 28 through December 31, the employees earned $1,754.00, so the following adjusting entry was made:

	20-1						
5	Dec.	31	Wages and Salaries Expense	1 7 5 4 00			5
6			Wages and Salaries Payable		1 7 5 4 00		6
7			To record accrued wages and salaries				7

The first pay period in 20-2 was on January 4. The totals line from Irina Company's payroll register for the week ended January 4, 20-2, was as follows:

PAYROLL

			EARNINGS				TAXABLE EARNINGS	
			REGULAR	OVERTIME	TOTAL	CUMULATIVE TOTAL	UNEMPLOYMENT COMPENSATION	SOCIAL SECURITY
1	Totals		3 3 5 0 00		3 3 5 0 00	3 3 5 0 00	3 3 5 0 00	3 3 5 0 00	1

REGISTER—WEEK ENDED January 4, 20-2

		DEDUCTIONS							NET PAY	
	FEDERAL INCOME TAX	SOCIAL SECURITY TAX	MEDICARE TAX	HEALTH INSURANCE	UNITED WAY	OTHER		TOTAL		
1	3 4 2 00	2 0 7 70	4 8 58	5 0 00	8 0 00			7 2 8 28	2 6 2 1 72	1

REQUIRED

1. Prepare the journal entry for the payment of the payroll on January 4, 20-2.

2. Prepare T accounts for Wages and Salaries Expense and Wages and Salaries Payable showing the beginning balance, January 4, 20-2, entry, and ending balance as of January 4, 20-2.

ANSWERS TO SELF-STUDY QUESTIONS AND EXERCISES

True/False Questions

1. F (does *not* work under control and direction)
2. T
3. F (is called wages)
4. T
5. T

Multiple Choice Questions

1. c **2.** d **3.** d **4.** b **5.** a

U REVU **Exercises**

1.
(a) 40 × $14 = $560
      5 × $14 × 1.5 =   105
           Gross pay $665
(b) $40

2. Wages and Salaries Expense	4,600.00	
Employee Income Tax Payable		417.00
Social Security Tax Payable		285.20
Medicare Tax Payable		66.70
State Income Tax Payable		46.00
Health Insurance Premiums Payable		181.00
Cash		3,604.10

## Chapter 9

Payroll Accounting: Employer Taxes and Reports

As competition has become more global, many challenges to businesses have developed. Learning how to function in many different languages and cultures is one of these challenges. Lingualinx is a full-service translation company that offers help with language issues. Founded in 2002, Lingualinx has offices in the United States, the United Kingdom, France, and China. It hires qualified professional linguists with skills tailored to provide services in more than 100 languages. Some examples of its capabilities include simple text translation, simultaneous interpretation, sign language, copywriting, and even Braille production. It can also provide on-site language instruction classes.

Lingualinx faces the same kinds of payroll issues as Intechra, the company described in the introduction to Chapter 8. But Lingualinx would face the added challenge of employees in multiple countries, so it would need to know the regulations in each location. In addition, you will learn in this chapter that employers must account for not just *employee* wages and taxes but also *employer* taxes. The complexity of payroll accounting is a major reason why many businesses hire an outside company to manage their payroll. You will also learn about two of these payroll service companies in this chapter's "A Broader View."

LEARNING OBJECTIVES

Careful study of this chapter should enable you to:

LO1 Describe and calculate employer payroll taxes.

LO2 Account for employer payroll taxes expense.

LO3 Describe employer reporting and payment responsibilities.

LO4 Describe and account for workers' compensation insurance.

LISEGAGNE/ISTOCKPHOTO.COM

The taxes we discussed in Chapter 8 had one thing in common—they all were levied on the employee. The employer withheld them from employees' earnings and paid them to the government. They did not add anything to the employer's payroll expenses.

In this chapter, we will examine several taxes that are imposed directly on the employer. All of these taxes represent additional payroll expenses. You will see that the total cost of employees includes not only wages but also payroll taxes and benefits such as vacation and sick pay.

EMPLOYER PAYROLL TAXES

LO1 Describe and calculate employer payroll taxes.

Most employers must pay FICA, FUTA (Federal Unemployment Tax Act), and SUTA (state unemployment tax) taxes.

EMPLOYER FICA TAXES

Employer FICA taxes are levied on employers at the same rates and on the same earnings bases as the employee FICA taxes. As explained in Chapter 8, we are assuming the Social Security component is 6.2% on maximum earnings of $106,800 for each employee. Since there is no maximum on the Medicare component, this tax is 1.45% on all earnings.

The payroll register we saw in Chapter 8 is a key source of information for computing employer payroll taxes. That payroll register is reproduced in Figure 9-1. The Taxable Earnings Social Security column shows that $4,835 of employee earnings were subject to Social Security tax for the pay period. The employer's Social Security tax on these earnings is computed as follows:

FIGURE 9-1 Payroll Register (left side)

PAYROLL

	NAME	ALLOWANCES	MARITAL STATUS	EARNINGS				TAXABLE EARNINGS		
				REGULAR	OVERTIME	TOTAL	CUMULATIVE TOTAL	UNEMPLOYMENT COMPENSATION	SOCIAL SECURITY	
1	Cadrain, Sarah	4	M	1 6 0 0 00	6 0 00	1 6 6 0 00	107 8 0 0 00	0 00	6 6 0 00	1
2	Gruder, James	1	S	7 6 0 00	1 4 0 00	9 0 0 00	43 4 0 0 00	0 00	9 0 0 00	2
3	Istone, Ken	4	M	5 4 5 00		5 4 5 00	27 0 2 5 00	0 00	5 4 5 00	3
4	Kuzmik, Helen	2	M	4 8 0 00	2 9 4 00	7 7 4 00	31 0 0 0 00	0 00	7 7 4 00	4
5	Lee, Hoseoup	3	M	4 4 0 00		4 4 0 00	22 3 4 0 00	0 00	4 4 0 00	5
6	Swaney, Linda	2	S	5 2 8 00	1 9 8 00	7 2 6 00	27 5 0 0 00	0 00	7 2 6 00	6
7	Tucci, Paul	3	M	4 9 0 00		4 9 0 00	25 0 5 0 00	0 00	4 9 0 00	7
8	Wiles, Harry	1	S	3 0 0 00		3 0 0 00	6 3 0 0 00	3 0 0 00	3 0 0 00	8
9				5 1 4 3 00	6 9 2 00	5 8 3 5 00	290 4 1 5 00	3 0 0 00	4 8 3 5 00	9
10										10

Time cards, pay rates

Prior period total + current period earnings

Current below $7,000 cumul. total

Current below $106,800 cumul. total

LEARNING KEY

Use the information in the payroll register to compute employer payroll taxes.

Social Security Taxable Earnings	×	Tax Rate	=	Tax
$4,835		0.062		$299.77

The Medicare tax applies to the total earnings of $5,835. The employer's Medicare tax on these earnings is computed as follows:

Total Earnings	×	Tax Rate	=	Tax
$5,835		0.0145		$84.61

These amounts plus the employees' Social Security and Medicare taxes withheld must be paid by the employer to the Internal Revenue Service (IRS).

SELF-EMPLOYMENT TAX

The self-employment tax rate is double the employee and employer Social Security and Medicare rates because the self-employed person is considered both the employer and employee.

Individuals who own and run their own business are considered self-employed. These individuals can be viewed as both employer and employee. They do not receive salary or wages from the business, but they do have earnings in the form of the business net income. **Self-employment income** is the net income of a trade or business run by an individual. Currently, persons earning net self-employment income of $400 or more must pay a **self-employment tax**. Self-employment tax is a contribution to the FICA program. The tax rates are double the Social Security and Medicare rates (12.4% + 2.9% = 15.3% total). They are applied to the same income bases as those used for the Social Security and Medicare taxes. *Publication 334, Tax Guide for Small Business*, contains helpful information for self-employed persons.

EMPLOYER FUTA TAX

The **FUTA (Federal Unemployment Tax Act) tax** is levied only on employers. It is not deducted from employees' earnings. The purpose of this tax is to raise funds to administer the combined federal/state unemployment compensation program. The maximum

FIGURE 9-1 Payroll Register (right side)

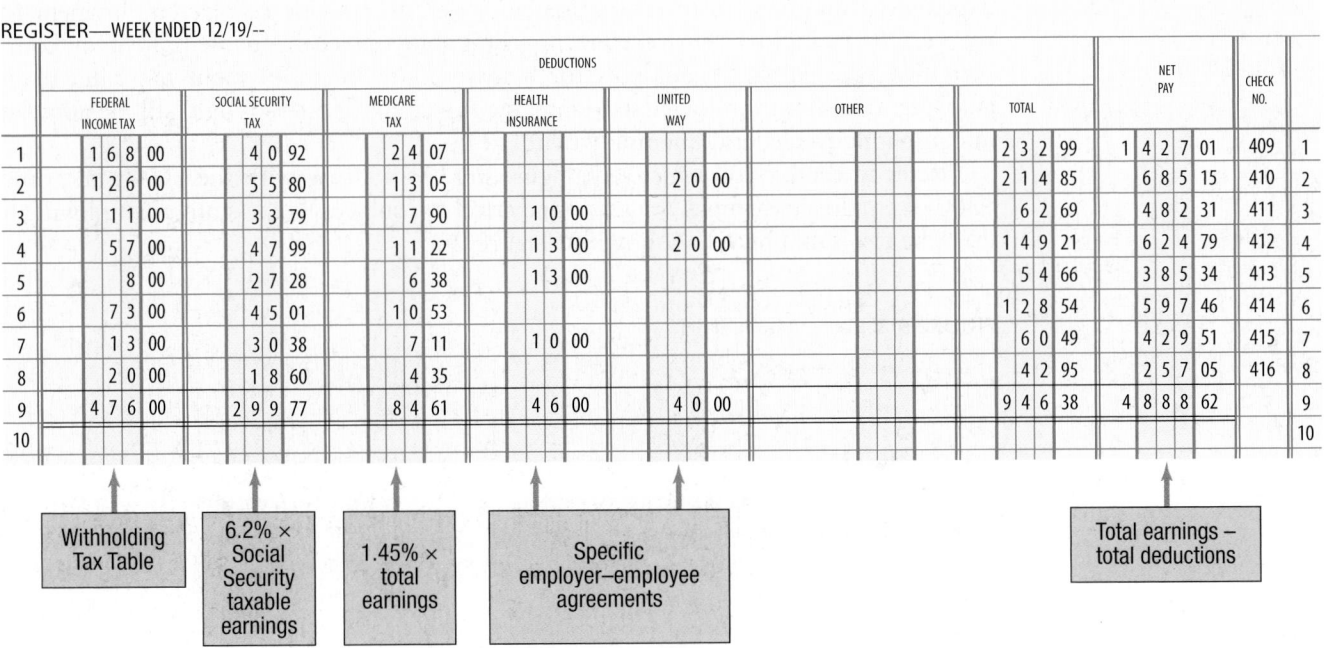

amount of earnings subject to the FUTA tax and the tax rate can be changed by Congress. The current rate is 6.2% applied to maximum earnings of $7,000 for each employee, but employers are allowed a credit of up to 5.4% for participation in state unemployment programs. Thus, the effective federal rate is commonly 0.8%.

Gross FUTA rate	6.2%
Credit for state unemployment taxes	5.4%
Net FUTA rate	0.8%

To illustrate the computation of the FUTA tax, refer to Figure 9-1. The Taxable Earnings Unemployment Compensation column shows that only $300 of employee earnings were subject to the FUTA tax. This amount is low because the payroll period is late in the calendar year (December 19, 20--). It is common for most employees to exceed the $7,000 earnings limit by this time. The FUTA tax is computed as shown in Figure 9-2.

FIGURE 9-2 Computation of FUTA Tax

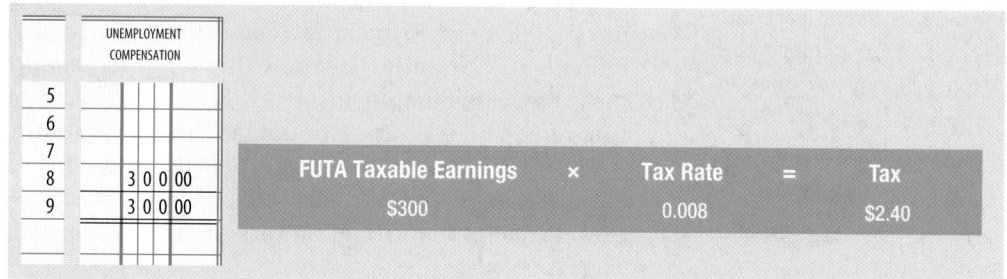

EMPLOYER SUTA TAX

State unemployment tax rates and maximum earnings amounts vary greatly. Current rates range from 5.4% to 11%. Maximum earnings amounts are $7,000 to $35,700.

The **SUTA** (**state unemployment tax**) **tax** is also levied only on employers in most states. The purpose of this tax is to raise funds to pay unemployment benefits. Tax rates and unemployment benefits vary among the states. A common rate is 5.4% applied to maximum earnings of $7,000 for each employee. Most states have an **experience-rating system** to encourage employers to provide regular employment to workers. If an employer has very few former employees receiving unemployment compensation, the employer qualifies for a lower state unemployment tax rate. If an employer qualifies for a lower state rate, the full credit of 5.4% would still be allowed in computing the federal unemployment tax due.

Refer to the payroll register in Figure 9-1. As we saw with the FUTA tax, only $300 of employee earnings for this pay period are subject to the state unemployment tax. The tax is computed as shown in Figure 9-3.

FIGURE 9-3 Computation of SUTA Tax

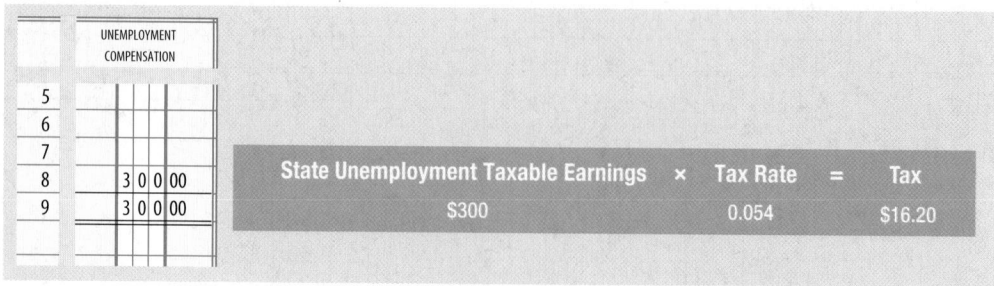

U REVU   Complete U REVU-1 on **page 339** to test your basic understanding of LO1.

ACCOUNTING FOR EMPLOYER PAYROLL TAXES

LO2 Account for employer payroll taxes expense.

Now that we have computed the employer payroll taxes, we need to journalize them. It is common to debit all employer payroll taxes to a single account—Payroll Taxes Expense. However, we usually credit separate liability accounts for Social Security, Medicare, FUTA, and SUTA taxes payable.

JOURNALIZING EMPLOYER PAYROLL TAXES

The employer payroll taxes computed in the previous section can be summarized as follows:

Employer's Social Security tax	$299.77
Employer's Medicare tax	84.61
FUTA tax	2.40
SUTA tax	16.20
Total employer payroll taxes	$402.98

These amounts provide the basis for the following journal entry:

5	Dec.	19	Payroll Taxes Expense	4 0 2 98			5
6			Social Security Tax Payable		2 9 9 77		6
7			Medicare Tax Payable		8 4 61		7
8			FUTA Tax Payable		2 40		8
9			SUTA Tax Payable		1 6 20		9
10			Employer payroll taxes for week ended Dec. 19				10

The steps needed to prepare this journal entry for employer payroll taxes are:

STEP 1 Obtain the total earnings and taxable earnings amounts from the Earnings—Total and Taxable Earnings columns of the payroll register. In this case, total earnings were $5,835; Social Security taxable earnings were $4,835; and Unemployment Compensation taxable earnings were $300.

STEP 2 Compute the amount of employer Social Security tax by multiplying the Social Security taxable earnings by 6.2%.

STEP 3 Compute the amount of employer Medicare tax by multiplying total earnings by 1.45%.

STEP 4 Compute the amount of FUTA tax by multiplying the Unemployment Taxable earnings by 0.8%.

STEP 5 Compute the amount of SUTA tax by multiplying the Unemployment Taxable earnings by 5.4%.

STEP 6 Prepare the appropriate journal entry using the amounts computed in steps 2–5.

To understand the journal entry for employer payroll taxes, let's use the accounting equation to examine the accounts involved. The five accounts affected by the payroll taxes entry above are shown in the accounting equation in Figure 9-4.

FIGURE 9-4 Accounting for Payroll Taxes

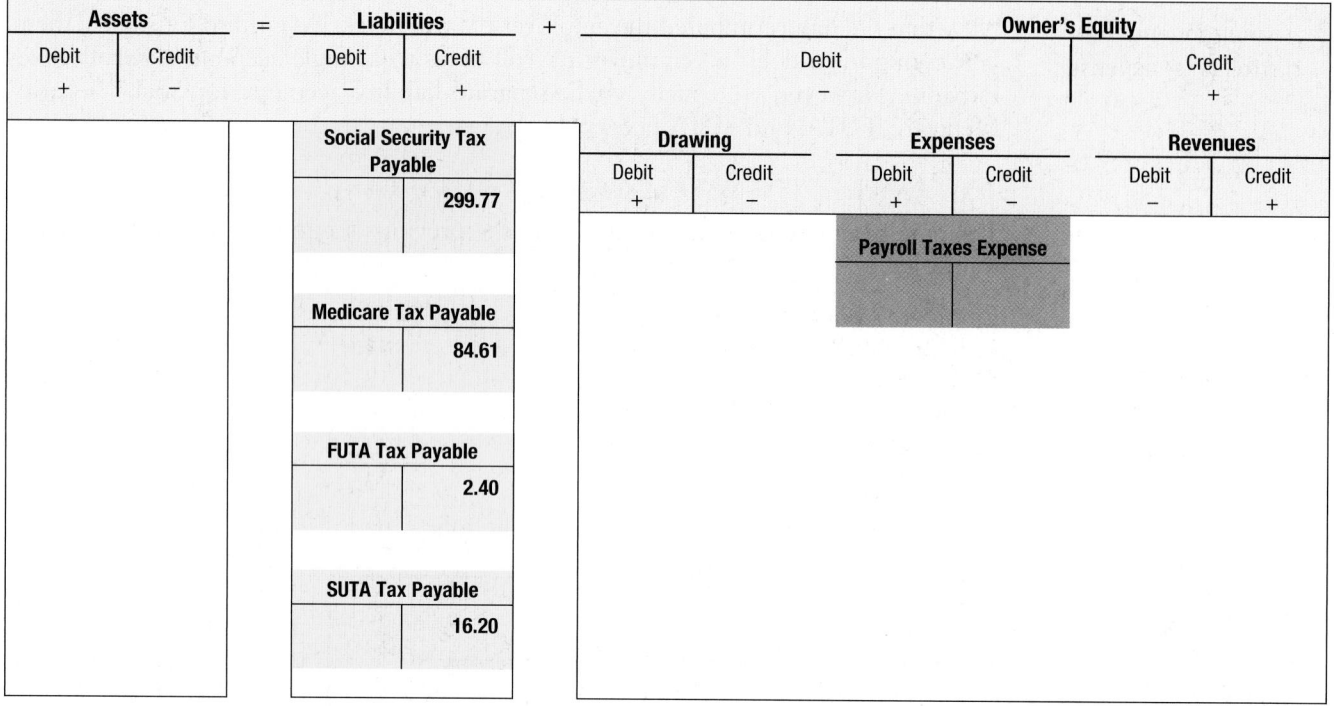

PAYROLL TAXES EXPENSE

The Social Security, Medicare, FUTA, and SUTA taxes imposed on the employer are expenses of doing business. Each of the employer taxes is debited to Payroll Taxes Expense.

Payroll Taxes Expense

Debit	Credit
Social Security, Medicare, FUTA, and SUTA taxes imposed on the employer	

SOCIAL SECURITY AND MEDICARE TAXES PAYABLE

These are the same liability accounts used in Chapter 8 to record the Social Security and Medicare taxes withheld from employees' earnings. The accounts are credited to enter the Social Security and Medicare taxes imposed on the employer. They are debited when the taxes are paid to the IRS. When all of the Social Security and Medicare taxes have been paid, the accounts will have zero balances.

LEARNING KEY

Employer and employee Social Security and Medicare taxes are credited to the same liability accounts because both of these taxes are due and will be paid to the IRS.

Social Security Tax Payable

Debit	Credit
Payment of Social Security tax	Social Security taxes (1) withheld from employees' earnings and (2) imposed on the employer

Medicare Tax Payable

Debit	Credit
Payment of Medicare tax	Medicare taxes (1) withheld from employees' earnings and (2) imposed on the employer

FUTA TAX PAYABLE

A separate liability account entitled FUTA Tax Payable is kept for the employer's FUTA tax. This account is credited for the tax imposed on employers under the Federal Unemployment Tax Act. The account is debited when this tax is paid. When all of the FUTA taxes have been paid, the account will have a zero balance.

FUTA Tax Payable

Debit	Credit
Payment of FUTA tax	FUTA tax imposed on the employer

SUTA TAX PAYABLE

A separate liability account entitled SUTA Tax Payable is kept for the state unemployment tax. This account is credited for the tax imposed on employers under the state unemployment compensation laws. The account is debited when this tax is paid. When all of the state unemployment taxes have been paid, the account will have a zero balance.

SUTA Tax Payable

Debit	Credit
Payment of SUTA tax	SUTA tax imposed on the employer

TOTAL PAYROLL COST OF AN EMPLOYEE

It is interesting to note what it really costs to employ a person. The employer must, of course, pay the gross wages of an employee. In addition, the employer must pay payroll taxes on employee earnings up to certain dollar limits.

To illustrate, assume that an employee earns $26,000 a year. The total cost of this employee to the employer is calculated as follows:

Gross wages	$26,000
Employer Social Security tax, 6.2% of $26,000	1,612
Employer Medicare tax, 1.45% of $26,000	377
State unemployment tax, 5.4% of $7,000	378
FUTA tax, 0.8% of $7,000	56
	$28,423

Thus, the total payroll cost of employing a person whose stated compensation is $26,000 is $28,423. Employer payroll taxes clearly are a significant cost of doing business. Employer-paid medical insurance and pension plans can further increase total payroll costs.

U REVU

Complete U REVU-2 on **page 339** to test your basic understanding of LO2.

REPORTING AND PAYMENT RESPONSIBILITIES

LO3 Describe employer reporting and payment responsibilities.

Employer payroll reporting and payment responsibilities fall into six areas:

1. Federal income tax withholding and Social Security and Medicare taxes
2. FUTA taxes
3. SUTA taxes
4. Employee Wage and Tax Statement (Form W-2)
5. Summary of employee wages and taxes (Form W-3)
6. Employment eligibility verification (Form I-9)

FEDERAL INCOME TAX WITHHOLDING AND SOCIAL SECURITY AND MEDICARE TAXES

Three important aspects of employer reporting and payment responsibilities for federal income tax withholding and Social Security and Medicare taxes are:

1. Determining when payments are due
2. Use of Form 8109, Federal Tax Deposit Coupon
3. Use of Form 941, Employer's Quarterly Federal Tax Return

When Payments Are Due

The date by which federal income tax withholding and Social Security and Medicare taxes must be paid depends on the amount of these taxes. Figure 9-5 summarizes the deposit rules stated in *Circular E—Employer's Tax Guide*. In general, the larger the amount that needs to be deposited, the more frequently payments must be made. For simplicity, we will assume that deposits must be made 15 days after the end of each month.

FIGURE 9-5 Summary of Deposit Rules

ACCUMULATED TAX LIABILITY	DEPOSIT DUE
1. Less than $2,500 at the end of the current quarter	1. Pay with Form 941 at end of the month following end of the quarter
2. $2,500 or more at the end of the current quarter and $50,000 or less in total during the lookback period*	2. Deposit 15 days after end of the month
3. $2,500 or more at the end of the current quarter and more than $50,000 in total during the lookback period*	3. Deposit every other Wednesday or Friday, depending on day of the week payroll payments are made
4. $100,000 or more on any day during the current quarter	4. Deposit by the end of the next banking day

*Lookback period is the four quarters beginning July 1, two years ago, and ending June 30, one year ago.

Form 8109

Deposits may be made using either the **Electronic Federal Tax Payment System (EFTPS)** or Form 8109. The EFTPS is an electronic funds transfer system for making federal tax deposits. Any taxpayer whose deposits in the prior year exceeded $200,000 is required to use this system. Deposits other than EFTPS are made at an authorized commercial bank using Form 8109, Federal Tax Deposit Coupon (Figure 9-6). The **Employer Identification Number (EIN)** shown on this form is obtained by the employer from the IRS. This number identifies the employer and must be shown on all payroll forms and reports filed with the IRS.

Taxpayers who are not required to make electronic deposits may voluntarily participate in EFTPS.

FIGURE 9-6 Federal Tax Deposit Coupon (Form 8109)

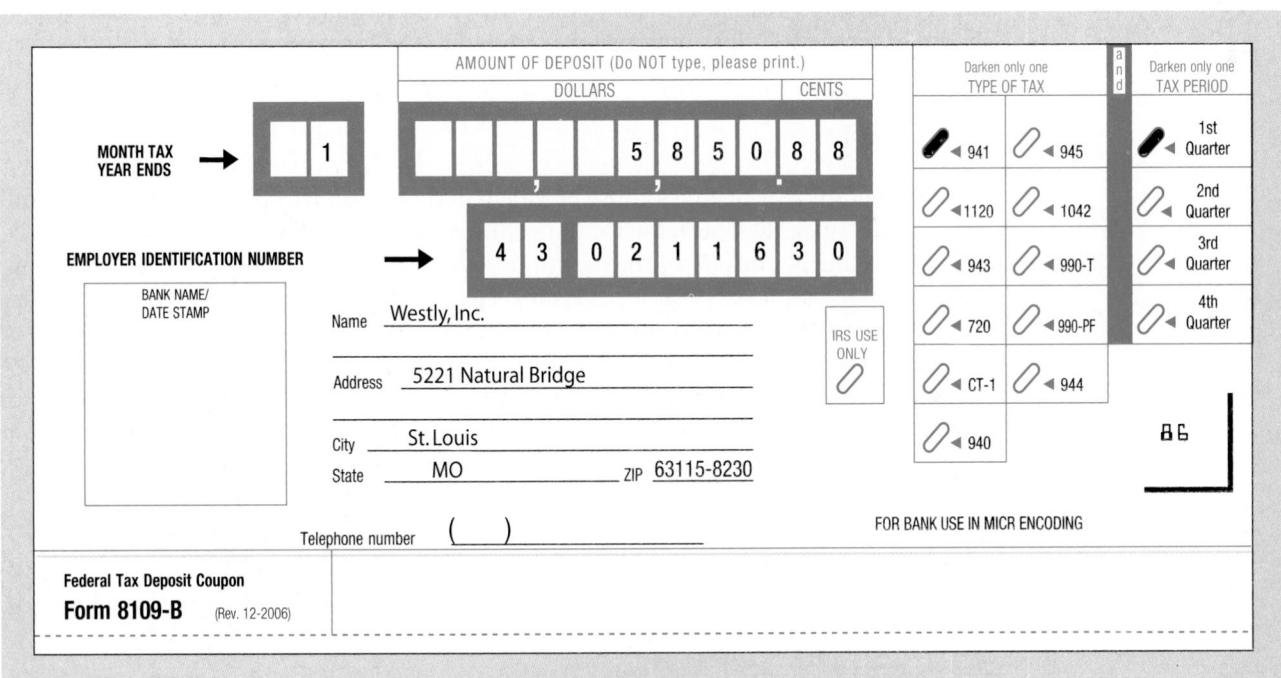

The $5,850.88 deposit shown in Figure 9-6 for Westly, Inc., was for the following taxes on wages paid in January:

Employees' income tax withheld from wages		$2,526.80
Social Security tax:		
Withheld from employees' wages	$1,346.24	
Imposed on employer	1,346.24	2,692.48
Medicare tax:		
Withheld from employees' wages	$ 315.80	
Imposed on employer	315.80	631.60
Amount of check		$5,850.88

The journal entry for this deposit would be as follows:

5	Feb.	15	Employee Income Tax Payable		2 5 2 6 80			5
6			Social Security Tax Payable		2 6 9 2 48			6
7			Medicare Tax Payable		6 3 1 60			7
8			Cash			5 8 5 0 88		8
9			Deposit of employee federal income tax and					9
10			Social Security and Medicare taxes					10

Form 941

Form 941, Employer's Quarterly Federal Tax Return, must be filed with the IRS at the end of the month following each calendar quarter. This form reports the following taxes for the quarter:

1. Employee federal income tax withheld

2. Employee Social Security and Medicare taxes withheld

3. Employer Social Security and Medicare taxes

A completed form for Westly, Inc., for the first quarter of the calendar year is shown in Figure 9-7. Instructions for completing the form are provided with the form and in *Circular E*.

FUTA TAXES

Federal unemployment taxes must be calculated on a quarterly basis. If the accumulated liability exceeds $500, the total must be paid to an authorized commercial bank. The total is due by the end of the month following the close of the quarter. If the liability is $500 or less, no deposit is necessary. The amount is simply added to the amount to be deposited for the next quarter. FUTA taxes are deposited using either EFTPS or Form 8109 (Figure 9-6).

Assume that an employer's accumulated FUTA tax liability for the first quarter of the calendar year is $508. The employer would use Form 8109 to deposit this amount on April 30. The journal entry for this transaction would be as follows:

15	Apr.	30	FUTA Tax Payable		5 0 8 00			15
16			Cash			5 0 8 00		16
17			Deposit of federal unemployment tax					17

FIGURE 9-7 Employer's Quarterly Federal Tax Return (Form 941)

Form **941 for 20--:**   **Employer's QUARTERLY Federal Tax Return**   950109
(Rev. January 20--)   Department of the Treasury — Internal Revenue Service   OMB No. 1545-0029

(EIN)
Employer identification number   4 3 – 0 2 1 1 6 3 0

Name (not your trade name)

Trade name (if any)   Westly, Inc.

Address   5221 Natural Bridge
Number   Street   Suite or room number

St. Louis   MO   63115-8230
City   State   ZIP code

Report for this Quarter of 20--
(Check one.)

[X] 1: January, February, March
[ ] 2: April, May, June
[ ] 3: July, August, September
[ ] 4: October, November, December

Read the separate instructions before you complete Form 941. Type or print within the boxes.

Part 1: Answer these questions for this quarter.

1	Number of employees who received wages, tips, or other compensation for the pay period including: *Mar. 12* (Quarter 1), *June 12* (Quarter 2), *Sept. 12* (Quarter 3), *Dec. 12* (Quarter 4)	1	8
2	Wages, tips, and other compensation	2	65,160.00
3	Income tax withheld from wages, tips, and other compensation	3	7,595.80 ← Employee federal income tax withheld
4	If no wages, tips, and other compensation are subject to social security or Medicare tax	[ ] Check and go to line 6.	
5	Taxable social security and Medicare wages and tips:		

	Column 1		Column 2	
5a Taxable social security wages	65,160.00	× .124 =	8,079.84	Employee and employer Social Security taxes
5b Taxable social security tips		× .124 =		
5c Taxable Medicare wages & tips	65,160.00	× .029 =	1,889.64	Employee and employer Medicare taxes

5d Total social security and Medicare taxes (*Column 2,* lines 5a + 5b + 5c = line 5d) .	5d	9,969.48
6	Total taxes before adjustments (lines 3 + 5d = line 6)	6	17,565.28
7	CURRENT QUARTER'S ADJUSTMENTS, for example, a fractions of cents adjustment. See the instructions.		
	7a Current quarter's fractions of cents		
	7b Current quarter's sick pay		
	7c Current quarter's adjustments for tips and group-term life insurance .		
	7d TOTAL ADJUSTMENTS. Combine all amounts on lines 7a through 7c	7d	.0
8	Total taxes after adjustments. Combine lines 6 and 7d	8	17,565.28
9	Advance earned income credit (EIC) payments made to employees	9	.0
10	Total taxes after adjustment for advance EIC (line 8 – line 9 = line 10) . . .	10	17,565.28
11	Total deposits for this quarter, including overpayment applied from a prior quarter and overpayment applied from Form 941-X or Form 944-X	17,565.28	
12a	COBRA premium assistance payments (see instructions) . . .		
12b	Number of individuals provided COBRA premium assistance reported on line 12a.		
13	Add lines 11 and 12a	13	17,565.28
14	Balance due. If line 10 is more than line 13, write the difference here	14	.0
	For information on how to pay, see the instructions.		[ ] Apply to next return.
15	Overpayment. If line 13 is more than line 10, write the difference here . .	Check one [ ] Send a refund.

▶ You **MUST** complete both pages of Form 941 and **SIGN** it.   Next ➡

For Privacy Act and Paperwork Reduction Act Notice, see the back of the Payment Voucher.   Cat. No. 17001Z   Form **941** (Rev. 1-20--)

FIGURE 9-7 Employer's Quarterly Federal Tax Return (Form 941) *(concluded)*

950209

Name *(not your trade name)*

Employer identification number (EIN)

Part 2: Tell us about your deposit schedule and tax liability for this quarter.

If you are unsure about whether you are a monthly schedule depositor or a semiweekly schedule depositor, see *Pub. 15 (Circular E)*, section 11.

16 **M O** Write the state abbreviation for the state where you made your deposits OR write "MU" if you made your deposits in multiple states.

17 **Check one:** ☐ Line 10 is less than $2,500. Go to Part 3.

☒ You were a monthly schedule depositor for the entire quarter. Enter your tax liability for each month. Then go to Part 3.

Tax liability:	Month 1	5,850.88
	Month 2	5,690.77
	Month 3	6,023.63
	Total liability for quarter	17,565.28	Total must equal line 10.

☐ You were a semiweekly schedule depositor for any part of this quarter. Complete *Schedule B (Form 941): Report of Tax Liability for Semiweekly Schedule Depositors,* and attach it to Form 941.

Part 3: Tell us about your business. If a question does NOT apply to your business, leave it blank.

18 If your business has closed or you stopped paying wages . . . . ☐ Check here, and

enter the final date you paid wages   /   / .

19 If you are a seasonal employer and you do not have to file a return for every quarter of the year . ☐ Check here.

Part 4: May we speak with your third-party designee?

Do you want to allow an employee, a paid tax preparer, or another person to discuss this return with the IRS? See the instructions for details.

☐ Yes. Designee's name and phone number   (   ) –

Select a 5-digit Personal Identification Number (PIN) to use when talking to the IRS. ☐ ☐ ☐ ☐ ☐

☒ No.

Part 5: Sign here. You MUST complete both pages of Form 941 and SIGN it.

Under penalties of perjury, I declare that I have examined this return, including accompanying schedules and statements, and to the best of my knowledge and belief, it is true, correct, and complete. Declaration of preparer (other than taxpayer) is based on all information of which preparer has any knowledge.

✗ Sign your name here *William P. Jones*

Print your name here *William P Jones*

Print your title here *Treasurer*

Date *4/ 30 /--*

Best daytime phone (   ) –

Paid preparer's use only

Check if you are self-employed . . . ☐

Preparer's name		Preparer's SSN/PTIN	
Preparer's signature		Date	/ /
Firm's name (or yours if self-employed)		EIN	
Address		Phone	( ) –
City		State		ZIP code	

Page **2**

Form **941** (Rev. 1-20--)

Form 940

In addition to making quarterly deposits, employers are required to file an annual report of federal unemployment tax using Form 940 (Figure 9-8). This form must be

FIGURE 9-8 Employer's Annual Federal Unemployment (FUTA) Tax Return (Form 940)

Form **940 for 20--:** Employer's Annual Federal Unemployment (FUTA) Tax Return   850108
Department of the Treasury — Internal Revenue Service
OMB No. 1545-0028

(EIN) Employer identification number   4 3 – 0 2 1 1 6 3 0

Name (not your trade name)

Trade name (if any)   Westly, Inc.

Address   5221 Natural Bridge
Number   Street   Suite or room number
St. Louis   MO   63115-8230
City   State   ZIP code

Type of Return
(Check all that apply.)

☐ **a.** Amended
☐ **b.** Successor employer
☐ **c.** No payments to employees in 20--
☐ **d.** Final: Business closed or stopped paying wages

Read the separate instructions before you fill out this form. Please type or print within the boxes.

Part 1: Tell us about your return. If any line does NOT apply, leave it blank.

1 If you were required to pay your state unemployment tax in ...

1a One state only, write the state abbreviation . . . **1a** M O
- OR -
1b More than one state (You are a multi-state employer) . . . . **1b** ☐ Check here. Fill out Schedule A.
Skip line 2 for 20-- and go to line 3.
2 If you paid wages in a state that is subject to CREDIT REDUCTION · . . . . . . **2** ☐ Check here. Fill out Schedule A (Form 940), Part 2.

Part 2: Determine your FUTA tax before adjustments for 20--. If any line does NOT apply, leave it blank.

3 Total payments to all employees **3**   258,954.00

4 Payments exempt from FUTA tax **4**

Check all that apply: **4a** ☐ Fringe benefits **4c** ☐ Retirement/Pension **4e** ☐ Other
4b ☐ Group-term life insurance **4d** ☐ Dependent care

5 Total of payments made to each employee in excess of $7,000 . . . . **5**   203,254.00

6 Subtotal (line 4 + line 5 = line 6) **6**   203,254.00

7 Total taxable FUTA wages (line 3 – line 6 = line 7) . . . . **7**   55,700.00   ← FUTA taxable wages

8 FUTA tax before adjustments (line 7 ×.008 = line 8) **8**   445.60

Part 3: Determine your adjustments. If any line does NOT apply, leave it blank.

9 If ALL of the taxable FUTA wages you paid were excluded from state unemployment tax, multiply line 7 by .054 (line 7 × .054 = line 9). Then go to line 12 . . . . . . **9**

10 If SOME of the taxable FUTA wages you paid were excluded from state unemployment tax, OR you paid ANY state unemployment tax late (after the due date for filing Form 940), fill out the worksheet in the instructions. Enter the amount from line 7 of the worksheet onto line 10 . **10**

Skip line 11 for 20-- and go to line 12.
11 If credit reduction applies, enter the amount from line 3 of Schedule A (Form 940) **11**

Part 4: Determine your FUTA tax and balance due or overpayment for 20--. If any line does NOT apply, leave it blank.

12 Total FUTA tax after adjustments (lines 8 + 9 + 10 + 11 = line 12) . . . . **12**   445.60   ← FUTA tax

13 FUTA tax deposited for the year, including any payment applied from a prior year . . . . **13**   427.60   ← FUTA tax paid

14 Balance due (If line 12 is more than line 13, enter the difference on line 14.)
• If line 14 is more than $500, you must deposit your tax.
• If line 14 is $500 or less, you may pay with this return. For more information on how to pay, see the separate instructions . . . . **14**   18.00   ← FUTA tax due

15 Overpayment (If line 13 is more than line 12, enter the difference on line 15 and check a box below.) **15**
Check one: ☐ Apply to next return.
☐ Send a refund.

▶ You **MUST** fill out both pages of this form and **SIGN** it.

Next ➡

For Privacy Act and Paperwork Reduction Act Notice, see the back of Form 940-V, Payment Voucher.   Cat. No. 11234O   Form **940** (20--)

FIGURE 9-8 Employer's Annual Federal Unemployment (FUTA) Tax Return (Form 940) (*concluded*)

850208

Name (*not your trade name*)	Employer identification number (EIN)

Part 5: Report your FUTA tax liability by quarter only if line 12 is more than $500. If not, go to Part 6.

16 Report the amount of your FUTA tax liability for each quarter; do NOT enter the amount you deposited. If you had no liability for a quarter, leave the line blank.

16a   **1st quarter** (January 1 – March 31) . . . .   **16a**   [.]

16b   **2nd quarter** (April 1 – June 30) . . . .   **16b**   [.]

16c   **3rd quarter** (July 1 – September 30) . . . . . .   **16c**   [.]

16d   **4th quarter** (October 1 – December 31) . . . . . .   **16d**   [.]

17   **Total tax liability for the year** (lines 16a + 16b + 16c + 16d = line 17) **17**   [.]   Total must equal line 12.

Part 6: May we speak with your third-party designee?

Do you want to allow an employee, a paid tax preparer, or another person to discuss this return with the IRS? See the instructions for details.

☐ **Yes.**   Designee's name and phone number   [ ]   ( ) –

      Select a 5-digit Personal Identification Number (PIN) to use when talking to IRS   ☐ ☐ ☐ ☐ ☐

☒ **No.**

Part 7: Sign here. You MUST fill out both pages of this form and SIGN it.

Under penalties of perjury, I declare that I have examined this return, including accompanying schedules and statements, and to the best of my knowledge and belief, it is true, correct, and complete, and that no part of any payment made to a state unemployment fund claimed as a credit was, or is to be, deducted from the payments made to employees. Declaration of preparer (other than taxpayer) is based on all information of which preparer has any knowledge.

✗ **Sign your name here**	*William P. Jones*	Print your name here	WILLIAM P. JONES
		Print your title here	TREASURER
Date	1/ 31 /–	Best daytime phone	( ) –

Paid preparer's use only   Check if you are self-employed . . ☐

Preparer's name		Preparer's SSN/PTIN	
Preparer's signature		Date	/ /
Firm's name (or yours if self-employed)		EIN	
Address		Phone	( ) –
City	State	ZIP code	

     Form **940** (20--)

filed with the IRS by the beginning of the second week of February. Figure 9-8 shows a completed Form 940 for Westly, Inc. If a balance is due, it may be paid using EFTPS or Form 940-V. Figure 9-9 shows a completed Form 940-V for Westly.

FIGURE 9-9 Payment Voucher (Form 940-V)

SUTA TAXES

Deposit rules and forms for state unemployment taxes vary among the states. Deposits usually are required on a quarterly basis. Assume that Westly's accumulated state unemployment liability for the first quarter of the calendar year is $2,754. The journal entry for the deposit of this amount with the state on April 30 would be as follows:

19	Apr.	30	SUTA Tax Payable	2 7 5 4 00		19
20			Cash		2 7 5 4 00	20
21			Deposit of state unemployment tax			21

EMPLOYEE WAGE AND TAX STATEMENT

By January 31 of each year, employers must furnish each employee with a Wage and Tax Statement, Form W-2 (Figure 9-10). This form shows the total amount of wages paid to the employee and the amounts of taxes withheld during the preceding taxable year. The employee earnings record contains the information needed to complete this form.

Multiple copies of Form W-2 are needed for the following purposes:

- Copy A—Employer sends to Social Security Administration
- Copy B—Employee attaches to federal income tax return
- Copy C—Employee retains for his or her own records
- Copy D—Employer retains for business records
- Copy 1—Employer sends to state or local tax department
- Copy 2—Employee attaches to state, city, or local income tax return

FIGURE 9-10 Wage and Tax Statement (Form W-2)

SUMMARY OF EMPLOYEE WAGES AND TAXES

Employers send Form W-3, Transmittal of Wage and Tax Statements (Figure 9-11), with Copy A of Forms W-2 to the Social Security Administration. Form W-3 must be filed by February 28 following the end of each taxable year. This form summarizes the employee earnings and tax information presented on Forms W-2 for the year. Information needed to complete Form W-3 is contained in the employee earnings records.

EMPLOYMENT ELIGIBILITY VERIFICATION

Every employee hired after November 6, 1986, must complete Form I-9, Employment Eligibility Verification. The purpose of this form is to document that each employee is authorized to work in the United States. The employee completes Section 1 of the form and provides the employer with evidence of the employee's identity and authorization to work. The employer completes Section 2 of the form indicating what evidence the employer examined.

Form I-9 is not filed with any government agency. Instead, it must be retained by the employer and made available for inspection if requested by the Department of Homeland Security or the Department of Labor.

SUMMARY OF TAXES, REPORTS, AND PAYMENTS

Keeping track of the many payroll taxes can be a challenge for an employer. Figure 9-12 summarizes the various employee and employer taxes we have discussed in Chapters 8 and 9. Figure 9-13 shows a calendar that highlights the due dates for the various reports and deposits. The calendar assumes the following for an employer:

1. Undeposited FIT (federal income tax) and Social Security and Medicare taxes of $2,500 at the end of each quarter and less than $50,000 during the lookback period.

2. Undeposited FUTA taxes of more than $500 at the end of each quarter.

3. SUTA taxes deposited quarterly.

The combination of payroll taxes, reports, deposit rules, and due dates can make payroll accounting rather complex. In fact, this is a major reason why small businesses often hire an accountant or an outside company to handle payroll.

FIGURE 9-11 Transmittal of Wage and Tax Statements (Form W-3)

DO NOT STAPLE

33333	**a** Control number	**For Official Use Only** ▶ OMB No. 1545-0008

b Kind of Payer ▶	941 ☐ Military ☐ 943 ☐ 944 ☐ CT-1 ☐ Hshld. emp. ☐ Medicare govt. emp. ☐ Third-party sick pay ☐	**1** Wages, tips, other compensation 276,917.00	**2** Federal income tax withheld 30,370.00

3 Social security wages   274,217.00   **4** Social security tax withheld   17,001.45

c Total number of Forms W-2   8   **d** Establishment number   **5** Medicare wages and tips   276,917.00   **6** Medicare tax withheld   4,015.30

e Employer identification number (EIN)   43-0211630   **7** Social security tips   **8** Allocated tips

f Employer's name   Westly, Inc.   **9** Advance EIC payments   **10** Dependent care benefits

5221 Natural Bridge
St. Louis, MO 63115-8230

11 Nonqualified plans   **12** Deferred compensation

13 For third-party sick pay use only

14 Income tax withheld by payer of third-party sick pay

g Employer's address and ZIP code

h Other EIN used this year

15 State MO   Employer's state ID number 21686001   **16** State wages, tips, etc.   276,917.00   **17** State income tax

18 Local wages, tips, etc.   **19** Local income tax

Contact person   Telephone number ( )   For Official Use Only

Email address   Fax number ( )

Under penalties of perjury, I declare that I have examined this return and accompanying documents, and, to the best of my knowledge and belief, they are true, correct, and complete.

Signature ▶   Title ▶   Date ▶

Form **W-3 Transmittal of Wage and Tax Statements** **20 - -** Department of the Treasury
Internal Revenue Service

FIGURE 9-12 Summary of Employee and Employer Taxes

	TAX APPLIES TO	
TAX	**EMPLOYEE**	**EMPLOYER**
Federal income tax	X	
State income tax	X	
Social Security	X	X
Medicare	X	X
FUTA		X
SUTA		X*

*Also applies to employees in some states.

FIGURE 9-13 Payroll Calendar

File Forms 940, 941, state unemployment tax report, and send W-2 to employees.	File Form 940	File form W-3 with CopyA ofW-2s.	File Form 941 and make FUTA and SUTA tax deposits.	Deposit FIT and Social Security and Medicare taxes from previous month.

January
S	M	T	W	T	F	S
			1	2	3	4
5	6	7	8	9	10	11
12	13	14	15	16	17	18
19	20	21	22	23	24	25
26	27	28	29	30	31	

February
S	M	T	W	T	F	S
						1
2	3	4	5	6	7	8
9	10	11	12	13	14	15
16	17	18	19	20	21	22
23	24	25	26	27	28	29

March
S	M	T	W	T	F	S
1	2	3	4	5	6	7
8	9	10	11	12	13	14
15	16	17	18	19	20	21
22	23	24	25	26	27	28
29	30	31				

April
S	M	T	W	T	F	S
			1	2	3	4
5	6	7	8	9	10	11
12	13	14	15	16	17	18
19	20	21	22	23	24	25
26	27	28	29	30		

May
S	M	T	W	T	F	S
					1	2
3	4	5	6	7	8	9
10	11	12	13	14	15	16
17	18	19	20	21	22	23
24	25	26	27	28	29	30
31						

June
S	M	T	W	T	F	S
	1	2	3	4	5	6
7	8	9	10	11	12	13
14	15	16	17	18	19	20
21	22	23	24	25	26	27
28	29	30				

July
S	M	T	W	T	F	S
			1	2	3	4
5	6	7	8	9	10	11
12	13	14	15	16	17	18
19	20	21	22	23	24	25
26	27	28	29	30	31	

August
S	M	T	W	T	F	S
						1
2	3	4	5	6	7	8
9	10	11	12	13	14	15
16	17	18	19	20	21	22
23	24	25	26	27	28	29
30	31					

September
S	M	T	W	T	F	S
		1	2	3	4	5
6	7	8	9	10	11	12
13	14	15	16	17	18	19
20	21	22	23	24	25	26
27	28	29	30			

October
S	M	T	W	T	F	S
				1	2	3
4	5	6	7	8	9	10
11	12	13	14	15	16	17
18	19	20	21	22	23	24
25	26	27	28	29	30	31

November
S	M	T	W	T	F	S
1	2	3	4	5	6	7
8	9	10	11	12	13	14
15	16	17	18	19	20	21
22	23	24	25	26	27	28
29	30					

December
S	M	T	W	T	F	S
		1	2	3	4	5
6	7	8	9	10	11	12
13	14	15	16	17	18	19
20	21	22	23	24	25	26
27	28	29	30	31		

A BROADER VIEW

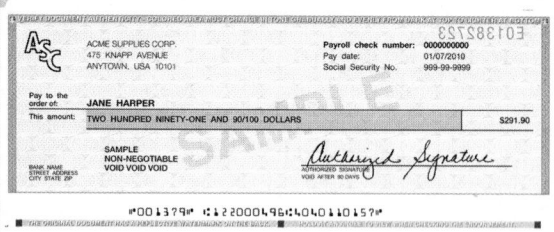

Dealing with Payroll Complexity—Let Someone Else Do It

A common way for both small and large businesses to deal with the complexity of payroll reports, deposit rules, and due dates is to hire an outside company to handle the payroll. Payroll processing companies have combined payroll expertise with the power of computers to create a major business enterprise based on the efficient and effective provision of payroll services.

The extent to which businesses use outside companies to handle payroll can be seen in the two largest payroll processing companies: Automatic Data Processing, Inc. (ADP) and Paychex, Inc. ADP has operations in 26 countries, provides payroll services to 585,000 clients (500,000 in the United States), and has revenues of $9 billion. Paychex has 100 locations nationwide, provides services to 572,000 clients, and has revenues of $2 billion. These companies prepare employee paychecks, journals, and summary reports; collect and remit funds for federal, state, and local payroll taxes; and file all required forms with government taxing authorities.

U REVU

Complete U REVU-3 on **page 339** to test your basic understanding of LO3.

WORKERS' COMPENSATION INSURANCE

LO4 Describe and account for workers' compensation insurance.

Most states require employers to carry workers' compensation insurance. **Workers' compensation insurance** provides insurance for employees who suffer a job-related illness or injury.

The employer usually pays the entire cost of workers' compensation insurance. The cost of the insurance depends on the number of employees, riskiness of the job, and the company's accident history. For example, the insurance premium for workers in a chemical plant could be higher than for office workers. Employers generally obtain the insurance either from the state in which they operate or from a private insurance company.

The employer usually pays the premium at the beginning of the year, based on the estimated payroll for the year. At the end of the year, after the actual amount of payroll is known, an adjustment is made. If the employer has overpaid, a credit is received from the state or insurance company. If the employer has underpaid, an additional premium is paid.

To illustrate the accounting for workers' compensation insurance, assume that Lockwood Co. expects its payroll for the year to be $210,000. If Lockwood's insurance premium rate is 0.2%, its payment for workers' compensation insurance at the beginning of the year would be $420.

Estimated Payroll	×	Rate	=	Estimated Insurance Premium
$210,000		0.002		$420.00

The journal entry for the payment of this $420 premium would be as follows:

7	Jan.	2	Workers' Compensation Insurance Expense		4 2 0 00			7
8			Cash			4 2 0 00		8
9			Paid insurance premium					9

If Lockwood's actual payroll for the year is $220,000, Lockwood would owe an additional premium of $20 at year-end.

Actual Payroll	×	Rate	=	Insurance Premium
$220,000		0.002		$440.00
Less premium paid				420.00
Additional premium due				$ 20.00

The adjusting entry at year-end for this additional expense would be as follows:

11	Dec.	31	Workers' Compensation Insurance Expense		2 0 00			11
12			Workers' Compensation Insurance Payable			2 0 00		12
13			Adjustment for insurance premium					13

In T account form, the total Workers' Compensation Insurance Expense of $440.00 would look like this.

Workers' Compensation Insurance Expense

Debit	Credit
420.00	
20.00	
440.00	

If Lockwood's actual payroll for the year is only $205,000, Lockwood would be due a refund of $10:

Payroll	×	Rate	=	Insurance Premium
$205,000		0.002		$410.00
Less premium paid				420.00
Refund due				$(10.00)

The adjusting entry at year-end for this refund due would be as follows:

16	Dec.	31	Insurance Refund Receivable			1 0 00		16
17			Workers' Compensation Insurance Expense				1 0 00	17
18			Adjustment for insurance premium					18

In T account form, the total Workers' Compensation Insurance Expense of $410 would look like this.

Workers' Compensation Insurance Expense

Debit	Credit
420.00	10.00
410.00	

U REVU

Complete U REVU-4 on **page 339** to test your basic understanding of LO4.

Profiles in Accounting

**Michael Burdish
Payroll Compliance
Auditor**

Michael Burdish graduated with an associate degree in accounting with honors from The College of Westchester. Michael excelled in his studies in accounting and knew this was the field for him. After graduation, Michael was hired as a payroll compliance auditor for an accounting firm. He is part of the team that audits companies and contractors that hire union members. The focus of the audits is to ensure that the correct amounts of benefits are paid. According to Michael he really enjoys his work. He especially likes meeting many new people and having new experiences. Michael intends to further his education and complete his baccalaureate degree in accounting.

LEARNING OBJECTIVES   Key Points to Remember

LO1 Describe and calculate employer payroll taxes.

LO2 Account for employer payroll taxes expense.

Employer payroll taxes include FICA, FUTA, and SUTA taxes. These taxes represent additional payroll expenses of the employer. The journal entry for payroll taxes is as follows:

8		Payroll Taxes Expense				x	x	x	xx							8
9		Social Security Tax Payable									x	x	x	xx		9
10		Medicare Tax Payable									x	x	x	xx		10
11		FUTA Tax Payable									x	x	x	xx		11
12		SUTA Tax Payable									x	x	x	xx		12

The steps to be followed in preparing this journal entry are as follows:

1. Obtain the total earnings and taxable earnings amounts from the Earnings—Total and Taxable Earnings columns of the payroll register.
2. Compute the amount of employer Social Security tax by multiplying the Social Security taxable earnings by 6.2%.
3. Compute the amount of employer Medicare tax by multiplying total earnings by 1.45%.
4. Compute the amount of FUTA tax by multiplying the Unemployment Taxable earnings by 0.8%.
5. Compute the amount of SUTA tax by multiplying the Unemployment Taxable earnings by 5.4%.
6. Prepare the appropriate journal entry using the amounts computed in steps 2–5.

LO3 Describe employer reporting and payment responsibilities.

Employer payroll reporting and payment responsibilities fall into six areas.

1. Federal income tax withholding and Social Security and Medicare taxes
2. FUTA taxes
3. SUTA taxes
4. Employee Wage and Tax Statement (Form W-2)
5. Summary of employee wages and taxes (Form W-3)
6. Employment eligibility verification (Form I-9)

Key forms needed in reporting and paying employer payroll taxes are as follows:

1. Form 8109, Federal Tax Deposit Coupon
2. Form 941, Employer's Quarterly Federal Tax Return
3. Form 940, Employer's Annual Federal Unemployment Tax Return

By January 31 of each year, employers must provide each employee with a Wage and Tax Statement, Form W-2.

By February 28 of each year, employers must file Form W-3 and Copy A of Form W-2 with the Social Security Administration.

LEARNING OBJECTIVES   Key Points to Remember

LO4 Describe and account for workers' compensation insurance.	Workers' compensation insurance provides insurance for employees who suffer a job-related illness or injury. Employers generally are required to carry and pay the entire cost of this insurance.

DEMONSTRATION PROBLEM

The Totals line from Hart Company's payroll register for the week ended December 31, 20--, is as follows:

(left side)

PAYROLL

	NAME	EMPLOYEE NUMBER	ALLOWANCES	MARITAL STATUS	EARNINGS				TAXABLE EARNINGS		
					REGULAR	OVERTIME	TOTAL	CUMULATIVE TOTAL	UNEMPLOYMENT COMPENSATION	SOCIAL SECURITY	
21	Totals				3 5 0 0 00	3 0 0 00	3 8 0 0 00	197 6 0 0 00	4 0 0 00	3 8 0 0 00	21

REGISTER—PERIOD ENDED December 31, 20--

(right side)

	DEDUCTIONS							NET PAY	CHECK NO.
	FEDERAL INCOME TAX	SOCIAL SECURITY TAX	MEDICARE TAX	HEALTH INSURANCE	UNITED WAY	OTHER	TOTAL		
21	3 8 0 00	2 3 5 60	5 5 10	5 0 00	1 0 0 00		8 2 0 70	2 9 7 9 30	21

Payroll taxes are imposed as follows: Social Security, 6.2%; Medicare, 1.45%; FUTA, 0.8%; and SUTA, 5.4%.

REQUIRED

1. a. Prepare the journal entry for payment of this payroll on December 31, 20--.

    b. Prepare the journal entry for the employer's payroll taxes for the period ended December 31, 20--.

2. Hart Company had the following balances in its general ledger *after* the entries for requirement (1) were made:

Employee Income Tax Payable	$1,620.00
Social Security Tax Payable	1,847.00
Medicare Tax Payable	433.00
FUTA Tax Payable	27.20
SUTA Tax Payable	183.60

    a. Prepare the journal entry for payment of the liabilities for employee federal income taxes and Social Security and Medicare taxes on January 15, 20--.

    b. Prepare the journal entry for payment of the liability for FUTA tax on January 31, 20--.

c. Prepare the journal entry for payment of the liability for SUTA tax on January 31, 20--.

3. Hart Company paid a premium of $280 for workers' compensation insurance based on estimated payroll as of the beginning of the year. Based on actual payroll as of the end of the year, the premium is $298. Prepare the adjusting entry to reflect the underpayment of the insurance premium.

Solution 1.

	DATE		DESCRIPTION	POST. REF.	DEBIT					CREDIT				
1	20-- Dec.	31	Wages and Salaries Expense		3	8	0	0	00					1
2			Employee Income Tax Payable							3	8	0	00	2
3			Social Security Tax Payable							2	3	5	60	3
4			Medicare Tax Payable								5	5	10	4
5			Health Insurance Premiums Payable								5	0	00	5
6			United Way Contributions Payable							1	0	0	00	6
7			Cash							2	9	7	9	30	7
8			To record Dec. 31 payroll											8
9														9
10		31	Payroll Taxes Expense			3	1	5	50					10
11			Social Security Tax Payable							2	3	5	60	11
12			Medicare Tax Payable								5	5	10	12
13			FUTA Tax Payable									3	20	13
14			SUTA Tax Payable								2	1	60	14
15			Employer payroll taxes for week ended Dec. 31											15

2. and 3.

	DATE		DESCRIPTION	POST. REF.	DEBIT					CREDIT				
18	Jan.	15	Employee Income Tax Payable		1	6	2	0	00					18
19			Social Security Tax Payable		1	8	4	7	00					19
20			Medicare Tax Payable			4	3	3	00					20
21			Cash							3	9	0	0	00	21
22			Deposit of employee federal income tax and											22
23			Social Security and Medicare taxes											23
24														24
25		31	FUTA Tax Payable				2	7	20					25
26			Cash								2	7	20	26
27			Paid FUTA tax											27
28														28
29		31	SUTA Tax Payable			1	8	3	60					29
30			Cash								1	8	3	60	30
31			Paid SUTA tax											31
32														32
33	Dec.	31	Workers' Compensation Insurance Expense				1	8	00					33
34			Workers' Compensation Insurance Payable								1	8	00	34
35			Adjustment for insurance premium											35

KEY TERMS

Electronic Federal Tax Payment System (EFTPS) (323)   An electronic funds transfer system for making federal tax deposits.

employer FICA taxes (316)   Taxes levied on employers at the same rates and on the same earnings bases as the employee FICA taxes.

Employer Identification Number (EIN) (323)   A number that identifies the employer on all payroll forms and reports filed with the IRS.

experience-rating system (318)   A system to encourage employers to provide regular employment to workers.

FUTA (Federal Unemployment Tax Act) tax (317)   A tax levied on employers to raise funds to administer the federal/state unemployment compensation program.

self-employment income (317)   The net income of a trade or business run by an individual.

self-employment tax (317)   A tax on the earnings of a self-employed person at double the Social Security and Medicare rates.

SUTA (state unemployment tax) tax (318)   A tax levied on employers to raise funds to pay unemployment benefits.

workers' compensation insurance (333)   Insurance carried by employers for employees who suffer a job-related illness or injury.

SELF-STUDY QUESTIONS AND EXERCISES

True/False Questions

1. LO1   Employer payroll taxes are deducted from the employee's pay.

2. LO1   The payroll register is a key source of information for computing employer payroll taxes.

3. LO1   Self-employment income is the net income of a trade or business owned and run by an individual.

4. LO1   The FUTA tax is levied only on the employees.

5. LO3   The W-4, which shows total annual earnings and deductions for federal and state income taxes, must be completed by the employer and given to the employee by January 31.

Multiple Choice Questions

1. LO2   The general ledger accounts commonly used to record the employer's Social Security, Medicare, FUTA, and SUTA taxes are classified as

   (a) assets.
   (b) liabilities.
   (c) expenses.
   (d) owner's equity.

2. LO2   Joyce Lee earns $30,000 a year. Her employer pays a matching Social Security tax of 6.2% on the first $106,800 in earnings, a Medicare tax of 1.45% on gross earnings, and a FUTA tax of 0.8% and a SUTA tax of 5.4%, both on the first $7,000 in earnings. What is the total cost of Joyce Lee to her employer?

   (a) $32,250
   (b) $30,000
   (c) $30,434
   (d) $32,729

3. LO3   The Form 941 tax deposit includes which of the following types of taxes withheld from the employee and paid by the employer?

   (a) Federal income tax and FUTA tax
   (b) Federal income tax and Social Security and Medicare taxes
   (c) Social Security and Medicare taxes and SUTA tax
   (d) FUTA tax and SUTA tax

4. LO4   Workers' compensation provides insurance for employees who

   (a) are unemployed due to a layoff.
   (b) are unemployed due to a plant closing.
   (c) are underemployed and need additional compensation.
   (d) suffer a job-related illness or injury.

5. LO4   The journal entry at the end of the year that recognizes an additional premium owed under workers' compensation insurance will include a

   (a) debit to Workers' Compensation Insurance Expense.
   (b) debit to Cash.
   (c) debit to Workers' Compensation Insurance Payable.
   (d) credit to Workers' Compensation Insurance Expense.

U REVU   **Exercises**

1. LO1   Total earnings for the employees of Gary's Grill for the week ended January 14, 20--, were $6,400. The following payroll taxes were levied on these earnings:

Social Security	6.2%
Medicare	1.45%
FUTA	0.8%
SUTA	5.4%

   Calculate Gary's payroll taxes expense for the week ended January 14, 20--.

2. LO2   Liu's Lounge had the following payroll taxes expense for the week ended February 10, 20--:

Social Security	$595.20
Medicare	139.20
FUTA	76.80
SUTA	518.40

   Prepare the journal entry for these payroll taxes.

3. LO3   ARC Co. owes the following amounts for payroll taxes and employees' withholding of Social Security, Medicare, and federal income tax as of April 15:

Social Security Tax Payable	$6,750.00
Medicare Tax Payable	1,575.00
FUTA Tax Payable	360.00
SUTA Tax Payable	2,646.00
Employee Income Tax Payable	4,095.00

   Prepare the journal entries for:
   (a)   Deposit of the employees' federal income taxes and the Social Security and Medicare taxes on April 15.
   (b)   Deposits of the FUTA and SUTA taxes on April 30.

4. LO4   LC Co. estimates that its total payroll for the year will be $260,000. LC's workers' compensation insurance premium rate is 0.22%. Calculate LC's estimated workers' compensation insurance premium and prepare the journal entry for the payment of this amount.

The answers to the Self-Study Questions and Exercises are at the end of the chapter (page 350).

APPLYING YOUR KNOWLEDGE

REVIEW QUESTIONS

LO1 1. Why do employer payroll taxes represent an additional expense to the employer, whereas the various employee payroll taxes do not?

LO1 2. At what rate and on what earnings base is the employer's Social Security tax levied?

LO1 3. What is the purpose of the FUTA tax, and who must pay it?

LO1 4. What is the purpose of the state unemployment tax, and who must pay it?

LO2 5. What accounts are affected when employer payroll tax expenses are properly recorded?

LO2 6. Identify all items that are debited or credited to Social Security Tax Payable and to Medicare Tax Payable.

LO2 7. Explain why an employee whose gross salary is $20,000 costs an employer more than $20,000 to employ.

LO3 8. What is the purpose of Form 8109, Federal Tax Deposit Coupon?

LO3 9. What is the purpose of Form 941, Employer's Quarterly Federal Tax Return?

LO3 10. What is the purpose of Form 940, Employer's Annual Federal Unemployment Tax Return?

LO3 11. What information appears on Form W-2, the employee's Wage and Tax Statement?

LO3 12. What is the purpose of Form I-9, Employment Eligibility Verification?

LO4 13. What is the purpose of workers' compensation insurance, and who must pay for it?

SERIES A EXERCISES

E 9-1A (LO1/2)

✓ Payroll taxes expense: $1,584.30

CALCULATION AND JOURNAL ENTRY FOR EMPLOYER PAYROLL TAXES
Portions of the payroll register for Barney's Bagels for the week ended July 15 are shown below. The SUTA tax rate is 5.4%, and the FUTA tax rate is 0.8%, both of which are levied on the first $7,000 of earnings. The Social Security tax rate is 6.2% on the first $106,800 of earnings. The Medicare rate is 1.45% on gross earnings.

Barney's Bagels
Payroll Register

Total Earnings	Total Taxable Earnings of All Employees	
	Unemployment Compensation	Social Security
$12,200	$10,500	$12,200

Calculate the employer's payroll taxes expense and prepare the journal entry to record the employer's payroll taxes expense for the week ended July 15 of the current year.

E 9-2A (LO1/2)

✓ Payroll taxes expense: $350.02

CALCULATION AND JOURNAL ENTRY FOR EMPLOYER PAYROLL TAXES
Earnings for several employees for the week ended March 12, 20--, are as follows:

Employee Name	Current Earnings	Taxable Earnings	
		Unemployment Compensation	Social Security
Aus, Glenn E.	$ 700	$200	$ 700
Diaz, Charles K.	350	350	350
Knapp, Carol S.	1,200	—	1,200
Mueller, Deborah F.	830	125	830
Yeager, Jackie R.	920	35	920

Calculate the employer's payroll taxes expense and prepare the journal entry as of March 12, 20--, assuming that FUTA tax is 0.8%, SUTA tax is 5.4%, Social Security tax is 6.2%, and Medicare tax is 1.45%.

E 9-3A (LO1/2)

✓ Payroll taxes expense: $886.86

CALCULATION OF TAXABLE EARNINGS AND EMPLOYER PAYROLL TAXES AND PREPARATION OF JOURNAL ENTRY Selected information from the payroll register of Raynette's Boutique for the week ended September 14, 20--, is as follows. Social Security tax is 6.2% on the first $106,800 of earnings for each employee. Medicare tax is 1.45% of gross earnings. FUTA tax is 0.8% and SUTA tax is 5.4% on the first $7,000 of earnings.

Employee Name	Cumulative Pay Before Current Earnings	Current Gross Pay	Taxable Earnings	
			Unemployment Compensation	Social Security
Burgos, Juan	$ 6,800	$1,250		
Ellis, Judy A.	6,300	1,100		
Lewis, Arlene S.	54,200	2,320		
Mason, Jason W.	53,900	2,270		
Yates, Ruby L.	27,650	1,900		
Zielke, Ronald M.	104,930	2,680		

Calculate the amount of taxable earnings for unemployment, Social Security, and Medicare taxes, and prepare the journal entry to record the employer's payroll taxes as of September 14, 20--.

E 9-4A (LO1/2)

✓ Total cost: $34,882.00

TOTAL COST OF EMPLOYEE J. B. Kenton employs Sharla Knox at a salary of $32,000 a year. Kenton is subject to employer Social Security taxes at a rate of 6.2% and Medicare taxes at a rate of 1.45% on Knox's salary. In addition, Kenton must pay SUTA tax at a rate of 5.4% and FUTA tax at a rate of 0.8% on the first $7,000 of Knox's salary.

Compute the total cost to Kenton of employing Knox for the year.

E 9-5A (LO3)

✓ 941 deposit: $20,700

JOURNAL ENTRIES FOR PAYMENT OF EMPLOYER PAYROLL TAXES Angel Ruiz owns a business called Ruiz Construction Co. He does his banking at Citizens National Bank in Portland, Oregon. The amounts in his general ledger for payroll taxes and the employees' withholding of Social Security, Medicare, and federal income tax payable as of April 15 of the current year are as follows:

Social Security tax payable (includes both employer and employee)	$11,250
Medicare tax payable (includes both employer and employee)	2,625
FUTA tax payable	600
SUTA tax payable	4,050
Employee income tax payable	6,825

(continued)

Journalize the payment of the employee federal income taxes and Social Security and Medicare taxes on April 15, 20--, and the payments of the FUTA and SUTA taxes on April 30, 20--.

E 9-6A (LO4)

✓ 2. Additional premium due: $14.00

WORKERS' COMPENSATION INSURANCE AND ADJUSTMENT General Manufacturing estimated that its total payroll for the coming year would be $425,000. The workers' compensation insurance premium rate is 0.2%.

REQUIRED

1. Calculate the estimated workers' compensation insurance premium and prepare the journal entry for the payment as of January 2, 20--.

2. Assume that General Manufacturing's actual payroll for the year is $432,000. Calculate the total insurance premium owed and prepare a journal entry as of December 31, 20--, to record the adjustment for the underpayment. The actual payment of the additional premium will take place in January of the next year.

SERIES A PROBLEMS

P 9-7A (LO1/2)

✓ Payroll taxes expense: $662.06

CALCULATING PAYROLL TAXES EXPENSE AND PREPARING JOURNAL ENTRY Selected information from the payroll register of Anderson's Dairy for the week ended July 7, 20--, is shown below. The SUTA tax rate is 5.4%, and the FUTA tax rate is 0.8%, both on the first $7,000 of earnings. Social Security tax on the employer is 6.2% on the first $106,800 of earnings, and Medicare tax is 1.45% on gross earnings.

			Taxable Earnings	
Employee Name	Cumulative Pay Before Current Earnings	Current Weekly Earnings	Unemployment Compensation	Social Security
Barnum, Alex	$ 6,750	$ 820		
Duel, Richard	6,340	725		
Hunt, J. B.	23,460	1,235		
Larson, Susan	6,950	910		
Mercado, Denise	105,450	3,520		
Swan, Judy	25,470	1,125		
Yates, Keith	28,675	1,300		

REQUIRED

1. Calculate the total employer payroll taxes for these employees.

2. Prepare the journal entry to record the employer payroll taxes as of July 7, 20--.

P 9-8A (LO2/3)

✓ Payroll taxes expense: $3,864.00

JOURNALIZING AND POSTING PAYROLL ENTRIES Cascade Company has four employees. All are paid on a monthly basis. The fiscal year of the business is June 1 to May 31.

The accounts kept by Cascade include the following:

Account Number	Title	Balance on June 1
101	Cash	$70,200
211	Employee Income Tax Payable	3,553
212	Social Security Tax Payable	5,103
213	Medicare Tax Payable	1,197
218	Savings Bond Deductions Payable	1,225
221	FUTA Tax Payable	574
222	SUTA Tax Payable	2,835
511	Wages and Salaries Expense	0
530	Payroll Taxes Expense	0

The following transactions relating to payrolls and payroll taxes occurred during June and July:

June 15 Paid $9,853 covering the following May taxes:

Social Security tax	$ 5,103
Medicare tax	1,197
Employee income tax withheld	3,553
Total	$ 9,853

30 June payroll:

Total wages and salaries expense		$42,000
Less amounts withheld:		
Social Security tax	$2,604	
Medicare tax	609	
Employee income tax	3,570	
Savings bond deductions	1,225	8,008
Net amount paid		$33,992

30 Purchased savings bonds for employees, $2,450

30 Employer payroll taxes expenses for June were:

Social Security	$2,604
Medicare	609
FUTA	84
SUTA	567
Total	$3,864

July 15 Paid $9,996 covering the following June taxes:

Social Security tax	$ 5,208
Medicare tax	1,218
Employee income tax withheld	3,570
Total	$ 9,996

31 Paid SUTA tax for the quarter, $3,402

31 Paid FUTA tax, $658

REQUIRED

1. Journalize the preceding transactions using a general journal.

2. Open T accounts for the payroll expenses and liabilities. Enter the beginning balances and post the transactions recorded in the journal.

P 9-9A (LO4)

✓ 3. Refund due: $48.00

WORKERS' COMPENSATION INSURANCE AND ADJUSTMENT Willamette Manufacturing estimated that its total payroll for the coming year would be $650,000. The workers' compensation insurance premium rate is 0.3%.

REQUIRED

1. Calculate the estimated workers' compensation insurance premium and prepare the journal entry for the payment as of January 2, 20--.

2. Assume that Willamette Manufacturing's actual payroll for the year was $672,000. Calculate the total insurance premium owed and prepare a journal entry as of December 31, 20--, to record the adjustment for the underpayment. The actual payment of the additional premium will take place in January of the next year.

3. Assume instead that Willamette Manufacturing's actual payroll for the year was $634,000. Prepare a journal entry as of December 31, 20--, for the total amount that should be refunded. The refund will not be received until the next year.

SERIES B EXERCISES

E 9-1B (LO1/2)

✓ Payroll taxes expense: $1,962.74

CALCULATION AND JOURNAL ENTRY FOR EMPLOYER PAYROLL TAXES Portions of the payroll register for Kathy's Cupcakes for the week ended June 21 are shown below. The SUTA tax rate is 5.4%, and the FUTA tax rate is 0.8%, both on the first $7,000 of earnings. The Social Security tax rate is 6.2% on the first $106,800 of earnings. The Medicare rate is 1.45% on gross earnings.

Kathy's Cupcakes
Payroll Register

Total Earnings	Total Taxable Earnings of All Employees	
	Unemployment Compensation	Social Security
$15,680	$12,310	$15,680

Calculate the employer's payroll taxes expense and prepare the journal entry to record the employer's payroll taxes expense for the week ended June 21 of the current year.

E 9-2B (LO1/2)

✓ Payroll taxes expense: $503.63

CALCULATION AND JOURNAL ENTRY FOR EMPLOYER PAYROLL TAXES Earnings for several employees for the week ended April 7, 20--, are as follows:

Employee Name	Current Earnings	Taxable Earnings	
		Unemployment Compensation	Social Security
Boyd, Glenda L.	$ 850	$300	$ 850
Evans, Sheryl N.	970	225	970
Fox, Howard J.	830	830	830
Jacobs, Phyllis J.	1,825	—	1,825
Roh, William R.	990	25	990

Calculate the employer's payroll taxes expense and prepare the journal entry as of April 7, 20--, assuming that FUTA tax is 0.8%, SUTA tax is 5.4%, Social Security tax is 6.2%, and Medicare tax is 1.45%.

E 9-3B (LO1/2)

✓ **Payroll taxes expense: $788.04**

CALCULATION OF TAXABLE EARNINGS AND EMPLOYER PAYROLL TAXES, AND PREPARATION OF JOURNAL ENTRY Selected information from the payroll register of Howard's Cutlery for the week ended October 7, 20--, is presented below. Social Security tax is 6.2% on the first $106,800 of earnings for each employee. Medicare tax is 1.45% on gross earnings. FUTA tax is 0.8% and SUTA tax is 5.4% on the first $7,000 of earnings.

Employee Name	Cumulative Pay Before Current Earnings	Current Gross Pay	Taxable Earnings	
			Unemployment Compensation	Social Security
Carlson, David J.	$ 6,635	$ 950		
Delgado, Luisa	6,150	1,215		
Lewis, Arlene S.	54,375	2,415		
Nixon, Robert R.	53,870	1,750		
Shippe, Lance W.	24,830	1,450		
Watts, Brandon Q.	105,400	2,120		

Calculate the amount of taxable earnings for unemployment, Social Security, and Medicare taxes, and prepare the journal entry to record the employer's payroll taxes as of October 7, 20--.

E 9-4B (LO1/2)

✓ **Total cost: $49,953.00**

TOTAL COST OF EMPLOYEE B. F. Goodson employs Eduardo Gonzales at a salary of $46,000 a year. Goodson is subject to employer Social Security taxes at a rate of 6.2% and Medicare taxes at a rate of 1.45% on Gonzales's salary. In addition, Goodson must pay SUTA tax at a rate of 5.4% and FUTA tax at a rate of 0.8% on the first $7,000 of Gonzales's salary.

Compute the total cost to Goodson of employing Gonzales for the year.

E 9-5B (LO3)

✓ **941 deposit: $19,058.00**

JOURNAL ENTRIES FOR PAYMENT OF EMPLOYER PAYROLL TAXES Francis Baker owns a business called Baker Construction Co. She does her banking at the American National Bank in Seattle, Washington. The amounts in her general ledger for payroll taxes and employees' withholding of Social Security, Medicare, and federal income tax payable as of July 15 of the current year are as follows:

Social Security tax payable (includes both employer and employee)	$9,563
Medicare tax payable (includes both employer and employee)	2,250
FUTA tax payable	504
SUTA tax payable	3,402
Employee federal income tax payable	7,245

Journalize the payment of the employee federal income taxes and Social Security and Medicare taxes on July 15, 20--, and the payments of the FUTA and state unemployment taxes on July 31, 20--.

E 9-6B (LO4)

✓ **2. Additional premium due: $22.00**

WORKERS' COMPENSATION INSURANCE AND ADJUSTMENT Columbia Industries estimated that its total payroll for the coming year would be $385,000. The workers' compensation insurance premium rate is 0.2%.

REQUIRED

1. Calculate the estimated workers' compensation insurance premium and prepare the journal entry for the payment as of January 2, 20--.

(continued)

2. Assume that Columbia Industries' actual payroll for the year is $396,000. Calculate the total insurance premium owed and prepare a journal entry as of December 31, 20--, to record the adjustment for the underpayment. The actual payment of the additional premium will take place in January of the next year.

SERIES B PROBLEMS

P 9-7B (LO1/2)

✓ Payroll taxes expense: $738.34

CALCULATING PAYROLL TAXES EXPENSE AND PREPARING JOURNAL ENTRY Selected information from the payroll register of Wray's Drug Store for the week ended July 14, 20--, is shown below. The SUTA tax rate is 5.4%, and the FUTA tax rate is 0.8%, both on the first $7,000 of earnings. Social Security tax on the employer is 6.2% on the first $106,800 of earnings, and Medicare tax is 1.45% on gross earnings.

| | | | Taxable Earnings | |
| | Cumulative Pay Before Current | Current Weekly | Unemployment | Social |
Employee Name	Earnings	Earnings	Compensation	Security
Ackers, Alice	$ 6,460	$ 645		
Conley, Dorothy	27,560	1,025		
Davis, James	6,850	565		
Lawrence, Kevin	52,850	2,875		
Rawlings, Judy	16,350	985		
Tanaka, Sumio	22,320	835		
Vadillo, Raynette	104,960	3,540		

REQUIRED

1. Calculate the total employer payroll taxes for these employees.

2. Prepare the journal entry to record the employer payroll taxes as of July 14, 20--.

P 9-8B (LO2/3)

✓ Payroll taxes expense: $2,105.33

JOURNALIZING AND POSTING PAYROLL ENTRIES Oxford Company has five employees. All are paid on a monthly basis. The fiscal year of the business is June 1 to May 31.

The accounts kept by Oxford Company include the following:

Account Number	Title	Balance on June 1
101	Cash	$69,500.00
211	Employee Income Tax Payable	2,018.00
212	Social Security Tax Payable	2,735.00
213	Medicare Tax Payable	641.00
218	Savings Bond Deductions Payable	787.50
221	FUTA Tax Payable	540.00
222	SUTA Tax Payable	1,380.00
511	Wages and Salaries Expense	0.00
530	Payroll Taxes Expense	0.00

The following transactions relating to payrolls and payroll taxes occurred during June and July:

June 15   Paid $5,394.00 covering the following May taxes:

Social Security tax	$2,735.00
Medicare tax	641.00
Employee income tax withheld	2,018.00
Total	$5,394.00

30   June payroll:

Total wages and salaries expense		$22,050.00
Less amounts withheld:		
Social Security tax	$1,367.10	
Medicare tax	319.73	
Employee income tax	1,920.00	
Savings bond deductions	787.50	4,394.33
Net amount paid		$17,655.67

30   Purchased savings bonds for employees, $1,575.00

30   Employer payroll taxes expenses for June were:

Social Security	$1,367.10
Medicare	319.73
FUTA	54.00
SUTA	364.50
Total	$2,105.33

July 15   Paid $5,293.66 covering the following June taxes:

Social Security tax	$ 2,734.20
Medicare tax	639.46
Employee income tax withheld	1,920.00
Total	$ 5,293.66

31   Paid SUTA tax for the quarter, $1,744.50

31   Paid FUTA tax, $594.00

REQUIRED

1.   Journalize the preceding transactions using a general journal.

2.   Open T accounts for the payroll expenses and liabilities. Enter the beginning balances and post the transactions recorded in the journal.

P 9-9B (LO4)

✓ 3. Refund due: $16.00

WORKERS' COMPENSATION INSURANCE AND ADJUSTMENT Multnomah Manufacturing estimated that its total payroll for the coming year would be $540,000. The workers' compensation insurance premium rate is 0.2%.

REQUIRED

1.   Calculate the estimated workers' compensation insurance premium and prepare the journal entry for the payment as of January 2, 20--.

2.   Assume that Multnomah Manufacturing's actual payroll for the year was $562,000. Calculate the total insurance premium owed and prepare a journal entry as of December 31, 20--, to record the adjustment for the underpayment. The actual payment of the additional premium will take place in January of the next year.

(continued)

3. Assume instead that Multnomah Manufacturing's actual payroll for the year was $532,000. Prepare a journal entry as of December 31, 20--, for the total amount that should be refunded. The refund will not be received until the next year.

MANAGING YOUR WRITING

The director of the art department at an advertising company, Wilson Watson, wants to hire new office staff. His boss tells him that to do so he must find in his budget not only the base salary for this position but an additional 30% for "fringe benefits." Wilson explodes: "How in the world can there be 30% in fringe benefits?" Write a memo to Wilson Watson explaining the costs that probably make up these fringe benefits.

ETHICS CASE

Bob Estes works at Cliffrock Company in the central receiving department. He unpacks incoming shipments and verifies quantities of goods received. Over the weekend, Bob pulled a muscle in his back while playing basketball. When he came to work on Monday and started unpacking shipments, his back started to hurt again. Bob called the human resources department and told them he hurt his back lifting a package at work. He was told to fill out an accident report and sent to an orthopedic clinic with a workers' compensation form. The doctor at the clinic told Bob not to lift anything heavy for two weeks and to stay home from work for at least one week.

1. Is Bob entitled to workers' compensation? Why or why not?

2. What effect will Bob's claim have on Cliffrock Company's workers' compensation insurance premium?

3. Write a short memo from the human resources department to Cliffrock Company's employees explaining the purpose of workers' compensation.

4. In small groups, discuss the job-related illness or injury risks of a computer input operator and measures an employer might take to minimize these risks.

MASTERY PROBLEM

✓ Payroll taxes expense: $730.75

The totals line from Nix Company's payroll register for the week ended March 31, 20--, is as follows:

(left side)

PAYROLL

	NAME	EMPLOYEE NUMBER	ALLOWANCES	MARITAL STATUS	EARNINGS			CUMULATIVE TOTAL	TAXABLE EARNINGS		
					REGULAR	OVERTIME	TOTAL		UNEMPLOYMENT COMPENSATION	SOCIAL SECURITY	
21	Totals				5 4 0 0 00	1 0 0 00	5 5 0 0 00	71 5 0 0 00	5 0 0 0 00	5 5 0 0 00	21

REGISTER—PERIOD ENDED March 31, 20--   (right side)

	DEDUCTIONS							NET PAY	CHECK NO.	
	FEDERAL INCOME TAX	SOCIAL SECURITY TAX	MEDICARE TAX	HEALTH INSURANCE	LIFE INSURANCE	OTHER	TOTAL			
21	5 0 0 00	3 4 1 00	7 9 75	1 6 5 00	2 0 0 00		1 2 8 5 75	4 2 1 4 25		21

Payroll taxes are imposed as follows: Social Security tax, 6.2%; Medicare tax, 1.45%; FUTA tax, 0.8%; and SUTA tax, 5.4%.

REQUIRED

1. a. Prepare the journal entry for payment of this payroll on March 31, 20--.

    b. Prepare the journal entry for the employer's payroll taxes for the period ended March 31, 20--.

2. Nix Company had the following balances in its general ledger before the entries for requirement (1) were made:

Employee income tax payable	$2,500
Social Security tax payable	2,008
Medicare tax payable	470
FUTA tax payable	520
SUTA tax payable	3,510

    a. Prepare the journal entry for payment of the liabilities for federal income taxes and Social Security and Medicare taxes on April 15, 20--.

    b. Prepare the journal entry for payment of the liability for FUTA tax on April 30, 20--.

    c. Prepare the journal entry for payment of the liability for SUTA tax on April 30, 20--.

3. Nix Company paid a premium of $420 for workers' compensation insurance based on the estimated payroll as of the beginning of the year. Based on actual payroll as of the end of the year, the premium is only $400. Prepare the adjusting entry to reflect the overpayment of the insurance premium at the end of the year (December 31, 20--).

CHALLENGE PROBLEM

This problem challenges you to apply your cumulative accounting knowledge to move a step beyond the material in the chapter.

✓ **Payroll taxes expense: $1,306.25**

Payrex Co. has six employees. All are paid on a weekly basis. For the payroll period ending January 7, total employee earnings were $12,500, all of which were subject to SUTA, FUTA, Social Security, and Medicare taxes. The SUTA tax rate in Payrex's state is 5.4%, but Payrex qualifies for a rate of 2.0% because of its good record of providing regular employment to its employees. Other employer payroll taxes are at the rates described in the chapter.

REQUIRED

1. Calculate Payrex's FUTA, SUTA, Social Security, and Medicare taxes for the week ended January 7.

2. Prepare the journal entry for Payrex's payroll taxes for the week ended January 7.

3. What amount of payroll taxes did Payrex save because of its good employment record?

ANSWERS TO SELF-STUDY QUESTIONS AND EXERCISES

True/False Questions

1. F (these taxes are paid by the employer)

2. T

3. T

4. F (FUTA tax is levied on employers)

5. F (this Form is W-2)

Multiple Choice Questions

1. b   **2.** d   **3.** b   **4.** d   **5.** a

U REVU   Exercises

1. Social Security $396.80
    Medicare   92.80
    FUTA   51.20
    SUTA   345.60
    Total $886.40

2. Payroll Taxes Expense   1,329.60
        Social Security Tax Payable   595.20
        Medicare Tax Payable   139.20
        FUTA Tax Payable   76.80
        SUTA Tax Payable   518.40
        Employer payroll taxes for week ended Feb. 10

3. (a) Social Security Tax Payable   6,750.00
        Medicare Tax Payable   1,575.00
        Employee Income Tax Payable   4,095.00
            Cash   12,420.00
            Deposit of employee federal income tax
            and Social Security and Medicare taxes

    (b) FUTA Tax Payable
            Cash   360.00
                Paid FUTA tax   360.00

        SUTA Tax Payable
            Cash   2,646.00
                Paid SUTA tax   2,646.00

4. Workers' Compensation Insurance Expense
        Cash   572.00
            Paid insurance premium   572.00

Accounting for a Merchandising Business

PART
3

Add Some Color to Your Learning!

Throughout the text, you will be introduced to many important terms and types of accounts. To help you learn the different terms and types of accounts, we have coded many of them using the following color key in Part 3:

- Assets
- Contra-Assets
- Liabilities
- Capital
- Drawing
- Revenues
- Contra-Revenues
- Expenses
- Contra-Costs (Contra-Purchases)
- Income Summary (Net Income/Net Loss)

## Chapter 10

Accounting for Sales and Cash Receipts

In recent years, we have seen increasing concern about how our actions affect the environment. Planet Shoes is an example of a young company whose business reflects this concern. Planet Shoes is an online shoe retailer specializing in eco-friendly shoes. It markets vegan shoes, shoes made from recycled chemicals, and a number of name brands such as Birkenstock, Clarks, Geox, and New Balance. At checkout, it even offers the option of carbon-free shipping and shoe recycling. And it donates 1% of its sales to environmental organizations.

Operating from Waltham, Massachusetts, Planet's revenues have grown from $541 thousand to $5.9 million in only 10 years. Planet must have a good system to manage and account for its high volume of sales. In addition, since all of its sales are via the Internet, it must know how to handle credit card sales. In this chapter, you will learn how to account for sales transactions, including credit card sales.

LEARNING OBJECTIVES

Careful study of this chapter should enable you to:

LO1 Describe merchandise sales transactions.

LO2 Describe and use merchandise sales accounts.

LO3 Describe and use the accounts receivable ledger.

LO4 Prepare a schedule of accounts receivable.

Over the last nine chapters, we have learned how to account for a service business. We are now ready to consider accounting for a different kind of business—merchandising. A **merchandising business** purchases merchandise such as clothing, furniture, or computers, and sells that merchandise to customers. For example, Planet Shoes buys shoes from vendors and manufacturers and sells them to its customers online.

This chapter examines how to account for the sale of merchandise using the accrual basis of accounting. We will learn how to use four new accounts and a subsidiary ledger.

MERCHANDISE SALES TRANSACTIONS

LO1 Describe merchandise sales transactions.

A **sale** is a transfer of merchandise from one business or individual to another in exchange for cash or a promise to pay cash. Sales procedures and documents vary greatly, depending on the nature and size of the business.

RETAILER

A retailer such as Planet Shoes makes all sales online. For Web-based transactions, companies use electronic forms that are similar to the paper documents described in this chapter.

Retail businesses generally sell to customers who enter the store, select the merchandise they want, and bring it to a salesclerk. The salesclerk enters the sale in some type of electronic cash register that generates a receipt for the customer. A copy of the receipt is retained in the register. Most registers can print a summary of the day's sales activity, like the one in Figure 10-1. This summary can be used to journalize sales in the accounting records.

FIGURE 10-1 Cash Register Tape Summary

```
            (1)
CASH SALES        327.79 *
            (3)
MCARD/VISA        550.62 *
            (6)
LAYAWAY            79.50 *
TOTAL CASH        957.91 *
            (2)
CHARGE SALES      543.84 *
            (5)
APPROVAL          126.58 *
TOTAL CHARGE      670.42 *

TOTAL SALES     1,628.33 G*
SALES TAX          81.42 *
                   81.42 *

REC'D ON ACCT.    324.51 *
                  324.51 *

PAID OUT           76.51 *
                   76.51 *

NO SALE             0.00 *
                    0.00 *

   *     SUB-TOTAL
   G*    GRAND TOTAL
```

An additional document often created as evidence of a sale in a retail business is a **sales ticket** (Figure 10-2). One copy of the sales ticket is given to the customer, and the other copy is sent to accounting.

FIGURE 10-2 Sales Ticket

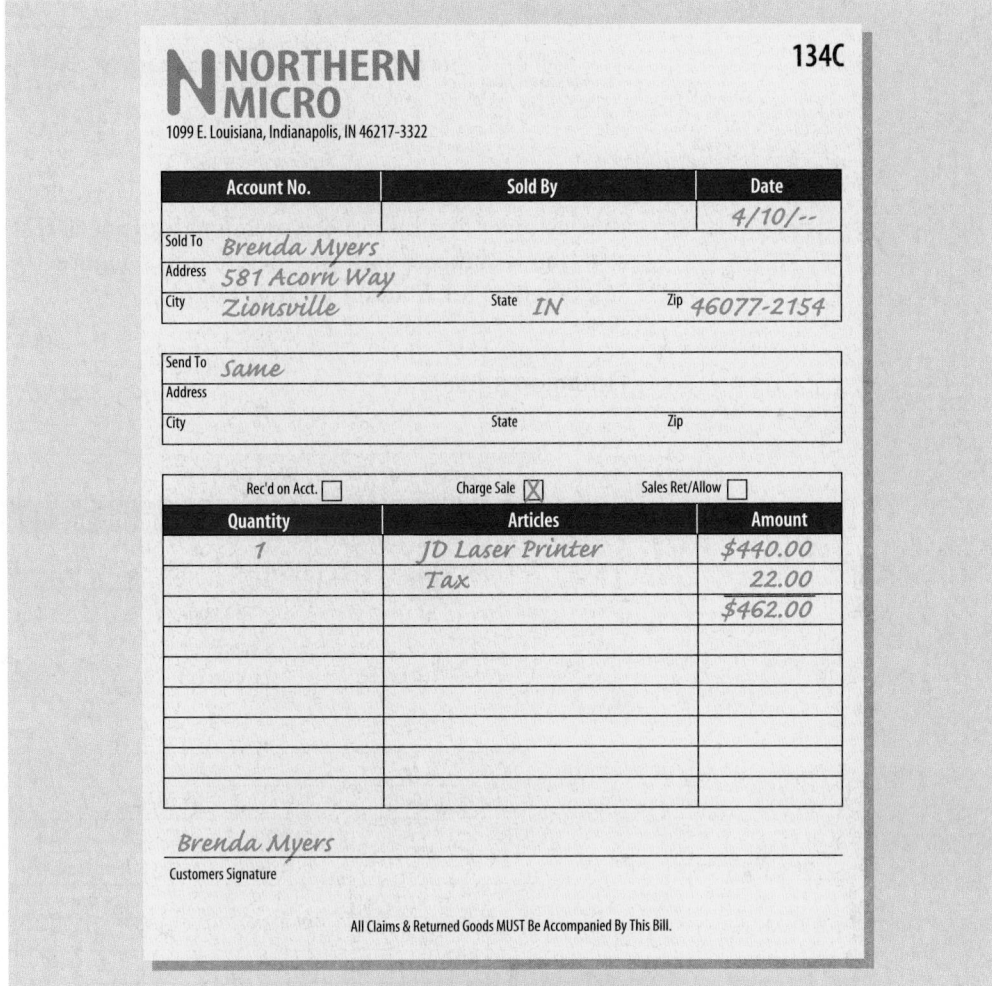

WHOLESALER

Figure 10-3 shows how the wholesaler plays a different role than the retailer in the marketing chain. Retailers usually sell to final consumers, whereas wholesalers tend to sell to retailers. This causes the wholesale sales transaction process to differ, as shown in Figure 10-4.

In a computerized system, customer orders can be submitted electronically. Even the credit approval process can be handled by the computer.

FIGURE 10-3 Marketing Chain

Customers commonly mail or fax written orders to buy merchandise from wholesalers. When the customer purchase order arrives, the customer name and items being ordered are determined. Since wholesalers typically make sales on account, credit approval is needed. Three copies of a **sales invoice** are then generated. One is sent to

FIGURE 10-4 Wholesale Sales Transaction Process

the customer as a bill for the merchandise, one is sent to accounting to record the sale, and one is shipped with the merchandise. Figure 10-5 shows the customer copy of a sales invoice for Aladdin Electric Supply.

FIGURE 10-5 Sales Invoice

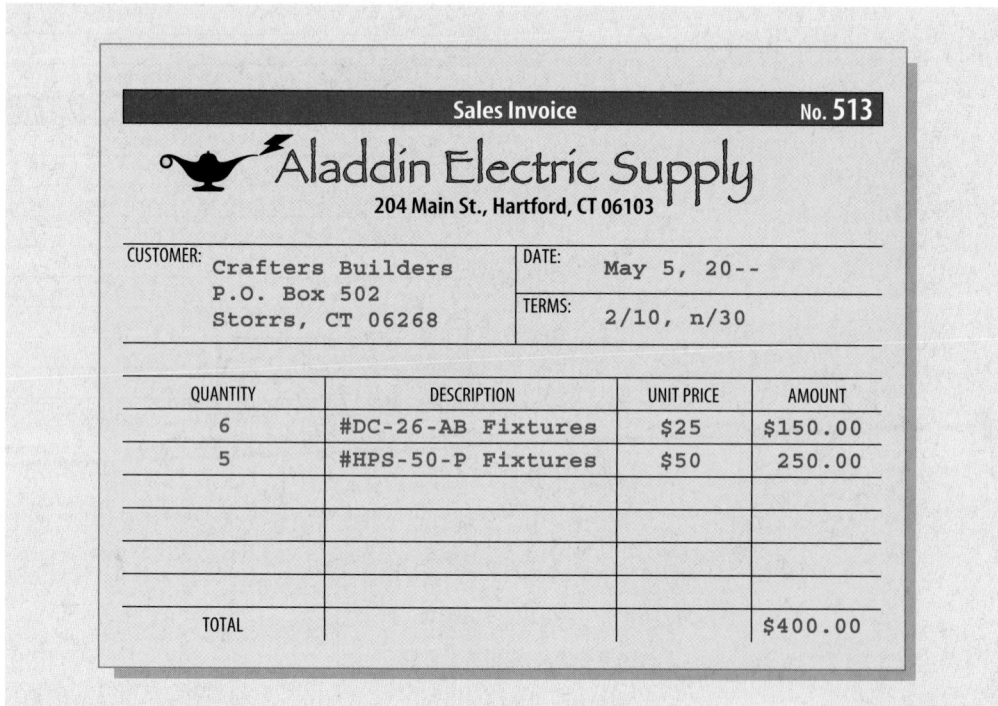

CREDIT MEMORANDUM

Both retailers and wholesalers sometimes have customers return goods or seek price reductions for damaged goods. Merchandise returned by a customer for a refund is called a **sales return**. Price reductions granted by the seller because of defects or other problems with the merchandise are called **sales allowances**. When credit is given for merchandise returned or for an allowance, a **credit memo** is issued for the amount involved. This document gets its name from the same debit and credit concepts you learned in Chapter 3. It is called a credit memo because the customer's account receivable is *credited* to reduce the amount the customer owes. One copy of the credit memo is given to the customer and one copy is sent to accounting. Figure 10-6 shows a credit memo issued by Northern Micro for merchandise returned by a customer.

FIGURE 10-6 Credit Memo

```
N NORTHERN                                    CREDIT # 72
  MICRO                                       MEMO
1099 E. Louisiana, Indianapolis, IN 46217-3322

Date      April 2, 20--
Sold To   Susan Chang
Address   337 Elm Street
City      Noblesville          State  IN      Zip  46060-3377

Sales Number                              OK
Cash        Mdse.      Charge     Gift        Amount
Refund      Order        ✓                       $42.00

   Quantity              Articles              Amount
      2            Printer Cartridges          $40.00
                         Tax                      2.00
                                                $42.00




Forty-two 00/100                                       Dollars

Reason    Not Needed

Rec'd Stock By   Laura Murphy

x  Susan Chang
Customer's Signature
```

U REVU   Complete U REVU-1 on **page 381** to test your basic understanding of LO1.

MERCHANDISE SALES ACCOUNTS

LO2 Describe and use merchandise sales accounts.

To account for merchandise sales transactions, we will use four new accounts:

1. Sales
2. Sales Tax Payable
3. Sales Returns and Allowances
4. Sales Discounts

The position of these accounts in the accounting equation and their normal balances are shown in Figure 10-7.

SALES ACCOUNT

The sales account is a revenue account used to record sales of merchandise. The account is credited for the selling price of merchandise sold during the period.

Sales

Debit	Credit
	to enter the selling price of merchandise sold

FIGURE 10-7 Accounting for Merchandise Sales Transactions

Assets		=	Liabilities		+	Owner's Equity			
Debit +	Credit −		Debit −	Credit +		Debit −		Credit +	

Sales Tax Payable: XXX (credit)

						Drawing		Expenses		Revenues	
						Debit +	Credit −	Debit +	Credit −	Debit −	Credit +

Sales: XXX (credit)

Sales Returns and Allowances: XXX (debit)

Sales Discounts: XXX (debit)

If a $100 sale is made for cash, the following entry is made:

5		Cash	1 0 0 00		5
6		Sales		1 0 0 00	6
7		Made cash sale			7

If the same sale is made on account, the entry is as follows:

The customer's name is placed after Accounts Receivable

5		Accounts Receivable/Customer	1 0 0 00		5
6		Sales		1 0 0 00	6
7		Made credit sale			7

Accounts Receivable is followed by a slash (/) and the name of the specific customer who owes the money. Accounts Receivable is the same account we first saw in Chapter 2. It is a general ledger account. The "Customer" name is for the customer's account in the accounts receivable ledger. This ledger is explained later in this chapter.

SALES TAX PAYABLE ACCOUNT

Most states require retailers to collect sales tax on sales to final consumers. When sales tax is imposed on merchandise sold, a separate account for Sales Tax Payable is kept. This is a liability account that is credited for the taxes imposed on sales. The account is debited for sales taxes paid to the proper taxing authority or for sales taxes on merchandise returned by customers. A credit balance in the account indicates the amount owed to the taxing authority for taxes collected.

Sales Tax Payable

Debit	Credit
to enter payment of tax to taxing authority or adjustment of tax on merchandise returned by customers	to enter tax imposed on sales

If a cash sale for $100 plus 5% sales tax (5% × $100 = $5) occurs, the following entry is made:

10	Cash		1 0 5 00		10
11	Sales			1 0 0 00	11
12	Sales Tax Payable			5 00	12
13	Made cash sale				13

If the same sale is made on account, the entry is as follows:

10	Accounts Receivable/Customer		1 0 5 00		10
11	Sales			1 0 0 00	11
12	Sales Tax Payable			5 00	12
13	Made credit sale				13

The debit to Accounts Receivable indicates that the amount owed by customers to the business has increased. Since the buyer has accepted the merchandise and promised to pay for it, revenue is recognized by crediting Sales. Sales Tax Payable is credited because the amount of sales tax owed to the taxing authority has increased.

SALES RETURNS AND ALLOWANCES ACCOUNT

Sales Returns and Allowances is a **contra-revenue account,** which has a debit balance and is deducted from the related revenue account. Sales returns and sales allowances are debited to this account. As shown in Figure 10-8, this account is reported as a deduction from Sales on the income statement. Returns and allowances are debited to a separate account rather than directly to Sales so that the business can more readily keep track of this activity.

Sales Returns and Allowances

Debit	Credit
to enter returns and allowances	

Look at the credit memo in Figure 10-6 on page 357. The entry for the return of these printer cartridges by Susan Chang would be as follows:

19	Sales Returns and Allowances		4 0 00		19
20	Sales Tax Payable		2 00		20
21	Accounts Receivable/Susan Chang			4 2 00	21
22	Returned merchandise — Credit Memo #72				22

FIGURE 10-8 Sales Returns and Allowances on the Income Statement

Sales				$38 5 0 0 00	
Less sales returns and allowances				2 0 0 00	
Net sales					$38 3 0 0 00

LEARNING KEY

To record returns and allowances, debit Sales Returns and Allowances for the amount of the sale excluding the sales tax.

Another type of discount sometimes offered between businesses is a trade discount. This discount is explained in Chapter 11.

Note carefully the parts of this entry. Sales Returns and Allowances is debited for the amount of the sale, *excluding* the sales tax. Sales Tax Payable is debited separately for the sales tax on the original sale amount. Accounts Receivable is credited for the total amount originally billed to Chang.

SALES DISCOUNTS ACCOUNT

Some businesses offer **cash discounts** to encourage prompt payment by customers who buy merchandise on account. When credit is tight and businesses are short of cash, it is particularly important to convert accounts receivable into cash as soon as possible. Prompt collection of accounts receivable also reduces the risk that those receivables will become uncollectible. Some possible credit terms are shown in Figure 10-9.

FIGURE 10-9 Credit Terms

TERMS	MEANING
2/10, n/30*	2% discount off sales price if paid within 10 days Total amount due within 30 days
1/10, n/30	Same as 2/10, n/30, except 1% discount instead of 2%
2/eom, n/60	2% discount if paid before end of month Total amount due within 60 days
3/10 eom, n/60	3% discount if paid within 10 days after end of month Total amount due within 60 days

*See Figure 10-5. A discount of $8 (2% × $400) is allowed if this invoice is paid by May 15 (invoice date of May 5 + 10 days).

To the seller, cash discounts are considered **sales discounts**. Sales Discounts is a contra-revenue account to which cash discounts allowed are debited. Like Sales Returns and Allowances, this account is reported as a deduction from Sales on the income statement, as shown in Figure 10-10.

Sales	
Debit	**Credit**
to enter cash discounts	

FIGURE 10-10 Sales Discounts on the Income Statement

Sales								$38	5	0	0	00		
Less: Sales returns and allowances				$	2	0	0	00						
Sales discounts					1	4	0	00		3	4	0	00	
Net sales												$38	1	6	0	00

If merchandise is sold for $100 with credit terms of 2/10, n/30, and cash is received within the discount period, two entries are made.

At time of sale:

26		Accounts Receivable/Customer			1	0	0	00					26
27		Sales							1	0	0	00	27
28		Made sale on account											28

At time of collection:

30		Cash			9	8	00					30
31		Sales Discounts			2	00						31
32		Accounts Receivable/Customer						1	0	0	00	32
33		Received cash on account										33

Figure 10-11 shows how (1) a sale on account followed by (2) collection with a cash discount affects the accounts receivable, sales, and cash accounts.

FIGURE 10-11 Sales on Account → Collection with Cash Discount

	(1)		(2)
	Credit Sale	2% Cash Discount	Cash Collection
Net Sales =	$100 −	$2 =	$98

ENTRY FOR CREDIT SALE

(1)	Accounts Receivable	1	0	0	00				
	Sales					1	0	0	00

ENTRY FOR CASH COLLECTION

(2)	Cash	9	8	00				
	Sales Discounts	2	00					
	Accounts Receivable				1	0	0	00

If any merchandise has been returned, the sales discount is calculated on the sale amount after deducting the return. For the above sale for $100, if $30 of merchandise had been returned, the discount on the remaining $70 collection would be 2% × $70 = $1.40. The journal entry for the collection is:

1		Cash			6	8	60					1
2		Sales Discount			1	40						2
3		Accounts Receivable						7	0	00		3
4		Received cash on account										4

If there is a sales tax, the discount is calculated on the sale amount excluding the sales tax. Assume merchandise is sold for $100 plus 5% sales tax (5% × $100 = $5), with credit terms of 2/10, n/30. At the time of the sale, the following entry is made:

1	Accounts Receivable	1 0 5 00		1
2	Sales		1 0 0 00	2
3	Sales Tax Payable		5 00	3
4	Made sale on account			4

If cash is received within the discount period, the discount is 2% × $100 = $2, and the entry is:

1	Cash	1 0 3 00		1
2	Sales Discounts	2 00		2
3	Accounts Receivable		1 0 5 00	3
4	Received cash on account			4

Note that this entry does not affect Sales Tax Payable. The sales tax is based on the amount of the sale, which is not affected by the timing of the collection on account.

U REVU

Complete U REVU-2 on page 381 to test your basic understanding of LO2.

JOURNALIZING AND POSTING SALES AND CASH RECEIPTS TRANSACTIONS

LO3 Describe and use the accounts receivable ledger.

To illustrate the journalizing and posting of sales and cash receipts transactions, we use Northern Micro, a retail computer business.

SALES

Assume the following sales transactions occurred during April 20--:

Apr. 4   Made Sale No. 133C on account to Enrico Lorenzo, $1,520 plus $76 sales tax.

10   Made Sale No. 134C on account to Brenda Myers, $440 plus $22 sales tax.

18   Made Sale No. 105D on account to Edith Walton, $980 plus $49 sales tax.

21   Made Sale No. 202B on account to Susan Chang, $620 plus $31 sales tax.

24   Made Sale No. 162A on account to Heidi Schwitzer, $1,600 plus $80 sales tax.

These transactions are entered in a general journal, as shown in Figure 10-12.

POSTING SALES TO THE GENERAL LEDGER

Sales transactions are posted from the general journal to the general ledger in the same manner as was illustrated in Chapter 4. Several steps are used, as indicated in Figure 10-13, for Northern Micro's April 4 and 10 sales transactions.

In the general ledger account:

STEP 1   Enter the date of the transaction in the Date column.

STEP 2   Enter the amount of the debit or credit in the Debit or Credit column.

STEP 3   Enter the new balance in the Balance columns under Debit or Credit.

STEP 4   Enter the journal page number from which each transaction is posted in the Posting Reference column.

FIGURE 10-12 Sales Entered in General Journal

4	Apr.	4	Accounts Receivable/E. Lorenzo	1 5 9 6 00		4
5			Sales		1 5 2 0 00	5
6			Sales Tax Payable		7 6 00	6
7			Sale No. 133C			7
8						8
9		10	Accounts Receivable/B. Myers	4 6 2 00		9
10			Sales		4 4 0 00	10
11			Sales Tax Payable		2 2 00	11
12			Sale No. 134C			12
13						13
14		18	Accounts Receivable/E. Walton	1 0 2 9 00		14
15			Sales		9 8 0 00	15
16			Sales Tax Payable		4 9 00	16
17			Sale No. 105D			17
18						18
19		21	Accounts Receivable/S. Chang	6 5 1 00		19
20			Sales		6 2 0 00	20
21			Sales Tax Payable		3 1 00	21
22			Sale No. 202B			22
23						23
24		24	Accounts Receivable/H. Schwitzer	1 6 8 0 00		24
25			Sales		1 6 0 0 00	25
26			Sales Tax Payable		8 0 00	26
27			Sale No. 162A			27

In the journal:

STEP 5 Enter the ledger account number in the Posting Reference column of the journal for each transaction that is posted.

Other sales transactions would be posted in the same manner.

POSTING SALES TO THE ACCOUNTS RECEIVABLE LEDGER

After all posting to the general ledger is completed, the accounts receivable, sales tax payable, and sales accounts in the general ledger are up to date. But at this point, Northern Micro has no complete record of the account receivable from *individual customers*. To run the business properly, Northern Micro needs this information.

A common approach to keeping a record of each customer's account receivable is to use an **accounts receivable ledger**. This is a separate ledger containing an individual account receivable for each customer. It is called a **subsidiary ledger**. A summary accounts receivable account called a **controlling account** is still maintained in the general ledger. The accounts receivable ledger is "subsidiary" to this account. If there are many customer accounts, it is good practice to assign each customer an account number. The subsidiary ledger accounts are kept in either alphabetical or numerical order, depending on whether customer accounts are identified by number. Figure 10-14 shows part of the accounts receivable ledger for Northern Micro.

Figure 10-14 illustrates the use of the accounts receivable ledger for Northern Micro's April 4 and 10 sales transactions. The accounts receivable ledger is posted

FIGURE 10-13 Posting Sales to the General Ledger

from the journal *daily* so that current information is available for each customer at all times. Note that including the individual customer name after Accounts Receivable in each journal entry helps in the posting process. Several steps are used to post from the general journal to the accounts receivable ledger, as shown in Figure 10-14.

In the accounts receivable ledger account:

STEP 1 Enter the date of the transaction in the Date column.

STEP 2 Enter the amount of the debit or credit in the Debit or Credit column.

STEP 3 Enter the new balance in the Balance column.

STEP 4 Enter the journal page number from which each transaction is posted in the Posting Reference column.

In the journal:

STEP 5 Enter a slash (/) followed by a check mark (✓) in the Posting Reference column of the journal for each transaction that is posted.

FIGURE 10-14 Posting Sales to the Accounts Receivable Ledger

A three-column account form is commonly used for customer accounts. Only one balance column is needed because the normal balance is a debit. If a credit balance occurs, the amount may be bracketed.

LEARNING KEY

When an accounts receivable ledger is used, the Posting Reference column in the general journal can serve two purposes. (1) The account number is inserted to indicate the general ledger account has been posted. (2) A slash (/) and a check mark (✓) can be inserted to indicate the accounts receivable ledger account has been posted.

The accounts receivable ledger also can be posted from the source document used to make the general journal entry. For example, Sales Ticket No. 134C (see Figure 10-2) could be used to post that sale to Brenda Myers' account in the accounts receivable ledger. In this case, 134C would be inserted in the Posting Reference column of her account.

Note the relationship between the general journal, accounts receivable ledger, and general ledger. Entries in the general journal are posted to the general ledger and accounts receivable ledger. After the posting of the accounts receivable ledger and the general ledger is completed, the total of the accounts receivable ledger balances should equal the Accounts Receivable balance in the general ledger. Remember, the accounts receivable ledger is simply a detailed listing of the same information that is summarized in Accounts Receivable in the general ledger.

SALES RETURNS AND ALLOWANCES

If a customer returns merchandise or is given an allowance for damaged merchandise, a general journal entry is required. On May 5, Susan Chang returned two printer cartridges costing $40 plus $2 sales tax (Figure 10-6, page 357). Figure 10-15 shows the general journal entry, general ledger posting, and accounts receivable ledger posting for this transaction.

The general journal entry is made in the usual manner. The general ledger is posted using the same five steps as were illustrated for sales transactions in Figure 10-13. The accounts receivable ledger is posted using the five steps below, as illustrated in Figure 10-15.

In the accounts receivable ledger account:

STEP 1 Enter the date of the transaction in the Date column.

STEP 2 Enter the amount of the debit or credit in the Debit or Credit column.

STEP 3 Enter the new balance in the Balance column.

STEP 4 Enter the journal page number from which each transaction is posted in the Posting Reference column.

In the journal:

STEP 5 Enter a slash (/) followed by a check mark (✓) in the Posting Reference column of the journal for each transaction that is posted.

CASH RECEIPTS

Like sales transactions, cash receipt transactions occur frequently in most businesses. Three common types of cash receipts from sales are collections on account, cash sales, and bank credit card sales.

Collections on Account

Sales on account lead to cash receipts, which are entered in the general journal. For example, assume that Northern Micro receives cash from Enrico Lorenzo for Sale No. 133C on April 14. The transaction is recorded in the general journal as follows:

25	Apr.	14	Cash		1	5	9	6	00							25
26			Accounts Receivable/E. Lorenzo								1	5	9	6	00	26
27			Received cash on account													27

Cash Sales

Most businesses also regularly make cash sales. The following entry shows cash sales of $500 recorded in the general journal on May 5:

3	May	5	Cash		5	0	0	00							3
4			Sales							5	0	0	00		4
5			Made cash sales												5

FIGURE 10-15 Accounting for Sales Returns and Allowances

Bank Credit Card Sales

An increasing amount of sales today are made using bank credit cards. In fact, consider Planet Shoes, the company in the chapter introduction. Planet operates totally online, so virtually all of its sales would be by bank credit card. Bank credit card sales are similar to cash sales because the cash is available to the business as soon as an electronic deposit is made at the end of the day. The credit card company makes the electronic deposit to the merchandiser's bank account for the gross amount of credit card sales less a processing fee. The fee is based on the gross amount of the sale, including the sales tax. Thus, on a sale of $100 plus sales tax of $5, the credit card fee at 4%

would be $4.20 (4% × $105). The following entry shows this credit card sale recorded on May 6:

8	May	6	Cash			1	0	0	80						8
9			Bank Credit Card Expense					4	20						9
10			Sales							1	0	0	00		10
11			Sales Tax Payable									5	00		11
12			Made credit card sale												12

A BROADER VIEW

IMAGE COPYRIGHT MORGAN LANE PHOTOGRAPHY,
2009/USED UNDER LICENSE FROM SHUTTERSTOCK
.COM

Is This Sale for Real?

U.S. businesses lose billions of dollars annually because of credit card fraud and bad checks. To reduce credit card fraud, cashiers should do two things: (1) Watch the customer sign the credit card slip and match it to the signature on the card. (2) Obtain an approval code on all credit card transactions. To reduce bad check losses, cashiers should accept only a driver's license as identification. They should compare the picture with the customer, watch the check being signed, and match the check signature with that on the driver's license.

JOURNALIZING CASH RECEIPTS

To illustrate the journalizing and posting of cash receipts transactions, we continue to use Northern Micro. Assume the following cash receipts transactions related to sales occurred during April 20--. (To simplify the illustration, cash sales and bank credit card sales for the month are summarized as single transactions at the end of the month.)

Apr. 14   Received cash on account from Enrico Lorenzo for Sale No. 133C, $1,596.

    20   Received cash on account from Brenda Myers for Sale No. 134C, $462.

    28   Received cash on account from Edith Walton for Sale No. 105D, $1,029.

    30   Cash sales for the month are $3,600 plus tax of $180.

    30   Bank credit card sales for the month are $2,500 plus tax of $125. Bank credit card expenses on these sales are $100.

These transactions are entered in a general journal as shown in Figure 10-16.

FIGURE 10-16 Cash Receipts Entered in General Journal

4	Apr.	14	Cash			1	5	9	6	00									4
5			Accounts Receivable/E. Lorenzo									1	5	9	6	00			5
6			Received cash on account																6
7																			7
8		20	Cash				4	6	2	00									8
9			Accounts Receivable/B. Myers										4	6	2	00			9
10			Received cash on account																10
11																			11
12		28	Cash			1	0	2	9	00									12
13			Accounts Receivable/E. Walton									1	0	2	9	00			13
14			Received cash on account																14
15																			15
16		30	Cash			3	7	8	0	00									16
17			Sales									3	6	0	0	00			17
18			Sales Tax Payable										1	8	0	00			18
19			Made cash sales																19
20																			20
21		30	Cash			2	5	2	5	00									21
22			Bank Credit Card Expense				1	0	0	00									22
23			Sales									2	5	0	0	00			23
24			Sales Tax Payable										1	2	5	00			24
25			Made credit card sales																25

POSTING CASH RECEIPTS TO THE GENERAL LEDGER AND ACCOUNTS RECEIVABLE LEDGER

Cash receipts transactions are posted to the general ledger in the same manner as was illustrated for sales transactions in Figure 10-13. To post cash receipts to the accounts receivable ledger, the steps below are used, as illustrated in Figure 10-17 for Northern Micro's April 14 and 20 cash receipts transactions.

In the accounts receivable ledger account:

STEP 1   Enter the date of the transaction in the Date column.

STEP 2   Enter the amount of the debit or credit in the Debit or Credit column.

STEP 3   Enter the new balance in the Balance column.

STEP 4   Enter the journal page number from which each transaction is posted in the Posting Reference column.

In the journal:

STEP 5   Enter a slash (/) followed by a check mark (✓) in the Posting Reference column of the journal for each transaction that is posted.

FIGURE 10-17 Posting Cash Receipts to the General Ledger and Accounts Receivable Ledger

GENERAL JOURNAL (Partial)   Page 8

Date		Description	Post. Ref.	Debit	Credit
20--					
Apr.	14	Cash	[5] 101	1,596.00	
		Accounts Receivable/E. Lorenzo	122/ ✓		1,596.00
		Received cash on account			
	20	Cash	[5] 101	462.00	
		Accounts Receivable/B. Myers	122/ ✓		462.00
		Received cash on account			

[2]

ACCOUNTS RECEIVABLE LEDGER (Partial)

NAME   Enrico Lorenzo
ADDRESS   5240 Tousley Court, Indianapolis, IN 46224-5678

Date		Item	Post. Ref.	Debit	Credit	Balance
20--						
Apr.	4		J8	1,596.00		1,596.00
[1]	14		[4] J8		1,596.00	[3] 0

NAME   Brenda Myers
ADDRESS   581 Acorn Way, Zionsville, IN 46077-2154

Date		Item	Post. Ref.	Debit	Credit	Balance
20--						
Apr.	10		J8	462.00		462.00
[1]	20		[4] J8		462.00	[3] 0

GENERAL LEDGER (Partial)

ACCOUNT   Cash   **ACCOUNT NO. 101**

Date		Item	Post. Ref.	Debit	Credit	Balance Debit	Balance Credit
20--							
Apr.	1	Bal.	✓			20,000.00	
	14		J8	1,596.00		21,596.00	
	20		J8	462.00		22,058.00	

ACCOUNT   Accounts Receivable   **ACCOUNT NO. 122**

Date		Item	Post. Ref.	Debit	Credit	Balance Debit	Balance Credit
20--							
Apr.	1	Bal.	✓			12,000.00	
	4		J8	1,596.00		13,596.00	
	10		J8	462.00		14,058.00	
	14		J8		1,596.00	12,462.00	
	18		J8	1,029.00		13,491.00	
	20		J8		462.00	13,029.00	

U REVU Complete U REVU-3 on **page 381** to test your basic understanding of LO3.

SCHEDULE OF ACCOUNTS RECEIVABLE

LO4 Prepare a schedule of accounts receivable.

At the end of the month, all postings to Accounts Receivable in the general ledger and to the accounts receivable ledger should be complete, as shown in Figure 10-18. At this point, the Accounts Receivable balance in the general ledger should equal the sum of the customer balances in the accounts receivable ledger.

To verify that the sum of the accounts receivable ledger balances equals the Accounts Receivable balance, a **schedule of accounts receivable** is prepared. This is an alphabetical or numerical listing of customer accounts and balances, usually prepared at the end of the month. Note that customers whose account balance is zero are not included. The schedule of accounts receivable for Northern Micro as of April 30 is illustrated in Figure 10-19.

This schedule is prepared from the list of customer accounts in the accounts receivable ledger. The total calculated in the schedule is compared with the balance in Accounts Receivable in the general ledger. Note that the $14,331 total listed in the schedule equals the Accounts Receivable balance shown in Figure 10-18. If the schedule total and the Accounts Receivable balance do not agree, the error must be located and corrected. To find the error, use the following procedures:

STEP 1   Verify the total of the schedule.

STEP 2   Verify the postings to the accounts receivable ledger.

STEP 3   Verify the postings to Accounts Receivable in the general ledger.

FIGURE 10-18 General Ledger and Accounts Receivable Ledger after Posting

ACCOUNTS RECEIVABLE LEDGER

NAME   Helen Avery

ADDRESS   1739 Woodsage Trace, Indianapolis, IN 46237-1199

Date	Item	Post. Ref.	Debit	Credit	Balance
20-- Apr. 1	Bal.	✓			2,302.00

NAME   Susan Chang

ADDRESS   337 Elm Street, Noblesville, IN 46060-3377

Date	Item	Post. Ref.	Debit	Credit	Balance
20-- Apr. 21		J9	651.00		651.00

NAME   Enrico Lorenzo

ADDRESS   5240 Tousley Court, Indianapolis, IN 46224-5678

Date	Item	Post. Ref.	Debit	Credit	Balance
20-- Apr. 4		J8	1,596.00		1,596.00
14		J8		1,596.00	0

NAME   Brenda Myers

ADDRESS   581 Acorn Way, Zionsville, IN 46077-2154

Date	Item	Post. Ref.	Debit	Credit	Balance
20-- Apr. 10		J8	462.00		462.00
20		J8		462.00	0

NAME   Heidi Schwitzer

ADDRESS   5858 Wildflower Cir., Bloomington, IN 47401-6209

Date	Item	Post. Ref.	Debit	Credit	Balance
20-- Apr. 1	Bal.	✓			1,883.00
24		J9	1,680.00		3,563.00

ACCOUNTS RECEIVABLE LEDGER (Continued)

NAME   Ken Ulmet

ADDRESS   5260 Eagle Creek, Indianapolis, I N 46254-8275

Date	Item	Post. Ref.	Debit	Credit	Balance
20-- Apr. 1	Bal.	✓			3,315.00

NAME   Edith Walton

ADDRESS   1113 Stones Crossing, Zionsville, IN 46077-6601

Date	Item	Post. Ref.	Debit	Credit	Balance
20-- Apr. 18		J8	1,029.00		1,029.00
28		J9		1,029.00	0

NAME   Vivian Winston

ADDRESS   124 MainSt., Zionsville, IN 46077-1358

Date	Item	Post. Ref.	Debit	Credit	Balance
20-- Apr. 1	Bal.	✓			4,500.00

GENERAL LEDGER (Partial)

ACCOUNT   Accounts Receivable   ACCOUNT NO. 122

Date	Item	Post. Ref.	Debit	Credit	Balance Debit	Balance Credit
20-- Apr. 1	Bal.	✓			12,000.00	
4		J8	1,596.00		13,596.00	
10		J8	462.00		14,058.00	
14		J8		1,596.00	12,462.00	
18		J8	1,029.00		13,491.00	
20		J8		462.00	13,029.00	
21		J9	651.00		13,680.00	
24		J9	1,680.00		15,360.00	
28		J9		1,029.00	14,331.00	

FIGURE 10-19 Schedule of Accounts Receivable

Northern Micro
Schedule of Accounts Receivable
April 30, 20--

Helen Avery	$ 2	3	0	2	00
Susan Chang		6	5	1	00
Heidi Schwitzer	3	5	6	3	00
Ken Ulmet	3	3	1	5	00
Vivian Winston	4	5	0	0	00
Total	$14	3	3	1	00

U REVU

Complete U REVU-4 on **page 381** to test your basic understanding of LO4.

SELF-STUDY

LO1 **Describe merchandise sales transactions.**

A merchandising business buys and sells merchandise. Retailers generally make sales in the store. Important accounting documents are cash register tapes and sales tickets. Wholesalers generally ship merchandise to retailers. A key accounting document is the sales invoice. When customers return merchandise or obtain price adjustments, a credit memo is issued.

LO2 **Describe and use merchandise sales accounts.**

Four accounts are used in accounting for merchandise sales transactions.
1. Sales
2. Sales Tax Payable
3. Sales Returns and Allowances
4. Sales Discounts

LO3 **Describe and use the accounts receivable ledger.**

To post sales transactions to the general ledger, use these five steps.

In the general ledger account:

STEP 1 Enter the date of the transaction in the Date column.

STEP 2 Enter the amount of the debit or credit in the Debit or Credit column.

STEP 3 Enter the new balance in the Balance columns under Debit or Credit.

STEP 4 Enter the journal page number from which each transaction is posted in the Posting Reference column.

In the journal:

STEP 5 Enter the ledger account number in the Posting Reference column of the journal for each transaction that is posted.

An accounts receivable ledger is a separate ledger containing an individual account receivable for each customer. To post sales transactions to the accounts receivable ledger, use these five steps.

In the accounts receivable ledger account:

STEP 1 Enter the date of the transaction in the Date column.

STEP 2 Enter the amount of the debit or credit in the Debit or Credit column.

STEP 3 Enter the new balance in the Balance column.

STEP 4 Enter the journal page number from which each transaction is posted in the Posting Reference column.

In the journal:

STEP 5 Enter a slash (/) followed by a check mark (✓) in the Posting Reference column of the journal for each transaction that is posted.

To post cash receipts transactions to the general ledger, use these five steps.

In the general ledger account:

STEP 1 Enter the date of the transaction in the Date column.

STEP 2 Enter the amount of the debit or credit in the Debit or Credit column.

STEP 3 Enter the new balance in the Balance columns under Debit or Credit.

(continued)

LEARNING OBJECTIVES   Key Points to Remember

LO3 (concluded)	STEP 4 Enter the journal page number from which each transaction is posted in the Posting Reference column. **In the journal:** STEP 5 Enter the ledger account number in the Posting Reference column of the journal for each transaction that is posted. To post cash receipts transactions to the accounts receivable ledger, use these five steps. **In the accounts receivable ledger account:** STEP 1 Enter the date of the transaction in the Date column. STEP 2 Enter the amount of the debit or credit in the Debit or Credit column. STEP 3 Enter the new balance in the Balance column. STEP 4 Enter the journal page number from which each transaction is posted in the Posting Reference column. **In the journal:** STEP 5 Enter a slash (/) followed by a check mark (✓) in the Posting Reference column of the journal for each transaction that is posted.
LO4 Prepare a schedule of accounts receivable.	The schedule of accounts receivable is used to verify that the sum of the accounts receivable ledger balances equals the Accounts Receivable balance.

DEMONSTRATION PROBLEM

Karen Hunt operates Hunt's Audio-Video Store. The books include a general journal, general ledger, and accounts receivable ledger. The following transactions related to sales on account and cash receipts occurred during April 20--:

Apr. 3   Sold merchandise on account to Susan Haberman, $159.50 plus tax of $11.17. Sale No. 41.

4   Sold merchandise on account to Goro Kimura, $299.95 plus tax of $21.00. Sale No. 42.

6   Received payment from Tera Scherrer on account, $69.50.

7   Issued Credit Memo No. 48 to Kenneth Watt for merchandise returned that had been sold on account, $42.75 including tax of $2.80.

10   Received payment from Kellie Cokley on account, $99.95.

11   Sold merchandise on account to Victor Cardona, $499.95 plus tax of $35.00. Sale No. 43.

14   Received payment from Kenneth Watt in full settlement of account, $157.00.

17   Sold merchandise on account to Susan Haberman, $379.95 plus tax of $26.60. Sale No. 44.

(continued)

Apr. 19 Sold merchandise on account to Tera Scherrer, $59.95 plus tax of $4.20. Sale No. 45.

21 Issued Credit Memo No. 49 to Goro Kimura for merchandise returned that had been sold on account, $53.45 including tax of $3.50.

24 Received payment from Victor Cardona on account, $299.95.

25 Sold merchandise on account to Kellie Cokley, $179.50 plus tax of $12.57. Sale No. 46.

26 Received payment from Susan Haberman on account, $250.65.

28 Sold merchandise on account to Kenneth Watt, $49.95 plus tax of $3.50. Sale No. 47.

30 Bank credit card sales for the month were $1,220.00 plus tax of $85.40. Bank credit card expense on these sales was $65.27.

30 Cash sales for the month were $2,000.00 plus tax of $140.00.

Hunt had the following general ledger account balances as of April 1:

Account Title	Account No.	General Ledger Balance on April 1
Cash	101	$5,000.00
Accounts Receivable	122	1,208.63
Sales Tax Payable	231	72.52
Sales	401	8,421.49
Sales Returns and Allowances	401.1	168.43
Bank Credit Card Expense	513	215.00

Hunt also had the following accounts receivable ledger account balances as of April 1:

Customer	Accounts Receivable Balance
Victor Cardona 6300 Washington Blvd. St. Louis, MO 63130-9523	$299.95
Kellie Cokley 4220 Kingsbury Blvd. St. Louis, MO 63130-1645	$99.95
Susan Haberman 9421 Garden Ct. Kirkwood, MO 63122-1878	$79.98
Goro Kimura 6612 Arundel Pl. Clayton, MO 63150-9266	$379.50
Tera Scherrer 315 W. Linden St. Webster Groves, MO 63119-9881	$149.50
Kenneth Watt 11742 Fawnridge Dr. St. Louis, MO 63131-1726	$199.75

REQUIRED

1. Open general ledger accounts and three-column accounts receivable ledger accounts for Hunt's Audio-Video Store as of April 1, 20--. Enter the April 1 balance in each of the accounts.

2. Enter each transaction in a general journal (page 7).

3. Post directly from the journal to the proper customers' accounts in the accounts receivable ledger. Each subsidiary ledger account should show the initial "J," followed by the appropriate journal page number as a posting reference for each transaction.

4. Post from the journal to the proper general ledger accounts. Each general ledger account should show the initial "J," followed by the appropriate journal page number as a posting reference for each transaction.

5. Prove the balance of the summary accounts receivable account by preparing a schedule of accounts receivable as of April 30, based on the accounts receivable ledger.

Solution 1. and 3.

ACCOUNTS RECEIVABLE LEDGER

NAME: Victor Cardona

DATE		ITEM	POST. REF.	DEBIT	CREDIT	BALANCE
20-- Apr.	1	Balance	✓			2 9 9 95
	11		J7	5 3 4 95		8 3 4 90
	24		J8		2 9 9 95	5 3 4 95

NAME: Kellie Cokley

DATE		ITEM	POST. REF.	DEBIT	CREDIT	BALANCE
20-- Apr.	1	Balance	✓			9 9 95
	10		J7		9 9 95	
	25		J8	1 9 2 07		1 9 2 07

NAME: Susan Haberman

DATE		ITEM	POST. REF.	DEBIT	CREDIT	BALANCE
20-- Apr.	1	Balance	✓			7 9 98
	3		J7	1 7 0 67		2 5 0 65
	17		J7	4 0 6 55		6 5 7 20
	26		J8		2 5 0 65	4 0 6 55

NAME: Goro Kimura

DATE		ITEM	POST. REF.	DEBIT	CREDIT	BALANCE
20-- Apr.	1	Balance	✓			3 7 9 50
	4		J7	3 2 0 95		7 0 0 45
	21		J8		5 3 45	6 4 7 00

(continued)

NAME: Tera Scherrer

DATE		ITEM	POST. REF.	DEBIT	CREDIT	BALANCE
20-- Apr.	1	Balance	✓			1 4 9 50
	6		J7		6 9 50	8 0 00
	19		J8	6 4 15		1 4 4 15

NAME: Kenneth Watt

DATE		ITEM	POST. REF.	DEBIT	CREDIT	BALANCE
20-- Apr.	1	Balance	✓			1 9 9 75
	7		J7		4 2 75	1 5 7 00
	14		J7		1 5 7 00	—
	28		J8	5 3 45		5 3 45

2., 3., and 4.

GENERAL JOURNAL PAGE 7

	DATE		DESCRIPTION	POST. REF.	DEBIT	CREDIT	
1	20-- Apr.	3	Accounts Receivable/Susan Haberman	122/✓	1 7 0 67		1
2			Sales	401		1 5 9 50	2
3			Sales Tax Payable	231		1 1 17	3
4			Sale No. 41				4
5							5
6		4	Accounts Receivable/Goro Kimura	122/✓	3 2 0 95		6
7			Sales	401		2 9 9 95	7
8			Sales Tax Payable	231		2 1 00	8
9			Sale No. 42				9
10							10
11		6	Cash	101	6 9 50		11
12			Accounts Receivable/Tera Scherrer	122/✓		6 9 50	12
13			Received cash on account				13
14							14
15		7	Sales Returns and Allowances	401.1	3 9 95		15
16			Sales Tax Payable	231	2 80		16
17			Accounts Receivable/Kenneth Watt	122/✓		4 2 75	17
18			Returned merchandise				18
19							19
20		10	Cash	101	9 9 95		20
21			Accounts Receivable/Kellie Cokley	122/✓		9 9 95	21
22			Received cash on account				22
23							23
24		11	Accounts Receivable/Victor Cardona	122/✓	5 3 4 95		24
25			Sales	401		4 9 9 95	25
26			Sales Tax Payable	231		3 5 00	26
27			Sale No. 43				27
28							28
29		14	Cash	101	1 5 7 00		29
30			Accounts Receivable/Kenneth Watt	122/✓		1 5 7 00	30
31			Received cash on account				31
32							32
33		17	Accounts Receivable/Susan Haberman	122/✓	4 0 6 55		33
34			Sales	401		3 7 9 95	34
35			Sales Tax Payable	231		2 6 60	35
36			Sale No. 44				36

2., 3., and 4.

	DATE		DESCRIPTION	POST. REF.	DEBIT				CREDIT				
			GENERAL JOURNAL									PAGE 8	
1	20-- Apr.	19	Accounts Receivable/Tera Scherrer	122/✓		6	4	15					1
2			Sales	401						5	9	95	2
3			Sales Tax Payable	231							4	20	3
4			Sale No. 45										4
5													5
6		21	Sales Returns and Allowances	401.1		4	9	95					6
7			Sales Tax Payable	231		3	50						7
8			Accounts Receivable/Goro Kimura	122/✓						5	3	45	8
9			Returned merchandise—Credit Memo #49										9
10													10
11		24	Cash	101	2	9	9	95					11
12			Accounts Receivable/Victor Cardona	122/✓					2	9	9	95	12
13			Received cash on account										13
14													14
15		25	Accounts Receivable/Kellie Cokley	122/✓	1	9	2	07					15
16			Sales	401					1	7	9	50	16
17			Sales Tax Payable	231						1	2	57	17
18			Sale No. 46										18
19													19
20		26	Cash	101	2	5	0	65					20
21			Accounts Receivable/Susan Haberman	122/✓					2	5	0	65	21
22			Received cash on account										22
23													23
24		28	Accounts Receivable/Kenneth Watt	122/✓		5	3	45					24
25			Sales	401						4	9	95	25
26			Sales Tax Payable	231							3	50	26
27			Sale No. 47										27
28													28
29		30	Cash	101	1	2	4	0	13				29
30			Bank Credit Card Expense	513		6	5	27					30
31			Sales	401					1	2	2	0	00	31
32			Sales Tax Payable	231						8	5	40	32
33			Credit card sales										33
34													34
35		30	Cash	101	2	1	4	0	00				35
36			Sales	401					2	0	0	0	00	36
37			Sales Tax Payable	231						1	4	0	00	37
38			Made cash sales										38

1. and 4.

GENERAL LEDGER (PARTIAL)

ACCOUNT: Cash   ACCOUNT NO. 101

DATE		ITEM	POST. REF.	DEBIT				CREDIT				BALANCE							
												DEBIT					CREDIT		
20-- Apr.	1	Balance	✓									5	0	0	0	00			
	6		J7		6	9	50					5	0	6	9	50			
	10		J7		9	9	95					5	1	6	9	45			
	14		J7	1	5	7	00					5	3	2	6	45			
	24		J8	2	9	9	95					5	6	2	6	40			
	26		J8	2	5	0	65					5	8	7	7	05			
	30		J8	1	2	4	0	13				7	1	1	7	18			
	30		J8	2	1	4	0	00				9	2	5	7	18			

(continued)

1. and 4.

ACCOUNT: Accounts Receivable ACCOUNT NO. 122

DATE		ITEM	POST. REF.	DEBIT	CREDIT	BALANCE DEBIT	BALANCE CREDIT
20-- Apr.	1	Balance	✓			1 2 0 8 63	
	3		J7	1 7 0 67		1 3 7 9 30	
	4		J7	3 2 0 95		1 7 0 0 25	
	6		J7		6 9 50	1 6 3 0 75	
	7		J7		4 2 75	1 5 8 8 00	
	10		J7		9 9 95	1 4 8 8 05	
	11		J7	5 3 4 95		2 0 2 3 00	
	14		J7		1 5 7 00	1 8 6 6 00	
	17		J7	4 0 6 55		2 2 7 2 55	
	19		J8	6 4 15		2 3 3 6 70	
	21		J8		5 3 45	2 2 8 3 25	
	24		J8		2 9 9 95	1 9 8 3 30	
	25		J8	1 9 2 07		2 1 7 5 37	
	26		J8		2 5 0 65	1 9 2 4 72	
	28		J8	5 3 45		1 9 7 8 17	

ACCOUNT: Sales Tax Payable ACCOUNT NO. 231

DATE		ITEM	POST. REF.	DEBIT	CREDIT	BALANCE DEBIT	BALANCE CREDIT
20-- Apr.	1	Balance	✓				7 2 52
	3		J7		1 1 17		8 3 69
	4		J7		2 1 00		1 0 4 69
	7		J7	2 80			1 0 1 89
	11		J7		3 5 00		1 3 6 89
	17		J7		2 6 60		1 6 3 49
	19		J8		4 20		1 6 7 69
	21		J8	3 50			1 6 4 19
	25		J8		1 2 57		1 7 6 76
	28		J8		3 50		1 8 0 26
	30		J8		8 5 40		2 6 5 66
	30		J8		1 4 0 00		4 0 5 66

ACCOUNT: Sales ACCOUNT NO. 401

DATE		ITEM	POST. REF.	DEBIT	CREDIT	BALANCE DEBIT	BALANCE CREDIT
20-- Apr.	1	Balance	✓				8 4 2 1 49
	3		J7		1 5 9 50		8 5 8 0 99
	4		J7		2 9 9 95		8 8 8 0 94
	11		J7		4 9 9 95		9 3 8 0 89
	17		J7		3 7 9 95		9 7 6 0 84
	19		J8		5 9 95		9 8 2 0 79
	25		J8		1 7 9 50		10 0 0 0 29
	28		J8		4 9 95		10 0 5 0 24
	30		J8		1 2 2 0 00		11 2 7 0 24
	30		J8		2 0 0 0 00		13 2 7 0 24

1. and 4.

ACCOUNT: Sales Returns and Allowances													ACCOUNT NO. 401.1			
DATE	ITEM	POST. REF.	DEBIT			CREDIT			BALANCE							
									DEBIT				CREDIT			
20-- Apr. 1	Balance	✓							1	6	8	43				
7		J7	3	9	95				2	0	8	38				
21		J8	4	9	95				2	5	8	33				

ACCOUNT: Bank Credit Card Expense													ACCOUNT NO. 513			
DATE	ITEM	POST. REF.	DEBIT			CREDIT			BALANCE							
									DEBIT				CREDIT			
20-- Apr. 1	Balance	✓							2	1	5	00				
30		J8	6	5	27				2	8	0	27				

5.

Hunt's Audio-Video Store Schedule of Accounts Receivable April 30, 20--					
Victor Cardona		5	3	4	95
Kellie Cokley		1	9	2	07
Susan Haberman		4	0	6	55
Goro Kimura		6	4	7	00
Tera Scherrer		1	4	4	15
Kenneth Watt			5	3	45
Total	1	9	7	8	17

KEY TERMS

accounts receivable ledger (363)   A separate ledger containing an individual account receivable for each customer, kept in either alphabetical or numerical order.

cash discounts (360)   Discounts to encourage prompt payment by customers who buy merchandise on account.

contra-revenue account (359)   An account with a debit balance that is deducted from the related revenue account.

controlling account (363)   A summary account maintained in the general ledger with a subsidiary ledger (for example, the accounts receivable ledger).

credit memo (356)   A document issued when credit is given for merchandise returned or for an allowance.

merchandising business (354)   A business that purchases merchandise such as clothing, furniture, or computers, and sells that merchandise to its customers.

sale (354)   A transfer of merchandise from one business or individual to another in exchange for cash or a promise to pay cash.

sales allowances (356)   Reductions in the price of merchandise granted by the seller because of defects or other problems with the merchandise.

sales discounts (360)   To the seller, cash discounts are considered sales discounts.

sales invoice (355)   A document that is generated to bill the customer to whom the sale was made.

sales return (356)   Merchandise returned by a customer for a refund.

sales ticket (355)   A document created as evidence of a sale in a retail business.

schedule of accounts receivable (370)   An alphabetical or numerical listing of customer accounts and balances, usually prepared at the end of the month.

subsidiary ledger (363)   A separate ledger made up of individual accounts that contain the detail for a controlling account.

SELF-STUDY QUESTIONS AND EXERCISES

True/False Questions

1. LO1   Reductions in the price of merchandise granted by the seller because of defects or other problems with the merchandise are called sales allowances.

2. LO2   All sales, for cash or on credit, can be recorded in the general journal.

3. LO2   Sales Tax Payable is a liability account that is credited for the amount of tax imposed on sales.

4. LO2   Sales Returns and Allowances is debited for the amount of the sale, including the sales tax on that amount.

5. LO2   Cash discounts are offered to encourage prompt payment by customers who buy on account.

Multiple Choice Questions

1. LO2   A credit sale of $250 plus a 6% sales tax would require a debit to Accounts Receivable of

    (a) $15.   (c) $30.
    (b) $280.   (d) $265.

2. LO2   When $25 of merchandise is returned for a credit on account, what is the amount of the credit to Accounts Receivable, assuming a 6% sales tax rate?

    (a) $1.50   (c) $26.50
    (b) $25.00 (d) $31.00

3. LO3   When $300, plus sales tax of 6%, is received for an amount previously owed, Cash is debited for what amount?

    (a) $18   (c) $300
    (b) $318   (d) $282

4. LO3   When credit sales are $325 plus sales tax of 5%, and there is a bank credit card fee of 3%, what is the debit to Bank Credit Card Expense?

    (a) $16.25 (c) $341.25
    (b) $10.24 (d) $331.01

5. LO3   Cash receipts should

    (a) be posted to customer accounts daily.
    (b) be posted to customer accounts weekly.
    (c) be posted to customer accounts at the end of the month.
    (d) not be posted.

U REVU   **Exercises**

1. **LO1**   The sales transaction process for a wholesale business is shown below.

| INPUT | PROCESSING | OUTPUT |

Customer Purchase Order

Complete the illustration by providing the missing information in the blank symbols.

2. **LO2**   Prepare journal entries for the following sales and cash receipts transactions.

  (a)   Merchandise is sold on account for $300 plus 3% sales tax, with 2/10, n/30 cash discount terms.
  (b)   Part of the merchandise sold in transaction (a) for $70 plus sales tax is returned for credit.
  (c)   The balance on account for the merchandise sold in transaction (a) is paid in cash within the discount period.

3. **LO3**   The following journal entries are for current sales and cash receipts transactions. Using T accounts, post these transactions to Cash, Accounts Receivable, Sales, Sales Returns and Allowances, and Sales Tax Payable in the general ledger, and to the customer account in the accounts receivable ledger.

(a)	Accounts Receivable/M. Schapiro	2 8 8 40	
	Sales		2 8 0 00
	Sales Tax Payable		8 40
	Made sale on account		

(b)	Sales Returns and Allowances	6 0 00	
	Sales Tax Payable	1 80	
	Accounts Receivable/M. Shapiro		6 1 80
	Returned merchandise		

(c)	Cash	2 2 6 60	
	Accounts Receivable/M. Shapiro		2 2 6 60
	Received on account		

4. **LO4**   On March 24, MS Company's Accounts Receivable consisted of the following customer balances:

S. Burton	$310
A. Tangier	240
J. Holmes	504
F. Fullman	110
P. Molty	90

During the following week, MS made a sale of $104 to Molty and collected cash on account of $207 from Burton and $360 from Holmes. Prepare a schedule of accounts receivable for MS at March 31, 20--.

The answers to the Self-Study Questions and Exercises are at the end of the chapter (pages 395–396).

REVIEW QUESTIONS

LO1 1. Identify the sales documents commonly used in retail and wholesale businesses.

LO1 2. What is the purpose of a credit memo?

LO2 3. Describe how each of the following accounts is used: (1) Sales, (2) Sales Tax Payable, (3) Sales Returns and Allowances, and (4) Sales Discounts.

LO3 4. What steps are followed in posting sales from the general journal to the general ledger?

LO3 5. What steps are followed in posting sales from the general journal to the accounts receivable ledger?

LO3 6. What steps are followed in posting sales returns and allowances from the general journal to the general ledger and accounts receivable ledger?

LO3 7. What steps are followed in posting cash receipts from the general journal to the general ledger?

LO3 8. What steps are followed in posting cash receipts from the general journal to the accounts receivable ledger?

LO4 9. If the total of the schedule of accounts receivable does not agree with the Accounts Receivable balance, what procedures should be used to search for the error?

SERIES A EXERCISES

E 10-1A (LO1)

SALES DOCUMENTS For each document or procedure listed below, indicate whether it would be used for a retail business or a wholesale business, as described in the chapter.

1. sales ticket
2. sales invoice
3. credit approval
4. cash register tape summary
5. credit memo
6. customer purchase order

E 10-2A (LO2)

✓ 3(d):

Sales Ret. & Allow.   35

   Accts. Rec.   35

SALES TRANSACTIONS AND T ACCOUNTS Using T accounts for Cash, Accounts Receivable, Sales Tax Payable, Sales, Sales Returns and Allowances, and Sales Discounts, enter the following sales transactions. Use a new set of accounts for each part, 1–5.

1. No sales tax.

  (a) Merchandise is sold for $300 cash.
  (b) Merchandise is sold on account for $285.
  (c) Payment is received for merchandise sold on account.

2. 5% sales tax.

  (a) Merchandise is sold for $300 cash plus sales tax.
  (b) Merchandise is sold on account for $285 plus sales tax.
  (c) Payment is received for merchandise sold on account.

3. Cash and credit sales, with returned merchandise.

    (a) Merchandise is sold for $325 cash.
    (b) $25 of merchandise sold for $325 is returned for refund.
    (c) Merchandise is sold on account for $350.
    (d) $35 of merchandise sold for $350 is returned for a credit.
    (e) Payment is received for balance owed on merchandise sold on account.

4. 5% sales tax, with returned merchandise.

    (a) Merchandise is sold on account for $400 plus sales tax.
    (b) Merchandise sold on account for $40 plus sales tax is returned for a credit.
    (c) Balance on account is paid in cash.
    (d) Merchandise is sold for $280 cash plus sales tax.
    (e) $20 of merchandise sold for $280 cash plus sales tax is returned for a refund.

5. Sales on account, with 2/10, n/30 cash discount terms.

    (a) Merchandise is sold on account for $350.
    (b) The balance is paid within the discount period.
    (c) Merchandise is sold on account for $290.
    (d) The balance is paid after the discount period.

E 10-3A (LO2)

✓ Net sales: $3,079

COMPUTING NET SALES Based on the following information, compute net sales.

Gross sales	$3,580
Sales returns and allowances	428
Sales discounts	73

E 10-4A (LO2)

✓ Aug 20:

Cash	135.20
Accts Rec/B.Feikert	135.20

JOURNALIZING SALES, SALES RETURNS AND ALLOWANCES, AND CASH RECEIPTS Prepare journal entries for the following transactions.

Aug. 4   Sold merchandise on account to F. Graves for $340 plus sales tax of 4%, with 2/10, n/30 cash discount terms.

6   Sold merchandise on account to B. Feikert for $180 plus sales tax of 4%.

10   F. Graves returned merchandise purchased on August 4 for $30 plus sales tax for credit.

13   F. Graves paid the balance due on her account.

15   B. Feikert returned merchandise purchased on August 6 for $50 plus sales tax for credit.

20   B. Feikert paid the balance due on his account.

E 10-5A (LO3)

✓ May 1:

A/R–J. Adams	2,120
Sales	2,000
Sales Tax Payable	120

JOURNALIZING SALES TRANSACTIONS Enter the following transactions in a general journal. Use a 6% sales tax rate.

May 1   Sold merchandise on account to J. Adams, $2,000 plus sales tax. Sale No. 488.

4   Sold merchandise on account to B. Clark, $1,800 plus sales tax. Sale No. 489.

8   Sold merchandise on account to A. Duck, $1,500 plus sales tax. Sale No. 490.

11   Sold merchandise on account to E. Hill, $1,950 plus sales tax. Sale No. 491.

E 10-6A (LO3)

✓ Ending Accts. Rec.
balance: $4,059

JOURNALIZING SALES RETURNS AND ALLOWANCES Enter the following transactions in a general journal and post them to the appropriate general ledger and accounts receivable ledger accounts. Use account numbers as shown in the chapter. Beginning balance in Accounts Receivable is $4,200. Beginning balances in selected customer accounts are Abramowitz, $850; Gruder, $428; and Perez, $1,018.

June 1　John B. Abramowitz returned merchandise previously purchased on account (Sale No. 329), $73.

　　　6　Marie L. Perez returned merchandise previously purchased on account (Sale No. 321), $44.

　　　8　L. B. Gruder returned merchandise previously purchased on account (Sale No. 299), $24.

E 10-7A (LO3)

✓ July 6:

Cash　　　　　643
　A/R–J. Adler　　643

JOURNALIZING CASH RECEIPTS Enter the following transactions in a general journal:

July 6　James Adler made payment on account, $643.

　　10　Cash sales for the week were $2,320.

　　14　Betty Havel made payment on account, $430.

　　15　J. L. Borg made payment on account, $117.

　　17　Cash sales for the week were $2,237.

E 10-8A (LO4)

✓ Accts. Rec. balance: $4,586

SCHEDULE OF ACCOUNTS RECEIVABLE From the accounts receivable ledger shown, prepare a schedule of accounts receivable for Pheng Co. as of August 31, 20--.

ACCOUNTS RECEIVABLE LEDGER

| NAME | B & G Distributors |
| ADDRESS | 2628 Burlington Avenue, Chicago, IL 60604-1329 |

DATE		ITEM	POST. REF.	DEBIT	CREDIT	BALANCE
20-- Aug.	3		J1	1 3 8 0 00		1 3 8 0 00
	8		J1		1 4 0 00	1 2 4 0 00

| NAME | M. Chang |
| ADDRESS | 1422 SW Pacific, Chicago, IL 60603-8596 |

DATE		ITEM	POST. REF.	DEBIT	CREDIT	BALANCE
20-- Aug.	5		J1	2 1 3 6 00		2 1 3 6 00
	11		J2		2 1 3 6 00	

| NAME | B. J. Hinschliff & Co. |
| ADDRESS | 133 College Blvd., Des Plaines, IL 60611-4431 |

DATE		ITEM	POST. REF.	DEBIT	CREDIT	BALANCE
20-- Aug.	15		J2	1 1 0 6 00		1 1 0 6 00
	21		J3	3 8 4 00		1 4 9 0 00

NAME	Sally M. Pitts																
ADDRESS	213 East 29th Place, Chicago, IL 60601-6287																
DATE		ITEM		POST. REF.		DEBIT					CREDIT				BALANCE		
20-- Aug.	21			J3		8	3	8	00						8	3	8	00

NAME	Trendsetters, Inc.																
ADDRESS	29 Industrial Way, Chicago, IL 60600-5918																
DATE		ITEM		POST. REF.		DEBIT					CREDIT				BALANCE		
20-- Aug.	28			J4	1	0	1	8	00					1	0	1	8	00

SERIES A PROBLEMS

P 10-9A (LO3)

✓ Accts. Rec. balance: $16,345.20

SALES TRANSACTIONS J. K. Bijan owns a retail business and made the following sales on account during the month of August 20--. There is a 6% sales tax on all sales.

Aug. 1   Sale No. 213 to Jung Manufacturing Co., $1,200 plus sales tax.

3   Sale No. 214 to Hassad Co., $3,600 plus sales tax.

7   Sale No. 215 to Helsinki, Inc., $1,400 plus sales tax. (Open a new account for this customer. Address is 125 Fishers Dr., Noblesville, IN 47870-8867.)

11   Sale No. 216 to Ardis Myler, $1,280 plus sales tax.

18   Sale No. 217 to Hassad Co., $4,330 plus sales tax.

22   Sale No. 218 to Jung Manufacturing Co., $2,000 plus sales tax.

30   Sale No. 219 to Ardis Myler, $1,610 plus sales tax.

REQUIRED

1.   Record the transactions in a general journal.

2.   Post from the journal to the general ledger and accounts receivable ledger accounts. Use account numbers as shown in the chapter.

P 10-10A (LO3)

✓ Accts. Rec. balance: $3,533.08

CASH RECEIPTS TRANSACTIONS Zebra Imaginarium, a retail business, had the following cash receipts during December 20--. The sales tax is 6%.

Dec. 1   Received payment on account from Michael Anderson, $1,360.

2   Received payment on account from Ansel Manufacturing, $382.

7   Cash sales for the week were $3,160 plus tax. Bank credit card sales for the week were $1,000 plus tax. Bank credit card fee is 3%.

8   Received payment on account from J. Gorbea, $880.

11   Michael Anderson returned merchandise for a credit, $60 plus tax.

14   Cash sales for the week were $2,800 plus tax. Bank credit card sales for the week were $800 plus tax. Bank credit card fee is 3%.

(continued)

Dec. 20 Received payment on account from Tom Wilson, $1,110.

21 Ansel Manufacturing returned merchandise for a credit, $22 plus tax.

21 Cash sales for the week were $3,200 plus tax.

24 Received payment on account from Rachel Carson, $2,000.

Beginning general ledger account balances were:

Cash	$9,862
Accounts Receivable	9,352

Beginning customer account balances were:

M. Anderson	$2,480
Ansel Manufacturing	982
J. Gorbea	880
R. Carson	3,200
T. Wilson	1,810

REQUIRED

1. Record the transactions in a general journal.

2. Post from the journal to the general ledger and accounts receivable ledger accounts. Use account numbers as shown in the chapter.

P 10-11A (LO3)

✓ Accts. Rec. balance: $8,133.33

SALES AND CASH RECEIPTS TRANSACTIONS Owens Distributors is a retail business. The following sales, returns, and cash receipts occurred during March 20--. There is an 8% sales tax. Beginning general ledger account balances were Cash, $9,741.00; and Accounts Receivable, $1,058.25. Beginning customer account balances included Thompson Group, $1,058.25.

Mar. 1 Sale on account No. 33C to Able & Co., $1,800 plus sales tax.

3 Sale on account No. 33D to R. J. Kalas, Inc., $2,240 plus sales tax.

5 Able & Co. returned merchandise from Sale No. 33C for a credit (Credit Memo No. 66), $30 plus sales tax.

7 Cash sales for the week were $3,160 plus sales tax.

10 Received payment from Able & Co. for Sale No. 33C less Credit Memo No. 66.

11 Sale on account No. 33E to Blevins Bakery, $1,210 plus sales tax.

13 Received payment from R. J. Kalas for Sale No. 33D.

14 Cash sales for the week were $4,200 plus sales tax.

16 Blevins Bakery returned merchandise from Sale No. 33E for a credit (Credit Memo No. 67), $44 plus sales tax.

18 Sale on account No. 33F to R. J. Kalas, Inc., $2,620 plus sales tax.

20 Received payment from Blevins Bakery for Sale No. 33E less Credit Memo No. 67.

21 Cash sales for the week were $2,400 plus sales tax.

25 Sale on account No. 33G to Blevins Bakery, $1,915 plus sales tax.

27 Sale on account No. 33H to Thompson Group, $2,016 plus sales tax.

28 Cash sales for the week were $3,500 plus sales tax.

REQUIRED

1. Record the transactions in a general journal.

2. Post from the journal to the general ledger and accounts receivable ledger accounts. Use account numbers as shown in the chapter.

P 10-12A (LO4)

✓ Accts. Rec. balance,
Thompson Group: $3,235.53

SCHEDULE OF ACCOUNTS RECEIVABLE Based on the information provided in Problem 10-11A, prepare a schedule of accounts receivable for Owens Distributors as of March 31, 20--. Verify that the accounts receivable account balance in the general ledger agrees with the schedule of accounts receivable total.

SERIES B EXERCISES

E 10-1B (LO1)

SALES DOCUMENTS Indicate whether each of the following documents or procedures is for a retail business or for a wholesale business, as described in the chapter.

1. A cash register receipt is given to the customer.

2. Credit approval is required since sales are almost always "on account."

3. Three copies of the sales invoice are prepared: one for shipping, one for the customer (as a bill), and one for accounting.

4. A sales ticket is given to a customer and another copy is sent to accounting.

5. The sales process begins with a customer purchase order.

6. The sales invoice itemizes what is sold, its cost, and the total amount owed.

E 10-2B (LO2)

✓ 3(d):
Sales Ret. & Allow.   24
  Accts. Rec.   24

SALES TRANSACTIONS AND T ACCOUNTS Using T accounts for Cash, Accounts Receivable, Sales Tax Payable, Sales, Sales Returns and Allowances, and Sales Discounts, enter the following sales transactions. Use a new set of accounts for each part, 1–5.

1. No sales tax.

   (a) Merchandise is sold for $250 cash.
   (b) Merchandise is sold on account for $225.
   (c) Payment is received for merchandise sold on account.

2. 6% sales tax.

   (a) Merchandise is sold for $250 cash plus sales tax.
   (b) Merchandise is sold on account for $225 plus sales tax.
   (c) Payment is received for merchandise sold on account.

3. Cash and credit sales, with returned merchandise.

   (a) Merchandise is sold for $481 cash.
   (b) $18 of merchandise sold for $481 is returned for a refund.
   (c) Merchandise is sold on account for $388.
   (d) $24 of merchandise sold for $388 is returned for a credit.
   (e) Payment is received for balance owed on merchandise sold on account.

(continued)

4.   6% sales tax, with returned merchandise.

   (a) Merchandise is sold on account for $480 plus sales tax.
   (b) Merchandise sold on account for $30 plus sales tax is returned.
   (c) The balance on the account is paid in cash.
   (d) Merchandise is sold for $300 cash plus sales tax.
   (e) $30 of merchandise sold for $300 cash plus sales tax is returned for a refund.

5.   Sales on account, with 2/10, n/30 cash discount terms.

   (a) Merchandise is sold on account for $280.
   (b) The balance is paid within the discount period.
   (c) Merchandise is sold on account for $203.
   (d) The balance is paid after the discount period.

E 10-3B (LO2)

✓ Net sales: $2,502

COMPUTING NET SALES Based on the following information, compute net sales:

Gross sales	$2,880
Sales returns and allowances	322
Sales discounts	56

E 10-4B (LO2)

✓ Oct. 20:

Cash	228.80	
Accts Rec/B. Farnsby		228.80

JOURNALIZING SALES, SALES RETURNS AND ALLOWANCES, AND CASH RECEIPTS Prepare journal entries for the following transactions.

Oct. 5   Sold merchandise on account to B. Farnsby for $280 plus sales tax of 4%.

8   Sold merchandise on account to F. Preetee for $240 plus sales tax of 4%, with 2/10, n/30 cash discount terms.

11   F. Preetee returned merchandise purchased on October 8 for $50 plus sales tax for credit.

17   F. Preetee paid the balance due on her account.

18   B. Farnsby returned merchandise purchased on October 5 for $60 plus sales tax for credit.

20   B. Farnsby paid the balance due on his account.

E 10-5B (LO3)

✓ Sept. 1:

A/R–K. Smith	1,890	
Sales		1800
Sales Tax Payable		90

JOURNALIZING SALES TRANSACTIONS Enter the following transactions in a general journal. Use a 5% sales tax rate.

Sept. 1   Sold merchandise on account to K. Smith, $1,800 plus sales tax. Sale No. 228.

3   Sold merchandise on account to J. Arnes, $3,100 plus sales tax. Sale No. 229.

5   Sold merchandise on account to M. Denison, $2,800 plus sales tax. Sale No. 230.

7   Sold merchandise on account to B. Marshall, $1,900 plus sales tax. Sale No. 231.

E 10-6B (LO3)

✓ Ending Accts. Rec. balance: $3,777

JOURNALIZING SALES RETURNS AND ALLOWANCES Enter the following transactions in a general journal and post them to the appropriate general ledger and accounts receivable ledger accounts. Use account numbers as shown in the chapter. Beginning balance in Accounts Receivable is $3,900. Beginning balances in selected customer accounts are Adams, $850; Greene, $428; and Phillips, $1,018.

June 1   Marie L. Phillips returned merchandise previously purchased on account (Sale No. 33), $43.

11   John B. Adams returned merchandise previously purchased on account (Sale No. 34), $59.

15   L. B. Greene returned merchandise previously purchased on account (Sale No. 35), $21.

E 10-7B (LO3)

✓ Nov. 1:

Cash	750	
A/R–J. Haghighat		750

JOURNALIZING CASH RECEIPTS Enter the following transactions in a general journal:

Nov. 1 Jean Haghighat made payment on account, $750.

12 Marc Antonoff made payment on account, $464.

15 Cash sales were $3,763.

18 Will Mossein made payment on account, $241.

25 Cash sales were $2,648.

E 10-8B (LO4)

✓ Accts. Rec. balance: $6,402

SCHEDULE OF ACCOUNTS RECEIVABLE From the accounts receivable ledger shown, prepare a schedule of accounts receivable for Gelph Co. as of November 30, 20--.

ACCOUNTS RECEIVABLE LEDGER

NAME James L. Adams Co.

ADDRESS 24481 McAdams Road, Dallas, TX 77001-3465

DATE		ITEM	POST. REF.	DEBIT	CREDIT	BALANCE
20-- Nov.	1		J1	3 1 8 0 00		3 1 8 0 00
	5		J1		1 8 0 00	3 0 0 0 00
	7		J2	2 0 0 00		3 2 0 0 00

NAME Trish Berens

ADDRESS 34 West 55th Avenue, Fort Worth, TX 76310-8182

DATE		ITEM	POST. REF.	DEBIT	CREDIT	BALANCE
20-- Nov.	3		J1	1 3 6 0 00		1 3 6 0 00

NAME M and T Jenkins, Inc.

ADDRESS 100 NW Richfield, Austin, TX 78481-3791

DATE		ITEM	POST. REF.	DEBIT	CREDIT	BALANCE
20-- Nov.	5		J1	2 6 2 8 00		2 6 2 8 00
	12		J2		2 6 2 8 00	—

NAME R & J Travis

ADDRESS 288 Beacon Street, Dallas, TX 79301-6642

DATE		ITEM	POST. REF.	DEBIT	CREDIT	BALANCE
20-- Nov.	22		J3	1 8 4 2 00		1 8 4 2 00

SERIES B PROBLEMS

P 10-9B (LO3)

✓ Accts. Rec. balance: $13,072.50

SALES TRANSACTIONS T. M. Maxwell owns a retail business and made the following sales on account during the month of July 20--. There is a 5% sales tax on all sales.

July 1 Sale No. 101 to Saga, Inc., $1,200 plus sales tax.

8 Sale No. 102 to Vinnie Ward, $2,100 plus sales tax.

15 Sale No. 103 to Dvorak Manufacturing, $4,300 plus sales tax.

21 Sale No. 104 to Vinnie Ward, $1,800 plus sales tax.

24 Sale No. 105 to Zapata Co., $1,600 plus sales tax. (Open a new account for this customer. Address is 789 N. Stafford Dr., Bloomington, IN 47401-6201.)

29 Sale No. 106 to Saga, Inc., $1,450 plus sales tax.

REQUIRED

1. Record the transactions in a general journal.

2. Post from the journal to the general ledger and accounts receivable ledger accounts. Use account numbers as shown in the chapter.

P 10-10B (LO3)

✓ Accts. Rec. balance: $2,744.45

CASH RECEIPTS TRANSACTIONS Color Florists, a retail business, had the following cash receipts during January 20--. The sales tax is 5%.

Jan. 1 Received payment on account from Ray Boyd, $880.

3 Received payment on account from Clint Hassell, $271.

5 Cash sales for the week were $2,800 plus tax. Bank credit card sales for the week were $1,200 plus tax. Bank credit card fee is 3%.

8 Received payment on account from Jan Sowada, $912.

11 Ray Boyd returned merchandise for a credit, $40 plus tax.

12 Cash sales for the week were $3,100 plus tax. Bank credit card sales for the week were $1,900 plus tax. Bank credit card fee is 3%.

15 Received payment on account from Robert Zehnle, $1,100.

18 Robert Zehnle returned merchandise for a credit, $31 plus tax.

19 Cash sales for the week were $2,230 plus tax.

25 Received payment on account from Dazai Manufacturing, $318.

Beginning general ledger account balances were:

Cash	$2,890.75
Accounts Receivable	6,300.00

Beginning customer account balances were:

R. Boyd	$1,400
Dazai Manufacturing	318
C. Hassell	815
J. Sowada	1,481
R. Zehnle	2,286

REQUIRED

1. Record the transactions in a general journal.

2. Post from the journal to the general ledger and accounts receivable ledger accounts. Use account numbers as shown in the chapter.

P 10-11B (LO3)

✓ Accts. Rec. balance: $6,104.25

SALES AND CASH RECEIPTS TRANSACTIONS Paul Jackson owns a retail business. The following sales, returns, and cash receipts are for April 20--. There is a 7% sales tax.

Apr. 1 Sale on account No. 111 to O. L. Meyers, $2,100 plus sales tax.

3 Sale on account No. 112 to Andrew Plaa, $1,000 plus sales tax.

6 O. L. Meyers returned merchandise from Sale No. 111 for a credit (Credit Memo No. 42), $50 plus sales tax.

7 Cash sales for the week were $3,240 plus sales tax.

9 Received payment from O. L. Meyers for Sale No. 111 less Credit Memo No. 42.

12 Sale on account No. 113 to Melissa Richfield, $980 plus sales tax.

14 Cash sales for the week were $2,180 plus sales tax.

17 Melissa Richfield returned merchandise from Sale No. 113 for a credit (Credit Memo No. 43), $40 plus sales tax.

19 Sale on account No. 114 to Kelsay Munkres, $1,020 plus sales tax.

21 Cash sales for the week were $2,600 plus sales tax.

24 Sale on account No. 115 to O. L. Meyers, $920 plus sales tax.

27 Sale on account No. 116 to Andrew Plaa, $1,320 plus sales tax.

28 Cash sales for the week were $2,800 plus sales tax.

29 Received payment from Melissa Richfield for $2,186.

Beginning general ledger account balances were:

Cash	$2,864.54
Accounts Receivable	2,726.25

Beginning customer account balances were:

K. Munkres	$ 482.00
M. Richfield	2,244.25

REQUIRED

1. Record the transactions in a general journal.

2. Post from the journal to the general ledger and accounts receivable ledger accounts. Use account numbers as shown in the chapter.

P 10-12B (LO4)

✓ Accts. Rec. balance, Melissa Richfield: $1,064.05

SCHEDULE OF ACCOUNTS RECEIVABLE Based on the information provided in Problem 10-11B, prepare a schedule of accounts receivable for Paul Jackson as of April 30, 20--. Verify that the accounts receivable account balance in the general ledger agrees with the schedule of accounts receivable total.

 MANAGING YOUR WRITING

You and your spouse have separate charge accounts at a local department store. When you tried to use your card last week, you were told that you were over your credit limit. This puzzled you because you had paid the entire account balance several weeks ago. When the monthly statements arrived yesterday, the error was clear. The store had credited your payment to your spouse's account.

(continued)

Your account was treated as over the limit, and the store charged you interest on the unpaid balance. You suspect that part of the problem is that you and your spouse use the same last name (Morales) and have similar first names (Carmen and Carmelo).

Write a letter to the store requesting correction of your accounts and suggesting a way to identify your accounts so that this error does not happen again.

ETHICS CASE

Wholesale Health Supply sells a variety of medical equipment and supplies to retailers. When a new retailer is approved for credit, one of the criteria is that the retailer must have been in business for at least six months. Good Earth Foods placed a large order with Wholesale Health Supply and requested credit terms. Wholesale Health Supply faxed a credit request form to Good Earth Foods, and the buyer at Good Earth Foods faxed the completed form back to Wholesale Health Supply. Robin Sylvester, the sales manager at Wholesale Health Supply, saw the credit application and noticed Good Earth Foods had only been in business for two months. Thinking she might lose the order if Good Earth Foods wasn't extended credit, Robin authorized the shipment. She figured by the time the credit department rejected the application, Good Earth Foods would have received the order and the vice president would override the rejection to keep a new customer. Robin was sure that everything would turn out alright.

1. Do you think Robin's decision to ship the order was unethical? Why or why not?

2. What would you have done if you were in Robin's position?

3. Write a memo from the credit department manager to Robin Sylvester explaining the reasoning behind requiring a new credit customer to be in business for at least six months.

4. In small groups, discuss ways to prevent a situation like this from happening.

MASTERY PROBLEM

✓ Accts. Rec. balance: $1,900.54

Geoff and Sandy Harland own and operate Wayward Kennel and Pet Supply. Their motto is, "If your pet is not becoming to you, he should be coming to us." The Harlands maintain a sales tax payable account throughout the month to account for the 6% sales tax. They use a general journal, general ledger, and accounts receivable ledger. The following sales and cash collections took place during the month of September:

Sept. 2   Sold a fish aquarium on account to Ken Shank, $125.00 plus tax of $7.50, terms n/30. Sale No. 101.

3   Sold dog food on account to Nancy Truelove, $68.25 plus tax of $4.10, terms n/30. Sale No. 102.

5   Sold a bird cage on account to Jean Warkentin, $43.95 plus tax of $2.64, terms n/30. Sale No. 103.

8   Cash sales for the week were $2,332.45 plus tax of $139.95.

10   Received cash for boarding and grooming services, $625.00 plus tax of $37.50.

11   Jean Warkentin stopped by the store to point out a minor defect in the bird cage purchased in Sale No. 103. The Harlands offered a sales allowance of $10.00 plus tax on the price of the cage which satisfied Warkentin.

Sept. 12   Sold a cockatoo on account to Tully Shaw, $1,200.00 plus tax of $72.00, terms n/30. Sale No. 104.

14   Received cash on account from Rosa Alanso, $256.00.

15   Rosa Alanso returned merchandise, $93.28 including tax of $5.28.

15   Cash sales for the week were $2,656.85 plus tax of $159.41.

16   Received cash on account from Nancy Truelove, $58.25.

18   Received cash for boarding and grooming services, $535.00 plus tax of $32.10.

19   Received cash on account from Ed Cochran, $63.25.

20   Sold pet supplies on account to Susan Hays, $83.33 plus tax of $5.00, terms n/30. Sale No. 105.

21   Sold three Labrador Retriever puppies to All American Day Camp, $375.00 plus tax of $22.50, terms n/30. Sale No. 106.

22   Cash sales for the week were $3,122.45 plus tax of $187.35.

23   Received cash for boarding and grooming services, $515.00 plus tax of $30.90.

25   Received cash on account from Ken Shank, $132.50.

26   Received cash on account from Nancy Truelove, $72.35.

27   Received cash on account from Joe Gloy, $273.25.

28   Borrowed cash to purchase a pet limousine, $11,000.00.

29   Cash sales for the week were $2,835.45 plus tax of $170.13.

30   Received cash for boarding and grooming services, $488.00 plus tax of $29.28.

Wayward had the following general ledger account balances as of September 1:

Account Title	Account No.	General Ledger Balance on Sept. 1
Cash	101	$23,500.25
Accounts Receivable	122	850.75
Notes Payable	201	2,500.00
Sales Tax Payable	231	909.90
Sales	401	13,050.48
Sales Returns and Allowances	401.1	86.00
Boarding and Grooming Revenue	402	2,115.00

Wayward also had the following accounts receivable ledger balances as of September 1:

Customer	Accounts Receivable Balance
Rosa Alanso 2541 East 2nd Street Bloomington, IN 47401-5356	$456.00
Ed Cochran 2669 Windcrest Drive Bloomington, IN 47401-5446	$63.25
Joe Gloy 1458 Parnell Avenue Muncie, IN 47304-2682	$273.25
Nancy Truelove 2300 E. National Road Cumberland, IN 46229-4824	$58.25

(continued)

New customers opening accounts during September were as follows:

All American Day Camp
3025 Old Mill Run
Bloomington, IN 47408-1080

Tully Shaw
3315 Longview Avenue
Bloomington, IN 47401-7223

Susan Hays
1424 Jackson Creek Road
Nashville, IN 47448-2245

Jean Warkentin
1813 Deep Well Court
Bloomington, IN 47401-5124

Ken Shank
6422 E. Bender Road
Bloomington, IN 47401-7756

REQUIRED

1. Enter the transactions for the month of September in a general journal. (Begin with page 7.)

2. Post the entries to the general and subsidiary ledgers. Open new accounts for any customers who did not have a balance as of September 1.

3. Prepare a schedule of accounts receivable.

4. Compute the net sales for the month of September.

CHALLENGE PROBLEM

This problem challenges you to apply your cumulative accounting knowledge to move a step beyond the material in the chapter.

✓ **June 14: Dr. Sales Discount , $12**

Enter the following transactions in a general journal:

June 4   Sold merchandise on account to T. Allen, $1,500.00 plus 6% sales tax, with 1/10, n/30 cash discount terms.

7   Sold merchandise on account to K. Bryant, $1,800.00 plus 6% sales tax, with 1/10, n/30 cash discount terms.

11   T. Allen returned merchandise totaling $300.00 from the June 4 sale, for credit.

14   T. Allen paid the balance due from the June 4 sale, less discount.

17   K. Bryant paid the balance due from the June 7 sale, less discount.

ANSWERS TO SELF-STUDY QUESTIONS AND EXERCISES

True/False Questions

1. T

2. T

3. T

4. F (the debit *excludes* the sales tax)

5. T

Multiple Choice Questions

1. d 2. c 3. b 4. b 5. a

U REVU   Exercises

1.

| INPUT | PROCESSING | OUTPUT |

Customer Purchase Order → Interpretation, Credit Approval, and Verification → Customer 1 Sales Invoice / Accounting 2 / Shipping 3

2.

(a)										
	Accounts Receivable			3	0	9	00			
	Sales							3	0 0	00
	Sales Tax Payable								9	00
	Made credit sale									

(b)										
	Sales Returns and Allowances			7	0	00				
	Sales Tax Payable				2	10				
	Accounts Receivable							7	2	10
	Returned merchandise									

(c)										
	Cash		2	3	2	30				
	Sales Discounts				4	60				
	Accounts Receivable							2	3 6	90
	Received cash on account									

3. **GENERAL LEDGER**

Cash

(c)	226.60		

Accounts Receivable

(a)	288.40	(b)	61.80
		(c)	226.60

Sales Tax Payable

(b)	1.80	(a)	8.40

Sales Returns and Allowances

(b)	60.00		

Sales

		(a)	280.00

Accounts Receivable Ledger
M. Schapiro

(a)	288.40	(b)	61.80
		(c)	226.60

4.   Schedule of Accounts Receivable
            March 31, 20--

S. Burton	$103
A. Tangier	240
J. Holmes	144
F. Fullman	110
P. Molty	194
Total	$791

## Chapter 11

CONSTRUCTION PHOTOGRAPHY/CORBIS

Accounting for Purchases and Cash Payments

In Chapter 10, we heard about Planet Shoes, the company whose eco-friendly shoes reflect a concern about the environment. Innovar Environmental is a different kind of company that addresses environmental issues in a totally different way. Innovar provides services to enable government and businesses to become green through construction and renovation. Its projects include lead paint, asbestos, and mold abatement; facilities demolition; site enhancements; green construction; natural disaster recovery; storage tank removal, and more.

Innovar was founded in 2000 and is based in Littleton, Colorado. It has benefited from the nationwide interest in going green, increasing its revenues in a recent four-year period by 400%, to $6.1 million. You might recall that one of Planet Shoes' biggest challenges was accounting for its high volume of sales activity. In contrast, Innovar has far fewer but larger sales transactions. Its challenge is accounting for the many purchases of items used in its major construction and renovation projects. In this chapter, you will learn how to account for purchases transactions, including various discounts, freight charges, and the return of items to the manufacturer.

LEARNING OBJECTIVES

Careful study of this chapter should enable you to:

LO1 Define merchandise purchases transactions.

LO2 Describe and use merchandise purchases accounts and compute gross profit.

LO3 Describe and use the accounts payable ledger.

LO4 Prepare a schedule of accounts payable.

Chapter 10 demonstrated how to account for sales in a merchandising business. This chapter continues the study of the merchandising business by examining how to account for merchandise purchases. We will learn how to use four new accounts and another subsidiary ledger.

MERCHANDISE PURCHASES TRANSACTIONS

LO1 Define merchandise purchases transactions.

In everyday language, purchases can refer to almost anything we have bought. For a merchandising business, however, **purchases** refers to merchandise acquired for resale. These are the goods a business buys for the sole purpose of selling them to its customers.

Purchasing procedures and documents vary, depending on the nature and size of a business. For example, in a small business, the owner or an employee might do the buying on a part-time basis. In a large business, there might be a separate purchasing department with a full-time manager and staff. In addition, the procedures and documents used can be affected by whether purchases are made on account or for cash.

The flowchart in Figure 11-1 shows some of the major documents used in the purchasing process of a merchandising business. In discussing the purchasing process, we will assume that the business makes purchases on account and has a purchasing department.

FIGURE 11-1 Purchasing Process Documents

Purchase Requisition → Purchase Order → Receiving Report → Purchase Invoice

In a computerized system, companies use electronic forms that are similar to the paper documents described in this chapter.

PURCHASE REQUISITION

A **purchase requisition** is a form used to request the purchase of merchandise or other property. Any authorized person or department can prepare this form and submit it to the purchasing department. Figure 11-2 shows a purchase requisition used by Northern Micro. One copy of this form is sent to the purchasing department, one goes to the accounting department, and one is kept by the department that prepared the requisition.

When purchase orders are submitted electronically, signals are sent to the vendor and the accounting and purchasing departments at the same time.

PURCHASE ORDER

The purchasing department reviews and approves the purchase requisition and prepares a purchase order. A **purchase order** is a written order to buy goods from a specific vendor (supplier). Figure 11-3 shows a purchase order prepared by Northern Micro based on the purchase requisition in Figure 11-2. One copy of the purchase order is sent to the vendor to order the goods, one goes to the accounting department, and one copy is kept in the purchasing department. Other copies may be sent to the department that prepared the purchase requisition and to the receiving area.

FIGURE 11-2 Purchase Requisition

FIGURE 11-3 Purchase Order

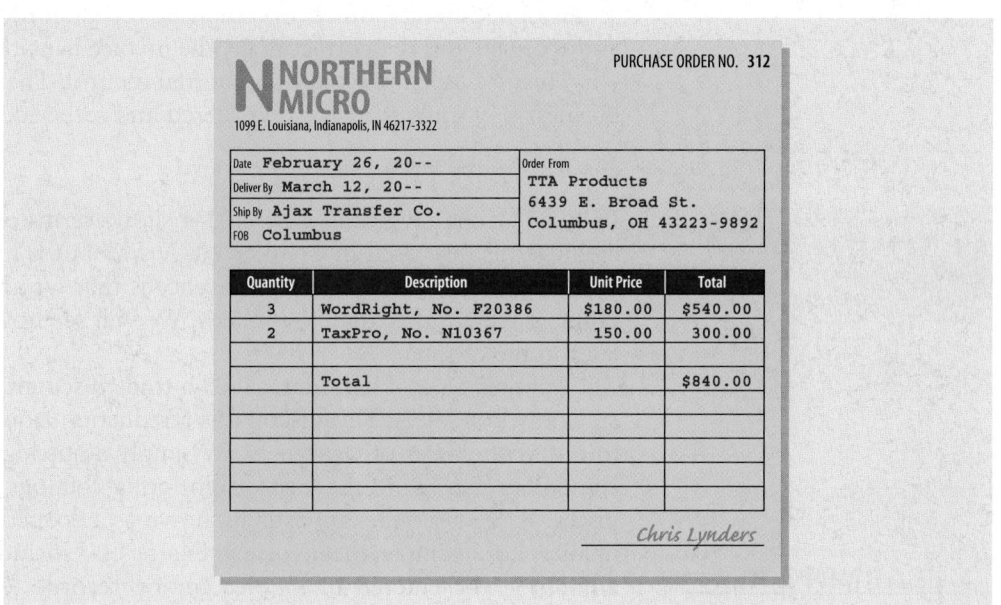

RECEIVING REPORT AND PURCHASE INVOICE

When the merchandise is received, a **receiving report** indicating what has been received is prepared. The receiving report can be a separate form, or one can be created from the vendor's purchase invoice. Figure 11-4 shows a vendor invoice on which a rubber stamp has been used to imprint a type of receiving report. The receiving clerk has indicated on the form the date and condition of the goods received.

An **invoice** is a document prepared by the seller as a bill for the merchandise shipped. To the seller, this is a sales invoice, as explained in Chapter 10. To the buyer, this is a **purchase invoice**. Figure 11-4 shows an invoice sent by TTA Products to Northern Micro for the goods ordered with the purchase order in Figure 11-3.

FIGURE 11-4 Purchase Invoice

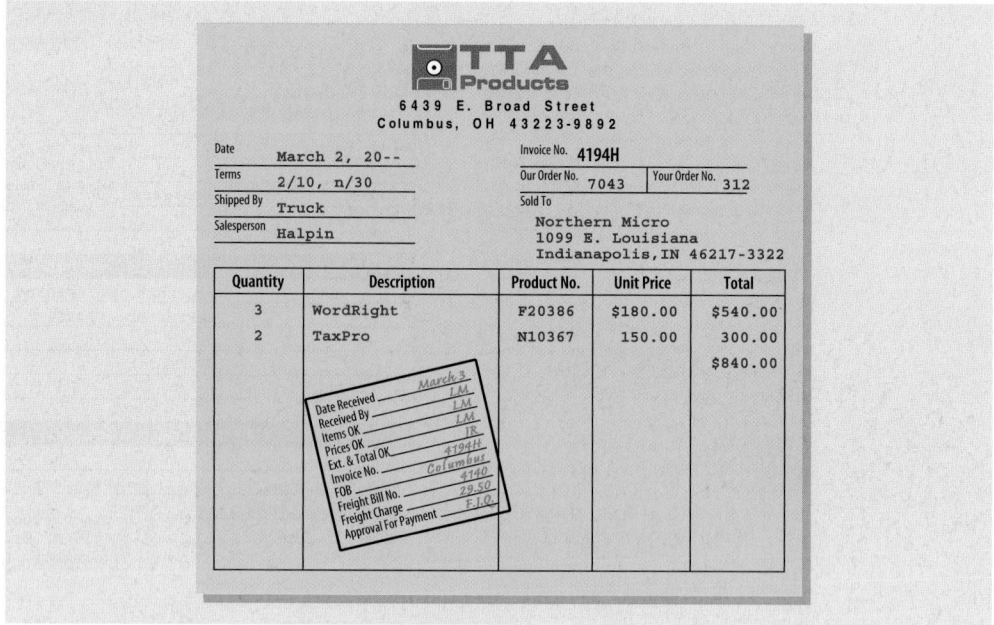

The accounting department compares the purchase invoice with the purchase requisition, purchase order, and receiving report. If the invoice is for the goods ordered and received and the correct price, the invoice is paid by the due date.

This is an example of good internal control. The procedure helps ensure that the business pays only for goods it ordered and received, and at the correct price.

CASH AND TRADE DISCOUNTS

Notice that the invoice in Figure 11-4 shows terms of 2/10, n/30. These are the same credit terms discussed in Chapter 10. A discount is available if the bill is paid within the discount period. The only difference is that we are now looking from the buyer's point of view rather than the seller's. We will see how to account for these discounts later in the chapter.

Another type of discount, called a **trade discount**, is often offered by manufacturers and wholesalers. This discount is a reduction from the list or catalog price offered to different classes of customers. By simply adjusting the trade discount percentages, companies can avoid the cost of reprinting catalogs every time there is a change in prices. Trade discounts are usually shown as a deduction from the total amount of the invoice. For example, the invoice in Figure 11-5 includes a trade discount of 10%. The amount to be entered in the accounting records for this invoice is $756, the net amount after deducting the trade discount of $84. Trade discounts represent a reduction in the price of the merchandise and should not be entered in the accounts of either the seller or the buyer.

We need to be careful in computing the cash discount when an invoice has both cash and trade discounts. The cash discount applies to the *net amount* after deducting the trade discount. For example, the cash discount and amount to be paid on the invoice in Figure 11-5 would be calculated as follows:

Gross amount	$840.00
Less 10% trade discount	84.00
Net amount	$756.00
Less 2% cash discount	15.12
Amount to be paid	$740.88

LEARNING KEY

Purchases and sales subject to trade discounts should be recorded in the accounting records at the *net amount* after deducting the trade discounts.

FIGURE 11-5 Purchase Invoice with Trade Discount

Complete U REVU-1 on **page 421** to test your basic understanding of LO1.

U REVU

MERCHANDISE PURCHASES ACCOUNTS

LO2 Describe and use merchandise purchases accounts and compute gross profit.

To account for merchandise purchases transactions, we will use four new accounts.

1. Purchases

2. Purchases Returns and Allowances

3. Purchases Discounts

4. Freight-In

The position of these accounts in the accounting equation and their normal balances are shown in Figure 11-6.

PURCHASES ACCOUNT

The purchases account is used to record the cost of merchandise purchased.

The approach to accounting for merchandise purchases shown in this chapter is known as the periodic method. Both the periodic and perpetual methods are covered in Chapter 13.

Purchases

Debit	Credit
to enter the cost of merchandise purchased	

FIGURE 11-6 Accounting for Merchandise Purchases Transactions

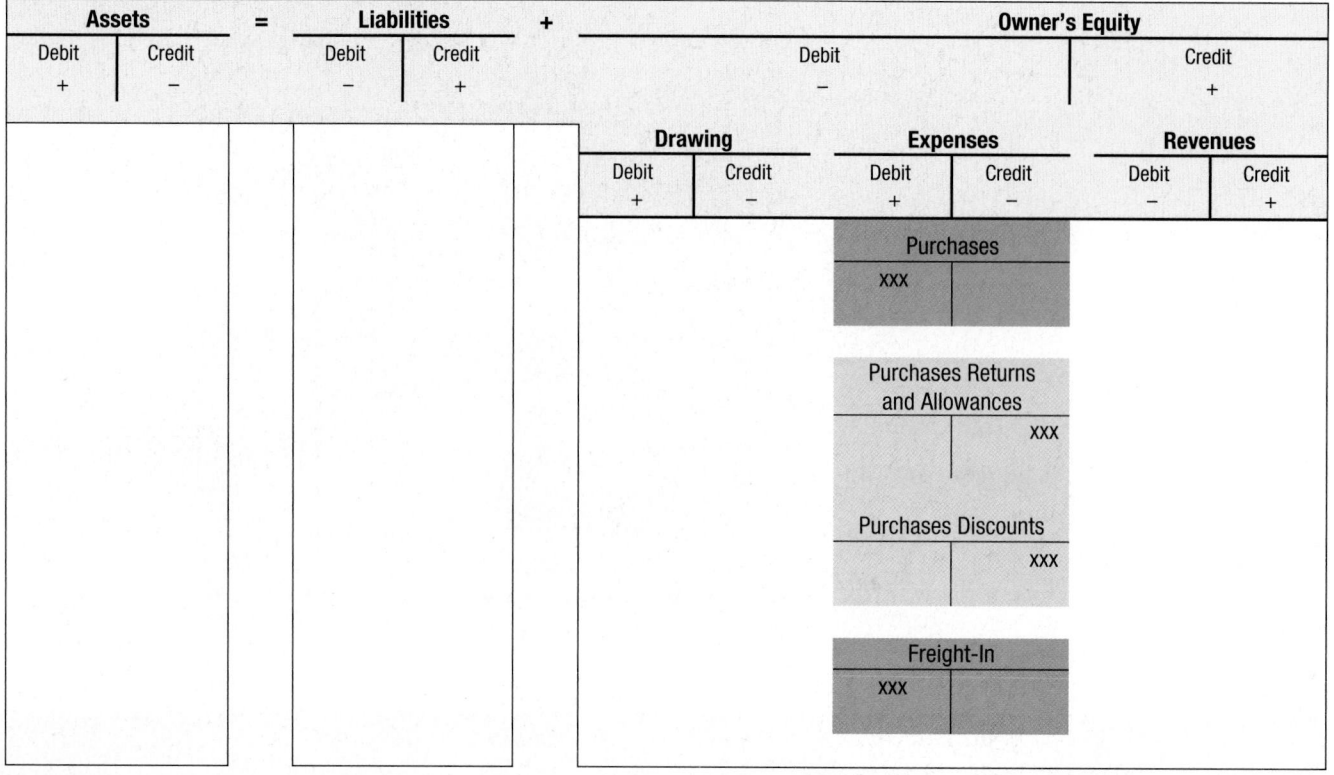

If a $100 purchase is made for cash, the following entry is made:

5		Purchases		1 0 0 00			5
6		Cash			1 0 0 00		6
7		Made cash purchase					7

If the same purchase is made on account, the entry is as follows:

The vendor's name is placed after Accounts Payable.

5		Purchases		1 0 0 00			5
6		Accounts Payable/Vendor			1 0 0 00		6
7		Made purchase on account					7

Accounts Payable is followed by a slash (/) and the name of the specific vendor to whom the purchaser owes money. The vendor name is for the vendor's account in the accounts payable ledger. This ledger is explained later in this chapter.

PURCHASES RETURNS AND ALLOWANCES ACCOUNT

Purchases	xxx
Less: Purch.	
ret. & all.	xx
Net purchases	xxx

Purchases Returns and Allowances is a **contra-cost** (or **contra-purchases**) **account,** which has a credit balance and is deducted from the related cost account. Purchases returns and purchases allowances are credited to this account. It is reported as a deduction from Purchases on the income statement to compute net purchases (see Figure 11-7 on page 407).

Purchases returns and allowances are similar to the sales returns and allowances we discussed in Chapter 10. We are simply looking at returns and allowances from the buyer's point of view. If merchandise is returned to a supplier, or the supplier grants a price reduction because of defects or other problems with merchandise purchased, Purchases Returns and Allowances is credited.

Purchases Returns and Allowances

Debit	Credit
	to enter returns and allowances

If merchandise that was purchased on account for $200 is defective and is returned to the supplier, the following entry is made:

9	Accounts Payable/Vendor	2 0 0 00		9
10	Purchases Returns and Allowances		2 0 0 00	10
11	Returned merchandise			11

If the same merchandise is retained but the supplier grants a price reduction of $45 because of the defects, the entry is as follows:

9	Accounts Payable/Vendor	4 5 00		9
10	Purchases Returns and Allowances		4 5 00	10
11	Allowance for defective merchandise			11

PURCHASES DISCOUNTS ACCOUNT

Purchases Discounts is a contra-purchases account used to record cash discounts allowed on purchases. Like Purchases Returns and Allowances, it is reported as a deduction from Purchases on the income statement to compute net purchases (see Figure 11-7).

Purchases	XXX
Less: Purchases	
discounts	XX
Net purchases	XXX

Purchases Discounts

Debit	Credit
	to enter cash discounts taken

If merchandise is purchased for $100 on account, with credit terms of 2/10, n/30, the following entry is made:

14	Purchases	1 0 0 00		14
15	Accounts Payable/Vendor		1 0 0 00	15
16	Made purchase on account			16

If payment for the merchandise is then made within the discount period, the entry is as follows:

18		Accounts Payable/Vendor		1	0	0	00						18
19		Cash							9	8	00		19
20		Purchases Discounts								2	00		20
21		Made payment on account											21

This approach to accounting for purchases discounts is known as the "gross-price method." The "net-price method" is described in the appendix.

Note the parts of this entry. Accounts Payable is debited for $100, the full amount of the invoice, because the entire debt has been satisfied. Cash is credited for only $98 because that is all that was required to pay the debt. The difference of $2 ($100 − $98) is credited to Purchases Discounts, which represents a reduction in the purchase price of the merchandise. That is why Purchases Discounts is deducted from Purchases on the income statement.

A BROADER VIEW

Cash Management—Those Discounts Matter

If a business makes a $2,000 purchase on account, with terms of 2/10, n/30, the available discount is only $40 ($2,000 × 0.02). On the surface, this seems unimportant, like "small change." But take a closer look. If the business does not pay $1,960 ($2,000 − $40) within 10 days, it must pay $2,000 within 30 days. This means that the business would pay $40 for the use of $1,960 for 20 more days. If we assume a 360-day year, the approximate annual interest rate for using the $1,960 for 20 days is 36%.

The innocent looking 2% cash discount represents a very high rate of interest. If a business regularly misses cash discount opportunities, the annual dollar cost can be substantial. For sound cash management, take advantage of discounts.

In Chapter 17, we discuss how to compute interest. There you will learn to compute the exact interest rate.

PHOTOLINK/PHOTODISC/GETTY IMAGES

FREIGHT-IN ACCOUNT

Freight-In is an adjunct-purchases account used to record transportation charges on merchandise purchases. It is added to net purchases on the income statement to compute cost of goods purchased (see Figure 11-7).

Freight-In

Debit	Credit
to enter transportation charges on merchandise purchases	

Net purchases	xxx
Add freight–in	xx
Cost of goods purchased	xxx

Transportation charges are expressed in FOB (free on board) terms that indicate who is responsible for paying the freight costs. **FOB shipping point** means that transportation charges are paid by the buyer. **FOB destination** means that transportation charges are paid by the seller. FOB terms also tell us who owns the inventory and who should count it in their inventory account. Under FOB shipping point, the buyer owns the inventory as soon as it is shipped and should count it in inventory. Under FOB destination, the seller owns the inventory until it is delivered to the buyer and should count it in inventory.

When the terms are FOB shipping point, either the freight charges will be listed separately on the purchase invoice or a separate freight bill will be sent. Assume Northern Micro receives an invoice for $400 plus freight charges of $38. The entry for this purchase is as follows:

25		Purchases		4	0	0	00						25
26		Freight-In			3	8	00						26
27		Accounts Payable/Vendor							4	3	8	00	27
28		Made purchase on account											28

Assume instead that Northern Micro receives an invoice for $400 for the same merchandise, shipped FOB shipping point. Northern Micro then receives a separate bill from the transportation company for $38. These two transactions are entered as follows:

30		Purchases		4	0	0	00						30
31		Accounts Payable/Vendor							4	0	0	00	31
32		Made purchase on account											32
33													33
34		Freight-In			3	8	00						34
35		Accounts Payable/Vendor								3	8	00	35
36		Freight charges on merchandise purchase											36

When the terms are FOB destination, generally no freight charges appear on the purchase invoice. The buyer simply records the purchase at the amount of the invoice. The freight-in account is not used in recording this purchase.

COMPUTATION OF GROSS PROFIT

An important step in determining net income for a merchandising business is the calculation of its gross profit. **Gross profit** (also called **gross margin**) is the difference between net sales and cost of goods sold. **Cost of goods sold** (also called **cost of merchandise sold**) is the difference between the goods available for sale and the ending inventory. It indicates the cost of the goods sold during the period. Gross profit provides very important information. It tells management the amount of sales dollars available to cover expenses, after covering the cost of the goods sold.

As a simple example, gross profit is computed as follows:

Net sales	$8,400
Cost of goods sold	5,300
Gross profit	$3,100

In a more realistic situation, we must compute net sales and cost of goods sold, in order to compute gross profit. Multiple steps are involved. To illustrate, we use three of the four new accounts described in Chapter 10, the four new accounts described in this chapter, and the merchandise inventory balances. Assume that Northern Micro has the following sales, purchases, and merchandise inventory balances for the year ended December 31, 20--:

From Chapter 10	Sales	$201,500
	Sales returns and allowances	1,200
	Sales discounts	1,000
From Chapter 11	Purchases	105,000
	Purchases returns and allowances	800
	Purchases discounts	1,000
	Freight-in	300
	Merchandise inventory, January 1, 20--	26,000
	Merchandise inventory, December 31, 20--	18,000

Figure 11-7 uses these balances to compute net sales, net purchases, cost of goods sold, and gross profit. The following four steps in computing gross profit are labeled in the figure:

STEP 1 Compute net sales.

(Sales – Sales Returns and Allowances – Sales Discounts)

STEP 2 Compute goods available for sale.

(Beginning Inventory + Cost of Goods Purchased)

STEP 3 Compute cost of goods sold.

(Goods Available for Sale – Ending Inventory)

STEP 4 Compute gross profit.

(Net Sales – Cost of Goods Sold)

LEARNING KEY

Cost of Goods Sold = Beginning Inventory + Net Purchases + Freight-In – Ending Inventory

Gross Profit = Net Sales – Cost of Goods Sold

FIGURE 11-7 Computation of Gross Profit on a Partial Income Statement

Income Statement (partial)									
Revenue from sales:									
Sales						$201 5 0 0 00			
Less: Sales returns and allowances			$ 1 2 0 0 00						
Sales discounts			1 0 0 0 00			2 2 0 0 00			
Step 1 ▸ Net sales								$199 3 0 0 00	
Cost of goods sold:									
Merchandise inventory, Jan. 1						$ 26 0 0 0 00			
Purchases			$105 0 0 0 00						
Less: Purchases returns and allowances	$ 8 0 0 00								
Purchases discounts	1 0 0 0 00		1 8 0 0 00						
Net purchases			$103 2 0 0 00						
Add freight-in			3 0 0 00						
Cost of goods purchased						103 5 0 0 00			
Step 2 ▸ Goods available for sale						$129 5 0 0 00			
Less merchandise inventory, Dec. 31						18 0 0 0 00			
Step 3 ▸ Cost of goods sold								111 5 0 0 00	
Step 4 ▸ Gross profit								$ 87 8 0 0 00	

U REVU

Complete U REVU-2 on **page 422** to test your basic understanding of LO2.

JOURNALIZING AND POSTING PURCHASES AND CASH PAYMENTS TRANSACTIONS

LO3 Describe and use the accounts payable ledger.

To illustrate the journalizing and posting of purchases transactions, we will continue with the transactions of Northern Micro.

PURCHASES

Assume the following purchases on account occurred during the month of April:

Apr. 4   Purchased merchandise from Compucraft, Inc., $3,300.
Invoice No. 631, dated April 2, terms, n/30.

8   Purchased merchandise from Datasoft, $2,500.
Invoice No. 927D, dated April 6, terms, n/30.

11   Purchased merchandise from EZX Corp., $8,700.
Invoice No. 804, dated April 9, terms, 1/15, n/30.

17   Purchased merchandise from Printpro Corp., $800.
Invoice No. 611, dated April 16, terms, n/30.

23   Purchased merchandise from Televax, Inc., $5,300.
Invoice No. 1465, dated April 22, terms, 1/10, n/30.

These transactions are entered in a general journal as shown in Figure 11-8.

FIGURE 11-8 Purchases Entered in General Journal

	DATE		DESCRIPTION	POST. REF.	DEBIT	CREDIT	
1	20-- Apr.	4	Purchases		3 3 0 0 00		1
2			Accounts Payable/Compucraft, Inc.			3 3 0 0 00	2
3			Invoice No. 631				3
4							4
5		8	Purchases		2 5 0 0 00		5
6			Accounts Payable/Datasoft			2 5 0 0 00	6
7			Invoice No. 927D				7
8							8
9		11	Purchases		8 7 0 0 00		9
10			Accounts Payable/EZX Corp.			8 7 0 0 00	10
11			Invoice No. 804				11
12							12
13		17	Purchases		8 0 0 00		13
14			Accounts Payable/Printpro Corp.			8 0 0 00	14
15			Invoice No. 611				15
16							16
17		23	Purchases		5 3 0 0 00		17
18			Accounts Payable/Televax, Inc.			5 3 0 0 00	18
19			Invoice No. 1465				19

GENERAL JOURNAL PAGE 6

POSTING PURCHASES TO THE GENERAL LEDGER

Purchases transactions are posted from the general journal to the general ledger in the same manner as was illustrated for sales in Chapter 10. The following steps are used, as indicated in Figure 11-9 for Northern Micro's April 4 and 8 purchases transactions:

In the general ledger account:

STEP 1 Enter the date of the transaction in the Date column.

STEP 2 Enter the amount of the debit or credit in the Debit or Credit column.

STEP 3 Enter the new balance in the Balance columns under Debit or Credit.

STEP 4 Enter the journal page number from which each transaction is posted in the Posting Reference column.

In the journal:

STEP 5 Enter the ledger account number in the Posting Reference column of the journal for each transaction that is posted.

Other purchases transactions would be posted in the same manner.

POSTING PURCHASES TO THE ACCOUNTS PAYABLE LEDGER

The Purchases and Accounts Payable resulting from merchandise purchases on account are now up to date in the general ledger. A record can be kept of the amount owed to each supplier by using an **accounts payable ledger**. This is a separate ledger containing an individual account payable for each supplier. It is similar to the accounts receivable ledger we saw in Chapter 10. A summary accounts payable account called

FIGURE 11-9 Posting Purchases to the General Ledger

GENERAL JOURNAL (Partial)   Page 6

Date		Description	Post. Ref.	Debit	Credit	
20--						
Apr.	4	Purchases	501	3,300.00		
		Accounts Payable/Compucraft, Inc.	202		3,300.00	
		Invoice No. 631				
	8	Purchases	501	2,500.00		
		Accounts Payable/Datasoft	202		2,500.00	
		Invoice No. 927D				

GENERAL LEDGER (Partial)

ACCOUNT   Accounts Payable   ACCOUNT NO. 202

Date		Item	Post. Ref.	Debit	Credit	Balance Debit	Balance Credit
20--							
Apr.	1	Bal.	✓				4,800.00
	4		J6		3,300.00		8,100.00
	8		J6		2,500.00		10,600.00

ACCOUNT   Purchases   ACCOUNT NO. 501

Date		Item	Post. Ref.	Debit	Credit	Balance Debit	Balance Credit
20--							
Apr.	1	Bal.	✓			17,400.00	
	4		J6	3,300.00		20,700.00	
	8		J6	2,500.00		23,200.00	

A three-column account form is commonly used for supplier accounts. Only one balance column is needed because the normal balance is a credit. If a debit balance occurs, the amount may be bracketed.

LEARNING KEY

When an accounts payable ledger is used, the Posting Reference column in the general journal serves two purposes. (1) The account number is inserted to indicate the general ledger account has been posted. (2) A slash (/) and a check mark (✓) are inserted to indicate the accounts payable ledger account has been posted.

a controlling account is maintained in the general ledger. The accounts payable ledger is "subsidiary" to this account. If there are many supplier accounts, it is a good practice to assign each supplier an account number. The subsidiary ledger accounts are kept in either alphabetical or numerical order, depending on whether the supplier accounts are identified by number.

Figure 11-10 illustrates the use of the accounts payable ledger for Northern Micro's April 4 and 8 purchases transactions. Note that the individual vendor name follows accounts payable in each journal entry affecting Accounts Payable. The following steps are used to post from the general journal to the accounts payable ledger, as shown in Figure 11-10:

In the accounts payable ledger account:

STEP 1 Enter the date of the transaction in the Date column.

STEP 2 Enter the amount of the debit or credit in the Debit or Credit column.

STEP 3 Enter the new balance in the Balance column.

STEP 4 Enter the journal page number from which each transaction is posted in the Posting Reference column.

In the journal:

STEP 5 Enter a slash (/) followed by a check mark (✓) in the Posting Reference column of the journal for each transaction that is posted.

FIGURE 11-10 Posting Purchases to the Accounts Payable Ledger

LEARNING KEY

The total of the accounts payable ledger balances must equal the Accounts Payable balance in the general ledger.

Note the relationship between the general journal, accounts payable ledger, and general ledger. All general journal entries are posted to both the general ledger and the accounts payable ledger. After the posting of the accounts payable ledger and general ledger is completed, the total of the accounts payable ledger balances should equal the Accounts Payable balance in the general ledger.

PURCHASES RETURNS AND ALLOWANCES

If a buyer returns merchandise or is given an allowance for damaged merchandise, a general journal entry is required. Assume that on May 4, Northern Micro returns $200 of merchandise to Televax, Inc. These goods were part of a purchase made on April 23. Figure 11-11 shows the general journal entry, general ledger posting, and accounts payable ledger posting for this transaction.

The general journal entry is made in the usual manner. The general ledger is posted using the same five steps as were illustrated for purchases transactions in Figure 11-9. The accounts payable ledger is posted using the following five steps, as illustrated in Figure 11-11:

In the accounts payable ledger account:

STEP 1 Enter the date of the transaction in the Date column.

STEP 2 Enter the amount of the debit or credit in the Debit or Credit column.

STEP 3 Enter the new balance in the Balance column.

STEP 4 Enter the journal page number from which each transaction is posted in the Posting Reference column.

In the journal:

STEP 5 Enter a slash (/) followed by a check mark (✓) in the Posting Reference column of the journal for each transaction that is posted.

FIGURE 11-11 Accounting for Purchases Returns and Allowances

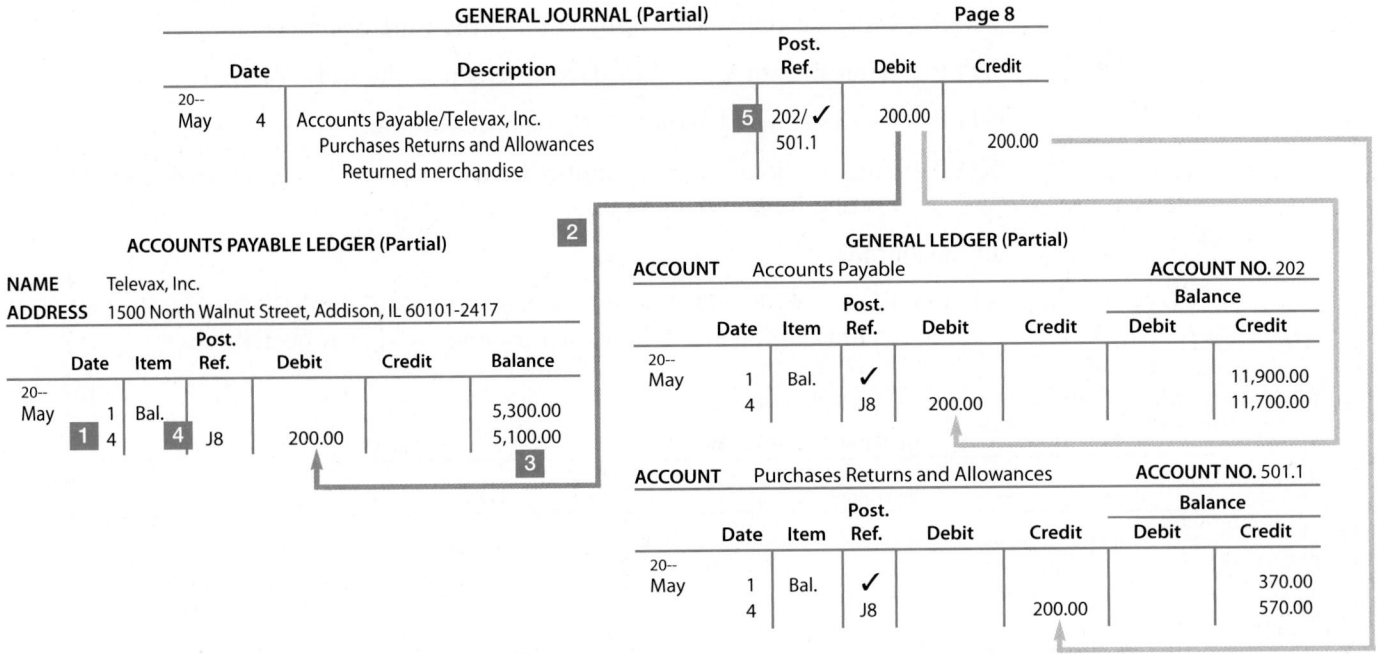

CASH PAYMENTS

To illustrate the journalizing and posting of cash payments, we will use Northern Micro's cash payment transactions. Assume Northern Micro made the following two payments on account during the month of April:

Apr. 10   Paid B. B. Small $4,800 for purchases made on account.

24   Paid EZX Corp. $8,700 less discount of 1% for purchases made on account.

These transactions are entered in a general journal as shown in Figure 11-12.

FIGURE 11-12 Cash Payments Entered in a General Journal

30	Apr.	10	Accounts Payable/B. B. Small		4	8	0	0	00							30
31			Cash								4	8	0	0	00	31
32			Made payment on account													32
33																33
34		24	Accounts Payable/EZX Corp.		8	7	0	0	00							34
35			Cash								8	6	1	3	00	35
36			Purchases Discounts										8	7	00	36
37			Made payment less discount on account													37

POSTING CASH PAYMENTS TO THE GENERAL LEDGER AND ACCOUNTS PAYABLE LEDGER

Cash payment transactions are posted to the general ledger in the same manner as was illustrated for purchases transactions in Figure 11-9. To post cash payments to the accounts payable ledger, the following steps are used, as indicated in Figure 11-13 for Northern Micro's April 10 and 24 cash payment transactions:

In the accounts payable ledger account:

STEP 1 Enter the date of the transaction in the Date column.

STEP 2 Enter the amount of the debit or credit in the Debit or Credit column.

STEP 3 Enter the new balance in the Balance column.

STEP 4 Enter the journal page number from which each transaction is posted in the Posting Reference column.

In the journal:

STEP 5 Enter a slash (/) followed by a check mark (✓) in the Posting Reference column of the journal for each transaction that is posted.

FIGURE 11-13 Posting Cash Payments to the General Ledger and Accounts Payable Ledger

U REVU   Complete U REVU-3 on **page 422** to test your basic understanding of LO3.

SCHEDULE OF ACCOUNTS PAYABLE

LO4 Prepare a schedule of accounts payable.

At the end of the month, all postings to Accounts Payable in the general ledger and to the accounts payable ledger should be complete, as shown in Figure 11-14. At this point, the Accounts Payable balance in the general ledger should equal the sum of the supplier balances in the accounts payable ledger.

FIGURE 11-14 General Ledger and Accounts Payable Ledger after Posting

ACCOUNTS PAYABLE LEDGER

NAME B. B. Small
ADDRESS 2323 High Street, Gurnee, IL 60031-5524

Date		Item	Post. Ref.	Debit	Credit	Balance
20--						
Apr.	1	Bal.	✓			4,800.00
	10		J6	4,800.00		—

NAME Compucraft, Inc.
ADDRESS 2100 West Main Street, Muncie, IN 47304-8139

Date		Item	Post. Ref.	Debit	Credit	Balance
20--						
Apr.	4		J6		3,300.00	3,300.00

NAME Datasoft
ADDRESS 210 Kirkwood, Bloomington, IN 47408-4346

Date		Item	Post. Ref.	Debit	Credit	Balance
20--						
Apr.	8		J6		2,500.00	2,500.00

NAME EZX Corp.
ADDRESS 2928 Rhodes Ave., Chicago, IL 60658-5036

Date		Item	Post. Ref.	Debit	Credit	Balance
20--						
Apr.	11		J6		8,700.00	8,700.00
	24		J6	8,700.00		—

NAME Printpro Corp.
ADDRESS 1200 Chambers Pike, Lincolnwood, IL 60648-2417

Date		Item	Post. Ref.	Debit	Credit	Balance
20--						
Apr.	17		J6		800.00	800.00

NAME Televax, Inc.
ADDRESS 1500 North Walnut Street, Addison, IL 60101-2417

Date		Item	Post. Ref.	Debit	Credit	Balance
20--						
Apr.	23		J6		5,300.00	5,300.00

GENERAL LEDGER (Partial)

ACCOUNT Accounts Payable   **ACCOUNT NO.** 202

Date		Item	Post. Ref.	Debit	Credit	Balance Debit	Balance Credit
20--							
Apr.	1	Bal.	✓				4,800.00
	4		J6		3,300.00		8,100.00
	8		J6		2,500.00		10,600.00
	10		J6	4,800.00			5,800.00
	11		J6		8,700.00		14,500.00
	17		J6		800.00		15,300.00
	23		J6		5,300.00		20,600.00
	24		J6	8,700.00			11,900.00

To verify that the sum of the accounts payable ledger balances equals the Accounts Payable balance, a **schedule of accounts payable** is prepared. This is an alphabetical or numerical listing of supplier accounts and balances, usually prepared at the end of the month. Figure 11-15 shows the schedule of accounts payable for Northern Micro as of April 30. Note that suppliers whose account balance is zero are not included.

This schedule is prepared from the list of supplier accounts in the accounts payable ledger. The total calculated in the schedule is compared with the balance in Accounts Payable in the general ledger. Note that the $11,900 total listed in the schedule equals

FIGURE 11-15 Schedule of Accounts Payable

Northern Micro
Schedule of Accounts Payable
April 30, 20--

Compucraft, Inc.		$ 3	3	0	0	00
Datasoft		2	5	0	0	00
Printpro Corp.			8	0	0	00
Televax, Inc.		5	3	0	0	00
		$11	9	0	0	00

the Accounts Payable balance shown in Figure 11-14. If the schedule total and the Accounts Payable balance do not agree, the error must be located and corrected. To find the error, use the following procedures:

STEP 1 Verify the total of the schedule.

STEP 2 Verify the postings to the accounts payable ledger.

STEP 3 Verify the postings to Accounts Payable in the general ledger.

U REVU

Complete U REVU-4 on page 422 to test your basic understanding of LO4.

SELF-STUDY

LEARNING OBJECTIVES	Key Points to Remember
LO1 Define merchandise purchases transactions.	For a merchandising business, purchases refers to merchandise acquired for resale. Major documents used in the purchasing process are the purchase requisition, purchase order, receiving report, and purchase invoice.
LO2 Describe and use merchandise purchases accounts and compute gross profit.	Four accounts are used in accounting for merchandise purchases transactions. 1. Purchases 2. Purchases Returns and Allowances 3. Purchases Discounts 4. Freight-In $$\text{Cost of Goods Sold} = \text{Beginning Inventory} + \text{Net Purchases} + \text{Freight-In} - \text{Ending Inventory}$$ $$\text{Gross Profit} = \text{Net Sales} - \text{Cost of Goods Sold}$$
LO3 Describe and use the accounts payable ledger.	To post purchases transactions to the general ledger: **In the general ledger account:** STEP 1 Enter the date of the transaction in the Date column. STEP 2 Enter the amount of the debit or credit in the Debit or Credit column. STEP 3 Enter the new balance in the Balance columns under Debit or Credit. STEP 4 Enter the journal page number from which each transaction is posted in the Posting Reference column. *(continued)*

LEARNING OBJECTIVES	Key Points to Remember

LO3 (concluded)

In the journal:

STEP 5 Enter the ledger account number in the Posting Reference column of the journal for each transaction that is posted.

An accounts payable ledger is a separate ledger containing an individual account payable for each supplier. To post from the general journal to the accounts payable ledger:

In the accounts payable ledger account:

STEP 1 Enter the date of the transaction in the Date column.

STEP 2 Enter the amount of the debit or credit in the Debit or Credit column.

STEP 3 Enter the new balance in the Balance column.

STEP 4 Enter the journal page number from which each transaction is posted in the Posting Reference column.

In the journal:

STEP 5 Enter a slash (/) followed by a check mark (✓) in the Posting Reference column of the journal for each transaction that is posted.

To post cash payments transactions to the general ledger:

In the general ledger account:

STEP 1 Enter the date of the transaction in the Date column.

STEP 2 Enter the amount of the debit or credit in the Debit or Credit column.

STEP 3 Enter the new balance in the Balance columns under Debit or Credit.

STEP 4 Enter the journal page number from which each transaction is posted in the Posting Reference column.

In the journal:

STEP 5 Enter the ledger account number in the Posting Reference column of the journal for each transaction that is posted.

To post cash payments transactions to the accounts payable ledger:

In the accounts payable ledger account:

STEP 1 Enter the date of the transaction in the Date column.

STEP 2 Enter the amount of the debit or credit in the Debit or Credit column.

STEP 3 Enter the new balance in the Balance column.

STEP 4 Enter the journal page number from which each transaction is posted in the Posting Reference column.

In the journal:

STEP 5 Enter a slash (/) followed by a check mark (✓) in the Posting Reference column of the journal for each transaction that is posted.

LO4 Prepare a schedule of accounts payable.

The schedule of accounts payable is used to verify that the sum of the accounts payable ledger balances equals the Accounts Payable balance.

DEMONSTRATION PROBLEM

Jodi Rutman operates a retail pharmacy called Rutman Pharmacy. The books include a general journal, a general ledger, and an accounts payable ledger. The following transactions are related to purchases and cash payments for the month of June 20--:

June 1	Purchased merchandise from Sullivan Co. on account, $234.20. Invoice No. 71 dated June 1, terms 2/10, n/30.
2	Issued Check No. 536 for payment of June rent (Rent Expense), $1,000.00.
5	Purchased merchandise from Amfac Drug Supply on account, $562.40. Invoice No. 196 dated June 2, terms 1/15, n/30.
7	Purchased merchandise from University Drug Co. on account, $367.35. Invoice No. 914A dated June 5, terms 3/10 eom, n/30.
9	Issued Check No. 537 to Sullivan Co. in payment of Invoice No. 71 less 2% discount.
12	Received a credit memo from Amfac Drug Supply for merchandise returned that was purchased on June 5, $46.20.
14	Purchased merchandise from Mutual Drug Co. on account, $479.40. Invoice No. 745 dated June 14, terms 2/10, n/30.
15	Received a credit memo from University Drug Co. for merchandise returned that was purchased on June 7, $53.70.
16	Issued Check No. 538 to Amfac Drug Supply in payment of Invoice No. 196 less the credit memo of June 12 and less 1% discount.
23	Issued Check No. 539 to Mutual Drug Co. in payment of Invoice No. 745 less 2% discount.
27	Purchased merchandise from Flites Pharmaceuticals on account, $638.47. Invoice No. 675 dated June 27, terms 2/10 eom, n/30.
29	Issued Check No. 540 to Dolgin Candy Co. for a cash purchase of merchandise, $270.20.
30	Issued Check No. 541 to Vashon Medical Supply in payment of Invoice No. 416, $1,217.69. No discount allowed.

REQUIRED

1. Enter the transactions in a general journal (start with page 7).

2. Post from the journal to the general ledger accounts and the accounts payable ledger. Account numbers and June 1 balances are as indicated in the accounts presented below. Then, update the account balances.

3. Prepare a schedule of accounts payable from the accounts payable ledger in the problem. Verify that the total of accounts payable in the schedule equals the June 30 balance of Accounts Payable in the general ledger.

Solution 1.

	DATE		DESCRIPTION	POST. REF.	DEBIT					CREDIT					
			GENERAL JOURNAL										Page 7		
1	20-- June	1	Purchases	501		2	3	4	20						1
2			Accounts Payable/Sullivan Co.	202/✓							2	3	4	20	2
3			Invoice No. 71												3
4															4
5		2	Rent Expense	521	1	0	0	0	00						5
6			Cash	101						1	0	0	0	00	6
7			Check No. 536												7
8															8
9		5	Purchases	501		5	6	2	40						9
10			Accounts Payable/Amfac Drug Supply	202/✓							5	6	2	40	10
11			Invoice No. 196												11
12															12
13		7	Purchases	501		3	6	7	35						13
14			Accounts Payable/University Drug Co.	202/✓							3	6	7	35	14
15			Invoice No. 914A												15
16															16
17		9	Accounts Payable/Sullivan Co.	202/✓		2	3	4	20						17
18			Cash	101							2	2	9	52	18
19			Purchases Discounts	501.2									4	68	19
20			Check No. 537												20
21															21
22		12	Accounts Payable/Amfac Drug Supply	202/✓			4	6	20						22
23			Purchases Returns and Allowances	501.1								4	6	20	23
24			Returned merchandise												24
25															25
26		14	Purchases	501		4	7	9	40						26
27			Accounts Payable/Mutual Drug Co.	202/✓							4	7	9	40	27
28			Invoice No. 745												28

	DATE		DESCRIPTION	POST. REF.	DEBIT					CREDIT					
			GENERAL JOURNAL										Page 8		
1	20-- June	15	Accounts Payable/University Drug Co.	202/✓			5	3	70						1
2			Purchases Returns and Allowances	501.1								5	3	70	2
3			Returned merchandise												3
4															4
5		16	Accounts Payable/Amfac Drug Supply	202/✓		5	1	6	20						5
6			Cash	101							5	1	1	04	6
7			Purchases Discounts	501.2									5	16	7
8			Check No. 538												8
9															9
10		23	Accounts Payable/Mutual Drug Co.	202/✓		4	7	9	40						10
11			Cash	101							4	6	9	81	11
12			Purchases Discounts	501.2									9	59	12
13			Check No. 539												13
14															14
15		27	Purchases	501		6	3	8	47						15
16			Accounts Payable/Flites Pharmaceuticals	202/✓							6	3	8	47	16
17			Invoice No. 675												17
18															18
19		29	Purchases	501		2	7	0	20						19
20			Cash	101							2	7	0	20	20
21			Check No. 540												21
22															22
23		30	Accounts Payable/Vashon Medical Supply	202/✓	1	2	1	7	69						23
24			Cash	101						1	2	1	7	69	24
25			Check No. 541												25

(continued)

2.

ACCOUNT: Cash   ACCOUNT NO. 101

DATE		ITEM	POST. REF.	DEBIT	CREDIT	BALANCE DEBIT	BALANCE CREDIT
20-- June	1	Balance	✓			9 1 8 0 00	
	2		J7		1 0 0 0 00	8 1 8 0 00	
	9		J7		2 2 9 52	7 9 5 0 48	
	16		J8		5 1 1 04	7 4 3 9 44	
	23		J8		4 6 9 81	6 9 6 9 63	
	29		J8		2 7 0 20	6 6 9 9 43	
	30		J8		1 2 1 7 69	5 4 8 1 74	

ACCOUNT: Accounts Payable   ACCOUNT NO. 202

DATE		ITEM	POST. REF.	DEBIT	CREDIT	BALANCE DEBIT	BALANCE CREDIT
20-- June	1	Balance	✓				1 2 1 7 69
	1		J7		2 3 4 20		1 4 5 1 89
	5		J7		5 6 2 40		2 0 1 4 29
	7		J7		3 6 7 35		2 3 8 1 64
	9		J7	2 3 4 20			2 1 4 7 44
	12		J7	4 6 20			2 1 0 1 24
	14		J7		4 7 9 40		2 5 8 0 64
	15		J8	5 3 70			2 5 2 6 94
	16		J8	5 1 6 20			2 0 1 0 74
	23		J8	4 7 9 40			1 5 3 1 34
	27		J8		6 3 8 47		2 1 6 9 81
	30		J8	1 2 1 7 69			9 5 2 12

ACCOUNT: Purchases   ACCOUNT NO. 501

DATE		ITEM	POST. REF.	DEBIT	CREDIT	BALANCE DEBIT	BALANCE CREDIT
20-- June	1	Balance	✓			13 8 2 6 25	
	1		J7	2 3 4 20		14 0 6 0 45	
	5		J7	5 6 2 40		14 6 2 2 85	
	7		J7	3 6 7 35		14 9 9 0 20	
	14		J7	4 7 9 40		15 4 6 9 60	
	27		J8	6 3 8 47		16 1 0 8 07	
	29		J8	2 7 0 20		16 3 7 8 27	

ACCOUNT: Purchases Returns and Allowances   ACCOUNT NO. 501.1

DATE		ITEM	POST. REF.	DEBIT	CREDIT	BALANCE DEBIT	BALANCE CREDIT
20-- June	1	Balance	✓				3 1 2 63
	12		J7		4 6 20		3 5 8 83
	15		J8		5 3 70		4 1 2 53

ACCOUNT: Purchases Discounts   ACCOUNT NO. 501.2

DATE		ITEM	POST. REF.	DEBIT	CREDIT	BALANCE DEBIT	BALANCE CREDIT
20-- June	1	Balance	✓				2 1 1 45
	9		J7		4 68		2 1 6 13
	16		J8		5 16		2 2 1 29
	23		J8		9 59		2 3 0 88

ACCOUNT: Rent Expense   ACCOUNT NO. 521

DATE		ITEM	POST. REF.	DEBIT	CREDIT	BALANCE DEBIT	BALANCE CREDIT
20-- June	1	Balance	✓			5 0 0 0 00	
	2		J7	1 0 0 0 00		6 0 0 0 00	

ACCOUNTS PAYABLE LEDGER

NAME: Amfac Drug Supply

DATE		ITEM	POST. REF.	DEBIT	CREDIT	BALANCE
20-- June	5		J7		5 6 2 40	5 6 2 40
	12		J7	4 6 20		5 1 6 20
	16		J8	5 1 6 20		

NAME: Flites Pharmaceuticals

DATE		ITEM	POST. REF.	DEBIT	CREDIT	BALANCE
20-- June	27		J8		6 3 8 47	6 3 8 47

NAME: Mutual Drug Co.

DATE		ITEM	POST. REF.	DEBIT	CREDIT	BALANCE
20-- June	14		J7		4 7 9 40	4 7 9 40
	23		J8	4 7 9 40		

NAME: Sullivan Co.

DATE		ITEM	POST. REF.	DEBIT	CREDIT	BALANCE
20-- June	1		J7		2 3 4 20	2 3 4 20
	9		J7	2 3 4 20		

NAME: University Drug Co.

DATE		ITEM	POST. REF.	DEBIT	CREDIT	BALANCE
20-- June	7		J7		3 6 7 35	3 6 7 35
	15		J8	5 3 70		3 1 3 65

NAME: Vashon Medical Supply

DATE		ITEM	POST. REF.	DEBIT	CREDIT	BALANCE
20-- June	1	Balance	✓			1 2 1 7 69
	30		J8	1 2 1 7 69		

(continued)

3.

Rutman Pharmacy Schedule of Accounts Payable June 30, 20--					
Flites Pharmaceuticals	$	6	3	8	47
University Drug Co.		3	1	3	65
	$	9	5	2	12
Proof					
Balance of Accounts Payable, June 30	$	9	5	2	12

KEY TERMS

accounts payable ledger (408)   A separate ledger containing an individual account payable for each supplier.

contra-cost account (402) An account with a credit balance that is deducted from the related cost account.

contra-purchases account (402) see contra-cost account.

cost of goods sold (405)   The difference between the goods available for sale and the ending inventory.

cost of merchandise sold (405)   See cost of goods sold.

FOB destination (405)   Shipping terms indicating that transportation charges are paid by the seller.

FOB shipping point (405)   Shipping terms indicating that transportation charges are paid by the buyer.

gross margin (405)   See gross profit.

gross profit (405)   The difference between net sales and cost of goods sold.

invoice (399)   A document prepared by the seller as a bill for the merchandise shipped. To the seller, this is a sales invoice. To the buyer, this is a purchase invoice.

purchase invoice (399)   A document prepared by the seller as a bill for the merchandise shipped. To the buyer, this is a purchase invoice.

purchase order (398)   A written order to buy goods from a specific vendor (supplier).

purchase requisition (398)   A form used to request the purchase of merchandise or other property.

purchases (398)   Merchandise acquired for resale to customers.

receiving report (399)   A report indicating what has been received.

schedule of accounts payable (413)   An alphabetical or numerical listing of supplier accounts and balances, usually prepared at the end of the month.

trade discount (400)   A reduction from the list or catalog price offered to different classes of customers.

SELF-STUDY QUESTIONS AND EXERCISES

True/False Questions

1. LO1   In the purchasing process, the purchase invoice is the first document prepared.

2. LO1   A sales invoice prepared by the seller is called a purchase invoice by the buyer.

3. LO1   A trade discount is a reduction from the list or catalog price offered to different classes of customers.

4. LO2   Purchases Returns and Allowances is debited when merchandise is returned for credit.

5. LO2   FOB shipping point means that transportation charges are paid by the seller.

Multiple Choice Questions

1. LO1   A purchase of merchandise for $300 with a trade discount of 10% would require a debit to Purchases of

   (a) $330.
   (b) $300.
   (c) $297.
   (d) $270.

2. LO2   In the income statement, Freight-In is

   (a) added to purchases.
   (b) subtracted from purchases.
   (c) added to sales.
   (d) subtracted from cost of goods sold.

3. LO2   The difference between net sales and cost of goods sold is called

   (a) gross profit.
   (b) net purchases.
   (c) goods available for sale.
   (d) the bottom line.

4. LO2   The difference between merchandise available for sale and the end-of-period merchandise inventory is called

   (a) gross profit.
   (b) net purchases.
   (c) net sales.
   (d) cost of goods sold.

5. LO2   A purchase invoice for $1,200 with credit terms 2/10, n/30, and a return of $300 received by the seller prior to payment, is paid within the discount period. A check should be sent for

   (a) $1,200.
   (b) $882.
   (c) $900.
   (d) $810.

U REVU   Exercises

1. LO1   Deering Housewares purchased merchandise for $1,200 less a 10% trade discount with credit terms of 1/10, n/30.

   a. Compute the trade discount.
   b. Compute the amount at which to record this purchase.
   c. Compute the cash discount if the payment for the merchandise is made within the discount period.

2. **LO2** Based on the following data for Dave's Supply House, determine the gross profit.

Net sales	$92,000
Merchandise inventory, January 1, 20--	27,000
Purchases during the year	60,800
Purchases returns and allowances during the year	3,100
Purchases discounts during the year	1,300
Merchandise inventory, December 31, 20--	24,000

3. **LO3** The following journal entries are for current purchases and cash payments transactions. Using T accounts, post these transactions to Cash, Accounts Payable, Purchases, Purchases Returns and Allowances, and Purchases Discounts in the general ledger, and the vendor account in the accounts payable ledger.

a. Purchases	350.00	
Accounts Payable/J. Bedas		350.00
b. Accounts Payable/J. Bedas	70.00	
Purchases Returns and Allowances		70.00
c. Accounts Payable/J. Bedas	280.00	
Cash		274.40
Purchases Discounts		5.60

4. **LO4** On June 23, Felini Plumbing's accounts payable consisted of the following vendor balances:

B. Sutton	$245
A. Gagne	703
L. Mohler	410
P. Luffman	190
Z. Quary	263

During the following week, Felini Plumbing made a purchase of $180 from Mohler and made cash payments on account of $375 to Gagne and $110 to Quary. Prepare a schedule of accounts payable for Felini Plumbing at June 30, 20--.

The answers to the Self-Study Questions and Exercises are at the end of the chapter (pages 434–435).

APPLYING YOUR KNOWLEDGE

REVIEW QUESTIONS

LO1 1. Identify the major documents commonly used in the purchasing process.

LO1 2. Distinguish between a cash discount and a trade discount.

LO2 3. Describe how each of the following accounts is used: (1) Purchases, (2) Purchases Returns and Allowances, (3) Purchases Discounts, and (4) Freight-In.

LO2 4. How are cost of goods sold and gross profit computed?

LO3 5. What steps are followed in posting purchases from the general journal to the general ledger?

LO3 6. What steps are followed in posting purchases from the general journal to the accounts payable ledger?

LO3 7. What steps are followed in posting purchases returns and allowances from the general journal to the general ledger and accounts payable ledger?

LO3 8. What steps are followed in posting cash payments from the general journal to the general ledger?

LO3 9. What steps are followed in posting cash payments from the general journal to the accounts payable ledger?

LO4 10. If the total of the schedule of accounts payable does not agree with the Accounts Payable balance, what procedures should be used to search for the error?

SERIES A EXERCISES

E 11-1A (LO1) **PURCHASING DOCUMENTS AND FLOWCHART LABELING** A partially completed flowchart showing some of the major documents commonly used in the purchasing function of a merchandise business is presented below. Identify documents 1, 3, and 4.

E 11-2A (LO1/2)

✓ 2: $1,764

TRADE DISCOUNT AND CASH DISCOUNTS Merchandise was purchased on account from Jacob's Distributors on May 17. The purchase price was $2,000, less a 10% trade discount and credit terms of 2/10, n/30.

1. Calculate the net amount to record the invoice, less the 10% trade discount.
2. Calculate the amount to be paid on this invoice within the discount period.
3. Journalize the purchase of the merchandise on May 17 in a general journal. Journalize the payment on May 27 (within the discount period).

E 11-3A (LO2)

✓ 3(c): Purchases Discounts: $70

PURCHASE TRANSACTIONS AND T ACCOUNTS Using T accounts for Cash, Accounts Payable, Purchases, Purchases Returns and Allowances, Purchases Discounts, and Freight-In, enter the following purchase transactions. Identify each transaction with its corresponding letter. Use a new set of T accounts for each set of transactions, 1–4.

1. Purchase of merchandise with cash.

   (a) Merchandise is purchased for cash, $1,500.
   (b) Merchandise listed at $3,500, less a trade discount of 15%, is purchased for cash.

(continued)

2. Purchase of merchandise on account with credit terms.

   (a) Merchandise is purchased on account, credit terms 2/10, n/30, $2,000.
   (b) Merchandise is purchased on account, credit terms 3/10, n/30, $1,200.
   (c) Payment is made on invoice (a) within the discount period.
   (d) Payment is made on invoice (b) too late to receive the cash discount.

3. Purchase of merchandise on account with return of merchandise.

   (a) Merchandise is purchased on account, credit terms 2/10, n/30, $4,000.
   (b) Merchandise is returned for credit before payment is made, $500.
   (c) Payment is made within the discount period.

4. Purchase of merchandise with freight-in.

   (a) Merchandise is purchased on account, $2,500 plus freight charges of $100. Terms of the sale were FOB shipping point.
   (b) Payment is made for the cost of merchandise and the freight charge.

E 11-4A (LO2)

✓ Cost of goods sold: $74,500

COMPUTING GROSS PROFIT The following data were taken from the accounts of Delhi Hardware, a small retail business. Determine the gross profit.

Sales	$113,500
Sales returns and allowances	800
Sales discounts	500
Merchandise inventory, January 1	34,000
Purchases during the period	76,000
Purchases returns and allowances during the period	4,000
Purchases discounts taken during the period	3,000
Freight-in on merchandise purchased during the period	1,500
Merchandise inventory, December 31	30,000

E 11-5A (LO3)

✓ May 9: Dr. Purchases, $2,300

JOURNALIZING PURCHASES TRANSACTIONS Journalize the following transactions in a general journal:

May 3   Purchased merchandise from Cintron, $6,500. Invoice No. 321, dated May 1, terms n/30.

9   Purchased merchandise from Mitsui, $2,300. Invoice No. 614, dated May 8, terms 2/10, n/30.

18   Purchased merchandise from Aloha Distributors, $4,200. Invoice No. 180, dated May 15, terms 1/15, n/30.

23   Purchased merchandise from Soto, $6,300. Invoice No. 913, dated May 22, terms 1/10, n/30.

E 11-6A (LO3)

✓ Ending Accounts Payable balance: $8,600

JOURNALIZING PURCHASES RETURNS AND ALLOWANCES AND POSTING TO GENERAL LEDGER AND ACCOUNTS PAYABLE LEDGER Using page 3 of a general journal and the following general ledger and accounts payable ledger accounts, journalize and post the following transactions:

July 7   Returned merchandise to Starcraft Industries, $700.

15   Returned merchandise to XYZ, Inc., $450.

27   Returned merchandise to Datamagic, $900.

General Ledger

Account No.	Account	Balance July 1, 20--
202	Accounts Payable	$10,650
501.1	Purchases Returns and Allowances	---

Accounts Payable Ledger

Name	Balance July 1, 20--
Datamagic	$2,600
Starcraft Industries	4,300
XYZ, Inc.	3,750

E 11-7A (LO3)

✓ Sept. 12: Cr. Cash, $6,930

JOURNALIZING CASH PAYMENTS TRANSACTIONS Enter the following cash payments transactions in a general journal:

Sept. 5   Issued Check No. 318 to Clinton Corp. for merchandise purchased August 28, $6,000, terms 2/10, n/30. Payment is made within the discount period.

12   Issued Check No. 319 to Mitchell Company for merchandise purchased September 2, $7,500, terms 1/10, n/30. A credit memo had been received on September 8 from Mitchell Company for merchandise returned, $500. Payment is made within the discount period after deduction for the return dated September 8.

19   Issued Check No. 320 to Expert Systems for merchandise purchased August 20, $4,100, terms n/30.

27   Issued Check No. 321 to Graphic Data for merchandise purchased September 17, $9,000, terms 2/10, n/30. Payment is made within the discount period.

E 11-8A (LO4)

✓ Total Accounts Payable: $14,370

SCHEDULE OF ACCOUNTS PAYABLE Ryan's Express, a retail business, had the following beginning balances and purchases and payments activity in its accounts payable ledger during October. Prepare a schedule of accounts payable for Ryan's Express as of October 31, 20--.

Accounts Payable Ledger

Name	Balance Oct. 1, 20--	Purchases	Payments
Columbia Products	$4,350	$3,060	$2,060
Favorite Fashions	4,910	1,970	2,600
Rustic Legends	5,130	2,625	3,015

SERIES A PROBLEMS

P 11-9A (LO3)

✓ Purchases balance: $20,790

PURCHASES TRANSACTIONS J. B. Speck, owner of Speck's Galleria, made the following purchases of merchandise on account during the month of September:

Sept. 3   Purchase Invoice No. 415, $2,650, from Smith Distributors.

8   Purchase Invoice No. 132, $3,830, from Michaels Wholesaler.

11   Purchase Invoice No. 614, $3,140, from J. B. Sanders & Co.

18   Purchase Invoice No. 329, $2,250, from Bateman & Jones, Inc.

(continued)

Sept. 23   Purchase Invoice No. 767, $4,160, from Smith Distributors.

27   Purchase Invoice No. 744, $1,980, from Anderson Company.

30   Purchase Invoice No. 652, $2,780, from Michaels Wholesaler.

REQUIRED

1. Record the transactions in a general journal.

2. Post from the general journal to the general ledger accounts and to the accounts payable ledger accounts. Use general ledger account numbers as shown in the chapter.

P 11-10A (LO3)

✓ Accounts Payable balance: $1,900

CASH PAYMENTS TRANSACTIONS Sam Santiago operates a retail variety store. The books include a general journal and an accounts payable ledger.

Selected account balances on May 1 are as follows:

General Ledger	
Cash	$40,000
Accounts Payable	20,000

Accounts Payable Ledger	
Fantastic Toys	$5,200
Goya Outlet	3,800
Mueller's Distributors	3,600
Van Kooning	7,400

The following are the transactions related to cash payments for the month of May:

May 1   Issued Check No. 426 in payment of May rent (Rent Expense), $2,400.

3   Issued Check No. 427 to Mueller's Distributors in payment of merchandise purchased on account, $3,600, less a 3% discount. Check was written for $3,492.

7   Issued Check No. 428 to Van Kooning in partial payment of merchandise purchased on account, $5,500. A cash discount was not allowed.

12   Issued Check No. 429 to Fantastic Toys for merchandise purchased on account, $5,200, less a 1% discount. Check was written for $5,148.

15   Issued Check No. 430 to City Power and Light (Utilities Expense), $1,720.

18   Issued Check No. 431 to A-1 Warehouse for a cash purchase of merchandise, $4,800.

26   Issued Check No. 432 to Goya Outlet for merchandise purchased on account, $3,800, less a 2% discount. Check was written for $3,724.

30   Issued Check No. 433 to Mercury Transit Company for freight charges on merchandise purchased (Freight-In), $1,200.

31   Issued Check No. 434 to Town Merchants for a cash purchase of merchandise, $3,000.

REQUIRED

1. Enter the transactions in a general journal.

2. Post from the general journal to the general ledger and the accounts payable ledger. Use general ledger account numbers as shown in the chapter.

P 11-11A (LO3)

✓ Cash balance: $11,805

PURCHASES AND CASH PAYMENTS TRANSACTIONS Freddy Flint owns a small retail business called Flint's Fantasy. The cash account has a balance of $20,000 on July 1. The following transactions occurred during July:

July 1   Issued Check No. 414 in payment of July rent, $1,500.

1   Purchased merchandise on account from Tang's Toys, Invoice No. 311, $2,700, terms 2/10, n/30.

3   Purchased merchandise on account from Sillas & Company, Invoice No. 812, $3,100, terms 1/10, n/30.

5   Returned merchandise purchased from Tang's Toys, receiving a credit memo on the amount owed, $500.

8   Purchased merchandise on account from Daisy's Dolls, Invoice No. 139, $1,900, terms 2/10, n/30.

11   Issued Check No. 415 to Tang's Toys for merchandise purchased on account, less return of July 5 and less 2% discount.

13   Issued Check No. 416 to Sillas & Company for merchandise purchased on account, less 1% discount.

15   Returned merchandise purchased from Daisy's Dolls, receiving a credit memo on the amount owed, $400.

18   Issued Check No. 417 to Daisy's Dolls for merchandise purchased on account, less return of July 15 and less 2% discount.

25   Purchased merchandise on account from Allied Business, Invoice No. 489, $2,450, terms n/30.

26   Purchased merchandise on account from Tang's Toys, Invoice No. 375, $1,980, terms 2/10, n/30.

29   Purchased merchandise on account from Sillas & Company, Invoice No. 883, $3,460, terms 1/10, n/30.

REQUIRED

1. Enter the transactions in a general journal.

2. Post from the journal to the general ledger and accounts payable ledger accounts. Use general ledger account numbers as shown in the chapter.

P 11-12A (LO4)

✓ Accounts Payable balance, Tang's Toys: $1,980

SCHEDULE OF ACCOUNTS PAYABLE Based on the information provided in Problem 11-11A, prepare a schedule of accounts payable for Flint's Fantasy as of July 31, 20--. Verify that the accounts payable account balance in the general ledger agrees with the schedule of accounts payable total.

SERIES B EXERCISES

E 11-1B (LO1)

PURCHASING DOCUMENTS AND FLOWCHART LABELING A flowchart showing some of the major documents commonly used in the purchasing function of a merchandise business is presented below. Briefly describe each document.

E 11-2B (LO1)

✓ 2: $4,365

TRADE DISCOUNT AND CASH DISCOUNTS Merchandise was purchased on account from Grant's Distributors on June 12. The purchase price was $5,000, less a 10% trade discount and credit terms of 3/10, n/30.

1. Calculate the net amount to record the invoice, less the 10% trade discount.
2. Calculate the amount to be paid on this invoice within the discount period.
3. Journalize the purchase of the merchandise on June 12 and the payment on June 22 (within the discount period) in a general journal.

E 11-3B (LO2)

✓ 3(c): Purchases Discounts, $100

PURCHASE TRANSACTIONS AND T ACCOUNTS Using T accounts for Cash, Accounts Payable, Purchases, Purchases Returns and Allowances, Purchases Discounts, and Freight-In, enter the following purchase transactions. Identify each transaction with its corresponding letter. Use a new set of T accounts for each set of transactions, 1–4.

1. Purchase of merchandise with cash.

   (a) Merchandise is purchased for cash, $2,300.
   (b) Merchandise listed at $4,000, less a trade discount of 10%, is purchased for cash.

2. Purchase of merchandise on account with credit terms.

   (a) Merchandise is purchased on account, credit terms 2/10, n/30, $4,000.
   (b) Merchandise is purchased on account, credit terms 3/10, n/30, $2,800.
   (c) Payment is made on invoice (a) within the discount period.
   (d) Payment is made on invoice (b) too late to receive the cash discount.

3. Purchase of merchandise on account with return of merchandise.

   (a) Merchandise is purchased on account, credit terms 2/10, n/30, $5,600.
   (b) Merchandise is returned for credit before payment is made, $600.
   (c) Payment is made within the discount period.

4. Purchase of merchandise with freight-in.

   (a) Merchandise is purchased on account, $3,800 plus freight charges of $200. Terms of the sale were FOB shipping point.
   (b) Payment is made for the cost of merchandise and the freight charge.

E 11-4B (LO2)

✓ Cost of goods sold: $76,700

COMPUTING GROSS PROFIT The following data were taken from the accounts of Burnside Bedknobs, a retail business. Determine the gross profit.

Sales	$116,900
Sales returns and allowances	1,100
Sales discounts	400
Merchandise inventory, January 1	30,000
Purchases during the period	100,000
Purchases returns and allowances during the period	2,000
Purchases discounts taken during the period	2,800
Freight-in on merchandise purchased during the period	1,500
Merchandise inventory, December 31	50,000

E 11-5B (LO3)

✓ Jan. 12: Dr. Purchases, $9,000

JOURNALIZING PURCHASES TRANSACTIONS Journalize the following transactions in a general journal:

Jan. 3   Purchased merchandise from Feng, $6,000. Invoice No. 416, dated January 1, terms 2/10, n/30.

     12   Purchased merchandise from Miranda, $9,000. Invoice No. 624, dated January 10, terms n/30.

Jan. 19   Purchased merchandise from J. B. Barba, $6,400. Invoice No. 190, dated January 18, terms 1/10, n/30.

26   Purchased merchandise from Ramirez, $3,700. Invoice No. 923, dated January 25, terms 1/15, n/30.

E 11-6B (LO3)

✓ Ending Accounts Payable balance: $6,950

JOURNALIZING PURCHASES RETURNS AND ALLOWANCES AND POSTING TO GENERAL LEDGER AND ACCOUNTS PAYABLE LEDGER Using page 3 of a general journal and the following general ledger accounts and accounts payable ledger accounts, journalize and post the following transactions:

Mar. 5   Returned merchandise to Tower Industries, $500.

11   Returned merchandise to A & D Arms, $625.

23   Returned merchandise to Mighty Mansion, $275.

General Ledger

Account No.	Account	Balance Mar 1, 20--
202	Accounts Payable	$8,350
501.1	Purchases Returns and Allowances	---

Accounts Payable Ledger

Name	Balance Mar 1, 20--
A & D Arms	$2,300
Mighty Mansion	1,450
Tower Industries	4,600

E 11-7B (LO3)

✓ Apr. 19: Cr. Cash, $4,950

JOURNALIZING CASH PAYMENTS TRANSACTIONS Enter the following cash payments transactions in a general journal:

Apr. 5   Issued Check No. 429 to Standard Industries for merchandise purchased March 27, $8,000, terms 2/10, n/30. Payment is made within the discount period.

19   Issued Check No. 430 to Finest Company for merchandise purchased April 10, $5,300, terms 1/10, n/30. A credit memo had been received on April 12 from Finest Company for merchandise returned, $300. Payment is made within the discount period after deduction for the return dated April 12.

21   Issued Check No. 431 to Funny Follies for merchandise purchased March 22, $3,250, terms n/30.

29   Issued Check No. 432 to Classic Data for merchandise purchased April 20, $7,000, terms 2/10, n/30. Payment is made within the discount period.

E 11-8B (LO4)

✓ Total accounts payable: $10,565

SCHEDULE OF ACCOUNTS PAYABLE Crystal's Candles, a retail business, had the following balances and purchases and payments activity in its accounts payable ledger during November. Prepare a schedule of accounts payable for Crystal's Candles as of November 30, 20--.

Accounts Payable Ledger

Name	Balance Nov. 1, 20--	Purchases	Payments
Carl's Candle Wax	$4,135	$ 955	$1,610
Handy Supplies	3,490	1,320	1,850
Wishy Wicks	3,300	1,905	1,080

SERIES B PROBLEMS

P 11-9B (LO3)

✓ Purchases balance: $18,515

PURCHASES TRANSACTIONS Ann Benton, owner of Benton's Galleria, made the following purchases of merchandise on account during the month of October:

Oct. 2   Purchase Invoice No. 321, $1,950, from Boggs Distributors.

7   Purchase Invoice No. 152, $2,915, from Wolfs Wholesaler.

10   Purchase Invoice No. 634, $3,565, from Komuro & Co.

16   Purchase Invoice No. 349, $2,845, from Fritz & McCord, Inc.

24   Purchase Invoice No. 587, $3,370, from Boggs Distributors.

26   Purchase Invoice No. 764, $2,240, from Sanderson Company.

31   Purchase Invoice No. 672, $1,630, from Wolfs Wholesaler.

REQUIRED

1.   Record the transactions in a general journal.

2.   Post from the general journal to the general ledger accounts and to the accounts payable ledger accounts. Use general ledger account numbers as shown in the chapter.

P 11-10B (LO3)

✓ Accounts Payable balance: $600

CASH PAYMENTS TRANSACTIONS Kay Zembrowski operates a retail variety store. The books include a general journal and an accounts payable ledger. Selected account balances on May 1 are as follows:

General Ledger

Cash	$40,000
Accounts Payable	20,000

Accounts Payable Ledger

Cortez Distributors	$4,200
Indra & Velga	6,800
Toy Corner	4,600
Troutman Outlet	4,400

The following transactions are related to cash payments for the month of May:

May 1   Issued Check No. 326 in payment of May rent (Rent Expense), $2,600.

4   Issued Check No. 327 to Cortez Distributors in payment of merchandise purchased on account, $4,200, less a 3% discount. Check was written for $4,074.

7   Issued Check No. 328 to Indra & Velga in partial payment of merchandise purchased on account, $6,200. A cash discount was not allowed.

11   Issued Check No. 329 to Toy Corner for merchandise purchased on account, $4,600, less a 1% discount. Check was written for $4,554.

15   Issued Check No. 330 to County Power and Light (Utilities Expense), $1,500.

19   Issued Check No. 331 to Builders Warehouse for a cash purchase of merchandise, $3,500.

25   Issued Check No. 332 to Troutman Outlet for merchandise purchased on account, $4,400, less a 2% discount. Check was written for $4,312.

May 30   Issued Check No. 333 to Rapid Transit Company for freight charges on merchandise purchased (Freight-In), $800.

31   Issued Check No. 334 to City Merchants for a cash purchase of merchandise, $2,350.

REQUIRED

1. Enter the transactions in a general journal.

2. Post from the general journal to the general ledger and the accounts payable ledger. Use general ledger account numbers as shown in the chapter.

P 11-11B (LO3)

✓ Cash balance: $12,790

PURCHASES AND CASH PAYMENTS TRANSACTIONS Debbie Mueller owns a small retail business called Debbie's Doll House. The cash account has a balance of $20,000 on July 1. The following transactions occurred during July:

July 1   Issued Check No. 314 for July rent, $1,400.

1   Purchased merchandise on account from Topper's Toys, Invoice No. 211, $2,500, terms 2/10, n/30.

3   Purchased merchandise on account from Jones & Company, Invoice No. 812, $2,800, terms 1/10, n/30.

5   Returned merchandise purchased from Topper's Toys receiving a credit memo on the amount owed, $400.

8   Purchased merchandise on account from Downtown Merchants, Invoice No. 159, $1,600, terms 2/10, n/30.

11   Issued Check No. 315 to Topper's Toys for merchandise purchased on account, less return of July 5 and less 2% discount.

13   Issued Check No. 316 to Jones & Company for merchandise purchased on account, less 1% discount.

15   Returned merchandise purchased from Downtown Merchants receiving a credit memo on the amount owed, $600.

18   Issued Check No. 317 to Downtown Merchants for merchandise purchased on account, less return of July 15 and less 2% discount.

25   Purchased merchandise on account from Columbia Products, Invoice No. 468, $3,200, terms n/30.

26   Purchased merchandise on account from Topper's Toys, Invoice No. 395, $1,430, terms 2/10, n/30.

29   Purchased merchandise on account from Jones & Company, Invoice No. 853, $2,970, terms 1/10, n/30.

REQUIRED

1. Enter the transactions in a general journal.

2. Post from the journal to the general ledger and accounts payable ledger accounts. Use general ledger account numbers as shown in the chapter.

P 11-12B (LO4)

✓ Accounts Payable balance, Topper's Toys: $1,430

SCHEDULE OF ACCOUNTS PAYABLE Based on the information provided in Problem 11-11B, prepare a schedule of accounts payable for Debbie's Doll House as of July 31, 20--. Verify that the accounts payable account balance in the general ledger agrees with the schedule of accounts payable total.

MANAGING YOUR WRITING

You are working as a summer intern at a rapidly growing organic food distributor. Part of your responsibility is to assist in the accounts payable department. You notice that most bills from suppliers are not paid within the discount period. The manager of accounts payable says the bills are organized by vendor, like the accounts payable ledger, and she is too busy to keep track of the discount periods. Besides, the owner has told her that the 1% and 2% discounts available are not worth worrying about.

Write a memo to the owner explaining why it is expensive not to take advantage of cash discounts on credit purchases. In addition, suggest a way to file (organize) supplier invoices so that they are paid within the discount period.

ETHICS CASE

Bob's Discount Auto Parts receives a cash discount of 2% from Auto Warehouse if it pays an invoice within 10 days. Bob, the owner, consistently sends payments 15 to 20 days after receiving the invoice and still deducts the amount of the discount. Last week, Bob received a call from Auto Warehouse reminding him that in order to get the discount, an invoice must be paid within 10 days. When Bob received the next invoice, he dated the check exactly 10 days from the date of the invoice but didn't mail the check for another week. The receivables manager from Auto Warehouse called Bob and again reminded him that the check should be mailed by the 10th day in order to receive the 2% discount. When Bob received the next invoice, he mailed it on time but post-dated the check for the following week.

1. Are Bob's attempts to extend the discount period unethical?

2. What alternatives can Auto Warehouse take to prevent Bob's Discount Auto Parts from stretching the discount period?

3. Write a short note from Auto Warehouse to Bob's Discount Auto Parts explaining cash discounts and credit terms.

4. In small groups, make a list of the advantages and disadvantages of offering cash discounts.

MASTERY PROBLEM

✓ Accounts Payable balance: $10,000

Michelle French owns and operates Books and More, a retail book store. Selected account balances on June 1 are as follows:

General Ledger

Cash	$32,200.00
Accounts Payable	2,000.00
M. French, Drawing	18,000.00
Purchases	67,021.66
Purchases Returns and Allowances	2,315.23
Purchases Discounts	905.00
Freight-In	522.60
Rent Expense	3,125.00
Utilities Expense	1,522.87

Accounts Payable Ledger

Northeastern Publishing Co.	$ 2,000.00

The following purchases and cash payments transactions took place during the month of June:

June 1   Purchased books on account from Irving Publishing Company, $2,100. Invoice No. 101, terms 2/10, n/30, FOB destination.

2   Issued Check No. 300 to Northeastern Publishing Co. for goods purchased on May 23, terms 2/10, n/30, $1,960 (the $2,000 invoice amount less the 2% discount).

3   Purchased books on account from Broadway Publishing, Inc., $2,880. Invoice No. 711, less a 20% trade discount, and invoice terms of 3/10, n/30, FOB shipping point.

3   Issued Check No. 301 to Mayday Shipping for delivery from Broadway Publishing, Inc., $250.

4   Issued Check No. 302 for June rent, $625.

8   Purchased books on account from Northeastern Publishing Co., $5,825. Invoice No. 268, terms 2/eom, n/60, FOB destination.

10   Received a credit memo from Irving Publishing Company, $550. Books had been returned because the covers were on upside down.

13   Issued Check No. 304 to Broadway Publishing, Inc., for the purchase made on June 3. (Check No. 303 was voided because an error was made in preparing it.)

28   Made the following purchases:

Invoice No.	Company	Amount	Terms
579	Broadway Publishing, Inc.	$2,350	2/10, n/30, FOB destination
406	Northeastern Publishing Co.	4,200	2/eom, n/60, FOB destination
964	Riley Publishing Co.	3,450	3/10, n/30, FOB destination

30   Issued Check No. 305 to Taylor County Utility Co. for June utilities, $325.

30   French withdrew cash for personal use, $4,500. Issued check no. 306.

30   Issued Check No. 307 to Irving Publishing Company for purchase made on June 1 less returns made on June 10.

30   Issued Check No. 308 to Northeastern Publishing Co. for purchase made on June 8.

30   Issued Check No. 309 for books purchased at an auction, $1,328.

REQUIRED

1. Enter the transactions in a general journal (start with page 16).

2. Post from the journal to the general ledger accounts and the accounts payable ledger. Use general ledger account numbers as indicated in the chapter.

3. Prepare a schedule of accounts payable.

4. If merchandise inventory was $35,523 on January 1 and $42,100 as of June 30, prepare the cost of goods sold section of the income statement for the six months ended June 30, 20--.

CHALLENGE PROBLEM

This problem challenges you to apply your cumulative accounting knowledge to move a step beyond the material in the chapter.

✓ May 14: Cr. Purchases Discounts, $9

Record the following transactions in a general journal:

May 4	Merchandise listed at $2,900, less a trade discount of 10%, is purchased on account, credit terms of 1/10, n/30, shipping terms FOB destination.
8	Merchandise purchased on May 4, listed at $520, is returned for credit.
14	Partial payment is made for the merchandise purchased on May 4, listed at $1,000, less 1% discount.
June 3	Payment is made of the balance due on the May 4 purchase.

ANSWERS TO SELF-STUDY QUESTIONS AND EXERCISES

True/False Questions

1. F (purchase requisition)
2. T
3. T
4. F (credited)
5. F (buyer)

Multiple Choice Questions

1. d **2.** a **3.** a **4.** d **5.** b

U REVU Exercises

1. a. $1,200 × 10% = $120
   b. $1,200 − $120 = $1,080
   c. $1,200 − $120 = $1,080 × 1% = $10.80

2.

Net sales			$92,000
Cost of goods sold:			
Merchandise inventory, Jan. 1		$27,000	
Purchases	$60,800		
Less: Purchases returns and allowances	$3,100		
Purchases discounts	1,300	4,400	
Cost of goods purchased		56,400	
Goods available for sale		$83,400	
Less merchandise inventory, Dec. 31		24,000	
Cost of goods sold			59,400
Gross profit			$32,600

3.

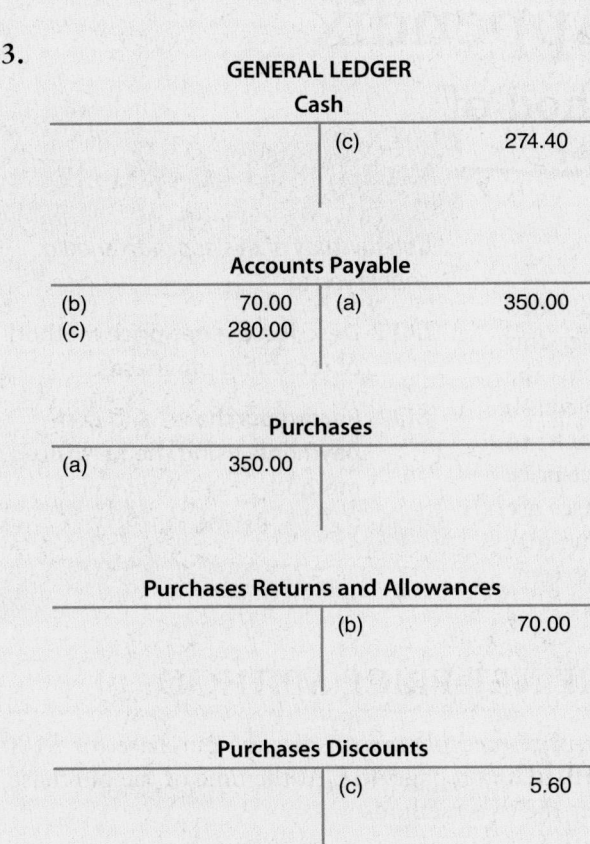

GENERAL LEDGER

Cash

		(c)	274.40

Accounts Payable

(b)	70.00	(a)	350.00
(c)	280.00		

Purchases

(a)	350.00		

Purchases Returns and Allowances

		(b)	70.00

Purchases Discounts

		(c)	5.60

Accounts Payable Ledger

J. Bedas

(b)	70.00	(a)	350.00
(c)	280.00		

4.

Felini Plumbing
Schedule of Accounts Payable
June 30, 20--

B. Sutton	$ 245
A. Gagne	328
L. Mohler	590
P. Luffman	190
Z. Quary	153
Total	$1,506

Chapter 11 Appendix

The Net-Price Method of Recording Purchases

LEARNING OBJECTIVES

Careful study of this appendix should enable you to:

LO1 Describe the net-price method of recording purchases.

LO2 Record purchases and cash payments using the net-price method.

NET-PRICE METHOD

LO1 Describe the net-price method of recording purchases.

In this chapter, purchases were recorded using the **gross-price method.** Under this method, purchases are recorded at the gross amount, regardless of available cash discounts. An alternative approach to accounting for purchases is the **net-price method.** Under this method, purchases are recorded at the net amount, assuming that all available cash discounts will be taken.

RECORDING WITH THE NET-PRICE METHOD

LO2 Record purchases and cash payments using the net-price method.

To compare the gross-price and net-price methods, reconsider the purchase for $100 on account, with credit terms of 2/10, n/30, on page 403. At the time of the purchase, the following entries are made under the two methods:

Gross-Price			Net-Price		
Purchases	100.00		Purchases	98.00*	
Accounts Payable		100.00	Accounts Payable		98.00

*$100—$2 (2% cash discount)

If the payment for the merchandise is made within the discount period, the entries are as follows:

Gross-Price			Net-Price		
Accounts Payable	100.00		Accounts Payable	98.00	
Cash		98.00	Cash		98.00
Purchases Discounts		2.00			

If payment for the merchandise is not made until after the discount period, the entries are as follows:

Gross-Price			Net-Price		
Accounts Payable	100.00		Accounts Payable	98.00	
Cash		100.00	Purchases Discounts Lost	2.00	
			Cash		100.00

Note that under the net-price method a new account, Purchases Discounts Lost, is used. Purchases Discounts Lost is a temporary owner's equity account used to record cash discounts lost on purchases. It is reported as an expense on the income statement.

Purchases Discounts Lost

Debit	Credit
to enter discounts lost because of late payment of invoices	

Purchases Discounts Lost represents a finance charge for postponing the payment for merchandise. If the balance in this account is large relative to the amount of gross purchases, management should review its cash payment procedures.

LEARNING OBJECTIVES   Key Points to Remember

LO1 Describe the net-price method of recording purchases.	Under the net-price method, purchases are recorded at the net amount, assuming all available cash discounts will be taken.
LO2 Record purchases and cash payments using the net-price method.	Assume a purchase is made for $100 on account, with credit terms of 2/10, n/30. Under the net-price method, the entry at the time of purchase is as follows:

Purchases	98.00	
Accounts Payable		98.00

If payment is made within the discount period, the entry is as follows:

Accounts Payable	98.00	
Cash		98.00

If payment is not made until after the discount period, the entry is as follows:

Accounts Payable	98.00	
Purchases Discounts Lost	2.00	
Cash		100.00

KEY TERMS

gross-price method (436)   Under this method, purchases are recorded at the gross amount.

net-price method (436)   Under this method, purchases are recorded at the net amount, assuming all available cash discounts are taken.

REVIEW QUESTIONS

LO1 1. At what amount are purchases recorded under the net-price method?

LO2 2. Under the net-price method, if payment for merchandise is not made within the discount period, what accounts are debited when the payment is made?

LO2 3. (a) What kind of an account is Purchases Discounts Lost?
(b) How is this item reported on the income statement?

SERIES A EXERCISE

E 11Apx-1A (LO2)

✓ 1. Apr. 11: Cr. Purchases
Discounts, $20

PURCHASES TRANSACTIONS—GROSS-PRICE AND NET-PRICE METHODS
Romero's Heating and Cooling had the following transactions during April:

Apr. 2   Purchased merchandise on account from Alanon Valve for $1,000, terms 2/10, n/30.

5   Purchased merchandise on account from Leon's Garage for $1,400, terms 1/10, n/30.

11   Paid the amount due to Alanon Valve for the purchase on April 2.

25   Paid the amount due to Leon's Garage for the purchase on April 5.

1. Prepare general journal entries for these transactions using the gross-price method.
2. Prepare general journal entries for these transactions using the net-price method.

SERIES B EXERCISE

E 11Apx-1B (LO2)

✓ 2. May 27: Dr. Purchases
Discounts Lost, $12

PURCHASES TRANSACTIONS—GROSS-PRICE AND NET-PRICE METHODS
Gloria's Repair Shop had the following transactions during May:

May 2   Purchased merchandise on account from Delgado's Supply for $900, terms 2/10, n/30.

6   Purchased merchandise on account from Goro's Auto Care for $1,200, terms 1/10, n/30.

11   Paid the amount due to Delgado's Supply for the purchase on May 2.

27   Paid the amount due to Goro's Auto Care for the purchase on May 6.

1. Prepare general journal entries for these transactions using the gross-price method.
2. Prepare general journal entries for these transactions using the net-price method.

## Chapter 12

RACHEL EPSTEIN/PHOTOEDIT

Special Journals

If you are an active health and fitness enthusiast, you might already know of NewHealth Nutrition, perhaps through its nutraplanet.com Web site. NewHealth Nutrition was founded in 2001 in Fayetteville, Georgia. In 2004, after a slow start operating from a traditional storefront, the company began selling on the Internet and the business took off. In the last four years, sales have quadrupled to more than $4 million.

NewHealth Nutrition sells a wide array of sports nutrition and health supplements. Many are targeted at bodybuilding, but its product categories include amino acids, carbohydrates, cardiovascular support, fat burners, herbs, joint support, and many others. Its products tend to be priced in the $13–$70 range. Most of the sales for a company like this probably would be for relatively small dollar amounts. This means the volume of transactions to generate annual sales of $4 million would be huge. NewHealth Nutrition would need a way to record all of this activity that is more efficient than the methods we have seen in Chapters 10 and 11. In Chapter 12, you will learn about a more efficient way to record transactions. In the "A Broader View Feature," you will see how computer software can add even greater efficiency.

LEARNING OBJECTIVES

Careful study of this chapter should enable you to:

LO1 Describe, explain the purpose of, and identify transactions recorded in special journals.

LO2 Describe and use the sales journal.

LO3 Describe and use the cash receipts journal.

LO4 Describe and use the purchases journal.

LO5 Describe and use the cash payments journal.

Chapters 10 and 11 demonstrated how to account for sales, cash receipts, purchases, and cash payments in a merchandising business. We also saw how to use accounts receivable and accounts payable ledgers to keep track of individual customer and supplier accounts. In this chapter, we continue to study how to account for sales, cash receipts, purchases, and cash payments, but our objective is to find a way to be more efficient. We will learn how to use four special journals that enable us to achieve this objective.

SPECIAL JOURNALS

LO1 Describe, explain the purpose of, and identify transactions recorded in special journals.

A **special journal** is a journal designed for recording only certain kinds of transactions. A special journal can be created for almost any kind of transaction. The types of special journals a business uses should depend on the types of transactions that occur most frequently for a business. The more transactions of a specific type that occur, the more likely a special journal of that type would be useful for the business.

The primary purpose of using special journals is to save time journalizing and posting transactions. In a general journal, we recorded transactions by writing the account names, debit and credit amounts, and an explanation for each transaction on several lines in the journal. In contrast, most transactions are entered in a special journal on a single line, with the debit and credit amounts indicated in special columns provided for each account. This enables substantial time saving. The posting process also is more efficient. Using the general journal, each transaction is posted separately to the appropriate general ledger accounts. With a special journal, summary postings of column totals are made to appropriate accounts on a periodic basis.

Of course, even if a business uses special journals, there still is a need for a general journal. For example, transactions that occur infrequently, and adjusting and closing entries, usually are recorded in the general journal.

Four special journals commonly used by businesses are as follows:

- Sales journal
- Cash receipts journal
- Purchases journal
- Cash payments journal

LEARNING KEY

The special journals and general journal are books of original entry. Each transaction is recorded in only <u>one</u> of these journals.

Figure 12-1 identifies the types of transactions recorded in each of the four special journals and the general journal. You might find it helpful to refer back to Figure 12-1 as the four special journals are introduced in this chapter.

FIGURE 12-1 Types of Journals and Transactions

TYPE OF JOURNAL	TYPE OF TRANSACTIONS RECORDED
Sales journal	All sales of merchandise on account
Cash receipts journal	All cash receipts
Purchases journal	All purchases of merchandise on account
Cash payments journal	All cash payments
General journal	All other transactions

In the following sections, we will examine the journalizing and posting process using each of the four special journals.

SALES JOURNAL

LO2 Describe and use the sales journal.

A **sales journal** is a special journal used to record only sales of merchandise on account. To illustrate the journalizing and posting of sales transactions in the sales journal, we use the following five sales transactions for Northern Micro from Chapter 10.

Apr. 4 Made Sale No. 133C on account to Enrico Lorenzo, $1,520, plus $76 sales tax.

10 Made Sale No. 134C on account to Brenda Myers, $440, plus $22 sales tax.

18 Made Sale No. 105D on account to Edith Walton, $980, plus $49 sales tax.

21 Made Sale No. 202B on account to Susan Chang, $620, plus $31 sales tax.

24 Made Sale No. 162A on account to Heidi Schwitzer, $1,600, plus $80 sales tax.

The general journal entries for these five transactions are shown in Figure 12-2.

FIGURE 12-2 Sales Entered in General Journal

4	Apr.	4	Accounts Receivable/E. Lorenzo		1	5	9	6	00							4
5			Sales							1	5	2	0	00		5
6			Sales Tax Payable									7	6	00		6
7			Sale No. 133C													7
8																8
9		10	Accounts Receivable/B. Myers			4	6	2	00							9
10			Sales								4	4	0	00		10
11			Sales Tax Payable									2	2	00		11
12			Sale No. 134C													12
13																13
14		18	Accounts Receivable/E. Walton		1	0	2	9	00							14
15			Sales								9	8	0	00		15
16			Sales Tax Payable									4	9	00		16
17			Sale No. 105D													17
18																18
19		21	Accounts Receivable/S. Chang			6	5	1	00							19
20			Sales								6	2	0	00		20
21			Sales Tax Payable									3	1	00		21
22			Sale No. 202B													22
23																23
24		24	Accounts Receivable/H. Schwitzer		1	6	8	0	00							24
25			Sales							1	6	0	0	00		25
26			Sales Tax Payable									8	0	00		26
27			Sale No. 162A													27

LEARNING KEY

Use a sales journal only for recording sales of merchandise on account.

Notice that each of these five entries involved the same three accounts. The same account titles were recorded five times. Similarly, to post these entries to the general ledger, five separate postings would be made to each of the three accounts, a total of 15 postings.

These transactions can be recorded more efficiently by using a sales journal. To illustrate, reconsider the five sales made on account by Northern Micro. They are entered in the sales journal in Figure 12-3. The sales journal provides separate columns for Accounts Receivable Debit, Sales Credit, and Sales Tax Payable Credit, the three accounts used repeatedly in the general journal in Figure 12-2. A sale is recorded in the sales journal by entering the following information:

1. Date

2. Sale number

3. Customer (to whom sold)

4. Dollar amounts

There is no need to enter any general ledger account titles, since they appear in the column headings.

FIGURE 12-3 Northern Micro Sales Journal

	DATE		SALE NO.	TO WHOM SOLD	POST. REF.	ACCOUNTS RECEIVABLE DEBIT					SALES CREDIT					SALES TAX PAYABLE CREDIT				
1	20-- Apr.	4	133C	Enrico Lorenzo		1	5	9	6	00	1	5	2	0	00		7	6	00	1
2		10	134C	Brenda Myers			4	6	2	00		4	4	0	00		2	2	00	2
3		18	105D	Edith Walton		1	0	2	9	00		9	8	0	00		4	9	00	3
4		21	202B	Susan Chang			6	5	1	00		6	2	0	00		3	1	00	4
5		24	162A	Heidi Schwitzer		1	6	8	0	00	1	6	0	0	00		8	0	00	5

SALES JOURNAL — PAGE 6

The sales journal in Figure 12-3 is designed for a company, like Northern Micro, that charges sales tax. For a wholesaler or any other company that does not charge sales tax, a sales journal like that in Figure 12-4 would be sufficient. In this case, there is only a single amount column headed Accounts Receivable Debit/Sales Credit. With no sales tax, the Accounts Receivable Debit and Sales Credit amounts are identical for each sale. Thus, only a single column is needed.

FIGURE 12-4 Sales Journal Without Sales Tax

DATE	SALE NO.	TO WHOM SOLD	POST. REF.	ACCOUNTS RECEIVABLE DEBIT/ SALES CREDIT	

SALES JOURNAL — PAGE 1

POSTING FROM THE SALES JOURNAL

Posting from the sales journal also is very efficient. Each general ledger account used in the sales journal requires only one posting each period. Figure 12-5 illustrates the general ledger posting process for Northern Micro's sales journal for the month of April.

The following steps are used to post from the sales journal to the general ledger at the end of each month, as indicated in Figure 12-5:

In the sales journal:

STEP 1 Total the amount columns, verify that the total of the debit column equals the total of the credit columns, and rule the columns.

In the ledger account:

STEP 2 Enter the date of the transaction in the Date column.

STEP 3 Enter the amount of the debit or credit in the Debit or Credit column.

STEP 4 Enter the new balance in the Balance columns under Debit or Credit.

STEP 5 Enter the initial "S" and the journal page number in the Posting Reference column.

In the sales journal:

STEP 6 Enter the ledger account number immediately below the column totals for each account that is posted.

FIGURE 12-5 Posting the Sales Journal to the General Ledger

					SALES JOURNAL			Page 6

SALES JOURNAL — Page 6

Date		Sale No.	To Whom Sold	Post. Ref.	Accounts Receivable Debit	Sales Credit	Sales Tax Payable Credit
20--							
Apr.	4	133C	Enrico Lorenzo		1,596.00	1,520.00	76.00
	10	134C	Brenda Myers		462.00	440.00	22.00
	18	105D	Edith Walton		1,029.00	980.00	49.00
	21	202B	Susan Chang		651.00	620.00	31.00
	24	162A	Heidi Schwitzer		1,680.00	1,600.00	80.00
					5,418.00	5,160.00	258.00
					(122)	(401)	(231)

1

6   3

GENERAL LEDGER (Partial)

ACCOUNT   Accounts Receivable   ACCOUNT NO. 122

Date		Item	Post. Ref.	Debit	Credit	Balance Debit	Balance Credit
20--							
Apr.	1	Bal.	✔			12,000.00	
	30	5	S6	5,418.00		17,418.00	

2 ... 4

ACCOUNT   Sales Tax Payable   ACCOUNT NO. 231

Date		Item	Post. Ref.	Debit	Credit	Balance Debit	Balance Credit
20--							
Apr.	30	5	S6		258.00		258.00

2 ... 4

ACCOUNT   Sales   ACCOUNT NO. 401

Date		Item	Post. Ref.	Debit	Credit	Balance Debit	Balance Credit
20--							
Apr.	1	Bal.	✔				27,000.00
	30	5	S6		5,160.00		32,160.00

2 ... 4

1 Debit total: $5,418

Credit total: $5,160
                    258
                  $5,418

LEARNING KEY

All special journal entries are posted to the general and subsidiary ledger accounts, *not* to the general journal.

As we saw in Chapter 10, Northern Micro also needs a record of the accounts receivable from *individual customers*. Figure 12-6 illustrates the use of the accounts receivable ledger. The accounts receivable ledger is posted *daily* so that current information is available for each customer at all times. The following steps are used to post the sales journal to the accounts receivable ledger, as shown in Figure 12-6:

FIGURE 12-6 Posting from the Sales Journal to the Accounts Receivable Ledger

SALES JOURNAL
Page 6

Date	Sale No.	To Whom Sold	Post. Ref.	Accounts Receivable Debit	Sales Credit	Sales Tax Payable Credit
20--						
Apr. 4	133C	Enrico Lorenzo	✔	1,596.00	1,520.00	76.00
10	134C	Brenda Myers	✔	462.00	440.00	22.00
18	105D	Edith Walton	✔	1,029.00	980.00	49.00
21	202B	Susan Chang	✔	651.00	620.00	31.00
24	162A	Heidi Schwitzer	✔	1,680.00	1,600.00	80.00
			5	5,418.00	5,160.00	258.00
				(122)	(401)	(231)

ACCOUNTS RECEIVABLE LEDGER

NAME Helen Avery
ADDRESS 1739 Woodsage Trace, Indianapolis, IN 46237-1199

Date	Item	Post. Ref.	Debit	Credit	Balance
20--					
Apr. 1	Bal.	✔			2,302.00

NAME Susan Chang
ADDRESS 337 Elm Street, Noblesville, IN 46060-3377

Date	Item	Post. Ref.	Debit	Credit	Balance
20--					
Apr. 21	4	S6	651.00		651.00

NAME Enrico Lorenzo
ADDRESS 5240 Tousley Court, Indianapolis, IN 46224-5678

Date	Item	Post. Ref.	Debit	Credit	Balance
20--					
Apr. 4	4	S6	1,596.00		1,596.00

NAME Brenda Myers
ADDRESS 581 Acorn Way, Zionsville, IN 46077-2154

Date	Item	Post. Ref.	Debit	Credit	Balance
20--					
Apr. 10	4	S6	462.00		462.00

NAME Heidi Schwitzer
ADDRESS 5858 Wildflower Cir., Bloomington, IN 47401-6209

Date	Item	Post. Ref.	Debit	Credit	Balance
20--					
Apr. 1	Bal.	✔			1,883.00
24	4	S6	1,680.00		3,563.00

NAME Ken Ulmet
ADDRESS 5260 Eagle Creek, Indianapolis, IN 46254-8275

Date	Item	Post. Ref.	Debit	Credit	Balance
20--					
Apr. 1	Bal.	✔			3,315.00

NAME Edith Walton
ADDRESS 1113 Stones Crossing, Zionsville, IN 46077-6601

Date	Item	Post. Ref.	Debit	Credit	Balance
20--					
Apr. 18	4	S6	1,029.00		1,029.00

NAME Vivian Winston
ADDRESS 124 Main St., Zionsville, IN 46077-1358

Date	Item	Post. Ref.	Debit	Credit	Balance
20--					
Apr. 1	Bal.	✔			4,500.00

GENERAL LEDGER (Partial)

ACCOUNT Accounts Receivable **ACCOUNT NO. 122**

Date	Item	Post. Ref.	Debit	Credit	Balance Debit	Balance Credit
20--						
Apr. 1	Bal.	✔			12,000.00	
30		S6	5,418.00		17,418.00	

ACCOUNT Sales Tax Payable **ACCOUNT NO. 231**

Date	Item	Post. Ref.	Debit	Credit	Balance Debit	Balance Credit
20--						
Apr. 30		S6		258.00		258.00

ACCOUNT Sales **ACCOUNT NO. 401**

Date	Item	Post. Ref.	Debit	Credit	Balance Debit	Balance Credit
20--						
Apr. 1	Bal.	✔				27,000.00
30		S6		5,160.00		32,160.00

In the accounts receivable ledger account:

STEP 1 Enter the date of the transaction in the Date column.

STEP 2 Enter the amount of the debit or credit in the Debit or Credit column.

STEP 3 Enter the new balance in the Balance column.

STEP 4 Enter the initial "S" and the journal page number in the Posting Reference column.

In the sales journal:

STEP 5 Enter a check mark (✓) in the Posting Reference column of the journal for each transaction that is posted.

The accounts receivable ledger also can be posted from the source document used to make the sales journal entry. For example, sales ticket #134C (see Figure 10-2) could be used to post that sale to Brenda Myers' account in the accounts receivable ledger. In this case, 134C would be inserted in the Posting Reference column of her account.

Note the relationship between the sales journal, accounts receivable ledger, and general ledger. All individual entries in the sales journal are posted to the accounts receivable ledger. The totals of all entries in the sales journal are posted to the general ledger accounts. After the posting of the accounts receivable ledger and the general ledger is completed, the total of the accounts receivable ledger balances should equal the Accounts Receivable balance in the general ledger.

LEARNING KEY

The total of the accounts receivable ledger balances must equal the Accounts Receivable balance in the general ledger.

U REVU

Complete U REVU-1 on **page 468** to test your basic understanding of LO2.

CASH RECEIPTS JOURNAL

LO3 Describe and use the cash receipts journal.

A **cash receipts journal** is a special journal used to record only cash receipts transactions. To illustrate its use, we continue with the transactions of Northern Micro. Northern Micro's cash receipts journal for the month of April is shown in Figure 12-7, with the following transactions:

Apr. 14 Received cash on account from Enrico Lorenzo for Sale No. 133C, $1,596.

20 Received cash on account from Brenda Myers for Sale No. 134C, $462.

28 Received cash on account from Edith Walton for Sale No. 105D, $1,029.

30 Made cash sales for the month of $3,600 plus tax of $180.

30 Made bank credit card sales for the month of $2,500 plus tax of $125. Bank credit card expenses on these sales are $100.

30 Received cash for rent revenue, $600.

30 Borrowed cash from the bank by signing a note, $3,000.

Northern Micro's cash receipts journal provides separate columns for Accounts Receivable Credit, Sales Credit, Sales Tax Payable Credit, Bank Credit Card Expense Debit, and Cash Debit. These are the accounts most frequently affected by Northern

FIGURE 12-7 Northern Micro Cash Receipts Journal

	DATE		ACCOUNT CREDITED	POST. REF.	GENERAL CREDIT					ACCOUNTS RECEIVABLE CREDIT					SALES CREDIT					SALES TAX PAYABLE CREDIT					BANK CREDIT CARD EXPENSE DEBIT					CASH DEBIT					
	20--																																		
1	Apr.	14	Enrico Lorenzo							1	5	9	6	00																1	5	9	6	00	1
2		20	Brenda Myers								4	6	2	00																	4	6	2	00	2
3		28	Edith Walton							1	0	2	9	00																1	0	2	9	00	3
4		30													3	6	0	0	00		1	8	0	00						3	7	8	0	00	4
5		30													2	5	0	0	00		1	2	5	00		1	0	0	00	2	5	2	5	00	5
6		30	Rent Revenue			6	0	0	00																						6	0	0	00	6
7		30	Notes Payable		3	0	0	0	00																					3	0	0	0	00	7
8																																			8

CASH RECEIPTS JOURNAL — PAGE 7

LEARNING KEY

Use a cash receipts journal to streamline journalizing and posting of cash receipts.

Micro's cash receipts transactions. In addition, a General Credit column is provided for credits to any other accounts affected by cash receipts transactions.

A cash receipt is recorded in the cash receipts journal by entering the following information:

1. Date

2. Account credited (if applicable)

3. Dollar amounts

The Account Credited column is used for two purposes.

1. To identify the customer name for any collection on account. This column is used whenever the Accounts Receivable Credit column is used.

2. To enter the appropriate account name whenever the General Credit column is used.

The Account Credited column is left blank whenever the entry is for cash sales or bank credit card sales.

The cash receipts journal in Figure 12-7 is designed for a company like Northern Micro, which charges sales tax, makes bank credit card sales, and offers no cash discounts. For a wholesaler that does not charge sales tax, makes no bank credit card sales, and offers cash discounts, a cash receipts journal like the one in Figure 12-8 would be used. Recall that a special journal should be designed with column headings for frequently used accounts. Thus, the cash receipts journal in Figure 12-8 has no Sales Tax Payable Credit or Bank Credit Card Expense Debit column. Instead, a Sales Discounts Debit column is provided. In this way, the common cash receipts transactions of the wholesaler can be easily and efficiently recorded.

FIGURE 12-8 Cash Receipts Journal Without Sales Tax

	DATE		ACCOUNT CREDITED	POST. REF.	GENERAL CREDIT	ACCOUNTS RECEIVABLE CREDIT	SALES CREDIT	SALES DISCOUNTS DEBIT	CASH DEBIT	
1										1

CASH RECEIPTS JOURNAL — PAGE 1

POSTING FROM THE CASH RECEIPTS JOURNAL

The cash receipts journal is posted to the general ledger in two stages, as illustrated in Figure 12-9. First, on a daily basis, the individual amounts in the General Credit column are posted. Second, at the end of the month, the totals of each of the other amount columns are posted.

FIGURE 12-9 Posting from the Cash Receipts Journal to the General Ledger

CASH RECEIPTS JOURNAL   Page 7

Date	Account Credited	Post. Ref.	General Credit	Accounts Receivable Credit	Sales Credit	Sales Tax Payable Credit	Bank Credit Card Expense Debit	Cash Debit
20-- Apr. 14	Enrico Lorenzo			1,596.00				1,596.00
20	Brenda Myers			462.00				462.00
28	Edith Walton			1,029.00				1,029.00
30		✔			3,600.00	180.00		3,780.00
30		✔			2,500.00	125.00	100.00	2,525.00
30	Rent Revenue	412	600.00					600.00
30	Notes Payable	201	3,000.00					3,000.00
			3,600.00	3,087.00	6,100.00	305.00	100.00	12,992.00
			(✔)	(122)	(401)	(231)	(513)	(101)

6 Debit total: $ 100
                        12,992
                      $13,092

Credit total: $ 3,600
                      3,087
                      6,100
                        305
                    $13,092

GENERAL LEDGER (Partial)

ACCOUNT   Cash   ACCOUNT NO. 101

Date	Item	Post. Ref.	Debit	Credit	Balance Debit	Balance Credit
20-- Apr. 1	Bal.	✔			20,000.00	
30		CR7	12,992.00		32,992.00	

ACCOUNT   Accounts Receivable   ACCOUNT NO. 122

Date	Item	Post. Ref.	Debit	Credit	Balance Debit	Balance Credit
20-- Apr. 1	Bal.	✔			12,000.00	
30		S6	5,418.00		17,418.00	
30		CR7		3,087.00	14,331.00	

ACCOUNT   Notes Payable   ACCOUNT NO. 201

Date	Item	Post. Ref.	Debit	Credit	Balance Debit	Balance Credit
20-- Apr. 1	Bal.	✔				6,000.00
30		CR7		3,000.00		9,000.00

ACCOUNT   Sales Tax Payable   ACCOUNT NO. 231

Date	Item	Post. Ref.	Debit	Credit	Balance Debit	Balance Credit
20-- Apr. 30		S6		258.00		258.00
30		CR7		305.00		563.00

ACCOUNT   Sales   ACCOUNT NO. 401

Date	Item	Post. Ref.	Debit	Credit	Balance Debit	Balance Credit
20-- Apr. 1	Bal.	✔				27,000.00
30		S6		5,160.00		32,160.00
30		CR7		6,100.00		38,260.00

ACCOUNT   Rent Revenue   ACCOUNT NO. 412

Date	Item	Post. Ref.	Debit	Credit	Balance Debit	Balance Credit
20-- Apr. 1	Bal.	✔				1,800.00
30		CR7		600.00		2,400.00

ACCOUNT   Bank Credit Card Expense   ACCOUNT NO. 513

Date	Item	Post. Ref.	Debit	Credit	Balance Debit	Balance Credit
20-- Apr. 1	Bal.	✔			430.00	
30		CR7	100.00		530.00	

To post the General Credit column, on a daily basis, use the following steps:

In the general ledger account:

STEP 1 Enter the date of the transaction in the Date column.

STEP 2 Enter the amount of the debit or credit in the Debit or Credit column.

STEP 3 Enter the new balance in the Balance columns under Debit or Credit.

STEP 4 Enter the initials "CR" and the journal page number in the Posting Reference column.

In the cash receipts journal:

STEP 5 Enter the ledger account number in the Posting Reference column for each account that is posted.

To post the other amount columns, at the end of the month, use the following steps:

In the cash receipts journal:

STEP 6 Total the amount columns, verify that the total of the debit columns equals the total of the credit columns, and rule the columns.

In the general ledger account:

STEP 7 Enter the date in the Date column.

STEP 8 Enter the amount of the debit or credit in the Debit or Credit column.

STEP 9 Enter the new balance in the Balance columns under Debit or Credit.

STEP 10 Enter the initials "CR" and the journal page number in the Posting Reference column.

In the cash receipts journal:

STEP 11 Enter the ledger account number immediately below the column totals for each account that is posted.

STEP 12 Enter a check mark (✓) in the Posting Reference column for the cash sales and bank credit card sales, and immediately below the General Credit column.

The general ledger accounts affected by the cash receipts transactions are now up to date. Postings to the accounts receivable ledger also must be made. These postings are made daily. Figure 12-10 illustrates the posting procedures, as follows:

In the accounts receivable ledger account:

STEP 1 Enter the date of the transaction in the Date column.

STEP 2 Enter the amount of the debit or credit in the Debit or Credit column.

STEP 3 Enter the new balance in the Balance column.

STEP 4 Enter the initials "CR" and the journal page number in the Posting Reference column.

In the cash receipts journal:

STEP 5 Enter a check mark (✓) in the Posting Reference column of the journal for each transaction that is posted.

FIGURE 12-10 Posting from the Cash Receipts Journal to the Accounts Receivable Ledger

CASH RECEIPTS JOURNAL — Page 7

Date	Account Credited	Post. Ref.	General Credit	Accounts Receivable Credit	Sales Credit	Sales Tax Payable Credit	Bank Credit Card Expense Debit	Cash Debit
20--								
Apr. 14	Enrico Lorenzo	✔		1,596.00				1,596.00
20	Brenda Myers	✔		462.00				462.00
28	Edith Walton	✔		1,029.00				1,029.00
30		✔			3,600.00	180.00		3,780.00
30		✔			2,500.00	125.00	100.00	2,525.00
30	Rent Revenue	412	600.00					600.00
30	Notes Payable	201	3,000.00					3,000.00
			3,600.00	3,087.00	6,100.00	305.00	100.00	12,992.00
			(✔)	(122)	(401)	(231)	(513)	(101)

(marker 5)

ACCOUNTS RECEIVABLE LEDGER

NAME Helen Avery
ADDRESS 1739 Woodsage Trace, Indianapolis, IN 46237-1199

Date	Item	Post. Ref.	Debit	Credit	Balance
20--					
Apr. 1	Bal	✔			2,302.00

NAME Susan Chang
ADDRESS 337 Elm Street, Noblesville, IN 46060-3377

Date	Item	Post. Ref.	Debit	Credit	Balance
20--					
Apr. 21		S6	651.00		651.00

NAME Enrico Lorenzo
ADDRESS 5240 Tousley Court, Indianapolis, IN 46224-5678

Date	Item	Post. Ref.	Debit	Credit	Balance
20--					
Apr. 4		S6	1,596.00		1,596.00
14		CR7		1,596.00	—

(markers 1, 4, 3)

NAME Brenda Myers
ADDRESS 581 Acorn Way, Zionsville, IN 46077-2154

Date	Item	Post. Ref.	Debit	Credit	Balance
20--					
Apr. 10		S6	462.00		462.00
20		CR7		462.00	—

(markers 1, 4, 3)

NAME Heidi Schwitzer
ADDRESS 5858 Wildflower Cir., Bloomington, IN 47401-6209

Date	Item	Post. Ref.	Debit	Credit	Balance
20--					
Apr. 1	Bal.	✔			1,883.00
24		S6	1,680.00		3,563.00

NAME Ken Ulmet
ADDRESS 5260 Eagle Creek, Indianapolis, IN 46254-8275

Date	Item	Post. Ref.	Debit	Credit	Balance
20--					
Apr. 1	Bal.	✔			3,315.00

NAME Edith Walton
ADDRESS 1113 Stones Crossing, Zionsville, IN 46077-6601

Date	Item	Post. Ref.	Debit	Credit	Balance
20--					
Apr. 18		S6	1,029.00		1,029.00
28		CR7		1,029.00	—

(markers 1, 4, 3)

NAME Vivian Winston
ADDRESS 124 Main St., Zionsville, IN 46077-1358

Date	Item	Post. Ref.	Debit	Credit	Balance
20--					
Apr. 1	Bal.	✔			4,500.00

(marker 2)

GENERAL LEDGER (Partial)

ACCOUNT Cash — ACCOUNT NO. 101

Date	Item	Post. Ref.	Debit	Credit	Balance Debit	Balance Credit
20--						
Apr. 1	Bal.	✔			20,000.00	
30		CR7	12,992.00		32,992.00	

ACCOUNT Accounts Receivable — ACCOUNT NO. 122

Date	Item	Post. Ref.	Debit	Credit	Balance Debit	Balance Credit
20--						
Apr. 1	Bal.	✔			12,000.00	
30		S6	5,418.00		17,418.00	
30		CR7		3,087.00	14,331.00	

ACCOUNT Notes Payable — ACCOUNT NO. 201

Date	Item	Post. Ref.	Debit	Credit	Balance Debit	Balance Credit
20--						
Apr. 1	Bal.	✔				6,000.00
30		CR7		3,000.00		9,000.00

ACCOUNT Sales Tax Payable — ACCOUNT NO. 231

Date	Item	Post. Ref.	Debit	Credit	Balance Debit	Balance Credit
20--						
Apr. 30		S6		258.00		258.00
30		CR7		305.00		563.00

ACCOUNT Sales — ACCOUNT NO. 401

Date	Item	Post. Ref.	Debit	Credit	Balance Debit	Balance Credit
20--						
Apr. 1	Bal.	✔				27,000.00
30		S6		5,160.00		32,160.00
30		CR7		6,100.00		38,260.00

ACCOUNT Rent Revenue — ACCOUNT NO. 412

Date	Item	Post. Ref.	Debit	Credit	Balance Debit	Balance Credit
20--						
Apr. 1	Bal.	✔				1,800.00
30		CR7		600.00		2,400.00

ACCOUNT Bank Credit Card Expense — ACCOUNT NO. 513

Date	Item	Post. Ref.	Debit	Credit	Balance Debit	Balance Credit
20--						
Apr. 1	Bal.	✔			430.00	
30		CR7	100.00		530.00	

A BROADER VIEW

Improving Efficiency—The Power of Computerized Bookkeeping

In this chapter, we see many examples of the ways in which special journals can make the bookkeeping process more efficient. Yet, these efficiency gains pale by comparison with the power of computerized bookkeeping. By means of a single keyboard entry, journals, general and subsidiary ledgers, customer and supplier accounts, periodic financial reports, and more can be updated. You can even pay bills when due electronically as part of the system.

Some good examples of computerized bookkeeping software are Peachtree® and QuickBooks®. Both of these software packages utilize the one entry-many reports feature. The user makes entries using the keyboard; then the system tracks the effects on the financial status of the business. The software can analyze accounts receivable and accounts payable, process payroll, print checks, and track expenses by vendor and revenues by customer. It can also produce income statements and balance sheets. It is even possible to customize the programs to match different business types.

U REVU

Complete U REVU-2 on **page 468** to test your basic understanding of LO3.

PURCHASES JOURNAL

LO4 Describe and use the purchases journal.

A **purchases journal** is a special journal used to record only purchases of merchandise on account. To illustrate the journalizing and posting of purchases transactions in the purchases journal, we continue with the transactions of Northern Micro. The following five purchases on account are from Chapter 11:

Apr. 4	Purchased merchandise from Compucraft, Inc., $3,300. Invoice No. 631, dated April 2, terms, n/30.
8	Purchased merchandise from Datasoft, $2,500. Invoice No. 927D, dated April 6, terms, n/30.
11	Purchased merchandise from EZX Corp., $8,700. Invoice No. 804, dated April 9, terms, 1/15, n/30.
17	Purchased merchandise from Printpro Corp., $800. Invoice No. 611, dated April 16, terms, n/30.
23	Purchased merchandise from Televax, Inc., $5,300. Invoice No. 1465, dated April 22, terms, 1/10, n/30.

🔑 LEARNING KEY

Use a purchases journal only for recording purchases of merchandise on account.

As we saw with sales transactions, these purchases transactions can be recorded efficiently in a special journal, in this case a purchases journal. To illustrate, the five purchases on account of Northern Micro are entered in the purchases journal in Figure 12-11. Northern Micro's purchases journal has a single column for Purchases Debit/Accounts Payable Credit, the two accounts used repeatedly when these

FIGURE 12-11 Northern Micro Purchases Journal

	DATE		INVOICE NO.	FROM WHOM PURCHASED	POST. REF.	PURCHASES DEBIT/ACCOUNTS PAYABLE CREDIT	
1	20-- Apr.	4	631	Compucraft, Inc.		3 3 0 0 00	1
2		8	927D	Datasoft		2 5 0 0 00	2
3		11	804	EZX Corp.		8 7 0 0 00	3
4		17	611	Printpro Corp.		8 0 0 00	4
5		23	1465	Televax, Inc.		5 3 0 0 00	5
6						20 6 0 0 00	6

transactions are recorded in a general journal. A purchase is recorded in the purchases journal by entering the following information:

1. Date
2. Invoice number
3. Supplier (from whom purchased)
4. Dollar amount

There is no need to enter any general ledger account titles, since they appear in the column heading.

The purchases journal in Figure 12-11 is designed for a company like Northern Micro, whose suppliers generally pay freight charges. For a company that frequently pays freight charges as part of the purchase price of merchandise, a purchases journal like the one in Figure 12-12 would be used. In this case, there are three columns: (1) Purchases Debit, (2) Freight-In Debit, and (3) Accounts Payable Credit.

> Remember that purchases returns and allowances are recorded in the general journal, as illustrated in Chapter 11, <u>not</u> in the purchases journal.

FIGURE 12-12 Purchases Journal with Freight-In Column

DATE	INVOICE NO.	FROM WHOM PURCHASED	POST. REF.	PURCHASES DEBIT	FREIGHT-IN DEBIT	ACCOUNTS PAYABLE CREDIT

POSTING FROM THE PURCHASES JOURNAL

Each general ledger account used in the purchases journal requires only one posting each period. Figure 12-13 illustrates the general ledger posting process for Northern Micro's purchases journal for the month of April.

The following steps are used to post from the purchases journal to the general ledger at the end of each month, as indicated in Figure 12-13:

In the purchases journal:

STEP 1 Total and rule the amount column.

In the general ledger account:

STEP 2 Enter the date in the Date column.

STEP 3 Enter the amount of the debit or credit in the Debit or Credit column.

STEP 4 Enter the new balance in the Balance columns under Debit or Credit.

STEP 5 Enter the initial "P" and the journal page number in the Posting Reference column.

> Step 1 is the main difference in posting the purchases journal to the general ledger. The remaining steps 2–6 are essentially the same as steps 1–5 used to post the general journal.

FIGURE 12-13 Posting from the Purchases Journal to the General Ledger

PURCHASES JOURNAL Page 8

Date	Invoice No.	From Whom Purchased	Post. Ref.	Purchases Debit/ Accounts Payable Credit
20--				
Apr. 4	631	Compucraft, Inc.		3,300.00
8	927D	Datasoft		2,500.00
11	804	EZX Corp.		8,700.00
17	611	Printpro Corp.		800.00
23	1465	Televax, Inc.		5,300.00
				20,600.00

(501) (202)

GENERAL LEDGER (Partial)

ACCOUNT   Accounts Payable   ACCOUNT NO. 202

| | | | | | | Balance | |
Date	Item	Post. Ref.	Debit	Credit		Debit	Credit
20--							
Apr. 1	Bal	✔					4,800.00
30		P8		20,600.00			25,400.00

ACCOUNT   Purchases   ACCOUNT NO.501

| | | | | | | Balance | |
Date	Item	Post. Ref.	Debit	Credit		Debit	Credit
20--							
Apr. 1	Bal	✔				17,400.00	
30		P8	20,600.00			38,000.00	

In the purchases journal:

STEP 6 Enter the Purchases and Accounts Payable account numbers immediately below the column total.

To maintain a record of the amount owed to each supplier, an accounts payable ledger is used. Figure 12-14 illustrates the use of the accounts payable ledger. The following steps are used to post from the purchases journal to the accounts payable ledger daily, as shown in Figure 12-14:

In the accounts payable ledger account:

STEP 1 Enter the date of the transaction in the Date column.

STEP 2 Enter the amount of the debit or credit in the Debit or Credit column.

STEP 3 Enter the new balance in the Balance column.

STEP 4 Enter the initial "P" and the journal page number in the Posting Reference column.

In the purchases journal:

STEP 5 Enter a check mark (✔) in the Posting Reference column of the journal for each transaction that is posted.

After the posting of the accounts payable ledger and general ledger is completed, the total of the accounts payable ledger balances should equal the Accounts Payable balance in the general ledger.

> If the accounts payable ledger is posted daily and the general ledger is posted at the end of the month, the accounts payable ledger total will equal the general ledger Accounts Payable total only at the end of the month.

FIGURE 12-14 Posting from the Purchases Journal to the Accounts Payable Ledger

PURCHASES JOURNAL   Page 8

Date	Invoice No.	From Whom Purchased	Post. Ref.	Purchases Debit/ Accounts Payable Credit
20--				
Apr. 4	631	Compucraft, Inc.	✔	3,300.00
8	927D	Datasoft	✔	2,500.00
11	804	EZX Corp.	✔	8,700.00
17	611	Printpro Corp.	✔	800.00
23	1465	Televax, Inc.	✔	5,300.00
			[5]	20,600.00

(501)   (202)

ACCOUNTS PAYABLE LEDGER (Partial)

NAME   B.B.Small
ADDRESS 2323 High Street, Gurnee, IL 60031-5524

Date	Item	Post. Ref.	Debit	Credit	Balance
20--					
Apr. 1	Bal.	✔			4,800.00

NAME   Compucraft, Inc.
ADDRESS 2100 West Main Street, Muncie, IN 47304-8139

Date	Item	Post. Ref.	Debit	Credit	Balance
20--					
Apr. 4	[4]	P8		3,300.00	3,300.00

NAME   Datasoft
ADDRESS 210 Kirkwood, Bloomington, IN 47408-4346

Date	Item	Post. Ref.	Debit	Credit	Balance
20--					
Apr. 8	[4]	P8		2,500.00	2,500.00

NAME   EZX Corp.
ADDRESS 2928 Rhodes Ave., Chicago, IL 60658-5036

Date	Item	Post. Ref.	Debit	Credit	Balance
20--					
Apr. 11	[4]	P8		8,700.00	8,700.00

NAME   Printpro Corp.
ADDRESS 1200 Chambers Pike, Lincolnwood, IL 60648-2417

Date	Item	Post. Ref.	Debit	Credit	Balance
20--					
Apr. 17	[4]	P8		800.00	800.00

NAME   Televax, Inc.
ADDRESS 1500 North Walnut Street, Addison, IL 60101-7328

Date	Item	Post. Ref.	Debit	Credit	Balance
20--					
Apr. 23	[4]	P8		5,300.00	5,300.00

GENERAL LEDGER (Partial)

ACCOUNT   Accounts Payable   ACCOUNT NO. 202

Date	Item	Post. Ref.	Debit	Credit	Balance Debit	Balance Credit
20--						
Apr. 1	Bal.	✔				4,800.00
30		P8		20,600.00		25,400.00

ACCOUNT   Purchases   ACCOUNT NO. 501

Date	Item	Post. Ref.	Debit	Credit	Balance Debit	Balance Credit
20--						
Apr. 1	Bal.	✔			17,400.00	
30		P8	20,600.00		38,000.00	

U REVU   Complete U REVU-3 on **page 468** to test your basic understanding of LO4.

CASH PAYMENTS JOURNAL

LO5 Describe and use the cash payments journal.

A **cash payments journal** is a special journal used to record only cash payments transactions. To illustrate its use, we will record the cash payments transactions of Northern Micro. Northern Micro's cash payments journal for the month of April is shown in Figure 12-15. Five types of cash payments transactions are shown as follows:

1. Payment of an expense (April 2)

2. Cash purchase (April 4)

3. Payment of an account payable (April 10 and 24)

4. Payment of a note payable (April 14)

5. Withdrawal by the owner (April 22)

FIGURE 12-15 Northern Micro Cash Payments Journal

CASH PAYMENTS JOURNAL

	DATE	CK. NO.	ACCOUNT DEBITED	POST. REF.	GENERAL DEBIT	ACCOUNTS PAYABLE DEBIT	PURCHASES DEBIT	PURCHASES DISCOUNTS CREDIT	CASH CREDIT	
1	Apr. 2	307	Rent Expense		2 4 0 0 00				2 4 0 0 00	1
2	4	308					1 4 0 0 00		1 4 0 0 00	2
3	10	309	B. B. Small			4 8 0 0 00			4 8 0 0 00	3
4	14	310	Notes Payable		2 0 0 0 00				2 0 0 0 00	4
5	22	311	Gary L. Fishel, Drawing		1 6 0 0 00				1 6 0 0 00	5
6	24	312	EZX Corp.			8 7 0 0 00		8 7 00	8 6 1 3 00	6
7					6 0 0 0 00	13 5 0 0 00	1 4 0 0 00	8 7 00	20 8 1 3 00	7

LEARNING KEY

Use a cash payments journal to streamline journalizing and posting of cash payments.

Northern Micro's cash payments journal provides separate columns for Accounts Payable Debit, Purchases Debit, Purchases Discounts Credit, and Cash Credit. These are the accounts most frequently affected by Northern Micro's cash payments transactions. In addition, a General Debit column is provided for debits to any other accounts affected by cash payments transactions. For good internal control over cash payments, all payments (except out of petty cash) should be made by check. Therefore, the cash payments journal also includes a Check No. column.

A cash payment is recorded in the cash payments journal by entering the following information:

1. Date

2. Check number

3. Account debited (if applicable)

4. Dollar amounts

The Account Debited column is used for two purposes:

1. To identify the supplier name for any payment on account. This column is used whenever the Accounts Payable Debit column is used.

2. To enter the appropriate account name whenever the General Debit column is used.

Note that the column is left blank if the entry is for cash purchases.

Posting from the Cash Payments Journal

The cash payments journal is posted to the general ledger in two stages, as illustrated in Figure 12-16. First, on a daily basis, the individual amounts in the General Debit column are posted. Second, at the end of the month, the totals of each of the other amount columns are posted.

To post the General Debit column, on a daily basis, the following steps are used:

In the general ledger account:

STEP 1   Enter the date of the transaction in the Date column.

STEP 2   Enter the amount of the debit or credit in the Debit or Credit column.

STEP 3   Enter the new balance in the Balance columns under Debit or Credit.

STEP 4   Enter the initials "CP" and the journal page number in the Posting Reference column.

In the cash payments journal:

STEP 5   Enter the ledger account number in the Posting Reference column for each account that is posted.

To post the other amount columns, at the end of the month, the following steps are used:

In the cash payments journal:

STEP 6   Total the amount columns, verify that the total of the debit columns equals the total of the credit columns, and rule the columns.

In the general ledger account:

STEP 7   Enter the date in the Date column.

STEP 8   Enter the amount of the debit or credit in the Debit or Credit column.

STEP 9   Enter the new balance in the Balance columns under Debit or Credit.

STEP 10   Enter the initials "CP" and the journal page number in the Posting Reference column.

In the cash payments journal:

STEP 11   Enter the ledger account number immediately below the column totals for each account that is posted.

STEP 12   Enter a check mark (✓) in the Posting Reference column for the cash purchases, and immediately below the General Debit column.

Postings from the cash payments journal to the accounts payable ledger also must be made. These postings are made daily. Posting procedures are as follows, as shown in Figure 12-17:

In the accounts payable ledger account:

STEP 1   Enter the date of the transaction in the Date column.

STEP 2   Enter the amount of the debit or credit in the Debit or Credit column.

STEP 3   Enter the new balance in the Balance column.

STEP 4   Enter the initials "CP" and the journal page number in the Posting Reference column.

In the cash payments journal:

STEP 5   Enter a check mark (✓) in the Posting Reference column of the journal for each transaction that is posted.

FIGURE 12-16 Posting from the Cash Payments Journal to the General Ledger

	Check		Post.	General	Accounts Payable	Purchases	Purchases Discounts	Cash
Date	No.	Account Debited	Ref.	Debit	Debit	Debit	Credit	Credit
20-- Apr. 2	307	Rent Expense	5 521	2,400.00				2,400.00
4	308		12 ✔			1,400.00		1,400.00
10	309	B. B. Small			4,800.00			4,800.00
14	310	Notes Payable	5 201	2,000.00				2,000.00
22	311	Gary L. Fishel, Drawing	5 312	1,600.00				1,600.00
24	312	EZX Corp.			8,700.00		87.00	8,613.00
				6,000.00	13,500.00	1,400.00	87.00	20,813.00	6
				(✔)	(202)	(501)	(501.2)	(101)	11
				12					

CASH PAYMENTS JOURNAL Page 12

6 Debit total: $ 6,000
13,500
1,400
$ 20,900

Credit total: $ 87
20,813
$ 20,900

GENERAL LEDGER (Partial)   8

ACCOUNT   Cash   ACCOUNT NO. 101

		Post.			Balance	
Date	Item	Ref.	Debit	Credit	Debit	Credit
20-- Apr. 1	Bal.	✔			20,000.00	
30		CR7	12,992.00		32,992.00	
30	10	CP12		20,813.00	12,179.00	9

ACCOUNT   Notes Payable   ACCOUNT NO. 201

		Post.			Balance	
Date	Item	Ref.	Debit	Credit	Debit	Credit
20-- Apr. 1	Bal.	✔				6,000.00
14	4	CP12	2,000.00			4,000.00	3

ACCOUNT   Accounts Payable   ACCOUNT NO. 202

		Post.			Balance	
Date	Item	Ref.	Debit	Credit	Debit	Credit
20-- Apr. 1	Bal.	✔				4,800.00
30		P8		20,600.00		25,400.00
30	10	CP12	13,500.00			11,900.00	9

ACCOUNT   Gary L. Fishel, Drawing   ACCOUNT NO. 312

		Post.			Balance	
Date	Item	Ref.	Debit	Credit	Debit	Credit
20-- Apr. 1	Bal.	✔			4,500.00	
22	4	CP12	1,600.00		6,100.00	3

ACCOUNT   Purchases   ACCOUNT NO. 501

		Post.			Balance	
Date	Item	Ref.	Debit	Credit	Debit	Credit
20-- Apr. 1	Bal.	✔			17,400.00	
30		P8	20,600.00		38,000.00	
30	10	CP12	1,400.00		39,400.00	9

ACCOUNT   Purchases Discounts   ACCOUNT NO. 501.2

		Post.			Balance	
Date	Item	Ref.	Debit	Credit	Debit	Credit
20-- Apr. 1	Bal.	✔				330.00
30	10	CP12		87.00		417.00	9

ACCOUNT   Rent Expense   ACCOUNT NO. 521

		Post.			Balance	
Date	Item	Ref.	Debit	Credit	Debit	Credit
20-- Apr. 1	Bal.	✔			6,600.00	
2	4	CP12	2,400.00		9,000.00	3

FIGURE 12-17 Posting from the Cash Payments Journal to the Accounts Payable Ledger

CASH PAYMENTS JOURNAL

Page 12

Date	Check No.	Account Debited	Post. Ref.	General Debit	Accounts Payable Debit	Purchases Debit	Purchases Discounts Credit	Cash Credit
20--								
Apr. 2	307	Rent Expense	521	2,400.00				2,400.00
4	308		✔			1,400.00		1,400.00
10	309	B. B. Small	✔		4,800.00			4,800.00
14	310	Notes Payable	201	2,000.00				2,000.00
22	311	Gary L. Fishel, Drawing	312	1,600.00				1,600.00
24	312	EZX Corp.	✔		8,700.00		87.00	8,613.00
				6,000.00	13,500.00	1,400.00	87.00	20,813.00
				(✔)	(202)	(501)	(501.2)	(101)

ACCOUNTS PAYABLE LEDGER (Partial)

NAME   B. B. Small
ADDRESS   2323 High Street, Gurnee, IL 60031-5524

Date	Item	Post. Ref.	Debit	Credit	Balance
20--					
Apr. 1	Bal.	✔			4,800.00
10		CP12	4,800.00		—

NAME   Compucraft, Inc.
ADDRESS   2100 West Main Street, Muncie, IN 47304-8139

Date	Item	Post. Ref.	Debit	Credit	Balance
20--					
Apr. 4		P8		3,300.00	3,300.00

NAME   Datasoft
ADDRESS   210 Kirkwood, Bloomington, IN 47408-4346

Date	Item	Post. Ref.	Debit	Credit	Balance
20--					
Apr. 8		P8		2,500.00	2,500.00

NAME   EZX Corp.
ADDRESS   2928 Rhodes Ave., Chicago, IL 60658-5036

Date	Item	Post. Ref.	Debit	Credit	Balance
20--					
Apr. 11		P8		8,700.00	8,700.00
24		CP12	8,700.00		—

NAME   Printpro Corp.
ADDRESS   1200 Chambers Pike, Lincolnwood, IL 60648-2417

Date	Item	Post. Ref.	Debit	Credit	Balance
20--					
Apr. 17		P8		800.00	800.00

NAME   Televax, Inc.
ADDRESS   1500 North Walnut Street, Addison, IL 60101-7328

Date	Item	Post. Ref.	Debit	Credit	Balance
20--					
Apr. 23		P8		5,300.00	5,300.00

GENERAL LEDGER (Partial)

ACCOUNT   Cash   ACCOUNT NO. 101

Date	Item	Post. Ref.	Debit	Credit	Balance Debit	Balance Credit
20--						
Apr. 1	Bal.	✔			20,000.00	
30		CR7	12,992.00		32,992.00	
30		CP12		20,813.00	12,179.00	

ACCOUNT   Notes Payable   ACCOUNT NO. 201

Date	Item	Post. Ref.	Debit	Credit	Balance Debit	Balance Credit
20--						
Apr. 1	Bal.	✔				6,000.00
14		CP12	2,000.00			4,000.00

ACCOUNT   Accounts Payable   ACCOUNT NO. 202

Date	Item	Post. Ref.	Debit	Credit	Balance Debit	Balance Credit
20--						
Apr. 1	Bal.	✔				4,800.00
30		P8		20,600.00		25,400.00
30		CP12	13,500.00			11,900.00

ACCOUNT   Gary L. Fishel, Drawing   ACCOUNT NO. 312

Date	Item	Post. Ref.	Debit	Credit	Balance Debit	Balance Credit
20--						
Apr. 1	Bal.	✔			4,500.00	
22		CP12	1,600.00		6,100.00	

ACCOUNT   Purchases   ACCOUNT NO. 501

Date	Item	Post. Ref.	Debit	Credit	Balance Debit	Balance Credit
20--						
Apr. 1	Bal.	✔			17,400.00	
30		P8	20,600.00		38,000.00	
30		CP12	1,400.00		39,400.00	

ACCOUNT   Purchases Discounts   ACCOUNT NO. 501.2

Date	Item	Post. Ref.	Debit	Credit	Balance Debit	Balance Credit
20--						
Apr. 1	Bal.	✔				330.00
30		CP12		87.00		417.00

ACCOUNT   Rent Expense   ACCOUNT NO. 521

Date	Item	Post. Ref.	Debit	Credit	Balance Debit	Balance Credit
20--						
Apr. 1	Bal.	✔			6,600.00	
2		CP12	2,400.00		9,000.00	

U REVU   Complete U REVU-4 on **page 468** to test your basic understanding of LO5.

LEARNING OBJECTIVES	Key Points to Remember
LO1 Describe, explain the purpose of, and identify transactions recorded in special journals.	A special journal is a journal designed for recording only certain kinds of transactions. The primary purpose of using special journals is to save time journalizing and posting transactions.
LO2 Describe and use the sales journal.	A sales journal is a special journal for recording sales of merchandise on account. A sale is recorded by entering the following: 1. Date 2. Sale number 3. Customer (to whom sold) 4. Dollar amounts To post from the sales journal to the general ledger, use the following steps: **In the sales journal:** STEP 1 Total the amount columns, verify that the total of the debit column equals the total of the credit columns, and rule the columns. **In the general ledger account:** STEP 2 Enter the date of the transaction in the Date column. STEP 3 Enter the amount of the debit or credit in the Debit or Credit column. STEP 4 Enter the new balance in the Balance columns under Debit or Credit. STEP 5 Enter the initial "S" and the journal page number in the Posting Reference column. **In the sales journal:** STEP 6 Enter the ledger account number immediately below the column totals for each account that is posted. To post from the sales journal to the accounts receivable ledger: **In the accounts receivable ledger account:** STEP 1 Enter the date of the transaction in the Date column. STEP 2 Enter the amount of the debit or credit in the Debit or Credit column. STEP 3 Enter the new balance in the Balance column. STEP 4 Enter the initial "S" and the journal page number in the Posting Reference column. **In the sales journal:** STEP 5 Enter a check mark (✓) in the Posting Reference column of the journal for each transaction that is posted.
LO3 Describe and use the cash receipts journal.	A cash receipts journal is a special journal for recording cash receipts. A cash receipt is recorded by entering the following: 1. Date 2. Account credited (if applicable) 3. Dollar amounts

(continued)

LEARNING OBJECTIVES   Key Points to Remember

LO3 (continued)

To post from the cash receipts journal to the general ledger:

To post the General Credit column, on a daily basis, use the following steps:

In the general ledger account:

STEP 1 Enter the date of the transaction in the Date column.

STEP 2 Enter the amount of the debit or credit in the Debit or Credit column.

STEP 3 Enter the new balance in the Balance columns under Debit or Credit.

STEP 4 Enter the initials "CR" and the journal page number in the Posting Reference column.

In the cash receipts journal:

STEP 5 Enter the ledger account number in the Posting Reference column for each account that is posted.

To post the other amount columns, at the end of the month, use the following steps:

In the cash receipts journal:

STEP 6 Total the amount columns, verify that the total of the debit columns equals the total of the credit columns, and rule the columns.

In the general ledger account:

STEP 7 Enter the date in the Date column.

STEP 8 Enter the amount of the debit or credit in the Debit or Credit column.

STEP 9 Enter the new balance in the Balance columns under Debit or Credit.

STEP 10 Enter the initials "CR" and the journal page number in the Posting Reference column.

In the cash receipts journal:

STEP 11 Enter the ledger account number immediately below the column totals for each account that is posted.

STEP 12 Enter a check mark (✓) in the Posting Reference column for the cash sales and bank credit card sales, and immediately below the General Credit column.

To post from the cash receipts journal to the accounts receivable ledger, use the following steps:

In the accounts receivable ledger account:

STEP 1 Enter the date of the transaction in the Date column.

STEP 2 Enter the amount of the debit or credit in the Debit or Credit column.

STEP 3 Enter the new balance in the Balance column.

STEP 4 Enter the initials "CR" and the journal page number in the Posting Reference column.

(continued)

LEARNING OBJECTIVES   Key Points to Remember

LEARNING OBJECTIVES	Key Points to Remember
LO3 (concluded)	**In the cash receipts journal:** STEP 5 Enter a check mark (✓) in the Posting Reference column of the journal for each transaction that is posted.
LO4 Describe and use the purchases journal.	A purchases journal is a special journal for recording purchases of merchandise on account. A purchase is recorded by entering the following: 1. Date 2. Invoice number 3. Supplier (from whom purchased) 4. Dollar amount To post from the purchases journal to the general ledger, use the following steps: **In the purchases journal:** STEP 1 Total and rule the amount column. **In the general ledger account:** STEP 2 Enter the date in the Date column. STEP 3 Enter the amount of the debit or credit in the Debit or Credit column. STEP 4 Enter the new balance in the Balance columns under Debit or Credit. STEP 5 Enter the initial "P" and the journal page number in the Posting Reference column. **In the purchases journal:** STEP 6 Enter the Purchases and Accounts Payable account numbers immediately below the column total. To post from the purchases journal to the accounts payable ledger, use the following steps: **In the accounts payable ledger account:** STEP 1 Enter the date of the transaction in the Date column. STEP 2 Enter the amount of the debit or credit in the Debit or Credit column. STEP 3 Enter the new balance in the Balance column. STEP 4 Enter the initial "P" and the journal page number in the Posting Reference column. **In the purchases journal:** STEP 5 Enter a check mark (✓) in the Posting Reference column of the journal for each transaction that is posted.
LO5 Describe and use the cash payments journal.	A cash payments journal is a special journal for recording cash payments. A cash payment is recorded by entering the following: 1. Date 2. Check number 3. Account debited (if applicable) 4. Dollar amounts

(continued)

LEARNING OBJECTIVES   Key Points to Remember

LO5 (concluded)

To post from the cash payments journal to the general ledger:

To post the General Debit column, on a daily basis, use the following steps:

In the general ledger account:

STEP 1 Enter the date of the transaction in the Date column.

STEP 2 Enter the amount of the debit or credit in the Debit or Credit column.

STEP 3 Enter the new balance in the Balance columns under Debit or Credit.

STEP 4 Enter the initials "CP" and the journal page number in the Posting Reference column.

In the cash payments journal:

STEP 5 Enter the ledger account number in the Posting Reference column for each account that is posted.

To post the other amount columns, at the end of the month, use the following steps:

In the cash payments journal:

STEP 6 Total the amount columns, verify that the total of the debit columns equals the total of the credit columns, and rule the columns.

In the general ledger account:

STEP 7 Enter the date in the Date column.

STEP 8 Enter the amount of the debit or credit in the Debit or Credit column.

STEP 9 Enter the new balance in the Balance columns under Debit or Credit.

STEP 10 Enter the initials "CP" and the journal page number in the Posting Reference column.

In the cash payments journal:

STEP 11 Enter the ledger account number immediately below the column totals for each account that is posted.

STEP 12 Enter a check mark (✓) in the Posting Reference column for the cash purchases, and immediately below the General Debit column.

To post from the cash payments journal to the accounts payable ledger, use the following steps:

In the accounts payable ledger account:

STEP 1 Enter the date of the transaction in the Date column.

STEP 2 Enter the amount of the debit or credit in the Debit or Credit column.

STEP 3 Enter the new balance in the Balance column.

STEP 4 Enter the initials "CP" and the journal page number in the Posting Reference column.

In the cash payments journal:

STEP 5 Enter a check mark (✓) in the Posting Reference column of the journal for each transaction that is posted.

DEMONSTRATION PROBLEM

During the month of May 20--, David's Specialty Shop engaged in the following transactions:

May 1   Sold merchandise on account to Molly Mac, $2,000, plus tax of $100. Sale No. 533.

2   Issued Check No. 750 to Kari Co. in partial payment of May 1 balance, $800, less 2% discount.

3   Purchased merchandise on account from Scanlan Wholesalers, $2,000. Invoice No. 621, dated May 3, terms 2/10, n/30.

4   Purchased merchandise on account from Simpson Enterprises, $1,500. Invoice No. 767, dated May 4, terms 2/15, n/30.

4   Issued Check No. 751 in payment of telephone expense for the month of April, $200.

8   Sold merchandise for cash, $3,600, plus tax of $180.

9   Received payment from Cody Slaton in full settlement of account, $2,500.

10   Issued Check No. 752 to Scanlan Wholesalers in payment of May 1 balance of $1,200.

12   Sold merchandise on account to Cody Slaton, $3,000, plus tax of $150. Sale No. 534.

12   Received payment from Kori Reynolds on account, $2,100.

13   Issued Check No. 753 to Simpson Enterprises in payment of May 4 purchase. Invoice No. 767, less 2% discount.

13   Cody Slaton returned merchandise for a credit, $1,000, plus sales tax of $50.

17   Returned merchandise to Johnson Essentials for credit, $500.

22   Received payment from Natalie Gabbert on account, $1,555.

27   Sold merchandise on account to Natalie Gabbert, $2,000, plus tax of $100. Sale No. 535.

29   Issued Check No. 754 in payment of wages (Wages Expense) for the four-week period ending May 30, $1,100.

Selected account balances as of May 1 were as follows:

Account	Account No.	Debit	Credit
Cash	101	$10,050.00	
Accounts Receivable	122	6,900.00	
Accounts Payable	202		$4,550.00

David's also had the following subsidiary ledger balances as of May 1:

Accounts Receivable:

Customer	Accounts Receivable Balance
Natalie Gabbert 12 Jude Lane Hartford, CT 06117	$1,821.00
Molly Mac 52 Juniper Road Hartford, CT 06118	279.00

Kori Reynolds
700 Hobbes Dr.
Avon, CT 06108 $2,300.00

Cody Slaton
5200 Hamilton Ave.
Hartford, CT 06111   2,500.00

Accounts Payable:

Vendor	Accounts Payable Balance
Johnson Essentials 34 Harry Ave. East Hartford, CT 05234	$2,350.00
Kari Co. 1009 Drake Rd. Farmington, CT 06082	1,000.00
Scanlan Wholesalers 43 Lucky Lane Bristol, CT 06007	1,200.00
Simpson Enterprises 888 Anders Street Newington, CT 06789	—

REQUIRED

1. Record the transactions in the sales journal, cash receipts journal, purchases journal, cash payments journal, and general journal. Total, verify, and rule the columns where appropriate at the end of the month.

2. Post from the journals to the general ledger, accounts receivable ledger, and accounts payable ledger accounts. Use account numbers as shown in the chapter.

Solution 1.

SALES JOURNAL   PAGE 7

	DATE	SALE NO.	TO WHOM SOLD	POST. REF.	ACCOUNTS RECEIVABLE DEBIT	SALES CREDIT	SALES TAX PAYABLE CREDIT	
1	20-- May 1	533	Molly Mac	✔	2 1 0 0 00	2 0 0 0 00	1 0 0 00	1
2	12	534	Cody Slaton	✔	3 1 5 0 00	3 0 0 0 00	1 5 0 00	2
3	27	535	Natalie Gabbert	✔	2 1 0 0 00	2 0 0 0 00	1 0 0 00	3
4					7 3 5 0 00	7 0 0 0 00	3 5 0 00	4
5					(1 2 2)	(4 0 1)	(2 3 1)	5

PURCHASES JOURNAL   PAGE 6

	DATE	INVOICE NO.	FROM WHOM PURCHASED	POST. REF.	PURCHASES DEBIT/ACCOUNTS PAYABLE CREDIT	
1	20-- May 3	621	Scanlan Wholesalers	✔	2 0 0 0 00	1
2	4	767	Simpson Enterprises	✔	1 5 0 0 00	2
3					3 5 0 0 00	3
4					(50 1) (2 02)	4

(continued)

GENERAL JOURNAL PAGE 5

	DATE		DESCRIPTION	POST. REF.	DEBIT	CREDIT	
1	20-- May	13	Sales Returns and Allowances	401.1	1 0 0 0 00		1
2			Sales Tax Payable	231	5 0 00		2
3			Accounts Receivable/Cody Slaton	122/✔		1 0 5 0 00	3
4			Accepted returned merchandise				4
5							5
6		17	Accounts Payable/Johnson Essentials	202/✔	5 0 0 00		6
7			Purchases Returns and Allowances	501.1		5 0 0 00	7
8			Returned merchandise				8
9							9

CASH PAYMENTS JOURNAL PAGE 11

	DATE		CK. NO.	ACCOUNT DEBITED	POST. REF.	GENERAL DEBIT	ACCOUNTS PAYABLE DEBIT	PURCHASES DEBIT	PURCHASES DISCOUNTS CREDIT	CASH CREDIT	
1	20-- May	2	750	Kari Co.	✔		8 0 0 00		1 6 00	7 8 4 00	1
2		4	751	Telephone Expense	525	2 0 0 00				2 0 0 00	2
3		10	752	Scanlan Wholesalers	✔		1 2 0 0 00			1 2 0 0 00	3
4		13	753	Simpson Enterprises	✔		1 5 0 0 00		3 0 00	1 4 7 0 00	4
5		29	754	Wages Expense	511	1 1 0 0 00				1 1 0 0 00	5
6						1 3 0 0 00	3 5 0 0 00		4 6 00	4 7 5 4 00	6
7						(✔)	(2 0 2)		(5 0 1 .2)	(1 0 1)	7

CASH RECEIPTS JOURNAL PAGE 10

	DATE		ACCOUNT CREDITED	POST. REF.	GENERAL CREDIT	ACCOUNTS RECEIVABLE CREDIT	SALES CREDIT	SALES TAX PAYABLE CREDIT	CASH DEBIT	
1	20-- May	8					3 6 0 0 00	1 8 0 00	3 7 8 0 00	1
2		9	C. Slaton	✔		2 5 0 0 00			2 5 0 0 00	2
3		12	K. Reynolds	✔		2 1 0 0 00			2 1 0 0 00	3
4		22	N. Gabbert	✔		1 5 5 5 00			1 5 5 5 00	4
5						6 1 5 5 00	3 6 0 0 00	1 8 0 00	9 9 3 5 00	5
6						(1 2 2)	(4 0 1)	(2 3 1)	(1 0 1)	6

2.

GENERAL LEDGER

ACCOUNT: Cash ACCOUNT NO. 101

DATE		ITEM	POST. REF.	DEBIT	CREDIT	BALANCE DEBIT	BALANCE CREDIT
20-- May	1	Balance	✔			10 0 5 0 00	
	31		CR10	9 9 3 5 00		19 9 8 5 00	
	31		CP11		4 7 5 4 00	15 2 3 1 00	

ACCOUNT: Accounts Receivable   ACCOUNT NO. 122

DATE		ITEM	POST. REF.	DEBIT	CREDIT	BALANCE DEBIT	BALANCE CREDIT
20-- May	1	Balance	✔			6 9 0 0 00	
	13		J5		1 0 5 0 00	5 8 5 0 00	
	31		S7	7 3 5 0 00		13 2 0 0 00	
	31		CR10		6 1 5 5 00	7 0 4 5 00	

ACCOUNT: Accounts Payable   ACCOUNT NO. 202

DATE		ITEM	POST. REF.	DEBIT	CREDIT	BALANCE DEBIT	BALANCE CREDIT
20-- May	1	Balance	✔				4 5 5 0 00
	17		J5	5 0 0 00			4 0 5 0 00
	31		P6		3 5 0 0 00		7 5 5 0 00
	31		CP11	3 5 0 0 00			4 0 5 0 00

ACCOUNT: Sales Tax Payable   ACCOUNT NO. 231

DATE		ITEM	POST. REF.	DEBIT	CREDIT	BALANCE DEBIT	BALANCE CREDIT
20-- May	13		J5	5 0 00		5 0 00	
	31		S7		3 5 0 00		3 0 0 00
	31		CR10		1 8 0 00		4 8 0 00

ACCOUNT: Sales   ACCOUNT NO. 401

DATE		ITEM	POST. REF.	DEBIT	CREDIT	BALANCE DEBIT	BALANCE CREDIT
20-- May	31		S7		7 0 0 0 00		7 0 0 0 00
	31		CR10		3 6 0 0 00		10 6 0 0 00

ACCOUNT: Sales Returns and Allowances   ACCOUNT NO. 401.1

DATE		ITEM	POST. REF.	DEBIT	CREDIT	BALANCE DEBIT	BALANCE CREDIT
20-- May	13		J5	1 0 0 0 00		1 0 0 0 00	

ACCOUNT: Purchases   ACCOUNT NO. 501

DATE		ITEM	POST. REF.	DEBIT	CREDIT	BALANCE DEBIT	BALANCE CREDIT
20-- May	31		P6	3 5 0 0 00		3 5 0 0 00	

ACCOUNT: Purchases Returns and Allowances   ACCOUNT NO. 501.1

DATE		ITEM	POST. REF.	DEBIT	CREDIT	BALANCE DEBIT	BALANCE CREDIT
20-- May	17		J5		5 0 0 00		5 0 0 00

ACCOUNT: Purchases Discounts   ACCOUNT NO. 501.2

DATE		ITEM	POST. REF.	DEBIT	CREDIT	BALANCE DEBIT	BALANCE CREDIT
20-- May	31		CP11		4 6 00		4 6 00

(continued)

ACCOUNT: Wages Expense **ACCOUNT NO.** 511

DATE	ITEM	POST. REF.	DEBIT	CREDIT	BALANCE DEBIT	BALANCE CREDIT
20-- May 29		CP11	1 1 0 0 00		1 1 0 0 00	

ACCOUNT: Telephone Expense **ACCOUNT NO.** 525

DATE	ITEM	POST. REF.	DEBIT	CREDIT	BALANCE DEBIT	BALANCE CREDIT
20-- May 4		CP11	2 0 0 00		2 0 0 00	

ACCOUNTS RECEIVABLE LEDGER

NAME: Natalie Gabbert
ADDRESS: 12 Jude Lane, Hartford, CT 06117

DATE	ITEM	POST. REF.	DEBIT	CREDIT	BALANCE
20-- May 1	Balance	✔			1 8 2 1 00
22		CR10		1 5 5 5 00	2 6 6 00
27		S7	2 1 0 0 00		2 3 6 6 00

NAME: Molly Mac
ADDRESS: 52 Juniper Road, Hartford, CT 06118

DATE	ITEM	POST. REF.	DEBIT	CREDIT	BALANCE
20-- May 1	Balance	✔			2 7 9 00
1		S7	2 1 0 0 00		2 3 7 9 00

NAME: Kori Reynolds
ADDRESS: 700 Hobbes Dr., Avon, CT 06108

DATE	ITEM	POST. REF.	DEBIT	CREDIT	BALANCE
20-- May 1	Balance	✔			2 3 0 0 00
12		CR10		2 1 0 0 00	2 0 0 00

NAME: Cody Slaton
ADDRESS: 5200 Hamilton Ave., Hartford, CT 06111

DATE	ITEM	POST. REF.	DEBIT	CREDIT	BALANCE
20-- May 1	Balance	✔			2 5 0 0 00
9		CR10		2 5 0 0 00	
12		S7	3 1 5 0 00		3 1 5 0 00
13		J5		1 0 5 0 00	2 1 0 0 00

ACCOUNTS PAYABLE LEDGER

NAME: Johnson Essentials

ADDRESS: 34 Harry Ave., East Hartford, CT 05234

DATE		ITEM	POST. REF.	DEBIT	CREDIT	BALANCE
20-- May	1	Balance	✔			2 3 5 0 00
	17		J5	5 0 0 00		1 8 5 0 00

NAME: Kari Co.

ADDRESS: 1009 Drake Rd., Farmington, CT 06082

DATE		ITEM	POST. REF.	DEBIT	CREDIT	BALANCE
20-- May	1	Balance	✔			1 0 0 0 00
	2		CP11	8 0 0 00		2 0 0 00

NAME: Scanlan Wholesalers

ADDRESS: 43 Lucky Lane, Bristol, CT 06007

DATE		ITEM	POST. REF.	DEBIT	CREDIT	BALANCE
20-- May	1	Balance	✔			1 2 0 0 00
	3		P6		2 0 0 0 00	3 2 0 0 00
	10		CP11	1 2 0 0 00		2 0 0 0 00

NAME: Simpson Enterprises

ADDRESS: 888 Anders Street, Newington, CT 06789

DATE		ITEM	POST. REF.	DEBIT	CREDIT	BALANCE
20-- May	1	Balance	✔			
	4		P6		1 5 0 0 00	1 5 0 0 00
	13		CP11	1 5 0 0 00		

KEY TERMS

cash payments journal (454)   A special journal used to record only cash payments transactions.

cash receipts journal (445)   A special journal used to record only cash receipts transactions.

purchases journal (450)   A special journal used to record only purchases of merchandise on account.

sales journal (441)   A special journal used to record only sales of merchandise on account.

special journal (440)   A journal designed for recording only certain kinds of transactions.

SELF-STUDY QUESTIONS AND EXERCISES

True/False Questions

1. LO1   The types of special journals a business uses should depend on the types of transactions it has most frequently.

2. LO1   If a business uses special journals, it generally will not need a general journal.

3. LO2   All sales, for cash or on credit, are recorded in the sales journal.

4. LO3   A cash receipts journal is used to record all cash receipts transactions.

5. LO4   Purchases returns and allowances are recorded in the general journal.

Multiple Choice Questions

1. LO2   The first step in posting the sales journal to the general ledger is to

   (a) total and verify the equality of the amount columns.
   (b) enter the date in the Date column of the ledger account.
   (c) enter the new balance in the Balance columns of the ledger account.
   (d) enter the ledger account number below the column totals in the journal.

2. LO3   In the cash receipts journal, each amount in the General Credit column is posted

   (a) daily.   (c) at the end of the month.
   (b) weekly.   (d) at the end of the year.

3. LO4   The journal that should be used to record the return of merchandise for credit is the

   (a) purchases journal.   (c) general journal.
   (b) cash payments journal.   (d) accounts payable journal.

4. LO4   A purchases journal is used to record all

   (a) purchases.   (c) purchases of merchandise on account.
   (b) cash purchases.   (d) purchases returns and allowances.

5. LO5   In the cash payments journal, each amount in the General Debit column is posted

   (a) daily.   (c) at the end of the month.
   (b) weekly.   (d) at the end of the year.

U REVU   Exercises

1. LO2   Enter the following transaction in a sales journal like the one illustrated in the chapter:

   June 1   Made Sale No. 214 on account to Erin Lucas, $840, plus $42 sales tax.

2. LO3   Enter the following transactions in a cash receipts journal like the one illustrated in the chapter:

   June 7   Received cash on account from Erin Lucas, $882.
        30   Made cash sales for the month of $2,150, plus sales tax of $107.50.
        30   Received cash for rent revenue, $750.

3. LO4   Enter the following transaction in a purchases journal like the one illustrated in the chapter:

   Apr. 6   Purchased merchandise from Clever, $1,680. Invoice No. 131, dated April 6, terms n/30.

4. LO5   Enter the following transactions in a cash payments journal like the one illustrated in the chapter:

   Aug. 2   Issued Check No. 193 in payment of August rent (Rent Expense), $2,200.

6   Issued Check No. 194 to Mason Hardware in payment of merchandise purchased on account, $1,700, less 2% discount. The check was written for $1,666.

10   Issued Check No. 195 to Augie's Wholesale for cash purchase of merchandise, $2,730.

The answers to the Self-Study Questions and Exercises are at the end of the chapter (page 485).

APPLYING YOUR KNOWLEDGE

REVIEW QUESTIONS

LO1 1. What is the primary purpose of using special journals?

LO2 2. List four items of information about each sale entered in the sales journal.

LO2 3. What steps are followed in posting from the sales journal to the general ledger?

LO2 4. What steps are followed in posting from the sales journal to the accounts receivable ledger?

LO3 5. List three items of information about each cash receipt entered in the cash receipts journal.

LO3 6. What steps are followed in posting from the cash receipts journal to the general ledger?

LO3 7. What steps are followed in posting from the cash receipts journal to the accounts receivable ledger?

LO4 8. List four items of information about each purchase entered in the purchases journal.

LO4 9. What steps are followed in posting from the purchases journal to the general ledger?

LO4 10. What steps are followed in posting from the purchases journal to the accounts payable ledger?

LO5 11. List four items of information about each cash payment entered in the cash payments journal.

LO5 12. What steps are followed in posting from the cash payments journal to the general ledger?

LO5 13. What steps are followed in posting from the cash payments journal to the accounts payable ledger?

SERIES A EXERCISES

E 12-1A (LO1)   **RECORDING TRANSACTIONS IN THE PROPER JOURNAL** Identify the journal (sales, cash receipts, purchases, cash payments, or general) in which each of the following transactions should be recorded:

(a) Sold merchandise on account.

(b) Purchased delivery truck on account for use in the business.

(continued)

(c) Received payment from customer on account.
(d) Purchased merchandise on account.
(e) Issued check in payment of electric bill.
(f) Recorded depreciation on factory building.

E 12-2A (LO2)

✓ May 1:Dr. Accounts Receivable/
J. Adams, $2,120

JOURNALIZING SALES TRANSACTIONS Enter the following transactions in a sales journal. Use a 6% sales tax rate.

May 1 Sold merchandise on account to J. Adams, $2,000, plus sales tax. Sale No 488.

4 Sold merchandise on account to B. Clark, $1,800, plus sales tax. Sale No. 489.

8 Sold merchandise on account to A. Duck, $1,500, plus sales tax. Sale No. 490.

11 Sold merchandise on account to E. Hill, $1,950, plus sales tax. Sale No. 491.

E 12-3A (LO3)

✓ July 6: Cr. Accounts Receivable/
J. Adler, $643

JOURNALIZING CASH RECEIPTS Enter the following transactions in a cash receipts journal:

July 6 James Adler made payment on account, $643.

10 Made cash sales for the week, $2,320.

14 Betty Havel made payment on account, $430.

15 J. L. Borg made payment on account, $117.

17 Made cash sales for the week, $2,237.

E 12-4A (LO4)

✓ May 9: Purchases Dr./Accounts
Payable Cr., $2,300

JOURNALIZING PURCHASES TRANSACTIONS Enter the following transactions in a purchases journal like the one below.

May 3 Purchased merchandise from Cintron, $6,500. Invoice No. 321, dated May 1, terms n/30.

9 Purchased merchandise from Mitsui, $2,300. Invoice No. 614, dated May 8, terms 2/10, n/30.

18 Purchased merchandise from Aloha Distributors, $4,200. Invoice No. 180, dated May 15, terms 1/15, n/30.

23 Purchased merchandise from Soto, $6,300. Invoice No. 913, dated May 22, terms 1/10, n/30.

		PURCHASES JOURNAL		PAGE
DATE	INVOICE NO.	FROM WHOM PURCHASED	POST. REF.	PURCHASES DEBIT/ACCOUNTS PAYABLE CREDIT

E 12-5A (LO5)

✓ Sept. 12: Cash Cr., $6,930

JOURNALIZING CASH PAYMENTS Landmark Industries uses a cash payments journal. Prepare a cash payments journal using the same format and account titles as illustrated in the chapter. Record the following payments for merchandise purchased:

Sept. 5 Issued Check No. 318 to Clinton Corp. for merchandise purchased August 28, $6,000, terms 2/10, n/30. Payment is made within the discount period.

12 Issued Check No. 319 to Mitchell Co. for merchandise purchased September 2, $7,500, terms 1/10, n/30. A credit memo had previously been received from Mitchell Co. for merchandise returned, $500. Payment is made within the discount period after deduction for the return dated September 8.

Sept. 19   Issued Check No. 320 to Expert Systems for merchandise purchased August 19, $4,100, terms n/30.

27   Issued Check No. 321 to Graphic Data for merchandise purchased September 17, $9,000, terms 2/10, n/30. Payment is made within the discount period.

SERIES A PROBLEMS

P 12-6A (LO2)

✓ Total Accounts Receivable Dr.: $16,345.20

SALES JOURNAL J. K. Bijan owns a retail business and made the following sales during the month of August 20--. There is a 6% sales tax on all sales.

Aug. 1   Sale No. 213 to Jung Manufacturing Co., $1,200, plus sales tax.

3   Sale No. 214 to Hassad Co., $3,600, plus sales tax.

7   Sale No. 215 to Helsinki, Inc., $1,400, plus sales tax. (Open a new account for this customer. Address is 125 Fishers Dr., Noblesville, IN 47870–8867.)

11   Sale No. 216 to Ardis Myler, $1,280, plus sales tax.

18   Sale No. 217 to Hassad Co., $4,330, plus sales tax.

22   Sale No. 218 to Jung Manufacturing Co., $2,000, plus sales tax.

30   Sale No. 219 to Ardis Myler, $1,610, plus sales tax.

REQUIRED

1. Record the transactions in the sales journal. Total and verify the column totals and rule the columns.

2. Post from the sales journal to the general ledger and accounts receivable ledger accounts. Use account numbers as shown in the chapter.

P 12-7A (LO3)

✓ Total Accounts Receivable Cr.: $5,732

CASH RECEIPTS JOURNAL Zebra Imaginarium, a retail business, had the following cash receipts during December 20--. The sales tax is 6%.

Dec. 1   Received payment on account from Michael Anderson, $1,360.

2   Received payment on account from Ansel Manufacturing, $382.

7   Made cash sales for the week, $3,160, plus tax. Bank credit card sales for the week, $1,000, plus tax. Bank credit card fee is 3%.

8   Received payment on account from J. Gorbea, $880.

11   Michael Anderson returned merchandise for a credit, $60, plus tax.

14   Made cash sales for the week, $2,800, plus tax. Bank credit card sales for the week, $800, plus tax. Bank credit card fee is 3%.

20   Received payment on account from Tom Wilson, $1,110.

21   Ansel Manufacturing returned merchandise for a credit, $22, plus tax.

21   Made cash sales for the week, $3,200, plus tax.

24   Received payment on account from Rachel Carson, $2,000.

(continued)

Beginning general ledger account balances were as follows:

Cash	$9,862
Accounts Receivable	9,352

Beginning customer account balances were as follows:

M. Anderson	$2,480
Ansel Manufacturing	982
J. Gorbea	880
R. Carson	3,200
T. Wilson	1,810

REQUIRED

1. Record the transactions in the cash receipts journal. Total and verify column totals and rule the columns. Use the general journal to record sales returns and allowances.

2. Post from the journals to the general ledger and accounts receivable ledger accounts. Use account numbers as shown in the chapter.

P 12-8A (LO2/3)

✓ Total Accounts Receivable

Dr.: $12,745.08

SALES JOURNAL, CASH RECEIPTS JOURNAL, AND GENERAL JOURNAL
Owens Distributors is a retail business. The following sales, returns, and cash receipts occurred during March 20--. There is an 8% sales tax. Beginning general ledger account balances were Cash, $9,741.00; and Accounts Receivable, $1,058.25. Beginning customer account balances were Thompson Group, $1,058.25.

Mar. 1 Sold merchandise to Able & Co., $1,800, plus sales tax. Sale No. 33C.

3 Sold merchandise to R. J. Kalas, Inc., $2,240, plus sales tax. Sale No. 33D.

5 Able & Co. returned merchandise from Sale No. 33C for a credit (Credit Memo No. 66), $30, plus sales tax.

7 Made cash sales for the week, $3,160, plus sales tax.

10 Received payment from Able & Co. for Sale No. 33C less Credit Memo No. 66.

11 Sold merchandise to Blevins Bakery, $1,210, plus sales tax. Sale No. 33E.

13 Received payment from R. J. Kalas for Sale No. 33D.

14 Made cash sales for the week, $4,200, plus sales tax.

16 Blevins Bakery returned merchandise from Sale No. 33E for a credit (Credit Memo No. 67), $44, plus sales tax.

18 Sold merchandise to R. J. Kalas, Inc., $2,620, plus sales tax. Sale No. 33F.

20 Received payment from Blevins Bakery for Sale No. 33E less Credit Memo No. 67.

21 Made cash sales for the week, $2,400, plus sales tax.

25 Sold merchandise to Blevins Bakery, $1,915, plus sales tax. Sale No. 33G.

27 Sold merchandise to Thompson Group, $2,016, plus sales tax. Sale No. 33H.

28 Made cash sales for the week, $3,500, plus sales tax.

REQUIRED

1. Record the transactions in the sales journal, cash receipts journal, and general journal. Total, verify, and rule the columns where appropriate at the end of the month.

2. Post from the journals to the general ledger and accounts receivable ledger accounts. Use account numbers as shown in the chapter.

P 12-9A (LO4)

✓ Total Purchases Dr.: $20,790

PURCHASES JOURNAL J. B. Speck, owner of Speck's Galleria, made the following purchases of merchandise on account during the month of September:

Sept. 3   Purchase Invoice No. 415, $2,650, from Smith Distributors.

8   Purchase Invoice No. 132, $3,830, from Michaels Wholesaler.

11   Purchase Invoice No. 614, $3,140, from J. B. Sanders & Co.

18   Purchase Invoice No. 329, $2,250, from Bateman & Jones, Inc.

23   Purchase Invoice No. 867, $4,160, from Smith Distributors.

27   Purchase Invoice No. 744, $1,980, from Anderson Company.

30   Purchase Invoice No. 652, $2,780, from Michaels Wholesaler.

REQUIRED

1. Record the transactions in the purchases journal. Total and rule the journal.

2. Post from the purchases journal to the general ledger and accounts payable ledger accounts. Use account numbers as shown in the chapter.

P 12-10A (LO4)

✓ Helmut's Hair Supply account balance: $4,240

PURCHASES JOURNAL, GENERAL LEDGER, AND ACCOUNTS PAYABLE LEDGER The purchases journal of Kevin's Kettle, a small retail business, is as follows:

		PURCHASES JOURNAL			PAGE 1	
	DATE	INVOICE NO.	FROM WHOM PURCHASED	POST. REF.	PURCHASES DEBIT/ACCOUNTS PAYABLE CREDIT	
1	20-- Jan. 2	101	Ruiz Imports		3 0 0 0 00	1
2	3	621	Helmut's Hair Supply		2 4 8 0 00	2
3	7	195	Viola's Boutique		4 3 6 0 00	3
4	12	267	Royal Flush		1 9 5 0 00	4
5	18	903	Maria's Melodies		4 7 0 0 00	5
6	25	680	Helmut's Hair Supply		1 7 6 0 00	6
7					18 2 5 0 00	7

REQUIRED

1. Post the total of the purchases journal to the appropriate general ledger accounts. Use account numbers as shown in the chapter.

2. Post the individual purchase amounts to the accounts payable ledger.

P 12-11A (LO5)

✓ Total Cash Cr.: $30,984

CASH PAYMENTS JOURNAL Sam Santiago operates a retail variety store. The books include a cash payments journal and an accounts payable ledger. All cash payments (except petty cash) are entered in the cash payments journal.

Selected account balances on May 1 are as follows:

General Ledger

Cash	$40,000
Accounts Payable	20,000

Accounts Payable Ledger

Fantastic Toys	$5,200
Goya Outlet	3,800
Mueller's Distributors	3,600
Van Kooning	7,400

The following are the transactions related to cash payments for the month of May:

May 1 Issued Check No. 426 in payment of May rent (Rent Expense), $2,400.

3 Issued Check No. 427 to Mueller's Distributors in payment of merchandise purchased on account, $3,600, less a 3% discount. Check was written for $3,492.

7 Issued Check No. 428 to Van Kooning in partial payment of merchandise purchased on account, $5,500. A cash discount was not allowed.

12 Issued Check No. 429 to Fantastic Toys for merchandise purchased on account, $5,200, less a 1% discount. Check was written for $5,148.

15 Issued Check No. 430 to City Power and Light (Utilities Expense), $1,720.

18 Issued Check No. 431 to A-1 Warehouse for a cash purchase of merchandise, $4,800.

26 Issued Check No. 432 to Goya Outlet for merchandise purchased on account, $3,800, less a 2% discount. Check was written for $3,724.

30 Issued Check No. 433 to Mercury Transit Company for freight charges on merchandise purchased (Freight-In), $1,200.

31 Issued Check No. 434 to Town Merchants for a cash purchase of merchandise, $3,000.

REQUIRED

1. Enter the transactions in a cash payments journal. Total, rule, and prove the cash payments journal.

2. Post from the cash payments journal to the general ledger and accounts payable ledger. Use general ledger account numbers as shown in the chapter.

P 12-12A (LO4/5)

✓ Total Cash Cr.: $11,170

PURCHASES JOURNAL, CASH PAYMENTS JOURNAL, AND GENERAL JOURNAL Freddy Flint owns a small retail business called Flint's Fantasy. The cash account has a balance of $20,000 on July 1. The following transactions occurred during July:

July 1 Issued Check No. 414 in payment of July rent, $1,500.

1 Purchased merchandise on account from Tang's Toys, Invoice No. 311, $2,700, terms 2/10, n/30.

July 3 Purchased merchandise on account from Sillas & Company, Invoice No. 812, $3,100, terms 1/10, n/30.

5 Returned merchandise purchased from Tang's Toys, receiving a credit memo on the amount owed, $500.

8 Purchased merchandise on account from Daisy's Dolls, Invoice No. 139, $1,900, terms 2/10, n/30.

11 Issued Check No. 415 to Tang's Toys for merchandise purchased on account, less return of July 5 and less 2% discount.

13 Issued Check No. 416 to Sillas & Company for merchandise purchased on account, less 1% discount.

15 Returned merchandise purchased from Daisy's Dolls, receiving a credit memo on the amount owed, $400.

18 Issued Check No. 417 to Daisy's Dolls for merchandise purchased on account, less return of July 15 and less 2% discount.

25 Purchased merchandise on account from Allied Business, Invoice No. 489, $2,450, terms n/30.

26 Purchased merchandise on account from Tang's Toys, Invoice No. 375, $1,980, terms 2/10, n/30.

29 Purchased merchandise on account from Sillas & Company, Invoice No. 883, $3,460, terms 1/10, n/30.

31 Freddy Flint withdrew cash for personal use, $2,000. Issued Check No. 418.

31 Issued Check No. 419 to Glisan Distributors for a cash purchase of merchandise, $975.

REQUIRED

1. Record the transactions in the purchases journal, cash payments journal, and general journal. Total and rule the purchases and cash payments journals. Prove the cash payments journal.

2. Post from the journals to the general ledger and accounts payable ledger accounts. Use general ledger account numbers as shown in the chapter.

SERIES B EXERCISES

E 12-1B (LO1)

RECORDING TRANSACTIONS IN THE PROPER JOURNAL Identify the journal (sales, cash receipts, purchases, cash payments, or general) in which each of the following transactions should be recorded.

(a) Issued credit memo to customer for merchandise returned.
(b) Sold merchandise for cash.
(c) Purchased merchandise on account.
(d) Issued checks to employees in payment of wages.
(e) Purchased factory supplies on account.
(f) Sold merchandise on account.

E 12-2B (LO2)

✓ Sept. 1: Dr. Accounts Receivable/
K. Smith, $1,890

JOURNALIZING SALES TRANSACTIONS Enter the following transactions in a sales journal. Use a 5% sales tax rate.

(continued)

Sept. 1	Sold merchandise on account to K. Smith, $1,800, plus sales tax. Sale No. 228.
3	Sold merchandise on account to J. Arnes, $3,100, plus sales tax. Sale No. 229.
5	Sold merchandise on account to M. Denison, $2,800, plus sales tax. Sale No. 230.
7	Sold merchandise on account to B. Marshall, $1,900, plus sales tax. Sale No. 231.

E 12-3B (LO3)

✓ Nov. 1: Cr. Accounts Receivable/
Jean Haghighat, $750

JOURNALIZING CASH RECEIPTS Enter the following transactions in a cash receipts journal:

Nov. 1	Jean Haghighat made payment on account, $750.
12	Marc Antonoff made payment on account, $464.
15	Made cash sales, $3,763.
18	Will Mossein made payment on account, $241.
25	Made cash sales, $2,648.

E 12-4B (LO4)

✓ Jan. 3: Purchases Dr./Accounts
Payable Cr., $6,000

JOURNALIZING PURCHASES TRANSACTIONS Enter the following transactions in a purchases journal like the one below.

Jan. 3	Purchased merchandise from Feng, $6,000. Invoice No. 416, dated January 1, terms 2/10, n/30.
12	Purchased merchandise from Miranda, $9,000. Invoice No. 624, dated January 10, terms n/30.
19	Purchased merchandise from J. B. Barba, $6,400. Invoice No. 190, dated January 18, terms 1/10, n/30.
26	Purchased merchandise from Ramirez, $3,700. Invoice No. 923, dated January 25, terms 1/15, n/30.

PURCHASES JOURNAL					PAGE
DATE	INVOICE NO.	FROM WHOM PURCHASED	POST. REF.	PURCHASES DEBIT/ACCOUNTS PAYABLE CREDIT	

E 12-5B (LO5)

✓ Apr. 19: Cash Cr., $4,950

JOURNALIZING CASH PAYMENTS Sandcastles Northwest uses a cash payments journal. Prepare a cash payments journal using the same format and account titles as illustrated in the chapter. Record the following payments for merchandise purchased:

Apr. 5	Issued Check No. 429 to Standard Industries for merchandise purchased April 3, $8,000, terms 2/10, n/30. Payment is made within the discount period.
19	Issued Check No. 430 to Finest Company for merchandise purchased April 10, $5,300, terms 1/10, n/30. A credit memo had previously been received from Finest Company for merchandise returned, $300. Payment is made within the discount period after deduction for the return dated April 12.
21	Issued Check No. 431 to Funny Follies for merchandise purchased March 21, $3,250, terms n/30.
29	Issued Check No. 432 to Classic Data for merchandise purchased April 20, $7,000, terms 2/10, n/30. Payment is made within the discount period.

SERIES B PROBLEMS

P 12-6B (LO2)

✓ Total Accounts Receivable

Dr.: $13,072.50

SALES JOURNAL T. M. Maxwell owns a retail business and made the following sales during the month of July 20--. There is a 5% sales tax on all sales.

July 1   Sale No. 101 to Saga, Inc., $1,200, plus sales tax.

8   Sale No. 102 to Vinnie Ward, $2,100, plus sales tax.

15   Sale No. 103 to Dvorak Manufacturing, $4,300, plus sales tax.

21   Sale No. 104 to Vinnie Ward, $1,800, plus sales tax.

24   Sale No. 105 to Zapata Co., $1,600, plus sales tax. (Open a new account for this customer. Address is 789 N. Stafford Dr., Bloomington, IN 47401–6201.)

29   Sale No. 106 to Saga, Inc., $1,450, plus sales tax.

REQUIRED

1. Record the transactions in the sales journal. Total and verify the column totals and rule the columns.

2. Post the sales journal to the general ledger and accounts receivable ledger accounts. Use account numbers as shown in the chapter.

P 12-7B (LO3)

✓ Total Accounts Receivable

Cr.: $3,481

CASH RECEIPTS JOURNAL Color Florists, a retail business, had the following cash receipts during January 20--. The sales tax is 5%.

Jan. 1   Received payment on account from Ray Boyd, $880.

3   Received payment on account from Clint Hassell, $271.

5   Made cash sales for the week, $2,800, plus tax. Bank credit card sales for the week, $1,200, plus tax. Bank credit card fee is 3%.

8   Received payment on account from Jan Sowada, $912.

11   Ray Boyd returned merchandise for a credit, $40, plus tax.

12   Made cash sales for the week, $3,100, plus tax. Bank credit card sales for the week, $1,900, plus tax. Bank credit card fee is 3%.

15   Received payment on account from Robert Zehnle, $1,100.

18   Robert Zehnle returned merchandise for a credit, $31, plus tax.

19   Made cash sales for the week, $2,230, plus tax.

25   Received payment on account from Dazai Manufacturing, $318.

Beginning general ledger account balances were as follows:

Cash	$2,890.75
Accounts Receivable	6,300.00

Beginning customer account balances were as follows:

R. Boyd	$1,400
Dazai Manufacturing	318
C. Hassell	815
J. Sowada	1,481
R. Zehnle	2,286

(continued)

REQUIRED

1. Record the transactions in the cash receipts journal. Total and verify the column totals and rule the columns. Use the general journal to record sales returns and allowances.

2. Post from the journals to the general ledger and accounts receivable ledger accounts. Use account numbers as shown in the chapter.

P 12-8B (LO2/3)

✓ Total Accounts Receivable

Dr.: $7,853.80

SALES JOURNAL, CASH RECEIPTS JOURNAL, AND GENERAL JOURNAL Paul Jackson owns a retail business. The following sales, returns, and cash receipts are for April 20--. There is a 7% sales tax.

Apr. 1 Sold merchandise to O. L. Meyers, $2,100, plus sales tax. Sale No. 111.

3 Sold merchandise to Andrew Plaa, $1,000, plus sales tax. Sale No. 112.

6 O. L. Meyers returned merchandise from Sale No. 111 for a credit (Credit Memo No. 42), $50, plus sales tax.

7 Made cash sales for the week, $3,240, plus sales tax.

9 Received payment from O. L. Meyers for Sale No. 111, less Credit Memo No. 42.

12 Sold merchandise to Melissa Richfield, $980, plus sales tax. Sale No. 113.

14 Made cash sales for the week, $2,180, plus sales tax.

17 Melissa Richfield returned merchandise from Sale No. 113 for a credit (Credit Memo No. 43), $40, plus sales tax.

19 Sold merchandise to Kelsay Munkres, $1,020, plus sales tax. Sale No. 114.

21 Made cash sales for the week, $2,600, plus sales tax.

24 Sold merchandise to O. L. Meyers, $920, plus sales tax. Sale No. 115.

27 Sold merchandise to Andrew Plaa, $1,320, plus sales tax. Sale No. 116.

28 Made cash sales for the week, $2,800, plus sales tax.

Beginning general ledger account balances were as follows:

Cash	$2,864.54
Accounts Receivable	2,726.25

Beginning customer account balances were as follows:

O. L. Meyers	$2,186.00
K. Munkres	482.00
M. Richfield	58.25

REQUIRED

1. Record the transactions in the sales journal, cash receipts journal, and general journal. Total, verify, and rule the columns where appropriate at the end of the month.

2. Post from the journals to the general ledger and accounts receivable ledger accounts. Use account numbers as shown in the chapter.

P 12-9B (LO4)

✓ Total Purchases Dr.: $18,515

PURCHASES JOURNAL Ann Benton, owner of Benton's Galleria, made the following purchases of merchandise on account during the month of October:

Oct. 2	Purchase Invoice No. 321, $1,950, from Boggs Distributors.
7	Purchase Invoice No. 152, $2,915, from Wolfs Wholesaler.
10	Purchase Invoice No. 634, $3,565, from Komuro & Co.
16	Purchase Invoice No. 349, $2,845, from Fritz & McCord, Inc.
24	Purchase Invoice No. 587, $3,370, from Boggs Distributors.
26	Purchase Invoice No. 764, $2,240, from Sanderson Company.
31	Purchase Invoice No. 672, $1,630, from Wolfs Wholesaler.

REQUIRED

1. Record the transactions in the purchases journal. Total and rule the journal.

2. Post from the purchases journal to the general ledger and accounts payable ledger accounts. Use account numbers as shown in the chapter.

P 12-10B (LO4)

✓ Amelia & Vincente account balance: $7,810

PURCHASES JOURNAL, GENERAL LEDGER, AND ACCOUNTS PAYABLE LEDGER The purchases journal of Ryan's Rats Nest, a small retail business, is as follows:

	DATE	INVOICE NO.	FROM WHOM PURCHASED	POST. REF.	PURCHASES DEBIT/ACCOUNTS PAYABLE CREDIT	
1	20-- Jan. 3	121	Sandra's Sweets		4 4 9 0 00	1
2	5	641	Amelia & Vincente		5 9 2 0 00	2
3	9	215	Nobuko's Nature Store		2 6 8 0 00	3
4	15	227	Smith and Johnson Company		6 5 6 0 00	4
5	21	933	Hidemi, Inc.		1 3 0 0 00	5
6	30	650	Amelia & Vincente		1 8 9 0 00	6
7					22 8 4 0 00	7

PURCHASES JOURNAL   PAGE 1

REQUIRED

1. Post the total of the purchases journal to the appropriate general ledger accounts. Use account numbers as shown in the chapter.

2. Post the individual purchase amounts to the accounts payable ledger.

P 12-11B (LO5)

✓ Total Cash Cr.: $29,890

CASH PAYMENTS JOURNAL Kay Zembrowski operates a retail variety store. The books include a cash payments journal and an accounts payable ledger. All cash payments (except petty cash) are entered in the cash payments journal. Selected account balances on May 1 are as follows:

General Ledger

Cash	$40,000
Accounts Payable	20,000

(continued)

Accounts Payable Ledger

Cortez Distributors	$4,200
Indra & Velga	6,800
Toy Corner	4,600
Troutman Outlet	4,400

The following transactions are related to cash payments for the month of May:

May 1   Issued Check No. 326 in payment of May rent (Rent Expense), $2,600.

4   Issued Check No. 327 to Cortez Distributors in payment of merchandise purchased on account, $4,200, less a 3% discount. Check was written for $4,074.

7   Issued Check No. 328 to Indra & Velga in partial payment of merchandise purchased on account, $6,200. A cash discount was not allowed.

11   Issued Check No. 329 to Toy Corner for merchandise purchased on account, $4,600, less a 1% discount. Check was written for $4,554.

15   Issued Check No. 330 to County Power and Light (Utilities Expense), $1,500.

19   Issued Check No. 331 to Builders Warehouse for a cash purchase of merchandise, $3,500.

25   Issued Check No. 332 to Troutman Outlet for merchandise purchased on account, $4,400, less a 2% discount. Check was written for $4,312.

30   Issued Check No. 333 to Rapid Transit Company for freight charges on merchandise purchased (Freight-In), $800.

31   Issued Check No. 334 to City Merchants for a cash purchase of merchandise, $2,350.

REQUIRED

1. Enter the transactions in a cash payments journal. Total, rule, and prove the cash payments journal.

2. Post from the cash payments journal to the general ledger and accounts payable ledger. Use general ledger account numbers as shown in the chapter.

P 12-12B (LO4/5)

✓ Total Cash Cr.: $10,760

PURCHASES JOURNAL, CASH PAYMENTS JOURNAL, AND GENERAL JOURNAL Debbie Mueller owns a small retail business called Debbie's Doll House. The cash account has a balance of $20,000 on July 1. The following transactions occurred during July:

July 1   Issued Check No. 314 for July rent, $1,400.

1   Purchased merchandise on account from Topper's Toys, Invoice No. 211, $2,500, terms 2/10, n/30.

3   Purchased merchandise on account from Jones & Company, Invoice No. 812, $2,800, terms 1/10, n/30.

5   Returned merchandise purchased from Topper's Toys receiving a credit memo on the amount owed, $400.

8   Purchased merchandise on account from Downtown Merchants, Invoice No. 159, $1,600, terms 2/10, n/30.

July 11	Issued Check No. 315 to Topper's Toys for merchandise purchased on account, less return of July 5 and less 2% discount.
13	Issued Check No. 316 to Jones & Company for merchandise purchased on account, less 1% discount.
15	Returned merchandise purchased from Downtown Merchants receiving a credit memo on the amount owed, $600.
18	Issued Check No. 317 to Downtown Merchants for merchandise purchased on account, less return of July 15 and less 2% discount.
25	Purchased merchandise on account from Columbia Products, Invoice No. 468, $3,200, terms n/30.
26	Purchased merchandise on account from Topper's Toys, Invoice No. 395, $1,430, terms 2/10, n/30.
29	Purchased merchandise on account from Jones & Company, Invoice No. 853, $2,970, terms 1/10, n/30.
31	Mueller withdrew cash for personal use, $2,500. Issued Check No. 318.
31	Issued Check No. 319 to Burnside Warehouse for a cash purchase of merchandise, $1,050.

REQUIRED

1. Record the transactions in the purchases journal, cash payments journal, and general journal. Total and rule the purchases and cash payments journals. Prove the cash payments journal.

2. Post from the journals to the general ledger and accounts payable ledger accounts. Use general ledger account numbers as shown in the chapter.

 ## MANAGING YOUR WRITING

You have a part-time job as a bookkeeper at a local office supply store. The accounting records consist of a general journal and general ledger. The manager is concerned about efficiency and feels that too much time is spent recording transactions. In addition, there sometimes is difficulty determining the amount owed to specific suppliers. The manager knows you are an accounting student and asks for your suggestions to improve the accounting function.

Write a memo to the manager describing how to increase efficiency and accuracy by using different accounting records.

ETHICS CASE

Judy Baresford, the store manager of Comfort Futons, noticed that the amount of time the two bookkeepers were spending on accounts receivable, accounts payable, and cash receipts was increasing due to the store's increase in sales. A friend of Judy's who is also a store manager suggested that she might want to have some special journals designed that would reduce the amount of work involved in the day-to-day bookkeeping at her store. Judy approached Jon Fortner and Sue Stavio, the bookkeepers, and asked them

(continued)

to come up with a proposal for special journals. During lunch, Jon told Sue he thought designing special journals would be a lot of work and it was not in his job description. Sue told him not to worry because she would just copy pages of special journals from her accounting textbook and they could submit these journals as their own design. Jon liked the idea and they agreed to meet the next night, scan the journals into Word, and submit them to Judy the following morning.

1.   Do you think Sue's suggestion is unethical? Why or why not?

2.   In using the generic special journals from Sue's accounting textbook, what possible problems can you foresee?

3.   If you were Judy, how would you respond to Sue and Jon's "plan"?

MASTERY PROBLEM

✓ Total Accounts Receivable Cr.:
$7,235

KLOOSTER
& ALLEN

During the month of October 20--, The Pink Petal flower shop engaged in the following transactions:

Oct. 1	Sold merchandise on account to Elizabeth Shoemaker, $1,000, plus tax of $50. Sale No. 222.
2	Issued Check No. 190 to Jill Hand in payment of October 1 balance of $500, less 2% discount.
2	Purchased merchandise on account from Flower Wholesalers, $4,000. Invoice No. 500, dated October 2, terms 2/10, n/30.
4	Purchased merchandise on account from Seidl Enterprises, $700. Invoice No. 527, dated October 4, terms 2/15, n/30.
5	Issued Check No. 191 in payment of telephone expense for the month of September, $150.
7	Sold merchandise for cash, $3,500, plus tax of $175.
9	Received payment from Leigh Summers in full settlement of account, $2,000.
11	Issued Check No. 192 to Flower Wholesalers in payment of October 1 balance of $1,500.
12	Sold merchandise on account to Leigh Summers, $2,000, plus tax of $100. Sale No. 223.
12	Received payment from Meg Johnson on account, $3,100.
13	Issued Check No. 193 to Seidl Enterprises in payment of October 4 purchase. Invoice No. 527, less 2% discount.
14	Meg Johnson returned merchandise for a credit, $300, plus sales tax of $15.
17	Returned merchandise to Vases Etc. for credit, $900.
24	Received payment from David's Decorating on account, $2,135.
27	Sold merchandise on account to David's Decorating, $3,000, plus tax of $150. Sale No. 224.
29	Issued Check No. 194 in payment of wages (Wages Expense) for the four-week period ending October 30, $900.

Selected account balances as of October 1 were as follows:

Account	Account No.	Debit	Credit
Cash	101	$18,225.00	
Accounts Receivable	122	9,619.00	
Accounts Payable	202		$5,120.00

The Pink Petal also had the following subsidiary ledger balances as of October 1:

Accounts Receivable:

Customer	Accounts Receivable Balance
David's Decorating 12 Jude Lane Hartford, CT 06117	$3,340.00
Elizabeth Shoemaker 52 Juniper Road Hartford, CT 06118	279.00
Meg Johnson 700 Hobbes Dr. Avon, CT 06108	4,000.00
Leigh Summers 5200 Hamilton Ave. Hartford, CT 06111	2,000.00

Accounts Payable:

Vendor	Accounts Payable Balance
Vases Etc. 34 Harry Ave. East Hartford, CT 05234	$3,120.00
Jill Hand 1009 Drake Rd. Farmington, CT 06082	500.00
Flower Wholesalers 43 Lucky Lane Bristol, CT 06007	1,500.00
Seidl Enterprises 888 Anders Street Newington, CT 06789	—

REQUIRED

1. Record the transactions in a sales journal (page 7), cash receipts journal (page 10), purchases journal (page 6), cash payments journal (page 11), and general journal (page 5). Total, verify, and rule the columns where appropriate at the end of the month.

2. Post from the journals to the general ledger, accounts receivable ledger, and accounts payable ledger accounts. Use account numbers as shown in the chapter.

CHALLENGE PROBLEM

✓ June 3: Cr. City Sales Tax
     Payable, $4.22

Screpcap Co. had the following transactions during the first week of June:

June 1   Purchased merchandise on account from Acme Supply, $2,700, plus freight charges of $160.

1   Issued Check No. 219 to Denver Wholesalers for merchandise purchased on account, $720, less 1% discount.

1   Sold merchandise on account to F. Colby, $246, plus 5% state sales tax plus 2% city sales tax.

2   Received cash on account from N. Dunlop, $315.

2   Made cash sale of $413 plus 5% state sales tax plus 2% city sales tax.

2   Purchased merchandise on account from Permon Co., $3,200, plus freight charges of $190.

3   Sold merchandise on account to F. Ayres, $211, plus 5% state sales tax plus 2% city sales tax.

3   Issued Check No. 220 to Ellis Co. for merchandise purchased on account, $847, less 1% discount.

3   Received cash on account from F. Graves, $463.

4   Issued Check No. 221 to Penguin Warehouse for merchandise purchased on account, $950, less 1% discount.

4   Sold merchandise on account to K. Stanga, $318, plus 5% state sales tax plus 2% city sales tax.

4   Purchased merchandise on account from Mason Milling, $1,630, plus freight charges of $90.

4   Received cash on account from O. Alston, $381.

5   Made cash sale of $319 plus 5% state sales tax plus 2% city sales tax.

5   Issued Check No. 222 to Acme Supply for merchandise purchased on account, $980, less 1% discount.

REQUIRED

1. Record the transactions in a general journal.

2. Assuming these are the types of transactions Screpcap Co. experiences on a regular basis, design the following special journals for Screpcap:

     (a)   Sales journal
     (b)   Cash receipts journal
     (c)   Purchases journal
     (d)   Cash payments journal

ANSWERS TO SELF-STUDY QUESTIONS AND EXERCISES

True/False Questions

1. T   **2.** F (general journal is still needed)   **3.** F (only credit sales)   **4.** T   **5.** T

Multiple Choice Questions

1. a   **2.** a   **3.** c   **4.** c   **5.** a

U REVU   Exercises

1.

	DATE	SALE NO.	TO WHOM SOLD	POST. REF.	ACCOUNT RECEIVABLE DEBIT	SALES CREDIT	SALES TAX PAYABLE CREDIT	
			SALES JOURNAL				PAGE 7	
1	June 1	214	Erin Lucas		8 8 2 00	8 4 0 00	4 2 00	1

2.

CASH RECEIPTS JOURNAL   PAGE

	DATE	ACCOUNT CREDITED	POST. REF.	GENERAL CREDIT	ACCOUNTS RECEIVABLE CREDIT	SALES CREDIT	SALES TAX PAYABLE CREDIT	CASH DEBIT	
1	June 7	Erin Lucas			8 8 2 00			8 8 2 00	1
2	30					2 1 5 0 00	1 0 7 50	2 2 5 7 50	2
3	30	Rent Revenue		7 5 0 00				7 5 0 00	3
4									4

3.

PURCHASES JOURNAL   PAGE

	DATE	INVOICE NO.	FROM WHOM PURCHASED	POST. REF.	PURCHASES DEBIT/ACCOUNTS PAYABLE CREDIT	
1	Apr. 6	131	Clever		1 6 8 0 00	1
2						2

4.

CASH PAYMENTS JOURNAL   PAGE

	DATE	CK NO.	ACCOUNT DEBITED	POST. REF.	GENERAL DEBIT	ACCOUNTS PAYABLE DEBIT	PURCHASES DEBIT	PURCHASES DISCOUNTS CREDIT	CASH CREDIT	
1	Aug. 2	193	Rent Expense		2 2 0 0 00				2 2 0 0 00	1
2	6	194	Mason Hardware			1 7 0 0 00		3 4 00	1 6 6 6 00	2
3	10	195					2 7 3 0 00		2 7 3 0 00	3
4										4

MARK LENNIHAN/AP PHOTO

PHOTO: © CARY BENBOW

Chapter 13

LEARNING OBJECTIVES

Careful study of this chapter should enable you to:

LO1 Explain the impact of merchandise inventory on the financial statements.

LO2 Describe the two principal systems of accounting for merchandise inventory—the periodic system and the perpetual system.

LO3 Compute the costs allocated to the ending inventory and cost of goods sold using different inventory methods.

LO4 Estimate the ending inventory and cost of goods sold by using the gross profit and retail inventory methods.

Accounting for Merchandise Inventory

With 11,000 employees serving 2 million customers weekly, Marsh operates 99 Marsh Supermarkets and five O'Malia's Food Markets in Indiana and Ohio. Headquartered in Indianapolis, Marsh also has 41 pharmacy locations, the largest pharmacy chain based in the state of Indiana. Known for its use of technology, Marsh has the distinction of being the first grocery store in the world to use electronic scanners to ring up purchases.

As you walk through a grocery store, have you ever wondered what the store paid for each item? It would be nice to know which items are "good buys" and which are "overpriced." What happens when management pays different amounts for identical products on the shelf? In this chapter, you will learn how merchandising firms determine which items were sold and which remain. That is, how they determine the cost of the goods sold and the cost of the goods remaining on the shelves at the end of the year.

In Chapters 10 and 11, you learned how to account for the purchase and sale of merchandise. One of the major reasons for keeping accounting records is to determine the net income (or net loss) of a business. A major component of net income is the gross profit. In Chapter 11, you learned how to compute gross profit. An abbreviated form of this calculation is shown below.

Calculation of Gross Profit		
Net sales		$110
Cost of goods sold		
Merchandise inventory, Jan. 1	$ 20	
Purchases	80	
Cost of goods available for sale	$100	
Less merchandise inventory, Dec. 31	30	
Cost of goods sold		70
Gross profit		$ 40

> The terms goods and merchandise mean the same thing and are used interchangeably.

For a merchandising business, the cost of goods available for sale ($100) during the accounting period must be divided between cost of goods sold ($70) and ending merchandise inventory ($30). In Chapter 11, the costs assigned to these accounts were provided. In this chapter, you will learn how to determine the dollar amounts assigned to cost of goods sold and ending merchandise inventory. In Chapter 14, we will illustrate the end-of-period adjustments required to bring the cost of goods sold and merchandise inventory accounts up to date to reflect their proper balances.

THE IMPACT OF MERCHANDISE INVENTORY ON FINANCIAL STATEMENTS

LO1 Explain the impact of merchandise inventory on the financial statements.

A company's ending inventory must be reported accurately. An error in the reported inventory will cause errors on the income statement, statement of owner's equity, and balance sheet. In addition, since this year's ending inventory becomes next year's beginning inventory, financial statements for the following year will also contain errors.

> This year's ending inventory becomes next year's beginning inventory.

Figure 13-1 illustrates the impact of an error in the *ending inventory*. The first pair of columns presents partial financial statements when the ending inventory is correct. For this illustration, sales, cost of goods sold, and operating expenses are assumed to be the same for 20-1 and 20-2. Thus, the same net income of $30 and beginning and ending merchandise inventories of $20 are reported for both years.

The second pair of columns in Figure 13-1 illustrates the effects of understating the ending inventory. Understating the ending inventory for 20-1 by $5 causes the cost of goods sold to be overstated by $5 and net income to be understated by $5. Since net income is reported on the statement of owner's equity, Erv Bultman's capital on December 31 is understated by $5. The understated capital also appears in the owner's equity section of the balance sheet. The understated ending inventory is reported in the current assets section of the balance sheet.

Even if the ending inventory for 20-2 is accurately reported, we still have a problem with the income statement. Since the ending inventory for 20-1 was understated, the beginning inventory for 20-2 is understated also ($15 instead of $20). This error causes cost of goods sold to be understated by $5 and net income to be overstated by $5.

LEARNING KEY

If the ending inventory for 20-1 is understated, net income for 20-1 is understated and net income for 20-2 is overstated.

FIGURE 13-1 Effect of Inventory Errors on Net Income

	ENDING INVENTORY FOR 20-1 IS CORRECT		ENDING INVENTORY FOR 20-1 IS UNDERSTATED		ENDING INVENTORY FOR 20-1 IS OVERSTATED	
	20-1	20-2	20-1	20-2	20-1	20-2
Income Statement						
Sales	80	80	80	80	80	80
Cost of goods sold:						
Beginning merchandise inventory	20	**20**	20	**15**	20	**25**
Add purchases (net)	40	40	40	40	40	40
Cost of goods available for sale	60	60	60	55	60	65
Less ending merchandise inventory	**(20)**	(20)	**(15)**	(20)	**(25)**	(20)
Cost of goods sold		(40)	(40)	(45)	(35)	(35)	(45)
Gross profit	40	40	35	45	45	35
Operating expenses	(10)	(10)	(10)	(10)	(10)	(10)
Net income	30	30	25	35	35	25
Statement of Owner's Equity						
Erv Bultman, capital, January 1	100	130	100	125	100	135
Net income	30	30	25	35	35	25
Erv Bultman, capital, December 31		130	160	125	160	135	160
Balance Sheet (Partial)						
Current assets:						
Merchandise inventory	20	20	15	20	25	20
Owner's equity:						
Erv Bultman, capital	130	160	125	160	135	160

LEARNING KEY

If the ending inventory for 20-1 is overstated, net income for 20-1 is overstated and net income for 20-2 is understated.

At this point, we can see that this inventory error "washes out" over the two-year period. The understated net income for 20-1 is offset by overstated net income in 20-2. Thus, Bultman's capital account as of December 31, 20-2, is reported accurately on the statement of owner's equity and balance sheet at $160. Assuming no future inventory errors, the financial statements for 20-3 and thereafter will be correct.

The third pair of columns in Figure 13-1 illustrates the effects of overstating the ending inventory in 20-1. This causes net income to be overstated in 20-1 and understated in 20-2. As previously discussed, these errors "wash out" by the end of 20-2. Thus, Bultman's capital account is correct in the 20-2 financial statements.

It is very important to have an accurate count and valuation for the ending inventory. Since errors in the ending inventory have a direct effect on net income for the period, managers may be tempted to manipulate this amount to achieve a desired result: to either increase net income to make the company look good, or decrease net income to reduce taxes or smooth earnings. For this reason, observing and verifying the ending inventory is an important aspect of an external auditor's job.

U REVU   Complete U REVU-1 on **page 506** to test your basic understanding of LO1.

TYPES OF INVENTORY SYSTEMS: PERIODIC AND PERPETUAL

LO2 Describe the two principal systems of accounting for merchandise inventory—the periodic system and the perpetual system.

The two principal systems of accounting for merchandise inventory are the periodic and the perpetual systems. Entries made for inventory transactions under these systems are illustrated in Figure 13-2. Chapter 11 illustrated the periodic inventory system. As shown in Figure 13-2, under the **periodic inventory system**, no entries are made to the merchandise inventory or cost of goods sold account during the year. Thus, the balance in the merchandise inventory account is based on the physical count of inventory taken at the end of the last accounting period. The merchandise inventory and the cost of goods sold for the current period are not determined until the end of the current accounting period, when a physical inventory is taken. At that time, the following formula is applied to calculate cost of goods sold.

LEARNING KEY

Under the periodic inventory system, the ending inventory and cost of goods sold are determined at the end of the accounting period, when a physical inventory is taken.

Beginning Inventory (based on last year's ending physical count)

+   Net Purchases (account balance at end of this year)
=   Cost of Goods Available for Sale

−   Ending Inventory (based on this year's ending physical count)
=   Cost of Goods Sold (for this year)

Adjusting entries are needed at the end of the fiscal year to update the merchandise inventory account and cost of goods sold. These entries are illustrated in Chapter 14.

FIGURE 13-2 Entries for Periodic and Perpetual Inventory Systems

TRANSACTION	PERIODIC SYSTEM		PERPETUAL SYSTEM	

1. Purchased merchandise on account, $100.	Purchases 100
	   Accounts Payable
		100	Merchandise Inventory 100
			   Accounts Payable
				100

2. Paid freight charge, $30.	Freight-In 30
	   Cash
		30	Merchandise Inventory 30
			   Cash
				30

3. Sold merchandise on account, $80.
     The cost of the merchandise was $50.
	Accounts Receivable 80
	   Sales
		80	Accounts Receivable 80
			   Sales
			Cost of Goods Sold 50
			   Merchandise Inventory
				80
				
				50

4. Merchandise costing $10 was returned to the supplier.	Accounts Payable 10
	   Purchases Ret. & Allow.
		10	Accounts Payable 10
			   Merchandise Inventory
				10

5. Customers returned merchandise sold for $20.
     The cost of the merchandise was $15.
	Sales Ret. and Allow. 20
	   Accounts Receivable
		20	Sales Ret. and Allow. 20
			   Accounts Receivable
			Merchandise Inventory 15
			   Cost of Goods Sold
				20
				
				15

6. Paid for merchandise costing $100. The supplier granted a 2% discount for prompt payment.	Accounts Payable 100
	   Purchases Discounts
	   Cash
		2
		98
			Accounts Payable 100
			   Merchandise Inventory
			   Cash
				2
				98

LEARNING KEY

Under the perpetual inventory system, cost of goods sold and the amount of merchandise inventory on hand are continually updated as merchandise is bought and sold.

As shown in Figure 13-2, under the **perpetual inventory system**, entries are made to the merchandise inventory and cost of goods sold accounts as transactions take place during the accounting period. The merchandise inventory account is debited for the cost of all goods purchased, including freight charges, and credited for the cost of all goods sold. In addition, this account is debited when customers return merchandise and is credited when suppliers grant returns, allowances, and discounts. Thus, the balance of the account represents the cost of goods on hand at all times. The cost of goods sold account is debited when merchandise is sold and credited when customers return merchandise. Thus, the balance of the account reflects the cost of goods sold at any point during the accounting period. No year-end adjusting entry is necessary as long as the physical inventory agrees with the amount reported in the merchandise inventory account. In Chapter 14, we will illustrate the proper adjustment if this is not true.

U REVU

Complete U REVU-2 on **page 506** to test your basic understanding of LO2.

ASSIGNING COST TO INVENTORY AND COST OF GOODS SOLD

LO3 Compute the costs allocated to the ending inventory and cost of goods sold using different inventory methods.

To determine the cost of goods sold and ending inventory, it is important to understand:

1. the purpose of a physical inventory,

2. the specific calculations used under the periodic and perpetual systems, and

3. the role of the lower-of-cost-or-market rule.

TAKING A PHYSICAL INVENTORY

Under the periodic system, the goods on hand at the end of the period are counted to allocate merchandise costs between sold and unsold goods. This process is called taking a **physical inventory**. A physical inventory is also important under the perpetual system. It verifies that the amount of merchandise actually held agrees with what is reported in the accounting records.

Taking a physical inventory can be a sizable task. Frequently, it is done after regular business hours. Some companies even close for a few days to take inventory. The ideal time to count the goods is when the quantity on hand is at its lowest level. A fiscal year that starts and ends at the time the stock of goods is normally at its lowest level is known as a **natural business year**. Such a year is used by many businesses for accounting purposes.

Various procedures are followed in taking an inventory to be sure that no items are missed and that no items are included more than once. Frequently, persons taking inventory work in pairs: one counts the items and the other records the information. Usually, this information is entered on a special form called an **inventory sheet**, like the one illustrated in Figure 13-3. The inventory sheet has columns for recording the description of each item, the quantity on hand, the cost per unit, and the extension.

Even under the perpetual inventory system, there will be differences between the actual inventory on the floor and the amount on the books. These differences are the result of breakage, spoilage, and theft. Thieves rarely yell "Debit Loss Due to Theft and credit Merchandise Inventory" as they attempt to leave the store with merchandise under their coats.

FIGURE 13-3 Inventory Sheet

INVENTORY Aug. 31 20 -- Page 1

Sheet No. 1
Called by L.M.M.
Entered by K.N.
Department A
Location Storeroom
Costed by C.M.H.
Extended by C.M.H.
Examined by C.J.C.

Description	Quantity	Unit	Unit Cost	Extensions	
Table Lamp	20	ea.	62.80	1,256.00	
Wall Rack	18	ea.	19.70	354.60	
Bookcase	7	ea.	88.10	616.70	
End Table	13	ea.	53.20	691.60	
Desk	6	ea.	158.30	949.80	
Total					6,465.10

A BROADER VIEW

The "Magic Wand" at Wal-Mart

At any given time, a typical Wal-Mart discount store has more than 70,000 standard items in stock. Every item must be inventoried and replenished in a timely way to avoid having too much or too little stock. Wal-Mart associates have the aid of the "Magic Wand," a handheld computer, linked by a radio-frequency network to in-store terminals. These high-tech devices provide up-to-the-minute information on inventory on hand, upcoming deliveries, and stock at Wal-Mart distribution centers.

ERMINGUT/ISTOCKPHOTO.COM

Only goods that are the property of the company should be included in a physical inventory. Two special situations that require care to determine ownership are (1) goods held for sale on **consignment** and (2) goods **in transit**. Sometimes one business will try to sell merchandise for another business or individual on a commission basis. This is called selling goods on consignment. Goods held on consignment remain the property of the shipper (**consignor**). They should not be included in the inventory of the company holding the goods (**consignee**).

To determine whether goods in transit at year-end should be included in inventory, we must know the FOB (free on board) terms. If goods are shipped FOB shipping point, the buyer pays for shipping and the goods belong to the buyer as soon as they are shipped. If goods are shipped FOB destination, the seller pays for shipping and the goods belong to the seller until they are received by the buyer.

After calculating the quantities of goods owned at the end of the period, the proper cost must be assigned to the inventory. In addition to the purchase price, we include delivery costs (freight-in), insurance, and, occasionally, storage fees. Therefore, cost means all necessary and reasonable costs incurred to get the goods to the buyer's place of business.

If all purchases of the same item were made at the same price per unit, computing the cost of the ending inventory would be simple. We would multiply the number of units by the cost per unit. In a world of changing prices, however, identical items are purchased at different times and at different costs per unit. Of the goods available for sale, how do we decide which units were sold and which units remain on the shelf? As shown in Figure 13-4, this decision affects the income statement and balance sheet. The following four inventory methods have become generally accepted for answering this question:

1. Specific identification

2. First-in, first-out (FIFO)

3. Weighted-average

4. Last-in, first-out (LIFO)

These methods may be applied under the periodic or perpetual inventory systems.

FIGURE 13-4 Allocation of Goods Available for Sale to Cost of Goods Sold and Ending Inventory

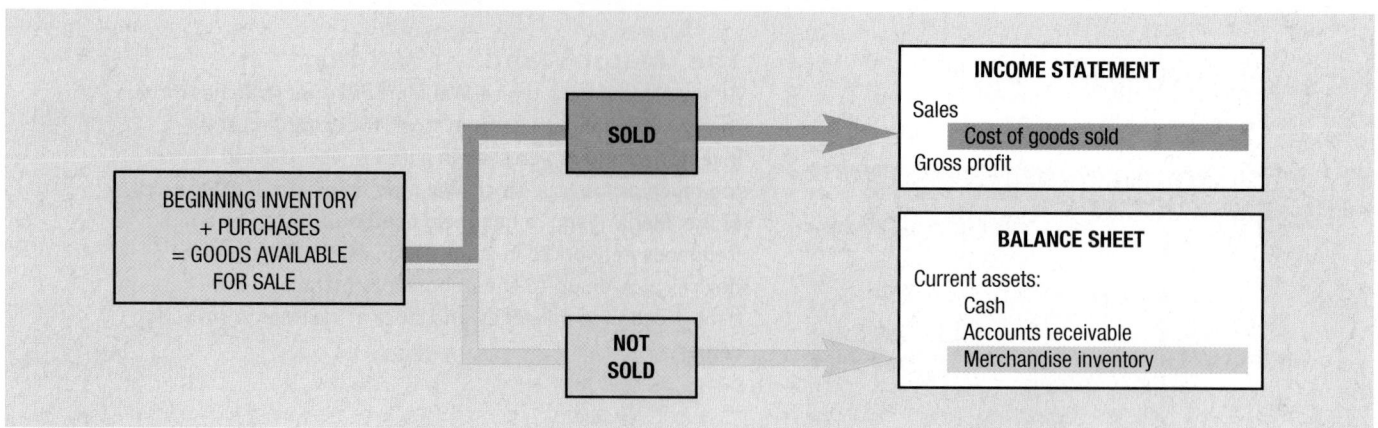

THE PERIODIC INVENTORY SYSTEM

Specific Identification Method

LEARNING KEY

The specific identification method requires that each inventory item have a distinguishing feature or marking to assure proper identification.

When each unit of inventory can be specifically identified, the **specific identification method** can be used. To use this method, inventory items must be physically different from each other, or they must have serial numbers. Examples include cars, motorcycles, furniture, appliances, and fine jewelry. When a unit is sold, its cost is determined from the supplier's invoice. Unless computerized, this method is practical only for businesses in which sales volume is relatively low and inventory unit value is relatively high. Otherwise, record keeping becomes expensive and time consuming.

To illustrate how specific identification costing works, assume the following data for an inventory of one specific model of children's bicycles:

Children's Bicycles (Model ZX007)

	Units	Unit Price	Total Cost
On hand at start of period	40	$62	$ 2,480
Purchased during period:			
1st purchase	60	65	3,900
2nd purchase	80	67	5,360
3rd purchase	70	68	4,760
Number of units available for sale	250		$16,500
On hand at end of period	50		
Number of units sold during period	200		

Of the 200 units sold during the period, the bicycle serial numbers show that 30 were from the beginning inventory, 50 were from the first purchase, 60 were from the second purchase, and 60 were from the last purchase. The cost of goods sold and the cost of inventory at the end of the period are determined as shown in Figure 13-5.

First-In, First-Out (FIFO) Method

LEARNING KEY

FIFO means **F**irst-**I**n, **F**irst-**O**ut.

Another widely used method of allocating merchandise cost is called the **first-in, first-out, or FIFO, method.** This costing method assumes that the first goods purchased were the first goods sold. Therefore, the latest goods purchased remain in inventory.

Whenever possible, a business will attempt to sell the older goods first. This is particularly true of businesses that sell perishable items or merchandise that may become obsolete. Grocery stores, fresh fruit stands, and computer software businesses are good examples. These businesses must rotate their stock forward. They pull the oldest bread,

FIGURE 13-5 Specific Identification Inventory Method

	COST OF GOODS SOLD			COST OF ENDING INVENTORY		
	Units	Unit Price	Total	Units	Unit Price	Total
Beginning inventory	30	$62	$ 1,860	10	$62	$ 620
1st purchase	50	65	3,250	10	65	650
2nd purchase	60	67	4,020	20	67	1,340
3rd purchase	60	68	4,080	10	68	680
Total	200		$13,210	50		$ 3,290
Alternative calculation if given goods available for sale and cost of goods sold or ending inventory.	Cost of goods available for sale Less cost of ending inventory Cost of goods sold		$16,500 (3,290) $13,210	Cost of goods available for sale Less cost of goods sold Cost of ending inventory		$16,500 (13,210) $ 3,290

milk, fruit, and vegetables to the front of the shelves and try to sell all copies of the current software before a new version arrives. FIFO costing is, therefore, widely used because it often follows the actual movement of goods. It assumes that the oldest units have been sold and the newest or freshest units are in the ending inventory.

Applying FIFO to the bicycle inventory data, the cost of goods sold and the cost of inventory at the end of the period are determined as shown in Figure 13-6.

FIGURE 13-6 FIFO Inventory Method

	COST OF GOODS SOLD			COST OF ENDING INVENTORY		
	Units	Unit Price	Total	Units	Unit Price	Total
Beginning inventory	40	$62	$ 2,480		$62	$ 0
1st purchase	60	65	3,900		65	0
2nd purchase	80	67	5,360		67	0
3rd purchase	20	68	1,360	50	68	3,400
Total	200		$ 13,100	50		$ 3,400
Alternative calculation if given goods available for sale and cost of goods sold or ending inventory.	Cost of goods available for sale Less cost of ending inventory Cost of goods sold		$ 16,500 (3,400) $ 13,100	Cost of goods available for sale Less cost of goods sold Cost of ending inventory		$ 16,500 (13,100) $ 3,400

LEARNING KEY

The consistency principle of accounting suggests that a business should use the same accounting techniques from year to year.

Note that the 50 items on hand at the end of the period are considered to be those most recently purchased.

FIFO costing is widely used because businesses have used this method for a long time. Accountants are reluctant to change a long-followed method of accounting when such a change would affect the comparability of their income calculations over a period of years. **Consistency** based on comparability is an important accounting principle.

Weighted-Average Method

Another method of allocating merchandise cost is called the **weighted-average method**, or **average cost method**. This costing method is based on the average cost of identical units.

Consider the bicycle inventory data again. The average cost of identical units is determined by dividing the total cost of units available for sale ($16,500) by the total number of units available for sale (250).

$$\frac{\$16,500 \text{ (cost of units available for sale)}}{250 \text{ (units available for sale)}} = \$66 \text{ weighted-average cost per unit}$$

The cost of goods sold and the cost of the end-of-period inventory are calculated as follows:

Cost of goods sold	200 units @ $66 =	$13,200
Cost of ending inventory	50 units @ $66 =	3,300
Total	250 units	$16,500

There is a logical appeal to the weighted-average method of allocating cost between goods sold and goods on hand. In this example, one-fifth (50) of the total units available (250) were unsold. The weighted-average method assigns one-fifth ($3,300) of the total cost ($16,500) to these goods.

LEARNING KEY

LIFO means **L**ast-**I**n, **F**irst-**O**ut.

Last-In, First-Out (LIFO) Method

A fourth method of allocating merchandise cost is called the **last-in, first-out**, or **LIFO, method**. It assumes that the sales in the period were made from the most recently purchased goods. Therefore, the earliest goods purchased remain in inventory.

This physical flow is associated with businesses selling products that are not perishable or likely to become obsolete, and may be difficult to handle. Imagine a large barrel of nails at a lumberyard. Customers take nails from the top of the barrel. When the supply gets low, new nails are simply piled on top of the old ones. There is no need to rotate the nails from the bottom to the top of the barrel.

Applying LIFO to the bicycle inventory data, the cost of goods sold and the cost of inventory at the end of the period are determined as shown in Figure 13-7.

FIGURE 13-7 LIFO Inventory Method

	COST OF GOODS SOLD			COST OF ENDING INVENTORY		
	Units	Unit Price	Total	Units	Unit Price	Total
Beginning inventory	0	$62	$ 0	40	$62	$ 2,480
1st purchase	50	65	3,250	10	65	650
2nd purchase	80	67	5,360		67	0
3rd purchase	70	68	4,760		68	0
Total	200		$13,370	50		$ 3,130
Alternative calculation if given goods available for sale and cost of goods sold or ending inventory.	Cost of goods available for sale		$16,500	Cost of goods available for sale		$16,500
	Less cost of ending inventory		(3,130)	Less cost of goods sold		(13,370)
	Cost of goods sold		$13,370	Cost of ending inventory		$ 3,130

Note that the 50 units on hand at the end of the period are considered to be the 40 units in the beginning inventory plus 10 of the units from the first purchase.

The LIFO method has been justified on the grounds that the physical movement of goods in some businesses is actually last-in, first-out. This is rarely the case, but the method has become popular for other reasons. One persuasive argument for the use of the LIFO method is that it matches the most current cost of items purchased against

Although LIFO is acceptable under U.S. GAAP and many U.S. companies use this method for financial reporting and tax purposes, it is not permitted under International Financial Reporting Standards.

LEARNING KEY

The inventory method used does not have to match the physical flow of goods.

the current sales revenue. When the most current costs of purchases are subtracted from sales revenue, the impact of changing prices on the resulting gross profit figure is minimized. In the opinion of many accountants, this is proper and desirable.

Another reason for the popularity of the LIFO method is its effect on income taxes. When prices are rising, net income calculated under the LIFO method is less than net income calculated under either the FIFO or the weighted-average method. Since the net income amount under LIFO is less, the related income tax will be less. The reverse would be true if prices were falling. However, periods of falling prices over the past two centuries have been few and brief.

Opponents of the LIFO method contend that its use causes old, out-of-date inventory costs to be shown on the balance sheet. The theoretical and practical merits of FIFO versus LIFO are the subject of much professional debate.

Physical Flows and Cost Flows

Of the four inventory costing methods described, only the specific identification costing method will necessarily reflect cost flows that match physical flows of goods. Each of the other three methods—FIFO, weighted-average, and LIFO—is based on assumed cost flows. The assumed cost flows *are not required to reflect the actual physical movement of goods* within the company. Any one of the three assumed cost flow methods could be used under any set of physical flow conditions. For example, a fresh fruit stand with an actual FIFO flow of inventory may use LIFO for accounting purposes. Similarly, a supplier of building materials that sells nails, lumber, and sand off the top of the pile may use FIFO even though the physical flow of goods is LIFO.

Comparison of Methods

To compare the results of the four inventory methods, let's assume that the 200 bicycle units in our example were sold for $18,000. Figure 13-8 contrasts the ending inventory, cost of goods sold, and gross profit under each of the four methods.

FIGURE 13-8 Comparison of Inventory Methods

	SPECIFIC IDENTIFICATION		FIFO		WEIGHTED AVERAGE		LIFO	
Sales		$18,000		$18,000		$18,000		$18,000
Cost of goods sold:								
Beginning inventory	$ 2,480		$ 2,480		$ 2,480		$ 2,480	
Purchases	14,020		14,020		14,020		14,020	
Goods available for sale	$16,500		$16,500		$16,500		$16,500	
Less ending inventory	3,290		3,400		3,300		3,130	
Cost of goods sold		13,210		13,100		13,200		13,370
Gross profit		$ 4,790		$ 4,900		$ 4,800		$ 4,630

During periods of rising prices, we can observe the following: LIFO generally produces the highest cost of goods sold, lowest gross profit, and lowest ending inventory. Since the most recent units purchased are assumed to have been sold, the most recent costs are matched against revenues and this provides the best measure of gross profit and net income. After all, the units sold must be replaced at current prices. However, under LIFO, the first units purchased are assumed to remain in inventory (FISH: First-In, Still Here). This means that units purchased many years ago may remain in the ending inventory. These dollar amounts are likely to have little meaning when measuring the firm's performance or financial health.

FIFO generally produces the lowest cost of goods sold, highest gross profit, and highest ending inventory. Since the last units purchased are assumed to be in ending inventory, these most recent costs provide the best inventory measure on the balance sheet (LISH: Last-In, Still Here). However, under FIFO, the first units purchased are assumed to have been sold. This means that somewhat older prices are used to compute cost of goods sold and gross profit than under LIFO. Thus, these measures are somewhat less useful than those computed under LIFO.

The weighted-average inventory method produces measures between LIFO and FIFO. The specific identification method will produce measures based on the actual units sold.

The Internal Revenue Service requires the use of the same inventory method for tax and financial reporting purposes. Since LIFO generally produces the highest cost of goods sold, lowest gross profit, and lowest tax liability, many firms use the LIFO inventory method to minimize federal income taxes. The tax dollars saved are then available for other purposes.

As discussed earlier, keep the following in mind when selecting the inventory method to be used by a business:

1. The physical flow of the inventory does not need to match the flow assumed by the inventory method.

2. The consistency principle requires that the same accounting methods be followed from period to period. Although it is acceptable to make changes, it is not appropriate to switch back and forth from FIFO to LIFO based on the desire to maximize or minimize earnings for a given year.

THE PERPETUAL INVENTORY SYSTEM

Under the perpetual inventory system, a continuous record is maintained for the quantities and costs of goods on hand at all times. The general ledger account for Merchandise Inventory under such a system is somewhat like the account for Cash. It provides a chronological record of each addition (purchase) and subtraction (sale). The balance of the account at any time shows the cost of goods that should be on hand.

When perpetual inventory records are kept, the merchandise inventory account in the general ledger is usually a controlling account. A subsidiary ledger is maintained with an account for each type of merchandise. These accounts are often recorded on cards or in computer files. As shown in Figure 13-9, the subsidiary accounts are designed to handle additions and subtractions and determine the new balance after each change. Goods sold usually are assigned cost on either a FIFO, moving-average, or LIFO basis. Procedures for applying the FIFO method in a perpetual inventory system are similar to those illustrated for a periodic system. The first merchandise purchased is treated as the first merchandise sold. The illustration in Figure 13-9 is based on the FIFO method. The specific techniques used to apply the moving-average and LIFO methods in a perpetual system are more complicated. They are illustrated in the chapter appendix.

LOWER-OF-COST-OR-MARKET METHOD OF INVENTORY VALUATION

It is a well-established tradition in accounting that gains should not be recognized unless a sale has occurred. If the value of an asset increases while it is being held, no formal entry of the gain is made on the books. On the other hand, if an asset's value declines while it is being held, it is generally considered proper to recognize a loss. This is in keeping with the accounting practice of **conservatism,** which states that when in doubt, the lower asset value and net income measure should be used. Thus, we should never anticipate gains, but we should always anticipate and account for losses.

FIGURE 13-9 Perpetual Inventory Record: FIFO Method

DATE	PURCHASES			COST OF GOODS SOLD				INVENTORY ON HAND				
	Units	Cost/ Unit	Total	Units	Cost/ Unit	CGS	Cumulative CGS	Layer	Units	Cost/ Unit	Layer Cost	Total
Jan. 1 (BI)								(1)	40	$62	$2,480	$2,480
Feb. 15				30	$62	$1,860	$1,860	(1)	10	$62	$620	$620
Mar. 1	60	$65	$3,900					(1)	10	$62	$620	
								(2)	60	65	3,900	$4,520
Apr. 1				10	$62	$620		(2)	30	$65	$1,950	
				30	$65	1,950	$4,430					$1,950
May 15	80	$67	$5,360					(2)	30	$65	$1,950	
								(3)	80	67	5,360	$7,310
June 30				30	$65	$1,950		(3)	20	$67	$1,340	
				60	67	4,020	$10,400					$1,340
Aug. 28	70	$68	$4,760					(3)	20	$67	$1,340	
								(4)	70	68	4,760	$6,100
Oct. 30				20	$67	$1,340		(4)	50	$68	$3,400	
				20	68	1,360	$13,100					$3,400
Cost of Goods Sold during 20--							$13,100					
BI: Beginning Inventory												

As applied to inventory, conservatism means that if the value of inventory declines while it is being held, the loss should be recognized in the period of the decline. The purpose of the **lower-of-cost-or-market method** is to recognize such losses on the income statement and to report the lower inventory valuation on the balance sheet.

In applying the lower-of-cost-or-market method, "**cost**" means the dollar amount calculated using one of the four inventory costing methods. "**Market**" means the cost to replace the inventory. It is the price in the market in which goods are purchased by the business—not the price in the market in which they are normally sold by the business. The lower-of-cost-or-market method assumes that a decline in the purchase (replacement) price of inventory is accompanied by a decline in the selling price. In this sense, a decline in the purchase (replacement) price signals a decline in the value of the inventory.

To illustrate the lower-of-cost-or-market method, assume the following end-of-period inventory data for three items:

LEARNING KEY

Under lower-of-cost-or-market, market represents the cost to replace the inventory item, not the selling price.

Item	Recorded Purchase Cost	End-of-Period Market Value	Lower-of-Cost-or-Market
1	$ 8,000	$ 7,000	$ 7,000
2	9,000	10,000	9,000
3	7,000	6,500	6,500
	$24,000	$23,500	$22,500

The illustration shows two ways to calculate the lower-of-cost-or-market. First, the lower-of-cost-or-market method can be applied to the total inventory. This involves comparing the $24,000 total cost with the $23,500 *total end-of-period market value*. Under the second approach, the method is applied to each item in inventory. This involves comparing the $24,000 total cost with the $22,500 lower-of-cost-or-market value determined by comparing cost with market value for *each item*. Either approach is acceptable, but the one chosen should be applied consistently across periods.

The difference between the cost and market value is considered a loss due to holding inventory. Normally, it is charged to an account such as **Loss on Write-Down of Inventory**. For example, based on application of the method to the total inventory in the previous illustration, a $500 loss ($24,000 − $23,500) is recognized as follows:

14	Loss on Write-Down of Inventory			5 0 0 00			14
15	Merchandise Inventory				5 0 0 00		15
16	To recognize loss in value of inventory held						16

The loss due to write-down of inventory should be reported on the income statement as an expense. Although not a preferred treatment, some businesses include it in cost of goods sold if the amounts are small.

U REVU

Complete U REVU-3 on page 506 to test your basic understanding of LO3.

ESTIMATING ENDING INVENTORY AND COST OF GOODS SOLD

LO4 Estimate the ending inventory and cost of goods sold by using the gross profit and retail inventory methods.

Many businesses prepare monthly or quarterly financial statements. To do this, the business must estimate the inventory at the end of the month or quarter and the cost of goods sold for the period. This is not a problem for businesses using the perpetual inventory method. Although these amounts need to be verified by a physical inventory at the end of the year, the unverified amounts are generally reliable estimates and can be used for these "interim" statements.

Businesses using the periodic inventory method must use other methods to estimate the ending inventory and cost of goods sold. Two generally accepted methods are the gross profit method and the retail inventory method.

GROSS PROFIT METHOD OF ESTIMATING INVENTORY

Under the **gross profit method**, a business's normal gross profit (net sales − cost of goods sold) is used to estimate the cost of goods sold and ending inventory. To illustrate the gross profit method, assume the following data with respect to Groomer Company:

Inventory, start of period	$80,000
Net purchases, first month	$70,000
Net sales, first month	$110,000
Normal gross profit as a percentage of sales	40%

The estimated cost of goods sold for the month and the estimated merchandise inventory at the end of the month would be determined as shown in Figure 13-10.

This calculation is appropriate only if the firm's normal gross profit as a percentage of net sales has been relatively stable over time. This type of calculation also can be used to test the reasonableness of the amount of inventory that was computed on the basis of a physical count. A large difference between the two amounts might indicate a mistake in the count, a mistake in the costing of the items, or a marked change

FIGURE 13-10 Steps for the Gross Profit Method

STEP 1	Compute the cost of goods available for sale.	Cost of goods available for sale:		
		Inventory, start of period	$ 80,000	
		Net purchases, first month	70,000	
		Cost of goods available for sale:		$150,000
STEP 2	Estimate cost of goods sold by deducting the normal gross profit from net sales.	Estimated cost of goods sold:		
		Net sales	$110,000	
		Normal gross profit	44,000	
		($110,000 × 40%)		
		Estimated cost of goods sold		66,000
STEP 3	Estimate the ending inventory by deducting cost of goods sold from the cost of goods available for sale.	Estimated end-of-month inventory		$ 84,000

in the gross profit rate. The gross profit procedure also can be used to estimate the cost of an inventory that was destroyed by fire or other casualty.

RETAIL METHOD OF ESTIMATING INVENTORY

Many retail businesses, such as department and clothing stores, use a variation of the gross profit method to calculate cost of goods sold and ending inventory. The procedure used, called the **retail method** of inventory, requires keeping records of both the cost and selling (retail) prices of all goods purchased. This information can be used to estimate cost of goods sold and ending inventory, as shown in Figure 13-11.

FIGURE 13-11 Steps in the Retail Inventory Method

			COST	RETAIL
STEP 1	Compute the cost of goods available for sale at cost and retail.	Inventory, start of period	$ 60,000	$ 85,000
		Net purchases during period	126,000	163,000
		Goods available for sale	$186,000	$248,000
STEP 2	Compute the ending inventory at retail by subtracting sales at retail from goods available for sale at retail.	Less net sales for period		180,000
		Inventory, end of period, at retail		$ 68,000
STEP 3	Compute the cost-to-retail ratio by dividing the cost of goods available for sale by the retail value of the goods available for sale.	Ratio of cost-to-retail prices of goods available for sale ($186,000 ÷ $248,000)		75%
STEP 4	Estimate the cost of the ending inventory by multiplying the ending inventory at retail (step 2) by the cost-to-retail ratio.	Inventory, end of period, at estimated cost (75% of $68,000)	(51,000)	
STEP 5	Estimate cost of goods sold by a. multiplying sales at retail by the cost-to-retail ratio, or b. subtracting the estimated ending inventory from the cost of goods available for sale.	Estimated cost of goods sold (or, sales of $180,000 × 75% = $135,000)	$135,000	

U REVU

Complete U REVU-4 on **page 506** to test your basic understanding of LO4.

LEARNING OBJECTIVES   Key Points to Remember

LO1 Explain the impact of merchandise inventory on the financial statements.

The cost of goods available for sale during the accounting period must be divided between the cost of goods sold and the ending merchandise inventory. Cost of goods sold is reported on the income statement and used to determine the gross profit for the period. The ending merchandise inventory is reported as a current asset on the balance sheet. Figure 13-12 illustrates the allocation of cost of goods available for sale into cost of goods sold and ending inventory.

FIGURE 13-12 Allocation of Goods Available for Sale to Cost of Goods Sold and Ending Inventory

LO2 Describe the two principal systems of accounting for merchandise inventory—the periodic system and the perpetual system.

There are two systems of accounting for merchandise.

Periodic Inventory System
1. The purchases account is debited for the cost of all goods purchased.
2. The sales account is credited for the selling prices of all goods sold.
3. At the end of the accounting period, a physical inventory is taken, and the following formula is applied to calculate cost of goods sold:

Beginning Inventory (last year's ending physical count)

+ <u>Net Purchases (account balance at end of this year)</u>
= Cost of Goods Available for Sale

− <u>Ending Inventory (this year's ending physical count)</u>
= Cost of Goods Sold (for this year)

Perpetual Inventory System
1. The merchandise inventory account is debited for all purchases.
2. The cost of goods sold account is debited, and the merchandise inventory account is credited for all sales.
3. Thus, the merchandise inventory account provides a running balance of the goods on hand.

LO3 Compute the costs allocated to the ending inventory and cost of goods sold using different inventory methods.

One of the following four inventory methods is generally used to determine the costs assigned to the goods sold and ending inventory:
- Specific identification
- FIFO: first-in, first-out
- Weighted-average
- LIFO: last-in, first-out

(continued)

LEARNING OBJECTIVES Key Points to Remember

LO3 (concluded)	The actual physical flow of inventory does not have to match the method used. During periods of rising prices, LIFO produces the lowest net income, and FIFO produces the highest net income.
LO4 Estimate the ending inventory and cost of goods sold by using the gross profit and retail inventory methods.	Firms using the periodic inventory method often need to estimate their inventory. Two methods are used for this purpose.

- **Gross Profit Method**—The firm's normal gross profit as a percentage of net sales is used to estimate cost of goods sold and ending inventory in three steps.
  1. Compute the cost of goods available for sale.
  2. Estimate cost of goods sold by deducting the normal gross profit (net sales × normal gross profit as percentage of net sales) from net sales.
  3. Estimate the ending inventory by deducting cost of goods sold from the cost of goods available for sale.
- **Retail Inventory Method**—The firm's ratio of cost-to-retail prices of goods available for sale is used to estimate ending inventory and cost of goods sold in five basic steps:
  1. Compute the cost of goods available for sale at cost and retail.
  2. Compute the ending inventory at retail by subtracting sales at retail from goods available for sale at retail.
  3. Compute the cost-to-retail ratio by dividing the cost of goods available for sale by the retail value of the goods available for sale.
  4. Estimate the cost of ending inventory by multiplying the ending inventory at retail (step 2) by the cost-to-retail ratio.
  5. Estimate cost of goods sold by:
     a. multiplying sales at retail by the cost-to-retail ratio, or
     b. subtracting the estimated ending inventory from the cost of goods available for sale.

DEMONSTRATION PROBLEM

Fialka Company's beginning inventory and purchases during the fiscal year ended October 31, 20-2, were as follows:

		Units	Unit Price	Total Cost
November 1, 20-1	Beginning inventory	500	$25.00	$ 12,500
November 12, 20-1	1st purchase	600	26.25	15,750
December 28, 20-1	2nd purchase	400	27.50	11,000
March 29, 20-2	3rd purchase	1,000	28.00	28,000
May 31, 20-2	4th purchase	750	28.50	21,375
July 29, 20-2	5th purchase	350	29.00	10,150
August 30, 20-2	6th purchase	675	30.00	20,250
October 21, 20-2	7th purchase	225	31.00	6,975
		4,500		$126,000

There are 1,600 units of inventory on hand on October 31, 20-2.

(continued)

REQUIRED

1. Calculate the total amount to be assigned to cost of goods sold for the fiscal year and ending inventory on October 31, 20-2, under each of the following periodic inventory methods:

   (a) FIFO
   (b) LIFO
   (c) Weighted-average cost (round calculations to two decimal places)

2. Assume that the market price per unit (cost to replace) of Fialka's inventory on October 31, 20-2, was $29. Calculate the total amount to be assigned to the ending inventory on October 31, 20-2, under each of the following methods:

   (a) FIFO lower-of-cost-or-market
   (b) Weighted-average lower-of-cost-or-market

3. Assume that a fire destroyed Fialka's store and all inventory on October 31, just prior to taking a physical inventory. Thus, Fialka must estimate the ending inventory and cost of goods sold. During the fiscal year ended October 31, 20-2, net sales of $134,000 were made. The normal gross profit rate is 40%. Use the gross profit method to estimate the cost of goods sold for the fiscal year ended October 31, 20-2, and the inventory on October 31, 20-2.

Solution 1a.

	FIFO INVENTORY METHOD						
Date		**Cost of Goods Sold**			**Cost of Ending Inventory**		
20-1/-2		**Units**	**Unit Price**	**Total**	**Units**	**Unit Price**	**Total**
Nov. 1	Beginning inventory	500	$25.00	$ 12,500		$25.00	$ 0
Nov. 12	1st purchase	600	26.25	15,750		26.25	0
Dec. 28	2nd purchase	400	27.50	11,000		27.50	0
Mar. 29	3rd purchase	1,000	28.00	28,000		28.00	0
May 31	4th purchase	400	28.50	11,400	350	28.50	9,975
July 29	5th purchase		29.00	0	350	29.00	10,150
Aug. 30	6th purchase		30.00	0	675	30.00	20,250
Oct. 21	7th purchase		31.00	0	225	31.00	6,975
	Total	2.900		$ 78,650	1,600		$ 47,350

Alternative calculation if given goods available for sale and cost of goods sold or ending inventory.	Cost of goods available for sale	$126,000	Cost of goods available for sale	$126,000
	Less cost of ending inventory	(47,350)	Less cost of goods sold	(78,650)
	Cost of goods sold	$ 78,650	Cost of ending inventory	$ 47,350

1b.

Date		LIFO INVENTORY METHOD					
		Cost of Goods Sold			Cost of Ending Inventory		
20-1/-2		Units	Unit Price	Total	Units	Unit Price	Total
Nov. 1	Beginning inventory		$25.00	$ 0	500	$25.00	$ 12,500
Nov. 12	1st purchase		26.25	0	600	26.25	15,750
Dec. 28	2nd purchase		27.50	0	400	27.50	11,000
Mar. 29	3rd purchase	900	28.00	25,200	100	28.00	2,800
May 31	4th purchase	750	28.50	21,375		28.50	0
July 29	5th purchase	350	29.00	10,150		29.00	0
Aug. 30	6th purchase	675	30.00	20,250		30.00	0
Oct. 21	7th purchase	225	31.00	6,975		31.00	0
	Total	2.900		$ 83,950	1,600		$ 42,050
Alternative calculation if given goods available for sale and cost of goods sold or ending inventory.		Cost of goods available for sale		$126,000	Cost of goods available for sale		$126,000
		Less cost of ending inventory		(42,050)	Less cost of goods sold		(83,950)
		Cost of goods sold		$ 83,950	Cost of ending inventory		$ 42,050

1c. Weighted-average method:
Average cost per unit: $126,000 ÷ 4,500 units = $28
Inventory, October 31, 20-2:

1,600 units @ $28 =	$44,800

Cost of goods sold for 20-1/-2:

2,900 units @ $28 =	$81,200

2a. FIFO lower-of-cost-or-market:

FIFO cost	$47,350
Market 1,600 units @ $29	46,400
Choose market	46,400

2b. Weighted-average lower-of-cost-or-market:

Weighted-average cost	$44,800
Market 1,600 units @ $29	46,400
Choose weighted-average cost	44,800

3. Estimated inventory on October 31, 20-2:

Inventory, November 1, 20-1	$ 12,500	
Net purchases, November 1, 20-1 through October 31, 20-2	113,500	
Cost of goods available for sale		$126,000
Estimated cost of goods sold:		
Net sales	$134,000	
Normal gross profit ($134,000 × 40%)	53,600	
Estimated cost of goods sold		80,400
Estimated inventory on October 31, 20-2		$ 45,600

KEY TERMS

average cost method (493)   See weighted-average method.

conservatism (496)   The accounting practice of conservatism states that we should never anticipate gains, but always anticipate and account for losses. As applied to inventory, conservatism means that if the value of inventory declines while it is being held, the loss should be recognized in the period of the decline.

consignee (491)   The company holding the merchandise of another business to be sold.

consignment (491)   Goods that are held by one business for sale but that are owned by another business.

consignor (491)   The owner of the merchandise that is held by another business.

consistency (493)   The principle that states that a business should use the same accounting methods from period to period. This improves the comparability of the financial statements over time.

cost (497)   In applying the lower-of-cost-or-market method, cost means the dollar amount calculated using one of the four inventory costing methods.

first-in, first-out (FIFO) method (492)   A method of allocating merchandise cost which assumes that the first goods purchased were the first goods sold and, therefore, that the latest goods purchased remain in inventory.

gross profit method (498)   A method of estimating inventory in which a business's normal gross profit percentage is used to estimate the cost of goods sold and ending inventory.

in transit (491)   Goods that are in the process of being shipped between the seller and the buyer.

inventory sheet (490)   A form used for recording inventory items. It has columns for recording the description of each item, the quantity on hand, the cost per unit, and the extension.

last-in, first-out (LIFO) method (494)   A method of allocating merchandise cost which assumes that the sales in the period were made from the most recently purchased goods. Therefore, the earliest goods purchased remain in inventory.

Loss on Write-Down of Inventory (498)   This account is debited when the market value (replacement cost) of the inventory is below cost when applying the lower-of-cost-or-market method of inventory valuation. It is reported on the income statement as an expense.

lower-of-cost-or-market method (497)   An inventory valuation method under which inventory is valued at the lower-of-cost-or-market value (replacement cost).

market (497)   In applying the lower-of-cost-or-market method, market means the cost to replace the inventory. It is the prevailing price in the market in which goods are purchased—not the prevailing price in the market in which they are normally sold.

natural business year (490)   A fiscal year that starts and ends at the time the stock of goods is normally at its lowest level.

periodic inventory system (489)   Under this system, the ending inventory and cost of goods sold are determined at the end of the accounting period, when a physical inventory is taken.

perpetual inventory system (489)   Under this system, the merchandise inventory and cost of goods sold accounts are updated when merchandise is bought and sold.

physical inventory (490)   A physical count of the goods on hand.

retail method (499)   A variation of the gross profit method that is used by many retail businesses, such as department and clothing stores, to estimate the cost of goods sold and ending inventory.

specific identification method (492)   A method of allocating merchandise cost in which each unit of inventory is specifically identified.

weighted-average method (493)   A method of allocating merchandise cost based on the average cost of identical units. The average cost of identical units is determined by dividing the total cost of units available for sale by the total number of units available for sale.

SELF-STUDY QUESTIONS AND EXERCISES

True/False Questions

1. LO1   An overstatement of ending inventory in the year 20-1 will cause net income to be overstated in the year 20-1.

2. LO1   An understatement of ending inventory in the year 20-1 will cause net income to be overstated in the year 20-2, assuming no other errors.

3. LO2   Under the perpetual system of accounting for inventory, the current merchandise inventory and the cost of goods sold are not determined until the end of the accounting period when a physical inventory is taken.

4. LO3   A fiscal year that starts and ends at the time the stock of goods is normally at its lowest level is known as a natural business year.

5. LO3   If goods are shipped FOB shipping point, the seller pays for the shipping costs.

Multiple Choice Questions

1. LO1   An understatement of ending inventory in the year 20-1 will cause the owner's equity account at the end of the year 20-2, assuming no other errors, to be

   (a) understated.
   (b) correctly stated.
   (c) overstated.
   (d) none of the above.

2. LO3   Goods held on consignment remain the property of the

   (a) consignee.
   (b) consignor.
   (c) buyer.
   (d) seller.

3. LO3   In times of rising prices, the inventory cost method that will yield the lowest net income is

   (a) FIFO.
   (b) weighted-average.
   (c) LIFO.
   (d) none of the above.

4. LO3   In times of rising prices, the inventory cost method that will yield the highest cost of goods sold is

   (a) LIFO.
   (b) weighted-average.
   (c) FIFO.
   (d) none of the above.

5. LO3   In the application of "lower-of-cost-or-market," market is the

   (a) lowest sales price.
   (b) highest sales price.
   (c) replacement cost.
   (d) average sales price.

U REVU   **Exercises**

1. **LO1** If the ending inventory is overstated by $10,000, indicate what, if anything, is incorrect about the following:

    Cost of goods sold   _____
    Gross profit   _____
    Net income   _____
    Ending owner's capital   _____

2. **LO2** Using the following information, compute the ending balance of the merchandise inventory account under the perpetual inventory system.

a.	Merchandise inventory, beginning balance	$ 20,000
b.	Purchased merchandise on account	200,000
c.	Sold merchandise on account	240,000
d.	Cost of merchandise sold in (c)	120,000
e.	Freight charges paid on inventory delivered to showroom	1,000
f.	Refund provided to customers for merchandise returned	800
g.	Cost of merchandise returned by customers	500

3. **LO3** Use the following information to compute cost of goods sold under the FIFO and LIFO inventory methods. The firm sold 200 units.

	Units	Unit Price	Total
Beginning inventory	50	$ 5	$ 250
1st purchase	100	8	800
2nd purchase	150	10	1,500

4. **LO4** Kulsrud Company would like to estimate the current inventory level. Using the gross profit method and the following information, estimate the current inventory level for Kulsrud Company.

Goods available for sale	$100,000
Net sales	150,000
Normal gross profit as a percent of sales	40%

The answers to the Self-Study Questions and Exercises are at the end of the chapter (pages 515–516).

APPLYING YOUR KNOWLEDGE

REVIEW QUESTIONS

LO1 1. What financial statements are affected by an error in the ending inventory?

LO2 2. What is the main difference between the periodic system of accounting for inventory and the perpetual system of accounting for inventory?

LO3 3. Is a physical inventory necessary under the periodic system? Why or why not?

LO3 4. Is a physical inventory necessary under the perpetual system? Why or why not?

LO3 5. In a period of rising prices, which inventory method will result in:

(a) the highest cost of goods sold?
(b) the lowest cost of goods sold?
(c) the highest ending inventory?

(d) the lowest ending inventory?

(e) the highest gross profit?

(f) the lowest gross profit?

LO3 6. What two factors are taken into account by the weighted-average method of merchandise cost allocation?

LO3 7. Which inventory method always follows the actual physical flow of merchandise?

LO3 8. When lower-of-cost-or-market is assigned to the items that comprise the ending merchandise inventory, what does "cost" mean? What does "market" mean?

LO4 9. List the three steps followed under the gross profit method of estimating inventory.

LO4 10. List the five steps followed under the retail method of estimating inventory.

SERIES A EXERCISES

E 13-1A (LO1)

INVENTORY ERRORS Assume that in year 1, the ending merchandise inventory is overstated by $50,000. If this is the only error in years 1 and 2, indicate which items will be understated, overstated, or correctly stated for years 1 and 2.

	Year 1	Year 2
Ending merchandise inventory	_____	_____
Beginning merchandise inventory	_____	_____
Cost of goods sold	_____	_____
Gross profit	_____	_____
Net income	_____	_____
Ending owner's capital	_____	_____

E 13-2A (LO2)

JOURNAL ENTRIES—PERIODIC INVENTORY Bill Diamond owns a business called Diamond Distributors. The following transactions took place during January of the current year. Journalize the transactions in a general journal using the periodic inventory method.

Jan. 5 Purchased merchandise on account from Prestigious Jewelers, $3,700.

8 Paid freight charge on merchandise purchased, $200.

12 Sold merchandise on account to Diamonds Unlimited, $4,900.

15 Received a credit memo from Prestigious Jewelers for merchandise returned, $600.

22 Issued a credit memo to Diamonds Unlimited for merchandise returned, $800.

E 13-3A (LO2)

JOURNAL ENTRIES—PERPETUAL INVENTORY Sandy Johnson owns a small variety store. The following transactions took place during March of the current year. Journalize the transactions in a general journal using the perpetual inventory method.

Mar. 3 Purchased merchandise on account from City Galleria, $2,700.

7 Paid freight charge on merchandise purchased, $175.

13 Sold merchandise on account to Amber Specialties, $3,000. The cost of the merchandise was $1,800.

18 Received a credit memo from City Galleria for merchandise returned, $500.

22 Issued a credit memo to Amber Specialties for merchandise returned, $400. The cost of the merchandise was $240.

E 13-4A (LO3)

✓ End. inv.: $45,500

ENDING INVENTORY COSTS Sandy Chen owns a small specialty store, named Chen's Chattel, whose year-end is June 30. Determine the total amount that should be included in Chen's Chattel's year-end inventory. A physical inventory taken on June 30 reveals the following:

Cost of merchandise on the showroom floor and in the warehouse	$37,800
Goods held on consignment (consignor is National Manufacturer)	6,400
Goods that Chen's Chattel, as the consignor, has for sale at the location of the Grand Avenue Vista	4,600
Sales invoices indicate that merchandise was shipped on June 29, terms FOB shipping point, delivered at buyer's receiving dock on July 3	3,800
Sales invoices indicate that merchandise was shipped on June 25, terms FOB destination, delivered at buyer's receiving dock on July 5	3,100

E 13-5A (LO3)

✓ 1. End. inv., FIFO: $300.00;
Weighted-avg.: $242.50

LOWER-OF-COST-OR-MARKET Stalberg Company's beginning inventory and purchases during the fiscal year ended December 31, 20--, were as follows:

		Units	Unit Price	Total Cost
Jan. 1	Beginning inventory	10	$20	$200
Mar. 5	1st purchase	10	22	220
Sept. 9	2nd purchase	10	25	250
Dec. 8	3rd purchase	10	30	300
		40		$970

There are 10 units of inventory on hand on December 31.

1. Calculate the total amount to be assigned to the ending inventory under each of the following periodic inventory methods:

    (a) FIFO
    (b) Weighted-average (round calculations to two decimal places)

2. Assume that the market price per unit (cost to replace) of Stalberg's inventory on December 31, 20--, was $26. Calculate the total amount to be assigned to the ending inventory on December 31 under each of the following methods:

    (a) FIFO lower-of-cost-or-market
    (b) Weighted-average lower-of-cost-or-market

3. What journal entry would be made under lower-of-cost-or-market for parts 2(a) and (b) above?

SERIES A PROBLEMS

P 13-6A (LO3)

✓ Cost of goods sold, FIFO: $77,100;
LIFO: $81,150; Weighted-avg.:
$79,050; Specific I.D.: $78,450

SPECIFIC IDENTIFICATION, FIFO, LIFO, AND WEIGHTED-AVERAGE Hamilton Company's beginning inventory and purchases during the fiscal year ended September 30, 20-2, were as follows:

		Units	Unit Price	Total Cost
October 1, 20-1	Beginning inventory	300	$20.00	$ 6,000
October 18	1st purchase	500	21.50	10,750
November 25	2nd purchase	400	22.00	8,800
January 12, 20-2	3rd purchase	800	23.00	18,400
March 17	4th purchase	900	23.50	21,150
June 2	5th purchase	600	24.00	14,400
August 21	6th purchase	500	25.00	12,500
September 27	7th purchase	400	25.75	10,300
		4,400		$102,300

Use the following information for the specific identification method.

There are 1,000 units of inventory on hand on September 30, 20-2. Of these 1,000 units:

100 are from October 18, 20-1	1st purchase
300 are from January 12, 20-2	3rd purchase
100 are from March 17	4th purchase
200 are from June 2	5th purchase
100 are from August 21	6th purchase
200 are from September 27	7th purchase

REQUIRED

Calculate the total amount to be assigned to cost of goods sold for the fiscal year ended September 30, 20-2, and ending inventory on September 30, 20-2, under each of the following periodic inventory methods:

1. FIFO

2. LIFO

3. Weighted-average (round calculations to two decimal places)

4. Specific identification

P 13-7A (LO3)

✓ 1. Ending inv., FIFO: $13,825;
LIFO: $8,000; Weighted-avg.: $10,500

COST ALLOCATION AND LOWER-OF-COST-OR-MARKET Douglas Company's beginning inventory and purchases during the fiscal year ended December 31, 20--, were as follows:

		Units	Unit Price	Total Cost
January 1, 20--	Beginning inventory	1,100	$ 8.00	$ 8,800
March 5	1st purchase	900	9.00	8,100
April 16	2nd purchase	400	9.50	3,800
June 3	3rd purchase	700	10.25	7,175
August 18	4th purchase	600	11.00	6,600
September 13	5th purchase	800	12.00	9,600
November 14	6th purchase	400	14.00	5,600
December 3	7th purchase	500	14.05	7,025
		5,400		$56,700

There are 1,000 units of inventory on hand on December 31.

REQUIRED

1. Calculate the total amount to be assigned to the ending inventory and cost of goods sold on December 31 under each of the following methods:

   (a) FIFO
   (b) LIFO
   (c) Weighted-average (round calculations to two decimal places)

2. Assume that the market price per unit (cost to replace) of Douglas's inventory on December 31 was $13. Calculate the total amount to be assigned to the ending inventory on December 31 under each of the following methods:

   (a) FIFO lower-of-cost-or-market
   (b) Weighted-average lower-of-cost-or-market

P 13-8A (LO4)

✓ Est. ending inv.: $80,800

GROSS PROFIT METHOD A fire completely destroyed all the inventory of Glisan Lumber Yard on August 5, 20--. Fortunately, the accounting records were not destroyed in the fire. The following information is provided by Glisan Lumber Yard for the time period January 1 through August 5:

Beginning inventory, **January 1, 20--**	$100,000
Net purchases, January 1 through August 5	420,000
Net sales, January 1 through August 5	732,000
Normal gross profit as a percentage of sales	40%

REQUIRED

Estimate the amount of merchandise inventory destroyed in the fire on August 5 using the gross profit method.

P 13-9A (LO4)

✓ Est. ending inv.: $39,000

RETAIL INVENTORY METHOD The following information is provided by Raynette's Pharmacy for the last quarter of its fiscal year ending on March 31, 20--:

	Cost	Retail
Inventory, start of period, January 1, 20--	$ 32,000	$ 52,000
Net purchases during the period	176,000	268,000
Net sales for the period		260,000

REQUIRED

1. Estimate the ending inventory as of March 31 using the retail inventory method.

2. Estimate the cost of goods sold for the time period January 1 through March 31 using the retail inventory method.

SERIES B EXERCISES

E 13-1B (LO1)

INVENTORY ERRORS Assume that in year 1, the ending merchandise inventory is understated by $40,000. If this is the only error in years 1 and 2, indicate which items will be understated, overstated, or correctly stated for years 1 and 2.

	Year 1	Year 2
Ending merchandise inventory	_____	_____
Beginning merchandise inventory	_____	_____
Cost of goods sold	_____	_____
Gross profit	_____	_____
Net income	_____	_____
Ending owner's capital	_____	_____

E 13-2B (LO2)

JOURNAL ENTRIES—PERIODIC INVENTORY Amy Douglas owns a business called Douglas Distributors. The following transactions took place during January of the current year. Journalize the transactions in a general journal using the periodic inventory method.

Jan.	5	Purchased merchandise on account from Elite Warehouse, $4,100.
	8	Paid freight charge on merchandise purchased, $300.
	12	Sold merchandise on account to Memories Unlimited, $5,200.
	15	Received a credit memo from Elite Warehouse for merchandise returned, $700.
	22	Issued a credit memo to Memories Unlimited for merchandise returned, $400.

E 13-3B (LO2)

JOURNAL ENTRIES—PERPETUAL INVENTORY Doreen Woods owns a small variety store. The following transactions took place during March of the current year. Journalize the transactions in a general journal using the perpetual inventory method.

Mar. 3 Purchased merchandise on account from Corner Galleria, $3,500.

7 Paid freight charge on merchandise purchased, $200.

13 Sold merchandise on account to Sonya Specialties, $4,250. The cost of the merchandise was $2,550.

18 Received a credit memo from Corner Galleria for merchandise returned, $900.

22 Issued a credit memo to Sonya Specialties for merchandise returned, $500. The cost of the merchandise was $300.

E 13-4B (LO3)

✓ Ending inv.: $53,700

ENDING INVENTORY COSTS Danny Steele owns a small specialty store, named Steele's Storeroom, whose year-end is June 30. Determine the total amount that should be included in Steele's Storeroom's year-end inventory. A physical inventory taken on June 30 reveals the following:

Cost of merchandise on the showroom floor and in the warehouse	$42,600
Goods held on consignment (consignor is Quality Manufacturer)	7,600
Goods that Steele's Storeroom, as the consignor, has for sale at the location of Midtown Galleria	8,300
Sales invoices indicate that merchandise was shipped on June 28, terms FOB shipping point, delivered at buyer's receiving dock on July 6	4,350
Sales invoices indicate that merchandise was shipped on June 26, terms FOB destination, delivered at buyer's receiving dock on July 1	2,800

E 13-5B (LO3)

✓ 1. Ending inv., FIFO: $800;

Weighted-avg.: $697.20

LOWER-OF-COST-OR-MARKET Bouie Company's beginning inventory and purchases during the fiscal year ended December 31, 20--, were as follows:

		Units	Unit Price	Total Cost
Jan. 1	Beginning inventory	20	$30	$ 600
Mar. 5	1st purchase	22	34	748
Sept. 9	2nd purchase	24	35	840
Dec. 8	3rd purchase	22	40	880
		88		$3,068

There are 20 units of inventory on hand on December 31.

1. Calculate the total amount to be assigned to the ending inventory under each of the following periodic inventory methods:

   (a) FIFO
   (b) Weighted-average (round calculations to two decimal places)

2. Assume that the market price per unit (cost to replace) of Bouie's inventory on December 31, 20--, was $39. Calculate the total amount to be assigned to the ending inventory on December 31 under each of the following methods:

   (a) FIFO lower-of-cost-or-market
   (b) Weighted-average lower-of-cost-or-market

3. What journal entry would be made under lower-of-cost-or-market for parts 2(a) and (b) above?

SERIES B PROBLEMS

P 13-6B (LO3)

✓ Ending inv., FIFO: $19,075; LIFO: $14,350; Weighted-avg.: $16,290; Specific I.D.: $17,000

SPECIFIC IDENTIFICATION, FIFO, LIFO, AND WEIGHTED-AVERAGE Boyce Company's beginning inventory and purchases during the fiscal year ended September 30, 20-2, were as follows:

		Units	Unit Price	Total Cost
October 1, 20-1	Beginning inventory	400	$15.00	$ 6,000
October 18	1st purchase	300	16.50	4,950
November 25	2nd purchase	600	17.00	10,200
January 12, 20-2	3rd purchase	700	17.25	12,075
March 17	4th purchase	800	18.00	14,400
June 2	5th purchase	400	19.00	7,600
August 21	6th purchase	300	21.00	6,300
September 27	7th purchase	500	21.75	10,875
		4,000		$72,400

Use the following information for the specific identification method.

There are 900 units of inventory on hand on September 30, 20-2. Of these 900 units:

50 are from October 18, 20-1	1st purchase
300 are from January 12, 20-2	3rd purchase
100 are from March 17	4th purchase
200 are from June 2	5th purchase
50 are from August 21	6th purchase
200 are from September 27	7th purchase

REQUIRED

Calculate the total amount to be assigned to the cost of goods sold for the fiscal year ended September 30, 20-2, and ending inventory on September 30, 20-2, under each of the following periodic inventory methods:

1. FIFO

2. LIFO

3. Weighted-average (round calculations to two decimal places)

4. Specific identification

P 13-7B (LO3)

✓ 1. Cost of goods sold, FIFO: $55,950; LIFO: $64,300; Weighted avg.: $60,475

COST ALLOCATION AND LOWER-OF-COST-OR-MARKET Hall Company's beginning inventory and purchases during the fiscal year ended December 31, 20--, were as follows:

		Units	Unit Price	Total Cost
January 1	Beginning inventory	800	$11.00	$ 8,800
March 5	1st purchase	600	12.00	7,200
April 16	2nd purchase	500	12.50	6,250
June 3	3rd purchase	700	14.00	9,800
August 18	4th purchase	800	15.00	12,000
September 13	5th purchase	900	17.00	15,300
November 14	6th purchase	400	18.00	7,200
December 3	7th purchase	500	20.30	10,150
		5,200		$76,700

There are 1,100 units of inventory on hand on December 31.

REQUIRED

1. Calculate the total amount to be assigned to the ending inventory and cost of goods sold on December 31 under each of the following methods:

   (a) FIFO
   (b) LIFO
   (c) Weighted-average (round calculations to two decimal places)

2. Assume that the market price per unit (cost to replace) of Hall's inventory on December 31 was $16. Calculate the total amount to be assigned to the ending inventory on December 31 under each of the following methods:

   (a) FIFO lower-of-cost-or-market
   (b) Weighted-average lower-of-cost-or-market

P 13-8B (LO4)

✓ Est. inv.: $82,500

GROSS PROFIT METHOD A flood completely destroyed all the inventory of Bayside Waterworks Company on July 1, 20--. Fortunately, the accounting records were not destroyed in the flood. The following information is provided by Bayside Waterworks for the time period January 1 through July 1, 20--.

Beginning inventory, January 1, 20--	$ 60,000
Net purchases, January 1 through July 1	380,000
Net sales, January 1 through July 1	650,000
Normal gross profit as a percentage of sales	45%

REQUIRED

Estimate the amount of merchandise inventory destroyed in the flood on July 1 using the gross profit method.

P 13-9B (LO4)

✓ Est. cost of goods sold: $193,750

RETAIL INVENTORY METHOD The following information is provided by Beverly's Basket Corner for the last quarter of its fiscal year ending on March 31, 20--:

	Cost	Retail
Inventory, start of period, January 1, 20--	$ 50,000	$ 80,000
Net purchases during the period	220,000	352,000
Net sales for the period		310,000

REQUIRED

1. Estimate the ending inventory as of March 31 using the retail inventory method.

2. Estimate the cost of goods sold for the time period January 1 through March 31 using the retail inventory method.

MANAGING YOUR WRITING

Most major grocery chains have optical scanning devices at the checkout stands and they certainly reduce the time required to check out. What benefits do they provide to the business? Next time you go to the grocery store, take a few minutes to chat with the manager. Ask the manager to describe the benefits of the scanning devices over the old machines that required the clerk to key in each purchase. Pay particular attention to the linkage between the scanning devices and the inventory systems. Be sure to ask whether the grocery store is on a periodic or perpetual system.

After your visit, write a memo to your instructor describing the benefits of the scanning devices and how they are linked with the inventory system.

ETHICS CASE

Electronics, Inc., is a high-volume, wholesale merchandising company. Most of its inventory turns over four or five times a year. The company has had 50 units of a particular brand of computers on hand for over a year. These computers have not sold and probably will not sell unless they are discounted 60 to 70%. The accountant is carrying them on the books at cost and intends to recognize the loss when they are sold. This way, she can avoid a significant write-down in inventory on the current year's financial statements.

1. Is the accountant correct in her treatment of the inventory? Why or why not?

2. If the computers cost $1,000 each and their market value is 40% of their cost, journalize the entry necessary for the write-down.

3. In a short paragraph, explain what is meant by conservatism and how it ties in with the lower-of-cost-or-market method of accounting for inventory.

4. In groups of three or four, make a list of reasons why inventories of electronic equipment might have to be written down.

MASTERY PROBLEM

✓ 1. Cost of goods sold, FIFO: $64,250; LIFO: $75,000; Weighted-avg.: $69,600

✓ 2. Ending inv., FIFO LCM: $21,600; Weighted-avg. LCM: $17,400

✓ 3. Estimated inv.: $22,000

Tiller Company's beginning inventory and purchases during the fiscal year ended December 31, 20-2, were as follows:

		Units	Unit Price	Total Cost
January 1, 20-2	Beginning inventory	1,500	$10.00	$15,000
January 12	1st purchase	500	11.50	5,750
February 28	2nd purchase	600	14.50	8,700
June 29	3rd purchase	1,200	15.00	18,000
August 31	4th purchase	800	16.50	13,200
October 29	5th purchase	300	18.00	5,400
November 30	6th purchase	700	18.50	12,950
December 21	7th purchase	400	20.00	8,000
		6,000		$87,000

There are 1,200 units of inventory on hand on December 31, 20-2.

REQUIRED

1. Calculate the total amount to be assigned to the cost of goods sold for 20-2 and ending inventory on December 31 under each of the following periodic inventory methods:

   (a) FIFO
   (b) LIFO
   (c) Weighted-average (round calculations to two decimal places)

2. Assume that the market price per unit (cost to replace) of Tiller's inventory on December 31 was $18. Calculate the total amount to be assigned to the ending inventory on December 31 under each of the following methods:

   (a) FIFO lower-of-cost-or-market
   (b) Weighted-average lower-of-cost-or-market

3. In addition to taking a physical inventory on December 31, Tiller decides to estimate the ending inventory and cost of goods sold. During the fiscal year ended December 31, 20-2, net sales of $100,000 were made at a normal gross profit rate of 35%. Use the gross profit method to estimate the cost of goods sold for the fiscal year ended December 31 and the inventory on December 31.

CHALLENGE PROBLEM

This problem challenges you to apply your cumulative accounting knowledge to move a step beyond the material in the chapter.

✓ FIFO CGS 20-2: $4,250;
LIFO CGS 20-2: $4,200

Bhushan Company has been using LIFO for inventory purposes because it would prefer to keep gross profits low for tax purposes. In its second year of operation (20-2), the controller pointed out that this strategy did not appear to work and suggested that FIFO cost of goods sold would have been higher than LIFO cost of goods sold for 20-2. Is this possible?

20-1	Units	Cost/Unit
Purchase 1	100	$1.00
Purchase 2	200	2.00
Purchase 3	300	3.00
Ending inventory	200	

20-2	Units	Cost/Unit
Beginning inventory	200	
Purchase 4	150	$4.00
Purchase 5	250	5.00
Purchase 6	350	6.00
Ending inventory	50	

REQUIRED

Using the information provided, compute the cost of goods sold for 20-1 and 20-2 comparing the LIFO and FIFO methods.

ANSWERS TO SELF-STUDY QUESTIONS AND EXERCISES

True/False Questions

1. T

2. T

3. F (this is true for the periodic method)

4. T

5. F (the buyer pays)

Multiple Choice Questions

1. b 2. b 3. c 4. a 5. c

U REVU　Exercises

1. Cost of goods sold   Understated by $10,000
    Gross profit   Overstated by $10,000
    Net income   Overstated by $10,000
    Ending owner's capital   Overstated by $10,000

2. Beginning inventory
    Merchandise inventory, beginning balance...................... $ 20,000
    Purchased merchandise on account.................................. 200,000
    Cost of merchandise sold .... (120,000)
    Freight charges paid on inventory delivered to showroom ... 1,000
    Cost of merchandise returned by customers 500
    Ending inventory $101,500

3. FIFO cost of goods sold:
    50 units @ $ 5 = $ 250
    100 units @ $ 8 =   800
    50 units @ $10 =   500
    FIFO cost of goods sold $1,550

    LIFO cost of goods sold:
    150 units @ $10 = $1,500
    50 units @ $ 8 =   400
    LIFO cost of goods sold $1,900

4. Estimated inventory using the gross profit method:
    Cost of goods available for sale .... $ 100,000
    Net sales $150,000
    Normal gross profit   60,000
     ($150,000 × 40% = $60,000)
    Estimated cost of goods sold... 90,000
    Estimated inventory .... $ 10,000

Chapter 13 Appendix

Perpetual Inventory Method: LIFO and Moving-Average Methods

LEARNING OBJECTIVES

Careful study of this appendix should enable you to:

LO1 Compute the costs allocated to the ending inventory and cost of goods sold using the perpetual LIFO inventory method.

LO2 Compute the costs allocated to the ending inventory and cost of goods sold using the perpetual moving-average inventory method.

In Chapter 13, you learned how to apply the LIFO and weighted-averge inventory methods under the periodic inventory system. Recall that all calculations under the periodic system are done at the end of the accounting period. Under the perpetual system, costs are computed every time merchandise is purchased and sold. These costs are used to maintain a running record of the cost of goods sold to date and the balance of inventory on hand.

PERPETUAL LIFO

LO1 Compute the costs allocated to the ending inventory and cost of goods sold using the perpetual LIFO inventory method.

When using the **perpetual LIFO inventory method**, every time inventory is purchased a new layer is formed. When inventory is sold, we assume that the most recently purchased layer is sold first. As those units are used up, units are taken from the next most recently purchased layer. To illustrate, let's assume that Phaler's Fishing Supplies has the following beginning inventory, purchases, and sales of one type of bobber during the month of June. Note that the beginning inventory also has layers based on the prices paid in earlier periods.

Date	Beginning Inventory and Purchases		Sales
	Units	Cost/Unit	Units
June 1 (BI)	20	$0.80	
	160	1.00	
	20	1.20	
June 4	300	1.50	
June 20			400
June 30	100	1.80	

BI: Beginning Inventory

As shown in Figure 13A-1, the beginning inventory of 200 units forms Phaler's first three layers of inventory. The purchase on June 4 forms a fourth layer (300 units @ $1.50 = $450). At this point, Phaler has a total of 500 units at a total cost of $650. On June 20, Phaler sells 400 units. Under perpetual LIFO, we assume that the 300 units purchased on June 4 are sold first, followed by 20 that cost $1.20 each and 80 units that cost $1.00 each from the beginning inventory. The cost of goods sold on June 20 is $554. The cost of the inventory on hand is $96. At this point, Phaler has 100 units remaining from the beginning inventory.

On June 30, Phaler purchases 100 units at $1.80 each. This forms a new fifth layer (100 @ $1.80 = $180). This layer is added to the two layers remaining from the beginning inventory for a total of 200 units at a total cost of $276 of inventory on hand on June 30. Note that the third ($1.20 layer) and fourth ($1.50 layer) layers of inventory are gone. They will never reappear. If Phaler makes additional sales before buying more inventory, they will come from the fifth layer at $1.80 each, followed by units from the second ($1.00) and then the first ($0.80) layers.

FIGURE 13A-1 Perpetual LIFO Inventory System

DATE	PURCHASES			COST OF GOODS SOLD				INVENTORY ON HAND				
	Units	Cost/Unit	Total	Units	Cost/Unit	CGS	Cumulative CGS	Layer	Units	Cost/Unit	Layer Cost	Total
Jan. 1 (BI)								(1)	20	$0.80	$ 16.00	
								(2)	160	1.00	160.00	
								(3)	20	1.20	24.00	$200.00
June 4								(1)	20	$0.80	$ 16.00	
								(2)	160	1.00	160.00	
								(3)	20	1.20	24.00	
	300	$1.50	$450.00				→	(4)	300	1.50	450.00	$650.00
June. 20				300	$1.50	$450.00		(1)	20	$0.80	$ 16.00	
				20	1.20	24.00		(2)	80	1.00	80.00	$ 96.00
				80	1.00	80.00	$554.00					
June 30								(1)	20	$0.80	$ 16.00	
								(2)	80	1.00	80.00	
	100	$1.80	$180.00				→	(5)	100	1.80	180.00	$276.00
Cost of Goods Sold for June						$554.00						

BI: Beginning Inventory

PERPETUAL MOVING-AVERAGE

LO2 Compute the costs allocated to the ending inventory and cost of goods sold using the perpetual moving-average inventory method.

When using the **perpetual moving-average inventory method**, every time inventory is purchased a new average cost per unit is calculated. When inventory is sold, the most recent average cost is used to measure cost of goods sold and the remaining inventory on hand. To illustrate, let's look again at the purchases and sales of Phaler's Fishing Supplies for the month of June.

Date	Beginning Inventory and Purchases		Sales
	Units	Cost/Unit	Units
June 1 (BI)	20	$0.80	
	160	1.00	
	20	1.20	
June 4	300	1.50	
June 20			400
June 30	100	1.80	

BI: Beginning Inventory

When using the moving average inventory method, it is best to do the calculations on a calculator or computer spreadsheet. Carry each calculation out to the number of decimal places allowed by the technology used. This will reduce rounding errors.

As shown in Figure 13A-2, a new average cost is calculated each time a purchase is made. The average cost of the June 1 beginning inventory is shown as $1.00 ($200 cost/200 units). To compute the average cost after buying more inventory on June 4, we take the cost of the inventory on hand ($200 + $450 = $650) and divide by the number of units on hand (200 + 300 = 500). Thus, the average cost of the inventory on hand on June 4 is $1.30 per unit. To compute the cost of the 400 units sold on June 20, multiply the 400 units by $1.30 to get the cost of goods sold of $520. The remaining cost of the inventory on hand is $130 ($650 − $520). The number of units on hand is reduced to 100 (500 − 400).

On June 30, 100 additional units are purchased. This increases the units on hand to 200 (100 + 100) and the cost of the inventory on hand to $310 ($130 + $180). Dividing the cost of the inventory on hand by the number of units on hand provides a new moving-average cost of $1.55 ($310 ÷ 200). If Phaler makes another sale before buying additional units, this average cost will be used to compute the cost of goods sold and determine the cost of the inventory remaining on hand. Note that selling inventory does not change the moving-average cost. This is because the units are being removed at the most recent average cost.

FIGURE 13A-2 Perpetual Moving-Average Inventory System

DATE	PURCHASES			COST OF GOODS SOLD				INVENTORY ON HAND AND AVG. COST/UNIT			
	Units	Cost/Unit	Total	Units	Cost/Unit	CGS	Cumulative CGS	Cost of Purchase or (Sale)	Cost of Inventory on Hand	Units on Hand	AVG. Cost/Unit
June 1 (BI)									$200.00	200.00	$1.0000
June 4	300.00	$1.50	$450.00					$450.00	650.00	500.00	1.3000
June 20				400.00	$1.30	$520.00	$520.00	(520.00)	130.00	100.00	1.3000
June 30	100.00	$1.80	$180.00					180.00	310.00	200.00	1.5500
Cost of Goods Sold during January							$520.00				
BI: Beginning Inventory											

LEARNING OBJECTIVES   Key Points to Remember

LO1	Compute the costs allocated to the ending inventory and cost of goods sold using the perpetual LIFO inventory method.	When using the perpetual LIFO inventory method, every time inventory is purchased, a new layer is formed. When inventory is sold, we assume the units were sold out of the most recent layer. As those units are used up, additional sales are taken from the next most recently purchased layer.
LO2	Compute the costs allocated to the ending inventory and cost of goods sold using the perpetual moving-average inventory method.	When using the perpetual moving-average inventory method, every time inventory is purchased, a new average cost per unit is calculated. When inventory is sold, the most recent average cost is used to measure cost of goods sold and the remaining inventory on hand.

KEY TERMS

perpetual LIFO inventory method (517)   A method of allocating merchandise cost which assumes that every time inventory is purchased, a new layer is formed. When inventory is sold, units are sold out of the most recent layer. As those units are used up, additional sales are taken from the next most recently purchased layer.

perpetual moving-average inventory method (518)   A method of allocating merchandise cost which assumes that every time inventory is purchased, a new average cost per unit is calculated. When inventory is sold, the most recent average cost is used to measure cost of goods sold and the remaining inventory on hand.

REVIEW QUESTION

LO1   1. Explain the primary difference between the periodic and perpetual inventory systems when calculating cost of goods sold and merchandise inventory.

SERIES A EXERCISE

E 13Apx-1A (LO1/2)

✓ CGS under perpetual LIFO: $3,345;
CGS under perpetual moving-average:
$3,250

PERPETUAL: LIFO AND MOVING-AVERAGE The beginning inventory, purchases, and sales for Myrl Sign Company for the month of April follow.

Date	Beginning Inventory and Purchases		Sales
	Units	Cost/Unit	Units
April 1 (BI)	100	$4.30	
	100	4.50	
	200	4.60	
April 20	400	5.50	
April 30			650

BI: Beginning Inventory

REQUIRED

Calculate the total amount to be assigned to cost of goods sold for April and the ending inventory on April 30, under each of the following methods:

1. Perpetual LIFO inventory method

2. Perpetual moving-average inventory method

SERIES A PROBLEM

P 13Apx-2A (LO1/2)

✓ CGS under perpetual LIFO: $1,900;
CGS under perpetual moving-average:
$1,856.64

PERPETUAL: LIFO AND MOVING-AVERAGE Kelley Company began business on January 1, 20-1. Purchases and sales during the month of January follow.

Date	Purchases		Sales
	Units	Cost/Unit	Units
Jan. 1	100	$1.00	
Jan. 4	400	1.10	
Jan. 5			300
Jan. 10	300	1.30	
Jan. 12			200
Jan. 15	200	1.35	
Jan. 18	500	1.60	
Jan. 22			800
Jan. 27			100
Jan. 31	300	1.80	

REQUIRED

Calculate the total amount to be assigned to cost of goods sold for January and the ending inventory on January 31, under each of the following methods:

1. Perpetual LIFO inventory method

2. Perpetual moving-average inventory method

SERIES B EXERCISE

E 13Apx-1B (LO1/2)

✓ CGS under perpetual LIFO: $5,435;
CGS under perpetual moving-average:
$5,395

PERPETUAL: LIFO AND MOVING-AVERAGE The beginning inventory, purchases, and sales for Harrington Equipment Company for the month of August follow.

Date	Beginning Inventory and Purchases		Sales
	Units	Cost/Unit	Units
Aug. 1 (BI)	100	$8.00	
	150	8.10	
	250	8.30	
Aug. 15	300	8.50	
Aug. 31			650

BI: Beginning Inventory

REQUIRED

Calculate the total amount to be assigned to cost of goods sold for August and the ending inventory on August 31, under each of the following methods:

1. Perpetual LIFO inventory method

2. Perpetual moving-average inventory method

SERIES B PROBLEM

P 13Apx-2B (LO1/2)

✓ CGS under perpetual LIFO: $3,720;
CGS under perpetual moving-average:
$3,665.25

PERPETUAL: LIFO AND MOVING-AVERAGE Vozniak Company began business on January 1, 20-1. Purchases and sales during the month of January follow.

Date	Purchases		Sales
	Units	Cost/Unit	Units
Jan. 1	100	$2.00	
Jan. 5	500	2.30	
Jan. 7			300
Jan. 12	300	2.40	
Jan. 15			300
Jan. 17	200	2.50	
Jan. 19	500	2.70	
Jan. 24			800
Jan. 28			100
Jan. 31	200	2.90	

REQUIRED

Calculate the total amount to be assigned to cost of goods sold for January and the ending inventory on January 31, under each of the following methods:

1. Perpetual LIFO inventory method

2. Perpetual moving-average inventory method

COURTESY OF THE SCRANTON/WILKES-BARRE YANKEES/WWW.SWBYANKEES.COM

PHOTO: DIGITAL IMAGING GROUP

Adjustments and the Work Sheet for a Merchandising Business

T he Scranton/Wilkes-Barre (Pa.) Yankees are the Class AAA affiliate of the New York Yankees. They play in the North Division of the International League with the Buffalo Bisons, Ottawa Lynx, Pawtucket Red Sox, Rochester Red Wings, and Syracuse Chiefs. The franchise was founded in 1989 when the Maine Guides moved to Pennsylvania. From 1989 to 2006, the team was the Class AAA International League affiliate of the Philadelphia Phillies known as the Red Barons.

The team is managed by Mandalay Sports Entertainment, which also operates several other Minor League teams. The Yankees play at PNC Field, which was built on Montage Mountain between Scranton and Wilkes-Barre and has a capacity of 10,310, including luxury suites with indoor and outdoor seating. It opened in 1989.

Often, we are expected to pay in advance for goods and services. This is true for season tickets for sporting events like the Scranton/Wilkes-Barre Yankees, magazine subscriptions, or tickets for popular operas or rock concerts. In return, we expect to receive the goods or services. In this chapter, you will learn proper accounting for cash receipts received in advance, which are known as unearned revenues.

LEARNING OBJECTIVES

Careful study of this chapter should enable you to:

LO1 Prepare an adjustment for merchandise inventory using the periodic inventory system.

LO2 Prepare an adjustment for unearned revenue.

LO3 Prepare a work sheet for a merchandising business.

LO4 Journalize adjusting entries for a merchandising business.

LO5 Prepare adjusting journal entries under the perpetual inventory system.

In Chapters 10 through 13, we learned how to account for the day-to-day transactions of a merchandising business. In this chapter, we focus on end-of-period adjustments and the preparation of the work sheet. Finally, in Chapter 15, we will complete the accounting cycle by preparing financial statements and closing entries.

A work sheet for a merchandising business is similar to the work sheet prepared for a service business (Chapter 5). It is used to prepare adjustments for supplies, prepaid insurance, wages earned but not paid, depreciation, and other necessary year-end adjustments. A merchandising business must also make an adjustment to properly report the amount of merchandise inventory held at the end of the accounting period. While revisiting the work sheet, we will also introduce a new adjustment for unearned revenue.

ADJUSTMENT FOR MERCHANDISE INVENTORY: PERIODIC INVENTORY SYSTEM

LO1 Prepare an adjustment for merchandise inventory using the periodic inventory system.

As discussed in Chapter 13, under the periodic inventory system when merchandise inventory is purchased, the purchases account is debited and Cash or Accounts Payable is credited. When inventory is sold, Cash or Accounts Receivable is debited and Sales is credited. Figure 14-1 provides a review of these entries.

FIGURE 14-1 Review of Entries for Purchase and Sale of Merchandise

TRANSACTION	ENTRY		
Purchase of merchandise	Purchases	xxx	
	Accounts Payable or Cash		xxx
Sale of merchandise	Accounts Receivable or Cash	xxx	
	Sales		xxx

Note that the merchandise inventory account is not debited or credited in either of these entries. Since sales and purchases have taken place during the year, the beginning balance of the merchandise inventory account no longer provides an accurate measure of the inventory held at the end of the year. Thus, an adjustment must be made. For other assets, like prepaid insurance, we would simply make an adjustment for the change in the asset account. *We do not follow this procedure for merchandise inventory.*

The adjustment for merchandise inventory is done in two steps.

1. Remove the beginning inventory from the merchandise inventory account by making the following entry:

Income Summary	old
Merchandise Inventory	old

2. Enter the ending inventory in the merchandise inventory account by making the following entry:

Merchandise Inventory	new
Income Summary	new

Periodic Inventory Adjustments:
1. Take out the old.
2. Bring in the new.

As discussed in Chapter 13, the quantity of inventory on hand at the end of the accounting period is determined by taking a physical count of the goods on hand. The cost of these goods is determined by using FIFO, LIFO, or another inventory method. Of course, this year's ending inventory becomes next year's beginning inventory.

To illustrate the adjustment for merchandise inventory, let's assume that Ponder's Bike Parts had a beginning merchandise inventory of $25,000. During the year, the entries shown in Figure 14-1 were made as merchandise was purchased and sold. At the end of the accounting period, a physical inventory of the merchandise determined that merchandise costing $30,000 was still on hand.

To appreciate the reason for the different adjustment process, recall the discussion in Chapter 13 of how the beginning and ending inventories are used when computing cost of goods sold. As shown in the bottom portion of Figure 14-2, the beginning inventory is added to purchases to compute cost of goods available for sale. The

FIGURE 14-2 Calculation of Cost of Goods Sold Using Information in the Income Statement Columns of the Work Sheet

Ponder's Bike Parts
Work Sheet (Partial)
For Year Ended December 31, 20 - -

	ACCOUNT TITLE	TRIAL BALANCE DEBIT	TRIAL BALANCE CREDIT	ADJUSTMENTS DEBIT	ADJUSTMENTS CREDIT	ADJUSTED TRIAL BALANCE DEBIT	ADJUSTED TRIAL BALANCE CREDIT	INCOME STATEMENT DEBIT	INCOME STATEMENT CREDIT	BALANCE SHEET DEBIT	BALANCE SHEET CREDIT	
1								Beginning	Ending			1
2								Inventory	Inventory			2
3												3
4	Merchandise Inventory	25 000 00		STEP 2 30 000 00	25 000 00 STEP 1	30 000 00				30 000 00		4
5	Income Summary			STEP 1 25 000 00	30 000 00 STEP 2	25 000 00	30 000 00	25 000 00	30 000 00			5
6	Purchases	80 000 00				80 000 00		80 000 00				6
7	Purchases Returns/Allowances		1 000 00				1 000 00		1 000 00 ← Purchases Returns & Allow.			7
8	Purchases Discounts		500 00				500 00	Purchases	500 00 ← Purchases Discounts			8
9	Freight-In	700 00				700 00		700 00				9
10												10
11								Freight-In				11
12												12
13												13
14												14

Step 1:	Remove beginning inventory	Income Summary	25,000	
		Merchandise Inventory		25,000
Step 2:	Insert ending inventory	Merchandise Inventory	30,000	
		Income Summary		30,000

Cost of goods sold:			
Merchandise inventory, January 1			$ 25 000 00
Purchases		$ 80 000 00	
Less: Purchases returns and allowances	$ 1 000 00		
Purchases discounts	500 00	1 500 00	
Net purchases		$ 78 500 00	
Add freight-in		700 00	
Cost of goods purchased			79 200 00
Goods available for sale			$104 200 00
Less merchandise inventory, December 31			30 000 00
Cost of goods sold			$ 74 200 00

ending inventory is subtracted from cost of goods available for sale to compute cost of goods sold.

Many firms use the work sheet to prepare financial statements. Thus, all of the information needed to compute cost of goods sold should be readily available in the Income Statement columns of the work sheet. To provide this information, we need an adjustment technique that results in the beginning inventory being extended into the Income Statement *Debit* column so it can be *added* to purchases. Further, we need the ending inventory extended into the Income Statement *Credit* column so it will be *subtracted* when computing cost of goods sold. As shown in Figure 14-2, this can be accomplished in two steps by using the income summary account.

STEP 1 The beginning inventory ($25,000) is removed by crediting Merchandise Inventory. Income Summary is debited because this amount is used in the calculation of cost of goods sold and net income.

STEP 2 The ending inventory ($30,000) is entered by debiting Merchandise Inventory. Income Summary is credited because this amount is also used in the calculation of cost of goods sold and net income.

Note that the debit *and* credit adjustments made to Income Summary are extended into the Adjusted Trial Balance and Income Statement columns. *This is the only time individual figures, rather than the net amount, are extended on the work sheet.* It is done in this case because the individual amounts are needed for the calculation of cost of goods sold on the income statement (beginning inventory + purchases − ending inventory = cost of goods sold). Note, also, that all of the information needed to compute cost of goods sold is readily available in the Income Statement columns of the work sheet.

🔑 LEARNING KEY

Both the debit and credit amounts on the income summary line are extended to the Income Statement columns.

U REVU

Complete U REVU-1 on **page 544** to test your basic understanding of LO1.

ADJUSTMENT FOR UNEARNED REVENUE

LO2 Prepare an adjustment for unearned revenue.

Some businesses require payment before delivering a product or performing a service. Examples include insurance companies, magazine publishers, apartment complexes, college food services, and professional sports and theater companies that sell season tickets. The cash received in advance is called **unearned revenue**. Since the cash has been received in advance, the company owes the customers the product or service, or must refund their money. Thus, unearned revenue is reported as a *liability* on the balance sheet.

🔑 LEARNING KEY

Remember, under the accrual basis of accounting, revenue is recorded when *earned* regardless of when cash is received.

To illustrate, let's assume that Brown County Playhouse sells season tickets for five plays produced throughout the year. Tickets sell for $10 for each play ($50 for a season ticket) and a maximum of 1,000 seats can be sold for each play. For simplicity, let's assume that all shows sell out during the first week that season tickets are available for sale. As shown below and in Figure 14-3, the sale of the tickets would be recorded as follows:

8		(1)	Cash			50	0	0	0	00									8
9			Unearned Ticket Revenue									50	0	0	0	00			9
10			Season ticket sales																10
11			($10 × 1,000 seats × 5 shows)																11

To prepare financial statements following production of the third show, an adjusting entry is needed to recognize that $30,000 ($10 × 1,000 seats × 3 shows) in ticket revenue has been earned. To do this, the following adjusting entry is made:

13		Adjusting Entries			13
14		Unearned Ticket Revenue	30 0 0 0 00		14
15		Ticket Revenue		30 0 0 0 00	15

The remaining balance of $20,000 in Unearned Ticket Revenue is reported as a current liability on the balance sheet.

FIGURE 14-3 Entries for Unearned Revenue

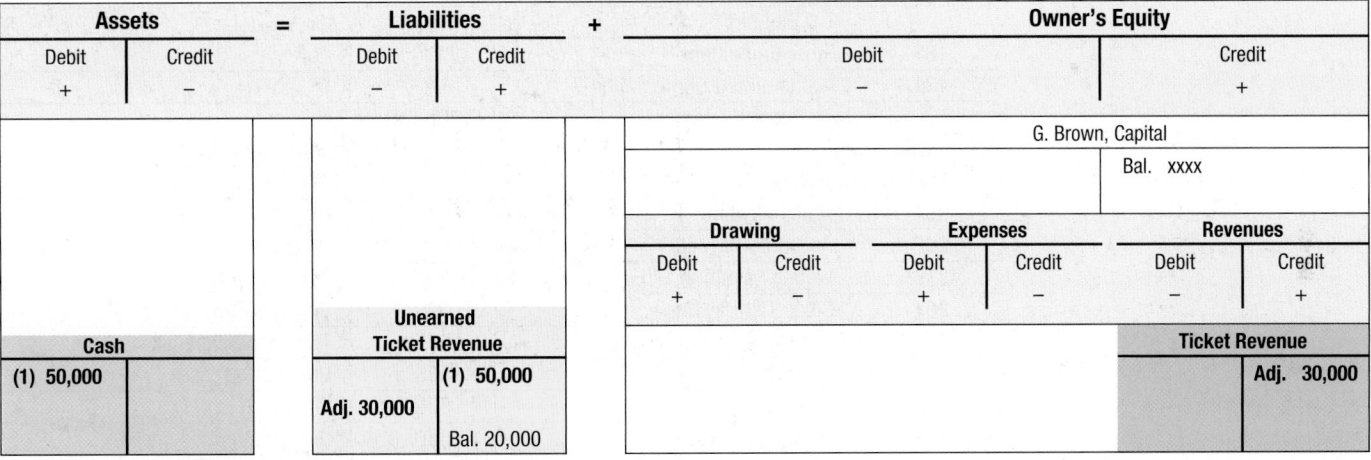

EXPANDED CHART OF ACCOUNTS

Let's take a look at where the new accounts for a merchandising business fit into a chart of accounts. Recall that the chart of accounts follows the form of the accounting equation (assets = liabilities + owner's equity + revenues – expenses). A chart of accounts for Northern Micro is provided in Figure 14-4. Note the classification of the new accounts introduced in Chapters 10 and 11 for a merchandising firm.

Merchandise Inventory is listed as a current asset. Since Northern Micro sells subscriptions to a computer magazine that it produces, Unearned Subscriptions Revenue is listed as a current liability, and Subscriptions Revenue is listed as a revenue. Sales Returns and Allowances and Sales Discounts are contra-revenue accounts. Recall, however, that Northern Micro does not offer sales discounts.

Purchases, Purchases Returns and Allowances, Purchases Discounts, and Freight-In are used to compute cost of goods sold. Thus, they are listed under this heading. Purchases Returns and Allowances and Purchases Discounts are often called contra-cost accounts or contra-purchases accounts.

Interest Expense is classified as "Other Expenses" instead of being listed under Operating Expenses. This is because it represents the expense of obtaining money to do business, rather than an expense directly associated with operating the business.

FIGURE 14-4 Chart of Accounts for Northern Micro

NORTHERN MICRO CHART OF ACCOUNTS			
Assets		**Revenue**	
Current Assets		401	Sales
101	Cash	401.1	Sales Returns and
122	Accounts Receivable		Allowances
131	Merchandise Inventory	**Other Revenue**	
141	Supplies	411	Interest Revenue
145	Prepaid Insurance	412	Rent Revenue
		413	Subscriptions Revenue
Property, Plant, and Equipment		**Expenses**	
161	Land	**Cost of Goods Sold**	
171	Building	501	Purchases
171.1	Accumulated Depreciation—	501.1	Purchases Returns and
	Building		Allowances
181	Store Equipment	501.2	Purchases Discounts
181.1	Accumulated Depreciation—	502	Freight-In
	Store Equipment	**Operating Expenses**	
Liabilities		511	Wages Expense
Current Liabilities		512	Advertising Expense
201	Notes Payable	513	Bank Credit Card
202	Accounts Payable		Expense
219	Wages Payable	521	Rent Expense
231	Sales Tax Payable	523	Supplies Expense
241	Unearned Subscriptions	525	Telephone Expense
	Revenue	533	Utilities Expense
Long-Term Liabilities		535	Insurance Expense
251	Mortgage Payable	540	Depreciation Expense—
			Building
Owner's Equity		541	Depreciation Expense—
311	Gary L. Fishel, Capital		Store Equipment
312	Gary L. Fishel, Drawing	549	Miscellaneous Expense
313	Income Summary		
		Other Expenses	
		551	Interest Expense

U REVU

Complete U REVU-2 on **page 544** to test your basic understanding of LO2.

PREPARING A WORK SHEET FOR A MERCHANDISING BUSINESS

LO3 Prepare a work sheet for a merchandising business.

The work sheet for a merchandising business is similar to the one shown in Chapter 5 for a service business. Recall the five steps taken to prepare a work sheet.

STEP 1 Prepare the trial balance.

STEP 2 Prepare the adjustments.

STEP 3 Prepare the adjusted trial balance.

STEP 4 Extend the adjusted trial balance amounts to the Income Statement and Balance Sheet columns.

STEP 5 Total the Income Statement and Balance Sheet columns to compute the net income or net loss.

The work sheet format and the five steps taken when preparing the work sheet are illustrated in Figure 14-5. Note that the new accounts introduced for a merchandising firm and the unearned revenue account are highlighted so that you can see their proper placement and extensions. (The abbreviation BI stands for beginning inventory; EI stands for ending inventory.) Pay particular attention to the extension of Income Summary. Both the debit and credit amounts for this account must be extended.

FIGURE 14-5 Overview of Work Sheet for a Merchandising Business

Name of Company
Work Sheet
For Year Ended December 31, 20 - -

	ACCOUNT TITLE	TRIAL BALANCE DEBIT	TRIAL BALANCE CREDIT	ADJUSTMENTS DEBIT	ADJUSTMENTS CREDIT	ADJUSTED TRIAL BALANCE DEBIT	ADJUSTED TRIAL BALANCE CREDIT	INCOME STATEMENT DEBIT	INCOME STATEMENT CREDIT	BALANCE SHEET DEBIT	BALANCE SHEET CREDIT	
1	― ― ― ― ― ― ― ― ― ― ―	Step 1:		Step 2:		Step 3:		Step 4:				1
2	― ― ― ― ― ― ― ― ― ― ―	Prepare a		Prepare the		Prepare the		Extend Adjusted				2
3	(Insert Ledger Account Titles)	Trial Balance		Adjustments		Adjusted Trial Balance		Account Balances				3
4		Assets				Assets				Assets		4
5		Mdse. Inv. (BI)		EI	BI	Mdse. Inv. (EI)				Mdse. Inv. (EI)		5
6			Liabilities				Liabilities				Liabilities	6
7			Unearned				Unearned				Unearned	7
8			Revenues				Revenues				Revenues	8
9												9
10			Capital				Capital				Capital	10
11		Drawing				Drawing				Drawing		11
12	― ― ― ― ― ― ― ― ― ― ―											12
13	Income Summary			BI	EI	BI	EI	BI	EI			13
14	― ― ― ― ― ― ― ― ― ― ―											14
15			Revenues				Revenues		Revenues			15
16			Sales				Sales		Sales			16
17		Sales R&A				Sales R&A		Sales R&A				17
18		Sales Discounts				Sales Discounts		Sales Discounts				18
19												19
20		Expenses				Expenses		Expenses				20
21		Purchases				Purchases		Purchases				21
22			Purch. R&A				Purch. R&A		Purch. R&A			22
23			Purch. Discounts				Purch. Discounts		Purch. Discounts			23
24		Freight-In				Freight-In		Freight-In				24
25								Step 5:				25
26								Complete the work sheet				26
27								(1) Sum columns				27
28								(2) Compute net income (loss)				28
29												29
30								Net	Net	Net	Net	30
31								Income	Loss	Loss	Income	31
32												32

BI = Beginning Inventory
EI = Ending Inventory

A BROADER VIEW

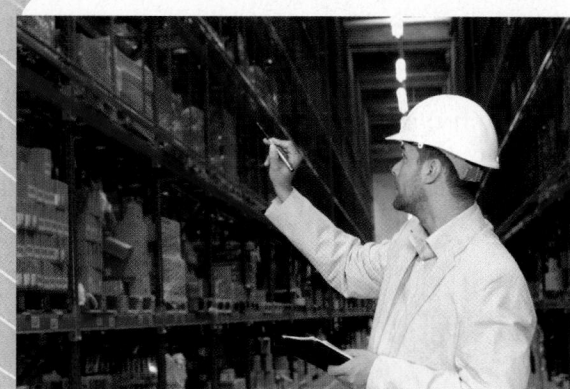

ENDOPACK/ISTOCKPHOTO.COM

The Importance of Inventory

Note the important role of the ending inventory in the calculation of cost of goods sold in Figure 14-2. If the ending inventory is overstated for any reason, net income will also be overstated. Given this important relationship, auditors observe and verify the accuracy of the physical inventory. However, unethical managers, desperate to improve profits, have on occasion found ways to mislead auditors.

In one case, managers overstated inventory counts for items that the auditors had not physically verified. In another case, auditors found a barrel whose contents had been valued by management at thousands of dollars. It actually contained floor sweepings. Finally, there was a case where management called the auditor, the day after the inventory audit, to report that additional inventory had arrived and should be included in the inventory count. The auditor never verified that the inventory was real. It turned out to be a scam that helped the company double its reported profits for the year. These unfortunate events highlight the reason auditors must exercise great care when conducting an inventory audit.

ADJUSTMENTS FOR NORTHERN MICRO

Before preparing a work sheet for Northern Micro, let's review the preparation of adjustments in T account form. Figure 14-6 provides year-end adjustment information for Northern Micro. Figure 14-7 shows adjusting entries based on this information. The unadjusted balances for these accounts were taken from Northern Micro's trial balance.

PREPARING A WORK SHEET FOR NORTHERN MICRO

Let's prepare a work sheet for Northern Micro following the five steps illustrated in Figure 14-5.

STEP 1 In Figure 14-8, the Trial Balance columns are completed by copying the balances of all accounts from the general ledger (not shown).

STEP 2 In Figure 14-9, the adjustments are entered. These entries are exactly the same as those made in T account form in Figure 14-7.

STEP 3 In Figure 14-10, extensions are made to the Adjusted Trial Balance columns. Note that both the debit and credit amounts for Income Summary are extended.

STEP 4 In Figure 14-11, the Adjusted Trial Balance amounts are extended to the Income Statement and Balance Sheet columns.

STEP 5 In Figure 14-11, the work sheet is completed by totaling the Income Statement and Balance Sheet columns. The difference between the debits and credits for each pair of columns represents the net income or net loss.

FIGURE 14-6 Year-End Adjustment Data for Northern Micro

YEAR-END ADJUSTMENT DATA FOR NORTHERN MICRO	
(a, b)	A physical count showed that merchandise inventory costing $18,000 is on hand as of December 31.
(c)	Supplies remaining at the end of the year, $400.
(d)	Unexpired insurance on December 31, $600.
(e)	Depreciation expense on the building for the year, $4,000.
(f)	Depreciation expense on the store equipment for the year, $3,000.
(g)	Wages earned but not paid as of December 31, $450.
(h)	Northern Micro publishes a computer magazine. Subscribers pay in advance. Unearned subscriptions revenue as of December 31, $2,000.

FIGURE 14-7 Adjusting Entries for Northern Micro

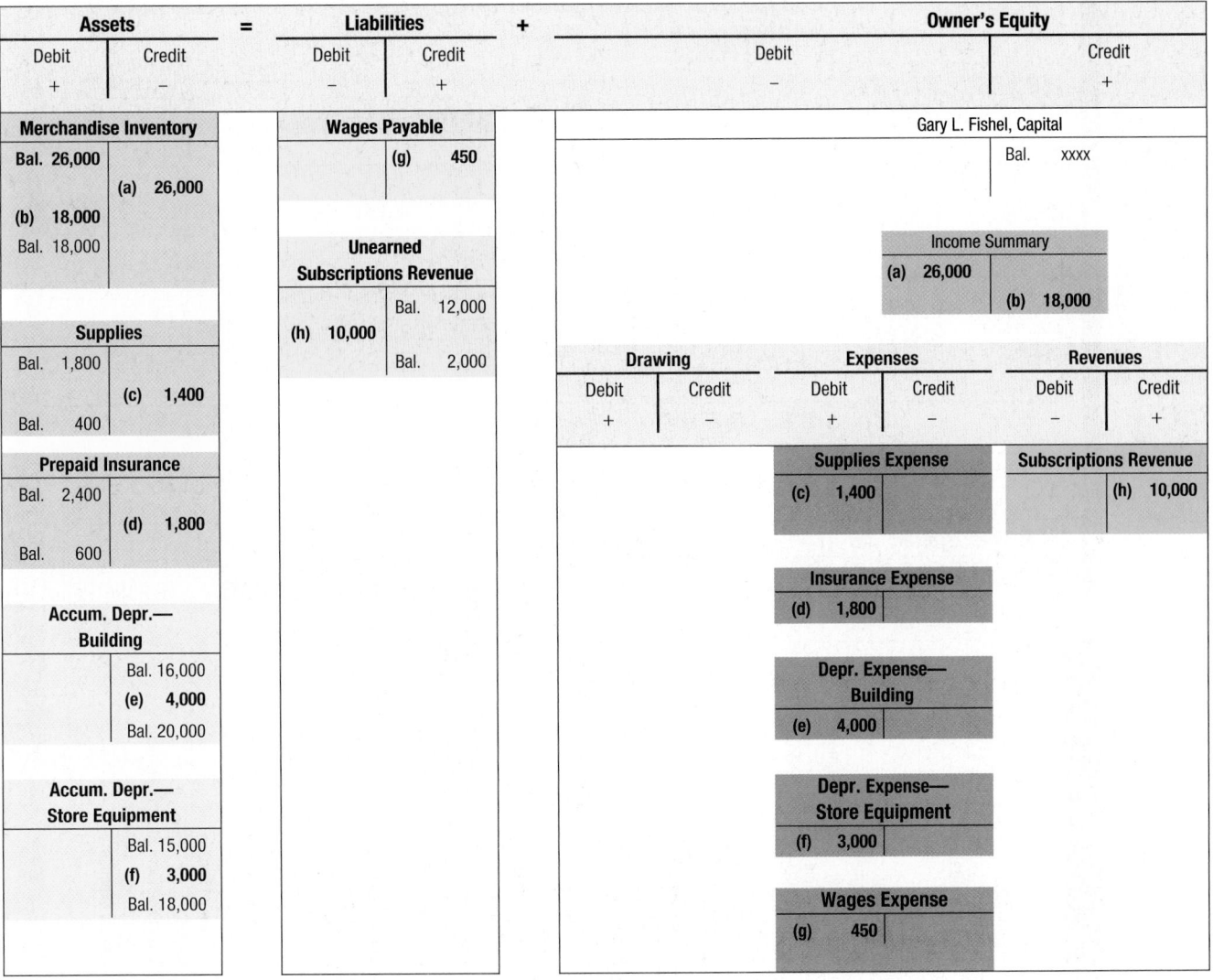

FIGURE 14-8 Step 1: Completion of the Trial Balance Columns

Northern Micro
Work Sheet
For Year Ended December 31, 20 - -

	ACCOUNT TITLE	TRIAL BALANCE DEBIT	TRIAL BALANCE CREDIT	ADJUSTMENTS DEBIT	ADJUSTMENTS CREDIT	ADJUSTED TRIAL BALANCE DEBIT	ADJUSTED TRIAL BALANCE CREDIT	INCOME STATEMENT DEBIT	INCOME STATEMENT CREDIT	BALANCE SHEET DEBIT	BALANCE SHEET CREDIT	
1	Cash	20 0 0 0 00										1
2	Accounts Receivable	15 0 0 0 00										2
3	Merchandise Inventory	26 0 0 0 00										3
4	Supplies	1 8 0 0 00										4
5	Prepaid Insurance	2 4 0 0 00										5
6	Land	10 0 0 0 00										6
7	Building	90 0 0 0 00										7
8	Accum. Depr.—Building		16 0 0 0 00									8
9	Store Equipment	50 0 0 0 00										9
10	Accum. Depr.—Store Equipment		15 0 0 0 00									10
11	Notes Payable		5 0 0 0 00									11
12	Accounts Payable		10 0 0 0 00									12
13	Wages Payable											13
14	Sales Tax Payable		1 5 0 0 00									14
15	Unearned Subscriptions Revenue		12 0 0 0 00									15
16	Mortgage Payable		30 0 0 0 00									16
17	Gary L. Fishel, Capital		114 4 0 0 00									17
18	Gary L. Fishel, Drawing	20 0 0 0 00										18
19	Income Summary											19
20	Sales		214 0 0 0 00									20
21	Sales Returns and Allowances	1 2 0 0 00										21
22	Interest Revenue		9 0 0 00									22
23	Rent Revenue		8 0 0 0 00									23
24	Subscriptions Revenue											24
25	Purchases	105 0 0 0 00										25
26	Purchases Returns and Allowances		8 0 0 00									26
27	Purchases Discounts		1 0 0 0 00									27
28	Freight‑	3 0 0 00										28
29	Wages Expense	42 0 0 0 00										29
30	Advertising Expense	2 5 0 0 00										30
31	Bank Credit Card Expense	1 5 0 0 00										31
32	Rent Expense	20 0 0 0 00										32
33	Supplies Expense											33
34	Telephone Expense	3 5 0 0 00										34
35	Utilities Expense	12 0 0 0 00										35
36	Insurance Expense											36
37	Depr. Expense—Building											37
38	Depr. Expense—Store Equipment											38
39	Miscellaneous Expense	2 2 5 0 00										39
40	Interest Expense	3 1 5 0 00										40
41		428 6 0 0 00	428 6 0 0 00									41
42												42

STEP 1

FIGURE 14-9 Step 2: Preparation of the Adjustments

Northern Micro
Work Sheet
For Year Ended December 31, 20 - -

	ACCOUNT TITLE	TRIAL BALANCE DEBIT	TRIAL BALANCE CREDIT	ADJUSTMENTS DEBIT	ADJUSTMENTS CREDIT	ADJUSTED TRIAL BALANCE DEBIT	ADJUSTED TRIAL BALANCE CREDIT	INCOME STATEMENT DEBIT	INCOME STATEMENT CREDIT	BALANCE SHEET DEBIT	BALANCE SHEET CREDIT
1	Cash	20 0 0 0 00									
2	Accounts Receivable	15 0 0 0 00									
3	Merchandise Inventory	26 0 0 0 00		(b) 18 0 0 0 00	(a) 26 0 0 0 00						
4	Supplie	1 8 0 0 00			(c) 1 4 0 0 00						
5	Prepaid Insurance	2 4 0 0 00			(d) 1 8 0 0 00						
6	Land	10 0 0 0 00									
7	Building	90 0 0 0 00									
8	Accum. Depr.—Building		16 0 0 0 00		(e) 4 0 0 0 00						
9	Store Equipment	50 0 0 0 00									
10	Accum. Depr.—Store Equipment		15 0 0 0 00		(f) 3 0 0 0 00						
11	Notes Payable		5 0 0 0 00								
12	Accounts Payable		10 0 0 0 00								
13	Wages Payable				(g) 4 5 0 00						
14	Sales Tax Payable		1 5 0 0 00								
15	Unearned Subscriptions Revenue		12 0 0 0 00	(h) 10 0 0 0 00							
16	Mortgage Payable		30 0 0 0 00								
17	Gary L. Fishel, Capital		114 4 0 0 00								
18	Gary L. Fishel, Drawing	20 0 0 0 00									
19	Income Summary			(a) 26 0 0 0 00	(b) 18 0 0 0 00						
20	Sales		214 0 0 0 00								
21	Sales Returns and Allowances	1 2 0 0 00									
22	Interest Revenue		9 0 0 00								
23	Rent Revenue		8 0 0 0 00								
24	Subscriptions Revenue				(h) 10 0 0 0 00						
25	Purchases	105 0 0 0 00									
26	Purchases Returns and Allowances		8 0 0 00								
27	Purchases Discounts		1 0 0 0 00								
28	Freight†	3 0 0 0 00									
29	Wages Expense	42 0 0 0 00		(g) 4 5 0 00							
30	Advertising Expense	2 5 0 0 00									
31	Bank Credit Card Expense	1 5 0 0 00									
32	Rent Expense	20 0 0 0 00									
33	Supplies Expense			(c) 1 4 0 0 00							
34	Telephone Expense	3 5 0 0 00									
35	Utilities Expense	12 0 0 0 00									
36	Insurance Expense			(d) 1 8 0 0 00							
37	Depr. Expense—Building			(e) 4 0 0 0 00							
38	Depr. Expense—Store Equipment			(f) 3 0 0 0 00							
39	Miscellaneous Expense	2 2 5 0 00									
40	Interest Expense	3 1 5 0 00									
41		428 6 0 0 00	428 6 0 0 00	64 6 5 0 00	64 6 5 0 00						
42											

Annotations (Adjustments column):
- ENDING INVENTORY → Merchandise Inventory debit (b) 18 0 0 0 00
- BEGINNING INVENTORY → Merchandise Inventory credit (a) 26 0 0 0 00
- BEGINNING INVENTORY → Income Summary debit (a) 26 0 0 0 00
- ENDING INVENTORY → Income Summary credit (b) 18 0 0 0 00

STEP 1   STEP 2

FIGURE 14-10 Step 3: Extensions to the Adjusted Trial Balance Columns

Northern Micro
Work Sheet
For Year Ended December 31, 20 - -

#	ACCOUNT TITLE	TRIAL BALANCE DEBIT	TRIAL BALANCE CREDIT	ADJUSTMENTS DEBIT	ADJUSTMENTS CREDIT	ADJUSTED TRIAL BALANCE DEBIT	ADJUSTED TRIAL BALANCE CREDIT
1	Cash	20 0 0 0 00				20 0 0 0 00	
2	Accounts Receivable	15 0 0 0 00				15 0 0 0 00	
3	Merchandise Inventory	26 0 0 0 00		(b)18 0 0 0 00	(a)26 0 0 0 00	18 0 0 0 00	
4	Supplies	1 8 0 0 00			(c) 1 4 0 0 00	4 0 0 00	
5	Prepaid Insurance	2 4 0 0 00			(d) 1 8 0 0 00	6 0 0 00	
6	Land	10 0 0 0 00				10 0 0 0 00	
7	Building	90 0 0 0 00				90 0 0 0 00	
8	Accum. Depr.—Building		16 0 0 0 00		(e) 4 0 0 0 00		20 0 0 0 00
9	Store Equipment	50 0 0 0 00				50 0 0 0 00	
10	Accum. Depr.—Store Equipment		15 0 0 0 00		(f) 3 0 0 0 00		18 0 0 0 00
11	Notes Payable		5 0 0 0 00				5 0 0 0 00
12	Accounts Payable		10 0 0 0 00				10 0 0 0 00
13	Wages Payable				(g) 4 5 0 00		4 5 0 00
14	Sales Tax Payable		1 5 0 0 00				1 5 0 0 00
15	Unearned Subscriptions Revenue		12 0 0 0 00	(h)10 0 0 0 00			2 0 0 0 00
16	Mortgage Payable		30 0 0 0 00				30 0 0 0 00
17	Gary L. Fishel, Capital		114 4 0 0 00				114 4 0 0 00
18	Gary L. Fishel, Drawing	20 0 0 0 00				20 0 0 0 00	
19	Income Summary			(a)26 0 0 0 00	(b)18 0 0 0 00	26 0 0 0 00	18 0 0 0 00
20	Sales		214 0 0 0 00				214 0 0 0 00
21	Sales Returns and Allowances	1 2 0 0 00				1 2 0 0 00	
22	Interest Revenue		9 0 0 00				9 0 0 00
23	Rent Revenue		8 0 0 00				8 0 0 00
24	Subscriptions Revenue				(h)10 0 0 0 00		10 0 0 0 00
25	Purchases	105 0 0 0 00				105 0 0 0 00	
26	Purchases Returns and Allowances		8 0 0 00				8 0 0 00
27	Purchases Discounts		1 0 0 0 00				1 0 0 0 00
28	Freight In	3 0 0 00				3 0 0 00	
29	Wages Expense	42 0 0 0 00		(g) 4 5 0 00		42 4 5 0 00	
30	Advertising Expense	2 5 0 0 00				2 5 0 0 00	
31	Bank Credit Card Expense	1 5 0 0 00				1 5 0 0 00	
32	Rent Expense	20 0 0 0 00				20 0 0 0 00	
33	Supplies Expense			(c) 1 4 0 0 00		1 4 0 0 00	
34	Telephone Expense	3 5 0 0 00				3 5 0 0 00	
35	Utilities Expense	12 0 0 0 00				12 0 0 0 00	
36	Insurance Expense			(d) 1 8 0 0 00		1 8 0 0 00	
37	Depr. Expense—Building			(e) 4 0 0 0 00		4 0 0 0 00	
38	Depr. Expense—Store Equipment			(f) 3 0 0 0 00		3 0 0 0 00	
39	Miscellaneous Expense	2 2 5 0 00				2 2 5 0 00	
40	Interest Expense	3 1 5 0 00				3 1 5 0 00	
41		428 6 0 0 00	428 6 0 0 00	64 6 5 0 00	64 6 5 0 00	454 0 5 0 00	454 0 5 0 00
42							

STEP 1 STEP 2 STEP 3

Ending Inventory (line 3)
Beginning Inventory (line 19)
Both the debit and credit are extended (line 19)
Ending Inventory (line 19)

FIGURE 14-11 Step 4: Extensions to the Income Statement and Balance Sheet Columns Step 5: Completing the Work Sheet and Computing Net Income

Northern Micro
Work Sheet
For Year Ended December 31, 20 --

#	Account Title	Trial Balance Debit	Trial Balance Credit	Adjustments Debit	Adjustments Credit	Adj. Trial Balance Debit	Adj. Trial Balance Credit	Income Statement Debit	Income Statement Credit	Balance Sheet Debit	Balance Sheet Credit	#
1	Cash	20 0 0 0 00				20 0 0 0 00				20 0 0 0 00		1
2	Accounts Receivable	15 0 0 0 00				15 0 0 0 00				15 0 0 0 00		2
3	Merchandise Inventory	26 0 0 0 00		(b)18 0 0 0 00	(a)26 0 0 0 00	18 0 0 0 00				18 0 0 0 00		3
4	Supplies	1 8 0 0 00			(c) 1 4 0 0 00	4 0 0 00				4 0 0 00		4
5	Prepaid Insurance	2 4 0 0 00			(d) 1 8 0 0 00	6 0 0 00				6 0 0 00		5
6	Land	10 0 0 0 00				10 0 0 0 00				10 0 0 0 00		6
7	Building	90 0 0 0 00				90 0 0 0 00				90 0 0 0 00		7
8	Accum. Depr.—Building		16 0 0 0 00		(e) 4 0 0 0 00		20 0 0 0 00				20 0 0 0 00	8
9	Store Equipment	50 0 0 0 00				50 0 0 0 00				50 0 0 0 00		9
10	Accum. Depr.—Store Equipment		15 0 0 0 00		(f) 3 0 0 0 00		18 0 0 0 00				18 0 0 0 00	10
11	Notes Payable		5 0 0 0 00				5 0 0 0 00				5 0 0 0 00	11
12	Accounts Payable		10 0 0 0 00				10 0 0 0 00				10 0 0 0 00	12
13	Wages Payable				(g) 4 5 0 00		4 5 0 00				4 5 0 00	13
14	Sales Tax Payable		1 5 0 0 00				1 5 0 0 00				1 5 0 0 00	14
15	Unearned Subscriptions Revenue		12 0 0 0 00	(h)10 0 0 0 00			2 0 0 0 00				2 0 0 0 00	15
16	Mortgage Payable		30 0 0 0 00				30 0 0 0 00				30 0 0 0 00	16
17	Gary L. Fishel, Capital		114 4 0 0 00				114 4 0 0 00				114 4 0 0 00	17
18	Gary L. Fishel, Drawing	20 0 0 0 00				20 0 0 0 00				20 0 0 0 00		18
19	Income Summary			(a)26 0 0 0 00	(b)18 0 0 0 00	26 0 0 0 00	18 0 0 0 00	26 0 0 0 00	18 0 0 0 00			19
20	Sales		214 0 0 0 00				214 0 0 0 00		214 0 0 0 00			20
21	Sales Returns and Allowances	1 2 0 0 00				1 2 0 0 00		1 2 0 0 00				21
22	Interest Revenue		9 0 0 00				9 0 0 00		9 0 0 00			22
23	Rent Revenue		8 0 0 0 00				8 0 0 0 00		8 0 0 0 00			23
24	Subscriptions Revenue				(h)10 0 0 0 00		10 0 0 0 00		10 0 0 0 00			24
25	Purchases	105 0 0 0 00				105 0 0 0 00		105 0 0 0 00				25
26	Purchases Returns and Allowances		8 0 0 0 00				8 0 0 0 00		8 0 0 0 00			26
27	Purchases Discounts		1 0 0 0 00				1 0 0 0 00		1 0 0 0 00			27
28	Freight-In	3 0 0 0 00				3 0 0 0 00		3 0 0 0 00				28
29	Wages Expense	42 0 0 0 00		(g) 4 5 0 00		42 4 5 0 00		42 4 5 0 00				29
30	Advertising Expense	2 5 0 0 00				2 5 0 0 00		2 5 0 0 00				30
31	Bank Credit Card Expense	1 5 0 0 00				1 5 0 0 00		1 5 0 0 00				31
32	Rent Expense	20 0 0 0 00				20 0 0 0 00		20 0 0 0 00				32
33	Supplies Expense			(c) 1 4 0 0 00		1 4 0 0 00		1 4 0 0 00				33
34	Telephone Expense	3 5 0 0 00				3 5 0 0 00		3 5 0 0 00				34
35	Utilities Expense	12 0 0 0 00				12 0 0 0 00		12 0 0 0 00				35
36	Insurance Expense			(d) 1 8 0 0 00		1 8 0 0 00		1 8 0 0 00				36
37	Depr. Expense—Building			(e) 4 0 0 0 00		4 0 0 0 00		4 0 0 0 00				37
38	Depr. Expense—Store Equipment			(f) 3 0 0 0 00		3 0 0 0 00		3 0 0 0 00				38
39	Miscellaneous Expense	2 2 5 0 00				2 2 5 0 00		2 2 5 0 00				39
40	Interest Expense	3 1 5 0 00				3 1 5 0 00		3 1 5 0 00				40
41		428 6 0 0 00	428 6 0 0 00	64 6 5 0 00	64 6 5 0 00	454 0 5 0 00	454 0 5 0 00	230 5 0 0 00	252 7 0 0 00	224 0 0 0 00	201 3 5 0 00	41
42	Net Income							22 6 5 0 00			22 6 5 0 00	42
43								252 7 0 0 00	252 7 0 0 00	224 0 0 0 00	224 0 0 0 00	43

STEP 1   STEP 2   STEP 3   STEPS 4 AND 5

U REVU Complete U REVU-3 on **page 544** to test your basic understanding of LO3.

ADJUSTING ENTRIES

LO4 Journalize adjusting entries for a merchandising business.

Recall that making the adjustments on the work sheet has no effect on the actual accounts in the general ledger. Journal entries must be made to enter the adjustments into the accounting system. Figure 14-12 shows the adjusting entries for Northern Micro.

LEARNING KEY

Recall that the work sheet is just a planning tool. The adjusting entries must be entered in the general journal.

FIGURE 14-12 Adjusting Entries for Northern Micro

	DATE		DESCRIPTION	POST. REF.	DEBIT	CREDIT	
1			Adjusting Entries				1
2	20-- Dec.	31	Income Summary		26 0 0 0 00		2
3			Merchandise Inventory			26 0 0 0 00	3
4							4
5		31	Merchandise Inventory		18 0 0 0 00		5
6			Income Summary			18 0 0 0 00	6
7							7
8		31	Supplies Expense		1 4 0 0 00		8
9			Supplies			1 4 0 0 00	9
10							10
11		31	Insurance Expense		1 8 0 0 00		11
12			Prepaid Insurance			1 8 0 0 00	12
13							13
14		31	Depr. Expense—Building		4 0 0 0 00		14
15			Accumulated Depr.—Building			4 0 0 0 00	15
16							16
17		31	Depr. Expense—Store Equipment		3 0 0 0 00		17
18			Accumulated Depr.—Store Equipment			3 0 0 0 00	18
19							19
20		31	Wages Expense		4 5 0 00		20
21			Wages Payable			4 5 0 00	21
22							22
23		31	Unearned Subscriptions Revenue		10 0 0 0 00		23
24			Subscriptions Revenue			10 0 0 0 00	24
25							25

GENERAL JOURNAL PAGE 3

U REVU Complete U REVU-4 on **page 544** to test your basic understanding of LO4.

ADJUSTING ENTRIES UNDER THE PERPETUAL INVENTORY SYSTEM

LO5 Prepare adjusting journal entries under the perpetual inventory system.

Under the perpetual inventory system, the merchandise inventory and cost of goods sold accounts are continually updated throughout the year to reflect purchases and sales of inventory. When inventory is purchased, the merchandise inventory account is

LEARNING KEY

Under the perpetual inventory system, cost of goods sold and the amount of merchandise inventory on hand are continually updated as merchandise is bought and sold.

debited and Cash or Accounts Payable is credited. When inventory is sold, two entries are made.

1. Cash or Accounts Receivable is debited and Sales is credited.

2. Cost of Goods Sold is debited and Merchandise Inventory is credited.

A comparison of the entries under the periodic and perpetual inventory systems is provided in Figure 14-13.

FIGURE 14-13 Entries for Periodic and Perpetual Inventory Systems

TRANSACTION	PERIODIC SYSTEM		PERPETUAL SYSTEM	
Purchased merchandise on account, $800.	Purchases Accounts Payable	800 800	Merchandise Inventory Accounts Payable	800 800
Sold merchandise on account, $400. The cost of the merchandise sold was $300.	Accounts Receivable Sales	400 400	Accounts Receivable Sales	400 400
			Cost of Goods Sold Merchandise Inventory	300 300

As discussed in Chapter 13, the perpetual inventory system does not eliminate the need for taking physical inventories. The perpetual records must be compared with the physical inventory to discover and correct any errors or losses of merchandise from theft, breakage, or spoilage. If a difference is found between the physical count and the amount in the perpetual inventory records, the records must be corrected by an adjusting entry. Some firms use Cost of Goods Sold to make this adjustment. A preferable approach is to use an account called **Inventory Short and Over**. For example, if the book balance is $3,840 and the physical count shows $3,710 worth of merchandise, the $130 shortage would be entered as follows:

					Adjusting Entry				
4		Inventory Short and Over			1 3 0 00				4
5		Merchandise Inventory					1 3 0 00		5
6		To adjust inventory per physical count							6

Similarly, if the book balance is $3,840 and the physical count shows $3,900 worth of merchandise, this $60 overage would be entered as follows:

					Adjusting Entry				
4		Merchandise Inventory			6 0 00				4
5		Inventory Short and Over					6 0 00		5
6		To adjust inventory per physical count							6

LEARNING KEY

A physical inventory is still important under the perpetual inventory system. It is used to verify the accuracy of the inventory records.

If Inventory Short and Over has a debit balance, the account is listed with other expenses on the income statement. If it has a credit balance, the account is listed with other revenues on the income statement.

Using a separate account, Inventory Short and Over, makes it easier for management to track inventory problems associated with errors, theft, breakage, and spoilage.

Further, it removes these items from the calculation of cost of goods sold and provides a better measure of the gross profit on sales.

A business that sells a wide selection of low-cost goods may not find it practical to keep a perpetual inventory. In contrast, a business that sells a few high-cost items (cars, fine jewelry, stereo equipment) can maintain such a record without incurring excessive processing costs. The increasing use of computers and optical scanning devices at the point of sale has enabled more businesses to switch from the periodic to the perpetual inventory system.

U REVU

Complete U REVU-5 on **page 544** to test your basic understanding of LO5.

SELF-STUDY

LEARNING OBJECTIVES   Key Points to Remember

LO1 Prepare an adjustment for merchandise inventory using the periodic inventory system.

Extra care is required for the end-of-period adjustment for merchandise inventory and the related extensions on the work sheet. The two-step adjustment process used on the work sheet is shown below. This technique is used so that all of the information required to compute cost of goods sold on the income statement is provided in the Income Statement columns of the work sheet.

ACCOUNT TITLE	TRIAL BALANCE DEBIT	TRIAL BALANCE CREDIT	ADJUSTMENTS DEBIT	ADJUSTMENTS CREDIT	ADJUSTED TRIAL BALANCE DEBIT	ADJUSTED TRIAL BALANCE CREDIT	INCOME STATEMENT DEBIT	INCOME STATEMENT CREDIT	BALANCE SHEET DEBIT	BALANCE SHEET CREDIT
							BI	EI		
Merchandise Inventory	20		STEP 2 30 / 20 STEP 1		30				30	
Income Summary			STEP 1 20 / 30 STEP 2		20	30	20	30		
Purchases	80						80			
							Purchases			

Step 1: Remove beginning inventory	Income Summary	20	
	Merchandise Inventory		20
Step 2: Insert ending inventory	Merchandise Inventory	30	
	Income Summary		30

BI: Beginning inventory ($20); EI: Ending inventory ($30)

Cost of goods sold:	
Merchandise inventory, January 1	$ 20
Purchases	80
Goods available for sale	$100
Less merchandise inventory, December 31	30
Cost of goods sold	$ 70

LO2 Prepare an adjustment for unearned revenue.

Some firms receive cash before providing a service or selling a product. The cash received in advance is considered a liability, unearned revenue, until earned. The adjusting entry to recognize that unearned revenue has become earned is as follows:

Unearned Revenue	xxx	
Revenue		xxx

LEARNING OBJECTIVES   Key Points to Remember

LO3 Prepare a work sheet for a merchandising business.	Steps to follow when preparing a work sheet are as follows: 1. Prepare the trial balance. 2. Prepare the adjustments. 3. Prepare the adjusted trial balance. 4. Extend the adjusted trial balance amounts to the Income Statement and Balance Sheet columns. 5. Total the Income Statement and Balance Sheet columns to compute the net income or net loss.
LO4 Journalize adjusting entries for a merchandising business.	The work sheet is a useful tool when preparing end-of-period adjustments and financial statements. Remember: The work sheet is NOT a formal part of the accounting system. Adjustments made on the work sheet must be entered in a journal and posted to the ledger.

LO5 Prepare adjusting journal entries under the perpetual inventory system.	Under the perpetual inventory system, the cost of goods sold and merchandise inventory accounts are updated whenever merchandise is purchased or sold. Thus, the firm knows how much inventory should be on hand at any given point in time. However, the balance of the merchandise inventory account must be verified with an actual physical count of the inventory before issuing financial statements. If there is a difference, an adjusting entry is made. If the balance in the inventory account is greater than the physical count, the following entry is made:
	
	Inventory Short and Over xxx
	    Merchandise Inventory xxx
	
	If the balance in the inventory account is less than the physical count, the following entry is made:
	
	Merchandise Inventory xxx
	    Inventory Short and Over xxx

DEMONSTRATION PROBLEM

Aaron Patton owns and operates Patton's Bait Shop and Boat Rental. A year-end trial balance is shown on the next page. Year-end adjustment data for Patton's Bait Shop and Boat Rental are as follows:

(a and b)   A physical count shows that merchandise inventory costing $15,000 is on hand as of December 31, 20--.

(c)   Supplies remaining at the end of the year, $200.

(d)   Unexpired insurance on December 31, $300.

(e)   Depreciation expense on the building for 20--, $2,000.

(f)   Depreciation expense on the store equipment for 20--, $1,500.

(g)   Wages earned but not paid as of December 31, $225.

(h)   Unearned boat rental revenue as of December 31, $1,000.

(continued)

REQUIRED

1. Prepare a year-end work sheet.

2. Journalize the adjusting entries.

3. Compute cost of goods sold using the work sheet prepared for part (1).

<table>
<tr><td colspan="11">Patton's Bait Shop and Boat Rental
Trial Balance
December 31, 20 - -</td></tr>
<tr><th>ACCOUNT TITLE</th><th colspan="5">DEBIT BALANCE</th><th colspan="5">CREDIT BALANCE</th></tr>
<tr><td>Cash</td><td>10</td><td>0</td><td>0</td><td>0</td><td>00</td><td></td><td></td><td></td><td></td><td></td></tr>
<tr><td>Accounts Receivable</td><td>7</td><td>5</td><td>0</td><td>0</td><td>00</td><td></td><td></td><td></td><td></td><td></td></tr>
<tr><td>Merchandise Inventory</td><td>19</td><td>0</td><td>0</td><td>0</td><td>00</td><td></td><td></td><td></td><td></td><td></td></tr>
<tr><td>Supplies</td><td></td><td>9</td><td>0</td><td>0</td><td>00</td><td></td><td></td><td></td><td></td><td></td></tr>
<tr><td>Prepaid Insurance</td><td>1</td><td>2</td><td>0</td><td>0</td><td>00</td><td></td><td></td><td></td><td></td><td></td></tr>
<tr><td>Land</td><td>5</td><td>0</td><td>0</td><td>0</td><td>00</td><td></td><td></td><td></td><td></td><td></td></tr>
<tr><td>Building</td><td>45</td><td>0</td><td>0</td><td>0</td><td>00</td><td></td><td></td><td></td><td></td><td></td></tr>
<tr><td>Accumulated Depreciation—Building</td><td></td><td></td><td></td><td></td><td></td><td>8</td><td>0</td><td>0</td><td>0</td><td>00</td></tr>
<tr><td>Store Equipment</td><td>25</td><td>0</td><td>0</td><td>0</td><td>00</td><td></td><td></td><td></td><td></td><td></td></tr>
<tr><td>Accumulated Depreciation—Store Equipment</td><td></td><td></td><td></td><td></td><td></td><td>7</td><td>5</td><td>0</td><td>0</td><td>00</td></tr>
<tr><td>Notes Payable</td><td></td><td></td><td></td><td></td><td></td><td>2</td><td>5</td><td>0</td><td>0</td><td>00</td></tr>
<tr><td>Accounts Payable</td><td></td><td></td><td></td><td></td><td></td><td>5</td><td>0</td><td>0</td><td>0</td><td>00</td></tr>
<tr><td>Wages Payable</td><td></td><td></td><td></td><td></td><td></td><td></td><td></td><td></td><td></td><td></td></tr>
<tr><td>Unearned Boat Rental Revenue</td><td></td><td></td><td></td><td></td><td></td><td>11</td><td>0</td><td>0</td><td>0</td><td>00</td></tr>
<tr><td>Aaron Patton, Capital</td><td></td><td></td><td></td><td></td><td></td><td>77</td><td>9</td><td>0</td><td>0</td><td>00</td></tr>
<tr><td>Aaron Patton, Drawing</td><td>10</td><td>0</td><td>0</td><td>0</td><td>00</td><td></td><td></td><td></td><td></td><td></td></tr>
<tr><td>Income Summary</td><td></td><td></td><td></td><td></td><td></td><td></td><td></td><td></td><td></td><td></td></tr>
<tr><td>Sales</td><td></td><td></td><td></td><td></td><td></td><td>100</td><td>2</td><td>5</td><td>0</td><td>00</td></tr>
<tr><td>Sales Returns and Allowances</td><td></td><td>6</td><td>0</td><td>0</td><td>00</td><td></td><td></td><td></td><td></td><td></td></tr>
<tr><td>Boat Rental Revenue</td><td></td><td></td><td></td><td></td><td></td><td></td><td></td><td></td><td></td><td></td></tr>
<tr><td>Purchases</td><td>52</td><td>5</td><td>0</td><td>0</td><td>00</td><td></td><td></td><td></td><td></td><td></td></tr>
<tr><td>Purchases Returns and Allowances</td><td></td><td></td><td></td><td></td><td></td><td></td><td>4</td><td>0</td><td>0</td><td>00</td></tr>
<tr><td>Purchases Discounts</td><td></td><td></td><td></td><td></td><td></td><td></td><td>5</td><td>0</td><td>0</td><td>00</td></tr>
<tr><td>Freight-In</td><td></td><td>1</td><td>5</td><td>0</td><td>00</td><td></td><td></td><td></td><td></td><td></td></tr>
<tr><td>Wages Expense</td><td>21</td><td>0</td><td>0</td><td>0</td><td>00</td><td></td><td></td><td></td><td></td><td></td></tr>
<tr><td>Advertising Expense</td><td>3</td><td>7</td><td>5</td><td>0</td><td>00</td><td></td><td></td><td></td><td></td><td></td></tr>
<tr><td>Supplies Expense</td><td></td><td></td><td></td><td></td><td></td><td></td><td></td><td></td><td></td><td></td></tr>
<tr><td>Telephone Expense</td><td>1</td><td>7</td><td>5</td><td>0</td><td>00</td><td></td><td></td><td></td><td></td><td></td></tr>
<tr><td>Utilities Expense</td><td>6</td><td>0</td><td>0</td><td>0</td><td>00</td><td></td><td></td><td></td><td></td><td></td></tr>
<tr><td>Insurance Expense</td><td></td><td></td><td></td><td></td><td></td><td></td><td></td><td></td><td></td><td></td></tr>
<tr><td>Depreciation Expense—Building</td><td></td><td></td><td></td><td></td><td></td><td></td><td></td><td></td><td></td><td></td></tr>
<tr><td>Depreciation Expense—Store Equipment</td><td></td><td></td><td></td><td></td><td></td><td></td><td></td><td></td><td></td><td></td></tr>
<tr><td>Miscellaneous Expense</td><td>3</td><td>6</td><td>2</td><td>5</td><td>00</td><td></td><td></td><td></td><td></td><td></td></tr>
<tr><td>Interest Expense</td><td></td><td></td><td>7</td><td>5</td><td>00</td><td></td><td></td><td></td><td></td><td></td></tr>
<tr><td></td><td>213</td><td>0</td><td>5</td><td>0</td><td>00</td><td>213</td><td>0</td><td>5</td><td>0</td><td>00</td></tr>
</table>

Solution 1.

Patton's Bait Shop and Boat Rental
Work Sheet
For Year Ended December 31, 20 --

#	ACCOUNT TITLE	Trial Balance Debit	Trial Balance Credit	Adjustments Debit	Adjustments Credit	Adjusted Trial Balance Debit	Adjusted Trial Balance Credit	Income Statement Debit	Income Statement Credit	Balance Sheet Debit	Balance Sheet Credit
1	Cash	10,000.00				10,000.00				10,000.00	
2	Accounts Receivable	7,500.00				7,500.00				7,500.00	
3	Merchandise Inventory	19,000.00		(b) 15,000.00	(a) 19,000.00	15,000.00				15,000.00	
4	Supplies	7,200.00			(c) 7,000.00	200.00				200.00	
5	Prepaid Insurance	1,200.00			(d) 900.00	300.00				300.00	
6	Land	5,000.00				5,000.00				5,000.00	
7	Building	45,000.00				45,000.00				45,000.00	
8	Accum. Depr.—Building		8,000.00		(e) 2,000.00		10,000.00				10,000.00
9	Store Equipment	25,000.00				25,000.00				25,000.00	
10	Accum. Depr.—Store Equipment		7,500.00		(f) 1,500.00		9,000.00				9,000.00
11	Notes Payable		2,500.00				2,500.00				2,500.00
12	Accounts Payable		5,000.00				5,000.00				5,000.00
13	Wages Payable				(g) 225.00		225.00				225.00
14	Unearned Boat Rental Revenue		11,000.00	(h) 10,000.00			1,000.00				1,000.00
15	Aaron Patton, Capital		77,900.00				77,900.00				77,900.00
16	Aaron Patton, Drawing	10,000.00				10,000.00				10,000.00	
17	Income Summary			(a) 19,000.00	(b) 15,000.00	19,000.00	15,000.00	19,000.00	15,000.00		
18	Sales		92,150.00				92,150.00		92,150.00		
19	Sales Returns and Allowances	6,000.00				6,000.00		6,000.00			
20	Boat Rental Revenue				(h) 10,000.00		10,000.00		10,000.00		
21	Purchases	39,450.00				39,450.00		39,450.00			
22	Purchases Returns and Allowances		4,000.00				4,000.00		4,000.00		
23	Purchases Discounts		5,000.00				5,000.00		5,000.00		
24	Freight-In	1,500.00				1,500.00		1,500.00			
25	Wages Expense	21,000.00		(g) 225.00		21,225.00		21,225.00			
26	Advertising Expense	3,750.00				3,750.00		3,750.00			
27	Supplies Expense			(c) 7,000.00		7,000.00		7,000.00			
28	Telephone Expense	1,750.00				1,750.00		1,750.00			
29	Utilities Expense	6,000.00				6,000.00		6,000.00			
30	Insurance Expense			(d) 900.00		900.00		900.00			
31	Depr. Expense—Building			(e) 2,000.00		2,000.00		2,000.00			
32	Depr. Expense—Store Equipment			(f) 1,500.00		1,500.00		1,500.00			
33	Miscellaneous Expense	3,625.00				3,625.00		3,625.00			
34	Interest Expense	75.00				75.00		75.00			
35		213,050.00	213,050.00	55,625.00	55,625.00	231,775.00	231,775.00	113,775.00	126,150.00	118,000.00	105,625.00
36	Net Income							12,375.00			12,375.00
37								126,150.00	126,150.00	118,000.00	118,000.00

(continued)

2.

			GENERAL JOURNAL						PAGE 3	
	DATE		DESCRIPTION	POST REF.	DEBIT		CREDIT			
1			Adjusting Entries							1
2	20-- Dec.	31	Income Summary		19 0 0 0 00					2
3			Merchandise Inventory				19 0 0 0 00			3
4										4
5		31	Merchandise Inventory		15 0 0 0 00					5
6			Income Summary				15 0 0 0 00			6
7										7
8		31	Supplies Expense		7 0 0 00					8
9			Supplies				7 0 0 00			9
10										10
11		31	Insurance Expense		9 0 0 00					11
12			Prepaid Insurance				9 0 0 00			12
13										13
14		31	Depreciation Expense—Building		2 0 0 0 00					14
15			Accumulated Depreciation—Building				2 0 0 0 00			15
16										16
17		31	Depreciation Expense—Store Equipment		1 5 0 0 00					17
18			Accumulated Depreciation—Store Equipment				1 5 0 0 00			18
19										19
20		31	Wages Expense		2 2 5 00					20
21			Wages Payable				2 2 5 00			21
22										22
23		31	Unearned Boat Rental Revenue		10 0 0 0 00					23
24			Boat Rental Revenue				10 0 0 0 00			24
25										25

3.

		Cost of goods sold:						
1		Cost of goods sold:						1
2		Merchandise inventory, January 1			$19 0 0 0 00			2
3		Purchases		$52 5 0 0 00				3
4		Less: Purchases returns and allowances	$ 4 0 0 00					4
5		Purchases discounts	5 0 0 00	9 0 0 00				5
6		Net purchases		$51 6 0 0 00				6
7		Add freight-in		1 5 0 00				7
8		Cost of goods purchased			51 7 5 0 00			8
9		Goods available for sale			$70 7 5 0 00			9
10		Less merchandise inventory, December 31			15 0 0 0 00			10
11		Cost of goods sold				$55 7 5 0 00		11

KEY TERMS

Inventory Short and Over (537)   An account used to adjust the perpetual inventory records when a difference exists between the physical count and the amount in the perpetual inventory records.

unearned revenue (526)   Cash received in advance of delivering a product or performing a service.

SELF-STUDY QUESTIONS AND EXERCISES

True/False Questions

1. LO1   Under the periodic inventory system, the beginning inventory is removed from the merchandise inventory account with a credit to Merchandise Inventory and a debit to Income Summary.

2. LO1   Under the periodic inventory system, the ending inventory is entered by debiting Merchandise Inventory and crediting Income Summary.

3. LO2   The cash received in advance before delivering a product or performing a service is called unearned revenue.

4. LO2   Unearned revenue is adjusted into an expense account at the end of the accounting period.

5. LO2   Sales Returns and Allowances is classified as a contra-cost account on the income statement.

Multiple Choice Questions

1. LO2   Purchases Returns and Allowances and Purchases Discounts are classified as _____ on the income statement.

    (a) expense accounts
    (b) contra-cost accounts
    (c) revenue accounts
    (d) contra-revenue accounts

2. LO3   The first step in preparing a work sheet is to

    (a) prepare the trial balance.
    (b) prepare the income statement.
    (c) prepare the adjustments.
    (d) prepare the balance sheet.

3. LO3   The last step in preparing a work sheet is to

    (a) prepare the adjusted trial balance.
    (b) total the Income Statement and Balance Sheet columns to compute net income or net loss.
    (c) prepare the adjustments.
    (d) extend the Adjusted Trial Balance columns.

4. LO3   Unearned Revenue is extended into the _____ on the work sheet.

    (a) Adjustments columns
    (b) Balance Sheet columns
    (c) Income Statement columns
    (d) Trial Balance columns

5. LO3   The most useful tool in preparing end-of-period adjustments and financial statements is the

(a) general ledger.   (c) general journal.
(b) work sheet.   (d) physical inventory.

U REVU   Exercises

1. LO1   Prepare the cost of goods sold section for Joseph's Gift Shop. The following amounts are known:

Beginning merchandise inventory	$ 20,000
Ending merchandise inventory	15,000
Purchases	171,000

2. LO2   The Venice Theatre sold and collected cash of $45,000 for season tickets. Upon collection of cash, Unearned Ticket Revenue was credited. At the end of the accounting period, $15,000 had been earned. Make the appropriate adjusting entry.

3. LO3   Information relating to inventory for Janie Par Gifts is provided below.

Beginning merchandise inventory	$120,000
Ending merchandise inventory	90,000
Purchases	250,000

1. Set up a work sheet similar to the one provided below.
2. Enter the appropriate information from above into the Trial Balance columns.
3. Prepare appropriate adjusting entries and extensions across the work sheet.

	ACCOUNT TITLE	TRIAL BALANCE		ADJUSTMENTS		ADJUSTED TRIAL BALANCE		INCOME STATEMENT		BALANCE SHEET		
		DEBIT	CREDIT	DEBIT	CREDIT	DEBIT	CREDIT	DEBIT	CREDIT	DEBIT	CREDIT	
1	Merchandise Inventory											1
2	Income Summary											2
3	Purchases											3

4. LO4   Using the partial work sheet provided below, prepare the adjusting entries for merchandise inventory.

	ACCOUNT TITLE	TRIAL BALANCE		ADJUSTMENTS		
		DEBIT	CREDIT	DEBIT	CREDIT	
1	Merchandise Inventory	50 0 0 0 00		(b) 60 0 0 0 00	(a) 50 0 0 0 00	1
2	Income Summary			(a) 50 0 0 0 00	(b) 60 0 0 0 00	2
3	Purchases	80 0 0 0 00				3

5. LO5   The following information is provided by Koffi Products:

Ending balance of merchandise inventory account	$50,000
Physical count of ending merchandise inventory	48,000

Prepare the appropriate adjusting entry under the perpetual inventory system.

The answers to the Self-Study Questions and Exercises are at the end of the chapter (page 562).

APPLYING YOUR KNOWLEDGE

REVIEW QUESTIONS

LO1 1. A firm is preparing to make adjusting entries at the end of the accounting period. The balance of the merchandise inventory account is $200,000. If the firm is using the periodic inventory system, what does this balance represent?

LO1 2. What work sheet amounts are used to compute cost of goods sold?

LO1 3. Why are both the debit and credit amounts in the Adjustments columns on the Income Summary line of the work sheet extended to the Adjusted Trial Balance columns?

LO2 4. What is an unearned revenue?

LO2 5. Give three examples of unearned revenue.

LO3 6. List the five steps taken to prepare a work sheet.

LO3 7. What does the difference between the totals of the Income Statement columns represent? What does the difference between the Balance Sheet column totals represent?

LO5 8. A firm is preparing to make adjusting entries at the end of the accounting period. The balance of the merchandise inventory account is $100,000. If the firm is using the perpetual inventory system, what does this balance represent?

SERIES A EXERCISES

E 14-1A (LO1)

ADJUSTMENT FOR MERCHANDISE INVENTORY USING T ACCOUNTS: PERIODIC INVENTORY SYSTEM Sam Baker owns a business called Sam's Sporting Goods. His beginning inventory as of January 1, 20--, was $47,000, and his ending inventory as of December 31, 20--, was $53,000. Set up T accounts for Merchandise Inventory and Income Summary and perform the year-end adjustment for Merchandise Inventory.

E 14-2A (LO1)

✓ Cost of goods sold: $65,200

CALCULATION OF COST OF GOODS SOLD: PERIODIC INVENTORY SYSTEM Prepare the cost of goods sold section for Adams Gift Shop. The following amounts are known:

Beginning merchandise inventory	$26,000
Ending merchandise inventory	23,000
Purchases	71,000
Purchases returns and allowances	3,500
Purchases discounts	5,500
Freight-in	200

E 14-3A (LO2)

ADJUSTMENT FOR UNEARNED REVENUES USING T ACCOUNTS Set up T accounts for Cash, Unearned Ticket Revenue, and Ticket Revenue. Post the following two transactions to the appropriate accounts, indicating each transaction by letter:

(a) Sold 1,500 season tickets at $30 each, receiving cash of $45,000.
(b) An end-of-period adjustment is needed to recognize that $35,000 in ticket revenue has been earned.

E 14-4A (LO3)

✓ Cost of goods sold: $75,500

WORK SHEET EXTENSIONS FOR MERCHANDISE INVENTORY ADJUST-MENTS: PERIODIC INVENTORY SYSTEM The following partial work sheet is taken from Kevin's Gift Shop for the year ended December 31, 20--. The ending merchandise inventory is $50,000.

1. Complete the Adjustments columns for the merchandise inventory.
2. Extend the merchandise inventory to the Adjusted Trial Balance and Balance Sheet columns.
3. Extend the remaining accounts to the Adjusted Trial Balance and Income Statement columns.
4. Prepare a cost of goods sold section from the partial work sheet.

Kevin's Gift Shop
Work Sheet (Partial)
For Year Ended December 31, 20 - -

	ACCOUNT TITLE	TRIAL BALANCE DEBIT	TRIAL BALANCE CREDIT	ADJUSTMENTS DEBIT	ADJUSTMENTS CREDIT	
1	Merchandise Inventory	40 0 0 0 00				1
12	Income Summary					12
13	Purchases	90 0 0 0 00				13
14	Purchases Returns and Allowances		2 0 0 0 00			14
15	Purchases Discounts		3 0 0 0 00			15
16	Freight-In	5 0 0 00				16
17						17
18						18

E 14-5A (LO3)

✓ Beg. inv.: $55,000

DETERMINING THE BEGINNING AND ENDING INVENTORY FROM A PARTIAL WORK SHEET: PERIODIC INVENTORY SYSTEM From the following partial work sheet, indicate the dollar amount of beginning and ending merchandise inventory:

	ACCOUNT TITLE	ADJUSTMENTS DEBIT	ADJUSTMENTS CREDIT	ADJUSTED TRIAL BALANCE DEBIT	ADJUSTED TRIAL BALANCE CREDIT	INCOME STATEMENT DEBIT	INCOME STATEMENT CREDIT	BALANCE SHEET DEBIT	BALANCE SHEET CREDIT	
1	Merchandise Inventory	(b) 60 0 0 0 00	(a) 55 0 0 0 00	60 0 0 0 00				60 0 0 0 00		1
2	Income Summary	(a) 55 0 0 0 00	(b) 60 0 0 0 00	55 0 0 0 00	60 0 0 0 00	55 0 0 0 00	60 0 0 0 00			2

E 14-6A (LO4)

✓ (a)

Inc. Sum.   45,000

  Mdse. Inv.   45,000

JOURNALIZE ADJUSTING ENTRIES FOR A MERCHANDISING BUSINESS The following partial work sheet is taken from the books of Kelly's Kittens, a local pet kennel, for the year ended December 31, 20--. Journalize the adjustments in a general journal.

Kelly's Kittens
Work Sheet (Partial)
For Year Ended December 31, 20 - -

	ACCOUNT TITLE	TRIAL BALANCE DEBIT	TRIAL BALANCE CREDIT	ADJUSTMENTS DEBIT	ADJUSTMENTS CREDIT	
1	Merchandise Inventory	45 0 0 0 00		(b) 50 0 0 0 00	(a) 45 0 0 0 00	1
2	Supplies	10 0 0 0 00			(d) 7 0 0 0 00	2
3	Building	60 0 0 0 00				3
4	Accum. Depr.—Building		15 0 0 0 00		(e) 5 0 0 0 00	4
5	Wages Payable				(f) 1 2 0 0 00	5
6	Unearned Grooming Revenue		3 0 0 0 00	(c) 2 0 0 0 00		6
7	Income Summary			(a) 45 0 0 0 00	(b) 50 0 0 0 00	7
8	Grooming Revenue		20 0 0 0 00		(c) 2 0 0 0 00	8
9	Wages Expense	37 0 0 0 00		(f) 1 2 0 0 00		9
10	Supplies Expense			(d) 7 0 0 0 00		10
11	Depr. Expense—Building			(e) 5 0 0 0 00		11
12				110 2 0 0 00	110 2 0 0 00	12
13						13

E 14-7A (LO5)

JOURNAL ENTRIES UNDER THE PERPETUAL INVENTORY SYSTEM Bhushan Building Supplies entered into the following transactions. Prepare journal entries under the perpetual inventory system.

June 1   Purchased merchandise on account from Brij Builder's Materials, $500,000.

3   Purchased merchandise for cash, $400,000.

5   Sold merchandise on account to Champa Construction for $20,000. The merchandise cost $15,000.

E 14-8A (LO5)

JOURNALIZE ADJUSTING ENTRY FOR A MERCHANDISING BUSINESS: PERPETUAL INVENTORY SYSTEM On December 31, Anup Enterprises completed a physical count of its inventory. Although the merchandise inventory account shows a balance of $350,000, the physical count comes to $325,000. Prepare the appropriate adjusting entry under the perpetual inventory system.

SERIES A PROBLEMS

P 14-9A (LO1/2/3/4)

✓ Adj. col. total: $78,600;

Net income: $39,390

COMPLETION OF A WORK SHEET SHOWING A NET INCOME The trial balance for the Seaside Kite Shop, a business owned by Joyce Kennington, is shown on page 548. Year-end adjustment information is as follows:

(a and b)   Merchandise inventory costing $30,000 is on hand as of December 31, 20--. (The periodic inventory system is used.)

(c)   Supplies remaining at the end of the year, $2,700.

(d)   Unexpired insurance on December 31, $2,900.

(e)   Depreciation expense on the building for 20--, $5,000.

(f)   Depreciation expense on the store equipment for 20--, $3,200.

(g)   Unearned rent revenue as of December 31, $2,200.

(h)   Wages earned but not paid as of December 31, $900.

(continued)

REQUIRED

1. Complete the Adjustments columns, identifying each adjustment with its corresponding letter.

2. Complete the work sheet.

3. Enter the adjustments in a general journal.

Seaside Kite Shop
Trial Balance
December 31, 20 --

ACCOUNT TITLE	DEBIT BALANCE	CREDIT BALANCE
Cash	20 0 0 0 00	
Accounts Receivable	14 0 0 0 00	
Merchandise Inventory	25 0 0 0 00	
Supplies	8 0 0 0 00	
Prepaid Insurance	5 4 0 0 00	
Land	30 0 0 0 00	
Building	50 0 0 0 00	
Accumulated Depreciation—Building		20 0 0 0 00
Store Equipment	35 0 0 0 00	
Accumulated Depreciation—Store Equipment		14 0 0 0 00
Accounts Payable		9 6 0 0 00
Wages Payable		
Sales Tax Payable		5 9 0 0 00
Unearned Rent Revenue		8 9 0 0 00
Mortgage Payable		45 0 0 0 00
J. Kennington, Capital		65 4 1 0 00
J. Kennington, Drawing	26 0 0 0 00	
Income Summary		
Sales		118 0 0 0 00
Sales Returns and Allowances	1 7 0 0 00	
Rent Revenue		
Purchases	27 0 0 0 00	
Purchases Returns and Allowances		1 4 0 0 00
Purchases Discounts		1 8 0 0 00
Freight-In	2 1 0 0 00	
Wages Expense	32 0 0 0 00	
Advertising Expense	3 6 0 0 00	
Supplies Expense		
Telephone Expense	1 3 5 0 00	
Utilities Expense	8 0 0 0 00	
Insurance Expense		
Depreciation Expense—Building		
Depreciation Expense—Store Equipment		
Miscellaneous Expense	8 6 0 00	
	290 0 1 0 00	290 0 1 0 00

P 14-10A (LO1/2/3/4)

✓ Adj. col. total: $72,650;

Net loss: $45,760

COMPLETION OF A WORK SHEET SHOWING A NET LOSS The trial balance for Cascade Bicycle Shop, a business owned by David Lamond, is shown below. Year-end adjustment information is as follows:

(a and b)   Merchandise inventory costing $22,000 is on hand as of December 31, 20--. (The periodic inventory system is used.)
(c)   Supplies remaining at the end of the year, $2,400.
(d)   Unexpired insurance on December 31, $1,750.
(e)   Depreciation expense on the building for 20--, $4,000.
(f)   Depreciation expense on the store equipment for 20--, $3,600.
(g)   Unearned storage revenue as of December 31, $1,950.
(h)   Wages earned but not paid as of December 31, $750.

Cascade Bicycle Shop
Trial Balance
December 31, 20 --

ACCOUNT TITLE	DEBIT BALANCE	CREDIT BALANCE
Cash	23 0 0 0 00	
Accounts Receivable	15 0 0 0 00	
Merchandise Inventory	31 0 0 0 00	
Supplies	7 2 0 0 00	
Prepaid Insurance	4 6 0 0 00	
Land	28 0 0 0 00	
Building	53 0 0 0 00	
Accumulated Depreciation—Building		17 0 0 0 00
Store Equipment	27 0 0 0 00	
Accumulated Depreciation—Store Equipment		9 0 0 0 00
Accounts Payable		3 8 0 0 00
Wages Payable		
Sales Tax Payable		3 0 5 0 00
Unearned Storage Revenue		5 6 0 0 00
Mortgage Payable		42 0 0 0 00
D. Lamond, Capital		165 7 6 0 00
D. Lamond, Drawing	33 0 0 0 00	
Income Summary		
Sales		51 0 0 0 00
Sales Returns and Allowances	2 4 0 0 00	
Storage Revenue		
Purchases	21 0 0 0 00	
Purchases Returns and Allowances		1 3 0 0 00
Purchases Discounts		1 9 0 0 00
Freight-In	1 8 0 0 00	
Wages Expense	35 0 0 0 00	
Advertising Expense	5 7 0 0 00	
Supplies Expense		
Telephone Expense	2 2 0 0 00	
Utilities Expense	9 6 0 0 00	
Insurance Expense		
Depreciation Expense—Building		
Depreciation Expense—Store Equipment		
Miscellaneous Expense	9 1 0 00	
	300 4 1 0 00	300 4 1 0 00

(continued)

REQUIRED

1. Complete the Adjustments columns, identifying each adjustment with its corresponding letter.

2. Complete the work sheet.

3. Enter the adjustments in the general journal.

P 14-11A (LO1/2/4)

✓ Adj. col. total: $88,155

WORKING BACKWARD FROM ADJUSTED TRIAL BALANCE TO DETERMINE ADJUSTING ENTRIES The partial work sheet shown below is taken from the books of Stark Street Computers, a business owned by Logan Cowart, for the year ended December 31, 20--.

Stark Street Computers
Work Sheet (Partial)
For Year Ended December 31, 20 --

	ACCOUNT TITLE	TRIAL BALANCE DEBIT	TRIAL BALANCE CREDIT	ADJUSTMENTS DEBIT	ADJUSTMENTS CREDIT	ADJUSTED TRIAL BALANCE DEBIT	ADJUSTED TRIAL BALANCE CREDIT	
1	Cash	18 0 0 0 00				18 0 0 0 00		1
2	Accounts Receivable	11 0 0 0 00				11 0 0 0 00		2
3	Merchandise Inventory	25 0 0 0 00				35 0 0 0 00		3
4	Supplies	8 0 0 0 00				2 8 2 0 00		4
5	Prepaid Insurance	5 4 0 0 00				1 2 2 5 00		5
6	Land	27 0 0 0 00				27 0 0 0 00		6
7	Building	48 0 0 0 00				48 0 0 0 00		7
8	Accum. Depr.—Building		20 0 0 0 00				27 0 0 0 00	8
9	Store Equipment	33 0 0 0 00				33 0 0 0 00		9
10	Accum. Depr.—Store Equipment		8 7 0 0 00				12 8 0 0 00	10
11	Accounts Payable		6 4 0 0 00				6 4 0 0 00	11
12	Wages Payable						1 3 0 0 00	12
13	Sales Tax Payable		5 7 0 0 00				5 7 0 0 00	13
14	Unearned Repair Revenue		8 2 0 0 00				1 8 0 0 00	14
15	Mortgage Payable		44 0 0 0 00				44 0 0 0 00	15
16	L. Cowart, Capital		80 0 2 5 00				80 0 2 5 00	16
17	L. Cowart, Drawing	35 0 0 0 00				35 0 0 0 00		17
18	Income Summary					25 0 0 0 00	35 0 0 0 00	18
19	Sales		122 0 0 0 00				122 0 0 0 00	19
20	Sales Returns and Allowances	2 2 5 0 00				2 2 5 0 00		20
21	Repair Revenue						6 4 0 0 00	21
22	Purchases	29 7 5 0 00				29 7 5 0 00		22
23	Purchases Returns and Allowances		1 8 5 0 00				1 8 5 0 00	23
24	Purchases Discounts		1 4 2 5 00				1 4 2 5 00	24
25	Freight-In	3 2 0 0 00				3 2 0 0 00		25
26	Wages Expense	37 0 0 0 00				38 3 0 0 00		26
27	Advertising Expense	4 1 2 5 00				4 1 2 5 00		27
28	Supplies Expense					5 1 8 0 00		28
29	Telephone Expense	1 6 5 0 00				1 6 5 0 00		29
30	Utilities Expense	9 1 5 0 00				9 1 5 0 00		30
31	Insurance Expense					4 1 7 5 00		31
32	Depr. Expense—Building					7 0 0 0 00		32
33	Depr. Expense—Store Equipment					4 1 0 0 00		33
34	Miscellaneous Expense	7 7 5 00				7 7 5 00		34
35		298 3 0 0 00	298 3 0 0 00			345 7 0 0 00	345 7 0 0 00	35

REQUIRED

1. Determine the adjusting entries by analyzing the difference between the adjusted trial balance and the trial balance.

2. Journalize the adjusting entries in a general journal.

P 14-12A (LO1/2/3/4)

✓ Adj. col. total: $92,335;
Cost of goods sold: $33,145

WORKING BACKWARD FROM THE INCOME STATEMENT AND BALANCE SHEET COLUMNS OF THE WORK SHEET TO DETERMINE ADJUSTED TRIAL BALANCE AND ADJUSTING ENTRIES The partially completed work sheet from the books of Lewis Music Store, a business owned by Hugo Lewis, for the year ended December 31, 20--, is shown on page 552.

REQUIRED

1. Analyze the work sheet and determine the adjusted trial balance and the adjusting entries by working backward from the Income Statement and Balance Sheet columns.

2. Journalize the adjusting entries in a general journal.

3. Prepare the cost of goods sold section of the income statement for Lewis Music Store.

SERIES B EXERCISES

E 14-1B (LO1)

ADJUSTMENT FOR MERCHANDISE INVENTORY USING T ACCOUNTS: PERIODIC INVENTORY SYSTEM Sandra Owens owns a business called Sandra's Sporting Goods. Her beginning inventory as of January 1, 20--, was $33,000, and her ending inventory as of December 31, 20--, was $36,000. Set up T accounts for Merchandise Inventory and Income Summary and perform the year-end adjustment for Merchandise Inventory.

E 14-2B (LO1)

✓ Cost of goods sold: $58,100

CALCULATION OF COST OF GOODS SOLD: PERIODIC INVENTORY SYSTEM Prepare the cost of goods sold section for Havens Gift Shop. The following amounts are known:

Beginning merchandise inventory	$29,000
Ending merchandise inventory	27,000
Purchases	62,000
Purchases returns and allowances	2,800
Purchases discounts	3,400
Freight-in	300

E 14-3B (LO2)

ADJUSTMENT FOR UNEARNED REVENUES USING T ACCOUNTS Set up T accounts for Cash, Unearned Ticket Revenue, and Ticket Revenue. Post the following two transactions to the appropriate accounts, indicating each transaction by letter:

(a) Sold 1,200 season tickets at $20 each, receiving cash of $24,000.
(b) An end-of-period adjustment is needed to recognize that $19,000 in ticket revenue has been earned.

PROBLEM 14-12A

Lewis Music Store
Work Sheet
For Year Ended December 31, 20 --

#	Account Title	Trial Balance Debit	Trial Balance Credit	Adjustments Debit	Adjustments Credit	Adjusted Trial Balance Debit	Adjusted Trial Balance Credit	Income Statement Debit	Income Statement Credit	Balance Sheet Debit	Balance Sheet Credit	#
1	Cash	27 0 0 0 00								27 0 0 0 00		1
2	Accounts Receivable	13 3 0 0 00								13 3 0 0 00		2
3	Merchandise Inventory	34 0 0 0 00								38 0 0 0 00		3
4	Supplies	5 3 0 0 00								1 5 0 0 00		4
5	Prepaid Insurance	6 1 0 0 00								1 7 8 5 00		5
6	Land	31 0 0 0 00								31 0 0 0 00		6
7	Building	52 0 0 0 00								52 0 0 0 00		7
8	Accum. Depr.—Building		17 0 0 0 00								21 1 4 5 00	8
9	Store Equipment	39 0 0 0 00								39 0 0 0 00		9
10	Accum. Depr.—Store Equipment		11 9 0 0 00								14 8 7 5 00	10
11	Accounts Payable		6 2 5 0 00								6 2 5 0 00	11
12	Wages Payable										8 7 5 00	12
13	Sales Tax Payable		6 2 0 0 00								6 2 0 0 00	13
14	Unearned Rent Revenue		7 4 0 0 00								3 1 7 5 00	14
15	Mortgage Payable		46 0 0 0 00								46 0 0 0 00	15
16	H. Lewis, Capital		111 6 2 0 00								111 6 2 0 00	16
17	H. Lewis, Drawing	37 0 0 0 00								37 0 0 0 00		17
18	Income Summary							34 0 0 0 00	38 0 0 0 00			18
19	Sales		136 0 0 0 00						136 0 0 0 00			19
20	Sales Returns and Allowances	3 5 0 0 00						3 5 0 0 00				20
21	Rent Revenue								4 2 2 5 00			21
22	Purchases	39 0 0 0 00						39 0 0 0 00				22
23	Purchases Returns and Allowances		2 5 3 0 00						2 5 3 0 00			23
24	Purchases Discounts		1 9 7 5 00						1 9 7 5 00			24
25	Freight-In	2 6 5 0 00						2 6 5 0 00				25
26	Wages Expense	42 0 0 0 00						42 8 7 5 00				26
27	Advertising Expense	4 1 7 5 00						4 1 7 5 00				27
28	Supplies Expense							3 8 0 0 00				28
29	Telephone Expense	1 9 8 0 00						1 9 8 0 00				29
30	Utilities Expense	7 9 4 5 00						7 9 4 5 00				30
31	Insurance Expense							4 3 1 5 00				31
32	Depr. Expense—Building							4 1 4 5 00				32
33	Depr. Expense—Store Equipment							2 9 7 5 00				33
34	Miscellaneous Expense	9 2 5 00						9 2 5 00				34
35		346 8 7 5 00	346 8 7 5 00					152 2 8 5 00	182 7 3 0 00	240 5 8 5 00	210 1 4 0 00	35
36	Net Income							30 4 4 5 00			30 4 4 5 00	36
37								182 7 3 0 00	182 7 3 0 00	240 5 8 5 00	240 5 8 5 00	37

E 14-4B (LO3)

✓ Cost of goods sold: $73,400

WORK SHEET EXTENSIONS FOR MERCHANDISE INVENTORY ADJUSTMENTS: PERIODIC INVENTORY SYSTEM The following partial work sheet is taken from Nicole's Gift Shop for the year ended December 31, 20--. The ending merchandise inventory is $37,000.

1. Complete the Adjustments columns for the merchandise inventory.
2. Extend the merchandise inventory to the Adjusted Trial Balance and Balance Sheet columns.
3. Extend the remaining accounts to the Adjusted Trial Balance and Income Statement columns.
4. Prepare a cost of goods sold section from the partial work sheet.

Nicole's Gift Shop
Work Sheet (Partial)
For Year Ended December 31, 20 --

	ACCOUNT TITLE	TRIAL BALANCE DEBIT	TRIAL BALANCE CREDIT	ADJUSTMENTS DEBIT	ADJUSTMENTS CREDIT	
1	Merchandise Inventory	30 0 0 0 00				1
12	Income Summary					12
13	Purchases	85 0 0 0 00				13
14	Purchases Returns and Allowances		2 2 0 0 00			14
15	Purchases Discounts		2 5 0 0 00			15
16	Freight-In	1 0 0 0 00				16
17						17
18						18

E 14-5B (LO3)

✓ Beg. inv.: $49,000

DETERMINING THE BEGINNING AND ENDING INVENTORY FROM A PARTIAL WORK SHEET: PERIODIC INVENTORY SYSTEM From the following partial work sheet, indicate the dollar amount of beginning and ending merchandise inventory.

	ACCOUNT TITLE	ADJUSTMENTS DEBIT	ADJUSTMENTS CREDIT	ADJUSTED TRIAL BALANCE DEBIT	ADJUSTED TRIAL BALANCE CREDIT	INCOME STATEMENT DEBIT	INCOME STATEMENT CREDIT	BALANCE SHEET DEBIT	BALANCE SHEET CREDIT	
1	Merchandise Inventory	(b) 45 0 0 0 00	(a) 49 0 0 0 00	45 0 0 0 00				45 0 0 0 00		1
2	Income Summary	(a) 49 0 0 0 00	(b) 45 0 0 0 00	49 0 0 0 00	45 0 0 0 00	49 0 0 0 00	45 0 0 0 00			2

E 14-6B (LO4)

✓ (b)
Mdse. Inv.   30,000
   Inc. Sum.   30,000

JOURNALIZE ADJUSTING ENTRIES FOR A MERCHANDISING BUSINESS The following partial work sheet is taken from the books of Carmen's Collies, a local pet kennel, for the year ended December 31, 20--. Journalize the adjustments in a general journal.

(continued)

Carmen's Collies
Work Sheet (Partial)
For Year Ended December 31, 20 - -

	ACCOUNT TITLE	TRIAL BALANCE DEBIT	TRIAL BALANCE CREDIT	ADJUSTMENTS DEBIT	ADJUSTMENTS CREDIT	
1	Merchandise Inventory	35 0 0 0 00		(b) 30 0 0 0 00	(a) 35 0 0 0 00	1
2	Supplies	4 5 0 0 00			(d) 3 1 0 0 00	2
3	Building	50 0 0 0 00				3
4	Accum. Depr.—Building		23 0 0 0 00		(e) 6 0 0 0 00	4
5	Wages Payable				(f) 1 3 0 0 00	5
6	Unearned Grooming Revenue		7 0 0 0 00	(c) 5 5 0 0 00		6
7	Income Summary			(a) 35 0 0 0 00	(b) 30 0 0 0 00	7
8	Grooming Revenue		24 0 0 0 00		(c) 5 5 0 0 00	8
9	Wages Expense	41 0 0 0 00		(f) 1 3 0 0 00		9
10	Supplies Expense			(d) 3 1 0 0 00		10
11	Depr. Expense—Building			(e) 6 0 0 0 00		11
12				80 9 0 0 00	80 9 0 0 00	12
13						13

E 14-7B (LO5)

JOURNAL ENTRIES UNDER THE PERPETUAL INVENTORY SYSTEM Sunita Computer Supplies entered into the following transactions. Prepare journal entries under the perpetual inventory system.

May 1 Purchased merchandise on account from Anju Enterprises, $200,000.

8 Purchased merchandise for cash, $100,000.

15 Sold merchandise on account to Salil's Pharmacy for $8,000. The merchandise cost $5,000.

E 14-8B (LO5)

JOURNALIZE ADJUSTING ENTRY FOR A MERCHANDISING BUSINESS: PERPETUAL INVENTORY SYSTEM On December 31, Anup Enterprises completed a physical count of its inventory. Although the merchandise inventory account shows a balance of $200,000, the physical count comes to $210,000. Prepare the appropriate adjusting entry under the perpetual inventory system.

SERIES B PROBLEMS

P 14-9B (LO1/2/3/4)

✓ Adj. col. total: $76,500;

Net income: $13,950

COMPLETION OF A WORK SHEET SHOWING A NET INCOME A trial balance for the Basket Corner, a business owned by Linda Palermo, is shown on page 567. Year-end adjustment information is provided below.

(a and b) Merchandise inventory costing $24,000 is on hand as of December 31, 20--. (The periodic inventory system is used.)
(c) Supplies remaining at the end of the year, $2,100.
(d) Unexpired insurance on December 31, $2,600.
(e) Depreciation expense on the building for 20--, $5,300.
(f) Depreciation expense on the store equipment for 20--, $3,800.
(g) Unearned decorating revenue as of December 31, $1,650.
(h) Wages earned but not paid as of December 31, $750.

REQUIRED

1. Complete the Adjustments columns, identifying each adjustment with its corresponding letter.

2. Complete the work sheet.

3. Enter the adjustments in a general journal.

Basket Corner
Trial Balance
December 31, 20 --

ACCOUNT TITLE	DEBIT BALANCE	CREDIT BALANCE
Cash	25 0 0 0 00	
Accounts Receivable	8 1 0 0 00	
Merchandise Inventory	32 0 0 0 00	
Supplies	7 1 0 0 00	
Prepaid Insurance	3 6 0 0 00	
Land	40 0 0 0 00	
Building	45 0 0 0 00	
Accumulated Depreciation—Building		16 0 0 0 00
Store Equipment	27 0 0 0 00	
Accumulated Depreciation—Store Equipment		5 5 0 0 00
Accounts Payable		3 6 0 0 00
Wages Payable		
Sales Tax Payable		6 2 0 0 00
Unearned Decorating Revenue		6 3 0 0 00
Mortgage Payable		36 0 0 0 00
L. Palermo, Capital		112 0 5 0 00
L. Palermo, Drawing	31 0 0 0 00	
Income Summary		
Sales		125 0 0 0 00
Sales Returns and Allowances	2 6 0 0 00	
Decorating Revenue		
Purchases	38 0 0 0 00	
Purchases Returns and Allowances		2 2 0 0 00
Purchases Discounts		1 7 0 0 00
Freight-In	1 9 0 0 00	
Wages Expense	38 0 0 0 00	
Advertising Expense	4 2 0 0 00	
Supplies Expense		
Telephone Expense	1 8 7 0 00	
Utilities Expense	8 4 0 0 00	
Insurance Expense		
Depreciation Expense—Building		
Depreciation Expense—Store Equipment		
Miscellaneous Expense	7 8 0 00	
	314 5 5 0 00	314 5 5 0 00

P 14-10B (LO1/2/3/4)

✓ Adj. col. total: $86,730;

Net loss: $53,630

COMPLETION OF A WORK SHEET SHOWING A NET LOSS The trial balance for Oregon Bike Company, a business owned by Craig Moody, is shown on page 556. Year-end adjustment information is provided below.

(a and b)   Merchandise inventory costing $26,000 is on hand as of December 31, 20--. (The periodic inventory system is used.)

(c) Supplies remaining at the end of the year, $2,500.

(d) Unexpired insurance on December 31, $1,820.

(continued)

(e) Depreciation expense on the building for 20--, $6,400.

(f) Depreciation expense on the store equipment for 20--, $2,800.

(g) Unearned rent revenue as of December 31, $2,350.

(h) Wages earned but not paid as of December 31, $1,100.

Oregon Bike Company
Trial Balance
December 31, 20 - -

ACCOUNT TITLE	DEBIT BALANCE	CREDIT BALANCE
Cash	27 0 0 0 00	
Accounts Receivable	12 0 0 0 00	
Merchandise Inventory	39 0 0 0 00	
Supplies	6 2 0 0 00	
Prepaid Insurance	5 8 0 0 00	
Land	32 0 0 0 00	
Building	58 0 0 0 00	
Accumulated Depreciation—Building		27 0 0 0 00
Store Equipment	31 0 0 0 00	
Accumulated Depreciation—Store Equipment		14 0 0 0 00
Accounts Payable		4 9 0 0 00
Wages Payable		
Sales Tax Payable		2 9 0 0 00
Unearned Rent Revenue		6 1 0 0 00
Mortgage Payable		49 0 0 0 00
C. Moody, Capital		169 5 0 0 00
C. Moody, Drawing	36 0 0 0 00	
Income Summary		
Sales		58 0 0 0 00
Sales Returns and Allowances	3 3 0 0 00	
Rent Revenue		
Purchases	19 0 0 0 00	
Purchases Returns and Allowances		9 0 0 00
Purchases Discounts		1 4 5 0 00
Freight-In	8 0 0 00	
Wages Expense	47 0 0 0 00	
Advertising Expense	6 2 0 0 00	
Supplies Expense		
Telephone Expense	1 8 6 0 00	
Utilities Expense	8 1 0 0 00	
Insurance Expense		
Depreciation Expense—Building		
Depreciation Expense—Store Equipment		
Miscellaneous Expense	4 9 0 00	
	333 7 5 0 00	333 7 5 0 00

REQUIRED

1. Complete the Adjustments columns, identifying each adjustment with its corresponding letter.

2. Complete the work sheet.

3. Enter the adjustments in a general journal.

P 14-11B (LO1/2/4)

✓ Adj. col. total: $88,805

WORKING BACKWARD FROM ADJUSTED TRIAL BALANCE TO DETERMINE ADJUSTING ENTRIES The partial work sheet shown below is taken from the books of Burnside Auto Parts, a business owned by Barbara Davis, for the year ended December 31, 20--.

Burnside Auto Parts
Work Sheet (Partial)
For Year Ended December 31, 20 - -

	ACCOUNT TITLE	TRIAL BALANCE DEBIT	TRIAL BALANCE CREDIT	ADJUSTMENTS DEBIT	ADJUSTMENTS CREDIT	ADJUSTED TRIAL BALANCE DEBIT	ADJUSTED TRIAL BALANCE CREDIT	
1	Cash	21 0 0 0 00				21 0 0 0 00		1
2	Accounts Receivable	8 3 0 0 00				8 3 0 0 00		2
3	Merchandise Inventory	32 0 0 0 00				36 0 0 0 00		3
4	Supplies	6 1 5 0 00				1 8 6 5 00		4
5	Prepaid Insurance	5 9 2 5 00				1 8 3 5 00		5
6	Land	41 7 5 0 00				41 7 5 0 00		6
7	Building	43 0 0 0 00				43 0 0 0 00		7
8	Accum. Depr.—Building		24 0 0 0 00				27 5 0 0 00	8
9	Store Equipment	25 4 0 0 00				25 4 0 0 00		9
10	Accum. Depr.—Store Equipment		12 4 0 0 00				14 7 5 0 00	10
11	Accounts Payable		8 1 0 0 00				8 1 0 0 00	11
12	Wages Payable						9 8 0 00	12
13	Sales Tax Payable		5 2 0 0 00				5 2 0 0 00	13
14	Unearned Rent-A-Junk Revenue		7 9 5 0 00				2 3 5 0 00	14
15	Mortgage Payable		26 0 0 0 00				26 0 0 0 00	15
16	B. Davis, Capital		109 1 3 0 00				109 1 3 0 00	16
17	B. Davis, Drawing	40 0 0 0 00				40 0 0 0 00		17
18	Income Summary			32 0 0 0 00	36 0 0 0 00			18
19	Sales		123 5 0 0 00				123 5 0 0 00	19
20	Sales Returns and Allowances	2 8 6 0 00				2 8 6 0 00		20
21	Rent-A-Junk Revenue						5 6 0 0 00	21
22	Purchases	32 5 2 5 00				32 5 2 5 00		22
23	Purchases Returns and Allowances		2 1 5 0 00				2 1 5 0 00	23
24	Purchases Discounts		2 4 0 0 00				2 4 0 0 00	24
25	Freight-In	3 1 7 5 00				3 1 7 5 00		25
26	Wages Expense	44 1 7 5 00				45 1 5 5 00		26
27	Advertising Expense	3 2 7 5 00				3 2 7 5 00		27
28	Supplies Expense					4 2 8 5 00		28
29	Telephone Expense	2 2 0 0 00				2 2 0 0 00		29
30	Utilities Expense	8 2 5 0 00				8 2 5 0 00		30
31	Insurance Expense					4 0 9 0 00		31
32	Depr. Expense—Building					3 5 0 0 00		32
33	Depr. Expense—Store Equipment					2 3 5 0 00		33
34	Miscellaneous Expense	8 4 5 00				8 4 5 00		34
35		320 8 3 0 00	320 8 3 0 00			363 6 6 0 00	363 6 6 0 00	35

REQUIRED

1. Determine the adjusting entries by analyzing the difference between the adjusted trial balance and the trial balance.

2. Journalize the adjusting entries in a general journal.

P 14-12B (LO1/2/3/4)

✓ Adj. col. total: $99,545;
Cost of goods sold: $31,975

WORKING BACKWARD FROM THE INCOME STATEMENT AND BALANCE SHEET COLUMNS OF THE WORK SHEET TO DETERMINE ADJUSTED TRIAL BALANCE AND ADJUSTING ENTRIES The partial work sheet shown on page 559 is taken from the books of Diamond Music Store, a business owned by Ned Diamond, for the year ended December 31, 20--.

REQUIRED

1. Analyze the work sheet and determine the adjusted trial balance and the adjusting entries by working backward from the Income Statement and Balance Sheet columns.

2. Journalize the adjusting entries in a general journal.

3. Prepare the cost of goods sold section of the income statement for Diamond Music Store.

 MANAGING YOUR WRITING

A friend of yours recently opened Abracadabra, a sportswear shop specializing in monogrammed athletic gear. Most merchandise is special ordered for customers. However, a small inventory is on hand. Your friend does not understand why a physical inventory is necessary before preparing the financial statements. She knows how much she paid for all merchandise purchased. Why not simply use this amount for cost of goods sold? After all, it has been paid for. Write a brief memo explaining the purpose of the physical inventory and why she should not use the cost of purchases as cost of goods sold.

PROBLEM 14-12B

Diamond Music Store
Work Sheet
For Year Ended December 31, 20- -

| | TRIAL BALANCE | | ADJUSTMENTS | | ADJUSTED TRIAL BALANCE | | INCOME STATEMENT | | BALANCE SHEET | |
ACCOUNT TITLE	DEBIT	CREDIT	DEBIT	CREDIT	DEBIT	CREDIT	DEBIT	CREDIT	DEBIT	CREDIT	
1 Cash	31 0 0 0 00								31 0 0 0 00		1
2 Accounts Receivable	11 9 8 0 00								11 9 8 0 00		2
3 Merchandise Inventory	33 6 0 0 00								39 1 0 0 00		3
4 Supplie	7 1 4 0 00								1 9 6 5 00		4
5 Prepaid Insurance	5 9 8 5 00								1 2 3 5 00		5
6 Land	36 2 0 0 00								36 2 0 0 00		6
7 Building	51 8 5 0 00								51 8 5 0 00		7
8 Accum. Depr.—Building		13 5 9 0 00								18 8 7 5 00	8
9 Store Equipment	32 6 7 5 00								32 6 7 5 00		9
10 Accum. Depr.—Store Equipment		10 2 9 0 00								14 7 5 5 00	10
11 Accounts Payable		5 8 9 5 00								5 8 9 5 00	11
12 Wages Payable										1 2 5 0 00	12
13 Sales Tax Payable		6 3 7 5 00								6 3 7 5 00	13
14 Unearned Rent Revenue		8 8 5 0 00								2 9 3 0 00	14
15 Mortgage Payable		42 4 0 0 00								42 4 0 0 00	15
16 N. Diamond, Capital		116 3 5 0 00								116 3 5 0 00	16
17 N. Diamond, Drawing	39 5 0 0 00								39 5 0 0 00		17
18 Income Summary							33 6 0 0 00	39 1 0 0 00			18
19 Sales		148 0 0 0 00						148 0 0 0 00			19
20 Sales Returns and Allowances	2 8 0 0 00						2 8 0 0 00				20
21 Rent Revenue								5 9 2 0 00			21
22 Purchases	40 7 0 0 00						40 7 0 0 00				22
23 Purchases Returns and Allowances		2 7 7 5 00						2 7 7 5 00			23
24 Purchases Discounts		2 3 2 5 00						2 3 2 5 00			24
25 Freight-I	1 8 7 5 00						1 8 7 5 00				25
26 Wages Expense	47 0 0 0 00						48 2 5 0 00				26
27 Advertising Expense	4 6 9 5 00						4 6 9 5 00				27
28 Supplies Expense							5 1 7 5 00				28
29 Telephone Expense	2 2 5 0 00						2 2 5 0 00				29
30 Utilities Expense	6 8 2 5 00						6 8 2 5 00				30
31 Insurance Expense							4 7 5 0 00				31
32 Depr. Expense—Building							5 2 8 5 00				32
33 Depr. Expense—Store Equipment							4 4 6 5 00				33
34 Miscellaneous Expense	7 7 5 00						7 7 5 00				34
35	356 8 5 0 00	356 8 5 0 00					161 4 4 5 00	198 1 2 0 00	245 5 0 5 00	208 8 3 0 00	35
36 Net Income							36 6 7 5 00			36 6 7 5 00	36
37							198 1 2 0 00	198 1 2 0 00	245 5 0 5 00	245 5 0 5 00	37

ETHICS CASE

Jason Tierro, an inventory clerk at Lexmar Company, is responsible for taking a physical count of the goods on hand at the end of the year. He has been performing this duty for several years. This year, Jason was very busy due to a shortage of personnel at the company, so he decided to just estimate the amount of ending inventory instead of doing an accurate count. He reasoned that he could come very close to the true amount because of his past experience working with inventory. Besides, he was sure that the sophisticated computer program that Lexmar had just invested in kept an accurate record of inventory on hand.

1. What is your opinion of Jason's reasoning?

2. If Jason underestimates the dollar amount of ending inventory, what effect will it have on net income for the current accounting period?

3. Write a short paragraph explaining why a physical inventory should be taken at least once a year.

4. In groups of three or four, make a list of possible reasons that the actual ending inventory might not agree with the ending inventory according to a computer system.

MASTERY PROBLEM

✓ Adj. T.B. col. total: $695,325;
Net income: $37,125

John Neff owns and operates Waikiki Surf Shop. A year-end trial balance is provided on page 561. Year-end adjustment data for the Waikiki Surf Shop are shown below.

(a and b) A physical count shows merchandise inventory costing $45,000 on hand as of December 31, 20--. Neff uses the periodic inventory system.
(c) Supplies remaining at the end of the year, $600.
(d) Unexpired insurance on December 31, $900.
(e) Depreciation expense on the building for 20--, $6,000.
(f) Depreciation expense on the store equipment for 20--, $4,500.
(g) Wages earned but not paid as of December 31, $675.
(h) Unearned boat rental revenue as of December 31, $3,000.

REQUIRED

1. Prepare a year-end work sheet.

2. Journalize the adjusting entries.

Waikiki Surf Shop Trial Balance December 31, 20 --										
ACCOUNT TITLE	DEBIT BALANCE					CREDIT BALANCE				
Cash	30	0	0	0	00					
Accounts Receivable	22	5	0	0	00					
Merchandise Inventory	57	0	0	0	00					
Supplies	2	7	0	0	00					
Prepaid Insurance	3	6	0	0	00					
Land	15	0	0	0	00					
Building	135	0	0	0	00					
Accumulated Depreciation—Building						24	0	0	0	00
Store Equipment	75	0	0	0	00					
Accumulated Depreciation—Store Equipment						22	5	0	0	00
Notes Payable						7	5	0	0	00
Accounts Payable						15	0	0	0	00
Wages Payable										
Unearned Boat Rental Revenue						33	0	0	0	00
J. Neff, Capital						233	7	0	0	00
J. Neff, Drawing	30	0	0	0	00					
Income Summary										
Sales						300	7	5	0	00
Sales Returns and Allowances	1	8	0	0	00					
Boat Rental Revenue										
Purchases	157	5	0	0	00					
Purchases Returns and Allowances						1	2	0	0	00
Purchases Discounts						1	5	0	0	00
Freight-In		4	5	0	00					
Wages Expense	63	0	0	0	00					
Advertising Expense	11	2	5	0	00					
Supplies Expense										
Telephone Expense	5	2	5	0	00					
Utilities Expense	18	0	0	0	00					
Insurance Expense										
Depreciation Expense—Building										
Depreciation Expense—Store Equipment										
Miscellaneous Expense	10	8	7	5	00					
Interest Expense		2	2	5	00					
	639	1	5	0	00	639	1	5	0	00

CHALLENGE PROBLEM

This problem challenges you to apply your cumulative accounting knowledge to move a step beyond the material in the chapter.

✓ **Net purchases in 20-1: $410,000**

Block Food's, a retail grocery store, has agreed to purchase all of its merchandise from Square Wholesalers. In return, Block receives a special discount on purchases. Over recent months, Square noticed that purchases by Block had been falling off. At first, Square simply thought that business might be down for Block and was hopeful that their purchases would pick up. When business with Block did not return to a normal level, Square requested financial statements from Block. Square's records indicate that Block purchased $300,000 worth of merchandise during 20-1, the most recent year.

(continued)

Selected information taken from Block's financial statements is as follows:

Balance Sheet	12/31/-1	12/31/-0
Inventory	$30,000	$20,000

Income Statement

Cost of goods sold	$400,000	

REQUIRED

Compute net purchases made by Block during 20-1. Does it appear that Block violated the agreement?

ANSWERS TO SELF-STUDY QUESTIONS AND EXERCISES

True/False Questions

1. T **2.** T **3.** T **4.** F (revenue is recognized) **5.** F (contra-revenue account)

Multiple Choice Questions

1. b **2.** a **3.** b **4.** b **5.** b

U REVU   Exercises

1.

Beginning merchandise inventory	$ 20,000
Purchases	171,000
Goods available for sale	$191,000
Less ending inventory	15,000
Cost of goods sold	$176,000

2.

Unearned Ticket Revenue	15,000	
Ticket Revenue		15,000

3.

	ACCOUNT TITLE	TRIAL BALANCE		ADJUSTMENTS		ADJUSTED TRIAL BALANCE		INCOME STATEMENT		BALANCE SHEET		
		DEBIT	CREDIT	DEBIT	CREDIT	DEBIT	CREDIT	DEBIT	CREDIT	DEBIT	CREDIT	
1	Merchandise Inventory	120 000 00		(b) 90 000 00	(a)120 000 00					90 000 00		1
2	Income Summary			(a)120 000 00	(b) 90 000 00			120 000 00	90 000 00			2
3	Purchases	250 000 00				250 000 00		250 000 00				3

4.

10		Income Summary	50 0 0 0 00			10
11		Merchandise Inventory		50 0 0 0 00		11
12		Merchandise Inventory	60 0 0 0 00			12
13		Income Summary		60 0 0 0 00		13

5.

8		Inventory Short and Over	2 0 0 0 00			8
9		Merchandise Inventory		2 0 0 0 00		9
10						10

Chapter 14 Appendix

Expense Method of Accounting for Prepaid Expenses

LEARNING OBJECTIVES

THE EXPENSE METHOD

LO1 Use the expense method of accounting for prepaid expenses.

Under the **expense method** of accounting for prepaid expenses, supplies and other prepaid items are entered as expenses when purchased. Under this method, we must adjust the accounts at the end of each accounting period to record the unused portions as assets. To illustrate, let's assume that the following entry was made when office supplies were purchased:

Careful study of this appendix should enable you to:

LO1 Use the expense method of accounting for prepaid expenses.

LO2 Make the appropriate adjusting entries when the expense method is used for prepaid expenses.

4		Office Supplies Expense		4 2 5 00		4
5		Cash			4 2 5 00	5
6		Purchased office supplies				6

In the next section, we will illustrate the proper adjusting entry when using the expense method.

ADJUSTING ENTRIES UNDER THE EXPENSE METHOD

LO2 Make the appropriate adjusting entries when the expense method is used for prepaid expenses.

Office Supplies Expense was debited for a total of $425 during the period. An inventory taken at the end of the period shows that supplies on hand amounted to $150. The following adjusting entry is made for supplies on hand:

8		Office Supplies		1 5 0 00		8
9		Office Supplies Expense			1 5 0 00	9
10						10

As shown in the T accounts below, after this entry is posted, the office supplies expense account has a debit balance of $275. This amount is reported on the income statement as an operating expense. The office supplies account has a debit balance of $150. It is reported on the balance sheet as a current asset.

Office Supplies		Office Supplies Expense	
Adj. 150		425	Adj. 150
		Bal. 275	

Let's consider another example of the use of the expense method. The following entry was made for the payment of $6,000 for a three-year insurance policy:

11		Insurance Expense		6 0 0 0 00		11
12		Cash			6 0 0 0 00	12
13		Paid insurance premium				13

At the end of the first year, one-third of the premium has expired and two-thirds remains. Thus, $2,000 for insurance expense should be reported on the income statement and $4,000 in prepaid insurance should be reported on the balance sheet. The following adjusting entry is made:

15		Prepaid Insurance		4 0 0 0 00		15
16		Insurance Expense			4 0 0 0 00	16
17						17

As shown in the T accounts below, after this entry is posted, the prepaid insurance account has a debit balance of $4,000. The insurance expense account has a debit balance of $2,000.

Prepaid Insurance			Insurance Expense		
Adj. 4,000			6,000	Adj. 4,000	
			Bal. 2,000		

The asset and expense methods of accounting for prepaid expenses give the same final result. In the **asset method**, the prepaid item is first debited to an asset account. At the end of each period, the amount consumed is debited to an expense account. In the expense method, the original amount is debited to an expense account. At the end of each accounting period, the portion not consumed is debited to an asset account.

LEARNING OBJECTIVES   Key Points to Remember

LO1 Use the expense method of accounting for prepaid expenses.	Under the expense method, an expense account is debited when prepaid items are acquired.
LO2 Make the appropriate adjusting entries when the expense method is used for prepaid expenses.	At the end of the accounting period, an asset must be recognized for the amount of the prepaid item remaining. The expense account must be credited so that the ending balance represents the amount of the item consumed.

KEY TERMS

asset method (564)   Under this method, the acquisition of a prepaid item is debited to an asset account.

expense method (563)   Under this method, the acquisition of a prepaid item is debited to an expense account.

SERIES A EXERCISE

E 14Apx-1A (LO1/2)

EXPENSE METHOD OF ACCOUNTING FOR PREPAID EXPENSES Davidson's Food Mart paid $1,200 in advance to the local newspaper for advertisements that will appear monthly. The following entry was made:

4		Advertising Expense		1 2 0 0 00			4
5		Cash			1 2 0 0 00		5
6		Paid prepaid advertising					6

At the end of the year, December 31, 20--, Davidson received notification that advertisements costing $800 had been run. Prepare the adjusting entry.

SERIES B EXERCISE

E 14Apx-1B (LO1/2)

EXPENSE METHOD OF ACCOUNTING FOR PREPAID EXPENSES Ryan's Fish House purchased supplies costing $3,000 for cash. This amount was debited to the supplies expense account. At the end of the year, December 31, 20--, an inventory showed that supplies costing $500 remained. Prepare the adjusting entry.

Chapter 15

woot!
Hi, are you new? Start here.   Log in   **today's woot**   blog   community   write us   what is woot?

Jawbone 2 Bluetooth Headset
$44.99 + $5 shipping
CONDITION: New, O.E.M.
PRODUCT: 1 Jawbone 2 Bluetooth Headset

DISCUSSION ON TODAY'S WOOT

djsegfault has some dislikes.

biggbill thinks beards are okay.

guitargoddsjm says, "The Jawbone 2 doesn't have multi-point pairing (a feature that a few recent motorola headsets have)."

casavista used some pliers to go upside down.

sdalinct ponders phone pairings.

theredlines thinks it's the only way to go.

j021294 inquires, "Will these work if you have a thick beard and sideburns or will all the hair block it from working correctly?" Bearded lady discrimination ensues.

Join This Discussion   207 comments

A POETIC EAR

And now, the Jawbone 2 Bluetooth Headset presents selected excerpts from the Bluetooth Anthology of 20th Century American Poetry.

The Blue Toothheadset
Carlos William Carlos

so much depends
upon

a blue toothhead
set

made from smooth

MAGGIANO'S
• LITTLE ITALY •

JOIN US FOR A
MEAL TONIGHT.
⊷⊶
TAKE A DIFFERENT
ONE HOME FOR
TOMORROW.

*Available at dinner,
through June 24th only.*

Click for reservations.

ADVERTISEMENT

YOUR DAILY WOOTCAST
▶   The Shanty of Bluetooth

$699 -- Ireland: 6 Nights at a Ritz-Carlton including Car & Air at Travelzoo

Discuss This Side Deal   4 comments

shirt.woot!   **wine.woot!**

Dark Secret   Caravel Gourmet Sea Salt Grinder Three - Pack

NEW IPHONE OS: 3.0 BAD APPLES SPOIL THE WHOLE PHONE
Landscape keyboard! Cut & paste! More new APIs than you can shake a developer

LEARNING OBJECTIVES

Careful study of this chapter should enable you to:

LO1 Prepare a single-step and multiple-step income statement for a merchandising business.

LO2 Prepare a statement of owner's equity.

LO3 Prepare a classified balance sheet.

LO4 Compute standard financial ratios.

LO5 Prepare closing entries for a merchandising business.

LO6 Prepare reversing entries.

Financial Statements and Year-End Accounting for a Merchandising Business

"Woot" was originally a truncated expression commonly used by players of Dungeons and Dragons for "Wow, loot!" "Woot, Inc.," is an online store, founded in 2003, that focuses on "selling cool stuff cheap." The company is known for its honest item descriptions and limited customer service. For example, the Web site explains that the company doesn't take calls because its 100 employees are busy finding new products and shipping orders. Further, don't try to return something until all other options have been exhausted. If you want cheap prices, don't expect great service. This candor is refreshing, but we suspect they will help you out if you need it. The company claims profitability is anticipated by 2043. "By then we should be retired; someone smarter might take over and jack up the prices." Clever, but with revenues increasing from $2.3 million to $117.4 million over a recent three-year period, we suspect the company is doing just fine. Probably the most unique characteristic of this merchandiser is that it sells only one product each day. It is available from 12:00 A.M. until sold out, or 11:59 P.M., when a different product is posted. Missed a cool product? Too bad. You can't buy yesterday's item.

Though clearly unique, this business must perform year-end accounting in the same manner as other retailers. In this chapter, you will learn how Woot and other merchandising firms prepare financial statements, compute financial ratios to evaluate performance, and prepare closing and reversing entries. No matter how unique, businesses must follow similar accounting procedures so that profitability and financial health can be compared across years and with other companies.

The first six chapters of this text illustrated the accounting cycle for a service business. In this chapter, we complete the accounting cycle for a merchandising business.

In Chapter 14, we prepared the year-end work sheet and adjusting entries for Northern Micro. In this chapter, we will prepare financial statements, look briefly at financial statement analysis, and demonstrate closing and reversing entries.

THE INCOME STATEMENT

LO1 Prepare a single-step and multiple-step income statement for a merchandising business.

As you know, a primary purpose of the work sheet is to serve as an aid in preparing the financial statements. Figure 15-1 shows the completed work sheet for Northern Micro. We will use it to prepare financial statements.

The purpose of an income statement is to summarize the results of operations during an accounting period. The income statement shows the sources of revenue, types of expenses, and the amount of the net income or net loss for the period. Two forms of the income statement commonly used are the single step and the multiple step. The **single-step income statement** lists all revenue items and their total first, followed by all expense items and their total. The difference, which is either net income or net loss, is then calculated. A single-step income statement for Northern Micro is illustrated in Figure 15-2.

The use of the work sheet to prepare a **multiple-step income statement** is illustrated in Figure 15-3. This type of income statement is commonly used for merchandising businesses. The term "multiple-step" is used because the final net income is calculated on a step-by-step basis. Gross sales is shown first, less sales returns and allowances and sales discounts. This difference is called **net sales**. (Many published income statements begin with the amount of net sales.) Cost of goods sold is subtracted next to arrive at **gross profit** (sometimes called **gross margin**).

Operating expenses are then listed and subtracted from the gross profit to compute **income from operations** (sometimes called **operating income**). Operating expenses are directly associated with providing the primary goods and services of the business. Some companies divide operating expenses into the following subcategories.

Selling expenses. These expenses are directly associated with selling activities. Examples include:

- Sales Salaries Expense
- Sales Commissions Expense
- Advertising Expense
- Bank Credit Card Expense
- Delivery Expense
- Depreciation Expense—Store Equipment and Fixtures

FIGURE 15-1 Northern Micro Work Sheet

Northern Micro
Work Sheet
For Year Ended December 31, 20 - -

ACCOUNT TITLE	TRIAL BALANCE DEBIT	TRIAL BALANCE CREDIT	ADJUSTMENTS DEBIT	ADJUSTMENTS CREDIT	ADJUSTED TRIAL BALANCE DEBIT	ADJUSTED TRIAL BALANCE CREDIT	INCOME STATEMENT DEBIT	INCOME STATEMENT CREDIT	BALANCE SHEET DEBIT	BALANCE SHEET CREDIT	
1 Cash	20 0 0 0 00				20 0 0 0 00				20 0 0 0 00		1
2 Accounts Receivable	15 0 0 0 00				15 0 0 0 00				15 0 0 0 00		2
3 Merchandise Inventory	26 0 0 0 00		(b) 18 0 0 0 00	(a) 26 0 0 0 00	18 0 0 0 00				18 0 0 0 00		3
4 Supplies	1 8 0 0 0 00			(c) 1 4 0 0 00	4 0 0 0 00				4 0 0 0 00		4
5 Prepaid Insurance	2 4 0 0 0 00			(d) 1 8 0 0 00	6 0 0 0 00				6 0 0 0 00		5
6 Land	10 0 0 0 00				10 0 0 0 00				10 0 0 0 00		6
7 Building	90 0 0 0 00				90 0 0 0 00				90 0 0 0 00		7
8 Accum. Depr.—Building		16 0 0 0 00		(e) 4 0 0 0 00		20 0 0 0 00				20 0 0 0 00	8
9 Store Equipment	50 0 0 0 00				50 0 0 0 00				50 0 0 0 00		9
10 Accum. Depr.—Store Equipment		15 0 0 0 00		(f) 3 0 0 0 00		18 0 0 0 00				18 0 0 0 00	10
11 Notes Payable		5 0 0 0 00				5 0 0 0 00				5 0 0 0 00	11
12 Accounts Payable		10 0 0 0 00				10 0 0 0 00				10 0 0 0 00	12
13 Wages Payable				(g) 4 5 0 00		4 5 0 00				4 5 0 00	13
14 Sales Tax Payable		1 5 0 0 00				1 5 0 0 00				1 5 0 0 00	14
15 Unearned Subscriptions Revenue		12 0 0 0 00	(h) 10 0 0 0 00			2 0 0 0 00				2 0 0 0 00	15
16 Mortgage Payable		30 0 0 0 00				30 0 0 0 00				30 0 0 0 00	16
17 Gary L. Fishel, Capital		114 4 0 0 00				114 4 0 0 00				114 4 0 0 00	17
18 Gary L. Fishel, Drawing	20 0 0 0 00				20 0 0 0 00				20 0 0 0 00		18
19 Income Summary			(a) 26 0 0 0 00	(b) 18 0 0 0 00	26 0 0 0 00	18 0 0 0 00	26 0 0 0 00	18 0 0 0 00			19
20 Sales		214 0 0 0 00				214 0 0 0 00		214 0 0 0 00			20
21 Sales Returns and Allowances	1 2 0 0 00				1 2 0 0 00		1 2 0 0 00				21
22 Interest Revenue		9 0 0 0 00				9 0 0 0 00		9 0 0 0 00			22
23 Rent Revenue		8 0 0 0 00				8 0 0 0 00		8 0 0 0 00			23
24 Subscriptions Revenue				(h) 10 0 0 0 00		10 0 0 0 00		10 0 0 0 00			24
25 Purchases	105 0 0 0 00				105 0 0 0 00		105 0 0 0 00				25
26 Purchases Returns and Allowances		8 0 0 0 00				8 0 0 0 00		8 0 0 0 00			26
27 Purchases Discounts		1 0 0 0 00				1 0 0 0 00		1 0 0 0 00			27
28 Freight-In	3 0 0 0 00				3 0 0 0 00		3 0 0 0 00				28
29 Wages Expense	42 0 0 0 00		(g) 4 5 0 00		42 4 5 0 00		42 4 5 0 00				29
30 Advertising Expense	2 5 0 0 00				2 5 0 0 00		2 5 0 0 00				30
31 Bank Credit Card Expense	1 5 0 0 00				1 5 0 0 00		1 5 0 0 00				31
32 Rent Expense	20 0 0 0 00				20 0 0 0 00		20 0 0 0 00				32
33 Supplies Expense			(c) 1 4 0 0 00		1 4 0 0 00		1 4 0 0 00				33
34 Telephone Expense	3 5 0 0 00				3 5 0 0 00		3 5 0 0 00				34
35 Utilities Expense	12 0 0 0 00				12 0 0 0 00		12 0 0 0 00				35
36 Insurance Expense			(d) 1 8 0 0 00		1 8 0 0 00		1 8 0 0 00				36
37 Depr. Expense—Building			(e) 4 0 0 0 00		4 0 0 0 00		4 0 0 0 00				37
38 Depr. Expense—Store Equipment			(f) 3 0 0 0 00		3 0 0 0 00		3 0 0 0 00				38
39 Miscellaneous Expense	2 2 5 0 00				2 2 5 0 00		2 2 5 0 00				39
40 Interest Expense	3 1 5 0 00				3 1 5 0 00		3 1 5 0 00				40
41	428 6 0 0 00	428 6 0 0 00	64 6 5 0 00	64 6 5 0 00	454 0 5 0 00	454 0 5 0 00	230 0 5 0 00	252 7 0 0 00	224 0 0 0 00	201 3 5 0 00	41
42 Net Income							22 6 5 0 00			22 6 5 0 00	42
43							252 7 0 0 00	252 7 0 0 00	224 0 0 0 00	224 0 0 0 00	43

FIGURE 15-2 Single-Step Income Statement

<table>
<tr><td colspan="11">Northern Micro
Income Statement
For Year Ended December 31, 20 - -</td></tr>
<tr><td>Revenues:</td><td></td><td></td><td></td><td></td><td></td><td></td><td></td><td></td><td></td><td></td></tr>
<tr><td>Net sales</td><td>$212</td><td>8</td><td>0</td><td>0</td><td>00</td><td></td><td></td><td></td><td></td><td></td></tr>
<tr><td>Interest revenue</td><td></td><td>9</td><td>0</td><td>0</td><td>00</td><td></td><td></td><td></td><td></td><td></td></tr>
<tr><td>Rent revenue</td><td>8</td><td>0</td><td>0</td><td>0</td><td>00</td><td></td><td></td><td></td><td></td><td></td></tr>
<tr><td>Subscriptions revenue</td><td>10</td><td>0</td><td>0</td><td>0</td><td>00</td><td></td><td></td><td></td><td></td><td></td></tr>
<tr><td>   Total revenues</td><td></td><td></td><td></td><td></td><td></td><td>$231</td><td>7</td><td>0</td><td>0</td><td>00</td></tr>
<tr><td>Expenses:</td><td></td><td></td><td></td><td></td><td></td><td></td><td></td><td></td><td></td><td></td></tr>
<tr><td>Cost of goods sold</td><td>$111</td><td>5</td><td>0</td><td>0</td><td>00</td><td></td><td></td><td></td><td></td><td></td></tr>
<tr><td>Wages expense</td><td>42</td><td>4</td><td>5</td><td>0</td><td>00</td><td></td><td></td><td></td><td></td><td></td></tr>
<tr><td>Advertising expense</td><td>2</td><td>5</td><td>0</td><td>0</td><td>00</td><td></td><td></td><td></td><td></td><td></td></tr>
<tr><td>Bank credit card expense</td><td>1</td><td>5</td><td>0</td><td>0</td><td>00</td><td></td><td></td><td></td><td></td><td></td></tr>
<tr><td>Rent expense</td><td>20</td><td>0</td><td>0</td><td>0</td><td>00</td><td></td><td></td><td></td><td></td><td></td></tr>
<tr><td>Supplies expense</td><td>1</td><td>4</td><td>0</td><td>0</td><td>00</td><td></td><td></td><td></td><td></td><td></td></tr>
<tr><td>Telephone expense</td><td>3</td><td>5</td><td>0</td><td>0</td><td>00</td><td></td><td></td><td></td><td></td><td></td></tr>
<tr><td>Utilities expense</td><td>12</td><td>0</td><td>0</td><td>0</td><td>00</td><td></td><td></td><td></td><td></td><td></td></tr>
<tr><td>Insurance expense</td><td>1</td><td>8</td><td>0</td><td>0</td><td>00</td><td></td><td></td><td></td><td></td><td></td></tr>
<tr><td>Depreciation expense—building</td><td>4</td><td>0</td><td>0</td><td>0</td><td>00</td><td></td><td></td><td></td><td></td><td></td></tr>
<tr><td>Depreciation expense—store equipment</td><td>3</td><td>0</td><td>0</td><td>0</td><td>00</td><td></td><td></td><td></td><td></td><td></td></tr>
<tr><td>Miscellaneous expense</td><td>2</td><td>2</td><td>5</td><td>0</td><td>00</td><td></td><td></td><td></td><td></td><td></td></tr>
<tr><td>Interest expense</td><td>3</td><td>1</td><td>5</td><td>0</td><td>00</td><td></td><td></td><td></td><td></td><td></td></tr>
<tr><td>   Total expenses</td><td></td><td></td><td></td><td></td><td></td><td>209</td><td>0</td><td>5</td><td>0</td><td>00</td></tr>
<tr><td>Net income</td><td></td><td></td><td></td><td></td><td></td><td>$ 22</td><td>6</td><td>5</td><td>0</td><td>00</td></tr>
</table>

LEARNING KEY

Although the formats for the single-step and multiple-step income statements are different, the reported net income is the same.

By showing other revenues and other expenses separately, it is possible to show income from operations. This makes it easier for the reader to see how the business is doing in its main activity.

General expenses. These expenses are associated with administrative, office, or general operating activities. Examples include:

- Rent Expense
- Office Salaries Expense
- Office Supplies Expense
- Telephone Expense
- Utilities Expense
- Insurance Expense
- Depreciation Expense—Office Equipment

Finally, other revenues are added and other expenses are subtracted to arrive at net income (or net loss). Note that the operating expenses are arranged according to the order given in the chart of accounts. They could also be listed by descending amount, with Miscellaneous Expense last.

FIGURE 15-3 Using a Work Sheet to Prepare a Multiple-Step Income Statement

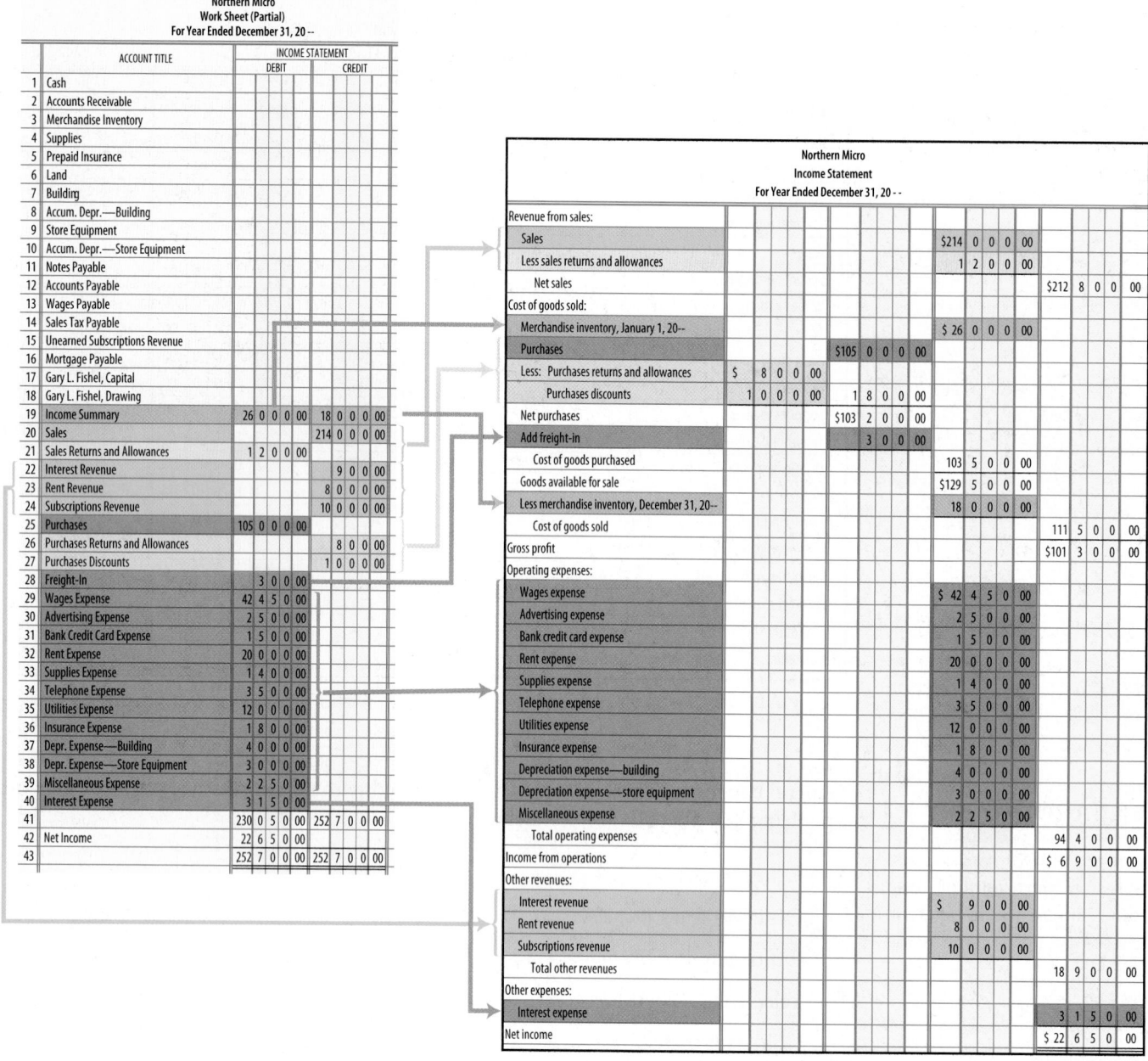

U REVU

Complete U REVU-1 on **page 592** to test your basic understanding of LO1.

THE STATEMENT OF OWNER'S EQUITY

LO2 Prepare a statement of owner's equity.

The statement of owner's equity summarizes all changes in the owner's equity during the period. It includes the net income or loss and any additional investments or withdrawals by the owner. These changes result in the end-of-period balance shown on this statement and the balance sheet.

To prepare the statement of owner's equity for Northern Micro, two sources of information are needed: (1) the work sheet, and (2) Gary Fishel's capital account (no. 311) in the general ledger. The work sheet (Figure 15-1) shows net income of $22,650 and withdrawals of $20,000 during the year. Fishel's capital account (Figure 15-4) shows a beginning balance of $104,400. An additional $10,000 was invested in the business in February of the current year. The statement of owner's equity for Northern Micro for the year ended December 31, 20--, is shown in Figure 15-5.

FIGURE 15-4 Capital Account for Gary L. Fishel

ACCOUNT: Gary L. Fishel, Capital										ACCOUNT NO. 311					
DATE		ITEM	POST. REF.	DEBIT				CREDIT			BALANCE				
											DEBIT		CREDIT		
20-- Jan.	1	Balance	✓										104 4 0 0 00		
Feb.	12		CR7					10 0 0 0 00					114 4 0 0 00		

FIGURE 15-5 Statement of Owner's Equity

The statement of owner's equity is the same for service and merchandising businesses.

Northern Micro Statement of Owner's Equity For Year Ended December 31, 20 - -								
Gary L. Fishel, capital, January 1, 20 --						$104	4 0 0	00
Add additional investments						10	0 0 0	00
Total investment						$114	4 0 0	00
Net income for the year	$22	6 5 0	00					
Less withdrawals for the year	20	0 0 0	00					
Increase in capital						2	6 5 0	00
Gary L. Fishel, capital, December 31, 20 - -						$117	0 5 0	00

U REVU

Complete U REVU-2 on **page 592** to test your basic understanding of LO2.

BALANCE SHEET

LO3 Prepare a classified balance sheet.

The use of the work sheet to prepare a report form classified balance sheet is illustrated in Figure 15-6. The balance sheet classifications used by Northern Micro are explained below.

CURRENT ASSETS

Current assets include cash and all other assets expected to be converted into cash or consumed within one year or the normal operating cycle of the business, whichever is longer. The **operating cycle** is the length of time generally required for a business to buy inventory, sell it, and collect the cash. This time period is generally less than a year. Thus, most firms use one year for classifying current assets. In a merchandising business, the current assets usually include cash, receivables (such as accounts receivable and notes receivable), and merchandise inventory. Since prepaid expenses, such as unused supplies and unexpired insurance, are likely to be consumed within a year, they also are reported as current assets.

LEARNING KEY

Note the use of the ending balance for merchandise inventory. It is reported on the income statement as part of the calculation of cost of goods sold. It also is reported on the balance sheet as a current asset.

FIGURE 15-6 Using a Work Sheet to Prepare a Report Form Classified Balance Sheet

Northern Micro
Work Sheet (Partial)
For Year Ended December 31, 20 --

	ACCOUNT TITLE	BALANCE SHEET DEBIT	BALANCE SHEET CREDIT
1	Cash	20 0 0 0 00	
2	Accounts Receivable	15 0 0 0 00	
3	Merchandise Inventory	18 0 0 0 00	
4	Supplies	4 0 0 00	
5	Prepaid Insurance	6 0 0 00	
6	Land	10 0 0 0 00	
7	Building	90 0 0 0 00	
8	Accum. Depr.—Building		20 0 0 0 00
9	Store Equipment	50 0 0 0 00	
10	Accum. Depr.—Store Equipment		18 0 0 0 00
11	Notes Payable		5 0 0 0 00
12	Accounts Payable		10 0 0 0 00
13	Wages Payable		4 5 0 00
14	Sales Tax Payable		1 5 0 0 00
15	Unearned Subscriptions Revenue		2 0 0 0 00
16	Mortgage Payable		30 0 0 0 00
17	Gary L. Fishel, Capital		114 4 0 0 00
18	Gary L. Fishel, Drawing	20 0 0 0 00	
19	Income Summary		
20	Sales		
21	Sales Returns and Allowances		
22	Interest Revenue		
23	Rent Revenue		
24	Subscriptions Revenue		
25	Purchases		
26	Purchases Returns and Allowances		
27	Purchases Discounts		
28	Freight-In		
29	Wages Expense		
30	Advertising Expense		
31	Bank Credit Card Expense		
32	Rent Expense		
33	Supplies Expense		
34	Telephone Expense		
35	Utilities Expense		
36	Insurance Expense		
37	Depr. Expense—Building		
38	Depr. Expense—Store Equipment		
39	Miscellaneous Expense		
40	Interest Expense		
41		224 0 0 0 00	201 3 5 0 00
42	Net Income		22 6 5 0 00
43		224 0 0 0 00	224 0 0 0 00

Northern Micro
Balance Sheet
December 31, 20 --

Assets				
Current assets:				
Cash			$20 0 0 0 00	
Accounts receivable			15 0 0 0 00	
Merchandise inventory			18 0 0 0 00	
Supplies			4 0 0 00	
Prepaid insurance			6 0 0 00	
Total current assets				$ 54 0 0 0 00
Property, plant, and equipment:				
Land			$10 0 0 0 00	
Building	$90 0 0 0 00			
Less accum. depr.—building	20 0 0 0 00	70 0 0 0 00		
Store equipment	$50 0 0 0 00			
Less accum. depr.—store equip.	18 0 0 0 00	32 0 0 0 00		
Total property, plant, and equipment				112 0 0 0 00
Total assets				$166 0 0 0 00
Liabilities				
Current liabilities:				
Notes payable	$ 5 0 0 0 00			
Accounts payable	10 0 0 0 00			
Wages payable	4 5 0 00			
Sales tax payable	1 5 0 0 00			
Unearned subscriptions revenue	2 0 0 0 00			
Mortgage payable (current portion)	5 0 0 00			
Total current liabilities		$19 4 5 0 00		
Long-term liabilities:				
Mortgage payable	$30 0 0 0 00			
Less current portion	5 0 0 00	29 5 0 0 00		
Total liabilities				$ 48 9 5 0 00
Owner's Equity				
Gary L. Fishel, capital				117 0 5 0 00*
Total liabilities and owner's equity				$166 0 0 0 00

*From statement of owner's equity.

Current assets are listed on the balance sheet from the most liquid to least liquid. **Liquidity** refers to the speed with which the company can convert the asset to cash. Cash is the most liquid asset and is always listed first. Notes Receivable, Accounts Receivable, and Merchandise Inventory often follow it on the balance sheet.

PROPERTY, PLANT, AND EQUIPMENT

Assets that are expected to be used for more than one year in the operation of a business are called **property, plant, and equipment**. Examples include land, buildings, office equipment, store equipment, and delivery equipment. Of these assets, only land is permanent; however, all of these assets have useful lives that are comparatively long. Typically, assets with longer useful lives are listed first.

The balance sheet of Northern Micro shows Land, Building, and Store Equipment. Land is not depreciated. Accumulated depreciation amounts are shown as deductions from the costs of the building and store equipment. The difference represents the **unde-preciated cost**, or **book value**, of the assets. This amount less any salvage value will be written off as depreciation expense in future periods.

CURRENT LIABILITIES

Current liabilities include those obligations that are due within one year or the normal operating cycle of the business, whichever is longer, and will require the use of current assets. As of December 31, the current liabilities of Northern Micro consist of Notes Payable, Accounts Payable, Wages Payable, Sales Tax Payable, Unearned Subscriptions Revenue, and the portion of Mortgage Payable that is due within the next year.

LONG-TERM LIABILITIES

Long-term liabilities include those obligations that will extend beyond one year or the normal operating cycle, whichever is longer. A common long-term liability is a mortgage payable.

A **mortgage** is a written agreement specifying that if the borrower does not repay a debt, the lender has the right to take over specific property to satisfy the debt. When the debt is paid, the mortgage becomes void. **Mortgage Payable** is an account that is used to reflect an obligation that is secured by a mortgage on certain property.

OWNER'S EQUITY

The permanent owner's equity accounts reported on the balance sheet are determined by the type of organization. The accounts for a sole proprietorship, a partnership, and a corporation differ. Northern Micro is a sole proprietorship and reports one owner's equity account, Gary L. Fishel, Capital. The balance of this account is taken from the statement of owner's equity. Partnerships are illustrated in Chapter 19 and corporations are discussed in Chapters 20 and 21.

> The current portion of long-term debt, the amount due within one year, is reported as a current liability. The remainder is reported under long-term liabilities.

U REVU ▷

Complete U REVU-3 on **page 592** to test your basic understanding of LO3.

FINANCIAL STATEMENT ANALYSIS

LO4 Compute standard financial ratios.

Both management and creditors are interested in using the financial statements to evaluate the financial condition and profitability of the firm. This can be done by making a few simple calculations.

BALANCE SHEET ANALYSIS

Recall the following:

1. Current assets include cash, items that will be converted to cash, and items that will be consumed within one year.

2. Current liabilities are obligations that will require the use of current assets.

Thus, the difference between current assets and current liabilities represents the amount of capital the business has available for current operations. This is called **working capital**.

Working Capital = Current Assets − Current Liabilities

The balance sheet in Figure 15-6 shows that Northern Micro has current assets of $54,000 and current liabilities of $19,450. Thus, the working capital at year end is $34,550 ($54,000 − $19,450). This amount should be more than adequate to satisfy current operating requirements.

Two measures of the firm's ability to pay its current liabilities are the **current ratio** and **quick ratio**. The formulas for calculating these ratios are as follows:

Northern Micro's current ratio of 2.8 to 1 is quite high, which indicates a favorable financial position. The traditional "rule of thumb" has been that a current ratio should be about 2 to 1, but many businesses operate successfully on a current ratio of 1.5 to 1. Although a rule of thumb is helpful, it is better to compare an individual company to industry averages, which are available in most public libraries or on the Internet.

Quick assets include cash and all other current assets that can be converted into cash quickly, such as accounts receivable and temporary investments. Temporary investments are discussed in more advanced textbooks. The balance sheet in Figure 15-6 shows total quick assets of $35,000 ($20,000 in cash + $15,000 in accounts receivable). This produces a quick ratio of 1.8 to 1. Quick assets appear to be more than adequate to meet current obligations. The traditional rule of thumb has been that a quick ratio should be about 1 to 1, but many businesses operate successfully on a quick ratio of 0.6 to 1.

INTERSTATEMENT ANALYSIS

Interstatement analysis provides a comparison of the relationships between selected income statement and balance sheet amounts. A good example of interstatement analysis is the ratio of net income to owner's equity in the business. This ratio is known as **return on owner's equity**.

$$\text{Return on Owner's Equity} = \frac{\text{Net Income}}{\text{Average Owner's Equity}} = \frac{\$22,650}{(\$104,400 + \$117,050) \div 2}$$

$$= \frac{\$22,650}{\$110,725}$$

$$= 20.5\%$$

The statement of owner's equity in Figure 15-5 shows that the owner's equity of Northern Micro was $104,400 on January 1 and $117,050 on December 31. The net income for the year of $22,650 is 20.5% of the average owner's equity. A comparison of this ratio with the return on owner's equity in prior years should be of interest to the owner. It may also be of interest to compare the return on owner's equity of Northern Micro with the same ratio for other businesses of comparable nature and size.

A second ratio involving both income statement and balance sheet accounts is a measure of the time required to collect cash from credit customers. This financial measure is often computed in two ways. The **accounts receivable turnover** is the number of times the accounts receivable "turned over," or were collected, during the accounting period. Of course, a higher number indicates that cash is collected more quickly. This ratio is calculated as follows:

🔑 LEARNING KEY

Ratio analysis is most informative when the ratios are compared with past performance and with those of similar businesses.

Information on industry averages is available in various publications from Dun & Bradstreet, Standard & Poor's, and Moody's.

$$\text{Accounts Receivable Turnover} = \frac{\text{Net Credit Sales for the Period}}{\text{Average Accounts Receivable}}$$

The accounts receivable turnover for Northern Micro for the year ended December 31 is computed as follows:

Net credit sales for the year (determined from the accounting records)	$110,000
Accounts receivable balance, January 1, 20-- (taken from last year's balance sheet)	10,000
Accounts receivable balance, December 31, 20--	15,000

Net credit sales is generally not reported in the financial statements. Use net sales, instead. As long as the proportion of cash and credit sales is reasonably stable over time, this ratio will provide a reasonable measure of the business's ability to collect receivables in a timely manner from year to year.

Northern Micro

$$\text{Average Accounts Receivable} = \frac{\text{Beginning Balance} + \text{Ending Balance}}{2} = \frac{\$10{,}000 + \$15{,}000}{2}$$
$$= \$12{,}500$$

$$\text{Accounts Receivable Turnover} = \frac{\text{Net Credit Sales for the Period}}{\text{Average Accounts Receivable}} = \frac{\$110{,}000}{\$12{,}500}$$
$$= 8.8$$

The **average collection period** is calculated by dividing the number of days in the year (365) by the rate of turnover to determine the number of days credit customers take to pay for their purchases. Northern Micro's customers are taking about 42 days.

365 days ÷ 8.8 = 41.5 days

Comparing the average collection period with a business's credit terms offers an indication of whether customers are paying within the terms. If Northern Micro allows credit terms of n/45, an average collection period of 41.5 days would suggest that customers are paying on a timely basis.

A third ratio involving both income statement and balance sheet accounts is the rate of **inventory turnover**. This is the number of times the merchandise inventory turned over, or was sold, during the accounting period. This ratio is calculated as follows:

$$\text{Inventory Turnover} = \frac{\text{Cost of Goods Sold for the Period}}{\text{Average Inventory}}$$

If inventory is taken only at the end of each accounting period, the average inventory for the period can be calculated by adding the beginning and ending inventories and dividing their sum by two. Northern Micro's turnover for the year ended December 31 is computed as follows:

Cost of goods sold for the period	$111,500
Beginning inventory	26,000
Ending inventory	18,000

Northern Micro

$$\text{Average Inventory} = \frac{\text{Beginning Inventory} + \text{Ending Inventory}}{2} = \frac{\$26{,}000 + \$18{,}000}{2}$$
$$= \$22{,}000$$

$$\text{Inventory Turnover} = \frac{\text{Cost of Goods Sold for the Period}}{\text{Average Inventory}} = \frac{\$111{,}500}{\$22{,}000}$$
$$= 5.1$$

The **average days to sell inventory** can be computed by dividing the number of days in the year (365) by the inventory turnover. For Northern Micro, it takes about two months.

365 days ÷ 5.1 = 71.6 days

The higher the rate of inventory turnover, the smaller the profit required on each dollar of sales to produce a satisfactory gross profit. This is because the increase in the number of units sold offsets the smaller amount of gross profit earned per unit. For example, grocery stores have a very small gross profit on each item sold, but make up for this with a rapid inventory turnover. Other types of businesses, jewelers for example, need a high gross profit on each item because their inventory turnover is quite slow. Evaluations of Northern Micro's rate of inventory turnover would require comparison with prior years, other companies, or its industry.

U REVU

Complete U REVU-4 on **pages 592–593** to test your basic understanding of LO4.

CLOSING ENTRIES

LO5 Prepare closing entries for a merchandising business.

Closing entries for a service business were illustrated in Chapter 6. The process is essentially the same for a merchandising business. All revenues and expenses reported on the income statement must be closed to Income Summary. Then, the income summary and drawing accounts are closed to the owner's capital account. Keep in mind, however, that a few new accounts were needed for a merchandising business. These include Sales Returns and Allowances, Sales Discounts, Purchases Returns and Allowances, and Purchases Discounts. Since these are temporary accounts reported on the income statement, they also must be closed. The easiest way to complete the closing process is by using the work sheet to prepare the closing entries in four basic steps, as illustrated in Figures 15-7 and 15-8.

FIGURE 15-7 The Closing Process

THE CLOSING PROCESS FOR A MERCHANDISING BUSINESS

STEP 1 All income statement accounts with credit balances are debited, with an offsetting credit to Income Summary.

STEP 2 All income statement accounts with debit balances are credited, with an offsetting debit to Income Summary.

STEP 3 The resulting balance in Income Summary, which is the net income or loss for the period, is transferred to the owner's capital account.

ACCOUNT: Income Summary   ACCOUNT NO. 331

DATE		ITEM	POST. REF.	DEBIT	CREDIT	BALANCE DEBIT	BALANCE CREDIT	Adjustments to:
20-- Dec.	31	Adjusting	J5	26 0 0 0 00		26 0 0 0 00		Remove Beg. Inventory
	31	Adjusting	J5		18 0 0 0 00	8 0 0 0 00		Enter End. Inventory
	31	Closing	J6		234 7 0 0 00		226 7 0 0 00	Closing step 1
	31	Closing	J6	204 0 5 0 00			22 6 5 0 00	Closing step 2
	31	Closing	J6	22 6 5 0 00				Closing step 3

STEP 4 The balance in the owner's drawing account is transferred to the owner's capital account.

FIGURE 15-8 Closing Entries for a Merchandising Business

Northern Micro
Work Sheet (Partial)
For Year Ended December 31, 20- -

	Account Title	Income Statement Debit	Income Statement Credit	Balance Sheet Debit	Balance Sheet Credit
17	Gary L. Fishel, Capital				114 4 0 0 00
18	Gary L. Fishel, Drawing			20 0 0 0 00	
19	Income Summary	26 0 0 0 00	18 0 0 0 00		
20	Sales		214 0 0 0 00		
21	Sales Returns and Allowances	1 2 0 0 0 00			
22	Interest Revenue		9 0 0 00		
23	Rent Revenue		8 0 0 0 00		
24	Subscriptions Revenue		10 0 0 0 00		
25	Purchases	105 0 0 0 00			
26	Purchases Returns and Allow.		8 0 0 0 00		
27	Purchases Discounts		1 0 0 0 00		
28	Freight-In	3 0 0 0 00			
29	Wages Expense	42 4 5 0 00			
30	Advertising Expense	2 5 0 0 00			
31	Bank Credit Card Expense	1 5 0 0 00			
32	Rent Expense	20 0 0 0 00			
33	Supplies Expense	1 4 0 0 00			
34	Telephone Expense	3 5 0 0 00			
35	Utilities Expense	12 0 0 0 00			
36	Insurance Expense	1 8 0 0 00			
37	Depr. Expense—Building	4 0 0 0 00			
38	Depr. Expense—Store Equip.	3 0 0 0 00			
39	Miscellaneous Expense	2 2 5 0 00			
40	Interest Expense	3 1 5 0 00			
41		230 0 5 0 00	252 7 0 0 00	224 0 0 0 00	201 3 5 0 00
42	Net Income	22 6 5 0 00			22 6 5 0 00
43		252 7 0 0 00	252 7 0 0 00	224 0 0 0 00	224 0 0 0 00
44					

GENERAL JOURNAL   PAGE 6

	Date	Description	Post. Ref.	Debit	Credit
1	20--	Closing Entries			
2	Dec. 31	Sales		214 0 0 0 00	
3		Interest Revenue		9 0 0 00	
4		Rent Revenue		8 0 0 0 00	
5		Subscriptions Revenue		10 0 0 0 00	
6		Purchases Returns and Allowances		8 0 0 0 00	
7		Purchases Discounts		1 0 0 0 00	
8		Income Summary			234 7 0 0 00
9					
10	31	Income Summary		204 0 5 0 00	
11		Sales Returns and Allowances			1 2 0 0 0 00
12		Purchases			105 0 0 0 00
13		Freight-In			3 0 0 0 00
14		Wages Expense			42 4 5 0 00
15		Advertising Expense			2 5 0 0 00
16		Bank Credit Card Expense			1 5 0 0 00
17		Rent Expense			20 0 0 0 00
18		Supplies Expense			1 4 0 0 00
19		Telephone Expense			3 5 0 0 00
20		Utilities Expense			12 0 0 0 00
21		Insurance Expense			1 8 0 0 00
22		Depreciation Exp.—Building			4 0 0 0 00
23		Depreciation Exp.—Store Equip.			3 0 0 0 00
24		Miscellaneous Expense			2 2 5 0 00
25		Interest Expense			3 1 5 0 00
26					
27	31	Income Summary		22 6 5 0 00	
28		Gary L. Fishel, Capital			22 6 5 0 00
29					
30	31	Gary L. Fishel, Capital		20 0 0 0 00	
31		Gary L. Fishel, Drawing			20 0 0 0 00
32					

POST-CLOSING TRIAL BALANCE

A trial balance of the general ledger accounts taken after the temporary owner's equity accounts have been closed is called a **post-closing trial balance**. The purpose of the post-closing trial balance is to prove that the general ledger is in balance at the beginning of a new accounting period, before any transactions for the new accounting period are entered. It should also confirm that all temporary accounts have zero balances. Figure 15-9 shows a post-closing trial balance for Northern Micro.

The post-closing trial balance must be prepared by taking the balances from the general ledger accounts. It should not be prepared from the balances on the work sheet. Using the general ledger accounts makes sure that all adjusting and closing entries were entered and posted correctly.

FIGURE 15-9 Post-Closing Trial Balance

Northern Micro
Post-Closing Trial Balance
December 31, 20 - -

ACCOUNT TITLE	ACCOUNT NO.	DEBIT BALANCE	CREDIT BALANCE
Cash	101	20 0 0 0 00	
Accounts Receivable	122	15 0 0 0 00	
Merchandise Inventory	131	18 0 0 0 00	
Supplies	141	4 0 0 00	
Prepaid Insurance	145	6 0 0 00	
Land	161	10 0 0 0 00	
Building	171	90 0 0 0 00	
Accumulated Depreciation—Building	171.1		20 0 0 0 00
Store Equipment	181	50 0 0 0 00	
Accumulated Depreciation—Store Equipment	181.1		18 0 0 0 00
Notes Payable	201		5 0 0 0 00
Accounts Payable	202		10 0 0 0 00
Wages Payable	219		4 5 0 00
Sales Tax Payable	231		1 5 0 0 00
Unearned Subscriptions Revenue	241		2 0 0 0 00
Mortgage Payable	251		30 0 0 0 00
Gary L. Fishel, Capital	311		117 0 5 0 00
		204 0 0 0 00	204 0 0 0 00

LESTER LEFKOWITZ/GETTY IMAGES

A BROADER VIEW

Who Cares About Tracking Financial Ratios?

Tracking a business's average collection period for receivables can help investors avoid making poor investments. Take the case of Kendall Square, a supercomputer maker. In an effort to increase sales and profits, Kendall Square recognized large amounts of revenues that had not actually been earned. Since no cash was received for these sales, accounts receivable increased dramatically (by 57%). Similarly, the average collection period increased to 157 days. Large increases in the average collection period should warn potential investors that something might be wrong. What happened at Kendall Square? Over $10 million of sales on account was never collected. This was equal to almost half of the revenues reported for the year. When eventually discovered, Kendall Square's stock price fell from $24.25 to $2.28 a share.

U REVU ▶   Complete U REVU-5 on **page 594** to test your basic understanding of LO5.

REVERSING ENTRIES

LO6 **Prepare reversing entries.**

Numerous adjusting entries are needed at the end of the accounting period to bring the account balances up to date for presentation in the financial statements. Although not required, some of these adjusting entries should be reversed at the beginning of the next accounting period. This is done to simplify the recording of transactions in the new accounting period. As its name implies, a **reversing entry** is the reverse or opposite of the adjusting entry.

ADJUSTING ENTRY

4	Dec.	31	Wages Expense			4	5	0	00				4
5			Wages Payable							4	5	0	00	5

REVERSING ENTRY (OPPOSITE)

7	Jan.	1	Wages Payable			4	5	0	00				7
8			Wages Expense							4	5	0	00	8

To see the advantage of using reversing entries, let's consider the effect of reversing Northern Micro's adjusting entry for wages earned, but not paid, at the end of the year. Figure 15-10 shows that accrued wages on December 31 were $450. These wages are for work performed by the employees on the last three days of the accounting period ($150 × 3 = $450). The employees will be paid on Friday, January 2, the normal payday.

Note that the adjusting and closing entries are the same, regardless of whether a reversing entry is made. However, the reversing entry on January 1 has an impact on the entry made when the employees are paid. **Without** a reversing entry, the payment on January 2, 20-2, must be split between reduction of the wages payable account for wages earned in 20-1 and Wages Expense for wages earned in 20-2. **With** a reversing entry, the bookkeeper simply debits Wages Expense and credits Cash, as is done on every other payday. Thus, the likelihood of error is reduced. Reversing entries are particularly important in large businesses where the individual recording the entry for wages may not even know what adjusting entries were made.

Not all adjusting entries should be reversed. To determine which adjusting entries to reverse, follow this rule: *Except for the first year of operations, reverse all adjusting entries that increase an asset or liability account from a zero balance.*

Except for the first year of operation, merchandise inventory, and contra-assets like accumulated depreciation, will have existing balances. Thus, they should never be reversed. The adjusting entries for Northern Micro are shown in Figure 15-11. Note that only the adjustment for accrued wages is reversed in Figure 15-12.

🔑 **LEARNING KEY**

Reverse all adjusting entries that increase an asset or liability account from a zero balance.

FIGURE 15-10 Adjusting, Closing, and Reversing Entries for Wages

		20-1		20-2	
	12/29/-1 Monday	12/30/-1 Tuesday	12/31/-1 Wednesday	1/1/-2 Thursday	1/2/-2 Friday
Wages Earned	150	150	150	150	150
Wages Paid	0	0	0	0	750
Total Earned			450		300
Total Paid			0		750
Accrued Wages on 12/31/-1			450		

Date	Without Reversing Entry		With Reversing Entry	
12/31/-1 Adj. Entry	Wages Expense 450 Wages Payable 450		Wages Expense 450 Wages Payable 450	
12/31/-1 Closing Entry	Income Summary 42,450 Wages Expense 42,450		Income Summary 42,450 Wages Expense 42,450	
1/1/-2 Rev. Entry	No Entry		Wages Payable 450 Wages Expense 450	
1/2/-2 Payment of Payroll	Wages Expense 300 Wages Payable 450 Cash 750		Wages Expense 750 Cash 750	

Description	Wages Expense	Description
Bal.	42,000	
12/31/-1 Adj.	450	
	42,450	12/31/-1 Close
1/2/-2 Payroll	300	

Description	Wages Expense	Description
Bal.	42,000	
12/31/-1 Adj.	450	
	42,450	12/31/-1 Close
	450	1/1/-2 Reversing
1/2/-2 Payroll	750	
Bal.	300	

	Wages Payable	
	450	12/31/-1 Adj.
1/2/-2 Payroll	450	

	Wages Payable	
	450	12/31/-1 Adj.
1/1/-2 Reverse	450	

	Cash	
	750	1/2/-2 Payroll

	Cash	
	750	1/2/-2 Payroll

FIGURE 15-11 Which Adjusting Entries to Reverse?

	DATE		DESCRIPTION	POST. REF.	DEBIT	CREDIT	
			GENERAL JOURNAL			PAGE 5	
1			Adjusting Entries				1
2	20-- Dec.	31	Income Summary		26 0 0 0 00		2
3			Merchandise Inventory			26 0 0 0 00	3
4							4
5		31	Merchandise Inventory		18 0 0 0 00		5
6			Income Summary			18 0 0 0 00	6
7							7
8		31	Supplies Expense		1 4 0 0 00		8
9			Supplies			1 4 0 0 00	9
10							10
11		31	Insurance Expense		1 8 0 0 00		11
12			Prepaid Insurance			1 8 0 0 00	12
13							13
14		31	Depr. Expense—Building		4 0 0 0 00		14
15			Accum. Depr.—Building			4 0 0 0 00	15
16							16
17		31	Depr. Expense—Store Equipment		3 0 0 0 00		17
18			Accum. Depr.—Store Equipment			3 0 0 0 00	18
19							19
20		31	Wages Expense		4 5 0 00		20
21			Wages Payable			4 5 0 00	21
22							22
23		31	Unearned Subscriptions Revenue		10 0 0 0 00		23
24			Subscriptions Revenue			10 0 0 0 00	24
25							25

SHOULD THE ADJUSTMENT BE REVERSED?

Never reverse adjustments for merchandise inventory.

Never reverse adjustments for merchandise inventory.

No. No asset or liability with a zero balance has been increased.

No. No asset or liability with a zero balance has been increased.

Never reverse adjustments for depreciation.

Never reverse adjustments for depreciation.

Yes. A liability account with a zero balance has been increased.

No. No asset or liability with a zero balance has been increased.

FIGURE 15-12 Reversing Entry for Northern Micro

	DATE		DESCRIPTION	POST. REF.	DEBIT	CREDIT	
			GENERAL JOURNAL			PAGE 7	
1			Reversing Entries				1
2	20-- Jan.	1	Wages Payable		4 5 0 00		2
3			Wages Expense			4 5 0 00	3
4							4
5							5

U REVU   Complete U REVU-6 on **page 594** to test your basic understanding of LO6.

LEARNING OBJECTIVES	Key Points to Remember

LO1 Prepare a single-step and multiple-step income statement for a merchandising business.

The general formats, for a single-step and multiple-step income statement are shown below.

Single-Step
Income Statement
For Year Ended December 31, 20--

Revenues:		
List all revenues	$xxx	
Total revenues		$xxx
Expenses:		
Cost of goods sold	$xxx	
List all other expenses	xxx	
Total expenses		xxx
Net income		$xxx

Multiple-Step
Income Statement
For Year Ended December 31, 20--

Revenue from sales:		
Sales	$xxx	
Less sales returns and allowances	xxx	
Net sales		$xxx
Cost of goods sold		xxx
Gross profit		$xxx
Operating expenses:		
List all operating expenses	$xxx	
Total operating expenses		xxx
Income from operations		$xxx
Other revenue:		
List all other revenue	$xxx	
Total other revenue		xxx
Other expenses:		
List all other expenses	$xxx	
Total other expenses		xxx
Net income		$xxx

LO2 Prepare a statement of owner's equity.

A statement of owner's equity has the following format:

Business Name
Statement of Owner's Equity
For Year Ended December 31, 20--

Capital, January 1, 20--		$xxx
Add additional investments		xxx
Total investment		$xxx
Net income for the year	$xxx	
Less withdrawals	xxx	
Increase in capital		xxx
Capital, December 31, 20--		$xxx

LEARNING OBJECTIVES   Key Points to Remember

LO3 **Prepare a classified balance sheet.**

A classified balance sheet has the following major headings:

Business Name
Balance Sheet
December 31, 20--

Assets

Current assets:

List all current assets	$xxx		
Total current assets		$xxx	

Property, plant, and equipment:

List all property, plant, and equipment	$xxx		
Less accumulated depreciation (if appropriate)	xxx	$xxx	
Total property, plant, and equipment			xxx
Total assets			$xxx

Liabilities

Current liabilities:

List all current liabilities	$xxx		
Total current liabilities		$xxx	

Long-term liabilities:

List all long-term liabilities	$xxx		
Total long-term liabilities		xxx	
Total liabilities			$xxx

Owner's Equity

Owner's capital	xxx
Total liabilities and owner's equity	$xxx

LO4 **Compute standard financial ratios.**

The following measures of financial condition may be computed from financial statement information:

Working Capital	=	Current Assets – Current Liabilities
Current Ratio	=	Current Assets ÷ Current Liabilities
Quick Ratio	=	Quick Assets ÷ Current Liabilities
Return on Owner's Equity	=	Net Income ÷ Average Owner's Equity
Accounts Receivable Turnover	=	$\dfrac{\text{Net Credit Sales for the Period}}{\text{Average Accounts Receivable}}$
Average Collection Period	=	$\dfrac{365}{\text{Accounts Receivable Turnover}}$
Inventory Turnover	=	$\dfrac{\text{Cost of Goods Sold for the Period}}{\text{Average Inventory}}$
Average Days to Sell Inventory	=	$\dfrac{365}{\text{Inventory Turnover}}$

LEARNING OBJECTIVES Key Points to Remember

LO5 Prepare closing entries for a merchandising business.	The four steps in the closing process for a merchandising business are as follows:

STEP 1 All income statement accounts with credit balances are debited, with an offsetting credit to Income Summary.

STEP 2 All income statement accounts with debit balances are credited, with an offsetting debit to Income Summary.

STEP 3 The resulting balance in Income Summary, which is the net income or loss for the period, is transferred to the owner's capital account.

STEP 4 The balance in the owner's drawing account is transferred to the owner's capital account.

LO6 Prepare reversing entries.

Use the following rule to determine which adjusting entries to reverse:

> Except for the first year of operations, reverse all adjusting entries that increase an asset or liability account from a zero balance.

DEMONSTRATION PROBLEM

Tom McKinney owns and operates McK's Home Electronics. He has a store where he sells and repairs televisions and stereo equipment. A completed work sheet for 20-1 is provided on page 585. McKinney made a $20,000 additional investment during 20-1. The current portion of Mortgage Payable is $1,000. Net credit sales for 20-1 were $200,000, and the balance of Accounts Receivable on January 1 was $26,000.

REQUIRED

1. Prepare a multiple-step income statement.

2. Prepare a statement of owner's equity.

3. Prepare a balance sheet.

4. Compute the following measures of performance and financial condition for 20-1:

   (a) current ratio
   (b) quick ratio
   (c) working capital
   (d) return on owner's equity
   (e) accounts receivable turnover and the average number of days required to collect receivables
   (f) inventory turnover and the average number of days required to sell inventory

5. Prepare adjusting entries and indicate which should be reversed and why.

6. Prepare closing entries.

7. Prepare reversing entries for the adjustments where appropriate.

McK's Home Electronics
Work Sheet
For Year Ended December 31, 20-1

	ACCOUNT TITLE	TRIAL BALANCE DEBIT	TRIAL BALANCE CREDIT	ADJUSTMENTS DEBIT	ADJUSTMENTS CREDIT	ADJUSTED TRIAL BALANCE DEBIT	ADJUSTED TRIAL BALANCE CREDIT	INCOME STATEMENT DEBIT	INCOME STATEMENT CREDIT	BALANCE SHEET DEBIT	BALANCE SHEET CREDIT	
1	Cash	10 000 00				10 000 00				10 000 00		1
2	Accounts Receivable	22 500 00				22 500 00				22 500 00		2
3	Merchandise Inventory	39 000 00		(b) 45 000 00	(a) 39 000 00	45 000 00				45 000 00		3
4	Supplies	2 700 00			(c) 2 100 00	6 00 00				6 00 00		4
5	Prepaid Insurance	3 600 00			(d) 2 700 00	9 00 00				9 00 00		5
6	Land	15 000 00				15 000 00				15 000 00		6
7	Building	135 000 00				135 000 00				135 000 00		7
8	Accum. Depr.—Building		24 000 00		(e) 6 000 00		30 000 00				30 000 00	8
9	Store Equipment	75 000 00				75 000 00				75 000 00		9
10	Accum. Depr.—Store Equipment		22 500 00		(f) 4 500 00		27 000 00				27 000 00	10
11	Notes Payable		7 500 00				7 500 00				7 500 00	11
12	Accounts Payable		15 000 00				15 000 00				15 000 00	12
13	Wages Payable				(g) 675 00		675 00				675 00	13
14	Sales Tax Payable		2 250 00				2 250 00				2 250 00	14
15	Unearned Repair Fees		18 000 00	(h) 15 000 00			3 000 00				3 000 00	15
16	Mortgage Payable		45 000 00				45 000 00				45 000 00	16
17	Tom McKinney, Capital		151 600 00				151 600 00				151 600 00	17
18	Tom McKinney, Drawing	30 000 00				30 000 00				30 000 00		18
19	Income Summary			(a) 39 000 00	(b) 45 000 00	39 000 00	45 000 00	39 000 00	45 000 00			19
20	Sales		300 750 00				300 750 00		300 750 00			20
21	Sales Returns and Allowances	1 000 00				1 000 00		1 000 00				21
22	Sales Discounts	800 00				800 00		800 00				22
23	Repair Fees				(h) 15 000 00		15 000 00		15 000 00			23
24	Interest Revenue		1 350 00				1 350 00		1 350 00			24
25	Purchases	157 500 00				157 500 00		157 500 00				25
26	Purchases Returns and Allowances		1 200 00				1 200 00		1 200 00			26
27	Purchases Discounts		1 500 00				1 500 00		1 500 00			27
28	Freight-In	4 500 00				4 500 00		4 500 00				28
29	Wages Expense	63 000 00		(g) 675 00		63 675 00		63 675 00				29
30	Advertising Expense	3 750 00				3 750 00		3 750 00				30
31	Supplies Expense			(c) 2 100 00		2 100 00		2 100 00				31
32	Telephone Expense	5 250 00				5 250 00		5 250 00				32
33	Utilities Expense	18 000 00				18 000 00		18 000 00				33
34	Insurance Expense			(d) 2 700 00		2 700 00		2 700 00				34
35	Depr. Expense—Building			(e) 6 000 00		6 000 00		6 000 00				35
36	Depr. Expense—Store Equipment			(f) 4 500 00		4 500 00		4 500 00				36
37	Miscellaneous Expense	3 375 00				3 375 00		3 375 00				37
38	Interest Expense	4 725 00				4 725 00		4 725 00				38
39		590 650 00	590 650 00	114 975 00	114 975 00	646 825 00	646 825 00	312 825 00	364 800 00	334 000 00	282 025 00	39
40	Net Income							51 975 00			51 975 00	40
41								364 800 00	364 800 00	334 000 00	334 000 00	41

(continued)

Solution 1.

McK's Home Electronics Income Statement For Year Ended December 31, 20 -1				
Revenue from sales:				
Sales			$300 7 5 0 00	
Less: Sales returns and allowances	$ 1 0 0 0 00			
Sales discounts	8 0 0 00		1 8 0 0 00	
Net sales				$298 9 5 0 00
Cost of goods sold:				
Merchandise inventory, January 1, 20-1			$ 39 0 0 0 00	
Purchases		$157 5 0 0 00		
Less: Purchases returns and allowances	$1 2 0 0 00			
Purchases discounts	1 5 0 0 00	2 7 0 0 00		
Net purchases		$154 8 0 0 00		
Add freight-in		4 5 0 00		
Cost of goods purchased			155 2 5 0 00	
Goods available for sale			$194 2 5 0 00	
Less merchandise inventory, December 31, 20-1			45 0 0 0 00	
Cost of goods sold				149 2 5 0 00
Gross profit				$149 7 0 0 00
Operating expenses:				
Wages expense			$ 63 6 7 5 00	
Advertising expense			3 7 5 0 00	
Supplies expense			2 1 0 0 00	
Telephone expense			5 2 5 0 00	
Utilities expense			18 0 0 0 00	
Insurance expense			2 7 0 0 00	
Depreciation expense—building			6 0 0 0 00	
Depreciation expense—store equipment			4 5 0 0 00	
Miscellaneous expense			3 3 7 5 00	
Total operating expenses				109 3 5 0 00
Income from operations				$ 40 3 5 0 00
Other revenues:				
Repair fees			$ 15 0 0 0 00	
Interest revenue			1 3 5 0 00	
Total other revenues				16 3 5 0 00
Other expenses:				
Interest expense				4 7 2 5 00
Net income				$ 51 9 7 5 00

2.

McK's Home Electronics Statement of Owner's Equity For Year Ended December 31, 20-1		
Tom McKinney, capital, January 1, 20-1		$131 6 0 0 00
Add additional investments		20 0 0 0 00
Total investment		$151 6 0 0 00
Net income for the year	$51 9 7 5 00	
Less withdrawals	30 0 0 0 00	
Increase in capital		21 9 7 5 00
Tom McKinney, capital, December 31, 20-1		$173 5 7 5 00

3.

McK's Home Electronics Balance Sheet December 31, 20 -1																			
Assets																			
Current assets:																			
Cash							$ 10	0	0	0	00								
Accounts receivable							22	5	0	0	00								
Merchandise inventory							45	0	0	0	00								
Supplies								6	0	0	00								
Prepaid insurance								9	0	0	00								
Total current assets												$ 79	0	0	0	00			
Property, plant, and equipment:																			
Land							$ 15	0	0	0	00								
Building	$135	0	0	0	00														
Less accumulated depreciation	30	0	0	0	00		105	0	0	0	00								
Store equipment	$ 75	0	0	0	00														
Less accumulated depreciation	27	0	0	0	00		48	0	0	0	00								
Total property, plant, and equipment												168	0	0	0	00			
Total assets												$247	0	0	0	00			
Liabilities																			
Current liabilities:																			
Notes payable	$ 7	5	0	0	00														
Accounts payable	15	0	0	0	00														
Wages payable		6	7	5	00														
Sales tax payable	2	2	5	0	00														
Unearned repair fees	3	0	0	0	00														
Mortgage payable (current portion)	1	0	0	0	00														
Total current liabilities							$ 29	4	2	5	00								
Long-term liabilities:																			
Mortgage payable	$ 45	0	0	0	00														
Less current portion	1	0	0	0	00		44	0	0	0	00								
Total liabilities												$ 73	4	2	5	00			
Owner's Equity																			
Tom McKinney, capital												173	5	7	5	00			
Total liabilities and owner's equity												$247	0	0	0	00			

4. (a) Current Ratio   = Current Assets ÷ Current Liabilities
        = $79,000 ÷ $29,425 = 2.68 to 1

   (b) Quick Ratio   = Quick Assets ÷ Current Liabilities
        = $32,500 ÷ $29,425 = 1.10 to 1

   (c) Working Capital = Current Assets − Current Liabilities
        = $79,000 − $29,425 = $49,575

   (d) Return on Owner's Equity = Net Income ÷ Average Owner's Equity

$$= \frac{\$51,975}{(\$131,600 + \$173,575) \div 2}$$

        = $51,975 ÷ $152,587.50

        = 34.1%

(continued)

(e) Accounts Receivable Turnover = $\dfrac{\text{Net Credit Sales for the Period}}{\text{Average Accounts Receivable}}$

$$= \dfrac{\$200,000}{(\$26,000 + \$22,500) \div 2}$$

$$= \$200,000 \div 24,250$$

$$= 8.25$$

Average number of days to collect an account receivable:
365 ÷ 8.25 = 44.24 days

(f) Inventory Turnover $= \dfrac{\text{Cost of Goods Sold for the Period}}{\text{Average Inventory}}$

$$= \dfrac{\$149,250}{(\$39,000 + \$45,000) \div 2}$$

$$= \$149,250 \div 42,000$$

$$= 3.6$$

Average number of days to sell inventory:
365 ÷ 3.6 = 101.39 days

5.

	DATE		DESCRIPTION	POST. REF.	DEBIT	CREDIT	
1			Adjusting Entries				1
2	20-1 Dec.	31	Income Summary		39 0 0 0 00		2
3			Merchandise Inventory			39 0 0 0 00	3
4							4
5		31	Merchandise Inventory		45 0 0 0 00		5
6			Income Summary			45 0 0 0 00	6
7							7
8		31	Supplies Expense		2 1 0 0 00		8
9			Supplies			2 1 0 0 00	9
10							10
11		31	Insurance Expense		2 7 0 0 00		11
12			Prepaid Insurance			2 7 0 0 00	12
13							13
14		31	Depr. Expense—Building		6 0 0 0 00		14
15			Accum. Depr.—Building			6 0 0 0 00	15
16							16
17		31	Depr. Expense—Store Equipment		4 5 0 0 00		17
18			Accum. Depr.—Store Equipment			4 5 0 0 00	18
19							19
20		31	Wages Expense		6 7 5 00		20
21			Wages Payable			6 7 5 00	21
22							22
23		31	Unearned Repair Fees		15 0 0 0 00		23
24			Repair Fees			15 0 0 0 00	24
25							25

GENERAL JOURNAL   PAGE 3

SHOULD THE ADJUSTMENT BE REVERSED?

Never reverse adjustments for merchandise inventory.

Never reverse adjustments for merchandise inventory.

No. No asset or liability with a zero balance has been increased.

No. No asset or liability with a zero balance has been increased.

Never reverse adjustments for depreciation.

Never reverse adjustments for depreciation.

Yes. A liability account with a zero balance has been increased.

No. No asset or liability with a zero balance has been increased.

6.

	DATE		DESCRIPTION	POST. REF.	DEBIT					CREDIT					
1			Closing Entries												1
2	20-1 Dec.	31	Repair Fees		15	0	0	0	00						2
3			Sales		300	7	5	0	00						3
4			Interest Revenue		1	3	5	0	00						4
5			Purchases Returns and Allowances		1	2	0	0	00						5
6			Purchases Discounts		1	5	0	0	00						6
7			Income Summary							319	8	0	0	00	7
8															8
9		31	Income Summary		273	8	2	5	00						9
10			Sales Returns and Allowances							1	0	0	0	00	10
11			Sales Discounts								8	0	0	00	11
12			Purchases							157	5	0	0	00	12
13			Freight-In								4	5	0	00	13
14			Wages Expense							63	6	7	5	00	14
15			Advertising Expense							3	7	5	0	00	15
16			Supplies Expense							2	1	0	0	00	16
17			Telephone Expense							5	2	5	0	00	17
18			Utilities Expense							18	0	0	0	00	18
19			Insurance Expense							2	7	0	0	00	19
20			Depr. Expense—Building							6	0	0	0	00	20
21			Depr. Expense—Store Equipment							4	5	0	0	00	21
22			Miscellaneous Expense							3	3	7	5	00	22
23			Interest Expense							4	7	2	5	00	23
24															24
25		31	Income Summary		51	9	7	5	00						25
26			Tom McKinney, Capital							51	9	7	5	00	26
27															27
28		31	Tom McKinney, Capital		30	0	0	0	00						28
29			Tom McKinney, Drawing							30	0	0	0	00	29
30															30

GENERAL JOURNAL — PAGE 4

7.

GENERAL JOURNAL — PAGE 5

	DATE		DESCRIPTION	POST. REF.	DEBIT				CREDIT				
1			Reversing Entries										1
2	20-2 Jan.	1	Wages Payable		6	7	5	00					2
3			Wages Expense						6	7	5	00	3
4													4

KEY TERMS

accounts receivable turnover (574)   The number of times the accounts receivable turned over, or were collected, during the accounting period. When 365 is divided by the turnover, this measure can be expressed in terms of the average number of days required to collect receivables.

average collection period (575)   The number of days in the year (365) divided by the accounts receivable turnover. Provides an indication of the number of days credit customers take to pay for their purchases.

average days to sell inventory (576)   The number of days in the year (365) divided by the inventory turnover. Provides an indication of the average number of days required to sell inventory.

book value (573)   See undepreciated cost.

current assets (571)   Cash and all other assets expected to be converted into cash or consumed within one year or the normal operating cycle of the business, whichever is longer.

current liabilities (573)   Those obligations that are due within one year or the normal operating cycle of the business, whichever is longer, and will require the use of current assets.

current ratio (574)   Current assets divided by current liabilities.

general expenses (569)   Those expenses associated with administrative, office, or general operating activities.

gross margin (567)   See gross profit.

gross profit (567)   Net sales minus cost of goods sold.

income from operations (567)   Gross profit minus operating expenses on a multiple-step income statement.

interstatement analysis (574)   Compares the relationship between certain amounts in the income statement and balance sheet.

inventory turnover (575)   The number of times the merchandise inventory turned over, or was sold, during the accounting period. When 365 is divided by the turnover, this measure can be expressed in terms of the average number of days required to sell inventory.

liquidity (572)   Refers to the speed with which an asset can be converted to cash.

long-term liabilities (573)   Those obligations that will extend beyond one year or the normal operating cycle, whichever is longer.

mortgage (573)   A written agreement specifying that if the borrower does not repay a debt, the lender has the right to take over specific property to satisfy the debt.

Mortgage Payable (573)   An account that is used to reflect an obligation that is secured by a mortgage on certain property.

multiple-step income statement (567)   This statement shows a step-by-step calculation of net sales, cost of goods sold, gross profit, operating expenses, income from operations, other revenues and expenses, and net income.

net sales (567)   Gross sales less sales returns and allowances and less sales discounts.

operating cycle (571)   The length of time generally required for a business to buy inventory, sell it, and collect the cash.

operating income (567)   See income from operations.

post-closing trial balance (578)   A trial balance taken after the temporary owner's equity accounts have been closed.

property, plant, and equipment (572)   Assets that are expected to be used for more than one year in the operation of a business.

quick assets (574)   Cash and all other current assets that can be converted into cash quickly, such as accounts receivable and temporary investments.

quick ratio (574)   Quick assets divided by current liabilities.

return on owner's equity (574)   Net income divided by average owner's equity.

reversing entry (579)   The opposite of the adjusting entry. It is made on the first day of the next accounting period and simplifies recording transactions in the new period.

selling expenses (567)   Those expenses directly associated with selling activities.

single-step income statement (567)   This statement lists all revenue items and their total first, followed by all expense items and their total.

undepreciated cost (573)   Cost of plant and equipment less the accumulated depreciation amounts. Also called book value.

working capital (573)   The difference between current assets and current liabilities, which represents the amount of capital the business has available for current operations.

SELF-STUDY QUESTIONS AND EXERCISES

True/False Questions

1. LO1   A multiple-step form of income statement calculates gross profit, before subtracting operating expenses.

2. LO3   Current assets include cash, items expected to convert into cash, and items that will be consumed during a year or the normal operating cycle, whichever is shorter.

3. LO3   Current assets are listed on the balance sheet in order of liquidity.

4. LO4   Working capital is the difference between current assets and current liabilities.

5. LO4   Accounts receivable turnover is the number of times merchandise inventory turned over or was sold during the accounting period.

Multiple Choice Questions

1. LO3   Which of these assets is *not* a current asset?

   (a) Cash
   (b) Accounts Receivable
   (c) Office Equipment
   (d) Merchandise Inventory

2. LO3   Which of these would be listed *first* on a balance sheet?

   (a) Accounts Receivable
   (b) Delivery Equipment
   (c) Accounts Payable
   (d) Prepaid Insurance

3. LO4   Which of these is considered a *quick asset*?

   (a) Merchandise Inventory
   (b) Accounts Receivable
   (c) Office Equipment
   (d) Prepaid Insurance

4. LO4   To calculate the accounts receivable turnover ratio, _____ is divided by average accounts receivable.

(a) Net sales   (c) Total sales
(b) Cost of goods sold   (d) Net credit sales

5. LO4   Inventory turnover is calculated by dividing cost of goods sold by

(a) average accounts receivable.
(b) average owner's equity.
(c) average inventory.
(d) accounts receivable turnover.

U REVU   Exercises

Use the following work sheet for Yoder's Cool Stuff for U REVU Exercises 1, 2, and 3.

Yoder's Cool Stuff
Work Sheet
For Year Ended December 31, 20 --

	ACCOUNT TITLE	TRIAL BALANCE DEBIT	TRIAL BALANCE CREDIT	ADJUSTMENTS DEBIT	ADJUSTMENTS CREDIT	ADJUSTED TRIAL BALANCE DEBIT	ADJUSTED TRIAL BALANCE CREDIT	INCOME STATEMENT DEBIT	INCOME STATEMENT CREDIT	BALANCE SHEET DEBIT	BALANCE SHEET CREDIT	
1	Cash	3 7 0 00				3 7 0 00				3 7 0 00		1
2	Accounts Receivable	6 5 0 00				6 5 0 00				6 5 0 00		2
3	Merchandise Inventory	2 0 0 0 00		(b) 4 0 0 0 00	(a) 2 0 0 0 00	4 0 0 0 00				4 0 0 0 00		3
4	Supplies	8 0 00			(c) 6 0 00	2 0 00				2 0 00		4
5	Prepaid Insurance	2 0 0 00			(d) 2 5 00	1 7 5 00				1 7 5 00		5
6	Delivery Equipment	8 0 0 0 00				8 0 0 0 00				8 0 0 0 00		6
7	Accum. Depr.—Delivery Equipment		2 0 0 0 00		(f) 1 0 0 0 00		3 0 0 0 00				3 0 0 0 00	7
8	Accounts Payable		1 8 0 0 00				1 8 0 0 00				1 8 0 0 00	8
9	Wages Payable				(e) 5 0 00		5 0 00				5 0 00	9
10	Pete Yoder, Capital		4 4 0 0 00				4 4 0 0 00				4 4 0 0 00	10
11	Pete Yoder, Drawing	1 5 0 00				1 5 0 00				1 5 0 00		11
12	Income Summary			(a) 2 0 0 0 00	(b) 4 0 0 0 00	2 0 0 0 00	4 0 0 0 00	2 0 0 0 00	4 0 0 0 00			12
13	Sales		12 6 5 0 00				12 6 5 0 00		12 6 5 0 00			13
14	Sales Returns and Allowances	5 0 0 00				5 0 0 00		5 0 0 00				14
15	Purchases	8 0 0 0 00				8 0 0 0 00		8 0 0 0 00				15
16	Wages Expense	6 5 0 00		(e) 5 0 00		7 0 0 00		7 0 0 00				16
17	Rent Expense	2 0 0 00				2 0 0 00		2 0 0 00				17
18	Supplies Expense			(c) 6 0 00		6 0 00		6 0 00				18
19	Telephone Expense	5 0 00				5 0 00		5 0 00				19
20	Insurance Expense			(d) 2 5 00		2 5 00		2 5 00				20
21	Depr. Expense—Delivery Equip			(f) 1 0 0 0 00		1 0 0 0 00		1 0 0 0 00				21
22		20 8 5 0 00	20 8 5 0 00	7 1 3 5 00	7 1 3 5 00	25 9 0 0 00	25 9 0 0 00	12 5 3 5 00	16 6 5 0 00	13 3 6 5 00	9 2 5 0 00	22
23								4 1 1 5 00			4 1 1 5 00	23
24								16 6 5 0 00	16 6 5 0 00	13 3 6 5 00	13 3 6 5 00	24
25												25

1. LO1   Prepare a multiple-step income statement for Yoder's Cool Stuff.

2. LO2   Prepare a statement of owner's equity for Yoder's Cool Stuff. Assume the beginning balance of Yoder's capital account was $3,400.

3. LO3   Prepare a balance sheet for Yoder's Cool Stuff.

4. LO4   Using the financial statements for Herman's Parts provided on page 593, compute the following ratios:

(a) Working capital   (c) Return on owner's equity
(b) Current ratio   (d) Inventory turnover

Herman's Parts
Income Statement
For Year Ended December 31, 20 - -

Revenue from sales:										
Sales	$28	0	0	0	00					
Less sales returns and allowances		5	0	0	00					
Net sales						$27	5	0	0	00
Cost of goods sold:										
Merchandise inventory, January 1, 20- -	$ 4	0	0	0	00					
Purchases	18	0	0	0	00					
Goods available for sale	$22	0	0	0	00					
Less merchandise inventory, December 31, 20--	6	0	0	0	00					
Cost of goods sold						16	0	0	0	00
Gross profit						$11	5	0	0	00
Operating expenses:										
Wages expense	$ 7	8	0	0	00					
Rent Expense		3	0	0	00					
Supplies expense		1	0	0	00					
Telephone expense			8	0	00					
Insurance expense			5	0	00					
Depr. expense—delivery equip.	1	0	0	0	00					
Total operating expenses						9	3	3	0	00
Net income						$ 2	1	7	0	00

Herman's Parts
Statement of Owner's Equity
For Year Ended December 31, 20 - -

Herman Gillespie, capital, January 1, 20--						$ 5	0	0	0	00
Add additional investment						1	0	0	0	00
Total investment						$ 6	0	0	0	00
Net income for the year	$ 2	1	7	0	00					
Less withdrawals for the year	1	0	0	0	00					
Increase in capital						1	1	7	0	00
Herman Gillespie, capital, December 31, 20--						$ 7	1	7	0	00

Herman's Parts
Balance Sheet
December 31, 20 - -

Assets										
Current assets:										
Cash	$	5	0	0	00					
Accounts receivable	1	9	2	0	00					
Merchandise inventory	6	0	0	0	00					
Supplies		2	0	0	00					
Prepaid insurance		4	0	0	00					
Total current assets						$ 9	0	2	0	00
Property, plant, and equipment:										
Delivery equipment	$6	0	0	0	00					
Less accumulated depreciation	3	0	0	0	00	3	0	0	0	00
Total assets						$12	0	2	0	00
Liabilities										
Current liabilities:										
Accounts payable	$3	8	0	0	00					
Wages payable	1	0	5	0	00					
Total current liabilities						$ 4	8	5	0	00
Owner's Equity										
Herman Gillespie, capital						7	1	7	0	00
Total liabilities and owner's equity						$12	0	2	0	00

5. LO5 Using the work sheet provided on page 592 for Yoder's Cool Stuff, prepare the closing entries.

6. LO6 Pinto Company made the following adjusting entries at the end of the year. It is Pinto's fifth year in operation. Prepare the appropriate reversing entry(ies).

Depreciation Expense—Delivery Equipment	500.00	
Accumulated Depreciation—Delivery Equipment		500.00
Interest Expense	1,000.00	
Interest Payable		1,000.00

The answers to the Self-Study Questions and Exercises are at the end of the chapter (pages 611–613).

APPLYING YOUR KNOWLEDGE

REVIEW QUESTIONS

LO1 1. Describe the nature of the two forms of an income statement.

LO4 2. Name and describe the calculation of two measures that provide an indication of a business's ability to pay current obligations.

LO4 3. Describe how to calculate the following ratios:

    (a) return on owner's equity
    (b) accounts receivable turnover
    (c) inventory turnover

LO5 4. Where is the information obtained that is needed in journalizing the closing entries?

LO5 5. Explain the function of each of the four closing entries made by Northern Micro.

LO5 6. What is the purpose of a post-closing trial balance?

LO6 7. What is the primary purpose of reversing entries?

LO6 8. What is the customary date for reversing entries?

LO6 9. What adjusting entries should be reversed?

SERIES A EXERCISES

E 15-1A (LO1)

✓ Net sales: $133,700

REVENUE SECTION, MULTIPLE-STEP INCOME STATEMENT Based on the information that follows, prepare the revenue section of a multiple-step income statement.

Sales	$140,000
Sales Returns and Allowances	3,500
Sales Discounts	2,800

E 15-2A (LO1)

✓ Cost of goods sold: $102,560

COST OF GOODS SOLD SECTION, MULTIPLE-STEP INCOME STATEMENT
Based on the information that follows, prepare the cost of goods sold section of a multiple-step income statement.

Merchandise Inventory, January 1, 20--	$ 34,000
Purchases	102,000
Purchases Returns and Allowances	4,200
Purchases Discounts	2,040
Freight-In	800
Merchandise Inventory, December 31, 20--	28,000

E 15-3A (LO1)

✓ Cost of goods sold: $87,860;
Net income: $15,634

MULTIPLE-STEP INCOME STATEMENT Use the following information to prepare a multiple-step income statement, including the revenue section and the cost of goods sold section, for Rau Office Supplies for the year ended December 31, 20--.

Sales	$148,300
Sales Returns and Allowances	1,380
Sales Discounts	2,166
Interest Revenue	240
Merchandise Inventory, January 1, 20--	26,500
Purchases	98,000
Purchases Returns and Allowances	2,180
Purchases Discounts	1,960
Freight-In	750
Merchandise Inventory, December 31, 20--	33,250
Wages Expense	23,800
Supplies Expense	900
Telephone Expense	1,100
Utilities Expense	7,000
Insurance Expense	1,000
Depreciation Expense—Equipment	3,100
Miscellaneous Expense	720
Interest Expense	3,880

E 15-4A (LO4)

✓ Current ratio: 4.64 to 1;
Return on owner's equity: 28.9%;
Inventory turnover: 3.13

FINANCIAL RATIOS Based on the financial statements for Jackson Enterprises (income statement, statement of owner's equity, and balance sheet) shown on the next pages, prepare the following financial ratios. All sales are credit sales. The Accounts Receivable balance on January 1, 20--, was $21,600.

1. Working capital
2. Current ratio
3. Quick ratio
4. Return on owner's equity
5. Accounts receivable turnover and average number of days required to collect receivables
6. Inventory turnover and average number of days required to sell inventory

(continued)

Jackson Enterprises
Income Statement
For Year Ended December 31, 20 - -

Revenue from sales:							
Sales				$184 2 0 0 00		
Less sales returns and allowances				2 1 0 0 00		
Net sales					$182 1 0 0 00
Cost of goods sold:							
Merchandise inventory, January 1, 20--				$ 31 3 0 0 00		
Purchases		$92 8 0 0 00				
Less: Purchases returns and allowances	$1 8 0 0 00				
Purchases discounts	1 8 5 6 00	3 6 5 6 00			
Net purchases		$89 1 4 4 00				
Add freight-in		9 3 3 00				
Cost of goods purchased				90 0 7 7 00		
Goods available for sale				$121 3 7 7 00		
Less merchandise inventory, December 31, 20--				28 1 7 7 00		
Cost of goods sold					93 2 0 0 00
Gross profit					$ 88 9 0 0 00
Operating expenses:							
Wages expense				$ 38 0 0 0 00		
Advertising expense				1 1 8 0 00		
Supplies expense				3 8 0 00		
Telephone expense				2 2 1 0 00		
Utilities expense				11 0 0 0 00		
Insurance expense				9 0 0 00		
Depreciation expense—building				4 0 0 0 00		
Depreciation expense—equipment				3 8 0 0 00		
Miscellaneous expense				5 3 0 00		
Total operating expenses					62 0 0 0 00
Income from operations					$ 26 9 0 0 00
Other revenues:							
Interest revenue				$ 1 8 0 0 00		
Other expenses:							
Interest expense				9 0 0 00	9 0 0 00
Net income					$ 27 8 0 0 00

Jackson Enterprises
Statement of Owner's Equity
For Year Ended December 31, 20 --

J. B. Gray, capital, January 1, 20--			$ 88 0 0 0 00
Net income for the year	$27 8 0 0 00		
Less withdrawals for the year	11 6 0 0 00		
Increase in capital			16 2 0 0 00
J. B. Gray, capital, December 31, 20--			$104 2 0 0 00

Jackson Enterprises
Balance Sheet
December 31, 20 --

Assets				
Current assets:				
Cash		$20 800 00		
Accounts receivable		18 900 00		
Merchandise inventory		28 177 00		
Supplies		1 323 00		
Prepaid insurance		900 00		
Total current assets				$ 70 100 00
Property, plant, and equipment:				
Building	$90 000 00			
Less accumulated depreciation—building	28 000 00	$62 000 00		
Equipment	$33 000 00			
Less accumulated depreciation—equipment	7 500 00	25 500 00		
Total property, plant, and equipment				87 500 00
Total assets				$157 600 00
Liabilities				
Current liabilities:				
Accounts payable	$12 600 00			
Wages payable	500 00			
Sales tax payable	1 200 00			
Mortgage payable (current portion)	800 00			
Total current liabilities		$15 100 00		
Long-term liabilities:				
Mortgage payable	$39 100 00			
Less current portion	800 00	38 300 00		
Total liabilities				$ 53 400 00
Owner's Equity				
J. B. Gray, capital				104 200 00
Total liabilities and owner's equity				$157 600 00

E 15-5A (LO5)   **CLOSING ENTRIES** From the work sheet on page 598, prepare the following:

1. Closing entries for Gimbel's Gifts and Gadgets in a general journal.
2. A post-closing trial balance.

E 15-6A (LO6)   **REVERSING ENTRIES** From the work sheet used in Exercise 15-5A, identify the adjusting entry(ies) that should be reversed and prepare the reversing entry(ies).

E 15-7A (LO5/6)   **ADJUSTING, CLOSING, AND REVERSING ENTRIES** Prepare entries for (a), (b), and (c) listed below using two methods. First, prepare the entries without making a reversing entry. Second, prepare the entries with the use of a reversing entry. Use T-accounts to assist your analysis.

(a) Wages paid during 20-1 are $20,800.
(b) Wages earned but not paid (accrued) as of December 31, 20-1, are $300.
(c) On January 3, 20-2, payroll of $800 is paid, which includes the $300 of wages earned but not paid in December.

EXERCISE 15-5A

Gimbel's Gifts and Gadgets
Work Sheet
For Year Ended December 31, 20-1

#	ACCOUNT TITLE	Trial Balance DEBIT	Trial Balance CREDIT	Adjustments DEBIT	Adjustments CREDIT	Adj. Trial Balance DEBIT	Adj. Trial Balance CREDIT	Income Statement DEBIT	Income Statement CREDIT	Balance Sheet DEBIT	Balance Sheet CREDIT
1	Cash	8 2 1 4 00				8 2 1 4 00				8 2 1 4 00	
2	Accounts Receivable	6 7 2 0 00				6 7 2 0 00				6 7 2 0 00	
3	Merchandise Inventory	14 2 1 0 00		(b) 16 8 0 0 00	(a) 14 2 1 0 00	16 8 0 0 00				16 8 0 0 00	
4	Supplies	6 8 0 00			(c) 3 8 0 00	3 0 0 00				3 0 0 00	
5	Prepaid Insurance	8 0 0 00			(d) 2 0 0 00	6 0 0 00				6 0 0 00	
6	Building	80 0 0 0 00				80 0 0 0 00				80 0 0 0 00	
7	Accum. Depr.—Building		13 6 0 0 00		(e) 4 0 0 0 00		17 6 0 0 00				17 6 0 0 00
8	Accounts Payable		5 2 8 0 00				5 2 8 0 00				5 2 8 0 00
9	Wages Payable				(f) 2 8 0 00		2 8 0 00				2 8 0 00
10	Sales Tax Payable		3 2 6 00				3 2 6 00				3 2 6 00
11	J. M. Gimbel, Capital		87 8 8 3 00				87 8 8 3 00				87 8 8 3 00
12	J. M. Gimbel, Drawing	8 0 0 0 00				8 0 0 0 00				8 0 0 0 00	
13	Income Summary			(a) 14 2 1 0 00	(b) 16 8 0 0 00	14 2 1 0 00	16 8 0 0 00	14 2 1 0 00	16 8 0 0 00		
14	Sales		86 0 0 0 00				86 0 0 0 00		86 0 0 0 00		
15	Sales Returns and Allowances	1 8 4 0 00				1 8 4 0 00		1 8 4 0 00			
16	Purchases	54 2 0 0 00				54 2 0 0 00		54 2 0 0 00			
17	Purchases Returns and Allowances		2 8 1 3 00				2 8 1 3 00		2 8 1 3 00		
18	Purchases Discounts		1 0 8 4 00				1 0 8 4 00		1 0 8 4 00		
19	Freight-In	8 0 0 00				8 0 0 00		8 0 0 00			
20	Wages Expense	16 8 0 0 00		(f) 2 8 0 00		17 0 8 0 00		17 0 8 0 00			
21	Advertising Expense	7 8 4 00				7 8 4 00		7 8 4 00			
22	Supplies Expense			(c) 3 8 0 00		3 8 0 00		3 8 0 00			
23	Telephone Expense	2 1 0 0 00				2 1 0 0 00		2 1 0 0 00			
24	Utilities Expense	1 3 1 0 00				1 3 1 0 00		1 3 1 0 00			
25	Insurance Expense			(d) 2 0 0 00		2 0 0 00		2 0 0 00			
26	Depr. Expense—Building			(e) 4 0 0 0 00		4 0 0 0 00		4 0 0 0 00			
27	Miscellaneous Expense	3 8 6 00				3 8 6 00		3 8 6 00			
28	Interest Expense	1 4 2 00				1 4 2 00		1 4 2 00			
29		196 9 8 6 00	196 9 8 6 00	35 8 7 0 00	35 8 7 0 00	218 0 6 6 00	218 0 6 6 00	97 4 3 2 00	106 6 9 7 00	120 6 3 4 00	111 3 6 9 00
30	Net Income							9 2 6 5 00			9 2 6 5 00
31								106 6 9 7 00	106 6 9 7 00	120 6 3 4 00	120 6 3 4 00

SERIES A PROBLEMS

P 15-8A (LO1/2/3)

✓ Cost of goods sold: $37,740;
Total assets: $39,850

INCOME STATEMENT, STATEMENT OF OWNER'S EQUITY, AND BALANCE SHEET Paulson's Pet Store completed the work sheet on page 600 for the year ended December 31, 20--. Owner's equity as of January 1, 20--, was $21,900. The current portion of Mortgage Payable is $500.

REQUIRED

1. Prepare a multiple-step income statement.

2. Prepare a statement of owner's equity.

3. Prepare a balance sheet.

P 15-9A (LO4)

✓ Working capital: $29,200;
Quick ratio: 2.78 to 1;
Accts. receivable turnover: 22.86

FINANCIAL RATIOS Use the work sheet and financial statements prepared in Problem 15-8A. All sales are credit sales. The Accounts Receivable balance on January 1, 20--, was $3,800.

REQUIRED

Prepare the following financial ratios:

(a) Working capital

(b) Current ratio

(c) Quick ratio

(d) Return on owner's equity

(e) Accounts receivable turnover and average number of days required to collect receivables

(f) Inventory turnover and average number of days required to sell inventory

P 15-10A (LO5/6)

✓ Net income: $10,610; Post-closing
trial bal. col. totals: $79,650

WORK SHEET, ADJUSTING, CLOSING, AND REVERSING ENTRIES Ellis Fabric Store shows the trial balance on page 601 as of December 31, 20-1.

At the end of the year, the following adjustments need to be made:

(a and b) Merchandise inventory as of December 31, $28,900.
(c) Unused supplies on hand, $1,350.
(d) Insurance expired, $300.
(e) Depreciation expense for the year, $500.
(f) Wages earned but not paid (Wages Payable), $480.
(g) Unearned revenue on December 31, 20-1, $1,000.

(continued)

PROBLEM 15-8A

Paulson's Pet Store
Work Sheet
For Year Ended December 31, 20 - -

| | TRIAL BALANCE | | ADJUSTMENTS | | ADJUSTED TRIAL BALANCE | | INCOME STATEMENT | | BALANCE SHEET | |
ACCOUNT TITLE	DEBIT	CREDIT	DEBIT	CREDIT	DEBIT	CREDIT	DEBIT	CREDIT	DEBIT	CREDIT	
1 Cash	15 8 6 0 00				15 8 6 0 00				15 8 6 0 00		1
2 Accounts Receivable	2 3 4 0 00				2 3 4 0 00				2 3 4 0 00		2
3 Merchandise Inventory	15 0 0 0 00		(b) 16 5 0 0 00	(a) 15 0 0 0 00	16 5 0 0 00				16 5 0 0 00		3
4 Supplies	8 0 0 00			(c) 2 0 0 00	6 0 0 00				6 0 0 00		4
5 Prepaid Insurance	6 0 0 00			(d) 1 5 0 00	4 5 0 00				4 5 0 00		5
6 Equipment	5 0 0 0 00				5 0 0 0 00				5 0 0 0 00		6
7 Accum. Depr.—Equipment		4 5 0 00		(e) 4 5 0 00		9 0 0 00				9 0 0 00	7
8 Accounts Payable		4 8 9 0 00				4 8 9 0 00				4 8 9 0 00	8
9 Wages Payable				(f) 3 0 0 00		3 0 0 00				3 0 0 00	9
10 Sales Tax Payable		8 6 0 00				8 6 0 00				8 6 0 00	10
11 Mortgage Payable		4 0 0 0 00				4 0 0 0 00				4 0 0 0 00	11
12 B. Paulson, Capital		23 9 0 0 00				23 9 0 0 00				23 9 0 0 00	12
13 B. Paulson, Drawing	1 2 0 0 00				1 2 0 0 00				1 2 0 0 00		13
14 Income Summary			(a) 15 0 0 0 00	(b) 16 5 0 0 00	15 0 0 0 00	16 5 0 0 00	15 0 0 0 00	16 5 0 0 00			14
15 Sales		71 5 1 0 00				71 5 1 0 00		71 5 1 0 00			15
16 Sales Returns and Allowances	1 3 4 0 00				1 3 4 0 00		1 3 4 0 00				16
17 Purchases	40 6 6 0 00				40 6 6 0 00		40 6 6 0 00				17
18 Purchases Returns and Allowances		1 0 2 0 00				1 0 2 0 00		1 0 2 0 00			18
19 Purchases Discounts		8 0 0 00				8 0 0 00		8 0 0 00			19
20 Freight-In	4 0 0 00				4 0 0 00		4 0 0 00				20
21 Wages Expense	22 3 0 0 00		(f) 3 0 0 00		22 6 0 0 00		22 6 0 0 00				21
22 Advertising Expense	3 0 0 00				3 0 0 00		3 0 0 00				22
23 Supplies Expense			(c) 2 0 0 00		2 0 0 00		2 0 0 00				23
24 Telephone Expense	6 8 4 00				6 8 4 00		6 8 4 00				24
25 Utilities Expense	7 1 6 00				7 1 6 00		7 1 6 00				25
26 Insurance Expense			(d) 1 5 0 00		1 5 0 00		1 5 0 00				26
27 Depr. Expense—Equipment			(e) 4 5 0 00		4 5 0 00		4 5 0 00				27
28 Miscellaneous Expense	1 5 0 00				1 5 0 00		1 5 0 00				28
29 Interest Expense	8 0 0 00				8 0 0 00		8 0 0 00				29
30	107 4 3 0 00	107 4 3 0 00	32 6 0 0 00	32 6 0 0 00	124 6 8 0 00	124 6 8 0 00	82 7 3 0 00	89 8 3 0 00	41 9 5 0 00	34 8 5 0 00	30
31 Net Income							7 1 0 0 00			7 1 0 0 00	31
32							89 8 3 0 00	89 8 3 0 00	41 9 5 0 00	41 9 5 0 00	32

Ellis Fabric Store
Trial Balance
For Year Ended December 31, 20-1

ACCOUNT TITLE	DEBIT BALANCE					CREDIT BALANCE				
Cash	28	0	0	0	00					
Accounts Receivable	14	2	0	0	00					
Merchandise Inventory	33	0	0	0	00					
Supplies	1	6	0	0	00					
Prepaid Insurance		9	0	0	00					
Equipment	6	6	0	0	00					
Accumulated Depreciation—Equipment						1	0	0	0	00
Accounts Payable						15	6	2	0	00
Wages Payable										
Sales Tax Payable							8	5	0	00
Unearned Revenue						5	0	0	0	00
W. P. Ellis, Capital						71	2	0	0	00
W. P. Ellis, Drawing	21	6	1	0	00					
Income Summary										
Sales						74	5	0	0	00
Sales Returns and Allowances	1	8	5	0	00					
Interest Revenue						1	2	0	0	00
Purchases	41	5	0	0	00					
Purchases Returns and Allowances						1	8	0	0	00
Purchases Discounts							8	3	0	00
Freight-In		6	6	0	00					
Wages Expense	14	8	8	0	00					
Advertising Expense		8	1	0	00					
Supplies Expense										
Telephone Expense	1	2	1	0	00					
Utilities Expense	3	2	4	0	00					
Insurance Expense										
Depreciation Expense—Equipment										
Miscellaneous Expense		9	2	0	00					
Interest Expense	1	0	2	0	00					
	172	0	0	0	00	172	0	0	0	00

REQUIRED

1. Prepare a work sheet.

2. Prepare adjusting entries.

3. Prepare closing entries.

4. Prepare a post-closing trial balance.

5. Prepare reversing entry(ies).

SERIES B EXERCISES

E 15-1B (LO1)

✓ Net sales: $82,196

REVENUE SECTION, MULTIPLE-STEP INCOME STATEMENT Based on the information that follows, prepare the revenue section of a multiple-step income statement.

Sales	$86,200
Sales Returns and Allowances	2,280
Sales Discounts	1,724

E 15-2B (LO1)

✓ Cost of goods sold: $59,442

COST OF GOODS SOLD SECTION, MULTIPLE-STEP INCOME STATEMENT

Based on the information that follows, prepare the cost of goods sold section of a multiple-step income statement.

Merchandise Inventory, January 1, 20--	$13,800
Purchases	71,300
Purchases Returns and Allowances	3,188
Purchases Discounts	1,460
Freight-In	390
Merchandise Inventory, December 31, 20--	21,400

E 15-3B (LO1)

✓ Cost of goods sold: $109,714;

Net income: $12,040

MULTIPLE-STEP INCOME STATEMENT

Use the following information to prepare a multiple-step income statement, including the revenue section and the cost of goods sold section, for Aeito's Plumbing Supplies for the year ended December 31, 20--.

Sales	$166,000
Sales Returns and Allowances	1,620
Sales Discounts	3,320
Interest Revenue	3,184
Merchandise Inventory, January 1, 20--	33,200
Purchases	111,300
Purchases Returns and Allowances	3,600
Purchases Discounts	2,226
Freight-In	640
Merchandise Inventory, December 31, 20--	29,600
Wages Expense	22,000
Supplies Expense	650
Telephone Expense	1,100
Utilities Expense	9,000
Insurance Expense	1,000
Depreciation Expense—Building	4,600
Depreciation Expense—Equipment	2,800
Miscellaneous Expense	214
Interest Expense	1,126

E 15-4B (LO4)

✓ Current ratio: 3.68 to 1;

Return on owner's equity: 42.6%;

Inventory turnover: 3.42

FINANCIAL RATIOS

Based on the financial statements, shown on pages 603–604, for McDonald Carpeting Co. (income statement, statement of owner's equity, and balance sheet), prepare the following financial ratios. All sales are credit sales. The balance of Accounts Receivable on January 1, 20--, was $6,800.

1. Working capital
2. Current ratio
3. Quick ratio
4. Return on owner's equity
5. Accounts receivable turnover and the average number of days required to collect receivables
6. Inventory turnover and the average number of days required to sell inventory

McDonald Carpeting Co.
Income Statement
For Year Ended December 31, 20 --

Revenue from sales:				
Sales			$122 8 0 0 00	
Less sales returns and allowances			1 1 0 0 00	
Net sales				$121 7 0 0 00
Cost of goods sold:				
Merchandise inventory, January 1, 20--			$ 19 3 0 0 00	
Purchases		$62 8 0 0 00		
Less: Purchases returns and allowances	$2 8 0 0 00			
Purchases discounts	1 9 4 4 00	4 7 4 4 00		
Net purchases		$58 0 5 6 00		
Add freight-in		9 4 4 00		
Cost of goods purchased			59 0 0 0 00	
Goods available for sale			$ 78 3 0 0 00	
Less merchandise inventory, December 31, 20--			16 7 0 0 00	
Cost of goods sold				61 6 0 0 00
Gross profit				$ 60 1 0 0 00
Operating expenses:				
Wages expense			$ 18 0 0 0 00	
Advertising expense			9 8 0 00	
Supplies expense			3 2 0 00	
Telephone expense			1 2 0 0 00	
Utilities expense			8 0 0 0 00	
Insurance expense			8 0 0 00	
Depreciation expense—building			3 5 0 0 00	
Depreciation expense—equipment			2 5 0 0 00	
Miscellaneous expense			2 0 0 00	
Total operating expenses				35 5 0 0 00
Income from operations				$ 24 6 0 0 00
Other revenues:				
Interest revenue			$ 2 8 0 0 00	
Other expenses:				
Interest expense			2 1 0 0 00	7 0 0 00
Net income				$ 25 3 0 0 00

McDonald Carpeting Co.
Statement of Owner's Equity
For Year Ended December 31, 20 - -

C. S. McDonald, capital, January 1, 20- -			$52 0 0 0 00
Net income for the year	$25 3 0 0 00		
Less withdrawals for the year	10 4 0 0 00		
Increase in capital			14 9 0 0 00
C. S. McDonald, capital, December 31, 20- -			$66 9 0 0 00

(continued)

McDonald Carpeting Co. Balance Sheet December 31, 20 - -																			
Assets																			
Current assets:																			
Cash										$10	4	0	0	00					
Accounts receivable										8	9	0	0	00					
Merchandise inventory										16	7	0	0	00					
Supplies										1	2	0	0	00					
Prepaid insurance											7	0	0	00					
Total current assets															$37	9	0	0	00
Property, plant, and equipment:																			
Building		$60	0	0	0	00													
Less accumulated depreciation—building		18	0	0	0	00	$42	0	0	0	00								
Equipment		$22	0	0	0	00													
Less accumulated depreciation—equipment		6	2	0	0	00	15	8	0	0	00								
Total property, plant, and equipment															57	8	0	0	00
Total assets															$95	7	0	0	00
Liabilities																			
Current liabilities:																			
Accounts payable		$ 8	4	0	0	00													
Wages payable			3	0	0	00													
Sales tax payable		1	0	0	0	00													
Mortgage payable (current portion)			6	0	0	00													
Total current liabilities							$10	3	0	0	00								
Long-term liabilities:																			
Mortgage payable		$19	1	0	0	00													
Less current portion			6	0	0	00	18	5	0	0	00								
Total liabilities															$28	8	0	0	00
Owner's Equity																			
C. S. McDonald, capital															66	9	0	0	00
Total liabilities and owner's equity															$95	7	0	0	00

E 15-5B (LO5)

CLOSING ENTRIES From the work sheet on page 605 prepare the following:

1. Closing entries for Balloons and Baubbles in a general journal.
2. A post-closing trial balance.

E 15-6B (LO6)

REVERSING ENTRIES From the work sheet in Exercise 15-5B, identify the adjusting entry(ies) that should be reversed and prepare the reversing entry(ies).

E 15-7B (LO5/6)

ADJUSTING, CLOSING, AND REVERSING ENTRIES Prepare entries for (a), (b), and (c) listed below using two methods. First, prepare the entries without making a reversing entry. Second, prepare the entries with the use of a reversing entry. Use T-accounts to assist your analysis.

(a) Wages paid during 20-1 are $20,080.
(b) Wages earned but not paid (accrued) as of December 31, 20-1, are $280.
(c) On January 3, 20-2, payroll of $840 is paid, which includes the $280 of wages earned but not paid in December.

EXERCISE 15-5B

Balloons and Baubbles
Work Sheet
For Year Ended December 31, 20-1

	ACCOUNT TITLE	TRIAL BALANCE DEBIT	TRIAL BALANCE CREDIT	ADJUSTMENTS DEBIT	ADJUSTMENTS CREDIT	ADJUSTED TRIAL BALANCE DEBIT	ADJUSTED TRIAL BALANCE CREDIT	INCOME STATEMENT DEBIT	INCOME STATEMENT CREDIT	BALANCE SHEET DEBIT	BALANCE SHEET CREDIT	
1	Cash	2 8 0 0 00				2 8 0 0 00				2 8 0 0 00		1
2	Accounts Receivable	4 2 0 0 00				4 2 0 0 00				4 2 0 0 00		2
3	Merchandise Inventory	8 6 0 0 00		(b) 7 5 0 0 00	(a) 8 6 0 0 00	7 5 0 0 00				7 5 0 0 00		3
4	Supplies	7 8 0 00			(c) 2 8 0 00	5 0 0 00				5 0 0 00		4
5	Prepaid Insurance	6 2 0 00			(d) 1 2 0 00	5 0 0 00				5 0 0 00		5
6	Equipment	3 0 0 0 00				3 0 0 0 00				3 0 0 0 00		6
7	Accum. Depr.—Equipment		6 0 0 00		(e) 3 0 0 00		9 0 0 00				9 0 0 00	7
8	Accounts Payable		1 8 0 0 00				1 8 0 0 00				1 8 0 0 00	8
9	Wages Payable				(f) 2 0 0 00		2 0 0 00				2 0 0 00	9
10	Sales Tax Payable		8 0 00				8 0 00				8 0 00	10
11	L. Marlow, Capital		12 2 0 0 00				12 2 0 0 00				12 2 0 0 00	11
12	L. Marlow, Drawing	2 0 0 0 00				2 0 0 0 00				2 0 0 0 00		12
13	Income Summary			(a) 8 6 0 0 00	(b) 7 5 0 0 00	8 6 0 0 00	7 5 0 0 00	8 6 0 0 00	7 5 0 0 00			13
14	Sales		31 0 0 0 00				31 0 0 0 00		31 0 0 0 00			14
15	Sales Returns and Allowances	8 0 0 00				8 0 0 00		8 0 0 00				15
16	Purchases	22 0 0 0 00				22 0 0 0 00		22 0 0 0 00				16
17	Purchases Returns and Allowances		1 8 0 0 00				1 8 0 0 00		1 8 0 0 00			17
18	Purchases Discounts		4 0 7 00				4 0 7 00		4 0 7 00			18
19	Freight-In	2 0 0 00				2 0 0 00		2 0 0 00				19
20	Wages Expense	1 2 0 0 00		(f) 2 0 0 00		1 4 0 0 00		1 4 0 0 00				20
21	Advertising Expense	3 0 0 00				3 0 0 00		3 0 0 00				21
22	Supplies Expense			(c) 2 8 0 00		2 8 0 00		2 8 0 00				22
23	Telephone Expense	7 0 0 00				7 0 0 00		7 0 0 00				23
24	Utilities Expense	4 8 0 00				4 8 0 00		4 8 0 00				24
25	Insurance Expense			(d) 1 2 0 00		1 2 0 00		1 2 0 00				25
26	Depr. Expense—Equipment			(e) 3 0 0 00		3 0 0 00		3 0 0 00				26
27	Miscellaneous Expense	1 1 0 00				1 1 0 00		1 1 0 00				27
28	Interest Expense	9 7 00				9 7 00		9 7 00				28
29		47 8 8 7 00	47 8 8 7 00	17 0 0 0 00	17 0 0 0 00	55 8 8 7 00	55 8 8 7 00	35 3 8 7 00	40 7 0 7 00	20 5 0 0 00	15 1 8 0 00	29
30	Net Income							5 3 2 0 00			5 3 2 0 00	30
31								40 7 0 7 00	40 7 0 7 00	20 5 0 0 00	20 5 0 0 00	31

SERIES B PROBLEMS

P 15-8B (LO1/2/3)

✓ Cost of goods sold: $75,350;
Total assets: $117,750

INCOME STATEMENT, STATEMENT OF OWNER'S EQUITY, AND BALANCE SHEET Backlund Farm Supply completed the work sheet on page 607 for the year ended December 31, 20--. Owner's equity as of January 1, 20--, was $50,000. The current portion of Mortgage Payable is $1,000.

REQUIRED

1. Prepare a multiple-step income statement.

2. Prepare a statement of owner's equity.

3. Prepare a balance sheet.

P 15-9B (LO4)

✓ Working capital: $43,230;
Quick ratio: 0.84 to 1;
Accts. receivable turnover: 4.35

FINANCIAL RATIOS Use the work sheet and financial statements prepared in Problem 15-8B. All sales are credit sales. The Accounts Receivable balance on January 1 was $38,200.

REQUIRED

Prepare the following financial ratios:

(a) Working capital

(b) Current ratio

(c) Quick ratio

(d) Return on owner's equity

(e) Accounts receivable turnover and the average number of days required to collect receivables

(f) Inventory turnover and the average number of days required to sell inventory

P 15-10B (LO5/6)

✓ Net income: $4,590; Post-closing trial
bal. columns: $53,500

WORK SHEET, ADJUSTING, CLOSING, AND REVERSING ENTRIES The trial balance for Darby Kite Store as of December 31, 20-1, is shown on page 608.

At the end of the year, the following adjustments need to be made:

(a and b) Merchandise inventory as of December 31, $23,600.
(c) Unused supplies on hand, $1,050.
(d) Insurance expired, $250.
(e) Depreciation expense for the year, $400.
(f) Wages earned but not paid (Wages Payable), $360.
(g) Unearned revenue on December 31, 20-1, $500.

REQUIRED

1. Prepare a work sheet.

2. Prepare adjusting entries.

(continued)

PROBLEM 15-8B

Backlund Farm Supply
Work Sheet
For Year Ended December 31, 20--

	ACCOUNT TITLE	TRIAL BALANCE DEBIT	TRIAL BALANCE CREDIT	ADJUSTMENTS DEBIT	ADJUSTMENTS CREDIT	ADJUSTED TRIAL BALANCE DEBIT	ADJUSTED TRIAL BALANCE CREDIT	INCOME STATEMENT DEBIT	INCOME STATEMENT CREDIT	BALANCE SHEET DEBIT	BALANCE SHEET CREDIT	
1	Cash	10 1 8 0 00				10 1 8 0 00				10 1 8 0 00		1
2	Accounts Receivable	26 4 2 0 00				26 4 2 0 00				26 4 2 0 00		2
3	Merchandise Inventory	42 1 6 0 00		(b) 44 3 0 0 00	(a) 42 1 6 0 00	44 3 0 0 00				44 3 0 0 00		3
4	Supplies	4 3 6 0 00			(c) 8 6 0 00	3 5 0 0 00				3 5 0 0 00		4
5	Prepaid Insurance	3 0 0 0 00			(d) 7 5 0 00	2 2 5 0 00				2 2 5 0 00		5
6	Equipment	38 0 0 0 00				38 0 0 0 00				38 0 0 0 00		6
7	Accum. Depr.—Equipment		6 0 0 0 00		(e) 9 0 0 00		6 9 0 0 00				6 9 0 0 00	7
8	Accounts Payable		41 2 0 0 00				41 2 0 0 00				41 2 0 0 00	8
9	Wages Payable				(f) 4 2 0 00		4 2 0 00				4 2 0 00	9
10	Sales Tax Payable		8 0 0 00				8 0 0 00				8 0 0 00	10
11	Mortgage Payable		8 0 0 0 00				8 0 0 0 00				8 0 0 0 00	11
12	J. Backlund, Capital		57 0 0 0 00				57 0 0 0 00				57 0 0 0 00	12
13	J. Backlund, Drawing	6 8 0 0 00				6 8 0 0 00				6 8 0 0 00		13
14	Income Summary			(a) 42 1 6 0 00	(b) 44 3 0 0 00	42 1 6 0 00	44 3 0 0 00	42 1 6 0 00	44 3 0 0 00			14
15	Sales		141 8 0 0 00				141 8 0 0 00		141 8 0 0 00			15
16	Sales Returns and Allowances	1 3 1 0 00				1 3 1 0 00		1 3 1 0 00				16
17	Purchases	81 3 0 0 00				81 3 0 0 00		81 3 0 0 00				17
18	Purchases Returns and Allowances		2 9 0 0 00				2 9 0 0 00		2 9 0 0 00			18
19	Purchases Discounts		1 5 1 0 00				1 5 1 0 00		1 5 1 0 00			19
20	Freight-In	6 0 0 00				6 0 0 00		6 0 0 00				20
21	Wages Expense	41 3 0 0 00		(f) 4 2 0 00		41 7 2 0 00		41 7 2 0 00				21
22	Advertising Expense	4 0 0 00				4 0 0 00		4 0 0 00				22
23	Supplies Expense			(c) 8 6 0 00		8 6 0 00		8 6 0 00				23
24	Telephone Expense	8 0 0 00				8 0 0 00		8 0 0 00				24
25	Utilities Expense	1 3 0 0 00				1 3 0 0 00		1 3 0 0 00				25
26	Insurance Expense			(d) 7 5 0 00		7 5 0 00		7 5 0 00				26
27	Depr. Expense—Equipment			(e) 9 0 0 00		9 0 0 00		9 0 0 00				27
28	Miscellaneous Expense	2 0 0 00				2 0 0 00		2 0 0 00				28
29	Interest Expense	1 0 8 0 00				1 0 8 0 00		1 0 8 0 00				29
30		259 2 1 0 00	259 2 1 0 00	89 3 9 0 00	89 3 9 0 00	304 8 3 0 00	304 8 3 0 00	173 3 8 0 00	190 5 1 0 00	131 4 5 0 00	114 3 2 0 00	30
31	Net Income							17 1 3 0 00			17 1 3 0 00	31
32								190 5 1 0 00	190 5 1 0 00	131 4 5 0 00	131 4 5 0 00	32

Darby Kite Store
Trial Balance
For Year Ended December 31, 20-1

ACCOUNT TITLE	DEBIT BALANCE	CREDIT BALANCE
Cash	11 7 0 0 00	
Accounts Receivable	11 2 0 0 00	
Merchandise Inventory	25 0 0 0 00	
Supplies	1 2 0 0 00	
Prepaid Insurance	8 0 0 00	
Equipment	5 4 0 0 00	
Accumulated Depreciation—Equipment		8 0 0 00
Accounts Payable		7 1 0 0 00
Wages Payable		
Sales Tax Payable		2 5 0 00
Unearned Revenue		3 0 0 0 00
M. D. Akins, Capital		50 0 0 0 00
M. D. Akins, Drawing	10 5 0 0 00	
Income Summary		
Sales		55 4 9 0 00
Sales Returns and Allowances	1 4 5 0 00	
Purchases	34 5 0 0 00	
Purchases Returns and Allowances		1 1 0 0 00
Purchases Discounts		6 3 0 00
Freight-In	3 6 0 00	
Wages Expense	10 8 8 0 00	
Advertising Expense	7 4 0 00	
Supplies Expense		
Telephone Expense	1 1 0 0 00	
Utilities Expense	2 3 0 0 00	
Insurance Expense		
Depreciation Expense—Equipment		
Miscellaneous Expense	3 2 0 00	
Interest Expense	9 2 0 00	
	118 3 7 0 00	118 3 7 0 00

3. Prepare closing entries.

4. Prepare a post-closing trial balance.

5. Prepare reversing entry(ies).

MANAGING YOUR WRITING

A friend of yours has the opportunity to invest in a small business. She has come to you for advice on how she might determine whether this would be a good investment. In particular, she is concerned about how long it takes to sell the merchandise and collect receivables. Draft a memo suggesting various ratios that should be computed to evaluate the business's profitability, ability to pay its current obligations, and time required to sell inventory and collect receivables.

ETHICS CASE

Brian Marlow recently was hired to prepare Louise Michener Consulting's year-end financial statements. Brian just earned his CPA certificate, and Louise Michener was one of his first clients. Louise employs a bookkeeper, Martha Halling, who does the daily journal entries and prepares a year-to-date trial balance at the end of each month. Martha gives the December 31 trial balance to a CPA to make the adjustments and generate the financial statements. As Brian was looking through Louise Michener's books, he noticed two things. First, in each of the last three years, a different CPA had prepared the financial statements. Second, the amount shown on the December 31 trial balance for miscellaneous expense was quite high this year compared to prior years. Brian called Martha to find out if she knew why miscellaneous expense had such a high balance. Martha's response was "I just do what Louise tells me to do. If she wants to charge personal expenses to the company, it's none of my business."

1. What should Brian do?

2. How might Brian's decision affect Martha? Has Martha done anything unethical?

3. Write a short letter from Brian to Louise explaining why personal items should not be charged to a business.

4. In small groups, discuss the ethical responsibilities of an accountant relating to a client's books.

MASTERY PROBLEM

✓ Net income: $21,350;
Total assets: $99,000;
Current ratio: 2.65 to 1;
Return on owner's equity: 28.1%

Dominique Fouque owns and operates Dominique's Doll House. She has a small shop in which she sells new and antique dolls. She is particularly well known for her collection of antique Ken and Barbie dolls. A completed work sheet for 20-3 is shown on the next page. Fouque made no additional investments during the year and the long-term note payable is due in 20-9. No portion of the long-term note is due within the next year. Net credit sales for 20-3 were $35,300, and receivables on January 1 were $2,500.

REQUIRED

1. Prepare a multiple-step income statement.

2. Prepare a statement of owner's equity.

3. Prepare a balance sheet.

4. Compute the following measures of performance and financial condition for 20-3:

   (a) Current ratio
   (b) Quick ratio
   (c) Working capital
   (d) Return on owner's equity
   (e) Accounts receivable turnover and average number of days required to collect receivables
   (f) Inventory turnover and the average number of days required to sell inventory

5. Prepare adjusting entries and indicate which should be reversed and why.

6. Prepare closing entries.

7. Prepare reversing entries for the adjustments where appropriate.

(continued)

MASTERY PROBLEM

Dominique's Doll House
Work Sheet
For Year Ended December 31, 20 -3

#	ACCOUNT TITLE	TRIAL BALANCE DEBIT	TRIAL BALANCE CREDIT	ADJUSTMENTS DEBIT	ADJUSTMENTS CREDIT	ADJUSTED TRIAL BALANCE DEBIT	ADJUSTED TRIAL BALANCE CREDIT	INCOME STATEMENT DEBIT	INCOME STATEMENT CREDIT	BALANCE SHEET DEBIT	BALANCE SHEET CREDIT
1	Cash	5 2 0 0 00				5 2 0 0 00				5 2 0 0 00	
2	Accounts Receivable	3 2 0 0 00				3 2 0 0 00				3 2 0 0 00	
3	Merchandise Inventory	22 3 0 0 00		(b) 24 6 0 0 00	(a) 22 3 0 0 00	24 6 0 0 00				24 6 0 0 00	
4	Office Supplies	8 0 0 00			(c) 6 0 0 00	2 0 0 00				2 0 0 00	
5	Prepaid Insurance	1 2 0 0 00			(d) 4 0 0 00	8 0 0 00				8 0 0 00	
6	Store Equipment	85 0 0 0 00				85 0 0 0 00				85 0 0 0 00	
7	Accum. Depr.—Store Equipment		15 0 0 0 00		(e) 5 0 0 0 00		20 0 0 0 00				20 0 0 0 00
8	Notes Payable		6 0 0 0 00				6 0 0 0 00				6 0 0 0 00
9	Accounts Payable		5 5 0 0 00				5 5 0 0 00				5 5 0 0 00
10	Wages Payable				(g) 2 0 0 00		2 0 0 00				2 0 0 00
11	Sales Tax Payable		8 5 0 00				8 5 0 00				8 5 0 00
12	Unearned Rent Revenue		1 0 0 0 00	(f) 7 0 0 00			3 0 0 00				3 0 0 00
13	Long-Term Note Payable		10 0 0 0 00				10 0 0 0 00				10 0 0 0 00
14	Dominique Fouque, Capital		75 8 0 0 00				75 8 0 0 00				75 8 0 0 00
15	Dominique Fouque, Drawing	21 0 0 0 00				21 0 0 0 00				21 0 0 0 00	
16	Income Summary			(a) 22 3 0 0 00	(b) 24 6 0 0 00	22 3 0 0 00	24 6 0 0 00	22 3 0 0 00	24 6 0 0 00		
17	Sales		130 5 0 0 00				130 5 0 0 00		130 5 0 0 00		
18	Sales Returns and Allowances	9 0 0 0 00				9 0 0 0 00		9 0 0 0 00			
19	Rent Revenue		25 0 0 0 00		(f) 7 0 0 00		25 7 0 0 00		25 7 0 0 00		
20	Purchases	72 0 0 0 00				72 0 0 0 00		72 0 0 0 00			
21	Purchases Discounts		7 5 0 00				7 5 0 00		7 5 0 00		
22	Freight-In	1 2 0 0 00				1 2 0 0 00		1 2 0 0 00			
23	Wages Expense	42 0 0 0 00		(g) 2 0 0 00		42 2 0 0 00		42 2 0 0 00			
24	Rent Expense	6 0 0 0 00				6 0 0 0 00		6 0 0 0 00			
25	Office Supplies Expense			(c) 6 0 0 00		6 0 0 00		6 0 0 00			
26	Telephone Expense	1 5 0 0 00				1 5 0 0 00		1 5 0 0 00			
27	Utilities Expense	7 6 0 0 00				7 6 0 0 00		7 6 0 0 00			
28	Insurance Expense			(d) 4 0 0 00		4 0 0 00		4 0 0 00			
29	Depr. Expense—Store Equipment			(e) 5 0 0 0 00		5 0 0 0 00		5 0 0 0 00			
30	Interest Expense	5 0 0 00				5 0 0 00		5 0 0 00			
31		270 4 0 0 00	270 4 0 0 00	53 8 0 0 00	53 8 0 0 00	300 2 0 0 00	300 2 0 0 00	160 2 0 0 00	181 5 0 0 00	140 0 0 0 00	118 6 5 0 00
32	Net Income							21 3 5 0 00			21 3 5 0 00
33								181 5 0 0 00	181 5 0 0 00	140 0 0 0 00	140 0 0 0 00

CHALLENGE PROBLEM

This problem challenges you to apply your cumulative accounting knowledge to move a step beyond the material in the chapter.

✓ **Average days to convert inventory to cash: 45.0 days**

John Byers owns and operates Byers Building Supplies. The following information was taken from his financial statements:

Balance Sheet	12/31/-2	12/31/-1
Accounts Receivable	$700	$500
Inventory	300	100

Income Statement		
Net Credit Sales	$7,200	
Cost of Goods Sold	5,000	

All sales are made on account.

REQUIRED

Based on the above information, on average, approximately how many days pass from the time Byers purchases inventory until he receives cash from customers?

ANSWERS TO SELF-STUDY QUESTIONS AND EXERCISES

True/False Questions

1. T
2. F (whichever is longer)
3. T
4. T
5. F (number of times accounts receivable turned over)

Multiple Choice Questions

1. c
2. a
3. b
4. d
5. c

U REVU   **Exercises**

1.

Yoder's Cool Stuff
Income Statement
For Year Ended December 31, 20 - -

Revenue from sales:														
Sales	$12	6	5	0	00									
Less sales returns and allowances		5	0	0	00									
Net sales						$12	1	5	0	00					
Cost of goods sold:														
Merchandise inventory, January 1, 20- -	$ 2	0	0	0	00									
Purchases	8	0	0	0	00									
Goods available for sale	$10	0	0	0	00									
Less merchandise inventory, December 31, 20--	4	0	0	0	00									
Cost of goods sold						6	0	0	0	00					
Gross profit						$ 6	1	5	0	00					
Operating expenses:														
Wages expense	$	7	0	0	00									
Rent expense		2	0	0	00									
Supplies expense			6	0	00									
Telephone expense			5	0	00									
Insurance expense			2	5	00									
Depr. expense—delivery equip.	1	0	0	0	00									
Total operating expenses						2	0	3	5	00					
Net income						$ 4	1	1	5	00					

2.

Yoder's Cool Stuff
Statement of Owner's Equity
For Year Ended December 31, 20 - -

Pete Yoder, capital, January 1, 20--						$ 3	4	0	0	00
Add additional investment						1	0	0	0	00
Total investment						$ 4	4	0	0	00
Net income for the year	$ 4	1	1	5	00					
Less withdrawls for the year		1	5	0	00					
increase in capital						3	9	6	5	00
Pete Yoder, capital, December 31, 20--						$ 8	3	6	5	00

3.

Yoder's Cool Stuff
Balance Sheet
December 31, 20 - -

Assets										
Current assets:										
Cash	$	3	7	0	00					
Accounts receivable		6	5	0	00					
Merchandise inventory	4	0	0	0	00					
Supplies			2	0	00					
Prepaid insurance		1	7	5	00					
Total current assets						$ 5	2	1	5	00
Property, plant, and equipment:										
Delivery equipment	$8	0	0	0	00					
Less accumulated depreciation	3	0	0	0	00	5	0	0	0	00
Total assets						$10	2	1	5	00
Liabilities										
Current liabilities:										
Accounts payable	$1	8	0	0	00					
Wages payable			5	0	00					
Total current liabilities						$ 1	8	5	0	00
Owner's Equity										
Pete Yoder, capital						8	3	6	5	00
Total liabilities and owner's equity						$10	2	1	5	00

4. a. Working capital:

Current assets	$9,020
– Current liabilities	4,850
	$4,170

b. Current ratio:

$$\frac{\text{Current Assets}}{\text{Current Liabilities}} = \frac{\$9,020}{\$4,850} = 1.86 \text{ to } 1$$

c. Return on owner's equity:

$$\frac{\text{Net Income}}{\text{Average Owner's Equity}} = \frac{\$2,170}{(\$5,000 + \$7,170)/2} = \frac{\$2,170}{\$6,085} = 35.7\%$$

d. Inventory turnover:

$$\frac{\text{Cost of Goods Sold}}{\text{Average Inventory}} = \frac{\$16,000}{(\$4,000 + \$6,000)/2} = \frac{\$16,000}{\$5,000} = 3.2$$

5.

	DATE	DESCRIPTION	POST. REF.	DEBIT	CREDIT	
1		Closing Entries				1
2		Sales		12 6 5 0 00		2
3		Income Summary			12 6 5 0 00	3
4						4
5		Income Summary		10 5 3 5 00		5
6		Sales Returns and Allowances			5 0 0 00	6
7		Purchases			8 0 0 0 00	7
8		Wages Expense			7 0 0 00	8
9		Rent Expense			2 0 0 00	9
10		Supplies Expense			6 0 00	10
11		Telephone Expense			5 0 00	11
12		Insurance Expense			2 5 00	12
13		Depr. Expense—Delivery Equip.			1 0 0 0 00	13
14						14
15		Income Summary		4 1 1 5 00		15
16		Pete Yoder, Capital			4 1 1 5 00	16
17						17
18		Pete Yoder, Capital		1 5 0 00		18
19		Pete Yoder, Drawing			1 5 0 00	19
20						20

6.

Interest Payable	1,000.00	
Interest Expense		1,000.00

Do not reverse the adjustment for depreciation expense. The adjusting entry does not increase an asset or liability from a zero balance and does not make the subsequent entry easier.

COMPREHENSIVE PROBLEM 2: ACCOUNTING CYCLE WITH SUBSIDIARY LEDGERS, PART 1

During the second half of December 20-1, TJ's Specialty Shop engaged in the following transactions:

Dec. 16   Received payment from Lucy Greene on account, $1,960.

16   Sold merchandise on account to Kim Fields, $160, plus sales tax of $8. Sale No. 640.

17   Returned merchandise to Evans Essentials for credit, $150.

18   Issued Check No. 813 to Evans Essentials in payment of December 1 balance of $1,250, less the credit received on December 17.

19   Sold merchandise on account to Lucy Greene, $620, plus tax of $31. Sale No. 641.

22   Received payment from John Dempsey on account, $1,560.

23   Issued Check No. 814 for the purchase of supplies, $120. (Debit Supplies)

24   Purchased merchandise on account from West Wholesalers, $1,200. Invoice No. 465, dated December 24, terms n/30.

26   Purchased merchandise on account from Nathen Co., $800. Invoice No. 817, dated December 26, terms 2/10, n/30.

27   Issued Check No. 815 in payment of utilities expense for the month of December, $630.

27   Sold merchandise on account to John Dempsey, $2,020, plus tax of $101. Sale No. 642.

29   Received payment from Martha Boyle on account, $2,473.

29   Issued Check No. 816 in payment of wages (Wages Expense) for the two-week period ending December 28, $1,100.

30   Issued Check No. 817 to Meyers Trophy Shop for a cash purchase of merchandise, $200.

As of December 16, TJ's account balances were as follows:

Account	Account No.	Debit	Credit
Cash	101	$ 9,705	
Accounts Receivable	122	10,256	
Merchandise Inventory	131	21,800	
Supplies	141	1,035	
Prepaid Insurance	145	1,380	
Land	161	8,700	
Building	171	52,000	
Accum. Depr.—Building	171.1		$ 9,200
Store Equipment	181	28,750	
Accum. Depr.—Store Equipment	181.1		9,300
Accounts Payable	202		3,600
Wages Payable	219		
Sales Tax Payable	231		1,378
Mortgage Payable	251		12,525
Tom Jones, Capital	311		90,000
Tom Jones, Drawing	312	8,500	
Income Summary	313		
Sales	401		124,900

Sales Returns and Allowances	401.1	$ 1,430	
Purchases	501	64,400	
Purchases Returns and Allowances	501.1		$ 460
Purchases Discounts	501.2		698
Freight-In	502	175	
Wages Expense	511	26,100	
Advertising Expense	512	4,700	
Supplies Expense	524		
Telephone Expense	525	2,180	
Utilities Expense	533	6,900	
Insurance Expense	535		
Depr. Expense—Building	540		
Depr. Expense—Store Equipment	541		
Miscellaneous Expense	549	2,700	
Interest Expense	551	1,350	
		$252,061	$252,061

TJ's also had the following subsidiary ledger balances as of December 16:

Accounts Receivable Ledger

Customer	Balance
Martha Boyle 12 Jude Lane Hartford, CT 06117	$3,796
Anne Clark 52 Juniper Road Hartford, CT 06118	2,100
John Dempsey 700 Hobbes Dr. Avon, CT 06108	1,560
Kim Fields 5200 Hamilton Ave. Hartford, CT 06117	—
Lucy Greene 236 Bally Lane Simsbury, CT 06123	2,800

Accounts Payable Ledger

Vendor	Balance
Evans Essentials 34 Harry Ave. East Hartford, CT 05234	$3,600
Nathen Co. 1009 Drake Rd. Farmington, CT 06082	—
Owen Enterprises 43 Lucky Lane Bristol, CT 06007	—
West Wholesalers 888 Anders Street Newington, CT 06789	—

At the end of the year, the following adjustments (a)–(g) need to be made:

(a, b) Merchandise inventory as of December 31, $19,700.

(c) Unused supplies on hand, $525.

(d) Unexpired insurance on December 31, $1,000.

(e) Depreciation expense on the building for the year, $800.

(f) Depreciation expense on the store equipment for the year, $450.

(g) Wages earned but not paid as of December 31, $330.

Requirements and working papers for this problem are provided in two versions: General Journal based and Special Journals based. Complete the version as directed by your instructor.

(continued)

REQUIRED—GENERAL JOURNAL

For those not using working papers:

1. If you are not using the working papers, open a general ledger, an accounts receivable ledger, and an accounts payable ledger as of December 16. Enter the December 16 balance of each of the accounts, with a check mark in the Posting Reference column.

REQUIRED—SPECIAL JOURNALS

For those not using working papers:

1. If you are not using the working papers:
   a. Open a general ledger, an accounts receivable ledger, and an accounts payable ledger as of December 16. Enter the following December 16 balances in the general ledger accounts and place a check mark in the Posting Reference column.

Cash	$ 11,500
Accounts Receivable	7,823
Accounts Payable	6,850
Sales Tax Payable	933
Sales	116,000
Purchases	60,500
Purchases Discounts	575

   b. Enter the December 16 balances in the rest of the general ledger accounts, as indicated in the trial balance, and place a check mark in the Posting Reference column.

   c. Enter the December 16 balances in the accounts receivable and accounts payable ledgers, as indicated in the subsidiary ledger account listings, and place a check mark in the Posting Reference column.

   d. Insert Dec. 1–15, Cumulative Amount, and the following amounts in the special journal columns.

   Sales Journal: Accounts Receivable Dr., 4,263; Sales Cr., 4,060; Sales Tax Payable Cr., 203.

   Cash Receipts Journal: Accounts Receivable Cr., 1,830; Sales Cr., 4,840; Sales Tax Pay. Cr., 242; Cash Dr., 6,912.

   Purchases Journal: Purchases Dr./Accts. Pay. Cr., 3,900.

   Cash Payments Journal: General Dr., 1,680; Accounts Payable Dr., 7,150; Purchases Discounts Cr., 123; Cash Cr., 8,707.

For working paper users and nonusers:

2. Enter transactions for the second half of December in the general journal. Post immediately to the accounts receivable and accounts payable ledgers.

3. Post from the journal to the general ledger.

For working paper users and nonusers:

2. Enter transactions for the second half of December in the proper journals. If you are using the working papers, the cumulative amount of entries in the special journals for December 1–15 has been entered in these journals for you. Post immediately to the accounts receivable and accounts payable ledgers.

3. Post from the journals to the general ledger. Post the journals in the following order: general, sales, purchases, cash receipts, and cash payments.

REQUIRED—GENERAL JOURNAL (*continued*)

4. Prepare schedules of accounts receivable and accounts payable.

5. Prepare a year-end work sheet, an income statement, a statement of owner's equity, and a balance sheet. The mortgage payable includes $600 that is due within one year.

6. Journalize and post adjusting entries.

7. Journalize and post closing entries. (*Hint*: Close all expense and revenue account balances listed in the Income Statement columns of the work sheet. Then, close Income Summary and Tom Jones, Drawing to Tom Jones, Capital.)

8. Prepare a post-closing trial balance.

9. Journalize and post reversing entries for the adjustments where appropriate, as of January 1, 20-2.

REQUIRED—SPECIAL JOURNALS (*continued*)

4. Prepare schedules of accounts receivable and accounts payable.

5. Prepare a year-end work sheet, an income statement, a statement of owner's equity, and a balance sheet. The mortgage payable includes $600 that is due within one year.

6. Journalize and post adjusting entries.

7. Journalize and post closing entries. (*Hint*: Close all expense and revenue account balances listed in the Income Statement columns of the work sheet. Then, close Income Summary and Tom Jones, Drawing to Tom Jones, Capital.)

8. Prepare a post-closing trial balance.

9. Journalize and post reversing entries for the adjustments where appropriate, as of January 1, 20-2.

COMPREHENSIVE PROBLEM 2: ACCOUNTING CYCLE WITH SUBSIDIARY LEDGERS, PART 2

During the month of January 20-2, TJ's Specialty Shop engaged in the following transactions:

Jan. 1   Sold merchandise on account to Anne Clark, $3,000, plus tax of $150. Sale No. 643.

2   Issued Check No. 818 to Nathen Co. in payment of January 1 balance of $800, less 2% discount.

3   Purchased merchandise on account from West Wholesalers, $1,500. Invoice No. 678, dated January 3, terms 2/15, n/30.

4   Purchased merchandise on account from Owen Enterprises, $2,000. Invoice No. 767, dated January 4, terms 2/10, n/30.

4   Issued Check No. 819 in payment of telephone expense for the month of January, $180.

8   Sold merchandise for cash, $3,600, plus tax of $180.

9   Received payment from Lucy Greene in full settlement of account, $1,491.

10   Issued Check No. 820 to West Wholesalers in payment of January 1 balance of $1,200.

12   Sold merchandise on account to Martha Boyle, $1,000, plus tax of $50. Sale No. 644.

12   Received payment from Anne Clark on account, $2,100.

12   Issued Check No. 821 in payment of wages (Wages Expense) for the two-week period ending January 11, $1,100.

13   Issued Check No. 822 to Owen Enterprises in payment of January 4 purchase. Invoice No. 767, less 2% discount.

13   Martha Boyle returned merchandise for a credit, $800, plus sales tax of $40.

17   Returned merchandise to Evans Essentials for credit, $300.

22   Received payment from John Dempsey on account, $2,121.

(*continued*)

Jan. 26   Issued Check No. 823 in payment of wages (Wages Expense) for the two-week period ending January 25, $1,100.

27   Issued Check No. 824 in payment of utilities expense for the month of January, $630.

27   Sold merchandise on account to John Dempsey, $2,000, plus tax of $100. Sale No. 645.

Late in January, TJ's agreed to sell the business to a competitor. To agree on a selling price, financial statements are needed as of January 31 and for the month of January 20-2. To prepare these financial statements, TJ's must perform the same procedures it normally does at year-end.

At the end of January, the following adjustments (a)–(g) need to be made:

(a, b)   Merchandise inventory as of January 31, $19,000.

(c)   Unused supplies on hand, $115.

(d)   Unexpired insurance on January 31, $968.

(e)   Depreciation expense on the building for the month, $67.

(f)   Depreciation expense on the store equipment for the month, $38.

(g)   Wages earned but not paid as of January 31, $330.

REQUIRED—GENERAL JOURNAL

For those not using working papers:

1. If you are not using the working papers, open a general ledger, an accounts receivable ledger, and an accounts payable ledger as of January 1. Enter the January 1 balance of each of the accounts, with a check mark in the Posting Reference column. The beginning balances for Part 2 are the same as the balances from your solution to Part 1 of Comprehensive Problem 2.

For working paper users and nonusers:

2. Enter transactions for the month of January in the general journal. Post immediately to the accounts receivable and accounts payable ledgers.

3. Post from the journal to the general ledger.

4. Prepare schedules of accounts receivable and accounts payable.

5. Prepare a month-end work sheet, income statement, statement of owner's equity, and balance sheet. The mortgage payable includes $600 that is due within one year.

6. Journalize and post adjusting entries.

7. Journalize and post closing entries. (*Hint*: Close all expense and revenue account balances listed in the Income Statement columns of the work sheet. Then close Income Summary and Tom Jones, Drawing to Tom Jones, Capital.)

8. Prepare a post-closing trial balance.

REQUIRED—SPECIAL JOURNALS

For those not using working papers:

1. If you are not using the working papers, open a general ledger, an accounts receivable ledger, and an accounts payable ledger as of January 1. Enter the January 1 balance of each of the accounts, with a check mark in the Posting Reference column. The beginning balances for Part 2 are the same as the balances from your solution to Part 1 of Comprehensive Problem 2.

For working paper users and nonusers:

2. Enter transactions for the month of January in the proper journals. Post immediately to the accounts receivable and accounts payable ledgers.

3. Post from the journals to the general ledger. Post the journals in the following order: general, sales, purchases, cash receipts, and cash payments.

4. Prepare schedules of accounts receivable and accounts payable.

5. Prepare a month-end work sheet, income statement, statement of owner's equity, and balance sheet. The mortgage payable includes $600 that is due within one year.

6. Journalize and post adjusting entries.

7. Journalize and post closing entries. (*Hint*: Close all expense and revenue account balances listed in the Income Statement columns of the work sheet. Then close Income Summary and Tom Jones, Drawing to Tom Jones, Capital.)

8. Prepare a post-closing trial balance.

Module Accounting for a Professional Service Business: The Combination Journal

Professional service businesses include law, dentistry, medicine, optometry, architecture, engineering, and accounting. As discussed in Chapter 5, many small professional service businesses do not need to prepare financial statements in strict compliance with generally accepted accounting principles (GAAP). This is because they don't need to raise large amounts of money from investors or creditors who expect GAAP financial statements. Thus, many of these businesses use the modified cash basis. This simplifies the accounting process and provides results similar to the accrual basis if receivables and payables are minimal. If at some point GAAP financial statements are needed, an accountant can convert the modified cash basis statements to the accrual basis which is required under GAAP.

Small professional service businesses may also use a combination journal as the book of original entry, instead of a general journal, or special journals (illustrated in Chapter 12). The purpose of this module is to illustrate accounting for a professional service business using the modified cash basis of accounting and a combination journal.

THE MODIFIED CASH AND ACCRUAL BASES OF ACCOUNTING

LO1 Explain the differences between the modified cash and accrual bases of accounting.

The modified cash and accrual bases of accounting are the same except for three types of events. The accounting differences for these three events are shown in Figure M-1. First, expenses for services received are not recorded until paid. Thus, accounts payable is not used under the modified cash basis for services received. Second, under the modified cash basis, accrued expenses are not recognized. Examples of accrued

FIGURE M-1 Modified Cash Basis vs. Accrual Basis of Accounting

DIFFERENCES BETWEEN MODIFIED CASH AND ACCRUAL BASES OF ACCOUNTING		
Event	**Accrual basis**	**Modified cash basis**
Expenses	Expense	No entry.
Bills for services received, but not yet paid.	Accounts Payable	(Record when paid.)
Wages earned by employees, but not yet paid.	Wages Expense	No entry.
	Wages Payable	(Record when paid.)
Revenues		
Services provided on account.	Accounts Receivable	No entry.
	Professional Fees	(Record when cash is received.)

The modified cash basis is the same as the accrual basis, except receivables and payables are not recognized for revenues and operating expenses.

expenses include wages that were earned by the employees, but not yet paid, and interest expense that has been incurred, but not yet paid. Thus, no end-of-period adjusting entries are made for these types of events. This means that other records must be used to maintain information on amounts owed for wages, interest, and other expenses. Typically, these bills are filed chronologically by due date.

Finally, under the modified cash basis, revenues from services performed on account are not recorded until cash is received. Thus, no accounts receivable are entered in the accounting system. This means that other records must be used to maintain information on amounts owed by clients and patients. These records generally include an appointment record and a client or patient ledger record. These records are illustrated in Figures M-2 and M-3.

FIGURE M-2 Appointment Record

Date: 6/4/--

Time	Patient	Medical Service	Fees	Payments
8:00	Dennis Rogan	OV	40.00	40.00
15				
30	Rick Cosier	OV;EKG	120.00	
45				
9:00	George Hettenhouse	OV;MISC	50.00	
15				
30	Sam Frumer	OV;LAB	75.00	75.00
45				
10:00	Dan Dalton	OV	40.00	
15				
30	Wally Bell	OV;X	65.00	
45				
11:00	Mike Groomer	X	40.00	40.00
15				
30				
45				
12:00				
15				
30				
45				
1:00	Mike Tiller	OV;LAB	80.00	
15				
30	Peggy Hite	OV;PHYS	190.00	
45				
2:00				
15				
30				
45				
3:00	Vivian Winston	OV;MISC	40.00	
15				
30				
45				
4:00	Hank Davis	OV	40.00	40.00
15				
30				
45				
	Bill Sharp			150.00
	Phil Jones			80.00
	Diane Gallagher			200.00
			780.00	625.00

FIGURE M-3 Client or Patient Ledger Account

Patient Name	Dennis Rogan				
Address	1542 Hamilton Avenue Cincinnati OH 45240-5524				
Phone Number	555-1683				
Date	Service Rendered	Time	Debit	Credit	Balance
20-- June 4	Office Visit	8:00	40.00		40.00
4				40.00	—

U REVU   Complete U REVU-1 on **page 638** to test your basic understanding of LO1.

ACCOUNTING FOR A PROFESSIONAL SERVICE BUSINESS

LO2 Describe special records for a professional service business using the modified cash basis.

The appointment record, shown in Figure M-2, is used to schedule appointments and to maintain a record of the services rendered, fees charged, and payments received. It also serves as a source document for the patient ledger records, shown in Figure M-3, which show the amount owed by each client or patient for services performed. A copy of this record may also be used for billing purposes.

THE COMBINATION JOURNAL

LO3 Describe and use a combination journal to record transactions of a professional service business.

The two-column general journal illustrated in Chapter 4 can be used to enter every transaction of a business. However, in most businesses, there are many similar transactions that involve the same account or accounts. Cash receipts and payments are good examples. Suppose that in a typical month there are 30 transactions that result in an increase in cash and 40 transactions that cause a decrease in cash. In a two-column general journal, this would require entering the account Cash 70 times, using a journal line each time.

A considerable amount of time and space is saved if a journal contains **special columns** for cash debits and cash credits. At the end of the month, the special columns for cash debits and credits are totaled. The total of the Cash Debit column is posted as one amount to the debit side of the cash account and the total of the Cash Credit column is posted as one amount to the credit side of the cash account. Thus, instead of receiving 70 postings, Cash receives only two: one debit and one credit. This method requires much less time and reduces the risk of making posting errors.

LEARNING KEY

The totals of special journal columns are posted as one amount to the account. This saves time and reduces the possibility of posting errors.

If other accounts are used frequently, special columns can be added for these accounts. **General Debit** and **General Credit columns** are used for accounts not affected by many transactions. A journal with such special and general columns is called a **combination journal**.

Many small professional enterprises use a combination journal to record business transactions. To demonstrate the use of a combination journal, let's consider the medical practice of Dr. Ray Bonita. Bonita uses the modified cash basis of accounting. The chart of accounts for his medical practice is shown in Figure M-4. The transactions for the month of June, his first month in practice, are provided in Figure M-5.

FIGURE M-4 Chart of Accounts

RAY BONITA, M.D. CHART OF ACCOUNTS			
Assets		**Revenue**	
101	Cash	401	Medical Fees
141	Medical Supplies		
142	Office Supplies	**Expenses**	
145	Prepaid Insurance	511	Wages Expense
182	Office Furniture	521	Rent Expense
182.1	Accum. Depr.—Office Furn.	523	Office Supplies Expense
185	Medical Equipment	524	Medical Supplies Expense
185.1	Accum. Depr.—Med. Equip.	525	Telephone Expense
		526	Laboratory Expense
Liabilities		535	Insurance Expense
202	Accounts Payable	541	Depr. Exp.—Office Furn.
		542	Depr. Exp.—Med. Equip.
Owner's Equity			
311	Ray Bonita, Capital		
312	Ray Bonita, Drawing		
313	Income Summary		

FIGURE M-5 Summary of Transactions for Ray Bonita's Medical Practice

June 1	Ray Bonita invested cash to start a medical practice, $50,000.
2	Paid for a one-year liability insurance policy, $6,000. Coverage began on June 1.
3	Purchased medical equipment for cash, $22,000.
4	Paid bill for laboratory work, $300.
5	Purchased office furniture on credit from Bittle's Furniture, $9,000.
6	Received cash from patients and insurance companies for medical services rendered, $5,000.
7	Paid June office rent, $2,000.
8	Paid part-time wages, $3,000.
9	Purchased medical supplies for cash, $250.
15	Paid telephone bill, $150.
15	Received cash from patients and insurance companies for medical services rendered, $10,000.
16	Paid bill for laboratory work, $280.
17	Paid part-time wages, $3,000.
19	Purchased office supplies for cash, $150.
20	Received cash from patients and insurance companies for medical services rendered, $3,200.
22	Paid the first installment to Bittle's Furniture, $3,300.
23	Purchased medical supplies for cash, $200.
24	Paid bill for laboratory work, $400.
25	Purchased additional furniture from Bittle's Furniture, $4,000. A down payment of $500 was made, with the remaining payments expected over the next four months.
27	Paid part-time wages, $2,500.
30	Received cash from patients and insurance companies for medical services rendered, $7,000.
30	Bonita withdrew cash for personal use, $10,000.

A combination journal for Bonita's medical practice is illustrated in Figure M-6. Note that special columns were set up for Cash (Debit and Credit), Medical Fees (Credit), Wages Expense (Debit), Laboratory Expense (Debit), Medical Supplies

FIGURE M-6 Combination Journal: Modified Cash Basis

COMBINATION JOURNAL   PAGE 1

Line	Date	Description	Post. Ref.	Cash Debit	Cash Credit	General Debit	General Credit	Medical Fees Credit	Wages Expense Debit	Laboratory Expense Debit	Medical Supplies Debit	Office Supplies Debit
1	20– June 1	Ray Bonita, Capital	311	50 0 0 0 00			50 0 0 0 00					
2	2	Prepaid Insurance	145		6 0 0 0 00	6 0 0 0 00						
3	3	Medical Equipment	185		22 0 0 0 00	22 0 0 0 00						
4	4				3 0 0 00					3 0 0 00		
5	5	Office Furniture	182			9 0 0 0 00						
6		Accounts Payable—Bittle's Furn.	202				9 0 0 0 00					
7	6			5 0 0 0 00				5 0 0 0 00				
8	7	Rent Expense	521		2 0 0 0 00	2 0 0 0 00						
9	8				3 0 0 0 00				3 0 0 0 00			
10					2 5 0 00						2 5 0 00	
11	15	Telephone Expense	525		1 5 0 00	1 5 0 00						
12	15			10 0 0 0 00				10 0 0 0 00				
13	16				2 8 0 00					2 8 0 00		
14	17				3 0 0 0 00				3 0 0 0 00			
15	19				1 5 0 00							1 5 0 00
16	20			3 2 0 0 00				3 2 0 0 00				
17	22	Accounts Payable—Bittle's Furniture	202		3 3 0 0 00	3 3 0 0 00						
18					2 0 0 00						2 0 0 00	
19	23				4 0 0 00					4 0 0 00		
20				7 0 0 0 00				7 0 0 0 00				
21	24	Office Furniture	182		5 0 0 00	4 0 0 0 00						
22		Accounts Payable—Bittle's Furn.	202				3 5 0 0 00					
23	30				2 5 0 0 00				2 5 0 0 00			
24	30	Ray Bonita, Drawing	312		10 0 0 0 00	10 0 0 0 00						
25				75 2 0 0 00	54 0 3 0 00	56 4 5 0 00	62 5 0 0 00	25 2 0 0 00	8 5 0 0 00	9 8 0 00	4 5 0 00	1 5 0 00
26				(1 0 1)	(1 0 1)	(✓)	(✓)	(4 0 1)	(5 1 1)	(5 2 6)	(1 4 1)	(1 4 2)

Proving the Combination Journal:

Debit columns:		Credit columns:	
Cash	75,200	Cash	54,030
General	56,450	General	62,500
Wages Expense	8,500	Medical Fees	25,200
Laboratory Expense	980		141,730
Medical Supplies	450		
Office Supplies	150		
	141,730		

Note: The account numbers in the Posting Reference column and at the bottom of the special columns are inserted as posting is completed. The same is true for the (✓) at the bottom of the General Debit and Credit columns.

(Debit), and Office Supplies (Debit). Special columns were set up for these accounts because they will be used frequently in this business. Other businesses might set up special columns for different accounts depending on the frequency of their use. Of course, General Debit and Credit columns for transactions affecting other accounts are also needed.

JOURNALIZING IN A COMBINATION JOURNAL

The following procedures were used to enter the transactions for Bonita for June:

General Columns

Enter transactions in the *general columns* in a manner similar to that used for the *general journal*. Look at the entry for June 5 in Figure M-6.

(a) Enter the name of the debited account (Office Furniture) first at the extreme left of the Description column.

(b) Enter the amount in the General Debit column.

(c) Enter the name of the account credited (Accounts Payable—Bittle's Furniture) on the next line, indented.

(d) Enter the amount in the General Credit column.

General and Special Accounts

Some transactions affect both a *general account and a special account*. Look at the entry for June 1 in Figure M-6.

(a) Enter the name of the general account in the Description column.

(b) Enter the amount in the General Debit or Credit column.

(c) Enter the amount of the debit or credit for the special account in the appropriate special column.

Enter all of this information on the same line.

Special Accounts

Many transactions affect only *special accounts*. Look at the entry for June 6 in Figure M-6.

(a) Enter the amounts in the appropriate special debit and credit columns.

(b) Do not enter anything in the Description column.

(c) Place a dash in the **Posting Reference column** to indicate that this amount is not posted individually. It will be posted as part of the total of the special column at the end of the month. (The posting process is described later in this chapter.)

Description Column

In general, the **Description column** is used for the following:

(a) To enter the account titles for the General Debit and General Credit columns.

(b) To identify specific creditors when assets are purchased on account (see entry for June 5).

   Note: For firms using the accrual basis of accounting, this column also would be used to identify specific customers receiving services on account (accounts receivable) and specific businesses that provided services on account (accounts payable).

(c) To identify specific creditors when payments are made on account (see entry for June 22).

(d) To identify adjusting, closing, and reversing entries.

(e) To identify amounts forwarded. When more than one page is required during an accounting period, amounts from the previous page are brought forward. In this situation, "Amounts Forwarded" is entered in the Description column on the first line.

PROVING THE COMBINATION JOURNAL

At the end of the accounting period, all columns of the combination journal should be totaled and ruled. The sum of the debit columns should be compared with the sum of the credit columns to verify that they are equal. The proving of Bonita's combination journal for the month of June is shown at the bottom of Figure M-6 on page 623.

U REVU

Complete U REVU-2 on **page 638** to test your basic understanding of LO3.

POSTING FROM THE COMBINATION JOURNAL

LO4 Post from the combination journal to the general ledger.

Accounts debited or credited in the general columns are posted individually throughout the month in the same manner followed for the general journal. A different procedure is used for special columns. Figure M-7 describes the procedures to follow in posting from the combination journal.

FIGURE M-7 Posting from a Combination Journal

GENERAL COLUMNS	Since a combination journal is being used, enter "CJ" and the page number in each general ledger account's **Posting Reference column**. Once the amount has been posted to the general ledger account, the account number is entered in the Posting Reference column of the combination journal. Accounts in the general column should be posted daily. The check marks at the bottom of the General Debit and Credit columns are entered at the end of the month and serve as a reminder that these totals should not be posted.
SPECIAL COLUMNS	1. Post the totals of the special columns to the appropriate general ledger accounts. 2. Once posted, enter the account number (in parentheses) beneath the column and "CJ" and the page number in each general ledger account's Posting Reference column.

🔑 **LEARNING KEY**

Amounts in the General column are posted individually. Only the totals of the special columns are posted.

Portions of the combination journal in Figure M-6 and general ledger accounts for Cash, Office Furniture, Accounts Payable, and Medical Fees are shown in Figure M-8 to illustrate the effects of this posting process. Note that the individual debits and credits in the General columns are posted individually throughout the month. Only the totals of the Special columns are posted at the end of the month.

To see the advantages of posting a combination journal compared with the general journal, simply compare the accounts in Figure M-8 with the same accounts in Chapter 4, Figure 4-12. Note the number of postings required for the general journal and combination journal.

FIGURE M-8 Posting the Combination Journal

	DATE		CASH DEBIT	CASH CREDIT	DESCRIPTION	POST. REF.	GENERAL DEBIT	GENERAL CREDIT	MEDICAL FEES CREDIT	
5	20-- June	5			Office Furniture	182	9 0 0 0 00			5
6					Accts. Payable—Bittle's Furn.	202		9 0 0 0 00		6
7		6	5 0 0 0 00			—			5 0 0 0 00	7
12		15	10 0 0 0 00			—			10 0 0 0 00	12
16		20	3 2 0 0 00			—			3 2 0 0 00	16
17		22		3 3 0 0 00	Accts. Payable—Bittle's Furn.	202	3 3 0 0 00			17
20		25		5 0 0 00	Office Furniture	182	4 0 0 0 00			20
21					Accts. Payable—Bittle's Furn.	202		3 5 0 0 00		21
23		30	7 0 0 0 00			—			7 0 0 0 00	23
25			75 2 0 0 00	54 0 3 0 00			56 4 5 0 00	62 5 0 0 00	25 2 0 0 00	25
26			(1 0 1)	(1 0 1)			(✓)	(✓)	(4 0 1)	26

GENERAL LEDGER

ACCOUNT: **Cash** ACCOUNT NO. **101**

DATE	ITEM	POST. REF.	DEBIT	CREDIT	BALANCE DEBIT	BALANCE CREDIT
20-- June 30		CJ1	75 2 0 0 00		75 2 0 0 00	
30		CJ1		54 0 3 0 00	21 1 7 0 00	

ACCOUNT: **Office Furniture** ACCOUNT NO. **182**

DATE	ITEM	POST. REF.	DEBIT	CREDIT	BALANCE DEBIT	BALANCE CREDIT
20-- June 5		CJ1	9 0 0 0 00		9 0 0 0 00	
25		CJ1	4 0 0 0 00		13 0 0 0 00	

ACCOUNT: **Accounts Payable** ACCOUNT NO. **202**

DATE	ITEM	POST. REF.	DEBIT	CREDIT	BALANCE DEBIT	BALANCE CREDIT
20-- June 5		CJ1		9 0 0 0 00		9 0 0 0 00
22		CJ1	3 3 0 0 00			5 7 0 0 00
25		CJ1		3 5 0 0 00		9 2 0 0 00

ACCOUNT: **Medical Fees** ACCOUNT NO. **401**

DATE	ITEM	POST. REF.	DEBIT	CREDIT	BALANCE DEBIT	BALANCE CREDIT
20-- June 30		CJ1		25 2 0 0 00		25 2 0 0 00

Color Key:
Red — Posting totals of Special columns.
Blue — Posting individual debits and credits in General columns.

	Number of Postings		
	General Journal	Combination Journal	
Cash	13	2	(Special columns for cash)
Delivery Equip./			
Office Furniture	3	2	(No special column)
Accounts Payable	3	3	(No special column)
Delivery/Medical Fees	3	1	(Special column for Medical Fees)

Clearly, using the combination journal can be quite efficient.

LEARNING KEY

Beginning cash balance
+ Cash debits to date
– Cash credits to date
Current cash balance

DETERMINING THE CASH BALANCE

The debits and credits to Cash are not posted until the end of the accounting period. Therefore, the cash balance must be computed when this information is needed. The cash balance may be computed at any time during the month by taking the beginning balance and adding total cash debits and subtracting total cash credits to date. Figure M-9 shows the calculation of Bonita's cash balance on June 15.

U REVU

Complete U REVU-3 on **page 638** to test your basic understanding of LO4.

PERFORMING END-OF-PERIOD WORK FOR A PROFESSIONAL SERVICE BUSINESS

LO5 Prepare a work sheet, financial statements, and adjusting and closing entries for a professional service business.

Once the combination journal has been posted to the general ledger, the end-of-period work sheet is prepared in the same way as described in Chapter 5. Recall that financial statements are prepared and end-of-period work is normally performed at the end of the fiscal year. For illustration purposes, we will perform these activities at the end of Bonita's first month of operations.

PREPARING THE WORK SHEET

Bonita's work sheet is illustrated in Figure M-10 on page 629. Adjustments were made for the following items:

(a) Medical supplies remaining on June 30, $350.

(b) Office supplies remaining on June 30, $100.

(c) Prepaid insurance expired during June, $500.

(d) Depreciation on office furniture for June, $200.

(e) Depreciation on medical equipment for June, $300.

PREPARING FINANCIAL STATEMENTS

Since this is the first month of Dr. Bonita's medical practice, we know the beginning balance of owner's equity is zero. We also know the $50,000 balance in the capital account on the work sheet is the result of his investment during June. With this information, we can prepare the financial statements directly from the work sheet. In future periods, the balance of the capital account on the work sheet will reflect the beginning balance plus any additional investments. Thus, we will need to examine Bonita's capital account for investments made during the period and report those separately on the statement of owner's equity. Bonita's financial statements are illustrated in Figure M-11 on page 630.

FIGURE M-9 Determining the Cash Balance

COMBINATION JOURNAL
PAGE 1

DATE		DESCRIPTION	POST. REF.	CASH DEBIT	CASH CREDIT	GENERAL DEBIT	GENERAL CREDIT	MEDICAL FEES CREDIT	WAGES EXPENSE DEBIT	LABORATORY EXPENSE DEBIT	MEDICAL SUPPLIES DEBIT	OFFICE SUPPLIES DEBIT	
20— June	1	Ray Bonita, Capital	311	50 0 0 0 00			50 0 0 0 00						1
	2	Prepaid Insurance	145		6 0 0 0 00	6 0 0 0 00							2
	3	Medical Equipment	185		22 0 0 0 00	22 0 0 0 00							3
	4		—		3 0 0 00					3 0 0 00			4
	5	Office Furniture	182			9 0 0 00							5
	6	Accounts Payable—Bittle's Furn.	202				9 0 0 00						6
	7		—	5 0 0 0 00				5 0 0 0 00					7
	8	Rent Expense	521		2 0 0 0 00	2 0 0 0 00							8
	9		—		3 0 0 0 00				3 0 0 0 00				9
	10		—		2 5 0 00						2 5 0 00		10
	11	Telephone Expense	525		1 5 0 00	1 5 0 00							11
	15		—	10 0 0 0 00				10 0 0 0 00					12
	15			65 0 0 0 00	33 7 0 0 00								13

Beginning balance	$ 0
Add cash debits	65,000
Total	$65,000
Less cash credits	33,700
Cash balance, June 15	$31,300

FIGURE M-10 Work Sheet for Ray Bonita, M.D.

Ray Bonita, M.D.
Work Sheet
For Month Ended June 30, 20- -

#	Account Title	Trial Balance Debit	Trial Balance Credit	Adjustments Debit	Adjustments Credit	Adjusted Trial Balance Debit	Adjusted Trial Balance Credit	Income Statement Debit	Income Statement Credit	Balance Sheet Debit	Balance Sheet Credit
1	Cash	21 1 7 0 00				21 1 7 0 00				21 1 7 0 00	
2	Medical Supplies	4 5 0 00			(a) 1 0 0 00	3 5 0 00				3 5 0 00	
3	Office Supplies	1 5 0 00			(b) 5 0 00	1 0 0 00				1 0 0 00	
4	Prepaid Insurance	6 0 0 00			(c) 5 0 00	5 5 0 00				5 5 0 00	
5	Office Furniture	13 0 0 0 00				13 0 0 0 00				13 0 0 0 00	
6	Accum. Depr.—Office Furniture				(d) 2 0 0 00		2 0 0 00				2 0 0 00
7	Medical Equipment	22 0 0 0 00				22 0 0 0 00				22 0 0 0 00	
8	Accum. Depr.—Medical Equipment				(e) 3 0 0 00		3 0 0 00				3 0 0 00
9	Accounts Payable		9 2 0 0 00				9 2 0 0 00				9 2 0 0 00
10	Ray Bonita, Capital		50 0 0 0 00				50 0 0 0 00				50 0 0 0 00
11	Ray Bonita, Drawing	10 0 0 0 00				10 0 0 0 00				10 0 0 0 00	
12	Medical Fees		25 2 0 0 00				25 2 0 0 00		25 2 0 0 00		
13	Wages Expense	8 5 0 0 00				8 5 0 0 00		8 5 0 0 00			
14	Rent Expense	2 0 0 0 00				2 0 0 0 00		2 0 0 0 00			
15	Office Supplies Expense			(b) 5 0 00		5 0 00		5 0 00			
16	Medical Supplies Expense			(a) 1 0 0 00		1 0 0 00		1 0 0 00			
17	Telephone Expense	1 5 0 00				1 5 0 00		1 5 0 00			
18	Laboratory Expense	9 8 0 00				9 8 0 00		9 8 0 00			
19	Insurance Expense			(c) 5 0 00		5 0 00		5 0 00			
20	Depr. Expense—Office Furniture			(d) 2 0 0 00		2 0 0 00		2 0 0 00			
21	Depr. Expense—Medical Equipment			(e) 3 0 0 00		3 0 0 00		3 0 0 00			
22		84 4 0 0 00	84 4 0 0 00	1 1 5 0 00	1 1 5 0 00	84 9 0 0 00	84 9 0 0 00	12 7 8 0 00	25 2 0 0 00	72 1 2 0 00	59 7 0 0 00
23	Net Income							12 4 2 0 00			12 4 2 0 00
24								25 2 0 0 00	25 2 0 0 00	72 1 2 0 00	72 1 2 0 00

FIGURE M-11 Financial Statements for Ray Bonita, M.D.

Ray Bonita, M.D. Income Statement For Month Ended June 30, 20 --										
Revenue:										
Medical fees						$25	2	0	0	00
Expenses:										
Wages expense	$8	5	0	0	00					
Rent expense	2	0	0	0	00					
Office supplies expense			5	0	00					
Medical supplies expense		1	0	0	00					
Telephone expense		1	5	0	00					
Laboratory expense		9	8	0	00					
Insurance expense		5	0	0	00					
Depreciation expense—office furniture		2	0	0	00					
Depreciation expense—medical equipment		3	0	0	00					
Total expenses						12	7	8	0	00
Net income						$12	4	2	0	00

Ray Bonita, M.D. Statement of Owner's Equity For Month Ended June 30, 20 --										
Ray Bonita, capital, June 1, 20 --						$				
Investment during June						50	0	0	0	00
Total investment						$50	0	0	0	00
Net income for June	$12	4	2	0	00					
Less withdrawals for June	10	0	0	0	00					
Increase in capital						2	4	2	0	00
Ray Bonita, capital, June 30, 20 --						$52	4	2	0	00

Ray Bonita, M.D. Balance Sheet June 30, 20 --										
Assets										
Current assets:										
Cash	$21	1	7	0	00					
Medical supplies		3	5	0	00					
Office supplies		1	0	0	00					
Prepaid insurance	5	5	0	0	00					
Total current assets						$27	1	2	0	00
Property, plant, and equipment:										
Office furniture	$13	0	0	0	00					
Less accumulated depreciation—office furniture		2	0	0	00	12	8	0	0	00
Medical equipment	$22	0	0	0	00					
Less accumulated depreciation—medical equipment		3	0	0	00	21	7	0	0	00
Total assets						$61	6	2	0	00
Liabilities										
Current liabilities:										
Accounts payable						$ 9	2	0	0	00
Owner's Equity										
Ray Bonita, capital						52	4	2	0	00
Total liabilities and owner's equity						$61	6	2	0	00

PREPARING ADJUSTING AND CLOSING ENTRIES

Adjusting and closing entries are made in the combination journal in the same manner demonstrated for the general journal in Chapter 6. We simply use the Description and General Debit and Credit columns. These posted entries are illustrated in Figures M-12 and M-13.

FIGURE M-12 Adjusting Entries

	DATE		CASH DEBIT	CASH CREDIT	DESCRIPTION	POST. REF.	GENERAL DEBIT	GENERAL CREDIT	
1					Adjusting Entries				1
2	20-- June	30			Medical Supplies Expense	524	1 0 0 00		2
3					Medical Supplies	141		1 0 0 00	3
4		30			Office Supplies Expense	523	5 0 00		4
5					Office Supplies	142		5 0 00	5
6		30			Insurance Expense	535	5 0 0 00		6
7					Prepaid Insurance	145		5 0 0 00	7
8		30			Depr. Expense—Office Furniture	541	2 0 0 00		8
9					Accum. Depr.—Office Furn.	182.1		2 0 0 00	9
10		30			Depr. Expense—Medical Equip.	542	3 0 0 00		10
11					Accum. Depr.—Medical Equip.	185.1		3 0 0 00	11

FIGURE M-13 Closing Entries

	DATE		CASH DEBIT	CASH CREDIT	DESCRIPTION	POST. REF.	GENERAL DEBIT	GENERAL CREDIT	
12									12
13					Closing Entries				13
14	20-- June	30			Medical Fees	401	25 2 0 0 00		14
15					Income Summary	313		25 2 0 0 00	15
16		30			Income Summary	313	12 7 8 0 00		16
17					Wages Expense	511		8 5 0 0 00	17
18					Rent Expense	521		2 0 0 0 00	18
19					Office Supplies Expense	523		5 0 00	19
20					Medical Supplies Expense	524		1 0 0 00	20
21					Telephone Expense	525		1 5 0 00	21
22					Laboratory Expense	526		9 8 0 00	22
23					Insurance Expense	535		5 0 0 00	23
24					Depr. Expense—Office Furn.	541		2 0 0 00	24
25					Depr. Expense—Med. Equip.	542		3 0 0 00	25
26		30			Income Summary	313	12 4 2 0 00		26
27					Ray Bonita, Capital	311		12 4 2 0 00	27
28		30			Ray Bonita, Capital	311	10 0 0 0 00		28
29					Ray Bonita, Drawing	312		10 0 0 0 00	29

U REVU   Complete U REVU-4 on **page 639** to test your basic understanding of LO5.

LEARNING OBJECTIVES   Key Points to Remember

LO1 Explain the differences between the modified cash and accrual bases of accounting.

As shown below, there are three basic differences between the modified cash and accrual bases of accounting.

DIFFERENCES BETWEEN MODIFIED CASH AND ACCRUAL BASES OF ACCOUNTING

EVENT	ACCRUAL BASIS	MODIFIED CASH BASIS
Expenses		
Bills for services received, but not yet paid.	Expense Accounts Payable	No entry. (Record when paid.)
Wages earned by employees, but not yet paid.	Wages Expense Wages Payable	No entry. (Record when paid.)
Revenues		
Services provided on account.	Accounts Receivable Professional Fees	No entry. (Record when cash is received.)

LO2 Describe special records for a professional service business using the modified cash basis.

Special records are required for a professional service business using the modified cash basis. Since accounts receivable are not entered in the accounting system, other records must be maintained to keep track of amounts owed by clients and patients. These records generally include an appointment record and a client or patient ledger record.

LO3 Describe and use a combination journal to record transactions of a professional service business.

A combination journal is used by some businesses to improve the efficiency of recording and posting transactions. It includes general and special columns. The headings for a typical combination journal for a doctor's office are shown below.

	CASH		DESCRIPTION	POST. REF.	GENERAL		MEDICAL FEES CREDIT	WAGES EXPENSE DEBIT	LABORATORY EXPENSE DEBIT	MEDICAL SUPPLIES DEBIT	OFFICE SUPPLIES DEBIT
DATE	DEBIT	CREDIT			DEBIT	CREDIT					

COMBINATION JOURNAL   PAGE 1

LO4 Post from the combination journal to the general ledger.

Rules for posting a combination journal are as follows:

1. Amounts entered in the general columns are posted individually to the general ledger on a daily basis.
2. The totals of the special columns are posted to the general ledger at the end of the month.

LO5 Prepare a work sheet, financial statements, and adjusting and closing entries for a professional service business.

The work sheet, financial statements, adjusting entries, and closing entries are prepared in the same manner as discussed in Chapters 5 and 6. Remember, however, that under the modified cash basis, adjustments are made only for prepaid items and depreciation of plant and equipment.

DEMONSTRATION PROBLEM

Maria Vietor is a financial planning consultant. She developed the following chart of accounts for her business:

Vietor Financial Planning
Chart of Accounts

Assets	Revenues
101 Cash	401 Professional Fees
142 Office Supplies	
	Expenses
Liabilities	511 Wages Expense
202 Accounts Payable	521 Rent Expense
	523 Office Supplies Expense
Owner's Equity	525 Telephone Expense
311 Maria Vietor, Capital	526 Automobile Expense
312 Maria Vietor, Drawing	533 Utilities Expense
313 Income Summary	534 Charitable Contributions Expense

Vietor completed the following transactions during the month of December of the current year:

Dec.   1   Vietor invested cash to start a consulting business, $20,000.

3   Paid December office rent, $1,000.

4   Received a check from Aaron Bisno, a client, for services, $2,500.

6   Paid Union Electric for December heating and light, $75.

7   Received a check from Will Carter, a client, for services, $2,000.

12   Paid Smith's Super Service for gasoline and oil purchases, $60.

14   Paid Comphelp for temporary secretarial services obtained through them during the past two weeks, $600.

17   Purchased office supplies on account from Cleat Office Supply, $280.

20   Paid Cress Telephone Co. for local and long-distance business calls during the past month, $100.

21   Vietor withdrew cash for personal use, $1,100.

24   Made donation to the National Multiple Sclerosis Society, $100.

27   Received a check from Ellen Thaler, a client, for services, $2,000.

28   Paid Comphelp for temporary secretarial services obtained through them during the past two weeks, $600.

29   Made payment on account to Cleat Office Supply, $100.

REQUIRED

1.   Enter the transactions in a combination journal. Establish special columns for Professional Fees, Wages Expense, and Automobile Expense. Vietor uses the modified cash basis of accounting. (Refer to the Chapter 4 Demonstration Problem to see how similar transactions were recorded in a general journal. Notice that the combination journal is much more efficient.)

2.   Prove the combination journal.

3.   Post these transactions to a general ledger.

4.   Prepare a trial balance.

(continued)

Solution 1. and 2.

COMBINATION JOURNAL
PAGE 1

DATE	No.	CASH DEBIT	CASH CREDIT	DESCRIPTION	POST. REF.	GENERAL DEBIT	GENERAL CREDIT	PROFESSIONAL FEES CREDIT	WAGES EXPENSE DEBIT	AUTOMOBILE EXPENSE DEBIT
20— Dec. 1	1	20,000 00		Maria Vietor, Capital	311		20,000 00			
3	2		1,000 00	Rent Expense	521	1,000 00				
4	3	2,500 00			—			2,500 00		
6	4		75 00	Utilities Expense	533	75 00				
7	5	2,000 00			—			2,000 00		
12	6		60 00		—					60 00
14	7		600 00						600 00	
17	8			Office Supplies	142	280 00				
	9			Accounts Payable—Cleat Office Supply	202		280 00			
20	10		100 00	Telephone Expense	525	100 00				
21	11		1,100 00	Maria Vietor, Drawing	312	1,100 00				
24	12		100 00	Charitable Contributions Expense	534	100 00				
	13				—					
27	14	2,000 00			—			2,000 00		
28	15		600 00						600 00	
29	16		100 00	Accounts Payable—Cleat Office Supply	202	100 00				
	17	26,500 00	3,735 00			2,755 00	20,280 00	6,500 00	1,200 00	60 00
		(101)	(101)			(✓)	(✓)	(401)	(511)	(526)
	18									

Proving the Combination Journal:

Debit columns:		Credit columns:	
Cash	26,500	Cash	3,735
General	2,755	General	20,280
Wages Expense	1,200	Professional Fees	6,500
Automobile Expense	60		30,515
	30,515		

3.

GENERAL LEDGER

ACCOUNT: Cash   ACCOUNT NO. 101

DATE		ITEM	POST. REF.	DEBIT	CREDIT	BALANCE	
						DEBIT	CREDIT
20-- Dec.	31		C J 1	26 5 0 0 00		26 5 0 0 00	
	31		C J 1		3 7 3 5 00	22 7 6 5 00	

ACCOUNT: Office Supplies   ACCOUNT NO. 142

DATE		ITEM	POST. REF.	DEBIT	CREDIT	BALANCE	
						DEBIT	CREDIT
20-- Dec.	17		C J 1	2 8 0 00		2 8 0 00	

ACCOUNT: Accounts Payable   ACCOUNT NO. 202

DATE		ITEM	POST. REF.	DEBIT	CREDIT	BALANCE	
						DEBIT	CREDIT
20-- Dec.	17		C J 1		2 8 0 00		2 8 0 00
	29		C J 1	1 0 0 00			1 8 0 00

ACCOUNT: Maria Vietor, Capital   ACCOUNT NO. 311

DATE		ITEM	POST. REF.	DEBIT	CREDIT	BALANCE	
						DEBIT	CREDIT
20-- Dec.	1		C J 1		20 0 0 0 00		20 0 0 0 00

ACCOUNT: Maria Vietor, Drawing   ACCOUNT NO. 312

DATE		ITEM	POST. REF.	DEBIT	CREDIT	BALANCE	
						DEBIT	CREDIT
20-- Dec.	21		C J 1	1 1 0 0 00		1 1 0 0 00	

ACCOUNT: Income Summary   ACCOUNT NO. 313

DATE		ITEM	POST. REF.	DEBIT	CREDIT	BALANCE	
						DEBIT	CREDIT
20--							

ACCOUNT: Professional Fees   ACCOUNT NO. 401

DATE		ITEM	POST. REF.	DEBIT	CREDIT	BALANCE	
						DEBIT	CREDIT
20-- Dec.	31		C J 1		6 5 0 0 00		6 5 0 0 00

ACCOUNT: Wages Expense   ACCOUNT NO. 511

DATE		ITEM	POST. REF.	DEBIT	CREDIT	BALANCE	
						DEBIT	CREDIT
20-- Dec.	31		C J 1	1 2 0 0 00		1 2 0 0 00	

(continued)

ACCOUNT: Rent Expense   ACCOUNT NO. 521

DATE	ITEM	POST. REF.	DEBIT	CREDIT	BALANCE DEBIT	BALANCE CREDIT
20-- Dec. 3		C J 1	1 0 0 0 00		1 0 0 0 00	

ACCOUNT: Office Supplies Expense   ACCOUNT NO. 523

DATE	ITEM	POST. REF.	DEBIT	CREDIT	BALANCE DEBIT	BALANCE CREDIT
20--						

ACCOUNT: Telephone Expense   ACCOUNT NO. 525

DATE	ITEM	POST. REF.	DEBIT	CREDIT	BALANCE DEBIT	BALANCE CREDIT
20-- Dec. 20		C J 1	1 0 0 00		1 0 0 00	

ACCOUNT: Automobile Expense   ACCOUNT NO. 526

DATE	ITEM	POST. REF.	DEBIT	CREDIT	BALANCE DEBIT	BALANCE CREDIT
20-- Dec. 31		C J 1	6 0 00		6 0 00	

ACCOUNT: Utilities Expense   ACCOUNT NO. 533

DATE	ITEM	POST. REF.	DEBIT	CREDIT	BALANCE DEBIT	BALANCE CREDIT
20-- Dec. 6		C J 1	7 5 00		7 5 00	

ACCOUNT: Charitable Contributions Expense   ACCOUNT NO. 534

DATE	ITEM	POST. REF.	DEBIT	CREDIT	BALANCE DEBIT	BALANCE CREDIT
20-- Dec. 24		C J 1	1 0 0 00		1 0 0 00	

4.

Vietor Financial Planning
Trial Balance
December 31, 20 - -

ACCOUNT TITLE	ACCOUNT NO.	DEBIT BALANCE	CREDIT BALANCE
Cash	101	22 7 6 5 00	
Office Supplies	142	2 8 0 00	
Accounts Payable	202		1 8 0 00
Maria Vietor, Capital	311		20 0 0 0 00
Maria Vietor, Drawing	312	1 1 0 0 00	
Professional Fees	401		6 5 0 0 00
Wages Expense	511	1 2 0 0 00	
Rent Expense	521	1 0 0 0 00	
Telephone Expense	525	1 0 0 00	
Automobile Expense	526	6 0 00	
Utilities Expense	533	7 5 00	
Charitable Contributions Expense	534	1 0 0 00	
		26 6 8 0 00	26 6 8 0 00

KEY TERMS

combination journal (621)   A journal with special and general columns.

Description column (624)   The column in the combination journal used to enter the account titles for the General Debit and General Credit columns; to identify specific creditors when assets are purchased, or payments made, on account; to identify amounts forwarded; and to identify adjusting, closing, and reversing entries.

General Credit column (621)   The column in the combination journal used to credit accounts that are used infrequently.

General Debit column (621)   The column in the combination journal used to debit accounts that are used infrequently.

Posting Reference column (624)   The column in the combination journal where the account number is entered after posting to accounts from the General Debit and Credit columns.

special columns (621)   Columns in combination journals for frequently used accounts.

SELF-STUDY QUESTIONS AND EXERCISES

True/False Questions

1. LO1   Under the accrual basis of accounting, revenues are recorded when earned.

2. LO1   The modified cash basis of accounting is used by most large businesses.

3. LO1   The modified cash basis uses the accrual basis when recording revenues and expenses.

4. LO1   Under the modified cash basis, interest expense is recorded when paid.

5. LO1   Many small professional service businesses use the modified cash basis.

Multiple Choice Questions

1. LO1   Using the modified cash basis, when a business provides services on account, _____ is debited.

    (a) no entry   (c) Cash
    (b) Accounts Receivable   (d) Owner's Equity

2. LO1   Using the modified cash basis, when wages are earned but not paid, _____ is debited.

    (a) Wages Expense   (c) Wages Payable
    (b) no entry   (d) Accrued Wages

3. LO3   Which of these would make the best "special column" in a combination journal?

    (a) Office Equipment   (c) Revenue
    (b) Prepaid Insurance   (d) Telephone Expense

4. **LO3** Verifying that debit column totals equal credit column totals is the process of

(a) debiting.   (c) closing.

(b) proving.   (d) adjusting.

5. **LO4** Posting from the combination journal is accomplished by placing " _____ "and the page number in the Posting Reference column of the general ledger account.

(a) G   (c) J

(b) DJ   (d) CJ

U REVU   **Exercises**

1. **LO1** Using the information provided below, compute net income using the accrual and modified cash bases.

a. Revenues earned for the year, $500,000.

b. Cash collected from patients and insurance companies during the year, $520,000.

c. Total expenses incurred during the year, $300,000.

d. Bills for services received this year (expenses), but not yet paid, $5,000.

e. Bills for services received last year, but paid this year, $3,000.

f. Wages earned by employees this year, but not yet paid, $10,000.

g. Wages earned by employees last year, but paid this year, $15,000.

2. **LO3** Tom Durkin, M.D., uses the modified cash basis and the combination journal provided below to record entries for his medical practice.

Date	Cash		Description	General		Medical Fees Credit	Wages Expense Debit	Laboratory Expense Debit	Medical Supplies Debit	Office Supplies Debit
	Debit	Credit		Debit	Credit					

Indicate which columns would be used for the debits and credits for the following transactions.

a. Medical services provided for cash.

b. Wages incurred, but not paid.

c. Cash paid for laboratory expenses.

d. Purchased medical supplies on account.

3. **LO4** Indicate the manner in which the information in the columns of the combination journal shown below is posted.

a. Insert an "a" at the bottom of the column if the individual transaction amounts are posted throughout the month.

b. Insert a "b" if the column total is posted at the end of the month.

Date	Cash		Description	General		Medical Fees Credit	Wages Expense Debit	Laboratory Expense Debit	Medical Supplies Debit	Office Supplies Debit
	Debit	Credit		Debit	Credit					

4. LO5   Using the information and combination journal provided below, prepare the June 30 adjusting entries for the following:

a. Medical supplies used, $4,000.
b. Depreciation on office furniture, $2,000.

Date	Cash		Description	General		Medical Fees Credit	Wages Expense Debit	Laboratory Expense Debit	Medical Supplies Debit
	Debit	Credit		Debit	Credit				

The answers to the Self-Study Questions and Exercises are at the end of the Module (pages 650–651).

APPLYING YOUR KNOWLEDGE

REVIEW QUESTIONS

LO1   1.   Explain when revenues are recorded under the modified cash basis and accrual basis of accounting.

LO1   2.   Explain when wages expense is recorded under the modified cash basis and accrual basis of accounting.

LO2   3.   Explain the purpose of an appointment record.

LO2   4.   Explain the purpose of a patient ledger account.

LO3   5.   Explain the purpose of a special column in the combination journal.

LO3   6.   Explain the purpose of the General columns in the combination journal.

LO3/4   7.   How does the use of the combination journal save time and space in entering cash transactions?

LO3   8.   Explain the purpose of the Description column in the combination journal.

LO3   9.   What is the purpose of proving the totals in the combination journal?

LO4   10.   When an entry is posted from the combination journal to a ledger account, what information is entered in the Posting Reference column of the combination journal? In the Posting Reference column of the ledger account?

SERIES A EXERCISES

E M-1A (LO1/3)

✓ **General Debit total: $2,715;**
Cash Debit total: $11,100

JOURNAL ENTRIES Jean Akins opened a consulting business. Journalize the following transactions that occurred during the month of January of the current year using the modified cash basis and a combination journal. Set up special columns for Consulting Fees (credit) and Wages Expense (debit).

(continued)

Jan. 1   Invested cash in the business, $10,000.

2   Paid office rent, $500.

3   Purchased office equipment on account from Business Machines, Inc., $1,500.

5   Received cash for services rendered, $750.

8   Paid telephone bill, $65.

10   Paid for a magazine subscription (miscellaneous expense), $15.

11   Purchased office supplies on account from Leo's Office Supplies, $300.

15   Paid for one-year liability insurance policy, $150.

18   Paid part-time help, $500.

21   Received cash for services rendered, $350.

25   Paid electricity bill, $85.

27   Withdrew cash for personal use, $100.

29   Paid part-time help, $500.

E M-2A (LO1/3)
✓ Total debits: $19,191

JOURNAL ENTRIES Bill Rackes opened a bicycle repair shop. Journalize the following transactions that occurred during the month of October of the current year. Use the modified cash basis and a combination journal with special columns for Repair Fees (credit) and Wages Expense (debit). Prove the combination journal.

Oct. 1   Invested cash in the business, $15,000.

2   Paid shop rental for the month, $300.

3   Purchased bicycle parts on account from Tracker's Bicycle Parts, $2,000.

5   Purchased office supplies on account from Downtown Office Supplies, $250.

8   Paid telephone bill, $38.

9   Received cash for services, $140.

11   Paid for a sports magazine subscription (miscellaneous expense), $15.

12   Made payment on account for parts previously purchased, $100.

14   Paid part-time help, $300.

15   Received cash for services, $350.

16   Paid electricity bill, $48.

19   Received cash for services, $250.

23   Withdrew cash for personal use, $50.

25   Made payment on account for office supplies previously purchased, $50.

29   Paid part-time help, $300.

SERIES A PROBLEMS

P M-3A (LO3/4/5)

✓ 2. Cash bal., 1/12: $10,310;

3. Total journal credits: $15,499;

5. Trial bal. total debits: $13,460

JOURNALIZING AND POSTING TRANSACTIONS AND PREPARING A TRIAL BALANCE Angela McWharton opened an on-call nursing services business. She rented a small office space and pays a part-time worker to answer the telephone. Her chart of accounts is shown below.

Angela McWharton Nursing Services
Chart of Accounts

Assets		Revenues	
101	Cash	401	Nursing Care Fees
142	Office Supplies		
181	Office Equipment	Expenses	
		511	Wages Expense
Liabilities		512	Advertising Expense
202	Accounts Payable	521	Rent Expense
		525	Telephone Expense
Owner's Equity		526	Transportation Expense
311	Angela McWharton, Capital	533	Electricity Expense
312	Angela McWharton, Drawing	549	Miscellaneous Expense
313	Income Summary		

McWharton's transactions for the first month of business are as follows:

Jan. 1   Invested cash in the business, $10,000.

1   Paid January rent, $500.

2   Purchased office supplies on account from Crestline Office Supplies, $300.

4   Purchased office equipment on account from Office Technology, Inc., $1,500.

6   Received cash for nursing services rendered, $580.

7   Paid telephone bill, $42.

8   Paid electricity bill, $38.

10   Received cash for nursing services rendered, $360.

12   Made payment on account for office supplies previously purchased, $50.

13   Reimbursed part-time worker for use of personal automobile (transportation expense), $150.

15   Paid part-time worker, $360.

17   Received cash for nursing services rendered, $420.

18   Withdrew cash for personal use, $100.

20   Paid for newspaper advertising, $26.

22   Paid for gas and oil, $35.

24   Paid subscription for journal on nursing care practices (miscellaneous expense), $28.

25   Received cash for nursing services rendered, $320.

27   Made payment on account for office equipment previously purchased, $150.

29   Paid part-time worker, $360.

30   Received cash for nursing services rendered, $180.

(continued)

REQUIRED

1. Journalize the transactions for January using the modified cash basis and page 1 of a combination journal. Set up special columns for Nursing Care Fees (credit), Wages Expense (debit), and Transportation Expense (debit).

2. Determine the cash balance as of January 12 (using the combination journal).

3. Prove the combination journal.

4. Set up general ledger accounts from the chart of accounts and post the transactions from the combination journal.

5. Prepare a trial balance.

P M-4A (LO3/4/5)

✓ 2. Cash bal., 11/12: $5,949; 3. Total journal credits: $6,499; 5. Trial Bal. total debits: $18,155; Adjusted Trial Bal. total debits: $18,455; Net income: $1,842; 7. Capital, 11/30: $6,772; Total assets, 11/30: $13,947

JOURNALIZING AND POSTING TRANSACTIONS AND PREPARING FINANCIAL STATEMENTS Sue Reyton owns a suit tailoring shop. She opened her business in September with a cash investment of $5,430. She rents a small work space and has an assistant to receive job orders and process claim tickets. Her trial balance shows her account balances for the first two months of business (September and October). No adjustments were made in September or October.

Sue Reyton Tailors
Trial Balance
October 31, 20 - -

ACCOUNT TITLE	ACCOUNT NO.	DEBIT BALANCE	CREDIT BALANCE
Cash	101	5 7 1 1 00	
Tailoring Supplies	141	1 0 0 0 00	
Office Supplies	142	4 8 5 00	
Prepaid Insurance	145	1 0 0 00	
Tailoring Equipment	188	3 8 0 0 00	
Accumulated Depreciation—Tailoring Equipment	188.1		
Accounts Payable	202		4 1 2 5 00
Sue Reyton, Capital	311		5 4 3 0 00
Sue Reyton, Drawing	312	5 0 0 00	
Tailoring Fees	401		3 6 0 0 00
Wages Expense	511	8 0 0 00	
Advertising Expense	512	3 3 00	
Rent Expense	521	6 0 0 00	
Telephone Expense	525	6 0 00	
Electricity Expense	533	4 4 00	
Miscellaneous Expense	549	2 2 00	
		13 1 5 5 00	13 1 5 5 00

Reyton's transactions for November are as follows:

Nov. 1   Paid November rent, $300.

2   Purchased tailoring supplies on account from Sew Easy Supplies, $150.

3   Purchased a new button hole machine on account from Seam's Sewing Machines, $3,000.

5   Earned first week's revenue: $400 in cash.

8   Paid for newspaper advertising, $13.

9   Paid telephone bill, $28.

10   Paid electricity bill, $21.

Nov. 12   Earned second week's revenue: $200 in cash, $300 on account.

15   Paid part-time worker, $400.

16   Made payment on account for tailoring supplies, $100.

17   Paid for magazine subscription (miscellaneous expense), $12.

19   Earned third week's revenue: $450 in cash.

21   Paid for prepaid insurance for the year, $500.

23   Received cash from customers (previously owed), $300.

24   Paid for newspaper advertising, $13.

26   Paid for special delivery fee (miscellaneous expense), $12.

29   Earned fourth week's revenue: $600 in cash.

Additional accounts needed are as follows:

313   Income Summary
523   Office Supplies Expense
524   Tailoring Supplies Expense
535   Insurance Expense
542   Depreciation Expense—Tailoring Equipment

November 30 adjustments are as follows:

(a) Tailoring supplies on hand, $450.
(b) Office supplies on hand, $285.
(c) Prepaid insurance expired over past three months, $150.
(d) Depreciation on tailoring equipment for the last three months, $300.

REQUIRED

1. Journalize the transactions for November using the modified cash basis and page 5 of a combination journal. Set up special columns for Tailoring Fees (credit), Wages Expense (debit), and Advertising Expense (debit).

2. Determine the cash balance as of November 12.

3. Prove the combination journal.

4. Set up general ledger accounts, including the additional accounts listed above, entering the balances as of November 1, 20--. Post the entries from the combination journal.

5. Prepare a work sheet for the three months ended November 30, 20--.

6. Record the adjusting entries on page 6 of the combination journal and post to the general ledger accounts.

7. Prepare an income statement and statement of owner's equity for the three months ended November 30, and a balance sheet as of November 30, 20--. (Assume that Reyton made an investment of $5,430 on September 1, 20--.)

8. Record closing entries on page 6 of the combination journal and post to the general ledger accounts.

SERIES B EXERCISES

E M-1B (LO1/3)

✓ **General Debit total: $2,129;**
Cash Debit total: $9,400.

JOURNAL ENTRIES Bill Miller opened a bookkeeping service business. Journalize the following transactions that occurred during the month of March of the current year. Use the modified cash basis and a combination journal with special columns for Bookkeeping Fees (credit) and Wages Expense (debit).

Mar. 1	Invested cash in the business, $7,500.
3	Paid March office rent, $500.
5	Purchased office equipment on account from Desk Top Office Equipment, $800.
6	Received cash for services rendered, $400.
8	Paid telephone bill, $48.
10	Paid for a magazine subscription (miscellaneous expense), $25.
11	Purchased office supplies, $200.
14	Received cash for services rendered, $520.
16	Paid for a one-year insurance policy, $200.
18	Paid part-time worker, $400.
21	Received cash for services rendered, $380.
22	Made payment on account for office equipment previously purchased, $100.
24	Paid electricity bill, $56.
27	Withdrew cash for personal use, $200.
29	Paid part-time worker, $400.
30	Received cash for services rendered, $600.

E M-2B (LO1/3)

✓ **Total debits: $14,349**

JOURNAL ENTRIES Amy Anjelo opened a delivery service. Journalize the following transactions that occurred in January of the current year. Use the modified cash basis and a combination journal with special columns for Delivery Fees (credit) and Wages Expense (debit). Prove the combination journal.

Jan. 1	Invested cash in the business, $10,000.
2	Paid shop rental for the month, $400.
3	Purchased a delivery cart on account from Walt's Wheels, $1,000.
5	Purchased office supplies, $250.
6	Paid telephone bill, $51.
8	Received cash for delivery services, $428.
11	Paid electricity bill, $37.
12	Paid part-time employee, $480.
13	Paid for postage stamps (miscellaneous expense), $29.
15	Received cash for delivery services, $382.
18	Made payment on account for delivery cart previously purchased, $90.
21	Withdrew cash for personal use, $250.

Jan. 24	Paid for a one-year liability insurance policy, $180.
26	Received cash for delivery services, $292.
29	Paid part-time employee, $480.

SERIES B PROBLEMS

P M-3B (LO3/4/5)

✓ 2. Cash bal., 7/14: $4,786; 3. Total journal credits: $9,472; 5. Trial bal. total debits: $8,190

JOURNALIZING AND POSTING TRANSACTIONS AND PREPARING A TRIAL BALANCE J. B. Hoyt opened a training center at the marina where he provides private water-skiing lessons. He rented a small building at the marina and has a part-time worker to assist him. His chart of accounts is shown below.

Water Walking by Hoyt
Chart of Accounts

Assets		Revenues	
101	Cash	401	Training Fees
142	Office Supplies		
183	Skiing Equipment	Expenses	
		511	Wages Expense
Liabilities		521	Rent Expense
202	Accounts Payable	525	Telephone Expense
		526	Transportation Expense
Owner's Equity		533	Electricity Expense
311	J. B. Hoyt, Capital	537	Repair Expense
312	J. B. Hoyt, Drawing	549	Miscellaneous Expense
313	Income Summary		

Transactions for the first month of business are as follows:

July 1	Invested cash in the business, $5,000.
2	Paid rent for the month, $250.
3	Purchased office supplies, $150.
4	Purchased skiing equipment on account from Water Fun, Inc., $2,000.
6	Paid telephone bill, $36.
7	Received cash for skiing lessons, $200.
10	Paid electricity bill, $28.
12	Paid part-time worker, $250.
14	Received cash for skiing lessons, $300.
16	Paid for gas and oil (transportation expense), $60.
17	Received cash for skiing lessons, $250.
20	Paid for repair to ski rope, $20.
21	Made payment on account for skiing equipment previously purchased, $100.
24	Received cash for skiing lessons, $310.
26	Paid for award certificates (miscellaneous expense), $18.
28	Paid part-time worker, $250.
30	Received cash for skiing lessons, $230.
31	Paid for repair to life jacket, $20.

(*continued*)

REQUIRED

1. Journalize the transactions for July using the modified cash basis and page 1 of a combination journal. Set up special columns for Training Fees (credit), Wages Expense (debit), and Repair Expense (debit).

2. Determine the cash balance as of July 14, 20--.

3. Prove the combination journal.

4. Set up general ledger accounts from the chart of accounts and post the transactions from the combination journal.

5. Prepare a trial balance.

P M-4B (LO3/4/5)

✓ 2. Cash bal., 6/12: $4,832;

3. Total journal credits: $4,587;

5. Trial Bal. total debits: $13,023;

Adjusted Trial Bal. total debits: $13,283;

Net income: $2,928;

7. Capital, 6/30: $7,028;

Total assets, 6/30: $9,008

KLOOSTER
& ALLEN

JOURNALIZING AND POSTING TRANSACTIONS AND PREPARING FINANCIAL STATEMENTS Molly Claussen owns a lawn care business. She opened her business in April with a cash investment of $5,000. She rents a small shop area where she stores her equipment and has an assistant to receive orders and process accounts. Her trial balance shows her account balances for the first two months of business (April and May). No adjustments were made at the end of April or May.

Molly Claussen's Green Thumb
Trial Balance
May 31, 20 - -

ACCOUNT TITLE	ACCOUNT NO.	DEBIT BALANCE	CREDIT BALANCE
Cash	101	4 6 0 4 00	
Lawn Care Supplies	141	5 8 8 00	
Office Supplies	142	2 4 3 00	
Prepaid Insurance	145	1 5 0 00	
Lawn Care Equipment	189	2 4 0 8 00	
Accumulated Depreciation—Lawn Care Equipment	189.1		
Accounts Payable	202		1 0 8 0 00
Molly Claussen, Capital	311		5 0 0 0 00
Molly Claussen, Drawing	312	8 0 0 00	
Lawn Care Fees	401		4 0 3 3 00
Wages Expense	511	6 0 0 00	
Rent Expense	521	4 0 0 00	
Telephone Expense	525	8 8 00	
Electricity Expense	533	6 2 00	
Repair Expense	537	5 0 00	
Gas and Oil Expense	538	1 2 0 00	
		10 1 1 3 00	10 1 1 3 00

Transactions for June are as follows:

June 1   Paid shop rent, $200.

2   Purchased office supplies, $230.

3   Purchased new landscaping equipment on account from Earth Care, Inc., $1,000.

5   Paid telephone bill, $31.

6   Received cash for lawn care fees, $640.

8   Paid electricity bill, $31.

10   Paid part-time worker, $300.

11   Received cash for lawn care fees, $580.

12   Paid for a one-year insurance policy, $200.

June 14   Made payment on account for landscaping equipment previously purchased, $100.

15   Paid for gas and oil, $40.

19   Paid for mower repairs, $25.

21   Received $310 cash for lawn care fees and earned $480 on account.

24   Withdrew cash for personal use, $100.

26   Paid for edging equipment repairs, $20.

28   Received cash from customers (previously owed), $480.

29   Paid part-time worker, $300.

Additional accounts needed are as follows:
313   Income Summary
523   Office Supplies Expense
524   Lawn Care Supplies Expense
535   Insurance Expense
542   Depreciation Expense—Lawn Care Equipment

June 30 adjustments are as follows:

(a) Office supplies on hand, $273.
(b) Lawn care supplies on hand, $300.
(c) Prepaid insurance expired over past three months, $100.
(d) Depreciation on lawn care equipment for past three months, $260.

REQUIRED

1. Journalize the transactions for June using the modified cash basis and page 5 of a combination journal. Set up special columns for Lawn Care Fees (credit), Repair Expense (debit), and Wages Expense (debit).

2. Determine the cash balance as of June 12.

3. Prove the combination journal.

4. Set up general ledger accounts including the additional accounts listed above, entering balances as of June 1, 20--. Post the entries from the combination journal.

5. Prepare a work sheet for the three months ended June 30, 20--.

6. Record the adjusting entries on page 6 of the combination journal and post to the general ledger accounts.

7. Prepare an income statement and statement of owner's equity for the three months ended June 30, and a balance sheet as of June 30, 20--. Assume that Claussen invested $5,000 on April 1, 20--.

8. Record the closing entries on page 6 of the combination journal and post to the general ledger accounts.

 MANAGING YOUR WRITING

Your friend is planning to start her own business and has asked you for advice. In particular, she is concerned about which method of accounting she should use. She has heard about the modified cash and accrual methods of accounting. However, she does not really understand the differences. Write a memo that explains each method and the type of business for which each method is most appropriate.

ETHICS CASE

Nancy Bowles, the owner of Bowles Services, a sole proprietorship, rushed into the office late Monday morning carrying a deposit receipt from the bank. Upon handing the receipt to Sarah, the accountant, she instructed her to debit Cash and credit Professional Fees for the full $10,000. When Sarah examined the source document, she saw that the cash had come from the account of Richard Bowles, Nancy's father. Nancy explained to Sarah that she was applying for a bank loan and needed to "show that her company earned more year-to-date income than it actually had." Nancy used the rationale that the company would earn at least $10,000 in revenue during the next few months but the financial statements the bank required were as of the end of this month.

1. Does Nancy's explanation make sense? Is it ethical?

2. How should this transaction be entered in Bowles Services' books? Does it matter whether the modified cash basis or accrual basis of accounting is used?

3. Make a written list of all the consequences Nancy might face as a result of recording this transaction as a debit to Cash and a credit to Professional Fees.

4. Break up into groups of two and role play Nancy's and Sarah's point of view in this situation.

MASTERY PROBLEM

✓ 1. Total debits to General Dr. col. of CJ: $112,705; 2. Total debits of CJ: $305,305; 4. Total debits on trial bal.: $232,200

John McRoe opened a tennis resort in June 20--. Most guests register for one week, arriving on Sunday afternoon and returning home the following Saturday afternoon. Guests stay at an adjacent hotel. The tennis resort provides lunch and dinner. Dining and exercise facilities are provided in a building rented by McRoe. A dietitian, masseuse, physical therapist, and athletic trainers are on call to assure the proper combination of diet and exercise. The chart of accounts and transactions for the month of June are provided below. McRoe uses the modified cash basis of accounting.

McRoe Tennis Resort
Chart of Accounts

Assets

101	Cash
142	Office Supplies
144	Food Supplies
184	Tennis Facilities
184.1	Accum. Depr.—Tennis Facilities
186	Exercise Equipment
186.1	Accum. Depr.—Exercise Equip.

Liabilities

202	Accounts Payable

Owner's Equity

311	John McRoe, Capital
312	John McRoe, Drawing
313	Income Summary

Revenue

401	Registration Fees

Expenses

511	Wages Expense
521	Rent Expense
523	Office Supplies Expense
524	Food Supplies Expense
525	Telephone Expense
533	Utilities Expense
535	Insurance Expense
536	Postage Expense
541	Depr. Exp.—Tennis Facilities
542	Depr. Exp.—Exercise Equip.

June 1	McRoe invested cash in the business, $90,000.
1	Paid for new exercise equipment, $9,000.
2	Deposited registration fees in the bank, $15,000.
2	Paid rent for month of June on building and land, $2,500.
2	Rogers Construction completed work on new tennis courts that cost $70,000. The estimated useful life of the facility is five years, at which time the courts will have to be resurfaced. Arrangements were made to pay the bill in July.
3	Purchased food supplies on account from Au Naturel Foods, $5,000.
5	Purchased office supplies on account from Gordon Office Supplies, $300.
7	Deposited registration fees in the bank, $16,200.
10	Purchased food supplies on account from Au Naturel Foods, $6,200.
10	Paid wages to staff, $500.
14	Deposited registration fees in the bank, $13,500.
16	Purchased food supplies on account from Au Naturel Foods, $4,000.
17	Paid wages to staff, $500.
18	Paid postage, $85.
21	Deposited registration fees in the bank, $15,200.
24	Purchased food supplies on account from Au Naturel Foods, $5,500.
24	Paid wages to staff, $500.
28	Deposited registration fees in the bank, $14,000.
30	Purchased food supplies on account from Au Naturel Foods, $6,000.
30	Paid wages to staff, $500.
30	Paid Au Naturel Foods on account, $28,700.
30	Paid utility bill, $500.
30	Paid telephone bill, $120.
30	McRoe withdrew cash for personal use, $1,500.

REQUIRED

1. Enter the transactions in a combination journal (page 1). Establish special columns for Registration Fees (credit), Wages Expense (debit), and Food Supplies (debit).

2. Prove the combination journal.

3. Post these transactions to a general ledger.

4. Prepare a trial balance as of June 30.

CHALLENGE PROBLEM

This problem challenges you to apply your cumulative accounting knowledge to move a step beyond the material in the module.

✓ **NI modified cash basis: $7,000;**
NI accrual basis: $7,300

Gerald Resler recently opened a financial consulting business. Summary transactions for the month of June, his second month of operation, are provided below.

1. Cash collected from clients for consulting fees, $10,000. $1,500 of the $10,000 was for consulting fees earned in May, but received in June.

2. Consulting fees earned in June, but to be received in July, $2,000.

3. Supplies on hand at the beginning of June amounted to $500. All purchases of supplies are made on account. Supplies purchased during June, $1,000. At the end of June, $600 worth of supplies remained unused.

4. Paid cash on account to suppliers during June, $800. $200 of the $800 was for purchases of supplies made in May.

5. Wages paid to an assistant, $2,000. Of this $2,000, $300 had been earned in May. In addition, the assistant earned $500 in June, which will be paid next month.

6. Purchased a laptop. Paid $1,200 cash in June and will pay the balance of $1,200 in July. Gerald expects to use the laptop for two years at which time he expects that it will be obsolete and have a zero salvage value.

REQUIRED

Prepare income statements for the month of June using the modified cash and accrual bases.

ANSWERS TO SELF-STUDY QUESTIONS AND EXERCISES

True/False Questions
1. T
2. F (Large businesses use the accrual basis.)
3. F (See Figure M-1)
4. T
5. T

Multiple Choice Questions
1. a
2. b
3. c
4. b
5. d

U REVU   Exercises

1.

	ACCRUAL BASIS	MODIFIED CASH BASIS
Revenues earned	$500,000	
Cash received from patients and insurance companies		$520,000
Expenses incurred	300,000	$300,000
Bills received, but not yet paid		(5,000)
Bills from last year, but paid this year		3,000
Wages earned this year, but not yet paid		(10,000)
Wages earned last year, but paid this year		15,000 303,000
	$200,000	$217,000

2.

	Debit	Credit
a.	Cash Debit	Medical Fees Credit
b.	No Entry	No Entry
c.	Laboratory Expense Debit	Cash Credit
d.	Medical Supplies Debit	General Credit

3.

Date	Cash		Description	General		Medical Fees Credit	Wages Expense Debit	Laboratory Expense Debit	Medical Supplies Debit	Office Supplies Debit
	Debit	Credit		Debit	Credit					
	b	b		a	a	b	b	b	b	b

4.

Date	Cash		Description	General		Medical Fees Credit	Wages Expense Debit	Laboratory Expense Debit	Medical Supplies Debit
	Debit	Credit		Debit	Credit				
20-- June			Adjusting Entries						
30			Medical Supplies Expense Medical Supplies	4,000	4,000				
30			Depr. Exp—Off. Furn. Accum. Depr—Off. Furn.	2,000	2,000				

*Page references in bold indicate defined terms.

NOTES

NOTES

NOTES

NOTES

NOTES

NOTES

Note: While for a specific company each account number used would have only one title, titles vary from company to company as needed. Particularly for the Owner's Equity accounts, the accounts used depends on the company ownership structure (proprietorship, partnership, or corporation).

Assets (100–199)

100s—Cash Related Accounts
101 Cash
105 Petty Cash

120s—Receivables
121 Notes Receivable
122 Accounts Receivable
122.1 Allowance for Bad Debts
123 Interest Receivable (Also Accrued Interest Receivable)

130s—Inventories
131 Merchandise Inventory
132 Raw Materials
133 Work in Process
134 Finished Goods

140s—Prepaid Items
141 Supplies (Specialty items like Medical, Bicycle, Tailoring, etc.)
142 Office Supplies
144 Food Supplies
145 Prepaid Insurance

150s—Long-Term Investments
153 Bond Sinking Fund

160s—Land
161 Land
162 Natural Resources
162.1 Accumulated Depletion

170s—Buildings
171 Buildings
171.1 Accumulated Depreciation—Buildings

180s—Equipment
181 Office Equipment (Also Store Equipment)
181.1 Accumulated Depreciation—Office Equipment (Also Store Equipment)
182 Office Furniture
182.1 Accumulated Depreciation—Office Furniture
183 Athletic Equipment (Also Tailoring, Lawn, Cleaning)
183.1 Accumulated Depreciation—Athletic Equipment (Also Tailoring, Lawn, Cleaning)
184 Tennis Facilities (Also Basketball Facilities)
184.1 Accumulated Depreciation—Tennis Facilities (Also Basketball Facilities)
185 Delivery Equipment (Also Medical, Van)
185.1 Accumulated Depreciation—Delivery Equipment (Also Medical, Van)

186 Exercise Equipment
186.1 Accumulated Depreciation—Exercise Equipment
187 Computer Equipment
187.1 Accumulated Depreciation—Computer Equipment

190s—Intangibles
191 Patents
192 Copyrights

Liabilities (200–299)

200s—Short-Term Payables
201 Notes Payable
201.1 Discount on Notes Payable
202 Accounts Payable (Also Vouchers Payable)
203 United Way Contribution Payable
204 Income Tax Payable
205 Common Dividends Payable
206 Preferred Dividends Payable
207 Interest Payable (Also Bond Interest Payable)

210s—Employee Payroll Related Payables
211 Employee Income Tax Payable
212 Social Security Tax Payable
213 Medicare Tax Payable
215 City Earnings Tax Payable
216 Health Insurance Premiums Payable
217 Credit Union Payable
218 Savings Bond Deductions Payable
219 Wages Payable

220s—Employer Payroll Related Payables
221 FUTA Tax Payable
222 SUTA Tax Payable
223 Workers' Compensation Insurance Payable

230s—Sales Tax
231 Sales Tax Payable

240s—Deferred Revenues and Current Portion of Long-Term Debt
241 Unearned Subscription Revenue (Also Unearned Ticket Revenue, Unearned Repair Fees)
242 Current Portion of Mortgage Payable

250s—Long-Term Liabilities
251 Mortgage Payable
252 Bonds Payable
252.1 Discount on Bonds Payable
253 Premium on Bonds Payable

generally accepted accounting principles (GAAP) (5)   Procedures and guidelines developed by the Financial Accounting Standards Board to be followed in the accounting and reporting process.

internal auditing (10)   Reviewing the operating and accounting control procedures adopted by management to make sure the controls are adequate and being followed; assuring that accurate and timely information is provided.

interpreting (5)   Deciding the meaning and importance of the information in various reports.

management advisory services (9)   Providing advice to businesses on a wide variety of managerial issues.

manufacturing business (7)   A business that makes a product to sell.

merchandising business (7)   A business that buys products to sell.

para-accountant (8)   A paraprofessional who provides many accounting, auditing, or tax services under the direct supervision of an accountant.

partnership (6)   A type of ownership structure in which more than one person owns the business.

public hearing (5)   Following the issuance of a discussion memorandum, public meetings are often held by FASB to gather opinions on the accounting issue.

recording (5)   Entering financial information about events affecting the company into the accounting system.

reporting (5)   Telling the results of the financial information.

Sarbanes-Oxley Act (SOX) (9)   An act passed by Congress to help improve reporting practices of public companies.

service business (7)   A business that provides a service.

sole proprietorship (6)   A type of ownership structure in which one person owns the business.

statement of financial accounting standards (SFAS) (6)   A standard issued by the Financial Accounting Standards Board. These standards must be followed when preparing financial statements.

summarizing (5)   Bringing the various items of information together to determine a result.

tax accounting (10)   Services focused on tax planning, preparing tax returns, and dealing with the Internal Revenue Service and other governmental agencies.

taxation (9)   See tax accounting.

APPLYING YOUR KNOWLEDGE

REVIEW QUESTIONS

LO1 1. What is the purpose of accounting?

LO1 2. Identify four user groups normally interested in financial information about a business.